32[∞]

D0326015

153865

Computer Communications

VOLUME I
PRINCIPLES

REMOVED FROM THE
ALVERNO COLLEGE LIBRARY

EDITOR

Wushow Chou
North Carolina State University

CONTRIBUTORS

Wushow Chou
Ira W. Cotton
Gilbert Falk
Simon S. Lam
Patrick V. McGregor
R. Andrew Pickens
Helen M. Wood

001.64404
c 738
v. 1

Alverno College
Library Media Center
Milwaukee, Wisconsin

Prentice-Hall, Inc. Englewood Cliffs, N.J. 07632

Library of Congress Cataloging in Publication Data

Main entry under title:

Computer communications.

   Includes bibliographies and index.
   Contents: v. 1. Principles.
   1. Computer networks.   2. Data transmission
systems.   I. Chou, W. (Wushow)
TK5105.5.C637   001.64'404   82-3833
ISBN 0-13-165043-2   (v. 1)   AACR2

© 1983 by Prentice-Hall, Inc., Englewood Cliffs, N.J. 07632

All rights reserved. No part of this book
may be reproduced in any form or
by any means without permission in writing
from the publisher.

Editorial/production supervision and interior design
   by *Aliza Greenblatt*
Cover design
   by *Debra Watson*
Manufacturing buyer
   Gordon Osbourne
Printed in the United States of America

10   9   8   7   6   5   4   3   2   1

ISBN 0-13-165043-2

PRENTICE-HALL INTERNATIONAL, INC., *London*
PRENTICE-HALL OF AUSTRALIA PTY. Limited, *Sydney*
PRENTICE-HALL CANADA, INC., *Toronto*
PRENTICE-HALL OF INDIA PRIVATE LIMITED, *New Delhi*
PRENTICE-HALL OF JAPAN, INC., *Tokyo*
PRENTICE-HALL OF SOUTHEAST ASIA PTE. LTD., *Singapore*
WHITEHALL BOOKS LIMITED, *Wellington, New Zealand*

Contents

Preface

The economy and convenience of extending the use of computing resources have promoted the development and expansion of communication-based computer systems. In 1970 there were fewer than 250,000 data terminals in the United States. Today there are more than 3 million, plus 200,000 facsimile machines. The expected growth rate in their numbers is over 20% per year. Present estimates are that there are 1 billion electronic messages per year generated or received by such devices. Within three years the number should almost double.

Another perspective on growth is that 70% of first-class mail is generated by computers. Almost all Fortune 500 companies are expected to have electronic mail systems in the next few years. Statistics indicate that we are inevitably heading toward an information society. This trend will be a continuing stimulation for new applications and new users. As a result, the rate of innovations in system design concepts, hardware features, and transmission services is accelerating; and as new applications become economically and operationally practical, demands increase and the cycle continues. The data terminals, or multimode terminals combining data, voice, and video capabilities, will outnumber the telephone sets used only for transmitting voice. Clearly, computer communication networks are needed.

One part of computer communication network design involves networking strategies. Volume I begins with a classification of networking alternatives (Chapter 1). Closely related are the control procedures used in the networks for managing traffic. Chapter 2 deals with control procedures at higher levels; IBM's System Network Architecture and ARPANET are used as examples.Chapter 3 addresses control procedures at the link level. Multiaccess schemes that allow a large number of terminals and computers to contend for a high-capacity channel are the topic in Chapter 4.

Another part of computer communication network design involves selection of digital transmission facilities. When common carriers provide all transmission facilities, people involved in planning computer communications systems do not need to understand the characteristics of the transmission facilities. The increasing need for wideband transmission facilities that are not provided by common carriers requires an understanding of the characteristics. Therefore, material on radio links, satellite channels, coaxial cables, and fiber optics is provided in Chapters 5, 6, and 7.

Control procedures are implemented in devices, and the devices are connected by transmission facilities to form networks. The communication devices and their functions are discussed in Chapter 8.

With the proliferation of equipment and use of computer communications, one issue that cannot be ignored is the security and integrity of the data flowing through various networks. Chapter 9 presents encryption possibilities, including data encryption standards and public key systems.

Two very important and interesting parts of computer communications network design deal with the problems of analysis and optimization of large teleprocessing networks. In Chapter 10 is a presentation of stochastic analytic methods for determining network performance, with emphasis placed on those that are practical, yet robust. A unified approach to the optimization of communication networks is given in Chapter 11. The unified approach combines exact and heuristic methods.

One of the most exciting aspects of computer communication technology is the emerging use of broadband facilities in networks. There will be wide use of satellite networks ranging from point-to-point to pervasive networks, cable networks that provide capacity for hundreds of megabits per second, and packet and cellular radio networks that can be used in situations where wired networks are less convenient. A possible scenario for new networks is that satellite channels be used as part of the backbone network, radio networks be included in the regional networks for local access or in place of telephone companies' local loops, and cable networks be used for limited-distance local networks. Examples of satellite networks, cable networks, and radio networks are given in Chapters 5, 6, and 7. Packet radio networks are discussed in Chapter 12.

The multiaccess schemes used on wideband facilities will make possible increased office automation and will be essential in the office of the future. The wide adaptation of limited-distance local networks, the topic of Chapter 13, will come first. The wide acceptance of the services available through local networks will prompt and accelerate the demand for communications and services that are not available locally. Users on one local network will be able to communicate with users on a geographically remote local network or access information and network services from a remote location.

For a user to access various possible network services not available locally or to communicate with another user at a remote site, there must be networks in between. Some of these networks will be in the form of public data networks. The discussion and comparison of several public data networks, as well as several private data networks, are given in Chapter 14. The issue of interconnecting the networks is considered in Chapter 15.

Another phenomenon is that of integration, that is, the integration of packet and circuit switching into the same architecture. Because of the growing conversion to computer-controlled digital switches, more telephone plants are converting from analog to digital. As a consequence, data, digitized voice, and other digital signals can be mixed in the same network, called an integrated services digital network. The integration of packet and circuit switching is addressed in Chapter 16. The combination of voice, data, still image, and video in the same network is addressed in Chapter 17.

While economy and convenience have resulted in the acceleration of demand in computer communication usage, they themselves are a direct consequence of advances in microelectronics, digitization techniques, and wideband digital transmission facilities. The availability of low-cost, high-performance microelectronic components allows the development of new applications of data communications usage and new data communication technologies which would otherwise be economically infeasible. The advancement of digitization techniques facilitates sharing of common transmission facilities for data, voice, and video traffic. Digitization techniques and the availability of wideband digital transmission facilities together open a new horizon for applications. Applications that require inexpensive, low-error-rate, high-bandwidth facilities, such as high-speed digital video transmission, are becoming practical. Chapter 18 presents these driving technologies that advance computer communications.

Many new network services will be developed to satisfy various application needs. A very important one is the access of distributed data bases. The issues of locating, managing, and coordinating distributed data bases are presented in Chapter 19.

Illustrated in Fig. A.1 are the interrelationships of topics covered in the book. However, each chapter is written to stand alone. Because of this, some overlap of material between certain chapters exists. Any apparent inconsistencies in terminology are attributable to the fact that definitions have not yet been agreed upon by all persons in the field of computer communications; conceptual differences may also exist between different individuals. No attempts have been made to unify definitions among the various authors. Indeed, the editor believes it is advantageous to be exposed to different definitions.

Wushow Chou
North Carolina State University

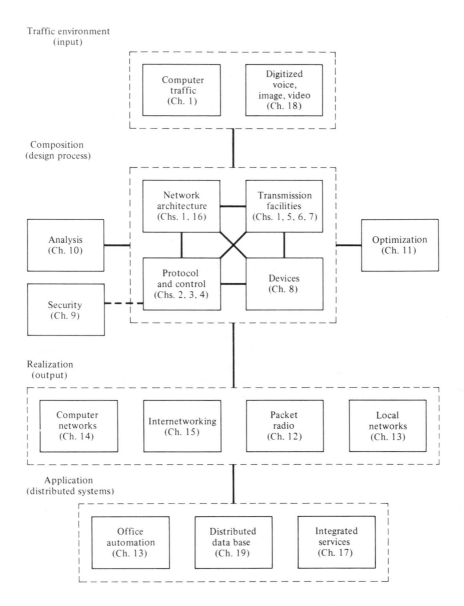

Traffic environment
(input)

Computer
traffic
(Ch. 1)

Digitized
voice,
image, video
(Ch. 18)

Composition
(design process)

Network
architecture
(Chs. 1, 16)

Transmission
facilities
(Chs. 1, 5, 6, 7)

Analysis
(Ch. 10)

Optimization
(Ch. 11)

Protocol
and control
(Chs. 2, 3, 4)

Devices
(Ch. 8)

Security
(Ch. 9)

Realization
(output)

Computer
networks
(Ch. 14)

Internetworking
(Ch. 15)

Packet
radio
(Ch. 12)

Local
networks
(Ch. 13)

Application
(distributed systems)

Office
automation
(Ch. 13)

Distributed
data base
(Ch. 19)

Integrated
services
(Ch. 17)

Figure A.1. Profile of computer communications.

1

Data/Computer Communications Network Structures

W. CHOU
North Carolina State University
Raleigh, North Carolina

1.1 INTRODUCTION

What is a computer communication network or system? Is there any distinction between data communications and computer communications? There has been no unique answer. The meaning of the term *computer communications* has been interpreted differently by various people. The different interpretations can be classified into three categories.

INTERPRETATION 1

"An interconnected group of independent computer systems which communicate with one another and share resources, such as programs, data, hardware, or software." With this definition, computers used solely for handling communications or controlling terminals are excluded.

INTERPRETATION 2

"An interconnected group of independent computers and data terminals which communicate with one another." With this definition, computers used for handling communications or controlling terminals, such as concentrators and terminal control units, are included.

INTERPRETATION 3

"Any data communication network which consists of at least one computer system." With this definition, there is almost no distinction between data communication and computer communication.

Historically, the term "computer communication" was first associated with packet switching. When used in a narrow sense, "computer communication" usually means packet switching. When the term *data communication* is used in a narrow sense, it usually means terminal-oriented networks where no computer-to-computer communication is involved. In this book we do not strictly distinguish between data and computer communications, but use the terms interchangeably. The basis of this chapter is an examination of the communication principles of different computer network architectures and structures, with a brief discussion of the elements of computer communication networks.

1.2   COMMUNICATING/SWITCHING PRINCIPLES

The most basic function of any data/computer communication network is the transfer of messages between communicating *data terminal equipment* (DTEs). (DTE is used here in a broad sense to represent any device that transmits or receives digital information. It might be a computer, data terminal, digital telephone, or digital facsimile or video equipment.) Message transfer can be achieved by direct connection, relaying, switching, or a combination of these. With *direct connection*, several DTEs share a communication channel and messages are transmitted from a source DTE directly to a destination DTE via the common communication channel without going through an intermediate device.

In the *relaying approach*, the DTEs are interfaced to certain communication devices that usually form a closed loop or ring. The path between the communication device interfacing the source DTE and the device interfacing the destination DTE may include additional intermediate devices. A message is relayed from one communication device to another until it reaches its destination.

For the *switching strategy*, DTEs are interfaced to switches that are interconnected to form a network. This network can assume any physical shape. Along the path from the source switch to the destination switch, each switch routes the message to one of its other lines for output.

1.2.1   Communication by Direct Connection

In a *direct-connection architecture*, multiple DTEs or users communicate with each other directly through a common channel. The common channel can be a cable, a pair of twisted wires, a terrestrial radio channel, or a satellite channel, for example. When one DTE transmits a message, all other DTEs that share the same channel and are within the range of the transmission receive the message at about the same time. The usually slight difference in receiving times at different DTEs is due to the difference in propagation delays between the transmitting DTE and the various receiving DTEs.

Except for devices that interface the DTEs and the transmission facilities, there are usually no intermediate devices. The one exception is when the intended destination DTE is beyond the range of the source DTE's transmitting power. In this case one or more switches or repeaters might be used. Since more than one DTE might attempt to use the common channel simultaneously, a control procedure must handle the contention problems. (In the limiting case, when only two DTEs are connected to a full-duplex channel in a point-to-point fashion, there is no contention problem.) Procedures for controlling access to a common channel by multiple DTEs are called *multiple-access* procedures.

Multiple access can be achieved by either static or dynamic allocation of the common channel. With static allocation, the channel is further divided into subchannels and each user has a dedicated subchannel. Subchannels can be assigned different capacities and can be created by *time-division multiplexing, frequency-division multiplexing*, or other appropriate multiplexing schemes. Once a subchannel is assigned to a DTE, other DTEs cannot send information through that subchannel even if it is idle, but any DTE can receive information from all subchannels. A static allocation broadcast approach, where every user is given a fixed allocation of the channel for transmission but may receive information from the whole channel, is sometimes called *channel-division multiple access.*

Subchannel dedication eliminates contention. Thus this approach may be viewed as *single access.* Examples familiar to all of us, although they do not necessarily involve data communications, are radio and television broadcasts. Radio and television stations are source DTEs and radio receivers and television sets in homes are destination DTEs.

When multiple access is achieved by dynamic allocation, the capacity and time duration assignments are determined dynamically to meet changing demands of the individual DTEs. A set of built-in rules schedule the traffic to optimize channel utilization and minimize conflicts. There are three classes of multiple-access schemes: polling, random access, and reservation.

With the *polling* scheme, one DTE is designated as the primary station and all other DTEs are secondary stations. This scheme is most commonly used in the teleprocessing environment. The primary station is the host computer, concentrator, front-end processor, or cluster controller, and the secondary stations are the terminals. A typical polling control scheme is outlined below.

The primary station polls the secondary stations, one by one, to inquire whether there is a message to send. If a polled secondary station has nothing to send, it indicates that in its response to the primary station. When a polled secondary station has a message to send, it responds positively by sending one complete message or a segment of the message. After the secondary station has responded, either negatively or positively, the next secondary station is polled. When the response to the input message is ready for output, the appropriate secondary station is "addressed." If that secondary station is ready to receive and responds positively to the "addressing" inquiry, the response is sent to it.

The polling scheme described above is sometimes called *discrete polling.* Slight variations of this scheme are *hub-go-ahead polling* and *string polling,* in which after a station is polled, the next station on the polling list is polled immediately (before the first station responds to the poll). If the first station responds positively, the polling message of the second station is immediately aborted. Otherwise, polling continues. This accelerates the polling when some terminals do not have messages to send. With hub-go-ahead polling, the polling message is passed from one station to the next; with string polling, the polling message is always sent directly from the primary station.

See [ANSI 76, IBM 70, IBM 75] for the descriptions of several common polling procedures. See Chap. 3 and [CHOU 80, MART 70, DOLL 78] for general discussions on polling.

With the *random-access* scheme, the DTEs seek access via interface devices to the same channel or the same set of channels independently. Random-access schemes can be further classified into slotted and unslotted schemes. In the *slotted* case, time is divided into slots and a DTE can access the channel only at the beginning of a time slot. In the *unslotted* case, a DTE can access the channel at any time with no slot framing restrictions. The slotted channel approach can achieve much better efficiency if the slot size closely matches the packet or message size. When the transmission of a packet or a message from one DTE overlaps that of another, as can happen in either the slotted or the unslotted case, the packets or messages from both DTEs collide and are lost and must be retransmitted after random delays. (Random delays are used to lower the chances of further collision.)

The random-access scheme is well suited to systems with DTEs that have mainly "bursty"-type traffic. (*Bursty traffic* is defined here to be traffic where the time interval needed for each transmission is very short relative to the interval between transmissions.) The random-access scheme first received recognition through its application in the ALOHA system at the University of Hawaii. Hence the unslotted scheme has been termed *pure ALOHA* and the slotted scheme, *slotted ALOHA*.

The channel efficiency of these two basic random-access schemes is rather low (approximately 18% for pure ALOHA and 37% for slotted ALOHA). CSMA/CD (carrier-sense multiple access/collision detection) is a modified version of the basic random-access schemes that can substantially improve channel utilization, to better than 95%. In this case, before a packet is sent, the DTE would first sense whether any other packet is using the carrier. The packet is sent only if the channel is idle. Because of the propagation delay, packets may still collide with another one after they have been sent on to the carrier. To minimize this impact, the DTE monitors the carrier after it has sent a packet to see whether there is collision. If so, the transmission is aborted and the packet is retransmitted later. Another modified version of the slotted random-access scheme is the R-ALOHA (reservation ALOHA), in which time is divided into frames and each frame is further divided into slots. A DTE acquires a slot by the regular slotted ALOHA scheme. Once it is successful in acquiring the slot, it "owns" the same slot in subsequent frames until it releases the slot.

The *reservation* scheme may be viewed as an extension of the slotted random scheme. With the reservation scheme, a DTE must make a reservation for one or more slots or for a channel before initiating transmission. The control scheme can be centralized or distributed. In a centralized control scheme, DTEs make reservation requests to one specific central station. The dynamic assignment of channels to the DTEs is made by the central station. In a distributed control scheme, the responsibi-

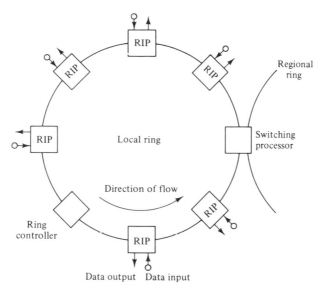

RIP = ring interface processor

Figure 1.1. Ring-shaped connection.

lity for accepting channel access requests and assigning channels is jointly held by all the DTEs that share a channel or channels. The reservation requests can be made by using TDMA or slotted ALOHA schemes in a portion of the channel specially set aside for such requests. The requests can also be made by random access or by piggyback on a data packet. The reservation schemes can achieve high efficiency in systems where there are a small number of stations with large volumes of (nonbursty) traffic and in systems where the ratio of propagation delay and packet transmission time is significant.

For more detailed discussion on random and reservation multiple-access schemes, see Chap. 4 and [LAM 79, TOBA 80, STAC 80, ROM 81, HANS 81].

1.2.2 Communication by Shifting or Relaying

A ring architecture has switch devices, called *ring interface processors* (RIPs), formed into one or several interlinked ring-shaped connections, as shown in Fig. 1.1. Each RIP is connected to the ring through a shift register bridging its input and output lines. A simplified schematic of a RIP is shown in Fig. 1.2. A DTE must connect to a RIP to communicate with others. Because of the physical appearance, this type of network is commonly called a *ring-switching, loop,* or *ring network.*

The traffic circulates around the ring as a continuous bit stream from one RIP to the next. If an input to a RIP is not addressed to one of its local DTEs, it is relayed immediately to the output through the shift register. It is in general not stored at the

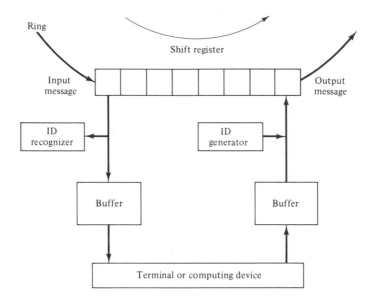

Figure 1.2. Simplified schematic of a basic RIP.

RIP, as contrasted to a store-and-forward architecture, in which every input message to a switch is always stored first before being output. If the input to a RIP does address a local DTE, it is relayed through the RIP. The RIP also relays outgoing messages from a local DTE to the ring.

The transmission mode can be synchronous or asynchronous. In the *synchronous* transmission mode, the bandwidth of the ring network is divided into equal-width time slots. The messages, or segments of the messages, are fitted into the slots for transmission. The synchronous mode is classified as *synchronous time-division multiplexing* (STDM) or *asynchronous time-division multiplexing* (ATDM). With STDM each slot is specifically dedicated to messages originating from a particular RIP. With ATDM the assignment of the slots to RIPs as they originate messages is determined dynamically. A common ATDM control scheme is to allow a RIP to transmit a message onto any time slot that is "empty" as it passes through the RIP. The same RIP clears the slot when it returns to the RIP.

In the *asynchronous* transmission mode, there are no fixed-sized time slots and the message sizes are not restricted. The asynchronous mode can use a fixed-length shift register or a variable-length shift register. With a fixed-length shift register, messages generated from different RIPs may overwrite each other if they are allowed to be forwarded onto the ring network simultaneously. A RIP may face the situation that, while it is relaying a message from a local DTE to its output line, a message in transit on the ring network arrives at the input side of the RIP and needs to be forwarded to the output. Thus a ring-switching network operated under the asynchronous mode with fixed-length shift registers either allows only one message to be outstanding at a time or faces the problem of overwriting. A method of control is to have a "token" circulating around the ring. A RIP must grab the token before it can transmit. It releases the token when its transmission is finished.

The use of a variable-length shift register allows more than one outstanding message but at the expense of additional hardware cost and complexity. If no locally generated messages are ready for output, a variable-length shift register functions like a fixed-length shift register that relays messages in transit on the ring from the input to the output side of the register. It functions like a storage register for a message in transit when a locally generated message is in the middle of transmission. The transient message is stored in the register until the transmission of the locally generated message is completed. Then the message is shifted to the output.

The schemes for controlling RIP access to the ring network can be roughly classified as being centralized or distributed. In a *centralized* control scheme, access is controlled by one or a small number of processors. In a *distributed* control system it is distributed to most, if not all, of the processors.

In practice, ring-switching networks have been in the form of single loops. Conceptually, however, one may consist of several interconnected loops or rings and form two or more hierarchical levels. When two or more ring networks are interconnected, the RIPs that connect the rings switch messages from one ring to the other. Local rings are connected to the regional rings and the regional rings are connected to a global ring. Two neighboring rings are interconnected by a switching processor. Messages are switched from one ring to another via the switch processor.

Descriptions of the different schemes can be found in [FARM 69, FARB 73, PIER 72, REAM 75, LIU 79]. A more detailed survey of ring-switching schemes can be found in [LIU 78]; some specific ring network examples are discussed in Chap. 13. A discussion of ring network's attributes can be found in [SALT 81].

1.2.3 Communication by Switching

In a switching architecture, each pair of communicating stations does not need to be directly connected. (A *communicating station* is the communication device that connects a DTE to the transmission facilities.) Transmission of a message from one station to another may be made through intermediate stations. In general, each station is connected to several input links and several output links. An intermediate station puts each input message on the output link that is determined by the network routing strategy. The stations are called *switches* and are either *circuit* or *store-and-forward* switches. Store-and-forward switching is generally known as *packet* or *message switching*.

1.2.3.1 Store-and-Forward Switching (Packet and Message Switching)

In a store-and-forward communication network, several geographically distributed communication processors are linked together to form a backbone network, which acts as a common user service to terminals, computers, or other DTEs.

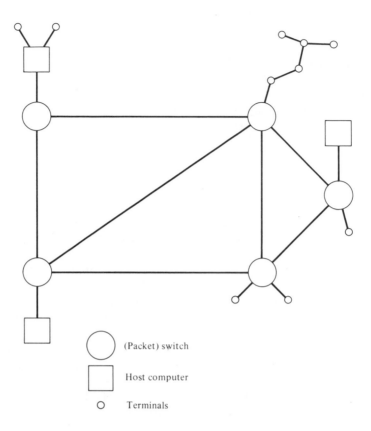

Figure 1.3. Mesh-shaped network.

DTEs requiring communications must first obtain access at a store-and-forward communication processor or switch. Messages are then sent through the network by the switches.

The topological structure of a general store-and-forward architecture is usually a mesh-shaped network, as shown in Fig. 1.3. Messages are routed from their source switches to their destinations along a communication path that can have other intermediate switches. The source switch, with respect to a message, is the one that is connected to the DTE that generates the message. At each of the switches along the path, an input message is first completely received and stored in the memory. Then, based on a routing table stored in the switch, it is routed or forwarded to the next switch on the path.

The basic conceptual difference between message switching and packet switching is that, in a *packet-switching* network, any message longer than a specified size is subdivided into segments not longer than the specified size before being transmitted. The message is reassembled at the destination. The segments are also called frames, blocks, or packets. The size of a full packet varies in different systems but is commonly

8

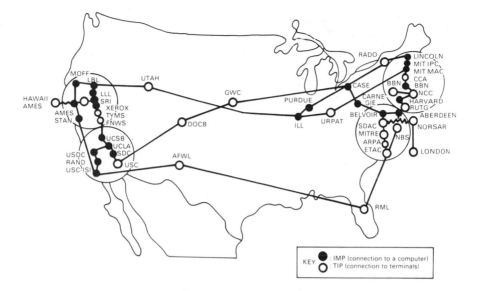

Figure 1.4. ARPANET.

128 or 256 characters. Packets less than full size can be transmitted. Small traffic units for packet switching give additional flexibility in design. The routing tables that determine the transmission path of a packet can be dynamically controlled based on traffic conditions instead of being preassigned. The packets can be stored in the main memory of the switches.

Message switching can be viewed as a special case of packet switching in which the segment size is as long as the longest possible message. Because of its message lengths and its operating environment, a conventional message-switching system uses a predetermined path, stores the messages in secondary memory devices (instead of main memory), and keeps a detailed journal of the messages. Only packet switching is considered in the remainder of this section.

Each switch in the network functions as a "local" network manager, deriving its management information from the network. To send a message, the source DTE precedes the text of its message with an address and delivers it to its local switch; this (mini)computer determines the best route, provides error control, and notifies the sender of message receipt. When a message is ready for transmission, the source DTE or its local switch divides the message into a set of one or more packets, each with appropriate header information. Each packet makes its way independently through the network to the destination switch or DTE, where the packets are reassembled. The best known packet-switching network is the ARPANET [DCA 78]. Fig. 1.4 shows its configuration. Several other well-known ones are GTE Telenet [ROBE 75], Tymnet [KOPF 77], DATAPAC [MCGI 78], Transpac [DANE 76], EPSS [HIGG 78], and Euronet [DAVI 78]. These and other operating packet/message networks are discussed in Chap. 14.

Not all packet-switching networks are the same or even react similarly under the same traffic environment. The elements that have the strongest impact on traffic environment and performance are the communication services provided, the flow/congestion control strategies, and the routing methodologies used in the network.

The four basic communication services provided by a packet-switching network are datagram, basic virtual channel, normal virtual channel, and circuit switching. With *datagram* service, the network picks up packets generated by source terminals or computers and delivers them to the destination terminals or computers on a packet-by-packet basis. Datagram service does not always guarantee the delivery of the packets, however. Neither does it always assure the correctness of any delivery. And the packets are not necessarily delivered in the same sequence as they were generated. Packets belonging to different messages but with the same destination may be delivered intermixed.

With a *basic virtual* circuit, the delivery and correctness of the packets are not guaranteed, but packets belonging to different messages are not intermixed at the destination. With a *normal virtual* channel, the network is responsible for delivering correctly sequenced packets at the destination. The network might break up a long message received from an originating user into packets but will reassemble them into the message before delivering it to the destination user. With *circuit-switching* service, a slot of bandwidth is dedicated on every link of a fixed path from the source switch to the destination. In this way, packet switching logically acts as circuit switching [FORG 77].

The flow/congestion control procedure of a communication network controls the rate at which messages are input to the network and the switches. It is responsible for avoiding the congestion that can occur from too many DTEs generating too much traffic to compete for limited resources, such as line capacities and buffers. Messages are usually not accepted by the network or the switches unless appropriate resources have been assigned to the DTE before its messages enter the network. Resources include buffers at the source and destination switches and a logical channel number between the source–destination switch pair. Resources required between the source–destination pair include store-and-forward buffers at the intermediate switches. For more information on flow/congestion control, refer to [CHOU 76B, SCHW 79, GERL 80, RUDI 79, GERL 82].

The routing strategy is a set of rules within all packet switches that determines when and through what intermediate switches a packet should be transmitted to minimize delays and optimize resource utilization. Routing strategies are classified as: deterministic, dynamic (or adaptive), or pipeline routing. With deterministic routing, the routing table that determines the output line on which input should be transmitted is preassigned and does not ordinarily vary with traffic conditions. In some cases, the routing table only provides one path between any pair of switches. In other cases, a secondary path is also provided. It is used when there is a failure or traffic congestion on the primary path.

With dynamic routing, the routing tables are periodically updated according to the traffic conditions. Under the virtual channel service, a combination of the dynamic and deterministic routing strategies may be used. A dynamic strategy is used to determine a path at the time the channel is initially set up. Afterwards, the packets flowing through the virtual channel are sent through this predetermined path.

With pipeline routing, more than one disjoint path can be used to simultaneously transmit the packets in a message in order to achieve a wider bandwidth and, therefore, faster message transmission. Although conceptually possible, no network has implemented pipeline routing. For more information on routing, refer to [MCQU 77, CHOU 79, MCQU 79, RUDI 79, MCQU 80, SCHW 80A, SCHW 80B, ROSE 80, ROSE 81, CHOU 81A, CHOU 81B].

When the concept of packet switching was first introduced, dynamic routing was viewed as one of its best features. However, few operational or planned networks use the pure dynamic routing scheme. (Two exceptions are the ARPANET and the planned AUTODIN II; refer to Chap. 14.)

A final comment is needed on the term "packet switching." Since in a broad sense any traffic unit, block, message, or character in the data communication environment can be viewed as a packet, the term "packet network" or even "packet-switching network" has been used loosely by many to encompass a large class of data/computer communication networks, including those using multiple-access or ring-switching techniques.

1.2.3.2 Circuit Switching

Note that in the store-and-forward switching environment when the source–destination path consists of more than one hop, the information unit (message or packet) is transmitted one hop at a time. The information unit is transmitted from the source switch to the first intermediate switch when a line from the source to this intermediate switch is available for transmission. It is transmitted whether other switches and lines on the path are busy or not. No other switch or line on the path is reserved for, or even aware of the existence of, this information unit. When the information reaches the intermediate switch, the line is immediately released. At this switch, the information seeks access to the line leading to the next switch on the path to the destination. It waits if that line is not immediately available.

In the circuit-switching environment, on the other hand, the whole path must be available and allocated between the source–destination pair before the transmission can be started. As long as the user does not release the path, the path is continuously dedicated and no other messages can use it whether it is busy with transmissions or not. (In the case where there are several circuits or channels of any hop on the path, one of the circuits or channels is dedicated instead of all of them.) The switches along the path do not intervene; information passing through them does not stop and is not stored.

The circuit-switching approach requires more time to set up a source–destination connection because every line on the path must be free before a connection can be made. It uses more network resources because the complete path must be reserved before the transmission begins, and because part or all of the path is dedicated even if there is no transmission. However, once a connection is made, no wait is required for the availability of a path each time there is information to send. Another advantage is that communication control overhead traffic is less.

If large volumes of information are to be transmitted in continuous streams, inefficient use of network resources during initial connections is relatively insignificant. Such traffic has no idle time during transmission to waste the network resource. With packet switching, the total overhead from control traffic can be substantial, and the accumulated waiting time for access to the lines can be very large. So for continuous and large streams of traffic, circuit switching may be better.

If the traffic is short and sporadic, the overhead involved in setting up a connection can be much greater than the overhead involved in controlling a packet. The additional delay along the path is less than the connection delay. So for short and sporadic traffic, packet switching may be better.

Note that, with circuit switching, there is no code, format, speed, or protocol conversion, and no intermediate device can intercept or alter the content of messages between the end users. Because of this transparent nature, a user does not need to be aware of or concerned about the existence of such a network.

For discussions on circuit switching, refer to [JOEL 79, FOLT 80].

1.3   Host-Computer-Oriented, Centrally Controlled Networks

In most switching networks, ring networks, random-access, or reservation multiple-access networks, the communication control responsibilities are spread equally among the communication devices or switches forming the networks. Thus these networks have been commonly viewed as networks with distributed control. However, most data communication networks are centrally controlled. The switching and communication functions are centrally controlled by a computer complex, which may consist of one or more computers and one or more front-end processors (FEPs). Part of the central functions may be delegated to remote processors or concentrators, or to intelligent DTEs. However, in the overall control procedures, these devices are usually subservient to the central site. Thus these types of networks may also be termed *host-oriented networks*.

The most common network architectures under this environment are summarized below.

Nonhierarchical

In the nonhierarchical case, DTEs are physically or logically directly connected to and controlled by a host computer or its FEP. (No concentrator-type devices are in the network; but there can be multiplexers, which are logically transparent. See Chap. 8 and [CHOU 76A].)

1. *Point-to-point (or star) connections.* The DTEs are connected directly, or through a multiplexer or FEP, to the host computer by direct dial-up or dedicated point-to-point connections as shown in Fig. 1.5. In essence, this is the single-access approach described in Sec. 1.2.

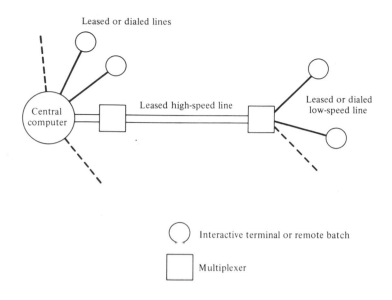

Figure 1.5. Point-to-point connections.

2. *Multipoint connections.* The DTEs are connected to the host computer directly or through a multiplexer or FEP by shared lines. These lines are usually formed into treelike structures, or, in some cases, into ring-shaped structures. A polling technique is used most commonly for resolving the multiple-access control problem.

Hierarchical

In a hierarchical architecture, DTEs are connected point to point or multipoint to concentrators, which are connected point to point or multipoint to the host computer or FEP. The terminals are controlled by the concentrators, which are in turn controlled by the host computer. This hierarchy of control gives the architecture its name. The connection linking the DTEs to the concentrators is the local access network, and the connection linking the concentrators to the host computers and FEPs is the backbone network. These connections are shown in Fig. 1.6. In a broad sense, when terminal control units (TCUs) are used and hardwired to "dumb" DTEs, the TCUs can be viewed as an additional layer in the hierarchy. Such a network architecture is the one most commonly used for distributed processing.

Fig. 1.7 represents the most general communication path between DTEs and a host computer. The path has the following sequence: DTE, to TCU, to multiplexer, to concentrator, to front-end processor, to host computer. The message flow on this path consists of the following steps:

13

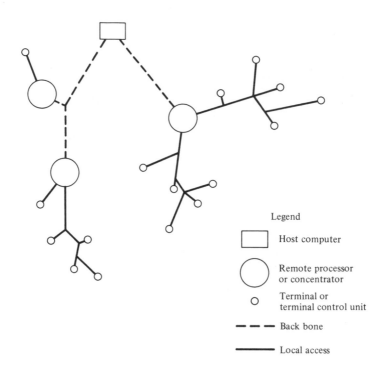

Legend

☐ Host computer

◯ Remote processor or concentrator

○ Terminal or terminal control unit

– – – Back bone

——— Local access

Figure 1.6. Tree-shaped hierarchically controlled data communication network architecture.

1. The input message is transmitted from the DTE to its TCU and is queued until it reaches the head of the queue.
2. The TCU is polled and "ACK" is returned. ("ACK" is a control message sent by the TCU to indicate that it has a message to send.)
3. The input message is transmitted from the TCU to the concentrator.
4. The concentrator processes the message.
5. The input message is queued and transmitted from the concentrator through the FEP to the host computer.
6. The input message is stored at the buffer staging area of the host computer while waiting to be processed.
7. The message is processed.
8. The reply is transmitted to the FEP and stored in the buffer to wait for transmission.
9. The reply is transmitted to the concentrator.
10. The reply is stored in a buffer at the concentrator.
11. The reply is processed by the concentrator.
12. The concentrator "addresses" the appropriate TCU.
13. The reply is transmitted from the concentrator to the TCU.
14. The reply is transmitted from the TCU to the DTE.

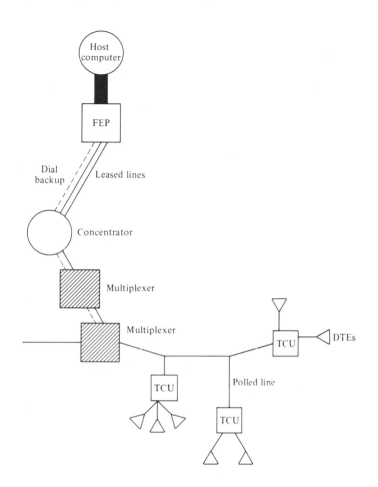

Figure 1.7. General communication path in a hierarchical network.

It can be observed from the descriptions above that, in general, a unique communication path exists between a DTE and its host computer. (However, there can be dial-up lines for backup when dedicated lines fail. Also, there can be parallel lines between two points, such as between the FEP and concentrator, for higher line throughout and better reliability. In this case, a message can be sent through any of the parallel lines.)

When concentrators are used, they perform simple store-and-forward switching functions. They pass messages between the host computer and the DTEs. The switching functions are a necessary consequence of concentration and are not switching in the full sense. Minicomputers used as concentrators and TCUs are quite underutilized. In some networks they have been used for local processing, local data-base accessing, or local switching. In other cases, residual capacities of remote processors are used for concentration. Sometimes such processing networks have been labeled "distributed," but in reality network control is centralized and host-

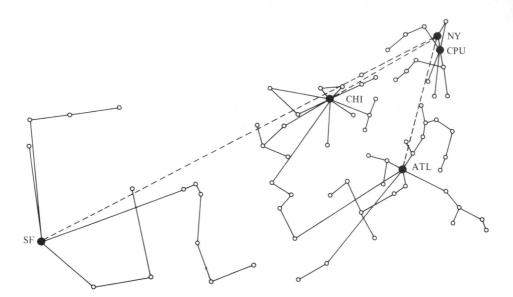

Figure 1.8. NASDAQ network.

computer oriented. An operating network of this type is the NASDAQ network (National Association of Security Dealers Automated Quotation). shown in Fig. 1.8.

Networks under IBM's SNA (System Network Architecture) are of this nature [CYPS 78].

1.4 Three Objectives: Three Networking Strategies

The basic objective of any data/computer communication network is to transport data from one location to another. But for some networks, the transportation of data is "the" objective, whereas for others it is a means to achieve another objective. *Common (shared)-user* switching networks are designed for transporting data. *Tele-processing* networks are designed to meet application needs. The common user switching networks may be classified as transporters of data between locations with a wide geographic distribution or between locations within limited distances. The term "teleprocessing" is used here in a broad sense to mean the ability of a computer system to collect/process remotely generated messages and requests, and to distribute messages and responses to the remote terminal devices. Thus applications such as point-of-sale and meter monitoring are all considered as teleprocessing. Note that the handling of transactions generated at remote points and the monitoring and reading of remote meters are the goals. Communication networks are a means of achieving the goals.

The physical elements that transport data are the switches and the transmission facilities. The cost of switches is in general independent of distance. Transmission facility costs are in general distance dependent. Thus for networks transporting data among locations within limited distances, the number of switches should be kept to a minimum of one or none; the capacity and number of transmission facilities is of less concern. For networks transporting data among geographically distributed locations, switches are used to economize the costs of the transmission facilities. Different traffic and application environments result in different numbers of switches being needed to minimize the total costs of switches and transmission facilities while still satisfying certain performance requirements. For teleprocessing networks, switches are usually not needed. Multiplexers, concentrators, modem sharing units, and so on, may be used to lower the costs of transmission facilities. (See [CHOU 76A] and Chap. 8. See also [SCHO 81, VISV 81].)

Teleprocessing

In a teleprocessing environment, all remote stations exhibit similar characteristics, have little or no processing and communication control capabilities, and communicate mainly with a single, or a few, computer sites. As such, it is natural that the main communication control function resides in the central computer site. The centrally controlled network described in Sec. 1.3 is most commonly used. Under limited circumstances, any of the network architectures described in Sec. 1.2 may also be used. For examples of such networks, refer to Chap. 14.

Local or Limited-Distance Networks

The objective of various local networks is to provide a data transport facility in a limited geographical area, most commonly within a building or a building complex. Data, telephone, FAX, and video DTEs can all be connected to such networks. All of the multiple-access strategies in Sec. 1.2.1 and the ring-switching strategies in Sec. 1.2.2 may be used to construct such networks. Other schemes discussed in Secs. 1.2 and 1.3 may also be used. However, for limited-distance environments, a host-oriented system is likely to be nonhierarchical (no concentrators); a switching network (message, packet, circuit) is likely to consist of only one switch. The architectures likely to be used in a limited-distance local network are centralized, single-channel multiple access, or ring. When multiple-access schemes or ring-switching schemes are used, the transmission facilities used will probably be of high speed: coaxial cable, CATV, optical fibers, radio links, microwave systems, laser, infrared, or simply twisted pairs of wires.

Some examples of local networks are: Ethernet [BOGG 76], which uses a contention multiple-access scheme called carrier-sense-multiple access/collision detection, and is intended to be used in the office information network environment; DCS (Distributed Computing System) [FARB 73], which uses a "token" ring-switching scheme and was originally designed for communications between minicomputers; and PRNET (Packet Radio Network) [KAHN 78], which uses the slotted Aloha multiple-access scheme to access a radio channel and covers a much broader geographical area than Ethernet or DCS. Because of their geographically limited nature, these networks generally serve a restricted community of common interest, not the general public. Further discussion on local networks and example networks can be found in Chaps. 13 and [FREE 79, MEIS 79, COTT 79, RAWS 79, HOPK 79,

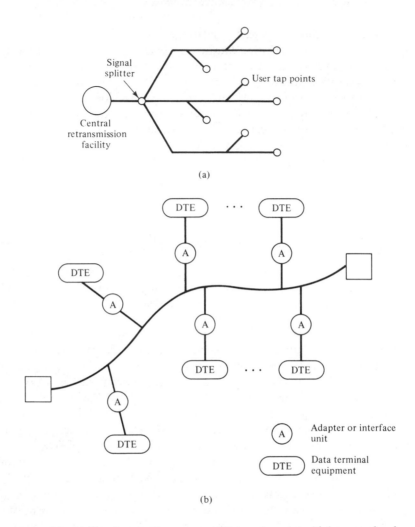

(a)

(b)

Figure 1.9. (a) Local network structure; (b) tree-shaped multiple-access local network.

LUDE 81, FREE 82, WILK 80, CRAV 81, BRAU 81]. Fig. 1.9 shows two typical configurations of a local network, and Fig. 1.10 shows a local network using optical fibers with a star coupler. Fig. 1.11 represents an application of the local network, an office of the future. Table 1.1 lists the network architecture alternatives. [NILS 80] has a discussion on a hierarchical packet radio architecture concept. [LUDE 81] describes a single switch, called DATAKIT, centrally controlled, local network.

Common-User Switching Networks for Geographically Distributed Locations

These networks serve as data communication "common carriers" and cover wide geographical areas. Through such networks, terminals at different locations may

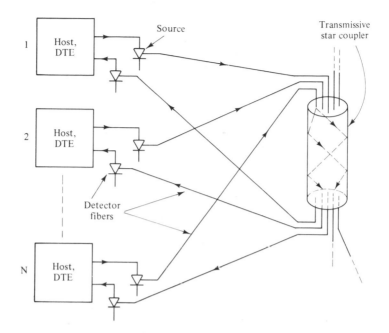

Figure 1.10. Fiber optic network. (From [RAWS 79]; with permission).

communicate with each other, as for electronic mail; terminals may access computers located at different locations, as in the time-sharing environment; dispersed computers may interface with each other, as for resource and load sharing; and terminals may access remote data bases, such as Vidcotex-type network services [BALL 80, MILL 81]. Even under the centralized teleprocessing environment, the messages between the terminals and the host computer can be transported via a common carrier type of network instead of a dedicated private network.

Terrestrial, satellite, or a combination of the two facilities may be used in the network. When terrestrial facilities are used, switching techniques (described in Sect. 1.2.3) are commonly used. If a satellite network is used, either a switching or a multiple-access scheme may be used. Some networks, such as GTE Telenet and Tymnet, serve the general public and may be viewed as public data networks; others, such as ARPANET and AUTODIN II, serve a limited community with common interests and may be viewed as private "public" networks.

For examples of such networks, refer to Chap. 14.

1.5 Taxonomy

Physical Structures

There are four basic physical structures: star, tree, loop, and mesh. The physical appearance is a *star* when each of the secondary stations is connected to the primary

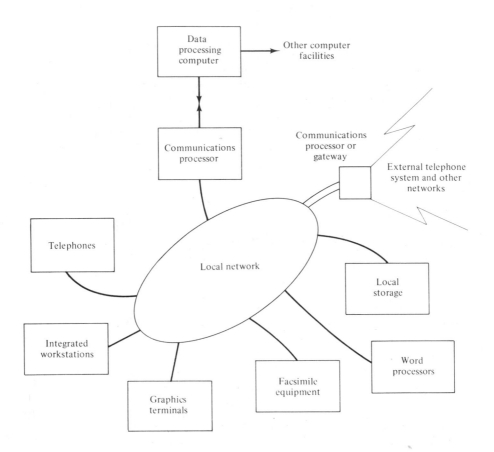

Figure 1.11. Model for the office of the future.

station via a separate link. For the case of multiple access, the stations that access the same channel are commonly linked in a *tree*-shaped form. (Note that the formation of a string of such stations is called a linear tree and is a special case.) Sometimes, the station links for multiple access can be formed into the shape of a *loop*. Ring-switching networks, of course, have the physical shape of loops. The switching networks—packet, message, or circuit—are usually *mesh*-shaped.

Although networks employing certain communication principles usually follow the fixed physical patterns just mentioned, the physical appearance and communication techniques employed in the networks are not in one-to-one correspondence. The possibility of a loop-shaped multiple-access network has already been noted. Other examples are that the physical appearance of a switching network can be in the shape of a tree or a loop, and interconnected rings can have the appearance of the meshes. Thus to classify data/computer communication networks based purely on physical appearance, as some have done, is meaningless.

Networks are not restricted to the star, tree, loop, or mesh structure. A

Table 1.1. *Common Network Architecture Alternatives for Local Networks.*

Centrally Controlled

- Host oriented
- Single circuit switch (PABX)
- Single message switch

Multiple Access

- Static allocation: Channel division multiple access dedicated subchannel for sending;
      broadcast for receiving

- Dynamic allocation: Centralized control - one DTE accepts request from DTE's for and
      allocates subchannels

   Distributed control -

      Random access (i) slotted
                     (ii) unslotted

      Carrier Sense Multiple Access/Collision Detection (CSMA/CD)

      Reservation (i) contention reservation
                  (ii) TDMA reservation

Ring Switching or Relaying (Conveyer Belt)

- Token
- Empty slot
- Buffering

composite network may have the appearance of a combination of more than one of the basic structures. For example, a tree-shaped multipoint polled network may terminate at a packet switch that is a part of a mesh-shaped packet-switching network.

Multiplexing Configurations

Multiplexing is a technique that allows one channel to be shared by different users. This is achieved by channel bandwidth sharing, in which different users are assigned different frequency subchannels and may access these subchannels simultaneously; or by time bandwidth sharing, in which different users must alternate their use of the channel or subchannel over time. A combination of the two strategies is also possible. Clearly, then, all the control schemes described for multiple accessing and ring switching can be viewed as multiplexing. Even packet switching can be viewed as multiplexing, since packets from different messages may be interleaved on the same link.

In this section we are not interested in the multiplexing achieved by these communication control schemes. Instead, we are addressing the cases where several subchannels are derived from a channel for certain pairs of locations and these

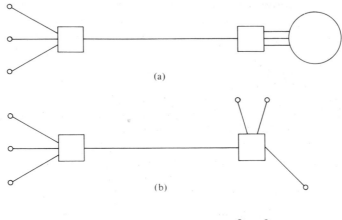

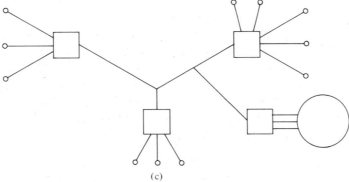

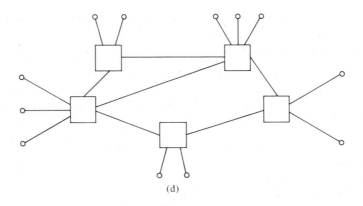

Figure 1.12. Four common multiplexing configurations: (a) fan-in or fan-out; (b) fan-in and fan-out; (c) multipoint; (d) distributed.

subchannels are viewed as parallel links between these pairs of locations. Thus the objective of this type of multiplexing is principally cost savings: paying the costs of one link, one pair of multiplexers, and one pair of high-speed modems to obtain the equivalence of several parallel links of lower speeds. This is cost effective only if extra hardware costs are less than the savings achievable from the transmission links.

To derive subchannels between a pair of locations, usually a multiplexer is placed at each site. The channel between the two multiplexers is high speed. Several low-speed lines are connected to each multiplexer on the side opposite the high-speed channel.

There are three types of multiplexing devices used in data/computer communication networks: frequency-division multiplexing (FDM), time-division multiplexing (TDM), and intelligent or statistical TDM (ITDM or STDM). With FDM, subchannels are derived by dividing the frequency bandwidth; with TDM, subchannels are derived by dividing time slots. In the FDM or TDM environment, each subchannel is dedicated to a separate low-speed input line. Since the chance that all these low-speed lines are busy transmitting is small, a larger number of the low-speed lines can share a smaller number of subchannels. The multiplexing function between the lines and the channels is ITDM or STDM. [VISV 81] For more detailed discussion on multiplexing devices, see [CHOU 76A] and Chap. 8.

There are four common multiplexing configurations: fan-in or fan-out, fan-in and fan-out, multipoint, and distributed. They are illustrated in Fig. 1.12. With *fan-in or fan-out*, the stations connected to one end of the multiplexer through the low-speed lines are not co-located with the multiplexer, whereas at the other end the multiplexer is co-located with the stations (such as the host computer). With *fan-in and fan-out*, stations at both ends are remotely located. With a *multipoint* configuration, several geographically dispersed multiplexers are connected on the same channel and each uses a different subset of subchannels. If some switching ability is built into the multiplexers, they can form a simple switching network and a *distributed* configuration. [SCHO 81]

Centralized and Distributed Control

The term *centralized network* is used customarily to mean a teleprocessing-type network. The term *distributed network* often refers to a packet-switching network. With the former, the control of communication is centralized; with the latter, the control is distributed to all switches. However, other network types can have centralized or distributed control. The circuit-switching, message-switching, and contention multiple-access networks can all be considered to have distributed control. Some control schemes of the reservation multiple-access and ring-switching types are distributed, and others are centralized.

Hierarchical and Hybrid Control

Because of the communication control scheme employed or the network size, some networks are organized hierarchically. In a centrally controlled network environment, the terminals are the lowest and the central computer site is the highest in the

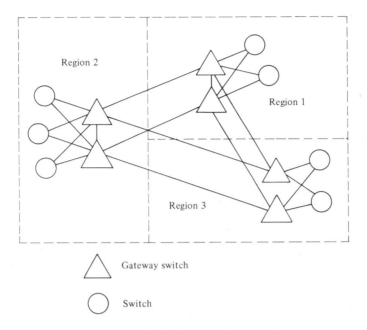

Region 2

Region 1

Region 3

△ Gateway switch

◯ Switch

Figure 1.13. Hierarchical packet-switching network.

communication control hierarchy. Just above the terminals in the hierarchy are the terminal control units (TCUs), if there are any, and above the TCUs are the remote concentrators (RCs), again if there are any.

When there are a large number of switches, the switches might be partitioned into regions. The regional networks are then interconnected through a global network. The switches in the global network consist of *gateway switches* from the regional networks. The communications between the regional and global networks are through gateway switches (called *tandem switches* by some). More than two levels of hierarchy are also possible. Fig. 1.13 is a packet-switching network with a hierarchy of two levels.

One possible way for geographically dispersed terminals and computers to communicate with each other is for those in geographical proximity to be connected into local networks using one of the direct-connection or shifting architectures; each of the local networks is then connected through a gateway-type device to a switch of a packet-switching network. This arrangement is a hybrid architecture in that two or more different communication architectures are used. The structure is also hierarchical. The local network is the lowest in the hierarchy and the packet-switching network is the highest. The gateway function may be housed completely in a separate gateway switch or may reside in a packet switch.

Another possible hybrid structure is to use a circuit-switching network as the backup for a packet- or message-switching network. When the lines do not have the capacities to handle the traffic, the packet/message switch dials up additional lines through a circuit-switching network. (Examples are DOD's AUTODIN I and AUTOVON, respectively a message- and a circuit-switching network.)

The portion of the network that is highest in the hierarchy is customarily called the *backbone network,* and each portion connecting the terminals is called a *local-access network.*

Integrated Switchng

Although the argument continues about whether packet switching outperforms circuit switching in all applications, it is generally agreed that each has its advantages and disadvantages. (Packet switching can give better line utilization and shorter delays for bursty-type traffic, and circuit switching is good for stream traffic.) The concept of integrating the two switching techniques into one network appears promising because they complement each other.

Two tactics are possible. One is to use separate transmission facilities for circuit and packet switching. Stations using packet switching and stations using circuit switching terminate at the same switches but are routed through different transmission facilities. The switches are a combination of a packet switch and a circuit switch. The second tactic is to use same facilities for both packet and circuit switching. Each line connecting the switches is multiplexed to two subchannels, one for circuit switching and the other for packet switching. The subchannels are further subdivided into slots. In the subchannel designated for the circuit switching, each of the slots corresponds to one circuit. The boundary between the two subchannels might vary depending on the amount of the traffic needing to be circuit switched. Chap. 16 gives a detailed discussion of the subject. See also [WEIN 80, COVI 75, MIYA 78, OCCH 77, KUMM 74, YU 80].

Internetworking

We have already mentioned that terminals on one local network may communicate with those on another by interconnecting with a packet-switching network. There can be also a need to interconnect packet-switching networks, possibly because the terminals and computers on one network need to access resources, terminals, and computers on another. Most packet-switching networks do not extend beyond a national boundary. So the need exists particularly for interconnecting the packet-switching networks to DTEs in different countries.

The interconnection of networks is not confined to the two situations described above. A local network within a building complex may be interconneted to another local network; or it may be connected to a regional network which may sprawl over the area of a city or a metropolitan area. The regional network may be connected to another local network, another regional network, or a backbone network, which may be a public data network extending to a much larger geographical area. Thus a DTE on one local network may talk to a remote DTE on another local network by sending messages through several intermediate networks.

The networks are interconnected through *adapters,* or *gateways.* There are two common strategies that may be used by the gateways to convert messages between

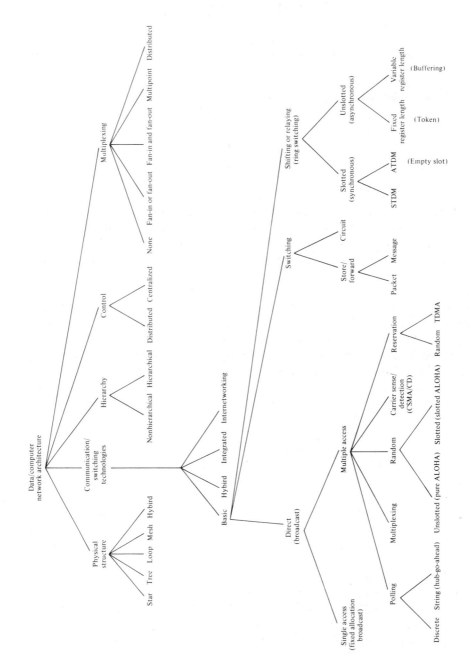

Figure 1.14. Taxonomy of data/computer networks.

two networks: mapping and bridging. With the *mapping* approach, the format of messages from one network is converted to that of another. For conversion it is necessary that the entities and functions of the two networks be in one-to-one correspondence. When a one-to-one mapping relation does not exist, the *bridging* approach may be used. In this case, a process that is able to communicate with the two communicating DTEs in the two networks is implemented in the gateway. The DTEs can then communicate through this process in the gateway.

For references on internetworking, see Chap. 15 and [SHOC 79, BOGG 80, POST 80A, CERF 80, POST 80B, ISO 80, EINE 81, UNSO 81, POST 81, SHOC 81, DEAT 81, RUTL 82].

Taxonomy Summary

Based on communication/switching principles, physical structures or appearance, multiplexing schemes, hierarchy, control, and other attributes discussed in this section, the taxonomy of data/computer communication network architectures can be summarized as shown in Fig. 1.14.

1.6 Elements of Computer Communication Networks

A computer communication network is composed of transmission facilities and communication hardware in addition to terminals and computers. There must also be a set of rules, implemented partly in software and partly in hardware or firmware, to ensure the orderly flow of traffic in the system and to utilize efficiently the resources of transmission facilities and communication hardware. So taken all together, a data/computer communication network can be viewed as consisting of three basic elements: transmission facilities, communication devices, and traffic management protocols. (Fed into the network is the traffic that is generated by terminals, computers, or other DTEs. A discussion of the traffic environment is given in Appendix 1.)

Transmission Facilities

Transmission facility is a general term used to mean any facility that carries data signals from one location to another. It can have one or a combination of transmission mediums, and can be provided by any of several groups of suppliers.

1. Media

    - Telephone plant facilities (analog, digital)
    - Satellite channels
    - Microwave facilities
    - Radio wave
    - Light wave (infrared, laser)
    - Cables (coaxial cables, optical fibers)
    - Wires

2. Suppliers

    • Common carriers (established telephone companies, primarily AT&T, its operating companies, and its affiliates)

    • Special common carriers [also called other common carriers (OCC)]

    • Satellite companies [e.g., American Satellite, Satellite Business Systems (SBS)]

    • Companies that provide specialized facilities and services, mainly leased ones [e.g., MIC Telecommunications, Southern Pacific Communications (SPC)]

    • Value-added common carriers
    Data signals are not only transmitted but are also processed. Thus additional services, or "values," are being added to the data, besides the transmission. They are mainly packet-switching-type networks (e.g., GTE Telenet, [ROBE 75], Tymnet [KOPF 77]).

    • CATV (Cable TV, Community Antenna TV)

    • Private networks

Technical discussions on the principles and properties of wideband facilities are given in Chaps. 5, 6 and 7.

Data Communication Devices

Data communication devices are used in data/computer communication systems to interface the data terminal equipment (DTE) with transmission facilities, to convert the DTE's signals to those recognizable by transmission facilities and vice versa, to reduce cost on transmission facilities, to relieve the load on the main computers by handling communication functions, to switch and control communication, or to monitor and diagnose the performance.

1. *Interfacing with transmission facilities:* modems, baseband modems, access controllers
2. *Saving communication costs:* multiplexers, concentrators
3. *Reducing processing load:* front-end processors, concentrators, terminal control units
4. *Switching and communication control:* ring switches, packet switches, message switches
5. *Diagnostic devices*

For more detailed discussion, see [CHOU 76A] and Chap. 8.

Control Procedures

In any communication system, especially in a data/computer communication system, it is essential to have a set of well-designed basic control procedures to ensure efficient, correct, and smooth transfer of information within the system. These procedures are usually implemented primarily in software, with a small fraction in hardware or firmware. Establishing control procedures may be viewed as a communication software problem. Control procedures are commonly called *protocols*. There is usually more than one set of protocols in a data/computer communication system: for example, line protocols, protocols between communicating host computers, terminal-computer protocols, and protocols between host computers and communication processors. The purposes of a protocol can be:

- To make the system convenient to use
- To use communication resources (lines, communication processors) in an efficient and orderly manner
- To control congestion and traffic flow
- To route and switch traffic
- To maintain message integrity (error detection, duplication detection, system component failure detection, error and failure recovery)

Discussion on protocol structures is given in Chap. 2, on internetworking protocols in Chap. 15, on data link control procedures in Chap. 3, and on multiple access procedures in Chap. 4. The framework that specifies the protocols is called *communication architecture*. Discussion of concepts of several popular communication architectures can be found in [IBM 81, DEC 80, LYON 80, SBS 81].

Acknowledgement

This work was supported by the National Science Foundation under Grant ENG-77-24110.

1

Appendix
Traffic Environment

The traffic environment created by each different application environment and set of operating requirements often exhibits unique characteristics. In order to determine the network design that can best match the traffic environment of the application, the characteristics of the traffic environment must be converted to a set of tangible and quantitative constraints and requirements, or parameters.

The process of quantifying the traffic environment is called the *traffic and requirement analysis*. Successful implementation of a data communication system depends to a great extent on the thoroughness of the data traffic analysis and the user requirement analysis.

Gathering traffic information is the most tedious part of planning. Traffic information should be collected from every user by means of current measurements and future projections. It can be almost impossible to measure and project traffic information accurately. It is often helpful if network planners and designers visit the users to assist them and to validate the information supplied by them.

A traffic environment can generally be specified by the following parameters: traffic characteristics, traffic volumes, number and geographic distributions of terminals and computers, distribution pattern of the traffic, and communication pattern.

Traffic Characteristics

Data traffic can be classified as: interactive traffic, real-time traffic, record transfer, and bulk transfer. *Interactive traffic* requires fast responses, generally a couple of seconds, but it can tolerate a large variance in response time. *Real-time traffic,* such as digitized voice, requires the variance of the response time to be small. For example, in the case of digitized voice, segments arriving at a destination with substantially different delays would result in unrecognizable noises. *Record transfer* messages are usually longer than interactive traffic message. It can tolerate longer delays than can interactive and real-time traffic, and can tolerate a large variance in response time. An example of such a message is an electronic mail message containing one or several screens of information displayed on a CRT. Response time in a couple of minutes is tolerable. *Bulk traffic* is for messages with large data volumes, such as file transfers, usually of the order of megabits. This type of traffic requires a wide bandwidth but can tolerate very long delays. If the messages consist of digital data, message integrity is important. If it is a digitized analog message, integrity is not important. Table 1.A.1 classifies the traffic types and lists their constraints.

Traffic Volume

Traffic volume is the amount of traffic to be generated per unit time at each location. The units can be in bits per second, kilobits per second, messages per hour,

Table 1.A.1. *Traffic Characteristics.*[a]

Minimum Constraints

Classification	Response Time Mean	Response Time Variance	Bandwidth	Message Integrity
Interactive	VS	S	S	I
Record	M	M	M	I
Batch	L	L	L	I
Real time	VS to M	VS	M to VL	NI/I

[a]VS, very short; S, short or small; M, medium; L, large; VL, very large; I, important; NI, not important.

mega-packets per year, and so on. The information on traffic volumes is usually given in terms of average arrival rates over certain time periods, such as over a business day or over a busy hour. Sometimes the distribution of the message interarrival time may also be provided. If not, the Poisson arrival pattern is usually assumed. A constant flow of high traffic between a pair of locations usually requires a network architecture that provides dedicated high-speed lines. On the other hand, a constant flow of low traffic or a sporadic flow of high traffic is more cost effective in network architectures that act like common carriers and make use of line sharing by all users of the network.

Number of DTEs

This is the number of computer sites, the number of terminal sites, and the numbers of computers and terminals at each site.

Geographic Distribution of DTEs

Terminals and computers of a computer communication system can be concentrated in a building complex or a locality, or can be dispersed over one or several states, over the continental United States, or across several countries. Within the geographic area that the terminals and computers span, they can be clustered at several localities or they can be distributed randomly. For locally concentrated systems, communication hardware costs dominate the system cost. In a widely dispersed system, line costs dominate.

Traffic Distribution Pattern

The traffic distribution pattern addresses the dependence of traffic volumes and characteristics on localities. It is closely related with traffic volume and the geographic distribution of terminals and computers. Certain locations might generate or receive substantially more traffic than other locations. There might be more traffic between locations near each other. Traffic generated by terminals in the same vicinity might have the same properties, such as the same response-time constraints, accessing the same files, and so on. Some systems have no such discernible patterns of traffic distribution.

Communication Pattern

In some applications, communication is necessary only between one or a few centralized locations and all other locations, for example, the credit card authorization systems. In other applications, communication is required between a large number or all of the location pairs. An example is the use of a computer network as a common carrier. For the former case, a centralized network is usually appropriate; for the latter case, the store-and-forward architecture of packet switching can be more cost effective under certain conditions.

REFERENCES

ANSI 76   "American National Standard Procedures for the Use of the Common Control Character of ASCII in Specified Communication Links," ANSI X3.28, 1976.

BALL 80   Ball, A. J. S., G. V. Bochmann, and J. Gecsei, "Videotex Networks," *Computer*, Vol. 13, No. 12, December 1980.

BARB 78   Barber, D. L. A., "The EIN Project: The End of the Beginning," *Proc. 4th Int. Conf. Comput. Commun.*, Kyoto, September 1978, pp. 33–38.

BOGG 76   Boggs, D. R., and R. M. Metcalfe, "Ethernet: Distributed Packet Switching for Local Communication Networks," *Commun. ACM*, Vol. 19, No. 7, 1976.

BOGG 80   Boggs, D. R., J. F. Shoch, E. A. Taft, and R. M. Metcalfe, "Pup: An Internetwork Architecture," *IEEE Trans. Commun.*, Vol. COM-28, No. 4, 1980, pp. 612–624.

BRAU 81   Braun, A. R., "Local Area Networks for the Automated Office — A Survey," *Proc. 7th Data Commun. Symp.*, October 1981.

CERF 80   Cerf, V. G., "Protocols for Interconnected Packet Networks," *Comput. Commun. Rev.*, Vol. 10, No. 4, October 1980, pp. 10–11.

CHOU 76A   Chou, W., and P. McGregor, "Computer Communications: Network Devices and Functions," *Comput. Commun. Rev.*, January 1976.

CHOU 76B   Chou, W., and M. Gerla, "A Unified Flow and Congestion Control Model for Packet Networks," *Proc. 3rd Int. Conf. Comput. Commun.*, August 1976.

CHOU 79   Chou, W., "Comparative Evaluation of Deterministic and Adaptive Routing," *Proc. Flow Control Comput. Networks*, Paris, February 1979, North-Holland, Amsterdam.

CHOU 80   Chou, W., and R. E. King, "Comparative Evaluation of Data Link Control Procedures under Multipoint Environment," *Proc. 1980 Symp. Appl. Trends: Comput. Network Protocols*, National Bureau of Standards, May 1980.

CHOU 81A   Chou, W., A. W. Bragg, and A. A. Nilsson, "The Need for Adaptive Routing in the Chaotic and Unbalanced Traffic Environment," *IEEE Trans. Commun.*, April 1981.

CHOU 81B   Chou, W., A. A. Nilsson, and A. W. Bragg, "The Need for Adaptive Routing in a Network Spanning Several Time Zones," *Proc. National Telecommun. Conf.*, November 29-December 3, 1981, New Orleans.

COTT 79   Cotton, I. W., "Technologies for Local Area Computer Networks," *Proc. Local Area Commun. Network Symp.*, May 1979, pp. 25–45.

COVI 75   Coviello, G., and P. A. Vena, "Integration of Circuit/Packet Switching in a SENET (Slotted Envelope NETwork) Concept," *Conf. Rec. Natl. Telecommun. Conf.*, New Orleans, December 1975, pp. 42-12 to 42-17.

CRAV 81   Cravis, H., "Local Networks for the 1980s," *Datamation*, Vol. 27, No. 3, March 1981.

CYPS 78   Cypser, R. J., *Communications Architecture For Distributed Systems*, Addison-Wesley, Reading, Mass., 1978.

DANE 76   Danet, A., R. Despres, A. LeRest, G. Pichon, and S. Ritzenthaler, "The French Public Packet Switching Service: The TRANSPAC Network," *Proc. 3rd Int. Conf. Comput. Commun.*, Toronto, August 1976, pp. 251–260.

DAVI 78   Davies, G. W. P., J. Y. Gresser, P. T. F. Kelly, and J. R. Thomas, "The EURONET Telecommunication and Information Network," *Proc. 4th Int. Conf. Comput. Commun.*, Kyoto, September 1978, pp. 189–194.

DCA 78   Defense Communications Agency, "ARPANET Information Brochure," revised March 1978.

DEAT 81   Deaton, G. A., Jr., and A. S. Barclay, "IBM Gives U.S. Users Ticket to X.25 Networks," *Data Commun.*, September 1981, pp. 83–93.

DEC 80   *Introduction to DECnet*, Digital Equipment Corporation, 1980.

DOLL 78   Doll, D. R., *Data Communications: Facilities, Networks, and Systems Design*, Wiley, New York, 1978.

EINE 81   Einert, D., and G. Glas, "Snatch Opens Manufacturers' Networks Through Gateways," *Proc. 7th Data Commun. Symp.*, October 1981.

FARB 73   Farber, D. J., J. Feldman, and F. R. Heinrich, "The Distributed Computing System," *Digest of Papers, COMPCON '73*, February 1973.

FARM 69   Farmer, W. D., and E. E. Newhall, "An Experimental Distributed Switching System to Handle Bursty Computer Traffic," *Proc. 1969 ACM Conf.*

FOLT 80   Folts, H. C., "Procedures for Circuit-Switched Service in Synchronous Public Data Networks," *IEEE Trans. Commun.*, Vol. COM-28, No. 4, 1980, pp. 489–496.

FORG 77   Forgie, J. W., and A. G. Nemeth, "An Efficient Packetized Voice/Data Network Using Statistical Flow Control," *ICC '77*, June 1977, pp. 38.2.44 to 38.2.48.

FREE 79   Freeman, H. A., and K. J. Thurber, "Issues in Local Computer Networks," *ICC '79*, June 1979, pp. 20.3.1 to 20.3.5.

GERL 80   Gerla, M., and L. Kleinrock, "Flow Control: A Comparative Survey," *IEEE Trans. Commun.*, Vol. COM-28, 1980, pp. 553–574.

HIGG 78   Higginson, P. L., and Z. Z. Fisher, "Experiences with the Initial EPSS Service," *Proc. Eurocomp.*, May 1978, pp. 581–600.

HOPK 79   Hopkins, G. T., "Multimode Communications on the MITRENET," *Proc. Local Area Commun. Network Symp.*, May 1979, pp. 169–177.

IBM 70   IBM Corp., *General Information — Binary Synchronous Communications*, GA27-3004-2, 1970.

IBM 75   IBM Corp., *IBM Synchronous Data Link Control — General Information*, GA27-3093-1, 1975.

IBM 81   *Systems Network Architecture: Concepts and Products*, IBM GC30-3072-0, January 1981.

ISO 80   *Open Systems Interconnection — Basic Reference Model*, ISO/TC97/SC16, December 3, 1980.

JOEL 79   Joel, A. E., Jr., "Circuit Switching: Unique Architecture and Applications,"
              Computer, June 1979, pp. 10–22.

KAHN 78   Kahn, R. E., S. A. Gronemeyer, J. Bruchfiel, and R. Kunzelman, "Advances
              in Packet Radio Technology," *Proc. of the IEEE, Special Issue on Packet
              Commun. Networks*, Vol. 66, No. 11, November 1978, pp. 146–149.

KOPF 77   Kopf, J. "TYMNET as a Multiplexed Packet Network," *Proc. AFIPS Natl.
              Comput. Conf.*, 1977, pp. 609–613.

KUMM 74   Kummerle, K., "Multiplexer Performance for Integrated Line- and Packet-
              Switched Traffic," *ICCC '74*, Stockholm, 1974.

LAM 79   Lam, S. S., "Satellite Packet Communication — Multiple Access Protocols
              and Performance," *IEEE Trans. Commun.*, Vol. COM-27, No. 10, 1979,
              pp. 1456–1466.

LIU 78   Liu, M. T., "Distributed Loop Computer Networks," *Advances in Compu-
              ters*, Vol. 17, Academic Press, New York, 1978, pp. 163–221.

LIU 79   Liu M. T., R. Pardo, D. Tsay, J. J. Wolf, B. W. Weide and C. P. Chou,
              "System Design of the Distributed Double-Loop Computer Network
              (DDLCN)," *Proc. First Int. Conf. Distributed Comput. Syst.*, October 1979.

LUDE 81   Luderer, G. W. R., H. Che, and W. T. Marshall, "A Virtual Circuit Switch as
              the Basis for Distributed Systems," *Proc. 7th Data Commun. Symp.*,
              October 1981.

LYON 80   Lyons, R. E., "A Total AUTODIN System Architecture," *IEEE Trans.
              Commun.*, Vol. COM-28, No. 9, September 1980.

MART 70   Martin, J., *Teleprocessing Network Organization*, Prentice-Hall, Englewood
              Cliffs, N.J., 1970.

MCGI 78   McGibbon, C. I., H. Gibbs, and S. C. K. Young, "DATAPAC — Initial
              Experiences with a Commercial Packet Network," *Proc. 4th Int. Conf.
              Comput. Commun.*, Kyoto, September 1978, pp. 103–108.

MCQU 74   McQuillan, J. M., "Adaptive Routing Algorithms for Distributed Networks,"
              Bolt, Beranek and Newman, Inc., Rep. No. 2831, May 1974.

MCQU 77   McQuillan, J. M., "Routing Algorithms for Computer Networks — A Sur-
              vey," *Proc. 1977 Natl. Telecommun. Conf.*, December 1977.

MCQU 79   McQuillan, J. M., I. Richer, and E. Rosen, "An Overview of the New Routing
              Algorithm for the ARPANET," *Proc. 6th Data Commun. Symp.*,
              November 1979.

MCQU 80   McQuillan, J. M., I. Richer, and E. Rosen, "The New Routing Algorithm for
              the ARPANET," *IEEE Trans. Commun.*, Vol. COM-28, 1980, pp. 711–719.

MEIS 79   Meisner, N. B. (Ed.), *Proc. MITRE/NBS Local Area Commun. Network
              Symp.*, May 1979.

MILL 81   Miller, D., "Where is Videotex Going?," *Data Commun.*, September 1981,
              pp. 97–105.

MIYA 78   Miyahara, H., and T. Hasegawa, "Integrated Switching with Variable Frame
              and Packet," *Conf. Rec. Int. Commun. Conf.*, Toronto, June 1978, pp. 20.3.1
              to 20.3.5.

NILS 80   Nilsson, A., W. Chou, and C. Graff, "A Packet Radio Communication
              Architecture in a Mixed Traffic and Dynamic Environment," *Proc. 1980
              Comput. Networking Symp.*, December 1980.

OCCH 77   Occhiogrosso, B., I. Gitman, W. Hsieh, and H. Frank, "Performance Analysis of Integrated Switching Communications Systems," *Conf. Rec. Natl. Telecommun. Conf.*, Los Angeles, December 1977, pp. 12.4.1 to 12.4.13.

PIER 72   Pierce, J. R., "How Far Can Data Loops Go?" *IEEE Trans. Commun.*, June 1972.

POST 80A   Postel, J. B., "Internetwork Protocol Approaches," *IEEE Trans. Commun.*, Vol. COM-28, No. 4, 1980, pp. 604–611.

POST 80B   Postel, J. B. (ed.), "DOD Standard Internet Protocol," Defense Advanced Research Projects Agency, Information Processing Techniques Office, RFC 760, IEN 128, January 1980.

POST 81   Postel, J. B., C. A. Sunshine, and D. Cohen, "The ARPA Internet Protocol," *Comput. Networks*, July 1981, pp. 261–271.

RAWS 79   Rawson, E. G., "Application of Fiber Optics to Local Networks," *Proc. Local Area Commun. Network Symp.*, May 1979, pp. 155–168.

REAM 75   Reams, C. C., and M. T. Liu, "A Loop Network for Simultaneous Transmission of Variable Length Messages," *Proc. 2nd Annu. Symp. Comput. Architecture*, 1975.

ROBE 75   Roberts, L. G., "Telenet: Principles and Practice," *Proc. Eurocomp.*, 1975, pp. 315–329.

ROM 81   Rom, R. and F. A. Tobagi, "Message-Based Priority Functions in Local Multiaccess Communication Systems," *Comput. Networks*, July 1981, pp. 273–286.

ROSE 80   Rosen, E. C., "The Updating Protocol of ARPANET's New Routing Algorithm," *Comput. Networks*, February 1980.

ROSE 81   Rosen, E. C., "Vulnerabilities of Network Control Protocols: An Example," *Comput. Commun. Rev.*, Vol. 11, No. 3, July 1981, pp. 10–16.

RUDI 79   Rudin, H., and H. Mueller, "On Routing and Flow Control," *Proc. Flow Control Comput. Networks*, J. L. Grange and M. Gien, eds., IFIP, North-Holland, Amsterdam, 1979, pp. 241–255.

RUDI 80   Rudin, H. and H. Mueller, "Dynamic Routing and Flow Control," *IEEE Trans. Commun.*, Vol. COM-28, No. 7, July 1980.

SALT 81   Saltzer, J. H., D. D. Clark, and K. T. Pogran, "Why a Ring?," *Proc. 7th Data Commun. Symp.*, October 1981.

SCHO 81   Scholl, T. H., "The New Breed — Switching Muxes," *Data Commun.*, June 1981.

SCHW 79   Schwartz, M., and S. Saad, "Analysis of Congestion Control Techniques in Computer Communication Networks," *Proc. Flow Control Comput. Networks*, J. L. Grange and M. Gien, eds., IFIP, North-Holland, Amsterdam, 1979, pp. 113–130.

SCHW 80A   Schwartz, M., and T. E. Stern, "Routing Techniques Used in Computer Communication Networks," *IEEE Trans. Commun.*, Vol. COM-28, 1980, pp. 539–552.

SCHW 80B   Schwartz, M., "Routing and Flow Control in Data Networks," *Proc. NATO Advanced Study Inst., New Concepts Multi-user Commun.*, Norwich, U.K., August 4-16, 1980.

SHOC 79   Shoch, J. F., and L. Stewart, "Interconnecting Local Networks via the Packet

Radio Network," *Proc. 6th Data Commun. Symp.*, November 1979, pp. 153–158.

SHOC 81   Shoch, J. F., D. Cohen, and E. A. Taft, "Mutual Encapsulation of Internetwork Protocols," *Comput. Networks*, July 1981, pp. 287–301.

STAC 80   Stack, T. R., and K. A. Dillencourt, "Protocols for Local Area Networks," *Proc. Trends Appl.: Comput. Network Protocols*, 1980, pp. 83–93.

TOBA 80   Tobagi, F. A., "Multiaccess Protocols in Packet Communication Systems," *IEEE Trans. Commun.*, Vol. COM-28, No. 4, 1980, pp. 468–488.

UNSO 81   Unsoy, M. S., and T. Shanahan, "X.75 Internetworking of Datapac and Telenet," *Proc. 7th Data Commun. Symp.*, October 1981.

VISV 81   Visvader, J., "The New Network Roles of the Statistical Mux," *Data Commun.*, June 1981.

WEIN 80   Weinstein, C. J., M. L. Malpass, and M. J. Fischer, "Data Traffic Performance of an Integrated, Circuit- and Packet-Switched Multiplex Structure," *IEEE Trans. Commun.*, Vol. COM-28, No. 6, 1980, pp. 873–878.

WILK 80   Wilkes, M. V., "The Impact of Wide-Band Local Area Communication Systems on Distributed Computing," *Computer*, Vol. 13, No. 9, September 1980.

YU 80   Yu, W., J. C. Majithia, and J. W. Wong, "Access Protocols for Circuit/Packet Switching Networks," *Comput. Networks*, December 1980.

2

The Structure
and Function
of Network Protocols

GILBERT FALK
Bolt, Beranek & Newman, Inc.
Cambridge, Massachusetts

2.1 INTRODUCTION

The increasing use of data communications as part of computer systems over the past several years has spawned a variety of network architectures to support requirements for distributed data processing. Network architectures have been developed by various R&D groups [ROBE 70, FARB 72, FRAS 75, BOGG 76, JACO 78A], by common carriers [HOVE 76, RIND 76, WORL 72, AT&T 78, KAPL 79], by minicomputer and mainframe manufacturers [WECK 76, MCFA 76], and by vendors of traditional communications hardware [FORN 76, DESM 76]. Network architectures identify physical and logical elements of a communication system and specify the interconnection and interactions among these elements that are permitted. The major part of each of these architectures is a set of communication protocols.

A communications protocol can be defined informally as a set of rules or conventions used to control data transfer in a computer communications system. We assume that data transfer is accomplished by a finite sequence of message exchanges. Protocols contain a precise specification of data and control message formats (e.g., headers, trailers, and maximum lengths). By defining procedures to control message flows (e.g., error handling and speed matching), protocols establish what can be viewed as logical communication paths between communicating entities. These logical paths may or may not correspond to direct physical connections. Protocol formats may be interpreted as defining protocol syntax and control procedures as defining protocol semantics and timing as described in [GREE 79]. Protocols are essential for providing basic network functionality and have a major impact on network performance and cost.

In this chapter the structure and functions of network protocols are described.

In Sec. 2.2 some global protocol design considerations are addressed. In Sec. 2.3 a taxonomy of network protocols is presented. Finally, in Sec. 2.4 the set of functions that are components of protocols are examined.

Although much of the following discussion is applicable to protocols in general, the type of communications systems emphasized in this chapter can best be characterized as packet-switching networks. By packet switching we mean that the logical data flow is transmitted from source to destination as a series of separately handled relatively short blocks called packets. In addition to the traditional packet networks (e.g., ARPANET [ROBE 70] and Telenet [ROBE 75], most computer vendor network architectures, such as Digital Equipment Corporation's DECNET [WECK 76, WECK 80] and IBM's SNA [MCFA 76], also fall within the scope of our broad definition of packet switching. Throughout this chapter numerous points are illustrated by examples taken from the ARPANET and SNA designs. The reason for this emphasis is the extensive literature available on these two major milestones in the evolution of computer networking. For those readers unfamiliar with either ARPANET or SNA, a brief overview of each as well as pointers to additional information is presented in Appendix 1.

2.2   GLOBAL PROTOCOL DESIGN CONSIDERATIONS

There are several global design considerations that are fundamental to the discussion of protocols in this chapter. These are examined briefly in the following sections.

2.2.1   Protocol Layering

A network architecture is a complex logical system. To facilitate understanding such systems for purposes of design, implementation, and maintenance, recently developed network architectures have been envisioned as assemblies of layers [TANE 81]. Structuring a system into layers provides a convenient partitioning of functions and facilitates sharing of common services. In the context of the present discussion, the important point is that a layered network architecture implies a hierarchy of network protocols. One view of this layered hierarchy is presented in Sec. 2.3. A slightly different view proposed by the International Standards Organization (ISO) [ISO 81, ZIMM 80] is illustrated in Fig. 2.1. Cypser [CYPS 78] presents yet a third view of the set of generic layers (see Fig. 2.A.2), which is contrasted with the ISO model in [CORR 79] and [TANE 81].

Each protocol layer of a network architecture is associated with communication between similar entities, referred to as "peers," in the set of interconnected systems. It is important to distinguish between these protocols and the interfaces between adjacent layers within a single-component system. Typically, a network architecture (e.g., SNA) specifies peer protocols, indicates the functional relationships between layers, and identifies information that must be passed between layers, but

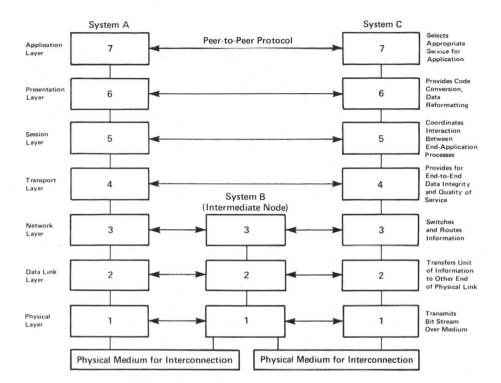

Figure 2.1. ISO open system interconnection reference model.

does not define the formats of interlayer exchanges. The specification of these formats is left open to provide flexibility to the implementer of products (e.g., a mainframe front-end processor or a terminal cluster controller) which adhere to the network architecture. Visibility of interlayer boundaries is required only at the boundary of a product in order to faciliate physical interconnection.

The advantages of a strictly layered approach need to be viewed in relation to the associated costs. Where all messages must be handled by distinct entities at every level, excessive processing overhead and delay may be introduced. A "worst-case" example of the costs of layering is suggested by Walden [WALD 75], where he describes a scenario of unnecessary translations associated with transmission of an array of floating-point numbers between two computers on the ARPANET. The user's view in this case was low throughout in spite of 50-kbps trunk circuits. Although one should not conclude from this example that all layering will prove unacceptable, special-purpose implementations that integrate the functions of several layers may be an attractive alternative in situations where high efficiency is essential. Special-purpose protocols can coexist and operate in parallel with a standard layered protocol hierarchy.

2.2.2 Protocol Symmetry

Closely related to the concept of protocol layering is the concept of protocol symmetry. The communicating entities at any level may stand in either a symmetric relationship (master to master, primary to primary) or an asymmetric relationship (master to slave, primary to secondary) with respect to one another. At upper levels of the protocol hierarchy, asymmetries may be associated with the logical differences between the communicating end users. For example, as discussed in Sec. 2.3.4, much of the actual use of a network can be viewed as communication between "user" and "server" processes. One does not expect that the commands sent by a user to a server will be the same as those sent from a server to a user. A quite different motivation for asymmetric protocol implementation has been the significant economic advantage to build nodes with only limited (secondary) capability. Such considerations are beginning to fade, however, due to recent advances in VLSI technology.

In general, symmetry of the normal data flow may be specified independent of the symmetry associated with protocol control procedures. Asymmetries in control may be advantageous in order to assign prime error recovery responsibility to one of the communicating entities. The entity with recovery responsibility should be able to respond to recovery requests from other parties with which it is communicating as well as initiating actions unilaterally.

2.2.3 Protocol Standardization

The last global issue that we wish to address is that of protocol standardization. To clarify the primary motivation for standardization, consider the case of N senders transmitting to M receivers. First assume that no standards are defined. Each pair of communicating entities develops its own special purpose design, resulting in NM distinct protocols. Moreover, there will be 2NM distinct protocol implementations. Obviously, this analysis is for the worst case, but it does point out the potential pitfalls of uncoordinated efforts. If a standard were developed and used for all data transfers, on the other hand, only a single protocol and N + M implementations will be required.

Standardization of communications protocols is not as clear cut as the argument above would indicate, however. First, in practical terms, it is difficult to get a group of individuals with potentially diverse communications requirements to agree on a single design. Furthermore, a standardized design is likely to support a superset of the requirements of each individual user, and the cost of this enhanced functionality may have to be paid by everyone. Finally, protocol standardization must be carried out with care to avoid being frozen into a design that is later recognized as being significantly suboptimal. Once a protocol has been implemented on a number of diverse systems, it is extremely costly to make major changes. A concrete example of this point is the ARPANET Host/Host protocol (see Sec. 2.3.3), which was implemented and subsequently seen to impose significant limitations on throughout [CERF 74A]. This does not suggest that standardization should be avoided, but that it should be carried out with great care and with an eye toward expandability. The

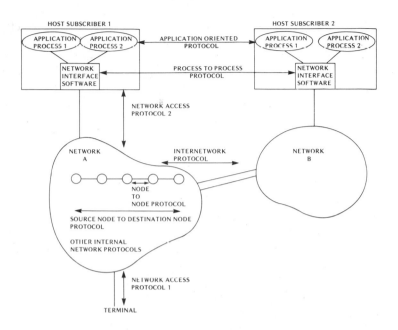

Figure 2.2. Relationship between network protocols.

SNA concept of "function subsets" of a standard protocol [CYPS 78] and the ARPANET concept of "option negotiation" [TELN 76] indicate that one can tailor a particular exchange between end users for efficiency while achieving the benefits of standardization. As noted earlier, there will be additional cases of a unique nature where existing standards prove inadequate. The system design should be flexible enough to admit the incorporation of special-purpose protocols.

2.3 A TAXONOMY OF NETWORK PROTOCOLS

Network protocols can be classified into one of the following five categories: internal network protocols, network access protocols, process-to-process protocols, application-oriented protocols, and internetwork protocols. The relationship of these protocols to one another is illustrated in Fig. 2.2. In this section each category is discussed in detail to provide a conceptual framework within which any protocol can be viewed.

2.3.1 Internal Network Protocols

The internal network protocols are those that the user of the network never sees. Their impact is noted only indirectly in terms of the level of network performance or functionality. Internal protocols have as their primary goal the reliable and efficient transfer of information. One can partition this class of protocols into two subclasses: data transfer protocols and network management protocols. *Data transfer protocols* are directly involved with the movement of user data. Individual blocks of information are wrapped in header/trailer envelopes defined by these protocols and sent from source to destination. *Network management protocols,* on the other hand, are not directly associated with the movement of user data but are necessary to maintain the network in a state where reliable information transfer can occur. These two classes of protocols are discussed separately in the next two sections.

2.3.1.1   Data Transfer Protocols

The nature of network data transfer protocols depends on the fundamental switching strategy employed. Two basic alternatives are the *datagram* (DG) strategy and the *virtual circuit* (VC) strategy. A DG strategy is one in which each block of information presented to the network by a subscriber is treated independently of each previous and each succeeding block. The French network Cyclades [POUZ 73] is an example of such a design. Typically, datagram networks make a reasonable attempt to ensure reliable transfer of information but do not guarantee error-free communication. Moreover, end-to-end sequencing (see Sec. 2.4.5) and flow control (see Sec. 2.4.6) of information is typically left to the user (or higher-level protocols) in datagram networks.

VC networks, on the other hand, make an attempt to provide more functions within the communications system. Typically, virtual circuit implementations provide stricter error control (see Sec. 2.4.4), flow control, and sequencing of data on internal logical connections. Conceptually, these logical connections are akin to the physical connections in traditional telephone systems. Logical connections, however, do not require permanent allocation of circuit bandwidth to calls. Virtual circuits can be switched or permanent. For switched virtual circuits, there is typically a call setup procedure, a data transfer phase, and a disconnect procedure. There has been considerable debate as to the relative merits of the datagram and virtual circuit approaches. The interested reader is referred to [POUZ 76] and [ROBE 78] for a discussion of the issues. In general, the enhanced functionality of virtual circuit networks will require more complex data transfer protocols than are required for datagram implementations.

Within the class of networks with internal virtual circuit implementations, one can distinguish two distinct subclasses: those in which the virtual circuit is known only by the entry/exit nodes and those where all nodes along the source-to-destination path are aware of the virtual circuit. The current ARPANET implementation [MCQU 75] is an example of the former. Tymnet's design [RIND 76] is an example of the latter. We refer to the former as a *pseudo-virtual circuit* implementation and the latter as a *true virtual circuit* implementation.

Node-to-Node Protocols

For both datagram and virtual circuit designs, node-to-node protocols support the transmission of data units from one node to the next on the path from source to destination. Node-to-node protocols can be viewed as consisting of two distinct layers. The lower layer is referred to as the link control layer. Link control protocols are responsible for establishing and terminating a logical connection between physical stations (nodes) and for managing the transfers of physical blocks of data between stations so as to ensure data integrity. The link may support two physical stations (point to point) or many stations (multipoint). The physical connection may be switched or nonswitched (dedicated) and it may be operated in either a synchronous or an asynchronous (start-stop) mode. High-speed high-performance communication generally employs synchronous transmission over dedicated transmission facilities.

For many years IBM's Binary Synchronous Communications (BSC) protocol [IBM 69] was the only widely accepted link control protocol for synchronous data transmission. Inherent BSC limitations and growing requirements for increased throughput, however, have recently led to the development of improved link-level standards. An ANSI standard referred to as ADCCP [ANSI 76] and a similar ISO standard referred to as HDLC [ISO 76, ISO 77] have been developed. Both of these standards are supersets of SDLC developed earlier by IBM for SNA [IBM 75]. Examples of other link-level protocols are DDCMP under DECNET [DIGI 78A] and the ARPANET IMP-to-IMP protocol [MCQU 77A]. The functions associated with link control protocols include framing and data transparency, connection establishment and termination, error control, flow control, sequencing, and addressing. The first four functions are supported as part of almost all link control procedures. The last two functions may be supported (e.g., SDLC) or may not (e.g., ARPANET IMP-to-IMP protocol). Each of these functions is defined and discussed in Sec. 2.4 as part of the general discussion on protocol functionality. Further discussion can be found in [GRAY 72, CYPS 78, HOUS 79, BERT 80, CONA 80, CARL 80, TOBA 80] and in Chap. 3 of this text, which is concerned with the details of link control procedures.

The node-to-node protocol supported by the link control layer is referred to as the *path control protocol*. Path control protocols serve to implement the nodal functions associated with packaging and routing of data units through the network. Destination address information is interpreted by path control in order to route each packet along the next leg of its journey. Data unit segmentation (see Sec. 2.4.1) and blocking of information into frames (see Sec. 2.4.3) are also path control functions. The control protocols that must be active in the background to support data packet routing are discussed in Sec. 2.3.1.2.

Source Node-to-Destination Node Protocols

If a network provides only datagram service, node-to-node protocols will be sufficient to transport data packets from one end of the network to the other. For virtual circuit designs, on the other hand, an additional source node-to-destination node protocol will be required to implement VC call establishment and termination, error control, flow control, sequencing, and out-of-band signaling. In the case of a single vendor architecture based on an integrated end-user/communication system implementation, a single protocol can serve both the packet transport system and the end-to-end conversations established between user processes (see Sec. 2.3.3). Under SNA, for example, the transmission control protocol provides the foundation for all end-to-end functions of the common transmission subsystem. If a network is designed to operate in a heterogeneous user environment, on the other hand, it may be desirable to provide both an internal source node-to-destination node protocol and an external process-to-process protocol even though there is some overlap in the message processing carried out at these two levels. A summary of the arguments pro and con is presented in [FALK 77A].

2.3.1.2   Network Management Protocols

Network management protocols, as indicated earlier, are only indirectly involved with the reliable transfer of data. They provide support necessary to guarantee that proper network state is maintained. Specific management protocols associated with routing, line status monitoring, and network control are discussed below.

Routing Protocols

Protocols that guarantee that proper information is available to path control for packet route selection (i.e., forwarding based on destination address) are prototypical of network control protocols. The wide variation in such routing protocols results from a diversity of routing strategies developed to date [MCQU 77B, CYPS 78, SCHW 80]. In the simplest case, routing tables used by path control are fixed (nonadaptive routing), and there is no need for a routing protocol. Static routing-table entries can be modified as required manually using remote network maintenance tools based on long-term measurements or estimates of traffic flows. Dynamic adaptive routing, on the other hand, requires protocols supporting the exchange of network state information between nodes (e.g., trunk or node up/down status and line loading). Significant state changes (e.g., trunk failures) are automatically reflected in real-time modification to the routing tables at each node under dynamic adaptive designs.

A major factor affecting adaptive routing protocols is whether route calculation is performed at a special routing center (e.g., Tymnet) or in a distributed fashion (e.g., ARPANET). In the centralized case, protocols must be defined to (1) control the flow of network state information to the routing center, (2) route path requests to the routing center, and (3) route specifications of paths from the center to locations making route requests. In general, the transfer of state information can either be initiated periodically or when a significant state change occurs. In the case of a distributed implementation, each node can either maintain complete network state information or only a subset of this information. The original ARPANET routing algorithm in use for almost a decade was based on each node maintaining information on the estimated best path delay to each destination via each incident trunk. Adjacent nodes exchanged best path information periodically [MCQU 78B]. This approach was subsequently modified so that each node keeps track of the delay on all network lines and generates an "event message" whenever a significant local change occurs. Event messages describe the nature of the local change and are broadcast to all other network nodes. A shortest-path computation run at each ARPANET node explicity computes the minimum delay path to all other nodes in the network to provide the basis for routing of data packets [MCQU 78C, MCQU 79, ROSE 79].

The routing mechanism used by SNA is a modified static strategy referred to as "explicit routing"[JUEN 76, AHUJ 79, ATKI 80]. Multiple physical paths referred to as *explicit routes* can be defined between any source-destination pair. Multiple *virtual routes* can share an explicit route and multiple logical conversations (sessions) can share a virtual route. Sessions are assigned to virtual routes based on the class of service requested (e.g., interactive or RJE). If a route being used by a session fails due to a link or node outage, all session ends using the failing route are notified so that sessions may be established over other operational routes. Protocol commands exist to activate and deactivate both explicit and virtual routes [AHUJ 79].

Line Status Monitoring Protocols

In order to establish the availability of internode trunks independent of data traffic flows (which may not exist at any instant), a second type of network management protocol may be used. In the case of the ARPANET, an exchange of HELLO and I-HEARD-YOU messages is used to determine the suitability of a line for data transmission (line up or line down). The obvious criterion is to define the line quality in terms of the errors experienced by the messages exchanged. An ideal set of line up/down procedures instantly bring a line down when it becomes bad and immediately bring a line up again when it is restored. Such goals cannot, however, be achieved. In practice, the goals are (1) to bring poor lines down quickly and keep them down longer than the period over which a line is usually bad, and (2) rarely to bring a good line down but to bring a good line up with reasonable speed. A more detailed discussion of line status monitoring protocols is presented in [MCQU 78C]. Under SNA, line status monitoring is integrated with the link control procedure SDLC [GRAY 77].

Network Control Protocols

A third set of management protocols are associated with functions coordinated from a central network location. Network operations personnel will generally be required to respond to exceptional conditions (e.g., certian node crashes or line outages), handle administrative matters (e.g., user billing), and implement both short-term and long-term network changes (e.g., add/delete a user/node or release new network software). Under SNA such functions are referred to as *network services* [CYPS 78] and are controlled by logical entities referred to as *system services control points* (SSCPs) distributed throughout the network. Each SSCP has a "domain" of responsibility and is responsible for interacting with network elements within its domain. Since there may be many SSCPs in a large SNA network (SSCPs generally exist in every IBM mainframe and many distributed processing systems), the SSCPs themselves may require coordination. IBM offers a program product, the Network Communications Control Facility (NCCF), for this purpose [BUDW 79, IBM 78D]. NCCF can support one or more operators with either disjoint or overlapping spans of control. NCCF in conjunction with another IBM program product, the Network Problem Determination Application (NPDA), implements protocols for collection, storage, and retrieval of error data related to lines, modems, terminals, and communications controllers [IBM 78C, WEIN 79].

Traditional packet networks such as the ARPANET and Telenet have operating personnel at a network control center (NCC). Physically, the NCC is a host computer supporting a variety of control terminal devices. Operating personnel at the NCC receive status reports from the network nodes and have facilities for initiating recovery procedures, carrying out remote diagnostics, and so on. Each of these activities requires a protocol exchange between the remote nodes and the central NCC computer. A more detailed discussion of NCC operations and protocols for the ARPANET can be found in [MCKE 75, SANT 76].

2.3.2   Network-Access Protocols

A network-access protocol is a protocol used by a subscriber (host or terminal) to communicate with the network node to which it is attached. Access protocols are particularly critical components of heterogeneous multivendor systems. Access protocols should be sufficiently general to permit the user to take full advantage of network functionality. On the other hand, the ease of attachment of a computer to a network is directly dependent on the complexity of the access protocol. Recognizing this area as one that must be addressed early, common carriers and post, telegraph, and telephone authorities (PTTs) supplying public data networks (especially Telenet, Datapac, and Transpac) have been strong supporters of the development of international access standards.

A significant result of these efforts has been the acceptance of Recommendation X.25 by the International Telegraph and Telephone Consultative Committee (CCITT). At present, Recommendation X.25 [CCIT 81A] is the only widely accepted international standard for access to public or private packet-switched data networks. The existence of this standard is likely to have a major impact in facilitating the implementation of true distributed processing systems. As mainframe and minicomputer manufactures begin to incorporate X.25 interface software into their computer communication systems, the problems of transferring data between dissimilar computers should be significantly reduced. The following section discusses X.25 in addition to some related device emulation interface standards. Sec. 2.3.2.2 identifies some nonstandard access protocols adopted by particular vendors and organizations.

2.3.2.1   International Interface Standards

Recommendation X.25 is a protocol specification that defines the communication across a computer [data terminating equipment (DTE)] to network [data circuit-terminating equipment (DCE)] interface. The X.25 standard consists of three distinct levels (or subprotocol layers). Level 1 specifies the physical interface between the DTE and DCE. In the X.25 specification document, level 1 is a reference to another international standard, CCITT Recommendation X.21 [CCIT 81A, BERT 80]. X.25 level 1 specifies a four-wire point-to-point synchronous electrically balanced connection. This connection runs at speeds between 600 and 48,000 bps and is made mechanically by a 15-pin connector. Level 2 of X.25 defines the link-level control procedure to be used for all frames passed between the DTE and DCE. It establishes a single full-duplex "error-free" (low residual error rate) access path between the subscriber and the network based on retransmission of packets received in error. The specification at level 2 is essentially a subset of the HDLC standard developed by the International Standards Organization (ISO) [ISO 76, ISO 77]. Level 3 of Recommendation X.25 defines mechanisms for multiplexing (superimposing) up to 4096 virtual circuits on the error-free path established by X.25 level 2 [RYBC 80]. Commands and responses exist at level 3 for call setup and clearing, flow control and reset, restart, and interrupt as well as normal data transfer.

In the original Telenet implementation, X.25 virtual circuits at the subscriber interface boundary were supported by ARPANET-style pseudo-virtual circuits within the network. Tymnet, which also provides X.25 access, on the other hand, is based on true virtual circuits internally. Recommendation X.25 was initially criticized for its inability to support transaction-oriented applications efficiently. Definitions for "datagram" and "fast select" interfaces have been developed to extend the X.25 specification and eliminate these apparent shortcomings [FOLT 80].

Although X.25 is a major step in the direction of standardized access procedures, it is primarily oriented toward multichannel (multiprocess) intelligent subscribers. To standardize the access to public data networks for single-channel unintelligent interactive terminals, using start-stop line control, a set of three additional specifications (Recommendations X.3, X.28, and X.29 [CCIT 81A, HOVE 77] have been adopted by CCITT. Recommendation X.3 defines a set of functions for a packet assembler-disassembler (PAD). PAD functions can be implemented either within the network user's terminal or terminal controller or within the nodes of a public or private data network. The X.3 PAD has responsibility for translating between packets, the language of the network, and character streams, the language of the unintelligent terminal. The PAD functions specify when packets should be forwarded (e.g., on carriage return, on buffer full, after N seconds), whether echoing should be performed by the network, whether print/display lines that are too long should be "folded" or truncated, and so on. Recommendation X.28 is the actual specification of the access protocol (command language) used between the terminal (human user) and the network (PAD). Recommendation X.29 is a specification of the protocol used to permit host computer control of the PAD. A single X.25 virtual circuit is associated with each terminal by the remote host computer. Two subchannels are multiplexed on this virtual circuit using the "qualified data bit" (Q-bit) defined within X.25 level 3. One subchannel is used for host-to-terminal data flow (Q = 0) and the other is used for host-to-PAD control (Q = 1). One can also view Recommendation X.29 as an example of an application-oriented terminal handling protocol as described in Secs. 2.3.4 and 2.3.4.1.

2.3.2.2   Nonstandard Access Interfaces

In spite of the growing acceptance of Recommendations X.25, X.3, X.28, and X.29 as the standards for accessing both public and private data networks, there are still a variety of other interfaces being used to connect computers and terminals to networks. We can identify several classes of such interfaces. The first class corresponds to those interfaces developed before the acceptance of X.25. An example of an interface in this category is the interface between a host and an IMP in the ARPANET [BOLT 78]. A major difference between the ARPANET host interface and X.25 is that the former defines a single host-to-network logical flow rather than multiple independent logical channels. Multiplexing of the single logical flow to the host is done as part of a process-to-process level protocol in the ARPANET (see Sec. 2.3.3).

A second class of nonstandard interfaces are the common device emulation interfaces. Because of the ubiquitous nature of IBM equipment and the de facto standards that such equipment defines, many networks provide plug-compatible support for polled 3270 terminal clusters and 2780/3780/Hasp RJE stations. To a host expecting to communicate with one of these resources, the network can present an interface that emulates the terminal's behavior and thus requires no hardware or software changes.

Manufacturer's network architectures constitute a third area where nonstandard interfaces are present [MCFA 76, WECK 76, SHAT 79]. Although many manufactures also support X.25 to facilitate access to public data networks, their native computer-to-network interface is different. In the case of IBM's SNA, the vehicle for communication between VTAM or TCAM, the most common communication system access software in the host, and NCP, the communication system software in the front end (node), is the Path Information Unit (PIU). Some communication system vendors have focused on this interface as the basis for providing an SNA-compatible network design.

A final class of nonstandard interfaces are those developed to support unique network requirements. Military systems are one example of this class. In the case of AUTODIN II developed by the Defense Communications Agency [DEFE 75, KULK 78, LYON 80], strict requirements on security, precedence, and closed communities of interest exist. In addition, a number of compatibility constraints are present due to the need to interoperate with existing systems (e.g., AUTODIN I [PAOL 75]). Packet-switched satellite networks designed to support integrated voice/data traffic also have unique access protocol requirements [JACO 78A].

2.3.3   Process-to-Process Protocols

One goal of the communications system is to provide a basic transport mechanism for data transmission between end users. These end users may be executing application programs or human users working at terminal devices. In both cases it is useful to model the end user as a process and, therefore, view the transport system as supporting process-to-process communication. In practice, each process typically interacts with a local control program (CP). Pairs of CPs interact according to a process-to-process protocol on behalf of their users. This level of protocol supports reliable controlled transmission of uninterpreted bit streams. It is the highest protocol level where the structure of the text portion of messages is ignored. Process-to-process protocols are sometimes referred to as end-to-end protocols or host-to-host protocols, although the latter name is somewhat misleading [WALD 79].

The functions provided by process-to-process protocols depend on the nature of the supporting services. A good tutorial exposition of these protocol interrelationships is presented in [CERF 78B]. Process-to-process protocols may define a larger address space than that defined as part of the network access protocol. This address space is used to provide common names by which to refer to host and terminal processes. Most process-to-process protocols in use are oriented toward virtual circuit operation and, therefore, define procedures for establishing and terminating end-to-end conversations. Both active establishment (where both ends simultaneously call each other) and passive establishment [where a service facility (server) end "listens" for calls] are possible. There is some variation in practice with regard to the implementation of error control and flow control at this level. An interrupt mechanism is often defined which permits the normal flow control to be bypassed (see Sec. 2.4.7).

Probably the earliest general-purpose process-to-process protocol was developed for the ARPANET [CARR 70, WALD 75, MCKE 76]. Within the ARPA community, this protocol has generally been referred to as the host-host protocol. Host-host protocol has also been called *NCP protocol* since its software realization is referred to as a *network control program* (no relation to IBM's SNA NCP). Host-host protocol is based on simplex logical connections between user processes. These simplex connections are derived from (multiplexed over) the single host-to-IMP connection discussed in Sec. 2.3.2.2. Because the protocol definition also requires distinct names for both ends of a connection, a relatively complex procedure referred to as the *initial connection protocol* (ICP) is required for associating users with service processes [POST 76]. The ICP works by having a service process continually listening for connections from users on a "well-known port." A user wishing to obtain the service connects to this well-known port and is subsequently switched by the server from the well-known port to another (pair of) port(s) which the server chooses. The server then continues to listen on the well-known port for calls from other remote users. Flow control, but not error control, is provided in host-host protocol. Effective throughout is limited due to an unfortunate specification of only a single outstanding message at a time per connection. A critique of some aspects of this protocol can be found in [CERF 74A].

Protocol designers have learned from the early mistakes of the ARPANET and have corrected the shortcomings noted above in more recent designs. The International Federation for Information Processing (IFIP) Working Group 6.1 submitted a proposal to CCITT for a general-purpose process-to-process protocol [CERF 78A]. In this design connections are full-duplex and multiple connections can share a common address at one end, thus eliminating the need for a complex initial connection procedure such as ICP. Both virtual circuit (Liaison) and datagram (Lettergram) operation is supported. Flow control is tied to message sequence numbers, which eliminates difficulties when flow control messages are themselves lost (see Sec. 2.4.6). Three levels of error protection are associated with three grades of end-to-end service. The IFIP protocol makes a minimal number of assumptions about the networks over which it will operate. It is designed to operate across either one network or several networks and to permit fragmentation as a message crosses from one network to another without requiring network reassembly at each step.

A protocol similar in motivation and direction to the IFIP protocol is the *transmission control protocol* (TCP) [INFO 80A] first described by Cerf and Kahn [CERF 74B]. One distinction between the IFIP and TCP protocols is that TCP is oriented only toward virtual circuit operation. Another distinction between the two is the fact that TCP views the transmission as a stream of bytes rather than as a sequence of letters. TCP is the end-to-end protocol used for internetworking experiments within the ARPA community and has been selected as the DOD standard for use in the AUTODIN II network.

Public data networks have not adopted a distinct process-to-process protocol. X.25 can be viewed as a proces-to-process protocol as well as an access protocol when end-to-end significance of control messages is enabled. At present, there is still some debate as to whether a process-to-process protocol on top of X.25 is useful [HERT 78, JACQ 78, RYBC 80].

SNA provides end-to-end error control and flow control (pacing) across the common transmission network as mentioned in Sec. 2.3.1.1. The most interesting difference between this level of protocol under SNA and the protocols described above is the fact that connections are established with the assistance of a central authority (SSCP) under SNA. This point is discussed further in Sec. 2.4.9.

2.3.4   Application-Oriented Protocols

All of the protocols based on process-to-process-level protocols will be referred to as *application-oriented protocols* in the following discussion. These protocols have also been referred to as "high-level protocols" [SPRO 78] or "function-oriented protocols" [CROC 72]. Protocols associated with ISO open-system architecture layers 5, 6, and 7 [ISO 81] also fall within this category. The difference between application-oriented protocols and lower-level protocols is their view of the data stream. All lower levels treat the text portion of a message as uninterpreted data. Application-level protocols, however, are concerned with the structure of these data and translations or transformations on them. As printed out by Sproull and Cohen [SPRO 78], application-level protocols are used in two slightly different ways in networks. In the first use, the basis for remote resource sharing [DAY 79], application-level protocols control services offered by resources in the network. Various sites in the network implement server processes that offer a specific service to any authorized user process which communicates a request. Examples of such protocols are terminal-handling protocols, file transfer protocols, and remote job entry protocols discussed below. A second use of application-level protocols is to coordinate the activities of various component processes within a single application [THOM 72].

2.3.4.1 Terminal-Handling Protocols

Terminal-handling protocols are intended to provide mechanisms that will facilitate the use of terminals for diverse applications in a network environment [DAY 80]. This is not possible at present due to variations in terminal characteristics, particularly higher-speed synchronous devices, and due to the terminal-specific support provided in most applications and operating systems. As pointed out by Day [DAY 79], two basic approaches to network terminal handling have emerged, the parametric approach and the virtual terminal approach. The parametric approach attempts to characterize the differences between terminals by a set of parameters. A host interacting with a terminal uses a protocol to inquire as to the capabilities of the terminal and to set parameters that will cause the host operation to be tailored to those capabilities. An example of this approach is the support of asynchronous terminals on X.25 public data networks using CCITT Recommendations X.3, X.28, and X.29 (see Sec. 2.3.2.1).

The virtual terminal approach is based on the notion that with a suitable level of abstraction, many differences between physical devices disappear and that a few generic terminal types can be defined and used by most applications. For example, the ability to contrast is an abstraction for various physical capabilities such as reverse video, blinking, or variable intensity. A mapping between a standard device which embodies such abstractions, called the virtual terminal, and whatever physical terminal is available can be realized in the software or firmware of a terminal controller or in the terminal itself. The virtual terminal is also the entity with which the host application converses. A *virtual terminal protocol* (VTP) defines the characteristics of a standard terminal and provides the specifications for driving it.

The definition of a virtual terminal makes an implicit selection of the actual terminals which are suited for emulation and on the applications that will be satisfied with the virtual terminal. A rudimentary "scroll-mode" virtual terminal capability is currently available in the ARPANET environment [DAVI 77, TELN 76] where a variety of asynchronous terminals are mapped into a standard ASCII "network virtual terminal" supported by many systems. A number of groups have developed virtual terminal specifications and protocols for more sophisticated "page-mode" virtual terminals and "data entry"-type devices [SCHI 77, BAUW 78, IFIP 78]. To facilitate interoperation between terminals and applications, the simpler virtual terminal models are defined as proper subsets of the more sophisticated ones. Scroll-mode operation provides a common language in which any terminal can potentially talk to any application.

The concept of a virtual terminal combines a number of functions that appear within different layers in the SNA design. For example, the notion of a terminal and application taking "turns" sending to one another is a function of the SNA Data Flow Control layer, while the notion of a common language (the SNA character string controls) and presentation services are associated with the Function Management layer [CYPS 78]. Some of the LU-type definitions in SNA are the conceptual equivalents of virtual terminal protocols. LU types 1 and 2, for example, correspond to the definition of data entry devices [IBM 78B, GRAY 79, IBM 79].

2.3.4.2   File Transfer Protocols

The primary objectives of a *file transfer protocol* (FTP) are to promote the sharing of files (programs as well as data), to shield user from variations in file storage between computer systems, and to transfer data reliably and efficiently. Although facilities for transmitting files between dissimilar computers (especially those from different vendors) are still at an early stage of development, a number of organizations have developed or are in the process of developing FTP designs [NEIG 76, CASH 76, GIEN 78, DIGI 78B, BUTS 79, FORS 79]. SNA's LU Type 6 architects a general capability for sending data base requests to remote locations in a heterogeneous single-vendor environment [GRAY 79A, GRAY 79B].

The general model of a network file transfer involves three parties. The *controller* is the user (host, process) that initiates and controls the file transfer. The *donor* is the host (process) at which the file to be transferred is stored. The *receiver* is the host (process) to which the file is to be transferred. The FTP coordinates the activity required to effect the transfer between donor and receiver. This three-party model reduces to a two-party model when the controller is also the donor or receiver.

File transfer can be separated into two subproblems. The first is concerned with the mechanics of moving files from one host to another. An FTP must provide a control structure to carry interhost commands and responses and must provide the means for two hosts to select a transmission format and agree on other specifics of file transmission. The second and more difficult file transfer subproblem has to do with file structure and data translation which may be required to store at one host a file that was created at another host. There are a variety of reasons for transferring a file from one host to another. The difficulty of the file translation problem depends on the reason a file is transferred as well as the differences between the two host systems involved in the transfer.

The translation problem is simplest when the host to which a file is moved is to be used only to store the file; that is, the file is never to be used at the destination host. In this case the responsibility of the source host is to translate the file into the format required for transmission. The responsibility of the destination host is to store the file in any format that will permit it subsequently to transmit the file back to the source host in the same format that was used when it received the file for storage.

The translation problem is more difficult when the file is to be used at the destination host and the file organizations supported by the two hosts are different. This can be a problem at a variety of levels. At a structural level, text files at some hosts may have a record structure while at other hosts they do not. At a lower level, the representations of data, such as floating-point numbers stored in a file, may differ. An FTP may be required to compensate for such differences. The extent to which general-purpose FTPs should become involved in file translations and transformation is a fundamental design decision.

2.3.4.3   Remote Job Entry Protocol

A remote job entry (RJE) protocol is a standard specifying the mechanisms that can be activated by a user at one location to cause a batch-processing job to be run at some other location. The protocol specifies the manner in which a remote user communicates over the network with a batch-processing server, causing that server to retrieve a job input file, to process the job, and to deliver the job's output file(s) to a remote location. An RJE protocol specifies a limited solution to the problem of job control in a network environment. For a more complete discussion of network job control issues, the reader is referred to [KIMB 76, RAYN 77, FORS 78, CRAB 78, SIMP 78].

The ARPANET RJE protocol (NETRJE) [BRES 76] is built on top of the VTP (Telnet) and FTP protocols. The RJE user establishes a Telnet control connection to the RJE server at the host where he wishes to submit his job. He then uses this connection to send NETRJE commands to the server to log in, to describe the location of his job, to describe how the job is to be transmitted to the server, and to describe what is to be done with the output when the execution of the job is complete. The RJE server on the foreign host initially uses FTP to get the input file and may use FTP after processing to deliver output back to the user. NETRJE protocol is general enough to allow job submission from one site, processing at another, and output at a third.

NETRJE has been criticized for not addressing the problem of moving parts of a file, for having security problems, and for requiring both unnecessary development effort and a large commitment of system resources. Improved designs have been proposed for the ARPANET environment by Day and Grossman [DAY 77] and Braden [BRAD 77]. Although SNA itself has not architected any protocol like NETRJE, the network job entry facility (NJE) for the JES subsystem which runs on SNA does provide similar capabilities in an IBM environment [SIMP 78].

2.3.4.4   Other Application-Oriented Protocols

The protocols described above provide the basis for many of the service activities that are currently of importance in a distributed processing environments. Other high-level protocols have been developed, however, and will become increasingly important in years to come. Electronic mail protocols have been used extensively over the past several years in the ARPANET environment [MYER 76] and are beginning to receive considerable national and international attention due to growth in the use of communicating word processors. CCITT has defined several standards for facsimile transmission over circuit-switched networks [JACO 78B] and one expects that protocols for use between facsimile devices on packet-switched networks will also begin to emerge shortly. Graphics protocols [THOM 76, SPRO 78], packet voice protocols [COHE 78, SPRO 78], and teleconferencing protocols [RUBI 78] have also been developed but, to date, have been used primarily in research environments.

2.3.5 Internetworking Protocols

There are a variety of models describing how communication between subscribers on different networks takes place. Each of these models has a direct impact on the nature of the protocols that will exist in the overall multinetwork system. The following paragraphs address this topic at a general level. A more detailed discussion of the issues involved in internetworking is the subject of Chap. 15 (Volume 2) of this text and [CERF 78C, POST 80].

In the simplest case, communication systems are completely compatible and one can interface all nodes at the link level. The internet arrangement is operated as a single network with an enlarged address space. The process-to-process protocol used for any of the component networks can be used as the process-to-process protocol for the composite network as well. No new protocol definition is required. This model may apply in a single-vendor environment where independently established communications systems are integrated into a single-networking arrangement. In a multi-vendor environment, however, this tightly coupled model is probably unrealistic, because of the diversity of existing designs and the requirement for network managers to have well-defined domains of responsibility.

Where variations in the internal capabilities of interconnected components exists and user access protocols differ, a logical approach is to provide a "gateway" function between networks. From the point of view of each component network, gateways are simply ordinary subscribers. The primary function of the gateway is to translate between the protocols and formats used in each component network. Gateways may also implement internetwork protocols to support internet addressing and data unit fragmentation/reassembly [INFO 80B]. Ideally, a common internet end-to-end protocol can be agreed on (such as the TCP or IFIP protocols described in Sec. 2.3.3). In this case gateway translation can be limited to incapsulation (decapsulation) of internet messages in the component network access protocol. Without internet standards, it will be necessary to provide end-to-end service as a concatenation of component services. This will increase the responsibilities of the gateways and may involve high-level and process-to-process level as well as access-level protocol translation. In general, gateways must participate in internetwork routing since the component networks do not necessarily have the ability to interpret internet addresses.

A special situation arises in the case of public packet-switched data networks (PDNs). Although the internal implementations of PDNs differ, all offer a common network access protocol, X.25. This can provide an attractive basis for internet communication [ROBE 76]. CCITT has followed this strategy with the adoption of Recommendation X.75 [CCIT 81B]. Recommendation X.75 defines the interface between two PDNs and is quite similar in both structure and detail to Recommendation X.25. X.75 level 1 defines the physical link between the signaling terminal equipment (STE) of the interconnected PDNs. Multiple links at 48 or 64 kilobits/sec. are permitted. X.75 level 2, which is based on the X.25 level 2 link access protocol LAP B, defines a single/multiple line reliable packet transfer procedure. Level 3 of

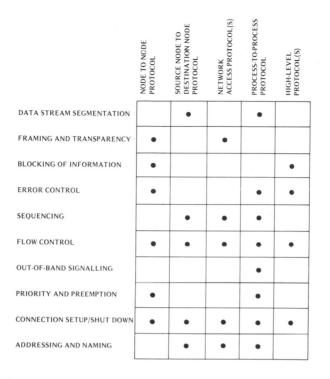

	NODE TO NODE PROTOCOL	SOURCE NODE TO DESTINATION NODE PROTOCOL	NETWORK ACCESS PROTOCOL(S)	PROCESS-TO-PROCESS PROTOCOL	HIGH-LEVEL PROTOCOL(S)
DATA STREAM SEGMENTATION		●		●	
FRAMING AND TRANSPARENCY	●		●		
BLOCKING OF INFORMATION	●				●
ERROR CONTROL	●			●	●
SEQUENCING		●	●	●	
FLOW CONTROL	●	●	●	●	●
OUT-OF-BAND SIGNALLING				●	
PRIORITY AND PREEMPTION	●			●	
CONNECTION SETUP/SHUT DOWN	●	●	●	●	●
ADDRESSING AND NAMING		●	●	●	

Figure 2.3. One possible association of protocol functions with protocol classes.

X.75 establishes the packet format and signaling procedures between PDN STEs. An end-to-end virtual circuit is comprised of a series X.25 and X.75 virtual circuits across and between the component networks.

2.4 PROTOCOL FUNCTIONS

The preceding sections have presented an overview of the hierarchy of cooperating network protocols. A single set of functions provides the basis for all of these protocols. The specific subset of functions that are components of a particular protocol at any level depend on the nature of the supporting communication system (e.g., lower-layer protocols) and the desired characteristics of the communications being implemented at the layer in question. Fig. 2.3 illustrates one possible association between protocol functions and protocol classes for a particular network. A mark indicates that the protocol function identified with the row is a feature of the protocol class indicated at the top of the column. A description of the data flow protocols for this network would consist of providing a detailed specification for each of the boxes marked in the figure. A comprehensive discussion of protocol functionality in general would necessarily involve many such tableaus; this is clearly beyond the scope of this chapter. Rather than attempt to discuss every function at each level for all possible assumptions of service and lower-level support, we restrict our attention in the sequel to a few important observations about each function.

2.4.1   Data-Stream Segmentation

The general problem being addressed by a communication system is the transfer of a stream of bytes from one entity to another. Because of practical limitations, it is typically the case that a data stream will be segmented into blocks of some maximum size. In the case of the ARPANET, user buffers are transmitted as a sequence of "messages" less than about 8000 bits in length. Messages are subsequently segmented into "packets" of up to 1000 bits within the source switching node (IMP). These packets are reassembled into messages by the destination IMP.

One can identify analogous segmentation of the data stream in networks supporting X.25 packet-mode access. The terminology is slightly confusing here since the "packets" delivered to an X.25 network correspond to the entities called "messages" in the case of the ARPANET. Telenet packets of up to 8000 bits are split into 1000-bit (sub)packets for transmission from source to destination. Recommendation X.25 also defines a mechanism for identifying logical data units larger than a single packet. By setting the "More Data Bit" in a data packet, a subscriber indicates that successive packets correspond to the same logical data unit. If the internal network packet size is larger than the access packet size, the network can combine multiple external packets into a single internal packet for efficiency of transmission. For X.25 networks with multiple external packet sizes, the network may also need to set the "More Data Bit" when transmitting a unit of logical data from a subscriber with a large external packet size to a subscriber with a smaller external packet size.

In the case of SNA, an application buffer of data can be segmented into a sequence of Request Units (RUs) for transmission. The maximum size of RUs is not fixed within the architecture but is established at the time a session is set up between two communicating Logical Units (LUs). Request Units can themselves be segmented into smaller data units (Buffer Information Unit segments) for more efficient transmission. Although the definition of SNA permits data unit segmentation to occur at each step of the source to destination path, repeated segmentation has not been implemented since no important advantage has been found to do so. Implementations of SNA have restricted data stream segmentation to the source and destination nodes [GRAY 79A]. Under SNA, a set of sequential RUs may be identified as a "chain." The chaining mechanism permits one to identify a series of RUs to the network as a single logical entity and to manage the recovery of the chain as a single unit. We note that this logical chaining is distinct from the physical blocking of information discussed in Sec. 2.4.3.

There are a variety of factors that influence the choice of internal packet size for a network. Delay considerations point to a smaller packet size. For interactive traffic, queuing delays may become intolerable if very large packets are permitted [KLEI 76]. With fixed-size packet buffers, very large packets also imply much wasted storage due to internal memory fragmentation, although very small packets are also quite inefficient in their use of storage due to fixed packet and buffer control information [SCHU 72, KLEI 74, KLEI 76]. Effective line bandwidth utilization involves a trade-off between large and small packets as well. Large packets are more likely to arrive at their destination in error and require retransmission, whereas small packets may result in an unacceptable level of line overhead due to header and trailer bits [METC 73, KIMB 75, TRAY 77A, TRAY 77B]. Finally, processing considerations within the nodes argue for larger packets since packet processing is often independent of packet length. The size of the entity presented to the network by the subscriber (i.e., message size for the ARPANET and packet size for Telenet) needs to be large as well since node processing associated with such entities can be significant and it may be undesirable for a subscriber to process many message interrupts [CROW 75].

2.4.2 Framing and Transparency

Protocol framing and transparency mechanisms support transmission of individual blocks of information across physical network links. Data flow on a link is realized by the transmission of a series of blocks (frames) of information separated by idle periods. To mark the beginning and end of a block, specific framing indicators are defined. The "start frame" and "end frame" marks may be the same or different. Recognition of these marks permits the receiver of a bit stream to maintain frame synchronization. In earlier "character-oriented" protocols, typified by IBM's Binary Synchronous Communication (BSC) protocol, control characters such as SOH/STX and ETB/ETX were placed at the beginning and end of a block, respectively. In the more recently defined "bit-oriented" link control procedures (HDLC, ADCCP, and SDLC) the single bit pattern (flag) 01111110 has been used for this purpose. Other framing flag patterns have been used in special environments to achieve improved efficiency [FORN 76].

Protocols may require that the information in a frame consist of only a sequence of elements from a specified alphabet or may permit any bit sequence to be transmitted transparently. If a block can contain arbitrary data, special attention must be paid to assure that random bit or character patterns in the middle of the information field are not confused with the framing indicators, causing a block to be considered complete prematurely. Under BSC, a technique referred to as *DLE doubling* is employed. Framing control characters are preceded with a single DLE when used with transparent mode. DLE characters appearing within the transparent text portion of a message are transmitted as two successive DLEs. The receiving interface is designed to delete one of these repeated characters before delivering the data to the receiver. HDLC-type protocols employ a technique called *bit stuffing* to achieve this same result. A zero bit is inserted in the data stream after any sequence of five 1 bits to distinguish the pattern from the flag sequence that delimits the frame. A different approach for supporting the transmission of arbitrary binary data is employed under Digital Equipment Corporation's DDCMP protocol [DIGI 78A]. Rather than indicating the end of a block by a marker, the size of the block is indicated by a count field in the block header. A more detailed discussion of the trade-offs associated with link level protocols can be found in Chap. 3.

2.4.3   Blocking of Information

In many networks the individual atomic entities that are moved across the network links consist of information from only a single logical source. For example, it is not possible to combine information from several users into a single ARPANET or Telenet packet. In other networks, however, this restriction is not imposed. The motivation for permitting this packing (blocking) of information from multiple source/destination streams is efficiency. Much of the processing associated with each link-level frame is independent of frame length. Moreover, the size of the link-level envelope that surrounds the text portion of a frame is also typically independent of frame length. If very small frames are permitted (e.g., single character frames for highly interactive applications), the line overhead per packet can be over 90% [FALK 77B]. This can be avoided if characters from many different users are packed together. Although there is clearly a processing cost associated with the task of packing and unpacking frames at each step along a path, some network designers have concluded that this cost is worth the more efficient use of other network resources.

Both SNA and Tymnet provide a capability for blocking of information within link-level frames. In the case of SNA, the elements blocked within the frame consist of Path Information Units (PIUs). The series of PIUs is called a Basic Transmission Unit (BTU). The BTU wrapped in its link control envelope is called a Basic Link Unit (BLU). At each node, the SNA Path Control function can examine the BTU, disassemble it, and route each component PIU according to its ultimate destination. If a number of small PIUs are again headed down the same line, a reblocking of those PIUs can take place. In practice, the blocking capabilities of path control under SNA are used only across mainframe I/O channel data links in order to reduce CPU cycle usage [GRAY 77]. This capability has apparently been more attractive in the case of Tymnet [RIND 76], where at times of significant traffic it is used to reduce the number of single character frames. Blocking of information is also an important feature of the Codex 6000 Intelligent Network Processors [FORN 76, VAND 76] and other statistical time-division multiplexer designs [DOLL 78, SCHW 77, SEID 78].

2.4.4   Error Control

There are several network failure modes that various protocol mechanisms are designed to address. Most obvious is the possibility that noise on the communication circuits will corrupt the transmitted bits. This can result in either a frame received with its text portion in error or a lost frame (if the noise happened to destroy some of the block framing). Data can also be corrupted while they are stored within the memory of a switching node or while being delivered to a node interface from node storage. Finally, node hardware can fail or latent software bugs may cause the node to crash in a way that requires a node reload or restart. This may result in loss of both data and state information.

Protocol mechanisms provided to handle the network failures described above can be classified as message identification techniques and checksumming techniques. Unique message identification allows a protocol to deal with lost and duplicate messages. For simplicity of implementation, identifiers attached to messages have typically taken the form of sequence numbers. Using sequence numbers for identifiers also allows the integration of error control, sequencing (ordering), and flow control, The same numbers can be used by all three functions (as described below).

Checksumming schemes are based on the concept of adding redundant control information to the user data being transmitted. If sufficient redundant information is added, error correction is possible based on only the received bit string. Error rates on most terrestrial communication circuits, however, make such "forward error correction" unattractive. The most common approaches used today are variations on the so-called automatic-repeat-request (ARQ) scheme. With ARQ schemes the checksum transmitted with the text portion of a message is adequate only for error detection (not for correction). Correctly received messages are acknowledged to the transmitter and incorrectly received messages are discarded. The transmitter times out the receipt of an acknowledgment (ACK) for each transmitted message and retransmits the message if necessary. Variations on this basic model are, of course, possible. For example, in some protocols the receiver can send the transmitter a negative acknowledgment (NAK) when an error is detected in order to speed up retransmission. Early horizontal and vertical parity checksums have largely been replaced with checksums based on cyclic codes [MART 70, BOUD 71, CYPS 78]. These cyclic codes are not only more powerful than parity check designs but can also be implemented quite efficiently in low-cost hardware.

In a network with multiple-link source-to-destination paths, error control can be applied on a link-by-link basis, on an end-to-end basis, or both. Link-by-link acknowledgment reduces the effective message delay over error-prone circuits [METC 73]. End-to-end control supports more complete error protection. A combined approach provides the advantages of both techniques but involves additional use of network resources (i.e., circuit bandwidth and node processing power).

There is much similarity among the error control mechanisms employed by present-day computer networks. Under SNA there is a single end-to-end session sequence number attached to each Request Unit (RU) transmitted by a process. This sequence number is generated by the Transmission Control (TC) function of the source node. It is passed back to the source process in order that acknowledgment and error recovery information associated with that Request Unit can be identified. Errors due to corruption of the data are handled by SDLC checksums on the links. In the ARPANET environment, a 12-bit message identifier passed between the host and its IMP can be used for identification of responses for outstanding messages. This identifier is also passed through to the destination host so that the host can detect lost and duplicate messages resulting from IMP network failures. In addition to standard link checksums, the ARPANET IMPs implement an end-to-end checksum in software to detect corruption of data occurring within the nodes. This software checksum is computed on each packet by the IMP as it comes in from the source host and is checked at each node along the end-to-end path.

It is important to keep the limitations as well as the capabilities of the ARQ protocols clearly in mind. Although they can successfully mask errors in the transmission medium, they cannot guarantee reliable transmission when part of the protocol itself is violated (e.g., due to a system crash). Proper state (sequence number) information must be maintained at both ends of a connection for correct operation. An independent higher-level checkpointing mechanism is likely to be required if recovery from protocol failures is also to be achieved [SUNS 75]. SNA LUs provide session restart facilities to do this via the Set and Test Sequence Number (STSN) command [EADE 77, CYPS 78].

2.4.5   Sequencing

Sequencing is that protocol function which permits delivery of data units to the destination in the same order that they were accepted from the source. Sequencing mechanisms are based on the use of sequence numbers attached to each message transmitted. Successive sequence numbers may be associated with each 8-bit data byte of a source-to-destination stream [CERF 74B] or may be associated with entire messages [CERF 78A]. In either case, the size of the sequence number space must be large enough so that an earlier message with sequence number N is not left within the system when the next incarnation of message number N is generated [POUZ 78]. In general, one will be safe if the maximum message lifetime is less than half the time to cycle through the sequence number space [CERF 74B]. Control messages as well as data messages can share the same set of sequence numbers or separate independently sequenced subchannels can be provided for control and data flows. A discussion of advantages and disadvantages of these two approaches can be found in [GARL 77].

Although protocols that support sequenced data flow are by far the most common, it is important to note that there are cases where sequencing is not only unnecessary but may, in fact, cause complications. Consider the case of an individual link between two adjacent switching nodes of a network. Since successive data frames flowing over this link will, in general, be associated with unrelated logical data flows, there is no reason to sequence the flow of these frames. Doing so may have the effect of reducing the effective node-to-node throughput and increasing effective packet delay and buffering requirements [FALK 78]. The ARPANET IMP-to-IMP protocol is an example of a link control procedure that does not provide sequenced delivery of frames [MCQU 77A].

2.4.6   Flow Control

The essence of the flow control problem is to match the rate of transmission by a sender to the rate of acceptance by a receiver. The communicating partners may be nodes talking over a physical circuit, processes conversing across a network, and so on. In the case of end-to-end traffic, we distinguish between flow control associated with a single logical flow and congestion control. Congestion control is a mechanism provided to deal with the competition between many logical flows for the limited resources of the network. The two concepts are certainly related, however, since without flow control a network very quickly becomes congested.

There are a variety of approaches that have been taken to solve or partially address the flow control problem [GERL 80]. In the simplest case the transmitter knows the fixed rate of acceptance of the receiver and may send data at precisely this rate. An example is listing a file on a local line printer. Unfortunately, the majority of receivers accept data at an unknown or variable rate. Another nonfeedback (open-loop) approach is to provide an infinite (very large) buffer at the receiver (e.g., a disk). This is the approach taken in traditional "message switching" systems. For general-purpose communication systems, however, this is not particularly attractive (by itself) since disks are relatively slow, unreliable, and expensive. Better solutions are available which involve the receiver informing the sender of its ability to accept data (closed-loop or feedback approaches).

In the simplest case, the receiver informs the sender of its inability to accept data indirectly by not acknowledging data it cannot accept. This approach relies on the error control mechanism to effect the retransmission. The disadvantage of this approach is that considerable processor and line bandwidth may be wasted and delay introduced by the transmission of unacceptable data. This can be avoided if the receiver explicitly gives the transmitter permission to send. The simplest exchange of this type involves the receiver sending STOP and START messages to the transmitter. The transmitter sends until it receives a STOP, at which time it suspends transmission until a subsequent START is received. The problem with this approach is that there may be a large time delay between the sender and receiver. If multiple outstanding messages are permitted, the receiver may still have to discard significant transmitted but unacknowledged data already in the communications channel. What is needed is a mechanism that explicitly allocates receiver buffer storage to the transmitter. In particular, the receiver can send the transmitter a message of the form "Send N More Data Units." These data units may be messages, bytes, bits, or a combination of these.

In the case of SNA, this type of flow control, called "pacing," is carried out within the Transmission Subsystem on a per session (LU-to-LU connection) basis. The receiver LU indicates to the transmitter LU that up to N more Request Units (RUs) may be transmitted. The number N is fixed for the duration of a session, but the pacing message may be sent by the receiver prior to the receipt of the previous N RUs in order to keep the end-to-end logical channel full. This supports high-throughput applications. In the case of the ARPANET, a similar type of flow control is used as part of the process-to-process level protocol but allocate messages take the form "Send M more Messages and B More Bits." In this case both M and B can vary from one allocate message to the next.

These ARPANET and SNA flow control mechanisms can both be described as incremental. This means that the receiver tells the sender that a certain number "more" data units of some type are allowed. It has been argued that incremental schemes have the potential to lose synchronization if allocation messages are lost within the communications system and no notification of the loss is provided.

Windowing schemes tied more tightly to end-to-end sequence numbers have more recently been proposed (e.g., in the TCP and IFIP end-to-end protocols described in Sec. 2.3.3). With these schemes an acknowledgment also specifies a sequence number beyond the last acknowledged frame. Only data within this variable-size window will be accepted by the receiver [GARL 77]. Such windowing schemes have the property that they are self-synchronizing. SNA, on the other hand, avoids loss of synchronization by guaranteed notification of message loss.

SNA session pacing is coupled with separate pacing on virtual routes (bundles of sessions). The purpose of virtual route pacing is global network congestion control rather than control of individual source/destination rates. There have been many papers written on the related subjects of flow control and congestion control in computer networks [KAHN 72, HERM 76, CHOU 76, LAM 79, RUDI 79, GERL 80]. The International Symposium on Flow Control in Computer Networks held in Versailles, February 1979, focused specifically on these two subjects [GRAN 79]. Much of the theory in this area will be tested over the next few years as large packet-switched networks carrying significant traffic become common.

2.4.7 Out-of-Band Signaling

Some form of flow control is associated with almost every network protocol. There are cases, however, where the normal flow control mechanisms need to be bypassed to ensure responsiveness to high-priority events. Consider the user of a time-sharing system who creates and begins the execution of a program which contains an erroneous infinite loop. When the user recognizes his error, he would like to instruct the time-sharing system to abort the execution of his program. If he is not locally connected to the time-sharing system, however, his "abort character" may be stuck in a buffer of some system other than its ultimate destination due to flow control constraints. What is needed is an out-of-band signal that is always passed and processed by the receiver even if its normal buffers are exhausted. Such a signal is often referred to as a protocol interrupt message. The interrupt message is most common in process-to-process level protocols for implementing the type of capability described above.

One possible interrupt capability for a process-to-process protocol involves the definition of a single interrupt control message. The interrupt message includes the interrupt code and a position sequence number in the data stream. When an interrupt signal arrives, the receiver discards any information currently buffered before the specified byte position in the data stream and transmits an interrupt to the receiving process. The need to discard information ahead of the interrupt is based on the following assumptions: (1) interrupts will be acknowledged, (2) acknowledgments implicitly acknowledge all previous sequence numbers, and (3) a single sequence number space is used for both control and data messages. To distinguish between different types of interrupts, it may be useful to allow an interrupt control message to contain a small amount of data. A further generalization of this type of interrupt capability is described in [GARL 77]. Such an approach may be necessary to avoid discarding certain control signals that might otherwise be blocked by flow control and flushed due to an interrupt. Under SNA, on the other hand, this situation does not arise since the interrupt capability supported by the "expedited flow" channel between LUs is not coupled via a sequence number to the normal LU-LU data flow. Coupling, if any, occurs at a higher level within the communicating application processes.

2.4.8 Priority and Preemption

Prioritizing the handling of various data and control messages is important for network performance. Defining more than one distinct priority level for data messages is useful in decreasing the queuing delay for important traffic or traffic associated with interactive applications. Beyond this, however, priority is important to ensure that the most critical network functions are not delayed. In the ARPANET implementation, routing messages are transmitted with highest priority followed by acknowledgments for received data messages. Furthermore, retransmissions of data are given priority over first transmissions to ensure that they do not get locked out indefinitely.

While priority is a desirable feature, preemption based on priority does not appear to be called for in most cases. Both node and link resources made available for processing and transmitting a data unit must be considered wasted when those data are preempted by higher-priority traffic. The result of message preemption is simply to trade reduced delay for degradation in useful bandwidth. Since the message delays in modern data communication systems are typically fractions of a second to begin with, any further improvement is often hardly worth the trouble. However, if one changes the focus from preemption of individual messages to preemption of conversations, the concept may be more attractive, particularly in a military environment [DEFE 75].

2.4.9 Establishment and Termination of Connections

A connection is an association between communicating entities. Data flow over a connection can be either simplex, half-duplex, or full-duplex. The connection establishment mechanism allows each end to assure itself that the other end exists, can be accessed, and can support the desired traffic flow. Connection establishment procedures also attempt to ensure that state information (e.g., next transmit and receive sequence numbers) at each end of the connection is consistent with state information at the other end. Connection initialization occurs at many levels in a typical communication system. Under X.25 level 2 (or HDLC in general) the two ends of each link exchange initialization commands Set Asynchronous Response Mode (SARM) or Set Asynchronous Balanced Mode (SABM). At level 3 under X.25, initialization is done on an individual basis for each DTE/DCE virtual circuit (e.g., Call Request/Call Connected). Connections are also established on an end-to-end basis between user processes. In the case of the ARPANET, request for connection commands

(RTS and STR) are sent from receiver to sender and from sender to receiver, respectively [MCKE 76]. In the case of SNA, a BIND command is sent from the primary LU to the secondary LU to establish LU-LU communication. Virtual route activation commands may also be required in an SNA network if no appropriate virtual route exists [AHUJ 79].

An important issue is whether or not a central authority must participate in the connection establishment procedure. In an SNA environment, session initiation for end users (LUs) involves communication with the SSCP. The SSCP carries out the functions of name-to-address mapping (see Sec. 2.4.10), access authorization, user profile lookup, and so on. A central authority is also involved in the connection setup with Tymnet, where the center also establishes the route to be dedicated to the connection. The Telenet and ARPANET designs, on the other hand, are similar in that only the two communicating entities are involved in the establishment of a communication path between one another.

The complexity of the connection establishment process depends to a large extent on the nature of the supporting communications system [CERF 78B]. If the underlying system is totally reliable and messages have a short maximum lifetime, the procedure can be quite straightforward. The two ends of the connection merely exchange Requests for Connection (RFCs), which cause the connection to be opened. RFC acknowledgments are not required. Each end of the connection goes through an "opening" state on its way from a "closed" state to an "open" state. The "opening" state corresponds to having only sent or received an RFC but not both. When two RFCs "rendezvous" at an end, the state of that end changes from "opening" to "open." The issue of rendezvous becomes quite important for end-to-end connections where there may be a significant delay between the arrival time for matching RFCs. RFCs must, in general, be queued either until the matching RFC arrives or until a system-specified timeout is exhausted. RFCs associated with certain service processes on a host system (e.g., the system LOGIN module, the file transfer package, etc.) are likely to be continuously queued "listening" for service requests.

Connection termination is also straightforward if the supporting system is totally reliable. When one or both of the communicating partners is finished, it sends a close to the other. A "closing" state analogous to the "opening" state is employed by each end to delay its closing of the connection until the other end agrees. A recovery strategy must be specified to handle the case where one end of the connection "crashes" and is unable to participate in the closing process.

Connection establishment becomes more complex if one takes a more pessimistic view of the underlying communication system with respect to its delay and reliability characteristics. Such pessimism may be appropriate in the case of process-to-process protocols which operate in multiple-network environments. One problem arises if a connection is opened, closed, and quickly reopened within the lifetime of messages in the network. Unless care is taken, it is possible that messages with sequence numbers from the old incarnation of the connection will be confused with messages having identical sequence numbers from the more recent incarnation. A similar problem may arise when one attempts to reestablish a connection after a protocol failure with loss of state information (e.g., caused by a system crash and restart). To avoid such problems, good methods for clearing out old duplicates (SNA) or for selecting initial nonconflicting sequence numbers and exchanging them between the two ends of a connection are required. It has been shown that a "three-way handshake" can guarantee a reliable exchange of starting sequence numbers without requiring either end to keep track of the other end's old sequence numbers [TOML 75, SUNS 75]. Using a "three-way handshake," the receiver of a request to reinitialize does not simply accept the request blindly, but asks for verification from the sender that the request is, in fact, the most current.

A variety of initial sequence number selection procedures have been proposed [TOML 75, DALA 75, GARL 77]. For networks where the maximum packet lifetime, T, is small, one can choose always to initialize both ends to zero. This may require delaying the establishment of a connection for T seconds to permit old duplicates to die out. If delaying the startup of all recently closed or unknown connections by T seconds adds too much delay, this procedure could be used only after a system crash. A connection table that remembers the last sequence number used on each closed connection (for T seconds) could be used to select an initial sequence number in the normal case. The connection establishment delay associated with system crashes can also be reduced using schemes that associate "incarnation numbers" with each restart of the host running the protocol module. The incarnation number may be stored in some form of nonvolatile memory or may be derived from a clock [TOML 75, GARL 77].

The only change in the connection termination strategy described earlier in the case of lossy networks is that close messages must be acknowledged.

2.4.10 Addressing and Naming

Addresses must be attached to messages that are transmitted over shared (multiplexed) facilities. Destination addresses provide information necessary for proper routing and delivery of data. Source addresses allow the receiver of a data unit to identify its origin. Addressing issues arise at every level of network protocol. At the link level, addresses are implicit if the configuration is point-to-point and explicit for polled multipoint or contention multipoint systems. At the subscriber interface level, networks provide an addressing structure to reference other subscribers. CCITT has agreed on a basic addressing structure of 12 binary-coded decimal (BCD) digits used to identify public data network subscribers (X.121, [CCIT 81B]). At the process-to-process level it is convenient to have a large address space for specifying communication ports within a subscriber. The ARPANET uses a 32-bit "socket" number for this purpose [MCKE 76]. Originally, SNA used a 16-bit network address for all process-to-process communication. The 16-bit field could be split into a subarea address and an element address within the subarea. The FID4 header defined for SNA Release 4.2 expanded this address space to support up to 48 bits, 32 bits of subarea and 16 bits within a subarea.

An important distinction should be made between logical addresses (names) and physical addresses (locations). A permanently assigned logical address can denote one or more physical addresses. If logical addresses are used, the sender of data need not know the physical location of the receiver and communicating entities can relocate without change of address. This is particularly important in the case of network failures where network recovery can be carried out transparently. In addition, logical addressing facilitates the support of mobile and multiple-connected subscribers, that is, systems connected to more than one network node in order to provide increased reliability and traffic-carrying capacity. Virtual circuit networks can support logical addressing mechanisms quite efficiently since the mapping from logical to physical addresses needs to be done only once per conversation and actual messages need contain only the physical address of the destination or an abbreviation for it. There are a variety of ways to establish a network-wide logical address structure in a heterogeneous operating environment and relate the global addresses to the local naming schemes used within component systems. Pouzin and Zimmerman discuss a number of possible approaches in [POUZ 78].

Typically, a single destination address will be associated with each piece of data. There are cases, however, where broadcast or multidestination addressing may be attractive. Broadcast addressing, where all other entities at the same level are to receive the message, has proved useful as part of certain routing algorithm protocols and as a means of informing system users of important changes in network status. Multidestination addressing, where a message carries a list of specific addresses, can improve the efficiency of certain applications such as electronic mail and teleconferencing. A variation on the concept of multidestination addressing is group addressing, where the message carries the name of the list of addresses rather than the list itself. In a virtual circuit network implementing only sessions (connections, conversations) between pairs of users, it is important to note that multidestination addressing implies the use of multiple sessions. A good discussion of a variety of issues related to enhanced network addressing capabilities can be found in [MCQU 78A].

2.5   CONCLUDING REMARKS

This chapter has attempted to provide the reader a framework in which to view the subject of data communications protocols. In Sec. 2.3, one view of the organization of protocols in an overall network architecture was presented. In Sec. 2.4 the set of functions that are components of the protocols identified earlier was discussed.

Although it was the intention of this presentation to be more descriptive than quantitative, it is important to emphasize the relationship of protocol design to overall network performance and efficiency. Protocol design must not only provide adequate functionality but must also take into account implications of providing the required level of service on the utilization of network resources. With the rapidly declining cost of processing power and memory, the cost of circuit bandwidth is often a driving force in protocol design at the communications system level. Delay is also a critical consideration for networks using satellite as well as terrestrial facilities.

We are currently at a point where interconnected networks are becoming available that can provide efficient, reliable, low-cost, data transport. The most important issues that remain are whether or not we will be able to capitalize on these facilities in terms of resource sharing, load sharing, and distributed data processing applications in multivendor environments. The current roadblock to achieving these goals is in the area of higher-level protocols. We believe that ongoing standards work in this area will have a major impact on the use of data communications systems over the next several years. The coming integration of diverse traffic types (e.g., data, voice, image) in a single communications system also presents some interesting challenges for the network protocol designer.

Appendix 1

The material in this appendix provides a brief overview of the ARPANET and IBM's Systems Network Architecture (SNA).

The ARPANET

The ARPANET is a packet-switching network originally developed by the Advanced Research Projects Agency (ARPA) of the Department of Defense [ROBE 70, HEAR 70, ORNS 72, MCQU 72, MCKE 75, MCQU 75, WALD 75, MCQU 77A]. Its design has been evolving over the past 12 years. The ARPANET is comprised of two main types of physical nodes: Interface Message Processors (IMPs) and Terminal Interface Message Processors (TIPs). The IMPs provide a store-and-forward switching function in addition to providing an interface for connecting host computers. A TIP is an IMP with an additional concentrator function providing network access for unintelligent asynchronous terminals. Arbitrary topological interconnection of IMPs and TIPs is permitted within the ARPANET design. A third type of node, referred to as the network control center (NCC), provides a central facility for network monitoring, diagnosis and maintenance.

The ARPANET is designed to provide reliable sequenced transfer of messages between pairs of host computers. An application buffer is delivered by a host to the network as a number of such messages, each less than 8000 bits in length. The IMP connected to the source host segments each message into up to eight packets. Packets can be up to 1000 bits in length. Packets of a message are routed independently through the network and are reassembled into the original message at the destination IMP, which assures ordered delivery of messages to the destination host. To provide process-to-process communication between end users, a Network Control Program (NCP) is typically added to the operating system of each attached host. The NCP multiplexes multiple conversations onto the single flow between host pairs supported by the interconnected IMPs. The terminal concentration function of the TIP can be thought of as a special-purpose network-supplied host. TIPs contain NCP software to support terminal-to-process communication.

The protocol hierarchy that supports the operation of the ARPANET is illustrated in Fig. 2.A.1. Adjacent IMPs forward data reliably between one another according to IMP-to-IMP protocol [MCQU 77A]. A source IMP-to-destination IMP protocol supports the packetizing, reassembling, and ordering of messages described above [MCQU 75]. The host-to-IMP protocol defines both a physical interface and a set of message formats for passing data between a host and its local IMP. For short distances a high-speed asynchronous bit serial interface is specified. An error-controlled link control procedure referred to as the very-distant-host interface is specified for distances of several thousand feet or more [BOLT 78]. Another access arrangement is defined for the connections of terminals to a TIP. This definition is comprised of both a physical interface and a terminal command language

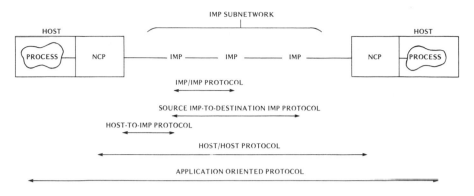

Figure 2.A.1. ARPANET protocol hierarchy.

[BOLT 75]. Finally, the process-to-process communication is supported by inter-communication between NCP software modules according to a protocol referred to as the host–host protocol [MCKE 76]. Process-to-process conversations can be established by pairs of processes exchanging "requests for connection" that specifically name one another or can be established between user processes and service process (e.g., the system logger, file transfer package, etc.) according to the initial connection protocol (ICP) [POST 76]. Host–host and ICP protocols form the foundation for a variety of application-oriented protocols in the ARPANET. These protocols are discussed in Sec. 2.3.4 and in [WALD 75]. The Transmission Control Protocol (TCP) [INFO 80A] is increasingly being used in the ARPANET as an alternative to the host–host and ICP protocols.

IBM Systems Network Architecture

Systems Network Architecture (SNA) was designed to provide a unifying system structure for the IBM teleprocessing environment [GRAY 77, CYPS 78, PIAT 77, MCFA 76, CULL 76, HOBG 76, ALBR 76, EADE 77, IBM 76, GRAY 79, ATKI 80, HOBE 80, IBM 78A]. Whereas the ARPANET is an actual implementation, SNA is a detailed template onto which all teleprocessing products must map. SNA leaves some mechanisms undefined (e.g., interlayer formats within nodes) to permit implementation flexibility while providing an adequate specification to ensure compatibility among different implementations (products).

SNA is designed to provide communication between logical entities referred to as Network Addressable Units (NAUs). Three types of NAUs exist. Logical Units (LUs) provide interface ports for SNA end users. End users may be either human operators at terminals or application programs. Physical Units (PUs) comprise a second set of network addressable units. A distinct PU is typically associated with each shared communications resource (host, cluster controller, etc.), in the network.

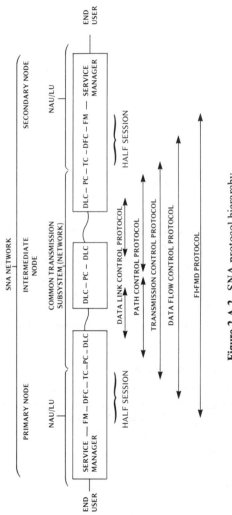

Figure 2.A.2. SNA protocol hierarchy.

The PU is the entity to which communication is directed when one wants to communicate with the associated physical device. Finally, each SNA network has one (or more in a multihost network) System Services Control Point (SSCP). The SSCP provides central monitoring, coordination, and control of its area of responsibility (domain) in the SNA network.

A number of functions exist within SNA nodes to support NAU-to-NAU communication. These functions comprise a hierarchy of protocols as illustrated in Fig. 2.A.2. At the lowest level, Data Link Control (DLC) elements in adjacent nodes support the reliable transmission of blocks called Path Information Units (PIUs) from one node to the next. Communicating Path Control (PC) elements in each node route PIUs onto the right links so as to direct each message toward its ultimate destination. PC elements are also involved with repackaging of data units. PIUs may be segmented into smaller pieces or blocked with other PIUs into larger units where delay or efficiency factors dictate. The PC and DLC layers taken together comprise what is termed the Common Transmission Subsystem. The Common Transmission Subsystem provides the foundation for Transmission Control (TC) elements within the source and destination nodes to implement virtual circuitlike end-to-end connections called sessions. The data units transmitted over sessions are called Request Units (RUs).

Sessions are the basis for all NAU-to-NAU communication under SNA. Higher-level protocols tailor general-purpose sessions to specific application requirements. The Data Flow Control (DFC) protocol layer works in concert with the TC elements to provide application specific control and synchronization of the data exchanges associated with a session. We note that DFC is not involved with the control of the sender and receiver rates. (Regulation of flow rate is a function of the TC elements called pacing.) At the highest level the Function Management elements, FI.FMDs, implement the protocols which for LU-to-LU sessions are primarily concerned with "presentation services." Presentation services format, edit, and translate data from one end user so that it will be more meaningful to the other end user. Data compression/decompression and command translation are examples of SNA presentation services. The FI.FMD, DFC, and TC elements at each end of an SNA session are referred to collectively as half-sessions and are the major entities comprising each LU. Different types of LU-to-LU sessions can be established corresponding to different selections of half-session functionality. Several canonical session types are defined within SNA and are referred to as LU types.

SNA is implemented in a large number of IBM products. The SNA software that runs in the communications controller nodes (e.g., the IBM 3705) is called the Advanced Communication Function/Network Control Program (ACF/NCP). The communications access method which runs on IBM mainframes (e.g., S/370, 303X, and 43XX hardware) is either the ACF Virtual Telecommunications Access Method (ACF/VTAM) or the ACF Telecommunications Access Method (ACF/TCAM). Some SNA functionality is also found in application-oriented subsystems such as the Customer Information Control System/Virtual Storage (CICS/VS) and program products such as the Network Communications Control Facility (NCCF) and the

Network Problem Determination Application (NPDA). The reader is directed to the most recent releases of IBM documentation on these software products for implementation details.

REFERENCES

AHUJ 79 Ahuja, V., "Routing and Flow Control in Systems Network Architecture," *IBM Syst. J.*, Vol. 18, No. 2, 1979, pp. 298–314.

ALBR 76 Albrecht, H. R., and K. D. Ryder, "The Virtual Telecommunications Access Method: A Systems Network Architecture Perspective," *IBM Sys. J.*, Vol. 15, No. 1, 1976, pp. 53–80.

ANSI 76 ANSI, "Proposed American National Standard for Advanced Data Communication Control Procedure," Sixth Draft, Task Group 4, Document X3S34/589, October 15, 1976.

ATKI 80 Atkins, J. D., "Path Control: The Transport Network of SNA," *IEEE Trans. Commun.*, Vol. COM-28, No. 4, April 1980, pp. 527–538.

AT&T 78 American Telephone and Telegraph Company, "Advanced Communications Service — Host and Terminal Functional Interface Description," Basking Ridge, N.J., September 1978.

BAUW 78 Bauwens, E., and F. Magnee, "Definition of the Virtual Terminal Protocol for the Belgian University Network," *Proc. Comput. Network Protocols Conf.*, (A. Danthine, Ed.) University of Liege, Belgium, February 1978, pp. D3-1 to D3-14.

BERT 80 Bertine, H. V., "Physical Level Protocols," *IEEE Trans. Commun.*, Vol. COM-28, No. 4, April 1980, pp. 433–444.

BOGG 76 Boggs, D. R., and R. M. Metcalfe "Ethernet: Distributed Packet Switching for Local Computer Networks," *Commun. ACM*, Vol. 19, No. 7, 1976, pp. 395–404.

BOLT 75 Bolt, Beranek and Newman, Inc., *Users Guide to the Terminal IMP*, BBN Rep. No. 2183, August 1975.

BOLT 78 Bolt, Beranek and Newman, Inc., "Specification for the Interconnection of a Host and IMP," BBN Rep. No. 1822, May 1978.

BOUD 71 Boudreau, P. E., and R. F. Steen, "Cyclic Redundancy Checking by Program," *AFIPS 1971 Conf. Proc.*, Vol. 39, pp. 9–15.

BRAD 77 Braden, R., "NETRJS Protocol," ARPA Network Working Group RFC #740, NIC #42423, November 22, 1977.

BRES 76 Bressler, R., and R. Guida "Remote Job Entry Protocol," in *ARPANET Protocol Handbook*, Network Information Center, Stanford Research Institute, Menlo Park, Calif., April 1976.

BUDW 79 Budway, J., "Software Tackles the Task of SNA Net Control," *Data Commun.*, May 1979, pp. 83–93.

BUTS 79 Butscher, B., and W. Heinze, "A File Transfer Protocol and Implementation," *Comput. Commun. Rev.*, Vol. 9, No. 3, 1979, pp. 2–12.

CARL 80 Carlson, D. E., "Bit-Oriented Data Link Control Procedures," *IEEE Trans.*

Commun., Vol. COM-28, No. 4, 1980, pp. 455–467.

CARR 70 Carr, S., S. D. Crocker, V. G. Cerf, "Host–Host Communication Protocol in the ARPA Network," *Proc. Spring Joint Comput. Conf.*, Vol. 36, Atlantic City, N.J., AFIPS Press, Montvale, N.J., 1970, pp. 589–598.

CASH 76 Cashman, P. M., and R. A. Faneuf, "File Package: The File Handling Facility for the National Software Works," Massachusetts Computer Associates, Inc., Document CADD-7612-2711, December 1976.

CCIT 81A CCITT, *Yellow Book*, Vol. VIII. 2: *International Telecommunications Union*, Geneva, 1981.

CCIT 81B CCITT, *Yellow Book*, Vol. VIII. 3: *International Telecommunications Union*, Geneva, 1981.

CERF 74A Cerf, V., "An Assessment of ARPANET Protocols," ARPANET Working Group, RFC 635, NIC 30489, April 1974.

CERF 74B Cerf, V., and R. E. Kahn, "A Protocol for Packet Network Interconnection," *IEEE Trans. Commun.*, Vol. COM-22, No. 5, 1974, pp. 637–648.

CERF 78A Cerf, V., A. McKenzie, R. Scantlebury, and H. Zimmermann, "Proposal for an Internetwork End-to-End Transport Protocol," *Proc. Comput. Network Protocol Conf.*, Liege, Belgium, February 1978, pp. H5 to H25.

CERF 78B Cerf, V., and J. McQuillan, *A Practical View of Computer Communication Protocols*, IEEE Press, New York 1978.

CERF 78C Cerf, V. G., and P. T. Kirstein, "Issues in Packet Network Interconnection," *Proc. IEEE*, Vol. 66, No. 11, 1978, pp. 1386–1408.

CHOU 76 Chou, W., and M. Gerla, "A Unified Flow and Congestion Control Model for Packet Networks," *Proc. 3rd Int. Conf. Comput. Commun.*, Toronto, Canada, August 1976, pp. 475–482.

COHE 78 Cohen, D., "A Protocol for Packet Switching Voice Communication," *Proc. Comput. Network Protocols Conf.*, Liege, Belgium, February 1978, D8-1 to D8-9.

CONA 80 Conard, J. W., "Character-Oriented Data Link Control Protocols," *IEEE Trans. Commun.*, Vol. COM-28, No. 4, 1980, pp. 445–454.

CORR 79 Corr, F. P., and D. H. Neal "SNA and Emerging International Standards," *IBM Syst. J.*, Vol. 18, No. 2, 1979, pp. 244–260.

CRAB 78 Crabtree, R. P., "Job Networking," *IBM Syst. J.*, Vol. 17, No. 3, 1978, pp. 206–220.

CROC 72 Crocker, S. D., J. F. Heafner, R. M. Metcalfe, and J. R. Postel, "Function-Oriented Protocols for the ARPA Computer Network," *AFIPS — Proc. SJCC*, Vol. 40, May 1972, pp. 271–279.

CROW 75 Crowther, W. R., F. E. Heart, A. A. McKenzie, J. M. McQuillan, and D. C. Walden, "Issues in Packet Switching Network Design," *Proc. Nat. Comput. Conf.*, Vol. 44, AFIPS Press, Montvale, N.J., 1975, pp. 161–175.

CULL 76 Cullum, P. G., "The Transmission Subsystem of Systems Network Architecture," *IBM Syst. J.*, Vol. 15, No. 1, 1976, pp. 24–38.

CYPS 78 Cypser, R. J., *Communications Architecture for Distributed Systems*, Addison-Wesley, Reading, Mass., 1978.

DALA 75   Dalal, Y. K., "More on Selective, Sequence Numbers," *Proc. ACM SIGCOMM/SIGOPS Interprocess Commun. Workshop*, March 24–25, 1975, Santa Monica, Calif. (*ACM Oper. Syst. Rev.*, Vol. 9, No. 3, 1975), pp. 11–23.

DAVI 77   Davidson, J., W. Hathaway, J. Postel, N. Mimno, R. Thomas, and D. Walden, "The ARPANET TELNET Protocol: Its Principles, Implementation, and Impact on Host Operating System Design," *Proc. 5th Data Commun. Symp.*, September 27–29, 1977, Snowbird, Utah, pp. 4.10 to 4.18.

DAY 77   Day, J. and G. R. Grossman, "An RJE Protocol for a Resource Sharing Network," *Comput. Commun. Rev.*, Vol. 7, No. 3, 1977, pp. 77–78.

DAY 79   Day, J. D., "Resource Sharing Protocols," *Computer*, Vol. 12, No. 9, 1979, pp. 47–56.

DAY 80   Day, J. D., "Terminal Protocols," *IEEE Trans. Commun.*, Vol. COM-28, No. 4, 1980, pp. 585–593.

DEFE 75   Defense Communications Agency, "System Performance Specification (Type A) for AUTODIN II Phase I," November 1975 (amended through 1977).

DESM 76   de Smet, J., and R. W. Sanders, "A Network Combining Packet Switching and Time Division Switching in a Common System," *Comput. Commun. Rev.*, Vol. 6, No. 1, 1976, pp. 38–62.

DIGI 78A   Digital Equipment Corporation, "DDCMP Specification," Version 4.0, Maynard, Mass., March 1978.

DIGI 78B   Digital Equipment Corporation, "Data Access Protocol (DAP)," Functional Specification, Version 4.1, Maynard, Mass., March 1978.

DOLL 78   Doll, D., *Data Communications Facilities, Networks and Systems Design*, Wiley-Interscience, New York, 1978.

EADE 77   Eade, D. J., P. Homan, and J. H. Jones, "CICS/VS and Its Role in Systems Network Architecture," *IBM Syst. J.*, Vol. 16, No. 3, 1977, pp. 258–286.

FALK 77A   Falk, G., and J. M. McQuillan "Alternatives for Data Network Architectures," *IEEE Comput.*, Vol. 10, No. 11, 1977, pp. 22–29.

FALK 77B   Falk, G., "Issues in Sizing Store and Forward Communication Switches," *Proc. Comput. Networking Symp.*, National Bureau of Standards, Gathersbury, Md., December 1977.

FALK 78   Falk, G., "A Comparison of Network Architectures — The ARPANET and SNA," *Proc. Nat. Comput. Conf.*, Vol. 47, AFIPS Press, Montvale, N.J., 1978, pp. 755–763.

FARB 72   Farber, D. J., and K. C. Larson, "The System Architecture of the Distributed Computer System — The Communications System," *Proc. Microwave Research Inst. Int. Symp. Comput. — Commun. Networks Teletraffic*, April 1972, pp. 21–27.

FOLT 80   Folts, H. C., "X.25 Transaction Oriented Features — Datagram and Fast Select," *IEEE Trans. Commun.*, Vol. COM-28, No. 4, 1980, pp. 496–500.

FORN 76   Forney, G. D., and J. E. Vander Mey, "The Codex Series of Intelligent Network Processors," *Comput. Commun. Rev.*, Vol. 6, No. 2, 1976, pp. 7–11.

FORS 78   Forsdick, H., R. Schantz, and R. H. Thomas, "Operating Systems for Computer Networks," *IEEE Comput.*, Vol. 11, No. 1, 1978, pp. 48–57.

FORS 79 Forsdick, H., and A. McKenzie, "FTP Functional Specification," Bolt, Beranek, and Newman Rep. No. 4051, August 1979.

FRAS 75 Fraser, A. G., "A Virtual Channel Network," *Datamation*, Vol. 21, No. 2, 1975, pp. 51–56.

GARL 77 Garlick, L. L., R. Rom, and J. B. Postel, "Reliable Host-to-Host Protocols: Problems and Techniques," *Proc. 5th ACM/IEEE Data Commun. Symp.*, Snowbird, Utah, September 1977, pp. 4/58 to 4/65.

GERL 80 Gerla, M., and L. Kleinrock, "Flow Control: A Comparative Survey," *IEEE Trans. Commun.*, Vol. COM-28, No. 4, 1980, pp. 553–574.

GIEN 78 Gien, M., "A Standard File Transfer Protocol," *Comput. Network Protocols Conf.*, Liege, Belgium, February 1978.

GRAN 79 Grange, J. L., and M. Gien, eds., *Flow Control in Computer Networks*, Proc. Int. Symp. Flow Control Comput. Networks, Versailles, France, February 12–14, 1979, North-Holland, New York, 1979.

GRAY 72 Gray, J. P., "Line Control Procedures," *Proc. IEEE*, Vol. 60, No. 11, 1972, pp. 1301–1312.

GRAY 77 Gray, J. P., "Network Services in System Network Architecture," *IEEE Trans. Commun.*, Vol. COM-25, No. 1, 1977, pp. 104–116.

GRAY 79A Gray, J. P., and T. B. McNeill, "SNA Multiple System Networking," *IBM Syst. J.*, Vol. 18, No. 2, 1979, pp. 263–297.

GRAY 79B Gray, J., "Services Provided to Users of SNA Networks," *Proc. 6th Data Commun. Symp.*, Monterey, Calif., November 1979.

GREE 79 Green, P. F., "An Introduction to Network Architectures and Protocols," *IBM Syst. J.*, Vol. 18, No. 2, 1979, pp. 202–222.

HEAR 70 Heart, F. E., R. Kahn, S. Ornstein, W. Crowther, and D. Walden, "The Interface Message Processor for the ARPA Computer Network," *AFIPS Conf. Proc. 36*, June 1970, pp. 551–567.

HERM 76 Herman, J., "Flow Control in the ARPA Network," *Comput. Networks*, Vol. 1, 1976, pp. 55–76.

HERT 78 Hertweck, F. R., E. Raubold, and F. Vogt, "X.25 Based Process–Process Communication," *Proc. Comput. Network Protocols Symp.*, Liege, Belgium, 1978.

HOBE 80 Hoberecht, V. L., "SNA Function Management," *IEEE Trans. Commun.*, Vol. COM-28, No. 4, 1980, pp. 594–603.

HOBG 76 Hobgood, W. S., "The Role of the Network Control Program in Systems Network Architecture," *IBM Syst. J.*, Vol. 15, No. 1, 1976, pp. 39–52.

HOUS 79 Housley, T., *Data Communications and Teleprocessing Systems*, Prentice-Hall, Englewood Cliffs, N.J., 1979.

HOVE 76 Hovey, R. B., "Packet-Switched Networks Agree on Standard Interface," *Data Commun.*, May–June 1976, pp. 25–39.

HOVE 77 Hovey, R. B., "Matching Teleprinters to X.25 Packet Switching Networks," *Data Commun.*, October 1977, pp. 63–69.

IBM 69 IBM Corp., "General Information — Binary Synchronous Communications," IBM Publ. GA27-3004, 1969.

IBM 75   IBM Corp., "Synchronous Data Link Control General Information," IBM Publ. GA27-3093-1, May 1975.

IBM 76   IBM Corp., "SNA Format and Protocol Reference Manual," IBM Form No. SC30-3112, 1976.

IBM 78A   IBM Corp., "Introduction to Advanced Communication Function," IBM Publ. GC30-3033-1, 1978.

IBM 78B   IBM Corp., "Systems Network Architecture: Types of Logical Unit Sessions," IBM Publ. GC-20-1869-0, June 1978.

IBM 78C   IBM Corp., "Network Problem Determination Application — General Information," IBM Publ. GC-34-2010-0, October 1978.

IBM 78D   IBM Corp., "Network Communications Control Facility," IBM Publ. GC-27-0429, 1978.

IBM 79   IBM Corp., "Systems Network Architecture: Logical Unit Types," IBM Publ. GC-20-1868-1, May 1979.

IFIP 78   IFIP/WG 6.1 — International Network Working Group, "Proposal for a Standard Virtual Terminal Protocol," *Proc. Comput. Network Protocols Conf.*, Liege, Belgium, February, 1978, pp. H27 to H49.

INFO 80A   Information Sciences Institute, "DoD Standard Transmission Control Protocol," University of Southern California, *IEN*, No. 129, 1980.

INFO 80B   Information Sciences Institute, "DoD Standard Internet Protocol," University of Southern California, *IEN*, No. 128, 1980.

ISO 76   International Standards Organization, "High Level Data Link Control — Frame Structure," IS 3309, 1976.

ISO 77   International Standards Organization, "High Level Data Link Control — Elements of Procedure," IS 4335, 1977.

ISO 81   International Standards Organization (ISO/TC 97/SC 16), "Data Processing — Open Systems Interconnection Basic Reference Model," Document N537 Revised, 1981.

JACO 78A   Jacobs, I. M., R. Binder, and E. V. Hoversten, "General Purpose Packet Satellite Networks," *Proc. IEEE*, Vol. 66, November 1978.

JACO 78B   Jacobson, C. L., "Digital Facsimile Standards," *Proc. Int. Conf. Commun.*, Toronto, Canada, 1978, pp. 48.2.1 to 48.2.3.

JACQ 78   Jacquemart, Y., "Network Interprocess Communication in an X.25 Environment," *Proc. Comput. Network Protocols Symp.*, Liege, Belgium, 1978.

JUEN 76   Jueneman, R. R., and G. S. Kerr, "Explicit Path Routing in Communication Networks," *Proc. 3rd Int. Conf. Comput. Commun.*, Toronto, Canada, August 1976.

KAHN 72   Kahn, R., and W. Crowther, "Flow Control in a Resource Sharing Computer Network," *IEEE Trans. Commun.*, Vol. COM-28, June 1972.

KAPL 79   Kaplan, G., and T. Mandey, "Data Communications: Three Systems Defined and Assessing the New Services," *IEEE Spectrum*, Vol. 16, October 1979, pp. 42–50.

KIMB 75   Kimbleton, S. R., and G. M. Schneider, "Computer Communications Networks: Approaches, Objectives and Performance Considerations," *ACM Comput. Surv.*, Vol. 7, No. 3, 1975, pp. 129–173.

KIMB 76 Kimbleton, S. R., and R. L. Mandell, "A Perspective on Network Operating Systems," *Proc. Natl. Comput. Conf.*, AFIPS Press, Montvale, N.J., 1976, pp. 551–559.

KLEI 74 Kleinrock, L., and W. Naylor, "On Measured Behavior of the ARPA Network," *AFIPS Conf. Proc. Natl. Comput. Conf.*, Vol. 43, 1974, pp. 767–780.

KLEI 76 Kleinrock, L., *Queuing Systems*, Vol. 2: *Computer Application*, Wiley Interscience, New York, 1976.

KULK 78 Kulkarni, V. R., and P. J. Sevcik, "Initial AUTODIN II Segment Interface Protocol (SIP) Specification," Western Union Technical Note 78-07.2, October 3, 1978.

LAM 79 Lam, S., and M. Reiser, "Congestion Control of Store-and-Forward Networks by Input Buffer Limits — An Analysis," *IEEE Trans. Commun.*, Vol. COM-27, No. 1, 1979, pp. 127–133.

LYON 80 Lyons, R. E., "A Total AUTODIN System Architecture," *IEEE Trans. Commun.*, Vol. COM-28, No. 9, 1980, pp. 1467–1471.

MART 70 Martin, J., *Teleprocessing Network Organization*, Prentice-Hall, Englewood Cliffs, N.J., 1970.

MCFA 76 McFadyen, J. H., "Systems Network Architecture: An Overview," *IBM Syst. J.*, Vol. 15, No. 1, 1976, pp. 4–23.

MCKE 75 McKenzie, A. A., "The ARPA Network Control Center," *Proc. 4th ACM Data Commun. Symp.*, Quebec City, Canada, October 1975, pp. 5-1 to 5-6.

MCKE 76 McKenzie, A., "Host/Host Protocol for the ARPA Network," in *ARPANET Protocol Handbook*, Network Information Center, Stanford Research Institute, Menlo Park, Calif., April 1976, pp. 7–37.

MCQU 72 McQuillan, J. M., F. E. Heart, W. R. Crowther, B. P. Cosell, and D. C. Walden, "Improvements in the Design and Performance of the ARPA Network," *AFIPS Conf. Proc. 41*, FJCC 1972, pp. 741–754.

MCQU 75 McQuillan, J. M., "The Evolution of Message Processing Techniques in the ARPA Network," *Network Systems and Software*, Infotech State-of-the-Art Report 24, Infotech Information, Ltd., Nicholson House, Maidenhead, Berkshire, England, pp. 541–578, 1975.

MCQU 77A McQuillan, J. M., and D. C. Walden, "ARPANET Design Decision," *Comput. Networks*, Vol. 1, No. 5, 1977.

MCQU 77B McQuillan, J. M., "Routing Algorithms for Distributed Networks — A Survey," *Proc. IEEE Natl. Telecommun. Conf.*, December 1977.

MCQU 78A McQuillan, J. M., Enhanced Addressing Capabilities for Computer Networks," *Proc. IEEE*, Vol. 66, No. 11, 1978, pp. 1517–1527.

MCQU 78B McQuillan, J. M., G. Falk, and I. Richer, "A Review of the Development and Performance of the ARPANET Routing Algorithm," *IEEE Trans. Commun.*, Vol. COM-26, No. 12, 1978, pp. 1802–1811.

MCQU 78C McQuillan, J. M., I. Richer, E. C. Rosen, "ARPANET Routing Algorithm Improvements — First Semi-Annual Technical Report," Bolt, Beranek, and Newman, Inc., Rep. No. 3803, Cambridge, Mass., April 1978.

MCQU 79 McQuillan, J. M., I. Richer, and E. Rosen, "An Overview of the New Routing

Algorithm for the Arpanet," *Proc. 6th Data Commun. Symp.*, Monterey, Calif., November 27–29, 1979.

METC 73   Metcalfe, R., "Packet Communications," MIT Project MAC Rep. MAC TR-114, Cambridge, Mass., 1973.

MYER 76   Myer, T. H., and D. A. Henderson, "Message Transmission Protocol," NIC 32116, in *ARPANET Protocol Handbook*, Network Information Center, Stanford Research Institute, Menlo Park, Calif., April 1976.

NEIG 76   Neigus, N., "File Transfer Protocol," in *ARPANET Protocol Handbook*, Network Information Center, Stanford Research Insitute, Menlo Park, Calif., April 1976.

ORNS 72   Ornstein, S. M., F. E. Heart, W. R. Crowther, S. B. Russell, H. K. Rising, and A. Michel, "The Terminal IMP for the ARPA Computer Network," *AFIPS Conf. Proc. 40*, June 1972, pp. 243–254.

PAOL 75   Paoletti, L. M., "AUTODIN," in *Computer Communication Networks*, R. L. Grimsdale and F. F. Kuo, eds. (Proc. NATO Advanced Study Inst. Comput. Commun. Networks, Sussex, U.K., 1975).

PIAT 77   Piatkowski, T. F., D. C. Hull, and R. J. Sundstrom, "Inside IBM's Systems Network Architecture," *Data Commun.*, February 1977, pp. 33–48.

POST 76   Postel, J., "Official Initial Connection Protocol," in *ARPANET Protocol Handbook*, Network Information Center, Stanford Research Institue, Menlo Park, Calif., April 1976, pp. 41–49.

POST 80   Postel, J., "Internetwork Protocol Approaches," *IEEE Trans. Commun.*, Vol. COM-28, No. 4, 1980, pp. 604–611.

POUZ 73   Pouzin, L., "Presentation and Major Design Aspects of the Cyclades Computer Network," *Proc. 3rd ACM Data Commun. Symp.*, November 1973, pp. 80–88.

POUZ 76   Pouzin, L., "Virtual Circuits vs. Datagrams; Technical and Political Problems," *Proc. Natl. Comput. Conf*, 1976, pp. 483–494.

POUZ 78   Pouzin, L., and H. Zimmerman, "A Tutorial on Protocols," *Proc. IEEE*, Vol. 66, No. 11, 1978, pp. 1346–1370.

RAYN 77   Rayner, D., "Where Next in Network Job Management?" *Proc. Natl. Comput. Symp.*, Park Cart Hotel, Lancaster Gate, London, September 1977.

RIND 76   Rinde, J., "Tymnet I: An Alternative of Packet Technology," *Proc. 3rd ICCC*, August 1976, pp. 268–273.

ROBE 70   Roberts, L. G., and B. D. Wessler, "Computer Network Development to Achieve Resource Sharing," *AFIPS Conf. Proc.*, Vol. 36, 1970, SJCC, pp. 543–549.

ROBE 75   Roberts, L. G., "Telenet: Principles and Practice," *Proc. Eur. Comput. Conf. Commun. Networks*, London, 1975, pp. 315–329.

ROBE 76   Roberts, L. G., International Interconnection of Public Packet Networks," *Int. Conf. Comput. Commun.*, 1976, pp. 239–245.

ROBE 78   Roberts, L. G., "The Evolution of Packet Switching," *Proc. IEEE*, Vol. 66, No. 11, 1978, pp. 1307–1313.

ROSE 79   Rosen, E., "The Updating Protocol of the ARPANET's New Routing Algorithm: A Case Study in Maintaining Identical Copies of a Changing Distributed Data Base," *Proc. 4th Berkeley Conf. Distributed Data Mgmt. Comput. Networks*, San Francisco, Calif., August 28–30, 1979, pp. 260–274.

RUBI 78   Rubin, D., E. Crarghill, and R. Rom, "Topics in the Design of a Natural Teleconferencing System," *Proc. Natl. Telecommun. Conf.*, Birmingham, Ala., 1978, pp. 12.4.1 to 12.4.5.

RUDI 79   Rudin, H. and H. Muller, "On Routing and Flow Control," *Proc. Int. Symp. Flow Control Comput. Networks*, Versailles, France, February 12–14, 1979.

RYBC 80   Rybczynski, A., "X.25 Interface and End-to-End Virtual Circuit Service Characteristics," *IEEE Trans. Commun.*, Vol. COM-28, No. 4, 1980, pp. 500–510.

SANT 76   Santos, P. J., "Software Instrumentation for Maintainability of Distributed Computer Networks," *Proc. 15th Ann. Tech. Symp.: Directions and Challenges*, National Bureau of Standards, Gaithersburg, Md., June 1976, pp. 143–148.

SCHI 77   Schicker, P., and A. Duenki, "The Virtual Terminal Definition," European Informatics Network Document, EIN/ZHR/77/018a, September 1977.

SCHU 72   Schultz, G. D., "A Stochastic Model for Message Assembly Buffering with a Comparison of Block Assignment Strategies," *J. ACM*, Vol. 19, No. 3, 1972, p. 483.

SCHW 77   Schwartz, M., *Computer Communication Network Design and Analysis*, Prentice-Hall, Englewood Cliffs, N.J., 1977.

SCHW 80   Schwartz, M., and T. E. Stern, "Routing Techniques Used in Computer Communication Networks," *IEEE Trans. Commun.*, Vol. COM-28, No. 4, 1980, pp. 539–552.

SEID 78   Seider, R., "How Statistical TDMs Let Network Lines Support More Terminals," *Data Commun.*, September 1978, pp. 95–108.

SHAT 79   Shatzer, R. R., L. C. Hartge, A. P. Russo, 3rd, and J. D. Chisholm, "HP's Network Concept Stresses Resource Sharing and Flexibility," *Data Commun.*, August 1979, pp. 73–82.

SIMP 78   Simpson, R. O., and G. H. Phillips, "Network Job Entry Facility for JES2," *IBM Syst. J.*, Vol. 17, No. 3, pp. 221–240, 1978.

SOLM 78   Soloman, J. V., "Datapac 3303 End-to-End Protocol," Serial No. NPD-100, Issue 1.1, July 1978.

SPRO 78   Sproull, R. F., and D. Cohen, "High-Level Protocols," *Proc. IEEE*, Vol. 66, No. 11, 1978, pp. 1371–1386.

SUNS 75   Sunshine, A., "Interprocess Communications Protocols for Computer Networks," Digital Systems Laboratory Tech. Rep. No. 105, Stanford University, Stanford, Calif., December 1975.

TANE 81   Tanenbaum, A. S., *Computer Networks*, Prentice-Hall, Englewood Cliffs, N.J., 1981.

TELN 76   "TELNET Protocol Specification," Network Working Group, ARPA Document NIC 18639, August 1973; also in *ARPANET Protocol Handbook*, Network Information Center, Stanford Research Institute, Menlo Park, Calif., April 1976.

THOM 72   Thomas, R. H., and D. A. Henderson, "McRoss — A Multi-computer Programming System," *AFIPS Conf. Proc.*, Vol. 40, June 1972, pp. 281–293.

THOM 76   Thomas, E., and R. Sproull, "Network Graphics Protocol," in *ARPANET Protocol Handbook*, Network Information Center, Stanford Research Institute, Menlo Park, Calif., April 1976.

TOBA 80   Tobagi, F. A., "Multiaccess Protocols in Packet Communication Systems," *IEEE Trans. Commun.*, Vol. COM-28, No. 4, 1980, pp. 468–488.

TOML 75   Tomlinson, R. S., "Selecting Sequence Numbers," *Proc. ACM SIGCOMM/ SIGOPS Interprocess Commun. Workshop*, March 24–25, 1975, Santa Monica, Calif., *ACM Oper. Syst. Rev.*, Vol. 9, No. 3, July 1975, pp. 11–23.

TRAY 77A   Traynham, K. C., and R. F. Steen, "Interpreting SDLC Throughput Efficiency, Part 1: 3 Models," *Data Commun.*, October 1977, pp. 43–51.

TRAY 77B   Traynham, K. C., and R. F. Steen, "Interpreting SDLC Throughput Efficiency, Part 2: Results," *Data Commun.*, November 1977, pp. 59–66.

VAND 76   Vander Mey, J. E., "The Architecture of a Transparent Intelligent Network," *Proc. Natl. Telecommun. Conf.*, 1976.

WALD 75   Walden, D. C., "Host-to-Host Protocols," in *Network Systems and Software*, Infotech State-of-the-Art Report 24, Infotech Information, Ltd., Nicholson House, Maidenhead, Berkshire, England, pp. 287–316, 1975.

WALD 79   Walden, D. C., and A. A. McKenzie, "The Evolution of Host–Host Protocol Technology," *Computer*, Vol. 12, No. 9, 1979, pp. 29–37.

WECK 76   Wecker, S., "The Design of DECNET — A General Purpose Network Base," *Proc. ELECTRO 76*, May 1976.

WECK 80   Wecker, S., "DNA: The Digital Network Architecture," *IEEE Trans. Commun.*, Vol. COM-28, No. 4, 1980, pp. 510–526.

WEIN 79   Weingarten, R. A., "An Integrated Approach to Centralized Communications Network Management," *IBM Syst. J.*, Vol. 18, No. 4, 1979, pp. 484–506.

WORL 72   Worley, A. R., "The Datran System," *Proc. IEEE*, Vol. 60, No. 11, 1972, pp. 1357–1368.

ZIMM 80   Zimmerman, H., "OSI Reference Model — The ISO Model of Architecture for Open Systems Interconnection," IEEE Trans. Commun., Vol. COM-28, No. 4, 1980, pp. 425–432.

3

Data Link Control Procedures

SIMON S. LAM
The University of Texas at Austin
Austin, Texas

3.1 INTRODUCTION

Data link control (DLC) protocols are concerned with the communication of data between different machines. Communication is considered to be accomplished if the intended receiver of a data message acquires access to the same serial stream of bits as that of the sender within some acceptable time delay. Thus "communication" is used throughout this chapter to mean *synchronization* of data.

Communication between "processes" within the same machine is easily accomplished with shared memory and an operating system that coordinates the communicating processes. When the communicating processes reside in different machines, however, several problems arise:

1. Communications facilities are needed to transport data from one machine to the other.
2. Coordination of the communicating processes can no longer rely on an operating system but needs to be done by the processes exchanging control messages directly between themselves.
3. The error rates of communications channels are such that comprehensive error detection and recovery techniques are needed to handle (1) and (2) properly.
4. The communications channel, especially over a long distance, is expensive and may need to be shared among concurrent "dialogues."

We next define some terminology. Machines that communicate include various kinds of terminals and computers. They are known as *data terminal equipment* (DTEs) in the protocol literature. Each DTE has a mechanism, which we shall call a *transceiver*, with the functional capability of sending and receiving bits serially over a communications channel. Examples of transceivers are modems in common-carrier communications facilities, line driver/receivers in in-house cable networks, and so on. Together, a DTE and its transceiver will be referred to as a *station*; see Fig. 3.1 for

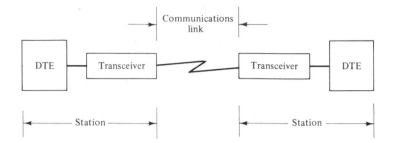

Figure 3.1. Two communicating stations.

illustration. A station is both a sender and a receiver of data messages (although not necessarily at the same time).

Although more than two stations may be involved in a "conference call" or "broadcast" mode of communication, present DLC protocols (of interest herein) deal mainly with dialogues between station pairs. To achieve communication between two stations, the synchronization functions required can be structured into a hierarchy of five levels of functions, to be referred to as the *hierarchical model* (see Fig. 3.2). Each level in the hierarchy depends on synchronism at the level below achieved over *finer grains of time*. Thus each level is offered a virtual (or real) communications channel by the level below, and in turn provides the level above with a virtual communications channel having improved characteristics. Together, the hierarchy of functions supplies the functional capabilities to bridge the gap between what is provided by communications channels and what is required for process-to-process communication.

The synchronization functions shown in Fig. 3.2 are defined in Sec. 3.2 and discussed in detail in Sec. 3.3 for the three major classes of DLC protocols: start–stop, character-oriented, and bit-oriented. Specifically, the hierarchical model is used as a framework for describing IBM's character-oriented BSC (Binary Synchronous Communication) protocol and bit-oriented SDLC (Synchronous Data Link Control) protocol. In Sec. 3.4 the different classes of DLC protocols are compared. For bit-oriented protocols, additional functional capabilities available in the protocol standards, HDLC (High-Level Data Link Control) and ADCCP (Advanced Data Communication Control Procedure), are discussed.

The objective of this chapter is to present DLC functional requirements using the hierarchical model as a framework and various existing protocols to illustrate solution techniques. For a detailed and complete description of these protocols, the reader should consult the latest manuals for up-to-date information.

Finally, we note that the hierarchical model introduced herein provides a structured representation of functional requirements for communication between two remote processes. Thus in addition to being a useful model for DLC protocols, it can be used to model higher-level communication protocol layers as well.

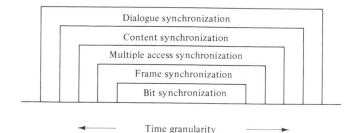

Time granularity

Figure 3.2. Hierarchy of communication functions.

3.2 SYNCHRONIZATION FUNCTIONS

We shall proceed from the bottom of the hierarchy shown in Fig. 3.2 upward.

Bit Synchronization

This level of functions deals with a receiver's ability to retrieve a stream of bits from an incoming analog signal by sampling for the bits at the proper times. The receiver needs to know (1) when to start sampling the first bit, and (2) the period (bit duration) between sampling consecutive bits.

Frame Synchronization

A frame is defined herein to be a stream of bits which is the basic unit of transfer of data and/or control information from a sender to a receiver. The frame synchronization level of functions establishes the conventions for a sender and receiver to delimit within a continuous stream of bits the beginning and the end of a frame. (We note that if the frame size is an integer multiple of the character size of a character-oriented system, character synchronization is also established.)

Another function at this level is error detection. Typically, to detect communication errors, redundancy is built into the bit stream to be transmitted using one of several coding techniques.

Multiple Access Synchronization

It is often necessary to share a physical communications channel among different concurrent sender–receiver pairs. In this case frames transmitted by different senders are interleaved in time. The multiple access synchronization level of functions is concerned with (1) control signals and protocols necessary to synchronize senders so as to avoid (or resolve) access conflicts, and (2) an addressing scheme for identifying senders and receivers. With multiple access synchronization, the higher-level protocol can then behave as if a dedicated (virtual) channel is provided for each sender–receiver pair.

The reader is referred to Chap. 4 for a tutorial treatment of multiple access protocols for channel sharing.

Content Synchronization

This level of functions is concerned with the information content of a frame transmitted from a sender to a receiver, in particular (1) how to differentiate between data and control information within the frame; (2) how to encode and decode control messages; (3) error control to ensure that a single error-free copy of each frame to be sent will arrive at the receiver within some acceptable duration of time; and (4) sequence control to ensure that when a data message is segmented and transported in multiple frames, the message segments are reassembled in the correct sequence.

Dialogue Synchronization

This level of functions is concerned with the initiation and subsequent termination of a dialogue between two stations during which the transfer of frames containing data can take place. Each station is both a sender and a receiver so that there are usually two sender–receiver pairs involved in a dialogue. Dialogue synchronization functions are also needed (1) to coordinate each station pair so that a sender transmits a frame only when it is in a state with the right to transmit and the receiver is in a state that can accept a new frame; and (2) to detect "nonsynchronous" conditions, attempt recovery upon detection of such conditions, and report unrecoverable conditions to higher-level protocols.

Examples of nonsynchronous conditions at the dialogue level are (1) incomplete protocol specification—a data or control message received is not among those expected by the receiver in its present state, and (2) deadlocks—mutual wait conditions between two stations.

In summary, we observe that bit and frame synchronization are necessary for the most rudimentary form of communication between two machines. Multiple access synchronization provides for the sharing of a communications channel by multiple sender–receiver pairs. Content synchronization provides for improved error characteristics, and the encoding of data and control information. Dialogue synchronization provides for data transfer in a mode of operation with desirable characteristics (flow control, interrupts, etc.)

3.3 ASYNCHRONOUS AND SYNCHRONOUS PROTOCOLS

The method for achieving bit synchronism between sender and receiver determines two basic forms of transmission: asynchronous and synchronous. In an asynchronous transmission system, bit synchronism is (in fact) maintained but only when data transmission is taking place and not during idle periods. The amount of data transmitted at a time is one character (5 to 8 bits). In a synchronous transmission system, bit synchronism is maintained at all times. DLC protocols normally used with

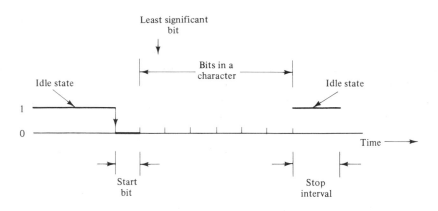

Figure 3.3. Asynchronous transmission.

a synchronous transmission system are said to be synchronous protocols, while DLC protocols normally used with an asynchronous transmission system are said to be asynchronous or start-stop protocols. We note that it is possible to use character-oriented protocols for both synchronous and asynchronous transmission systems. An example is the ANSI (American National Standards Institute) X3.28 protocol standard [ANSI 75], which is akin to the character-oriented BSC protocol to be described. However, both are much more sophisticated than early start-stop DLC protocols and will be classified as synchronous protocols in our discussions below.

3.3.1 Asynchronous Protocols [MCNA 77]

The history of start–stop protocols lies in early teleprinter systems. Consider a communications line connecting a sender to a receiver. By convention, the line is idle when current is flowing in it, which is called the 1 state or MARK condition. The no-current state is called the 0 state or SPACE condition. To start transmitting, the line is brought to the 0 state for one bit time; this is called the *start bit*. For the next 5 to 8 bits (the number depending on the character code being used) the line is brought to the 1 or 0 state as necessary to represent the character being sent. After each character, the line is maintained at the 1 state for a minimum duration of time (equal to 1, 1.5, or 2 bit times) before the transmission of another character can begin; this is the *stop interval* (see Fig. 3.3). Thus transmission is one character at a time, with the bits representing each character preceded by a start bit and succeeded by a stop interval. The stop interval ensures that a transition occurs at the beginning of each start bit, which is used by the receiver to acquire bit synchronization.

Start–stop protocols are said to be asynchronous because a new character can be transmitted at any time (thus asynchronously) following the stop interval of the previous character. Bit synchronism, however, is maintained during the transmission of each character. The receiver determines the initial sampling time from the 1-to-0 transition of the start bit. (This can be accomplished, for example, by a "16 x clock" which samples the incoming signal at 16 times the transmission bit rate.) The sampling period between bits is known from the transmission bit rate. However, since clocks in different machines may differ slightly, the sampling of the last bit in a character may be somewhat off center. This can be corrected in the reception of the next character by retiming the 1-to-0 transition of its start bit.

Start–stop protocols are based upon the use of a character code (Baudot, ASCII, etc.) for representing control messages and data. The start bit and stop interval, in addition to providing bit synchronization, also provides character synchronization (i.e., how to partition a stream of bits into characters). Most character codes provide for some control characters which are used for various DLC control functions (mentioned above) as well as necessary device control functions.

Typically, start–stop protocols are used for terminal devices with a keyboard, with no message buffer, and little intelligence; characters are sent one at a time as keys are struck. The terminal device is controlled remotely by its "host" computer. Start–stop protocols were mostly developed in the past in conjunction with the development of terminal devices. Each terminal type would have its own protocol. Such protocols are often incompatible between terminal types.

Although a significant portion of terminal devices currently in use are nonintelligent start–stop devices, we shall not dwell on start–stop protocols much more. First, for pedagogic reasons; start–stop protocols do not provide a good illustration of the hierarchy of DLC functions discussed in Sec. 3.2. Second, the technological trend is toward more intelligent terminals which can accommodate synchronous protocols having more sophisticated functions.

3.3.2   Synchronous Protocols

The proliferation of start–stop protocols associated with numerous terminal types is a problem. Another disadvantage of asynchronous transmission is the overhead of a start bit and a stop interval associated with each character transmitted. With synchronous transmission the overhead above is eliminated by keeping bit synchronism between receiver and sender at all times, including idle periods. Most synchronous protocols are intended for terminal devices which have more buffering and processing capability than start–stop devices and therefore can implement more functions.

Bit Synchronization

When the receiver and transmitter are in proximity, bit synchronism can be maintained by a single shared clock for both the transmitter and the receiver. In other cases, bit timing will have to be recovered from the data signal at the receiver. To do so necessitates some provisions to ensure transitions in the data signal. Specifically, when a transmitter is first connected to a receiver, some number of initial transitions are necessary to establish bit synchronization. The sampling period between bits is known approximately from the data transmission rate but needs to be checked and adjusted periodically with the help of transitions in the data signal. This implies that certain bit streams may not be acceptable or that additional bits may have to be inserted to ensure an adequate number of transitions for reliable clock recovery. In most systems, the transceiver is a synchronous modem, which will recover symbol timing and provide bit timing to the DTE in a received data timing lead. (The transmit data timing may be provided by either the DTE or modem. Some synchronous modems do not need data link control to provide transitions in the data signal; for example, some have scrambler–descrambler circuits that create transitions in the data signal.)

The subject of modulation–demodulation and clock recovery are classical communication problems at a lower level of detail and are beyond the scope of this chapter. The reader is referred to [DAVE 72]. We shall only discuss bit synchronism in terms of certain DLC functions provided for preventing the transmission of transitionless data.

Two Classes of Synchronous Protocols

There are two main classes of synchronous protocols: character-oriented and bit-oriented. A main distinction between them, as suggested by the names, is the technique for accomplishing frame synchronization. But as we shall see, they differ in their methods for multiple access synchronization, content synchronization, and dialogue synchronization as well.

Character-oriented protocols include the X3.28 standard of ANSI and IBM's BSC protocol. They are very similar and the latter is used widely by industry. In Sec. 3.3.2.1, we shall describe the main features of BSC as documented in [IBM 70] to illustrate this class of protocols.

Bit-oriented protocols include ADCCP, which is a standard of ANSI; HDLC, which is a standard of ISO (International Standards Organization); and IBM's SDLC protocol. In Sec. 3.3.2.2 we describe the version of SDLC as documented in [IBM 75] to illustrate this class of protocols.[1] We note that SDLC, HDLC, and ADCCP are basically of the same genre; the two protocol standards have evolved out of IBM's submissions to the respective standards organizations. However, additional functions have been defined (or proposed) for HDLC and ADCCP, which are not present in the current version of SDLC [IBM 75]. These functions are discussed in Sec. 3.4.

Other computer manufacturers have also proposed similar DLC protocols, including BDLC of Burroughs, UDLC of Sperry-Univac, and DDCMP of Digital Equipment Corporation. DDCMP is byte-count oriented. An excellent discussion of DDCMP may be found in [MCNA 77].

3.3.2.1 Description of a Character-Oriented Protocol—BSC [IBM 70]

Suppose that bit synchronism is maintained between a receiver and a transmitter. Since both data and control must be encoded and transported in packages of bits called frames,[2] the synchronization problem at the next level involves the following:

---

[1]Excellent discussions of SDLC concepts may be found in [CYPS 78, DONN 74].

[2]The term "frame" has been defined in this chapter but is not defined in [IBM 70].

Bit positions 4, 5, 6, 7		Bit positions 0, 1, 2, 3															
		0000	0001	0010	0011	0100	0101	0110	0111	1000	1001	1010	1011	1100	1101	1110	1111
	Hex	0	1	2	3	4	5	6	7	8	9	A	B	C	D	E	F
0000	0	NUL	DLE	DS		SP	&	—						{	}	\	0
0001	1	SOH	DC1	SOS						a	j	~		A	J		1
0010	2	STX	DC2	FS	SYN					b	k	s		B	K	S	2
0011	3	ETX	DC3							c	l	t		C	L	T	3
0100	4	PF	RES	BYP	PN					d	m	u		D	M	U	4
0101	5	HT	NL	LF	RS					e	n	v		E	N	V	5
0110	6	LC	BS	EOB/ETB	UC					f	o	w		F	O	W	6
0111	7	DEL	IL	PRE/ESC	EOT					g	p	x		G	P	X	7
1000	8		CAN							h	q	y		H	Q	Y	8
1001	9	RLF	EM							i	r	z		I	R	Z	9
1010	A	SMM	CC	SM		¢	!	$\mid$	:								
1011	B	VT				.	$	,	#								
1100	C	FF	IFS		DC4	<	*	%	@								
1101	D	CR	IGS	ENQ	NAK	(	)	_	'								
1110	E	SO	IRS	ACK		+	;	>	=								
1111	F	SI	IUS	BEL	SUB			¬	?	"							

Duplicate assignment

Figure 3.4. EBCDIC character assignments.

(1) upon reception of a sequence of bits, to determine which bit is the beginning and which bit is the end of a frame; and (2) error detection.

In character-oriented protocols, all data and control information are encoded as characters. The IBM manual lists three character-code sets that can be used for BSC. They are EBCDIC with 8 bits per character for 256 assignments, USASCII with 7 bits plus a parity bit per character for 128 assignments, and 6-bit Transcode with 64 assignments. As an example the EBCDIC assignments are illustrated in Fig. 3.4.

Frame Synchronization

With a character-code set, BSC data and control characters are represented by unique bit sequences. (We discuss below how transparent data, i.e., an arbitrary stream of bits, can be transmitted.) In particular, the bit sequence representing the character SYN is unique. Because of the serial-by-character nature of transmission, frame synchronization and character synchronization are accomplished at the same time. Each frame transmitted is always preceded by two or more SYN characters. The receiver will hunt for the bit pattern of SYN SYN. (We use the shorthand notation of $\emptyset$ for SYN SYN as in [IBM 70].) When the receiver detects a sequence of two or more SYN characters in an incoming signal, the bits immediately following (6 or 8 bits, depending on the code set) will form the first character of the frame.[3] The receiver may detect more than two SYN characters in a row because SYN is also used to fill any idle time in between frames. If the frame contains data characters, it ends with either one of the following control characters: ITB, ETB, or ETX followed by two BCC characters for error detection. (See below for further explanation of these control characters.) If the frame contains only control information, one or more control characters may be present, representing one of a well-defined set of control messages.

We said earlier that bit synchronism may be maintained by the transceiver or DTE in a station. If it is done by the DTE, a special bit synchronization pattern needs to precede the frame synchronization pattern $\emptyset$. (This bit synchronization pattern can be the hex '55' '55' or the SYN SYN SYN SYN pattern that provides for the 16 transitions necessary for bit synchronization.) Bit synchronism will be assumed from now on.

To ensure that the first and last characters of a frame are properly transmitted by the transceiver, which may turn on and off abruptly, BSC requires the addition of a pad character immediately before the synchronization characters of a frame and immediately afterward. [The leading pad character may consist of alternating 0 and 1 bits (hex '55') or a SYN character. The trailing pad character consists of all 1 bits (hex 'FF').] With the frame synchronization method, BSC frames containing data and/or control information from a sender to a receiver will be in one of the following two formats:

PAD $\emptyset$ [heading and/or data] BCC BCC PAD

PAD $\emptyset$ [control] PAD

The two BCC characters are for error detection. The exact nature of the heading, control, and data fields in the frame formats above will be clarified in our discussions below on multiple access synchronization and content synchronization. For simplicity, we drop the leading and trailing PAD characters in our notation from now on.

Another function at the frame synchronization level is to detect the presence of

---

[3]Note that this procedure is subject to errors. First, the $\emptyset$ sequence may be missed because of bit errors in it. On the other hand, the two-character bit pattern of $\emptyset$ is not unique and may appear in the middle of certain three-character sequences.

errors within transmitted frames. Depending on the character-code set selected, one or more of the following three error-checking methods may be used for BSC:

VRC   Vertical redundancy checking

LRC   Longitudinal redundancy checking

CRC   Cyclic redundancy checking

With each method, two BCC characters are generated at the sender and are included at the end of each data frame. They are used for error detection at the receiver. Note from the frame formats above that BSC control messages are not protected by error checking.

CRC is a much more powerful technique for error detection than VRC or LRC and can detect many types of multiple errors. It is to be preferred since errors in communications transmission systems tend to occur in bursts [BURT 72]. CRC is available with all three BSC character-code sets. For a detailed description of LRC, VRC, and the CRC coding algorithm, the reader is referred to [MART 70, MCNA 77].

Multiple Access Synchronization

The multiple access synchronization function determines which of a population of transmitters may access a shared communications channel. If the communications channel is dedicated to a single sender–receiver pair, the problem is trivially solved. Otherwise, some multiple access protocol is required.

The method for multiple access depends on the communications link configuration. BSC permits two types of communications link configurations between stations: point to point and multipoint. We consider first a point-to-point communications link between two stations. Remember that each station is both a sender and a receiver. BSC requires a *half-duplex* mode of operation such that only one station can be transmitting at a time. Half-duplex operation is required even if the communications link consists of two separate communications channels, one for each of the two directions of transmission. Note that whenever the line "turns around," reversing the direction of transmission, character synchronization (and possibly bit synchronization) need to be reestablished.

A point-to-point communications link is shared via a *contention* protocol. If a station wants to acquire control of the line, it sends the initialization sequence

Ø ENQ

The other station replies with

Ø ACK0   if ready to receive

Ø NAK   if not ready to receive

Ø WACK   if temporarily not ready to receive (try again later!)

Since it is possible that both stations bid for the line at about the same time, to avoid

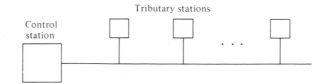

Figure 3.5. Multipoint link configuration.

any deadlock each station is designated to be primary or secondary. The primary station has high priority. When bidding for the line, the primary, but not the secondary, can continue to retry (up to a certain limit) until it gets an affirmative response.

The station with control of the line is the *transmitting station* and can transmit frames containing data to the *receiving station*. Following each such frame transmitted, the line may turn around for the receiving station to send a reply. The reply is a control message (ACK, NAK, etc.) and may not contain any data, except in the limited conversational mode (see below). A station relinquishes control of the line with the control message ∅ EOT. For 3 seconds the other station can bid for the line without competition. After 3 seconds, both stations may bid for control of the line.

BSC also permits a multipoint communications link configuration (see Fig. 3.5), with a control station and many tributary stations sharing the same line. Data flow is always between the control station and one of the tributary stations. The communications method is again half-duplex, so that transmission of data can take place in only one direction at a time, either from the control station to a tributary or from a tributary to the control station. There are two additional functions required: (1) sharing of the line among the tributary stations; and (2) addresses for identifying the tributary stations.

The communications link is shared among the tributary stations via *polling* and *selection* protocols under the supervision of the control station. The control station directs its incoming traffic by sequentially polling each tributary station. When polled, a tributary station has control of the line and assumes the role of the transmitting station with the control station acting as the receiving station, such as previously described for a point-to-point line. The control station directs its outgoing traffic by first selecting a tributary station as the receiving station. The control station then acts as the transmitting station. In both cases, the transmitting–receiving relationship is ended when the transmitting station sends the message ∅ EOT. If the transmitting station is a tributary station, control of the line is passed back to the control station.

The following sequence is used by the control station to poll or select a tributary station:

∅ EOT PAD ∅ [polling or selection address] ENQ

The polling or selection address sequence consists of one to seven characters. It gives the tributary station address (and also a specific device address if the station has several available). The possible replies from a polled tributary station are:

1. A frame containing data
2. Ø EOT: negative reply when the station has nothing to send
3. Ø STX ENQ: temporary text delay (TTD) when the station is unable to transmit its initial data within 2 seconds; this permits the polled station to retain control of the line and avoid being timed out by the control station

The possible replies from a selected tributary station are:

1. Ø ACK0: affirmative, ready to receive
2. Ø NAK: negative, not ready to receive
3. Ø WACK: temporarily not ready to receive

Content Synchronization

With multiple access synchronization, two processes can send frames of bits to each other. The next level of functions is to enable a receiver to interpret correctly the content of a frame. There are three functions involved here:

1. To differentiate between control and data information within a frame; for control information, the receiver and sender must also agree on the encoding of a set of control messages.
2. To distinguish an arbitrary bit stream of data (transparent data), although some of the bits may be the same as control characters.
3. To remedy errors so as to ensure that a single error-free copy of each frame at the sender will arrive in sequence at the receiver within a reasonable amount of time.

Encoding of Data and Control.   The separation of data and control is solved in BSC with the use of a character-code set. Data transfer is always in the form of a serial stream of characters. Characters in the code set are reserved to represent either data or control. BSC control characters are for DLC control functions as well as other high-level control functions, such as device control. (The mixing of control functions at different levels is one of the frequent criticisms of BSC.) Specifically, control of the data link is achieved through use of the following control characters and two-character sequences:

SYN	Synchronous Idle
SOH	Start of Heading
STX	Start of Text
ITB	End of Intermediate Transmission Block
ETB	End of Transmission Block
ETX	End of Text
EOT	End of Transmission
ENQ	Enquiry

ACK0/ACK1	Alternating Affirmative Acknowledgments
WACK	Wait-Before-Transmit Positive Acknowledgment
NAK	Negative Acknowledgment
DLE	Data-Link Escape
RVI	Reverse Interrupt
TTD	Temporary Text Delay
DLE EOT	Disconnect Sequence for a Switched Line

Several of the above are not defined in the character code sets but are represented as two-character control sequences. They are ACK0, ACK1, WACK, RVI, and TTD. Some minor variations in the designation of the characters and compositions of the character sequences exist among the different code sets. For example, ACK0 and ACK1 correspond to the two-character sequences DLE 0 and DLE 1 in USASCII but are coded as DLE '70' and DLE / in EBCDIC. On the other hand, TTD is represented by STX ENQ in all code sets.

BSC frames have the following formats:

$\emptyset$ SOH [heading] STX [data] ETX BCC BCC

$\emptyset$ [control character sequence]

Frames containing data or heading are sent only by a transmitting station to a receiving station. In these frames, SOH marks the beginning of a heading containing control information for high-level (non-DLC) functions such as message identification, routing, device control, and priority. STX marks the beginning of the data section. Either SOH [heading] or STX [data] may be absent in a frame. Each frame is terminated by one of the control characters ETX, ETB, or ITB. In all cases it is followed by two BCC characters for error detection.

Both ETX and ETB terminate frames started by STX or SOH and cause the communications channel to turn around and require a reply from the receiving station. ETX terminates a data message at the data processing level. At the DLC level, a data message may be segmented into *transmission blocks* for ease of processing and more efficient error control. Each transmission block begins with STX and ends with ETB, except for the last block of a data message, which ends with ETX.

The "SOH [heading] STX [data]" portion, where [data] can be either a complete data message or a transmission block, can be further segmented into *intermediate blocks* for increased reliability in error detection. When an intermediate block is sent in a frame, the frame is terminated by ITB, again followed by two BCC characters. The last intermediate block in a sequence is terminated by ETB or ETX as appropriate. After the first intermediate block, succeeding ones need not be preceded by STX or SOH in a frame (except in the case of transparent data to be discussed below). Frames terminated by ITB do not cause a line turnaround or require a reply from the receiver. Each sequence of intermediate blocks, comprising a data message or a transmission block, is treated as a whole by the receiving station. All BSC stations must have the ability to receive intermediate blocks. The ability to send intermediate blocks is an option.

Frames containing control information only have the format

$\emptyset$ [control character sequence]

We have seen the use of some of these control messages for multiple access synchronization. We shall encounter some others in the following discussions.

Transparent Data. So far in our description of BSC, the characters that can be sent in the data portion of a frame have been assumed to be limited to a subset of the characters in the character-code set. To send an arbitrary stream of characters (transparent data) without some of the characters taking on any control meaning, BSC provides the *transparent text mode* of operation within a frame. During the transparent text mode, any control characters transmitted must be preceded by DLE to be recognized as denoting a control function. In particular, the transparent text mode is initiated by DLE STX and is terminated by any of DLE ETX, DLE ETB, or DLE ITB. (In the last case, if the succeeding intermediate block is also transparent, that intermediate block must begin with DLE STX. Recall that a beginning STX is not required of intermediate blocks in the nontransparent mode of operation if that intermediate block is not the first one.) Thus a frame in a transparent text mode may look like

$\emptyset$ DLE STX [transparent data] DLE ETX BCC BCC

If a control character is needed within the transparent data, a DLE character is inserted in front of it. Also, if a DLE character appears in the transparent data (with no control meaning), an additional DLE must also be inserted in front of it lest it be misinterpreted as preceding a control character. The inserted DLC characters need to be stripped off at the receiver. The following procedure may be used by the receiver:

Step 1.   Hunt for a DLE character in the input stream. When a DLE is received, discard it and go to Step 2.

Step 2.   *If* the next character is a DLE *then* accept it as a data character and go to Step 1,

else accept the next character as a control character and go to Step 1.

Error Control. One of the content synchronization functions is to recover from transmission errors. BSC does so with an automatic-repeat-request (ARQ) technique. When a transmitting station ends a frame containing data with ETB or ETX, a reply is required of the receiving station. It can reply with $\emptyset$ ACK0 or $\emptyset$ ACK1, indicating "data accepted, ready for more," or $\emptyset$ NAK, indicating "data not accepted, retransmission necessary." The line then turns around again for the transmitting station to send a frame. If necessary, retransmission of a frame of data is attempted a number of times following the initial NAK, after which recovery action is required. If the transmitting station receives no reply after sending a frame of data, due to either the frame or the reply being garbled, the transmitting station can request a reply from the receiving station by sending the control message ∅ ENQ. The receiving station repeats the previous response: NAK, ACK0, or ACK1, as appropriate.

Two positive acknowledgment responses are used for the following reason. ACK0 is used as an affirmative response to the transmitting station's initial ENQ and for an affirmative response to all even-number transmission blocks. ACK1 is used for all odd-number transmission blocks. The odd or even count of a block does not change even when it is retransmitted. As a result the alternating affirmative replies enable the sender to detect the loss of a transmission block. Also, since transmission blocks are sent one at a time until successfully received and acknowledged, the original sequence of transmission blocks at the sender is preserved at the receiver. However, a transmission block does not actually contain a bit indicating it to be even or odd. It is thus not possible for the receiver to detect a duplicate transmission block. (A duplicate would be sent if, for instance, an ACK was garbled and turned into a NAK.)

Recall that only frames containing heading/data are protected by error detection. Control messages are not checked. The BSC manual mentions some provisions for using trailing pad characters for format checking which serves as a limited means of error detection.

The "accumulation" for the BCC characters begins right after the first STX or SOH character following either a line turnaround or a previous ITB termination of an intermediate block. All characters following that, including control characters, are used in the accumulation, with the exception of SYN idle characters inserted for bit and character synchronization considerations (see below).

Dialogue Synchronization

With content synchronization, it is now possible to send frames containing data from one station to another. There also exists a set of control messages which can be used for coordinating the actions and responses of two communicating stations in a dialogue fashion. The dialogue level functions consist of:

1. Initial dialogue synchronization
2. Recovery methods in the event of loss of synchronism and
3. Dialogue termination

Initial dialogue synchronization in BSC is trivially accomplished once multiple access synchronization has been established, with one station being in the "transmit" state and the other in the "receive" state.

In the case of switched-network (dial-up) operation, additional initial synchronization procedures are needed immediately following the establishment of a communications circuit. The calling station sends either one of the following messages:

∅ ENQ   Who are you?

∅ α...ENQ   I am α.... Who are you?

The called station replies positively with

$\emptyset \; \alpha \ldots$ ACK0

where the called station identity $\alpha \ldots$ is optional. The called station replies negatively with

$\emptyset$ NAK

$\emptyset$ WACK

The identity sequences $\alpha \ldots$ may be 2 to 15 characters long. The minimum two-character sequence must consist of the same character transmitted twice (for reliability).

A dial-up call between two stations can be terminated by either one of the stations transmitting the disconnect message

$\emptyset$ DLE EOT

A call may also be disconnected by the disconnect timeout to be described below. Apart from the transmit and receive states, the stations may transit to other states as a result of the following control messages.

TTD (Temporary Text Delay). The TTD control sequence is sent by a transmitting station when it wishes to retain control of the line but is not ready to transmit data. It is sent after approximately 2 seconds to avoid the 3-second receive timeout at the receiving station. The receiving station responds NAK and waits for transmission to begin again. TTD can be repeated one or more times. TTD can also be used to abort a transmission. If following the receiving station's reply of NAK, the transmitting station sends EOT, the transmit–receive relationship is terminated. (This is called the forward abort sequence.)

RVI (Reverse Interrupt). RVI is a positive acknowledgment used in place of ACK0 or ACK1 (depending on the current odd–even count). RVI is transmitted by a receiving station to request termination of the current transmit–receive relationship. The transmitting station treats RVI as a positive acknowledgment (0 to 1 as appropriate) and proceeds to transmit all data that might prevent it from becoming a receiving station. The ability to receive RVI is mandatory, but the ability to transmit RVI is optional.

WACK (Wait-Before-Transmit Positive Acknowledgment). WACK allows a receiving station to indicate a "temporarily not ready to receive" condition to the transmitting station. The normal transmitting station response to WACK is ENQ. The receiving station may continue to respond with WACK. The transmitting station has the option of terminating the dialogue by EOT or disconnecting a circuit with DLE EOT. The ability to receive WACK is mandatory. The ability to send WACK is optional.

Timeouts. Timeouts are used to attempt recovery from possible nonsynchronous conditions. There are four specific timeouts used in BSC:

1. *Transmit timeout.* This is a nominal 1-second timeout that establishes the rate at which synchronous idles are automatically inserted into frames containing heading and data. Ordinarily, SYN SYN is inserted every second. For transparent data, DLE SYN is inserted instead. These insertions permit character synchronization to be checked and in the case of SYN SYN, reestablished. If bit synchronism is maintained by the DTE, insertion of DLE SYN is required at least every 84 characters to ensure bit synchronism amid transitionless data. The inserted synchronous idle characters are not included in BCC accumulation for error detection.

2. *Receive timeout.* This is a nominal 3-second timeout and is used to limit the waiting time tolerated by a station to receive a reply as well as for other functions.

3. *Disconnect timeout.* This timeout is used optionally on switched network connections. It is used to prevent a station from holding on to a connection for a prolonged period of inactivity. After 20 seconds of inactivity, the station will disconnect from the switched network.

4. *Continue timeout.* This is a nominal 2-second timeout associated with the control messages TTD and WACK.

Additional BSC Features

1. A frame containing heading/data can be terminated prematurely by using an ENQ character which signals the receiving station to disregard the current frame. NAK is always the reply from the receiving station.

2. BSC permits a "limited conversational mode" whereby a frame containing heading/data can be sent in place of a positive acknowledgment by the receiving station as a reply to a frame that ended with ETX or DLE ETX. The transmitting station must then reply with a control message and not with another conversational reply.

Comments on the Structure of BSC

We have given a description of the BSC protocol using the hierarchical functional levels in Fig. 3.2 as a framework for elaboration. Ideally, a well-structured protocol should have minimal interfaces defined between adjacent functional levels so that functions and implementation techniques at one level can be changed without affecting adjacent levels if the interfaces are maintained to be the same. Since BSC was not originally designed with the hierarchical functional levels in mind, the decomposition of BSC functions into different levels such as we have done is somewhat awkward at places. We illustrate this observation by pointing out some dependencies between the BSC functional levels described earlier in this section.

1. The half-duplex mode of operation facilitates the logical design of dialogue

interactions betwen two communicating stations. Its effect pervades all functional levels. For instance, bit and character synchronization need to be reestablished whenever a line turns around. The stop-and-wait form of ARQ technique is used for error control.

2. The transmit–receive coordination of two communicating stations at the dialogue level is directly coupled to the transmit–receive coordination at the multiple access level of all stations sharing a multipoint link. The dialogue-level control messages WACK and TTD are used as an integral part of the multiple access protocol.

3.3.2.2 Description of a Bit-Oriented Protocol —SDLC [IBM 75]

The SDLC protocol will also be described in terms of the hierarchy of synchronization functional levels in Fig. 3.2; however, techniques used in SDLC for solving these synchronization problems are different from BSC and other character-oriented protocols.

Again, we begin on the premise that bit synchronism is maintained by the transceivers or the DTE. In either case, our description of data link control will be concerned only with avoiding the transmission of transitionless data.

Frame Synchronization

A bit-oriented protocol, as its name suggests, deals with a stream of bits rather than a stream of characters. A character-code set is therefore not required. To delimit the beginning and end of a frame, a unique sequence of 8 bits 01111110 called a flag, denoted by F, is used. So each frame looks like

F [control and data] FCS F

where FCS consists of 16 CRC bits for error detection. The ending F may be followed by a frame, by another F, or by an idle condition. A series of contiguous F's may be transmitted to maintain bit synchronism and to maintain the data link in an active state. An idle state is perceived by the receiver when he receives a succession of 15 or more consecutive binary ones.

The F bit sequence 01111110 is made unique by zero insertion at the transmitting station and zero deletion at the receiving station, performed as part of the DLC protocol. The transmitter inserts a binary zero after any succession of five consecutive 1's inside a frame following the beginning F. The receiver removes a zero that follows a received sequence of five continuous 1's. We shall see below that with unique flags, the transmission of transparent data is always possible rather than handled as a special case.

The contents of every SDLC frame, with the exception of the beginning and ending flags, are protected by cyclic redundancy checking. Specifically, the generating polynomial, $x^{16} + x^{12} + x^5 + 1$, which is a CCITT standard, is used for generating the error detection bits [MCNA 77]. These bits are put into the FCS field immediately preceding the ending flag of a frame. Note, however, that the computation of the FCS bits at the sender is done before the zero insertion operation. Therefore, the inserted zeros are not protected by FCS. At the receiver, the deletion of inserted zeros is performed before the FCS computation.

When data signal transitions are needed by the DTE or transceiver for bit synchronism considerations, SDLC specifies the zero complementing NRZI (Non-Return-to-Zero-Inverted) coding method, with which, to send a binary 1 in the data, the signal on the line remains in the same state. The signal switches to the opposite state to send a binary 0 in the data. Thus an extended period of binary zeros in the data is transmitted as continuous transitions in the channel. A long period of binary 1's in the data will have transitions in the channel as a result of the zero insertion requirement to make the flags unique. If NRZI is used, it must be used by all DTEs on the data link.

Multiple Access Synchronization

The basic data link configurations that are currently supported by the SDLC protocol are:

1. Point-to-point half-duplex line, switched or nonswitched
2. Point-to-point duplex line, nonswitched
3. Multipoint duplex line, nonswitched
4. Unidirectional loop consisting of point-to-point simplex line segments

where

- Simplex means data-carrying ability in one direction only
- Half-duplex means data-carrying ability in both directions but not at the same time
- Duplex means simultaneous bidirectional data-carrying ability

In any of the SDLC data link configurations, exactly one of the stations is designated to be the primary station of the data link. Thus each data link has a primary station and one or more secondary stations. Communication of data always takes place between the primary station and a secondary station. Secondary stations, if more than one is present, cannot communicate with each other. We remind the reader that sometimes a station has the capability to implement only half-duplex protocols, even if a full-duplex line is available. In a multipoint configuration, it is often the case that only the primary station operates duplex, while secondary stations operate half-duplex. Thus the primary may be transmitting to one secondary while simultaneously receiving from another secondary station.

With a point-to-point duplex line, both transmitter–receiver pairs have their own dedicated channels. In this case, multiple access synchronization is not necessary.

For all other configurations, sharing of a channel by multiple transmitter–receiver pairs is involved and multiple access synchronization is needed for conflict resolution. In SDLC, the encoding of control messages used for multiple access, content, and dialogue synchronization levels is integrated. Therefore, it is necessary for us to consider now the format of an SDLC frame.

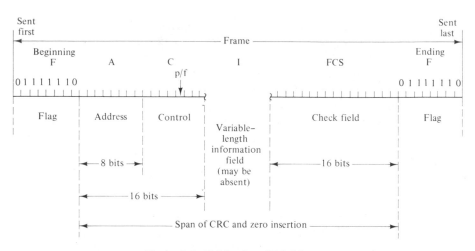

Figure 3.6. Fields of an SDLC frame.

With character-oriented DLC protocols, the character-code set usually provides for control characters. A sequence of one or more such control characters forms a control message. This approach necessitates special handling of transparent data.

Bit-oriented protocols separate control and data information by putting them in different parts of a frame. This approach, called *positional significance*, is possible because the beginning and ending flags can be uniquely identified (through zero insertion and deletion at the frame synchronization level) and thus provide reference points for locating data and control fields. Specifically, a frame consists of the fields shown in Fig. 3.6. For multiple-access synchronization we are presently interested only in the address field and the p/f-bit in the control field.[4]

In each of the SDLC data link configurations, there is a primary station and one or more secondary stations. The primary station acts as a central controller for data link access. It carries out this function using the address (A) field and the poll/final (p/f) bit in the control field. Since there is only one primary station, it never needs to be identified. The address of the secondary station in communication with the primary is always indicated in the address field (see Fig. 3.6). If the frame is from secondary to primary, the A field identifies the sender. If the frame is from primary to secondary, the A field identifies the intended receiver. In frames from the primary, a common address may be used for a group of secondary stations. In particular, an all-1's address field is often used as a broadcast or all-stations address.

In frames sent by the primary, the p/f-bit is a *poll bit*. In frames sent by a secondary station, the p/f-bit is a *final bit*. When the primary sends a frame to a secondary station with the poll bit turned on, it demands a response from the secondary station. Access right is also automatically granted to that secondary station for using the data link. The secondary station can then send a sequence of frames on the data link; the number of frames is limited only by error and sequence control

---

[4]We use lowercase letters p and f to avoid confusion with F, which denotes a flag.

100

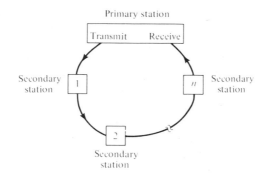

Figure 3.7. Loop configuration.

considerations to be addressed later. The secondary station relinquishes its access right when it sends a frame with the final bit turned on.

This use of the poll/final bit is adhered to for all primary–secondary dialogues even for a point-to-point full-duplex data link configuration where each transmitter–receiver pair has its own dedicated channel (see the discussion of the normal response mode in the dialogue synchronization section below).

In a point-to-point half-duplex line, the primary and secondary stations alternate use of the shared data link. In a multipoint full-duplex line, the primary-to-secondary channel is dedicated to the primary transmitter, which can send frames to any one of the secondary stations by identifying it in the address field. The secondary-to-primary channel is shared by the secondary stations and access right to the shared channel is controlled by the primary station via polling using the poll bit.

An SDLC loop consists of a series of point-to-point simplex lines. Each secondary station ordinarily acts as a repeater. Bits sent out of the primary station are relayed from one secondary station to the next one downstream until they return to the primary station (see Fig. 3.7). Such a loop is therefore unidirectional and half-duplex procedures between the primary and a secondary are used. The primary transmits a frame to any one of the secondary stations by identifying it in the address field. Or it may command a response from a secondary station by polling it.

The poll may be specific, as in point-to-point and multipoint configurations, with the poll bit turned on in a primary-to-secondary frame. Or the poll may be for a group of secondary stations with a common address. In the latter case the primary station polls by first sending an NSP (nonsequenced poll) control message with a common address in the address field (see below for the encoding of NSP and other control messages). After the NSP, the primary sends a binary zero followed by continuous 1's, which starts a *polling cycle*. If the poll bit in the NSP frame is also turned on, the addressed secondary stations are required to respond. If the poll bit is off, the addressed secondary stations are only invited to transmit. The response to an NSP control message requires turning on the final bit only if the command had the poll bit turned on.

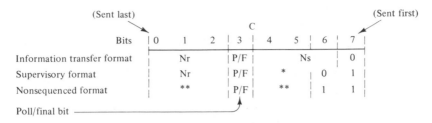

*Codes for supervisory commands/responses
**Codes for nonsequenced commands/responses

Figure 3.8. SDLC control field formats.

Thus a polling cycle begins with the transmission of an NSP control frame by the primary, followed by a "go-ahead" pattern consisting of a binary zero followed by continuous 1's. The first down-loop secondary station that has been polled receives the go-ahead when it has counted a zero and seven consecutive 1's in its input signal. It repeats the first six 1's and changes the seventh one to a binary zero. Thus an SDLC flag is generated. That secondary station then suspends the repeater function and transmits from itself to the primary station one or more frames. When it is finished, it resumes the repeater function. The ending binary zero in the ending flag of the last frame followed by continuous 1's now creates a go-ahead pattern again. The access right to the shared channel is then passed on to the next downstream secondary station that has been polled. Finally, when the primary station receives seven or more continuous 1's, the polling cycle is complete and the primary station is back in control of the data link.

Content Synchronization

As before, the functions included in this functional layer are: the separation of data and control, the encoding of control messages, error control, and the sequencing of frames.

The first function is provided using the positional significance approach discussed earlier: control and data are transmitted in different fields of a frame. The positions of these fields are measured from the beginning and end of the frame marked by unique flags. Unlike character-oriented protocols, the data transmitted are always considered to be transparent data and no special handling is required.

Depending on the values of bits 6 and 7 in the control field of a frame, SDLC defines three different kinds of frames with different formats:

Information transfer (I) frames
Supervisory (S) frames
Nonsequenced (NS) frames

The control field formats of these three kinds of frames are shown in Fig. 3.8, where bit 7 differentiates between I-frames and the others; bit 6 differentiates between S-

Format (note 1)	Sent last — Binary configuration — Sent first			Acronym	Command	Response	I-Field prohibited	Resets Nr and Ns	Confirms frames through Nr-1	Defining characteristics
NS	000	P/F	0011	NSI	X	X				Command or response that requires nonsequenced information
	000	F	0111	RQI		X	X			Initialization needed; expect SIM
	000	P	0111	SIM	X		X	X		Set initialization mode; the using system prescribes the procedures
	100	P	0011	SNRM	X		X	X		Set normal response mode; transmit on command
	000	F	1111	ROL		X	X			This station is off line
	010	P	0011	DISC	X		X			Do not transmit or receive information
	011	F	0011	NSA		X	X			Acknowledge NS commands
	100	F	0111	CMDR		X				Nonvalid command received; must receive SNRM, DISC, or SIM
	101	P/F	1111	XID	X	X				System identification in I field
	001	0/1	0011	NSP	X		X			Response optional if no P-bit
	111	P/F	0011	TEST	X	X				Check pattern in I field
S	Nr	P/F	0001	RR	X	X	X		X	Ready to receive
	Nr	P/F	0101	RNR	X	X	X		X	Not ready to receive
	Nr	P/F	1001	REJ	X	X	X		X	Transmit or retransmit, starting with frame Nr
I	Nr	P/F	Ns 0	I	X	X			X	Sequenced I-frame

Note 1: NS = nonsequenced, S = supervisory, I = information

Figure 3.9. Summary of SDLC commands and responses

and NS-frames. The p/f-bit in the control field has been encountered earlier for multiple-access synchronization. It is also used for some dialogue synchronization functions. The bit sequences N_r and N_s are for error and sequence control of I-frames. The remaining bits (marked * and ** in Fig. 3.8) are used to encode various control messages. The rest of the frame for all three formats are identical except for the I-field (see Fig. 3.6). In I-frames, the I-field can accommodate an arbitrarily long sequence of data bits, which must be a multiple of 8 bits. Otherwise, its length is subject only to error detection performance considerations. The I-field is not permitted in S-frames, while the I-field may be used to transmit link management data in NS-frames.

A listing of the encoding of SDLC control messages defined in [IBM 75] is shown in Fig. 3.9. We note that not all the bit sequences have been assigned. Hence additional control messages may be defined in the future as it becomes necessary.

A significant advantage of bit-oriented protocols over character-oriented protocols is the ease with which the set of control messages can be expanded. Recall that in BSC, the character-code set determines the available control characters. To define additional control messages one must employ longer and longer sequences of control characters. Character-oriented protocols are inefficient since only a very small number of the 8-bit sequences in a character is used for encoding control information. While with the positional significance approach in bit-oriented protocols, theoretically all 2^8 possible bit sequences can be used to encode control information.

We talk next about the error and sequence control functions of SDLC. Recall that error detection is performed for all frames. In addition, all I-frames are numbered in sequence. Sequence numbering is used to detect lost (garbled) frames or duplicated frames so as to guarantee that I-frames are delivered in their original order.

Recall that in BSC, data frames must be transmitted and acknowledged one at a time. Hence their order is preserved. Furthermore, the use of ACK0 and ACK1 for odd- and even-numbered transmission blocks ensures that a missing frame will be detected.

In SDLC, a transmitter can transmit up to seven I-frames before receiving positive acknowledgment. This is possible because the sequence numbering fields N_S and N_r are 3-bit sequences and have a counting capacity of 8.

Each station sequentially numbers every I-frame it transmits. This count is known as N_S, which is the sequence number (modulo 8) of the transmitted frame. The same station also keeps track, sequentially, of error-free I-frames it has received. N_r is the sequence number (modulo 8) of the next I-frame that it expects.

Consider two communicating stations, 1 and 2, with transmit and receive counts $V_S(1)$ and $V_r(1)$ at station 1, $V_S(2)$ and $V_r(2)$ at station 2. Suppose that an I-frame is sent from station 1 to station 2. It contains $N_S(1) = V_S(1)$, which is the sequence number of that particular I-frame. $V_S(1)$ is then incremented by 1. At station 2, if an error is detected in the frame, that frame is simply rejected. Suppose that it is error free. $N_S(1)$ is then compared to $V_r(2)$, which is the sequence number expected by station 2. If they agree, the frame is accepted and $V_r(2)$ is incremented by 1. If $N_S(1) \neq V_r(2)$, the received frame is rejected. [There are two possible cases. $N_S(1) < V_r(2)$ means that the received frame is a duplicate. On the other hand, $N_S(1) > V_r(2)$ means that the received frame is out of sequence and some I-frames are missing. Since $N_S(1)$ and $V_r(2)$ are modulo 8 numbers, the two cases cannot really be distinguished. However, the ability to distinguish the two cases is not necessary to achieve the objective of error and sequence control.]

Next consider the $N_r(1)$ field in the I-frame from station 1 to station 2. $N_r(1)$ is set equal to $V_r(1)$ and is a positive acknowledgment from station 1 to station 2 confirming correct reception of previously sent I-frames, from station 2 to station 1, with contiguous sequence numbers (modulo 8) up to and including $N_r(1) - 1$. The positive acknowledgment indicated by $N_r(1)$ is accepted as long as the I-frame is error free, even though it may be out of sequence. Buffers containing acknowledged frames may then be released.

We note several things regarding error and sequence control:

1. On a duplex data link, a transmitter can transmit I-frames continuously as long as it receives positive acknowledgments from incoming I-frames so that it does not have seven outstanding unacknowledged I-frames. On a half-duplex data

link, at most seven I-frames can be transmitted at a time before the line turns around for an acknowledgment.

2. A single positive acknowledgment can acknowledge up to seven frames at the same time. This is unlike BSC, in which data frames must be acknowledged individually.

3. If an error is detected in any I-frame, all I-frames following it need to be retransmitted even if they have been correctly received. This protocol ensures that the original order of the I-frames is preserved at the receiver.

4. Supervisory and nonsequenced frames are not numbered. They are not therefore protected by sequence numbering against loss, duplication, or out-of-order reception. All frames, however, have CRC error detection.

5. Supervisory frames have the N_r field and can therefore be used to provide positive acknowledgments.

6. In the discussion above, the $N_r(1)$ count received by station 2 acknowledges correct reception of I-frames up to and including $N_r(1) - 1$. Note that this serves as a positive acknowledgment. Alternatively, the supervisory frame REJ can be used by station 1 to demand station 2 to transmit or retransmit starting with frame $N_r(1)$. In this respect, REJ is like a negative acknowledgment.

Dialogue Synchronization

In both multipoint and loop configurations, there are multiple secondary stations which may be engaging in concurrent dialogues with a single primary station. However, having achieved multiple access synchronization, we can consider each dialogue individually. A dialogue involves only two stations: a primary and a secondary. Control messages from primary to secondary are called *commands*. Control messages from secondary to primary are called *responses*. The primary always transmits first to initiate a dialogue, although on a switched data link either one may call the other first to make the physical connection. We note that in a network environment, a station may be attached to more than one data link; it can be a primary on one data link but a secondary on another data link.

The responses of a secondary depend on its "mode" status. The primary station of a dialogue can command one of three modes at the secondary station:

> Normal disconnected mode (NDM)
> Initialization mode
> Normal response mode (NRM)

A secondary station that receives a DISC command assumes NDM; it also assumes NDM when power is turned on or when a switched connection is initially made.

Valid commands with the p-bit turned on cause a disconnected secondary station to respond with a request for on-line status (ROL) or, if needed, a request for initialization (RQI). In the latter case, the command SIM is expected, which causes the secondary to enter initialization mode and starts predefined initialization procedures stored at the secondary. The command SNRM puts the secondary in the NRM and subordinates the secondary to the primary; a secondary cannot transmit unless it has been polled by the primary. The primary and secondary transmit–receive counts V_r and V_s are reset to 0. The secondary station remains in NRM until it receives a DISC or SIM command. NSA is the affirmative response to the mode-setting commands SNRM, DISC, or SIM.

In SDLC, data transfer between primary and secondary takes place when the secondary is in NRM. In this mode, the secondary has access right to transmit only after it has received a frame from the primary with the p-bit turned on. It can then transmit one or more frames and relinquishes its access right when it turns the f-bit on in its last frame. (An exception to this procedure using the p/f-bit is the polling of secondary stations on a loop with the NSP command.) For the sequence control considerations discussed earlier, each station can have only up to seven unacknowledged I-frames outstanding. In a half-duplex link, to get a positive acknowledgment, the line must turn around. Therefore, the p- and f-bits also serve to turn the line around, thus alternating control of the line between primary and secondary. In a full-duplex link, the p- and f-bits serve only to assign and relinquish the access right of the secondary.

We have so far encountered one control message encoded in supervisory frames, REJ. There are two other control messages encoded in supervisory frames, which are used for flow control. They are RR (receive ready) and RNR (receive not ready). They can be sent by a receiver, either primary or secondary, to control the flow from the sender.

A dialogue may get out of synchronization when one or both stations become uncertain of the status of the other. Nonsynchronous conditions could occur because of lost frames, and frames received out of sequence. Timeouts and retries are the means for recovering synchronization. Some of the SDLC conditions for timeouts and retries are:

1. When the primary station transmits a frame with the p-bit turned on, response is expected within a certain time. The absence of a response may be due to no transmission from the secondary ("idle detect" condition) or garbled transmissions from the secondary ("nonproductive receive" condition). Timeouts are needed for both conditions to initiate recovery action at the primary. We note that a secondary cannot retry if there is no acknowledgment to its last frame with the f-bit turned on, since it has just given up its access right. In a loop, however, the secondary can retry following an NSP polling command.

2. Retries are made to obtain acknowledgment of a command. For example, NSA is the expected acknowledgment for SNRM, DISC, and SIM.

3. Retries are made to resume communication with a busy station following reception of RNR. Retries may be attempted by a primary or a secondary station.

4. Retries are made to achieve initial on-line status at a secondary station (ROL response).

5. Retries are made to initiate active communication at a secondary station (RQI response).

6. For a switched data link, an inactivity timeout of 20 seconds is used to alert stations of link disuse. If the timeout expires at either station, that station may attempt to alert the other station. After a user-specified number of unsuccessful attempts, the station disconnects the switched circuit.

If a nonsynchronous condition cannot be recovered by the specified number of retries, help from protocols at a level above data link control will be necessary. The type of intervention required depends on the decision-making power available beyond that of data link control. At a terminal, for example, operator intervention may be needed. Some other conditions also require help from protocols at a level above data link control:

1. If a primary station transmits a command that is not valid for the receiving secondary station, the secondary responds with a CMDR frame. The I-field of the frame contains secondary station status data that the primary needs for appropriate recovery action. Intervention from a higher level is required to analyze and act on the secondary status report. The secondary then expects a mode-setting command from the primary station.

2. If a secondary station's response, XID, to the exchange of station identification contains the wrong identification, intervention from a higher level is required to analyze and act on the situation.

Additional SDLC Features

1. Apart from I-frames, SDLC provides another vehicle for either primary or secondary to send data to each other. These are the NSI frames of the nonsequenced format. NSI frames are not sequenced nor are they acknowledged at the DLC level.

2. A transmitter, primary or secondary, may abort the transmission of a frame by sending eight consecutive binary 1's with no zero insertion. This abort pattern terminates a frame without an FCS field or ending flag. The abort pattern may be followed by seven additional binary 1's, which will idle the data link, or it may be followed by a flag. An aborting secondary station may not start another frame until it receives a command from the primary. In the case of a loop, a loop secondary station may abort by first transmitting the abort pattern or by simply resuming the repeater function (thus propagating continuous 1's).

Comments on the Structure of SDLC

We found that the SDLC protocol can be decomposed to fit into the hierarchical functional levels in Fig. 3.2 very well with one obvious exception. That is the shared use of the p/f–bit by different levels. At the multiple–access level, the p/f–bit is used to effect the sharing of a data link by multiple secondary stations. At the dialogue level, the p/f–bit is used to effect the NRM dialogue interactions. The p/f–bit may also be used to provide a check point for error recovery action.

3.4 THE EVOLUTION OF DLC PROTOCOLS

In this chapter we have examined the main classes of data link control protocols in the chronological order of their development; first asynchronous or start–stop protocols, then synchronous character–oriented protocols, and finally synchronous bit-oriented protocols. Generally, synchronous protocols have a lot more functional capability than asynchronous protocols and are intended for computers and terminal devices that are intelligent and have memory for buffering relatively long messages.

Start–stop protocols were originally designed for nonintelligent unbuffered terminal devices. A significant percentage of terminals in use today are still of this type and start–stop protocols are still the only protocols that they are capable of using. However, both technological and marketing trends are pointing toward the use of more and more intelligent buffered terminal devices. Furthermore, the development of packet–switching networks poses new DLC requirements for communication between computers as equals (in addition to the traditional master–slave mode of operation). Bit-oriented synchronous protocols have been developed to meet these requirements and to take advantage of hardware capabilities not heretofore available. The importance of such protocols is emphasized by the emergence of the protocol standards.

In this section we first provide a critical review of the different classes of protocols described earlier. We then summarize functional capabilities in HDLC and ADCCP that are not available in the current version of SDLC described above.

Recall that communication has been defined herein as synchronization of data between different machines. We found that the synchronization problem can be structured into a hierarchy of functional levels, each level in the hierarchy depending on synchronism at the level below achieved over finer grains of time. The synchronization functional levels in the hierarchy are (in decreasing granularity of time):

Dialogue synchronization
Content synchronization
Multiple access synchronization
Frame synchronization
Bit synchronization

The most basic requirements are bit and frame synchronization, so that bits of data and control information can be transported as a package (frame) from one machine to another.

Start–stop protocols generally rely on a character-code set which defines data characters and some control characters. Both control and data are transmitted one character at a time. The start bit and stop interval accomplish both bit and character synchronization. The latter can be regarded as the equivalent of frame synchronization since characters are transmitted one at a time. Start–stop protocols have limited functions in the higher levels of the hierarchy and are typically specific to terminal device types. There has been a proliferation of start–stop protocols designed for different code sets and different terminal devices, resulting in a serious compatability problem. Nonintelligent terminals often have to be remotely controlled by the computers they are communicating with. As a result, device control in addition to data link control characters and sequences are intermixed with data in dialogue exchanges. Data link configurations are typically point-to-point half-duplex. Not only is there little sharing of communications facilities, but often an operator needs multiple terminals to interact with different application programs even though they reside within the same host computer. Finally, the irreducible overhead of a start bit and a stop interval associated with the transmission of every character is another decided disadvantage. These are some of the reasons that prompted the development of synchronous protocols for communication between computers and sophisticated data terminals or other computers.

Synchronous protocols, both character- and bit-oriented, avoid many of the deficiencies of asynchronous protocols, and provide essentially the complete hierarchy of functions identified earlier. Character-oriented protocols, such as BSC described earlier, still depend on a character–code set. Some of the frequent criticisms of BSC (and similar character-oriented protocols) are:

1. The character–code set contains both data link control and device control characters. There is no clear separation between data link control, device control, and various high-level source–destination control functions, which need to be decoded at the data link control level.

2. Control frames with control and address information are not protected by error checking. (Some format checking is done using pad characters as a rudimentary form of error detection. For example, the control characters EOT and NAK must be followed by a trailing pad character of all 1 bits. This is done to reduce the probability of a transmission line error converting a positive acknowledgment response into an EOT or NAK response.)

3. New control messages need to be defined as sequences of existing control characters. Upward compatibility is difficult as new functions are defined.

4. Also as a result of using a character–code set, transparent data are handled as a special case, using the transparent text mode described earlier.

5. Communication is always half-duplex even if a full-duplex communications line is used. Only one unacknowledged data frame can be outstanding at a time; each such data frame is individually acknowledged. As a result, frequent turnarounds of the communications line are necessary for data transfer, giving rise to inefficient utilization of the communications line, especially when the application calls for short transmission blocks.

6. A transmitting station, with control of the line, can continue to transmit indefinitely, thus monopolizing it; the receiving station can send only control messages in reply. Some partial remedies, however, are provided; such as the limited conversational mode and the reverse interrupt (RVI) control message.

Bit-oriented protocols, such as SDLC described above, provide improvements over character-oriented protocols with more functional capabilities and better solution techniques to the synchronization problems. The positional significance approach provides not only separation of control and data but also facilitates a clean separation of DLC from high-level communications protocol layers. This is consistent with the layering approach in communications network architecture, in which each protocol layer is associated with a positionally significant header and trailer of a frame [ZIMM 80]. Data link control, being the lowest protocol layer[5] in the communications network architecture, provides the outermost header and trailer of a frame. High-level functions (such as device control and session control) are encoded in headers and trailers which are treated as part of the "information field" of a frame by data link control protocols and are thus invisible to data link control facilities.

With positionally significant control and data fields within a frame, growth in functional requirements can be accommodated by expanding the size of the control field. (See the discussion of HDLC and ADCCP below.) Transparent data are also handled as a rule rather than an exception. All control and data information are contained within frames all of which are error checked.

Communication between SDLC stations can be full or half duplex. SDLC link configurations consist of loops, in addition to point-to-point and multipoint lines (available with BSC). Up to seven information frames can be transmitted before a positive acknowledgment is required. The considerations described above all contribute toward more efficient utilization of the communications facilities than do start–stop and BSC techniques. In a half-duplex configuration, the maximum of seven outstanding unacknowledged information frames also prevents a station from monopolizing the communications line.

Additional Functional Capabilities in HDLC
and ADCCP [ANSI 79, ISO 79, CYPS 78]

SDLC, as described above, and the protocol standards HDLC and ADCCP are compatible protocols with the current version of SDLC [IBM 75] having only a subset of the repertoire of commands and capabilities adopted for HDLC and ADCCP. We discuss some of these extended capabilities in this section.[6] First we note that some of the control messages are called by different names in the protocol standards. In particular, the terminology "unnumbered" is used throughout in place of "nonsequenced"; thus NSI becomes UI (unnumbered information), NSA becomes UA (unnumbered acknowledgment), and NSP becomes UP (unnumbered poll). Also, the term FRMR (frame reject) is used instead of the SDLC term of CMDR (command reject).

HDLC and ADCCP provide for the use of an extended control field of 16 bits. Additional bits are available in supervisory and nonsequenced formats for encoding

---

[5] According to the OSI Reference Model [ZIMM 80], physical control, which is concerned with electrical characteristics, is actually the lowest functional layer.

[6] Since many of these extended capabilities were proposed by IBM to the standards organizations, it seems reasonable to expect that SDLC will be upgraded in the future to include them.

new control messages. Seven-bit fields are used for N_s and N_r counts, thus permitting the transmission of up to 127 information frames before positive acknowledgment. This is desirable for efficient utilization of very high speed communications channels and satellite links which have a large propagation delay (since the mean number of frames that can be enroute from a sender to a receiver is equal to the throughput rate times the average delay from the sender to the receiver). HDLC and ADCCP also include provisions for an extended address field.

An additional supervisory frame, SREJ (selective reject), is defined in the protocol standards. SREJ is a negative acknowledgment that indicates rejection of the information frame with the sequence number contained in the N_r field (but acceptance of frames numbered up to and including $N_r - 1$). However, unlike REJ, SREJ demands retransmission of only the specific information frame numbered N_r, and not subsequent frames that have also been sent. We note that this provision may alter the sequence ordering of information frames delivered from the transmitting station to the receiving station. If the original sequence of the information frames needs to be reestablished, it will have to be performed by protocols at a level higher than that of DLC. We note that in packet-switching networks, the frames exchanged by two packet-switching nodes typically belong to different "virtual circuits" and preservation of ordering is not important at the data link control level.

In the current version of SDLC, data transfer can take place only with the secondary station in the normal response mode. HDLC and ADCCP provide two additional secondary station modes for the transfer of information frames. An SARM (set asynchronous response mode) command places a secondary station in a mode in which it can initiate transmissions without having been polled first; otherwise the primary–secondary relationship between the stations is essentially the same as in NRM. The SABM (set asynchronous balanced mode) command is used to make stations into equals with identical command and response capabilities. The stations are called *combined stations* rather than primary and secondary stations. Each combined station is, in effect, a combination of a primary and a secondary station. The asynchronous balanced mode is intended primarily for point-to-point full-duplex links; note that in a packet network environment, a true full-duplex communications capability is important.

High-Level Communications Protocols

We have attempted to present data link control protocols as a structured set of functions. The hierarchical model introduced herein provides a structured representation of functional requirements for remote processes to communicate. Thus it can be used to model high-level communications protocol layers as well. In most network architectures (see, e.g., [ZIMM 80]) data link control constitutes just the lowest layer of a larger hierarchy of communications protocol layers. If we examine the functions in the hierarchy, we find that those functions within the high-level protocol layers can also be structured into functions for multiple-access synchronization, content synchronization, and dialogue synchronization, similar to what we have encountered at the data link control layer.

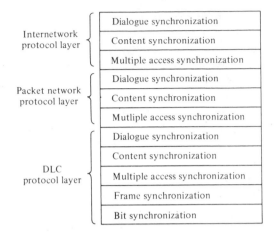

Figure 3.10. Communications protocol layers and their functional requirements.

We illustrate this idea in Fig. 3.10 by considering a somewhat simplified communications architecture for internetworking with three protocol layers. Note that the functional levels of dialogue, content, and multiple-access synchronization are reiterated three times: once in the DLC protocol layer, then in the packet network protocol layer, and finally in the internetwork protocol layer. Although the functional requirements are the same in the three protocol layers, the end points and the characteristics of the communications channel (virtual or real) assumed by different protocol layers are different. Consequently, the degrees of importance associated with various synchronization functions will not be the same in different protocol layers and the solution techniques will thus be different. Consider the end-to-end transport protocol layer of a packet-switching network. The multiple-access synchronization functional level again deals with the sharing of communications facilities by multiple sender–receiver pairs. But with a mesh topology and store-and-forward nodes, the multiple-access synchronization problems are: routing and the synchronization of routing information, congestion control, and so on, which are not the same as before for DLC. The dialogue and content synchronization levels still deal with flow control, error and sequence control, and so on, as described earlier for DLC. The specific protocols for solving these problems, however, are somewhat different because the characteristics of a packet network are different from those of a data link (at a lower level in the network). For example, flow control is probably more important for dialogue synchronization at the network level than at the DLC level, while error control is probably more important at the DLC level than at the network level (because the network transport protocols can count on reliable data links provided by DLC at the lower level). Finally, when different packet-switching networks are interconnected via gateways, it is not hard to see that the multiple access synchronization, content synchronization, and dialogue synchronization functions are needed again in internetworking protocols [CERF 78] for the network of gateways.

ACKNOWLEDGMENTS

This work was supported by the National Science Foundation under Grant ECS78-01803. The author would like to thank Wushow Chou of North Carolina State University and Vint Cerf of the Defense Advanced Research Projects Agency for their helpful comments. He is particularly indebted to an anonymous reviewer who painstakingly read an early draft, pointed out many errors, and made numerous valuable suggestions for improvement.

REFERENCES

ANSI 75	American National Standards Institute, "Procedures for the Use of the Communication Control Characters of American National Standard Code for Information Interchange in Specified Data Communication Links," ANSI X3.28-1976, December 1975.
ANSI 79	American National Standards Institute, "American National Standard for Advanced Data Communication Control Procedures (ADCCP)," ANSI X3.66-1979, January 1979.
BURT 72	Burton, H. O., and D. D. Sullivan, "Errors and Error Control," *Proc. IEEE*, November 1972.
CERF 78	Cerf, V. G., and P. T. Kirstein, "Issues in Packet-Network Interconnection," *Proc. IEEE*, Vol. 66, November 1978.
CYPS 78	Cypser, R. J., *Communications Architecture for Distributed Systems*, Addison-Wesley, Reading, Mass., 1978.
DAVE 72	Davey, J. R., "Modems," *Proc. IEEE*, November 1972.
DONN 74	Donnan, R. A., and J. R. Kersey, "Synchronous Data Link Control: A Perspective," *IBM Syst. J.*, May 1974.
IBM 70	IBM Corp., *General Information — Binary Synchronous Communications*, Manual No. GA27-3004-2, 3rd. ed., October 1970.
IBM 75	IBM Corp., *Synchronous Data Link Control — General Information*, Manual No. GA27-3093-1, May 1975.
ISO 79	International Standards Organization, "Data Communication — High-Level Data Link Control Procedures — Frame Structure," Ref. No. ISO 3309-1979; "Data Communication — High-Level Data Link Control Procedures — Elements of Procedures," Ref. No. ISO 4335-1979, 1979.
MART 70	Martin, J., *Teleprocessing Network Organization*, Prentice-Hall, Englewood Cliffs, N.J., 1970.
MCNA 77	McNamara, J. E., *Technical Aspects of Data Communication*, Digital Equipment Corp., Maynard, Mass., 1977.
ZIMM 80	Zimmermann, H., "OSI Reference Model — The ISO Model of Architecture for Open Systems Interconnection," *IEEE Trans. Commun.*, April 1980.

4

Multiple Access Protocols

SIMON S. LAM
The University of Texas at Austin
Austin, Texas

4.1 INTRODUCTION

Packet-broadcasting networks may be defined as packet-switching networks in which the connectivity requirements of the network users are furnished by a broadcast medium (channel). Two examples of broadcast media are satellite and terrestrial radio channels. A less obvious example is that of a multipoint cable. Although multipoint networks have been in use for many years as broadcast networks, it was the ALOHANET using radio channels and a novel contention protocol [ABRA 70, BIND 75a] that first called attention to the concept of packet broadcasting as we know it now. This concept clearly emerged with the packet satellite project [ABRA 73, KLEI 73, ROBE 73, CROW 73, BUTT 74, JACO 77, JACO 78, WEIS 78] and the packet radio project [KAHN 77, KAHN 78] of the Advanced Research Projects Agency. Currently, packet broadcasting networks appear to be important in two areas. The first is satellite data networks. The rapid pace of development of commercial satellite systems in recent years has enabled substantial reductions in satellite system costs [ABRA 75]. Meanwhile, another marketplace is expanding rapidly: local area networks, which although outside the computer room, are confined to local environments (e.g., office complex, manufacturing plant, etc.). Such networks, based on CATV technology, are said to offer real advantages to computing facilities which serve many terminals and/or employ distributed processing [WILL 74, THOR 75, DEMA 76, METC 76, WEST 78]. An extensive bibliography of local computer networks can be found in [CLAR 78, THUR 79].

Of interest in this chapter are protocols for sharing a single broadcast channel by a population of users. The users have random traffic requirements as well as delay constraints. The central problem is that of *conflict resolution* among users desiring channel access. The methods for conflict resolution will be referred to as *multiple access protocols*. We present a classification of such protocols, illustrate each class with description of specific protocols, and compare their performance under various traffic and channel assumptions. To delimit the scope of this chapter, we consider only networks in which everyone in the population of users can "hear" everyone else over the broadcast channel (i.e., we have a one-hop broadcast network). Multi-hop networks with packet repeaters such as those described in [KAHN 78, LAM 80b] are not considered.

The key measure of performance of a multiple access (MA) protocol is its channel throughput versus average delay trade-off characteristic. The throughput of a channel is defined as follows. Let C be the channel transmission rate in bits per second (bps) and let there be on the average P bits in a transmitted block of data. The *channel throughput S* is defined to be the ratio of the rate of successfully transmitted data blocks to the rate C/P. Thus channel throughput is a normalized quantity between 0 and 1. It includes as useful throughput overhead bits contained in data blocks for bit synchronization, addressing, error control, and other network control functions; these overheads are not, however, directly attributable to the MA protocol. Other overheads that are directly attributable to the implementation of an MA protocol are accounted for in the calculation of channel throughput; the maximum achievable channel throughput is thus less than 1 and is of interest as a gross measure of performance.

We next discuss briefly traditional multiple access protocols which are channel-oriented rather than packet-oriented (of interest here). A model for characterizing traffic sources is then presented. Following that, the characteristics of different categories of multiple access protocols are surveyed. Specific protocols and their performance are examined in some detail in Secs. 4.2, 4.3, and 4.4.

4.1.1 Traditional Techniques

The problem of multiple access in the design of satellite systems, for example, has been solved in the past with voice communications in mind. The design objective is to maximize the number of (voice-grade) channels for given constraints of power and bandwidth. The common satellite multiple access techniques are frequency-division multiple access (FDMA), time-division multiple access (TDMA), and code-division multiple access (CDMA) [SCHW 73]. CDMA is also called spread-spectrum multiple access. It is by far the least efficient and has been used mainly for military systems with antijam and security requirements. TDMA is generally more efficient than FDMA; the price paid is an increase in the cost and complexity of the equipment of each user [PRIT 77].

Multiple access protocols have traditionally been channel-oriented. The transmission capacity available is subdivided into separate channels (with FDMA or TDMA). The basic unit for allocation is thus a channel. Channels can be either (1) fixed assigned, or (2) demand assigned to users. With demand assignment, a channel needs to be set aside for signaling among users. (Access to the signaling channel is another multiple access problem! A typical solution for this is TDMA with fixed assignment.) Demand assignment can then be accomplished with either a central controller or a distributed control algorithm [PRIT 77, PUEN 71].

The channel-oriented MA protocols are suitable for voice traffic and may also be suitable for some data traffic. Data communications in general, however, have very diverse requirements, ranging from inquiry–response systems with intermittent traffic to file transfers with large volumes of data. In this chapter we are interested mainly in the class of new packet-oriented MA protocols for time sharing a single broadcast channel. The broadcast channel under consideration for the shared use of a population of users may possibly have been derived at a higher level of resource allocation via FDMA, TDMA, or CDMA. (The allocation scheme at this level will be of no concern to us.) We concentrate on the conflict resolution aspect of the multiple access problem and its performance in terms of throughput and delay. Other aspects of the multiple access problem (such as modulation, coding, and clock synchronization) are classical problems and are beyond the scope of this chapter; see, for example, [ELLI 73, JACO 74, GARD 80].

4.1.2 Traffic Model

The following model will be used to represent the traffic characteristics and transmission requirements of users of a message (or packet)-oriented communication network. Examples of users are human operators of computer terminals, computer programs interacting with such human operators or with other programs/data bases in other machines, and data concentrators for a multiplicity of such traffic sources. We view a user simply as a traffic source that can be modeled as a random point process with instants of message arrivals being the points of interest. A message is defined to be a block of data that has a time-delay constraint associated with it for delivery to a destination user. (In a packet-oriented network, a message may be transported in one or more packets.) The definition above is quite general. For example, a message may be a computer data file that needs to be delivered within a period of hours. It may be a line of characters in an inquiry–response system that needs to be delivered in a fraction of a second. It may be a digital voice sample (8 bits) that has a delay constraint dictated by the real-time voice sampling rate (e.g., 8000 samples per second).

Computer data traffic sources are often described as "bursty." Traffic burstiness is an important characteristic that influences the design of packet communication systems. This concept is briefly reviewed and a quantitative measure of burstiness, called the *bursty factor*, as defined in [LAM 78A], is presented below.

The bursty nature of a data traffic source stems from more than just randomness in message generation time and size. The user-specified message delay constraints to be met for these traffic sources are actually the single most important factor in determining if data traffic sources behave in a bursty manner. Suppose that we are given a traffic source with

$$T = \text{average interarrival time between messages}$$

and

$$\delta = \text{average message delay constraint}$$

where δ can be estimated in practice from the performance specifications of the intended network users. Generally, a user-specified source–destination delay constraint can be broken up into several parts, each part becoming a constraint for a segment of the communication path. δ is defined here to be the constraint for the message transmission time plus any necessary conflict resolution and queueing delays; it excludes, however, propagation delays through the network as well as message-processing delays at the source and destination.

The bursty factor β of the traffic source is defined to be

$$\beta = \frac{\delta}{T} \tag{4.1}$$

Note that β depends only on δ and T, which are inherent user characteristics. (The delay constraint δ is indeed an inherent source characteristic in the eyes of the network designer. Failing to satisfy it means that the user will take his business elsewhere!) Next consider a traffic source that is formed by merging together N sources with different statistics and delay constraints. The bursty factor of the aggregate source is defined to be the sum of the bursty factors of the individual sources:

$$\beta = \beta_1 + \beta_2 + \ldots + \beta_N \tag{4.2}$$

The usefulness of β is due to the following observation [LAM 78A]. Suppose that a communication channel is dedicated to a traffic source with bursty factor β and that all delay constraints are met. Then the resulting ratio of peak to average channel data rates (PAR) satisfies

$$\text{PAR} \geq \frac{1}{\beta} \tag{4.3}$$

and the channel throughput S satisfies

$$S \leq \beta \tag{4.4}$$

In other words, β gives an upper bound on the duty cycle of a traffic source. This information is useful to the network designer and is available independent of the communication system eventually provided. A traffic source with a small β ($\ll 1$) is said to be *bursty*.

The result above also says that for bursty users, channel-oriented MA protocols using either fixed assignment or demand assignment (over a period of time $\gg \delta$) are going to be very inefficient ($S \ll \delta$ 1). To improve the throughput of a broadcast channel shared by users with random bursty traffic, it is desirable to dynamically allocate transmission capacity on a per message (or packet) basis. This benefits from the multiplexing effect of Eq. (4.2) as well as the scaling effect of large systems discussed in [KLEI 76, sec. 5.1]. The key to realizing these gains is to design MA protocols for resolving channel-access conflicts without excessive overhead.

We note that the definition of bursty factor in Eq. (4.1) does not involve the

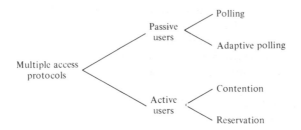

Figure 4.1. Classification of multiple access protocols.

average length of messages generated by a traffic source. Thus it is possible for a traffic source to generate very long messages but is still considered to be very bursty by definition. This average-message-length parameter, we shall see, also strongly affects the performance of MA protocols.

4.1.3 Network Assumptions

We consider a population of N users sharing use of a single broadcast channel. The ith user has a message generation rate of λ_i messages per second. Each message may give rise to one or more fixed-length packets with a mean number of L. Each packet carries a destination address so that when the packet is transmitted over the channel, with no interference from another user, it will be received by the proper addressee(s). Errors due to channel noise will be ignored. Such errors affect MA protocols equally and their effect can be evaluated separately. Notice that the specific connectivity requirements of the population of users are relevant only indirectly through the resulting set of message rates. Given the set of λ_i, it does not matter, for example, whether users want to communicate with each other or they all want to talk to a specific central site. Thus our only concern is the access problem of the broadcast channel.

Each user is capable of sending and receiving data at the channel transmission rate of C bps. In a number of MA protocols, the users are time synchronized so that the channel can be viewed as a sequence of time slots (just as in TDMA). Each time slot can accommodate one data packet. Minislots may also be interleaved with the data slots to accommodate small control packets.

When given access to the broadcast channel, a user can send data to any other user. Thus the MA protocol is simply an algorithm (possibly distributed as well as nondeterministic) for determining the channel-access rights of the users. In some protocols, the access right is not uniquely determined and it is possible for packet transmissions from different users to "collide" in the channel. It is assumed that the collisions are always destructive and that none of the packets involved in a collision can be correctly received. Each packet contains parity bits for error detection.

Suppose that it takes R seconds following a packet transmission for a user to find out whether it suffered a collision. R will be referred to as the *collision detection time*. In many systems [ABRA 73, METC 76], the user can find out the outcome of a transmission for himself by monitoring the broadcast channel. In this case, R is approximately equal to the propagation delay of the channel. (The propagation delay is always taken to be the maximum value between any pair of sender and receiver in the network.) If this collision detection mechanism is not possible, then R corresponds to the timeout period of a positive acknowledgment protocol [ABRA 70, BIND 75A].

4.1.4 A Classification of Protocols

The gamut of packet-oriented MA protocols can be classified as shown in Fig. 4.1 and may be illustrated by the following analogy.* Consider a group of students in a classroom who want to say something. Assume that if two or more students talk at the same time, the resulting speech will be unintelligible.

Passive versus Active Talkers

The students may be "passive." A student will talk only when specifically asked to do so by a teacher acting as a central controller. The teacher determines who wants to talk by polling the students one by one. Or the students may be "active." Whoever has something to say will try to do something about getting the opportunity to talk. Among protocols for active talkers, we further differentiate between two categories as follows.

Contention versus Reservation Protocols

Under a contention protocol, there is no attempt to coordinate the talkers. Each student tries to talk whenever he has something to say. In doing so, he might exercise some caution to try to minimize interference with other talkers by observing past activities in the room. The alternative is to use reservation protocols which may use one of the following two types of control.

Centralized versus Distributed Control

Under a reservation protocol, each student who wants to talk raises his hand to signal a request to talk. A teacher may be present to serve as a central controller to determine who should talk next. Alternatively, each student monitors the requests of all students and exercises a distributed algorithm to determine who should talk next.

In the next three sections we illustrate each class of protocols introduced above with descriptions of specific protocols. Performance implications of various channel and traffic parameters are discussed. In particular, a number of the protocols rely upon a short channel propagation delay for their efficiency and are thus not suitable for satellite channels.

---

*Another way to classify MA protocols, discussed in [LAM 80A] is to think of users desiring channel access as customers forming a distributed queue. The objective of a MA protocol is to identify such customers.

4.2 PROTOCOLS FOR PASSIVE USERS

This class of protocols is commonly known as *polling protocols*. The presence of a central controller is required. Users are passive in the sense that they may access the channel only when specifically polled by the central controller. The controller has two functions: (1) to identify users with data to send (the *ready users*), and (2) to schedule use of the channel by these users.

4.2.1 Conventional Polling Protocols

In conventional polling protocols, the central controller performs the foregoing two functions by polling the population of users one after the other. Upon the arrival of a polling message, the user polled transmits all messages accumulated in his buffer. The time needed to poll every user once and transmit their accumulated data is said to be the polling cycle time t_c. This is just the time between successive polls of a specific user.

A very important parameter determining the efficiency of polling protocols is the total "walk time" in a polling cycle. This is the portion of cycle time attributable to necessary overheads such as channel propagation delay, transmission time of polling and response messages, modem synchronization time, and so on. A detailed breakdown of time elements in a polling cycle can be found in [MART 72].

Minor implementation variations of the foregoing description exist, such as, prioritized polling list, some users polled more than once in a cycle, the amount of data that a user can transmit at a time is limited, and others [MART 72]. These will not be considered.

The two conventional polling protocols most widely used are: roll-call polling and hub polling [SCHW 77, chap. 12]. In *roll-call polling*, the central controller sends a polling message to the user polled. The user transmits his waiting data (if any) and passes control back to the central controller before the next user is polled. In *hub polling*, the central controller initiates a polling cycle by polling the user at the top of its polling list. The user transmits his waiting data (if any) and passes the polling message on to the next user directly. The user at the bottom of the list passes control back to the central controller to complete a polling cycle. The obvious advantage of hub polling over roll-call polling is that the average walk time $\bar{w}$ between users is typically less. However, the individual users need to be more intelligent and reliable than those of roll-call polling.

To illustrate the key performance trade-offs in the design of polling protocols, we consider here some results from a queueing model of N identical users [KONH 74]. The same model applies to both roll-call and hub polling. (A detailed analysis of polling that takes into account various system features and response-time elements can be found in [CHOU 78].)

Suppose that each user has an arrival rate of λ messages per second and an average message transmission time of $1/\mu$ sec.

120

Define

$$\rho = \frac{\lambda}{\mu}$$

Let $\bar{w}$ be the average walk time between users and $\bar{t}_c$ be the average cycle time. Then it can be shown that [KONH 74]

$$\bar{t}_c = \frac{N\bar{w}}{1 - N\rho} \tag{4.5}$$

The waiting time of a message is defined here to be the interval from its time of arrival to the start of its transmission. An expression for the average waiting time W is derived in [KONH 74]. It can be easily shown that

$$W \geq \frac{\bar{t}_c}{2} (1 - \rho)$$

Thus the simple expression in Eq. (4.5) can be used as an indirect measure of the average delay of a message, which is

$$D = W + \frac{1}{\mu}$$

Equation (4.5) has the usual queueing theory form, with $N\rho$ being the traffic intensity of the broadcast channel. We have in the limit $\bar{t}_c \uparrow \infty$ as $N\rho \uparrow 1$. Observe that $\bar{t}_c$ is also directly proportional to the total walk time $N\bar{w}$ in a polling cycle. Consequently, the delay performance may be greatly degraded if $\bar{w}$ is large (e.g., satellite channel) or N is large.

We next consider a performance booby trap of polling protocols. Suppose that N is increased but a higher-speed channel is used such that the channel utilization $N\rho$ remains the same. This change will in general tend to decrease the average delay D as a result of the scaling effect [KLEI 76, sec. 5.1]. However, with a conventional polling protocol, the same change will affect D adversely as well as follows. Increasing N while keeping $N\rho$ constant increases the $\bar{t}_c/2$ portion of the average delay due to the increased polling overhead $N\bar{w}$!

So far we have assumed users with plenty of buffer capacity (i.e., infinite waiting room for queues). Under this assumption the maximum channel throughput of polling is 1 in the limit of infinite queues.

Consider now users that have limited buffering capacity, so that each user can transmit at most one message at a time. One consequence is that $\bar{t}_c$ is always finite. In addition, the channel throughput S can be easily shown to be bounded as follows:

$$S \leq \frac{1/\mu}{\bar{w} + (1/\mu)} \tag{4.6}$$

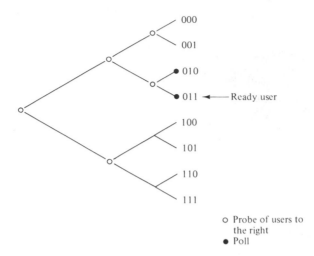

Figure 4.2. Inquiries (probe or poll) needed in an example of eight users.

The upper bound in Eq. (4.6) is the maximum channel throughput of polling for such users. In this case polling becomes extremely inefficient when the traffic consists of very short messages (e.g., terminals doing character-at-a-time transmission [WEST 72]).

4.2.2 Adaptive Polling

With conventional polling, when the network is lightly loaded, it is still necessary to poll every one of the users, although few users are *ready* (have data to send). The mean delay D in this situation is mainly determined by the polling overhead and not by the channel traffic intensity!

For a lightly loaded network, an adaptive polling protocol has been proposed by Hayes [HAYE 78] which significantly reduces the polling overhead. The key idea introduced is called *probing*. When a group of (two or more) users are probed, a polling message is sent by the central controller to all users in the group. Any users with data to send respond by transmitting some signal in the channel. To avoid cancellation by interference, the signal can be some noise energy. Note that if a group of users is probed and none responds, the whole group can be ignored until the next polling cycle. Thus when the network is lightly loaded, significant polling overhead reduction results through probing groups of users. The following implementation is suggested [HAYE 78].

Assume a total of $N = 2^n$ users. Each user is addressed by an n-bit binary number. The central controller can probe a group of users by sending the common prefix of the addresses of the users. At the beginning of each polling cycle, the central controller divides the users into 2^{n-j} groups of 2^j users each. The determination of j will be discussed later. Each of the 2^{n-j} groups is probed separately. If probing a group produces a positive response, each group is divided into two groups, which are then probed separately. This process is repeated until all ready users are identified and serviced.

A poll (of a single user) or a probe (of two or more users) will both be referred to as an *inquiry*. An example is illustrated in Fig. 4.2 with a group of eight users. Only one of them (address 011) is ready. Starting with probing all users ($j = 0$), a total of seven inquiries (five probes and two polls) are needed to complete the polling cycle.

Returning to our general problem, let us consider the following special cases.

Case 1. Pure polling, $j = 0$. The number of inquiries required is 2^n, which is independent of the number of ready users.

Case 2. Pure probing, $j = n$. Pure probing is excellent under very light loading. For instance, if there is exactly one ready user, the number of inquiries is $2n + 1$. However, pure probing is penalized under heavy loading. If all users are ready, the number of inquiries will be $2^{n+1} - 1$.

From these extreme cases, we see that the group size 2^j to be selected at the beginning of each polling cycle is crucial to the performance of the protocol. It should be chosen to minimize the expected number of inquiries in the current polling cycle. Let

$$p = \text{Prob [a user has data to send in the current polling cycle]}$$

and

$$\bar{I}(j) = E[\text{number of inquiries}/j]$$

We want to determine j^* such that

$$\bar{I}(j^*) = \min_{0 \le j \le n} \bar{I}(j)$$

Let us compare the probing of a group of 2^j users and probing two groups of 2^{j-1} users. If we probe 2^j users, the probability that none will respond to the probe is

$$\text{Prob[no response}/j] = (1 - p)^{2^j}$$

In this event, the choice of j instead of $j - 1$ saves one inquiry. On the other hand, in the event that there is a positive response from the group of 2^j users, the choice of j instead of $j - 1$ spends one more inquiry. Thus we have

$$\begin{aligned}\Delta\bar{I}(j) &= \bar{I}(j) - \bar{I}(j - 1)\\ &= 2^{n-j}[(-1)(1 - p)^{2^j} + (1 - (1 - p)^{2^j})]\\ &= 2^{n-j}[1 - 2(1 - p)^{2^j}]\end{aligned}$$

for $j = 1, \ldots, n$. Note that the term $1 - 2(1 - p)^{2^j}$ increases monotonically with j. Thus $\bar{I}(j)$ is minimized by the largest j such that[1]

---

[1] This is a simpler proof than the one found in [HAYE 78]. It is interesting to note that in general if addresses use base m numbers so that each node of the tree in Fig. 4.2 has m branches, the optimality condition is $(1 - p)^{m^j} > 1/m$.

$$1 - 2(1 - p)^{2^j} < 0$$

or

$$(1 - p)^{2^j} > \frac{1}{2} \tag{4.7}$$

Equation (4.7) tells the central controller how to determine j at the beginning of each polling cycle as a function of p. An estimate of p is

$$p = 1 - e^{-\lambda t_c} \tag{4.8}$$

where λ is the Poisson rate of message arrivals to a user, and t_c is the duration of the last polling cycle. Equation (4.8) assumes that messages arriving during one polling cycle do not respond positively to an inquiry until the next polling cycle. (This gives a pessimistic view of the operation of the system.) From Eqs. (4.7) and (4.8), we have

$$2^j < \frac{\ln 2}{\lambda t_c} \tag{4.9}$$

At the beginning of each polling cycle, the central controller can determine j^* as a function of λ and t_c using Eq. (4.9)

Performance Summary

The mean cycle time for the adaptive polling protocol is still basically Eq. (4.5) but with the polling overhead term $N\overline{w}$ considerably reduced, especially under light loading. For instance, if there is only one ready user in a polling cycle, the number of inquiries is $2(\log_2 N) + 1$ instead of N. The adaptivity in the protocol assures that there is no penalty during periods of heavy load. These above observations are illustrated in Fig. 4.3, which compares the mean number of inquiries per polling cycle as a function of p for pure polling, pure probing, and the optimum adaptive strategy using Eq. (4.7).

4.3 PROTOCOLS FOR ACTIVE USERS

We consider next two classes of protocols that require ready users to seek channel access actively instead of waiting to be polled. These are called contention and reservation protocols. Under *contention protocols*, there is no attempt to coordinate the ready users to avoid collisions entirely. Instead, each ready user makes his own decision regarding when to access the channel: he exercises caution, however, to minimize interference with other ready users as much as possible. Under *reservation protocols*, a reservation channel is provided for ready users to communicate among themselves such that only one ready user is scheduled for channel access at a time. Since users are geographically distributed, the multiple access problem has not really disappeared; it now exists in the access of the reservation channel for the transmission of small reservation requests.

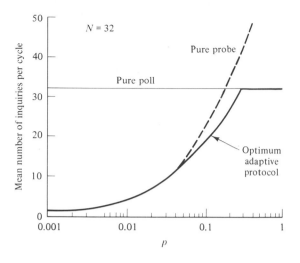

Figure 4.3. Performance of adaptive polling.

4.3.1 Contention Protocols

Unlike polling protocols, the overhead incurred by contention protocols for assigning channel access to ready users is independent of N but instead is dependent on the level of channel traffic. Thus pure contention protocols are suitable for a large population of bursty users (i.e., $N \uparrow \infty$ as $\beta \downarrow 0$ for each user but $N\beta$ remains constant). For a lightly loaded network, the delay performance of contention protocols can be far superior to polling protocols. Below we describe two pure contention protocols (ALOHA and slotted ALOHA), two contention protocols which include elements of reservation (R-ALOHA and CSMA), and an adaptive protocol (URN). We discuss, in the context of slotted ALOHA, the stability problem of contention protocols and the need for adaptive control in these protocols. We then describe a tree algorithm for resolving contention which guarantees channel stability. The algorithm is based on essentially the same idea as that of the adaptive polling algorithm described earlier.

4.3.1.1 The ALOHA Protocol [ABRA 70, BIND 75A]

Under the ALOHA protocol, users are not synchronized in any way. Each user transmits a data packet whenever one is ready. In the event that two or more packets collide (i.e., overlap in time), each user involved realizes this after R seconds (the collision detection time) and retransmits his packet after a randomized delay. As we discuss below, this randomized delay turns out to be crucial to the stability behavior and thus the throughput-delay performance of all contention-based protocols.

In [ABRA 70], Abramson first derived the maximum channel throughput of the ALOHA protocol in the limit of an infinite user population ($N \uparrow \infty$ and for each user $\beta \downarrow 0$). All messages consist of single packets. Hence the aggregate packet "birth process" is a Poisson process at a rate of S packets per packet transmission time.

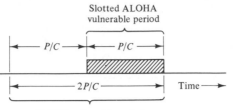

Figure 4.4. ALOHA and slotted ALOHA vulnerable periods of a transmitted packet.

Abramson also made the assumption that the sum of new transmissions and retransmissions in the channel (called *channel traffic*) can be approximated as a Poisson process at a rate of G packets per packet time. Furthermore, statistical equilibrium is assumed. The probability that a transmitted packet is successful is

$$\frac{S}{G} = e^{-2G}$$

(4.10)

which is obtained from consideration of Fig. 4.4; each transmitted packet has a vulnerable period of two packet time durations. It will be successful only if no other packet begins transmission within the vulnerable period.

From Eq. (4.10) the maximum possible ALOHA channel throughput is obtained at $G = 0.5$ and for an infinite-user population model (under the foregoing assumptions) is

$$C_A = \frac{1}{2e} \simeq 0.184$$

(4.11)

4.3.1.2 The Slotted ALOHA Protocol
[ROBE 72, ABRA 73, KLEI 73]

The slotted ALOHA protocol is just like ALOHA with the additional requirement that the channel is slotted in time. Users are required to synchronize their packet transmissions into fixed-length channel time slots. By requiring synchronization of packet start times, packet collisions due to partial overlaps are avoided and the vulnerable period of a transmitted packet is just the duration of a time slot (see Fig. 4.4). Under the same assumptions given above for ALOHA, we have

$$\frac{S}{G} = e^{-G}$$

(4.12)

where S is maximized at $G = 1$. The resulting slotted ALOHA maximum channel throughput for an infinite-user population model is twice that of the unslotted case:

$$C_{SA} = \frac{1}{e} \simeq 0.368$$

(4.13)

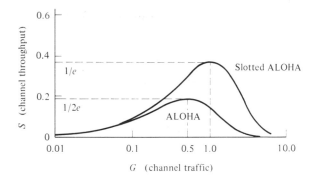

Figure 4.5. ALOHA and slotted ALOHA throughout curves.

Equations (4.10) and (4.12) are plotted in Fig. 4.5.

Two methods of scheduling retransmissions following the detection of a collision have been considered [METC 73, LAM 74]:

1. *Geometrically distributed delay.* A collided packet is retransmitted in a time slot with probability $p < 1$. With probability $1 - p$, the packet is delayed and the Bernoulli trial is repeated in the next time slot.
2. *Uniformly distributed delay.* A time slot is selected for retransmitting a collided packet from the next K time slots chosen equally likely.

For purposes of performance modeling, simulation studies indicate that in many cases the mean value $\bar{k}$ (instead of the exact probability distribution) of the retransmission delay is sufficient for predicting the behavior of a slotted ALOHA channel [LAM 74].

4.3.1.3 Performance Considerations

The analysis of ALOHA and slotted ALOHA given above was based upon three assumptions: (A1) statistical independence of channel traffic, (A2) infinite user population, and (A3) statistical equilibrium. More detailed studies of slotted ALOHA investigated the validity of these assumptions. In particular, it was shown that a necessary condition for (A1) is that the mean randomized delay $\bar{k}$ for retransmissions must be large ($\bar{k} \rightarrow \infty$). However, simulations showed that the maximum channel throughput results given by Eqs. (4.11) and (4.13) are robust; they are already quite accurate if $N \geq 10$ and $\bar{k} \geq 5$ [KLEI 73, LAM 74]. In these same references, the delay performance of slotted ALOHA was first studied for finite values of $\bar{k}$. When the traffic distribution is unbalanced with a mixture of high-rate as well as low-rate users, it was shown that the slotted ALOHA maximum channel throughput of $1/e$ can be considerably improved [ABRA 73].

The validity of assumption (A3) was also examined. It was shown that the slotted ALOHA protocol, without adaptive control, is potentially unstable [METC 73, LAM 74, KLEI 74, KLEI 75A]. (We might have deduced this from the curves in Fig. 4.5, which show two equilibrium values of G for each value of S!) Statistical fluctuations may cause the channel to drift into a saturation state—the channel is filled up with collisions resulting in zero throughput. For an unstable channel, equilibrium conditions assumed earlier exist only for a finite period of time before channel saturation occurs. A Markov chain formulation of the infinite population slotted ALOHA model shows that it is always unstable, in the sense that a stationary probability distribution does not exist [LAM 74, KLEI 75A, FAYO 77].

Fortunately, N must be finite in a real network. In this case slotted ALOHA channels may exhibit stable or unstable behavior, depending upon the parameters N, $\bar{k}$, and S (channel input rate). In [LAM 74, KLEI 74, KLEI 75A], a theory of channel stability behavior is formulated. Specifically, a method for characterizing stable and unstable channels and a quantitative measure of instability for unstable channels are introduced. A theoretical treatment of the adaptive control of unstable channels using a Markov decision model can be found in [LAM 75A]. Various heuristic control algorithms and their performance are presented in [LAM 75B, LAM 79A, LAM 80A]. Several effective feedback control algorithms are proposed in [GERL 77A]. Simulations showed that these techniques are effective means of achieving stability, for initially unstable channels, at the expense of a small amount of delay-throughput performance degradation relative to lower-bound values.

Control algorithms for preventing channel saturation are based upon one or both of the following mechanisms: (1) reducing the probability of retransmitting a collided packet in a time slot (thus increasing the effective $\bar{k}$), and (2) revoking the access right of some users for a period of time (thus reducing the effective N). These two mechanisms have been referred to as retransmission control and input control, respectively [LAM 74, LAM 75A]. Recall that the slotted ALOHA channel throughput S is maximized when the channel traffic rate is 1. The goal of most adaptive control algorithms is to achieve the $G = 1$ condition in the channel. The main difficulty is the acquisition of global network status information by individual users. If, for example, the total number n of ready users can be made known to individual users instantaneously, then an adaptive strategy for realizing the $G = 1$ condition is to have each ready user transmit into the next time slot with probability $1/n$ (provided that $n \geq 1$).

Next we observe that the delay-throughput performance of contention protocols is not entirely independent of N, as we said earlier. When N is increased (accompanied by a decrease in β), slotted ALOHA channels tend to be less stable [LAM 74, KLEI 75A], which affects the delay-throughput performance. However, this is only a second-order effect.

We have discussed the stability problem and adaptive control techniques within the context of slotted ALOHA, which is a pure contention protocol. However, the stability problem is present in all contention-based protocols (many to be described in this section as well as the next section on reservation protocols) and must not be forgotten.

4.3.1.4   The R-ALOHA Protocol [CROW 73, LAM 78B, LAM 80C]

The traffic environment suitable for ALOHA and slotted ALOHA is that of a large population of low-rate bursty users with short messages (one packet per message). The R-ALOHA protocol was originally proposed by Crowther et al. [CROW 73] and is suitable for users who generate long multipacket messages or users with steady input traffic and queueing capability.

The R-ALOHA protocol requires, in addition to time slotting, that time slots are organized into frames. Time slots are identified by their positions in the frame. The duration of a frame must be greater than the maximum channel propagation time between any two users in the network. (This is of concern in practice only for a satellite channel.) Consequently, each user is aware of the usage status of time slots in the previous frame. The network operates without any central control but requires each user to execute the same set of rules for transmitting packets into a time slot depending on the outcome in the same time slot of the previous frame.

A time slot in the previous frame is *unused* if it was empty or contained a collision. Slots unused in the previous frame are available for contention by ready users in exactly the same manner as slotted ALOHA. A slot that had a successful transmission by a user in the previous frame is *used* and is reserved for the same user in the current frame. As a result, such a user now has the equivalent of an assigned TDMA channel for as long as he has traffic to send in it.

We further differentiate between two slightly different protocols depending on whether an end-of-use flag is included in the header of the last packet before a user gives up his reserved slot:

(P1) end-of-use flag not included

(P2) end-of-use flag included

Under (P1), a time slot is always wasted when a user gives up his reserved slot. The trade-off for adopting (P2) is some additional packet processing overhead by each user.

Under the assumption of equilibrium conditions, the channel throughput S_{RA} of R-ALOHA can be expressed in terms of the slotted ALOHA throughput S_{SA} for the contention portion of the channel [LAM 80C]:

$$S_{RA} = \frac{S_{SA}}{S_{SA} + 1/\bar{v}} \qquad \text{under (P1)}$$

or

$$S_{RA} = \frac{S_{SA}}{S_{SA} + [(1 - S_{SA})/\bar{v}]} \qquad \text{under (P2)} \tag{4.14}$$

where $\bar{v}$ is the average number of packets that a user transmits before he gives up a

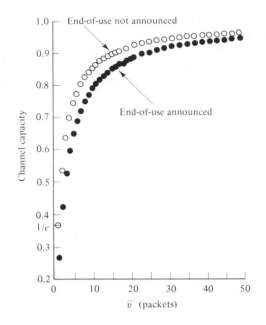

Figure 4.6. Maximum channel throughput versus v for R-ALOHA.

reserved slot. Note that S_{RA} is a monotonic function of S_{SA}, so that the maximum channel throughput of R-ALOHA is

$$C_{RA} = \frac{C_{SA}}{C_{SA} + 1/\bar{v}} \qquad \text{under (P1)}$$

or

$$C_{RA} = \frac{C_{SA}}{C_{SA} + [(1 - C_{SA})/\bar{v}]} \qquad \text{under (P2)}$$

Assuming that $C_{SA} = 1/e$, C_{RA} is plotted in Fig. 4.6 as a function of $\bar{v}$. Note that $\bar{v}$ range from 1 to infinity; thus we have

$$\frac{1}{1 + e} \leq C_{RA} \leq 1 \qquad \text{under (P1)}$$

or

$$\frac{1}{e} \leq C_{RA} \leq 1 \qquad \text{under (P2)}$$

Notice that the R-ALOHA protocol adapts itself to the nature of the traffic. At one extreme, it behaves like slotted ALOHA when the users are bursty ($\bar{v} = 1$). At the other extreme, the channel throughput of R-ALOHA approaches 1 in the $\bar{v} \to \infty$

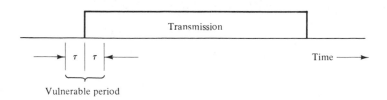

Figure 4.7. Unslotted CSMA vulnerable period.

limit; this is the case for high-rate users who can accommodate very long queues. The reader is referred to [LAM 78B, LAM 79A, LAM 80C] for a queueing and message delay analysis of R-ALOHA as well as simulation results.

4.3.1.5 *CSMA Protocols* [TOBA 74, KLEI 75B, METC 76, HANS 77, LAM 79B, LAM 80A, TOBA 79]

For broadcast channels with a *short propagation delay*, collisions in the channel can be significantly reduced by requiring each user to sense the channel for the presence of any ongoing transmission before accessing it, hence the name Carrier-Sense Multiple Access (CSMA). A ready user (user with data to send) transmits his data into the channel only if the channel has been sensed idle. Let τ seconds be the amount of time from the start of transmission by one user to when all users sense the presence of this transmission. It is equal to the maximum propagation delay between two users in the network plus carrier detection time. (The latter depends on the modulation technique and channel bandwidth. It was found to be negligible relative to the propagation delay in some cases [KLEI 75B].)

Given that a user sensed the channel to be idle and began a transmission, the vulnerable period of that transmission to collisions is 2τ seconds (see Fig. 4.7). In a short propagation delay environment, this vulnerable period is significantly smaller that those of ALOHA and slotted ALOHA. The channel may also be slotted into minislots of duration τ seconds each, thereby reducing the vulnerable period further to just τ seconds. (Note, however, that τ is the absolute minimum time-slot duration. A larger value is necessary in practice. The reader is referred to [ELLI 73, GARD 80] for a discussion of some techniques for time-synchronizing distributed users.)

Suppose that $\bar{x}$ is the average duration of a successful transmission. The maximum channel throughput of a CSMA protocol depends strongly upon the ratio

$$\alpha = \tau/\bar{x}$$

Specifically, we find out below that C_{CSMA} goes up to 1 if α is decreased to zero (by either letting $\tau \downarrow 0$ or $\bar{x} \uparrow \infty$; see below).

CSMA protocols have been studied extensively in the past within a packet radio network environment by Kleinrock and Tobagi [KLEI 75B, TOBA 74] and later by Hansen and Schwartz [HANS 77]. CSMA protocols were also implemented and analyzed within a multipoint cable network environment [METC 76, WEST 78,

131

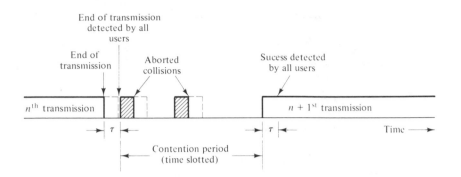

Figure 4.8. Illustration of the CSMA protocol.

LAM 79B, LAM 80A, TOBA 79].The main difference between the two environments is as follows. In cable networks, collisions in the broadcast channel can be detected easily. Thus users involved in a collision can abort their transmissions immediately upon detecting the collision. Mechanisms for detecting collisions and aborting transmissions have been implemented in at least two networks [METC 76, WEST 78]. It appears, however, that this "collision abort" capability is not easily implementable in packet radio networks of interest in [TOBA 74, KLEI 75B].

We present next the CSMA protocol defined and analyzed in [LAM 80A] This particular version of CSMA clearly shows the relationship of CSMA to the slotted ALOHA protocol (in pretty much the same manner as R-ALOHA is related to slotted ALOHA). The analysis of this CSMA protocol is fairly complete. In addition to maximum channel throughput, explicit formulas for average message delay as well as the moment generating function of the number of ready users are available.

A description of the protocol follows; (see also Fig. 4.8). Network users are time synchronized so that following each successful transmission, the channel is slotted in time. To implement the collision abort capability discussed above, the minimum duration of a time slot is 2τ, so that within a time slot if a collision is detected and the collided transmissions are aborted immediately, the channel will be clear of any transmission at the beginning of the next time slot. (In practice, the duration of a time slot needs to be larger than 2τ. The slotted channel assumption is made mainly to facilitate the analysis. In a real network, either a slotted or unslotted channel may be implemented.) The protocol is defined by the two possible courses of action by ready users:

(C1) Following a successful transmission, each ready user transmits with probability 1 into the next time slot.

(C2) Upon detection of a collision, each ready user exercises an adaptive algorithm for selecting its transmission probability (less than 1) in the next time slot.

The adaptive algorithm in (C2) is not specified. Howevewever, it should be clear that the contention problem in the minislots is exactly the slotted ALOHA problem. An adaptive control algorithm (such as those considered for slotted ALOHA) is needed to guarantee that a successful transmission occurs within a finite number of slots following a collision. The first successful transmission terminates the contention period (see Fig. 4.8).

The maximum channel throughput of the CSMA protocol defined can be obtained as a function of the equilibrium slotted ALOHA throughput S_{SA}. Let C_{SA} be the maximum achievable value of S_{SA}. It is shown in [LAM 80A] that

$$C_{CSMA} = \frac{C_{SA}}{2\alpha + C_{SA}(1 + \alpha)} \tag{4.15}$$

We note that C_{CSMA} is equal to one in the $\alpha \downarrow 0$ limit. Recall that $\alpha = \tau/\bar{x}$. In both ground radio and cable environments, τ is typically very short, say 0.001 to 0.1 of a packet transmission time. Furthermore, if we consider users who are capable of accommodating long queues, so that $\bar{x}$ is now the average time to empty a user's queue instead of a single packet transmission time, the channel throughput will be one in the $\bar{x} \rightarrow \infty$ limit.

The CSMA protocol defined above has the desirable property that when the channel is lightly utilized, the delay in identifying and assigning channel access to a ready user is extremely short and is independent of N (unlike polling and probing, considered earlier also for a short-propagation-delay environment). In particular, when there is exactly one ready user, the delay is zero.

In Fig. 4.9 we plot the fraction of transmissions that incur zero delay in gaining channel access (given that the channel is free) as a function of α and channel throughput. These are analytic results obtained with $S_{SA} = 1/e$ in [LAM 80A], where a queueing and message delay analysis of the foregoing CSMA protocol can be found. A comparison of the delay-throughput performance of CSMA and polling is shown in Fig. 4.14 and discussed in Sec. 4.4. The stability problem and adaptive control of CSMA have also been addressed [TOBA 77, HANS 77]. An alternative method of solution to these problems is to view the contention periods as a slotted ALOHA channel; this is the approach taken here as well as in [METC 76].

4.3.1.6 The URN Protocol [KLEI 78, YEMI 78]

The slotted ALOHA protocol is an important component of both R-ALOHA and CSMA protocols. We also learned earlier that the slotted ALOHA protocol needs to be adaptively controlled. Furthermore, the goal of most adaptive control algorithms is to achieve the $G = 1$ condition in the channel. Let us assume for the moment that the number n of ready users at any time is in fact known to individual users instantaneously. (We discuss later how to estimate n.) Then an adaptive strategy for achieving the $G = 1$ condition is to have each ready user transmit into the next time slot with probability $1/n$, where $n \geq 1$.

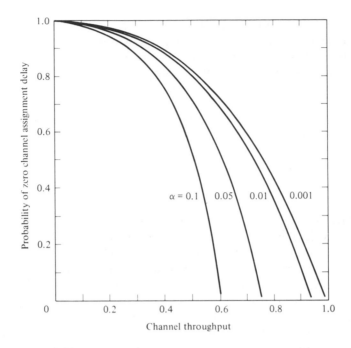

Figure 4.9. Probability of zero channel assignment delay versus throughput.

Kleinrock and Yemini [KLEI 78] proposed an alternative "pure" strategy for ready users to determine whether or not to transmit in the next time slot: the probability of transmission is either 1 or 0. In other words, some users have full channel-access rights, whereas others have none. (Consequently, the URN protocol is said to be *asymmetric*.) A user who has a channel-access right and is also ready transmits into the next time slot. It is possible to prove that optimal strategies are always pure strategies and therefore asymmetric [YEMI 78].

The URN protocol is described using the following URN model. Consider each user as a colored ball in an urn: black for ready, white for not ready. The access protocol is essentially a rule to sample balls from the urn. Let k be the number of balls drawn from the urn. The probability of a successful transmission (throughput) is that of getting exactly one black ball in the sample. The probability is

$$\text{Prob [throughput]} = \frac{\binom{n}{1}\binom{N-n}{k-1}}{\binom{N}{k}}$$

(4.16)

where N is the number of balls, and n is the number black balls. Equation (4.16) is maximized when $k = \lfloor N/n \rfloor$ where $\lfloor x \rfloor$ gives the integer part of x. Not only does this value of k maximize the probability of selecting exactly one black ball, but it also gives that the average number of black balls selected is equal to 1 (i.e., $G = 1$).

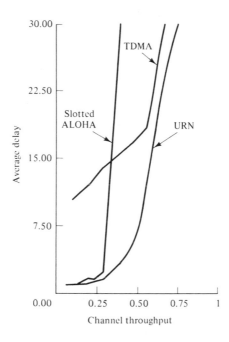

Figure 4.10. Simulated delay-throughput performance of URN.

The URN protocol adapts smoothly to network load fluctuations. When the network is lightly loaded, a large number of users get channel access rights. For instance, $n = 1$ gives risk to $k = N$; all users get access rights, but only one (the lone ready user) is going to make use of it. As the network load increases, n increases and the number k of users getting access rights is reduced. When $n > N/2$, then $k = 1$ and the URN protocol becomes effectively a TDMA protocol (which is most suitable for a heavy load). The maximum channel throughput of URN is thus unity. In Fig. 4.10 simulated delay-throughput results of URN obtained in [KLEI 78] are shown, illustrating the desirable traffic adaptivity of the protocol.

Two questions arise in the implementation of the URN protocol: How does an individual user obtain the up-to-date value of n? How does the protocol obtain coordination of the distributed decisions of individual users?

A solution for estimating n with high accuracy at the expense of a small overhead is proposed in the references. Briefly, it consists of a binary erasure reservation subchannel. An idle user who becomes ready (n increases by 1) sends a message of a few bits in the subchannel. When a ready user turns idle (n decreases by 1), the condition is detected by other users from examining his last packet or its positive acknowledgment in the broadcast channel. An erasure (collision) in the subchannel means that two or more users become ready in the same time slot. In this case, the increase in n is assumed to be 2 (an approximation). The resulting error in the estimate of n was found to be negligible since the probability of more than two users

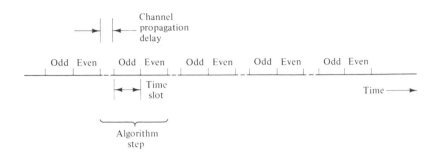

Figure 4.11. Tree algorithm steps.

becoming ready in the same time slot is very small. Furthermore, the estimate of n is corrected every time the network goes idle ($n = 0$). Other heuristic algorithms for estimating n can be found in [LAM 74, LAM 75A, LAM 75B].

Implementation of the URN protocol must also ensure that individual users agree on k, the number of users with access rights, as well as their identity. The optimal $k = \lfloor N/n \rfloor$ to be used is determined by each user from n estimated as described above. The selection of which k users should get access rights may be achieved via identical pseudo-random number generators at individual users, or via a window mechanism as well as other methods. The reader should consult the references for details.

4.3.1.7 A Tree Algorithm for Contention Resolution [CAPE 77, CAPE 79]

A tree algorithm for scheduling retransmission of packets involved in a collision was proposed by Capetanakis [CAPE 77]. A very desirable property of the algorithm is channel stability. The key idea of the algorithm is similar to that of adaptive polling considered earlier. The difference between the two is in implementation. Adaptive polling relies on a central controller probing passive users for status information. On the other hand, implementation of the tree algorithm is distributed, thus requiring users to be able to observe outcomes in the broadcast channel and make decisions. To do so, the channel needs to be time slotted. Furthermore, each algorithm step requires at least a channel propagation time plus two time slots to execute. The channel propagation time in each algorithm step is necessary to enable users to find out the outcomes of the previous algorithm step (see Fig. 4.11). For a satellite channel, some special technique is needed to avoid wasting the large propagation time interval between slot pairs. One method is to time multiplex the channel into subchannels that can be used independently by different user populations. For example, if P/C is the duration of a time slot, R is the channel propagation time, and m is an integer such that

$$\frac{2mP}{C} > R$$

then the satellite channel can be time multiplexed into $m + 1$ subchannels, each accessed by a population of users with the tree algorithm. For a high-speed satellite channel (m is large), much of the benefit from statistically averaging user demands discussed in Sec. 4.1.2 will be lost. Another idea suggested in the reference is to use a tree algorithm on $1/(m + 1)$ of the channel to make reservations for the other $m/(m + 1)$ of the channel (see Sec. 4.3.2).

The binary tree algorithm is described next. Suppose that each user corresponds to a leaf in a binary tree, such as that illustrated in Fig. 4.2 earlier (in the context of probing). Each user handles at most one packet at a time. The number of users can be finite or infinite. An infinite user population corresponds to a Poisson source of packet arrivals; in this case the binary tree extends to infinity. Time slots in the channel are paired into odd and even slots as shown in Fig. 4.11. To facilitate description of the algorithm, a last-in-first-out stack is assumed. (It is obviously not necessary.) Each algorithm step consists of the following three action steps. Initially, the stack is empty and step 3 is executed.

1. Remove the binary tree (or subtree) from top of stack and divide it into two subtrees. Users with access rights in the first subtree transmit in the odd slot; users with access rights in the second subtree transmit in the even slot.
2. Observe outcomes in the two slots. For each slot, discard the subtree if the slot is empty or contains a successful transmission; put the subtree back on the stack if the slot contains a collision.
3. If the stack is empty, give access rights to all new packets that have arrived in the meantime and put the entire tree on stack; go to step 1.

Note that new packet arrivals are only given access rights when the stack empties, which marks the end of one "epoch" and the beginning of the next. Arrivals during one epoch must wait to be served in the next epoch.

We make two observations. First, the objective of the algorithm is to divide the population of users into partitions, each containing at most one contending user. Therefore, the order of the tree search is not important. (In other words, the stack does not have to be last-in-first-out.) Second, the assignment of binary addresses to users does not have to be predetermined. Specifically, following a collision, a contending user may with equal probability join any one of the two resulting subtrees.

For the Poisson source model, Capetanakis [CAPE 77] showed that the tree that minimizes the number of time slots to process η packets, where η is a Poisson random variable, is binary everywhere except for the root node. The optimum degree $d_0{}^*$ of the root node depends on the mean value of η.

An adaptive version of the tree algorithm (analogous to adaptive polling) can be designed to adjust dynamically the degree of the root node at the beginning of each epoch as a function of the mean number of accumulated packets λh where h is the number of time slots in the previous epoch and λ is the Poisson source rate. The optimum degree of the root node is

$$d_0^* \begin{cases} \dfrac{1}{n} & \lambda h \leq 1.70 \\ & 1.70 + 1.15(n-2) < h \leq 1.70 + 1.15(n-1) \end{cases}$$

The adaptive tree algorithm has a maximum channel throughput of 0.430 packet per slot and guarantees channel stability if $\lambda < 0.430$ packet per slot.

The tree algorithm can be used for contention resolution in CSMA instead of adaptively controlled random retransmission delays for ready users. The trade-off is the tree algorithm's requirement for time slotting; time-synchronizing distributed users to achieve small time slots is a nontrivial problem [ELLI 73, GARD 80].

4.3.1.8 Concluding Remarks

In this section we began with pure contention protocols (ALOHA, slotted ALOHA) and then moved on to more sophisticated contention-based protocols (R-ALOHA, CSMA, URN) with improved delay-throughput performance. A tree algorithm for contention resolution was also shown. These protocols all have distributed control. Each user makes his own decision regarding channel access based solely on observable outcomes in the broadcast channel. In the URN protocol implementation, however, a reservation subchannel is provided for users to communicate with each other in a limited fashion. In Sec. 4.3.2 we describe reservation protocols that require users to cooperate with each other to avoid collisions entirely through use of a reservation subchannel.

4.3.2 Reservation Protocols

The objective of reservation protocols is to avoid collisions entirely. Since users are distributed, a reservation subchannel is necessary for users to communicate with each other. There are two key problems to be solved for most reservation protocols: (1) implementation of the reservation subchannel, and (2) implementation of a queue for the entire population of distributed users (distributed global queue). We also examine some protocols for a short propagation delay environment which do not require a global queue.

4.3.2.1 The Reservation Channel

The original broadcast channel can be either time or frequency multiplexed into a reservation channel and a data channel. An advantage of time-multiplexed channels is that the partition may be variable. With a variable partition, the maximum throughput of data messages can be made very close to one under a heavy network load when users have long queues. With a fixed partition, the overhead lost to the reservation channel is a fixed fraction of the original channel capacity.

With a global queue, there is no conflict in the use of the data channel. However, the multiple access problem of the distributed users has not disappeared. It exists now in the access of the reservation channel. Any of the previously described multiple access protocols can be used. However, for simplicity, most proposed reservation protocols adopt either a fixed assigned TDMA protocol or some version of the slotted

ALOHA protocol. We are faced with the same trade-off as before. A TDMA protocol performs poorly for a large population of bursty users. On the other hand, a slotted ALOHA protocol is independent of N but needs to be adaptively controlled for stable operation.

The high achievable channel throughput of reservation protocols (relative to pure contention) comes about from substantially reducing the volume of traffic requiring conflict resolution, and the concomitant overhead; the reduction is from the totality of data messages to just one short reservation packet per data message (or less). Note that R-ALOHA and CSMA derive their efficiency from essentially the same principle.

Part of the price that one pays for the gain in channel throughput of reservation protocols over contention protocols is an increase in message delay. The minimum delay incurred by a message, excluding message transmission time, is more than twice the channel propagation time. This consideration is important for satellite channels. The minimum delay can be reduced, however, if one can anticipate future arrivals and make reservations in advance! One possible example is packetized digital speech traffic.

4.3.2.2 The Distributed Global Queue

There are two approaches to implement a global queue of requests for a population of distributed users. One is to employ a central controller which tells the ready users when to access the channel; an additional subchannel for controller-to-user traffic is typically required. On the other hand, a distributed control implementation is more interesting and probably more desirable. In this approach each user maintains information on the status of the global queue and makes his own decision as to when is his turn to access the channel. An important problem here is the synchronization of queue status information of all users. This means that reservation packets broadcasted in the reservation channel need to be received correctly by *all* users. In the event of an error, an individual user must be able to detect the presence of error in his queue status information. Any such user who is out of synchronization, as well as new users who have just joined the network, must be able to acquire *queue synchronization* from observing the reservation and data channels within a reasonable duration of time.

Various queue disciplines may be used for the global queue [e.g., random selection, first-in-first-out (FIFO), round-robin, priority based upon type or delay constraint, etc.]. The processing requirement of a sophisticated scheduling algorithm may be quite substantial.

4.3.2.3 A Protocol with Distributed Control
[ROBE 73]

The ideas of a reservation subchannel and a distributed global queue were first proposed by Roberts [ROBE 73]. A satellite channel was considered; the reservation protocol proposed, however, is applicable to other broadcast media. It is assumed that the channel is time slotted and that time slots are organized into frames. Each frame consists of a data subframe and a reservation subframe; each slot in the reservation subframe is further subdivided into V smaller slots. The small slots are for reservation packets as well as possibly positive acknowledgment packets and small data packets, to be used on a contention basis with the slotted ALOHA protocol.[2]

Roberts' protocol makes use of the broadcast capability of the channel; a reservation packet successfully transmitted with no interference is received by all users. Each reservation request is for a position in the global queue for a group of packets. The queue discipline proposed by Roberts is FIFO according to the order reservation requests are received. We shall refer to this as the *FIFO protocol*. Each user maintains his copy of the queue status information. It is sufficient for each user to record only the queue length (in number of packets) as well as the queue positions of his own reservations.

It is necessary for a currently inactive user who wants to join the queue, to acquire queue synchronization. In this protocol the queue length information may be supplied in the header of each data packet transmitted. Alternatively, it may be announced periodically by a "master" controller. Note that such queue length information is one propagation delay old when received. To acquire queue synchronization, a user must update the queue length information so received with reservation requests received within a channel propagation time just prior to receiving the queue-length information.

To maintain synchronization among the users, it is necessary and sufficient that each reservation packet that is received correctly by any user be received correctly by all users. This condition may be assured by properly encoding the reservation requests. A simple strategy proposed by Roberts is to send parity-checked copies of requests in triplicate within a reservation packet.

As a result of the distributed nature of queue management, the impact of an error in a user's queue status is to cause some collisions in data slots and to delay some data packets momentarily. However, no catastrophic failure occurs. Users involved in such collisions must declare themselves to be out of synchronization. A user who receives a reservation packet with unrecoverable error must also do the same. Users who are out of synchronization discard their acquired reservations and reacquire queue synchronization in the same fashion as newly activated users described above.

4.3.2.4   Maximum Channel Throughput

The maximum channel throughput of a reservation protocol is $1 - \gamma$, where γ is the minimum fraction of the original channel capacity needed to accommodate the reservation request traffic. Consider the FIFO protocol above. Let L be the average number of data packets per reservation request. Since there are V small slots in a data slot, the ratio of data bits to reservation request bits transmitted is equal to

---

[2] Our description varies slightly from the reference. In Roberts' original proposal, each reservation subframe is just one data slot long. He also considered a technique for adaptively changing the ratio of the subframe sizes as a function of traffic load. When the queue length is zero, the whole frame is used for making reservations.

$$\bar{v} = VL$$

Suppose that the reservation channel is used by reservation packets only (excluding acknowledgment and small data packets mentioned above) and its maximum channel throughput is C_{SA} under the slotted ALOHA protocol. It can be easily shown that in this case

$$\gamma = \frac{1}{1 + C_{SA}\bar{v}} \tag{4.17}$$

The maximum channel throughput of the reservation protocol is $1 - \gamma$. We make several observations. First, the maximum throughput expression is the same as that for R-ALOHA, with just a slightly different interpretation for $\bar{v}$. Second, it is independent of N. Third, $\bar{v}$ is assumed to be a fixed parameter; thus the maximum channel throughput value is fixed and strictly less than 1.

Now suppose that the partition between data and reservation slots in a frame can be dynamically varied. Also, reservation requests can be piggybacked in the header of scheduled data packets. In this case, when the network is heavily loaded with long message queues at individual users, $\bar{v}$ will become very large; the maximum channel throughput becomes 1 in the $\bar{v} \to \infty$ limit.

Alternatively, if the frame is fixed partitioned and a fixed assignment TDMA protocol is used for the reservation subchannel, we have

$$\gamma = \frac{N}{MV} \tag{4.18}$$

where N is the number of users and M is the number of data slots in a frame.

A fixed assignment TDMA protocol is sometimes preferable to slotted ALOHA for the reservation subchannel since it is simple to implement; unlike slotted ALOHA, adaptive control is not needed. However, Eq. (4.18) shows that it is applicable only for a small user population. One can always increase M to increase channel throughput; a large M is undesirable, however, since the delay of reservation packets becomes large and hence the message delay as well.

The maximum throughput $1 - \gamma$ is plotted in Fig. 4.12 versus N for the two cases given by Eqs. (4.17) and (4.18).

4.3.2.5 Other Protocols with Distributed Control

Another reservation protocol with distributed control was proposed by Binder [BIND 75B]. The channel is divided into time slots which are organized into frames. Let M be the number of slots in a frame. The frame duration is required to be larger than the channel propagation time. Also, the number N of users is required to be less than or equal to M. Each user is fixed assigned a time slot within the frame and sends information concerning his current queue length in the header of each data packet

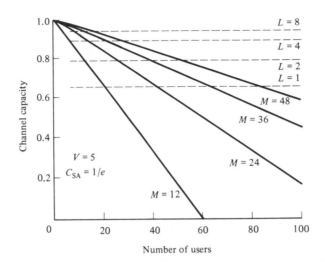

Figure 4.12. Maximum channel throughput versus number of users for reservation protocols.

that he transmits into his fixed assigned slot. Note that this is equivalent to a fixed assigned TDMA reservation subchannel.

The global queue is implemented via distributed control. The global queue status consists of the queue lengths of all ready users (those with nonempty queues). Each user exercises the following rules for channel access. A user may send data in his fixed assigned slot at any time. Any unassigned as well as unused slots (assigned to currently idle users) within a frame are used by the ready users in a round-robin fashion. A user who has been idle can transmit in his fixed assigned (owned) slot to deliberately generate a collision. Such a collision is noted by all users. Another rule dictates that following a collision, only the owner of the slot can use it in the next frame. Thus a special feature of this protocol is that even if a user is in the process of acquiring queue synchronization, he still has the use of a fixed assigned TDMA channel. A disadvantage is that the number of users N must be less than M. The problems of maintaining and acquiring queue synchronization are similar to those of the FIFO protocol above.

Recently, the PODA (Priority-Oriented Demand Assignment) protocol was proposed and implemented in SATNET, a prototype packet satellite network [JACO 77, JACO 78, WEIS 78]. Logically, PODA is an extension of Roberts' FIFO protocol with a much more sophisticated scheduling algorithm designed to handle the requirements of a general-purpose packet satellite network. These requirements include: multiple delay constraints, multiple priority levels, variable message length, fairness, efficient message acknowledgments, and the accommodation of "stream traffic." Stream traffic denotes a class of traffic sources typified by digital voice. Each such traffic source generates a stream of messages with a small interarrival-time variance. Also, the maximum acceptable delay for each message is only slightly larger than the channel propagation time. These characteristics are quite different from what we have considered so far. Thus stream traffic requires special handling apart from individual data messages (datagrams).

Like the FIFO protocol, PODA divides channel time into frames. Each frame consists of an information subframe and a reservation subframe. If slotted ALOHA is used for multiple access in the reservation subframe, the protocol is said to be contention-based and is called CPODA; if fixed assignment TDMA is used, the protocol is called FPODA. In addition to using the reservation subframe, a reservation request can also be piggybacked into the header of a scheduled message. While the total frame size is fixed, the reservation subframe is allowed to grow or shrink according to network loading. If the global queue is empty, the reservation subframe occupies the entire frame. The two types of traffic are distinguished when reservations are made. An explicit reservation is sent for each datagram while a reservation is sent only once for all messages of a particular stream. Each stream reservation contains information defining the stream repetition interval, desired maximum delay relative to this interval, and priority. Whenever the interval starting time is near, a reservation is automatically created and entered into the scheduling queue. The scheduling discipline of the global queue is very elaborate and depends on explicit priority, urgency, and fairness. Some measurement and simulation performance results of CPODA are reported in [GERL 77B, CHU 78]. Queue synchronization is addressed in [HSU 78, WEIS 78]. More on reservation protocols can be found in [BALA 79, BORG 77, BORG 78].

4.3.2.6 Short-Propagation-Delay Environment

The reservation protocols described above all maintain a global queue of reservations, one reservation for a group of packets, for channel access. Consider now networks with a very short propagation delay relative to the transmission time of a packet. Instead of a global queue, the following approach for conflict resolution has been proposed for a ground radio network environment by Kleinrock and Scholl [KLEI 77].

The broadcast channel is divided into minislots interleaved with data slots. Each data slot is preceded by N minislots, where N is the user population size. We shall refer to this class of protocols as the *minislotted protocols*. Before the start of every data slot, a priority ordering exists among the N users. Three priority disciplines were considered in [KLEI 77]: alternating priorities, round robin, and random order. The priority ordering determines the assignment of minislots: one per user. Ready users make their presence known by transmitting (carrier only) into their assigned minislots while idle users keep quiet. The first ready user appearing in a minislot gets the following data slot. Since there are N minislots associated with every data slot, the maximum channel throughput is

$$\frac{1}{1 + N\alpha}$$

where α is the ratio of minislot to data slot duration. Obviously, the performance of this class of protocols is acceptable only if $N\alpha \ll 1$. The delay-throughput-performance of minislotted protocols was found to be inferior to roll-call polling in many cases [KLEI 77].

To reduce the number of minislots needed for each data slot, the MSAP protocol was proposed. At the end of a packet transmission, the protocol operates as follows:

1.   The user who transmitted the last packet is given priority.
2.   The priority user can transmit immediately; other users defer via carrier sensing.
3.   If the priority user is sensed idle, then one minislot later, access priority is passed on to the next user in sequence, and steps 2 and 3 are repeated.

The number of minislots in between contiguous packet transmissions ranges from 0 to N - 1. It should be clear that MSAP is analogous to conventional polling in its scheduling discipline but has distributed control and active users instead of centralized control and passive users. However, a minislot of duration τ (same as that in CSMA) in MSAP is typically much smaller than the corresponding average walk time $\bar{w}$ in polling. This is because the transmission time of a polling message needs to be included in $\bar{w}$ but no corresponding overhead is needed in τ. The delay-throughput performance of MSAP was found to be better than roll-call polling in all cases considered in [KLEI 77]. However, MSAP requires the nontrivial task of time synchronizing users to implement minislots.

Independently, a similar idea was explored by Rothhauser and Wild [ROTH 76] for a bit-synchronous broadcast channel (e.g., a data bus). As a result of bit synchronism, a single bit is sufficient for a user to indicate his status (ready or idle). With a population of N users, N bits are sufficient for identifying all ready users immediately preceding each data transfer phase using the "one-out-of-N" code. During the data transfer phase, ready users can transmit according to a priority sequence known to all users. A multilevel code structure was also proposed in [ROTH 76] that can substantially reduce the number of bits for identifying ready users [to a minimum of ln (N) bits when only one ready user is present]. This protocol is called *multilevel multiple access* (MLMA). A closer look shows that the multilevel code structure is based on the same "tree search" idea as Hayes' algorithm and the tree algorithm described earlier.

No provision for traffic adaptivity was mentioned in the MLMA proposal. Traffic adaptivity was found to be necessary for efficiency in times of heavy traffic in the other two algorithms.

4.3.2.7 *Protocols with Centralized Control*

The presence of a central controller eliminates the queue synchronization problem discussed earlier for distributed control protocols. Instead, the central controller manages the global queue, accepts reservations, and informs users when to access the channel. An additional subchannel is typically required for controller-to-user traffic. Since the multiple access problem of the reservation subchannel remains essentially the same as discussed above for distributed control protocols, we will not describe specific protocols.

Protocols with centralized control have been proposed and studied by Tobagi and Kleinrock for radio networks [TOBA 76], by Mark for a data bus [MARK 78], and by Ng and Mark for a satellite network with on-board processing that serves as the central controller [NG 77]. Recently, Mark and Ng proposed a coding scheme, called CMAP, that offers significant overhead reduction over the one-out-of-N code for identifying ready users [MARK 79].

4.4 PERFORMANCE COMPARISONS

Our focus in this chapter is mainly on the sharing and conflict resolution aspect of the multiple access problem. A broadcast channel of C bps is assumed. The performance criteria of interest are channel throughput and message delay. Engineering considerations such as modulation, clock synchronization, coding, and random-noise errors are not within the scope of this chapter. Different broadcast media are differentiated mainly by the effect of their channel propagation delay on an MA protocol's delay-throughput performance. (We note, however, that some protocols do have special requirements and can be implemented in some broadcast media but not others.)

Even within our limited scope of performance, it should be clear to the reader by now that there is no single protocol that is optimum. The performance of a multiple access protocol is strongly dependent on the traffic model and network loading. In general, some traffic characteristics do favor one class of protocols more than others. We list some of them below.

Traffic Model	Multiple Access Protocols Favored
Nonbursty users	Fixed assigned channels (TDMA, FDMA)
Bursty users, short messages	Pure contention
Bursty users, long messages, large N	Reservation protocols with contention reservation channel
Bursty users, long messages, small N	Reservation protocols with fixed TDMA reservation channel

For traffic models that are a fixed or time-varying combination of the models above, "mixed" protocols (such as R-ALOHA, CSMA) and adaptive protocols (such as URN, adaptive polling) may be suitable. To illustrate some of the observations above, we show the delay-throughput performance of representatives of the different classes of protocols under various specific traffic assumptions.

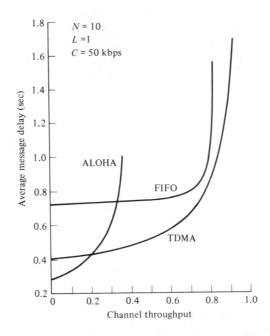

Figure 4.13. Delay-throughput trade-off for 10 users and short messages (one packet per message).

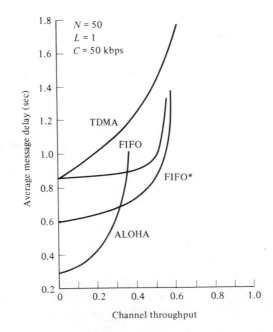

Figure 4.14. Delay-throughput trade-off for 50 users and short messages (one packet per message).

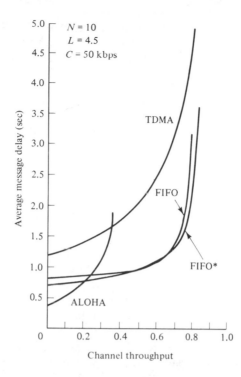

Figure 4.15. Delay-throughput trade-off for 10 users and multipacket messages.

In Figs. 4.13, to 4.15, four protocols are considered: (1) fixed assigned TDMA channels, (2) slotted ALOHA, (3) FIFO modified to use a fixed TDMA reservation channel, and (4) FIFO with a slotted ALOHA reservation channel; they are labeled as TDMA, ALOHA, FIFO, and FIFO*, respectively, in the figures. Delay formulas for TDMA and slotted ALOHA from [LAM 77B, KLEI 73] are used. The expected delay of a message for the reservation protocols is taken to be the sum of the expected delay D_1 incurred by the reservation request and the expected delay D_2 incurred by the message itself after the reservation has been made. To calculate D_1 and D_2, we regard the original broadcast channel at C bps to be split up into two separate channels: a data channel at $(1 - \gamma)C$ bps and a reservation channel at γC bps. D_1 and D_2 are then calculated separately.

In Fig. 4.13 we show results obtained assuming 10 users sharing a 50-kbps satellite channel with a propagation delay of 0.27 second. All messages consist of single packets of 1125 bits each. In the case of FIFO, a frame size $M = 12$ is assumed with $V = 5$ and $\gamma = 1/6$. Observe that the performance of fixed assigned TDMA is the best for this traffic model except when the channel throughput is less than 0.2, where slotted ALOHA gives a smaller delay.

Now suppose that we consider a larger population of more bursty users than the traffic model above. Let N be increased from 10 to 50 (so that the bursty factor of each user is now $1/5$ of that of the model above). Figure 4.14 shows that TDMA has the worst performance for this new traffic model. FIFO, with $M = 24$ and $\gamma = 5/12$, also has poor performance, due to the large reservation channel overhead needed for 50 users. FIFO*, with $\gamma = 0.4$ assuming $C_{SA} = 0.3$, has better performance than FIFO, but the reservation channel overhead is still quite large since each message consists of a single packet only. The delay-throughput performance of slotted ALOHA is independent of the change from the first to the second traffic model and appears to be the most suitable protocol for the second traffic model, provided that a channel throughput of about 0.3 or less is acceptable. If a channel throughput of more than 0.3 is desired, FIFO* should be employed.

Now suppose that we are back to having 10 users but that the data traffic consists of long messages (eight packets each) as well as short messages (one packet each) in equal number. The average message length L is increased from 1 to 4.5 packets. Delay-throughput results for the four protocols are shown in Fig. 4.15. The delay curve for slotted ALOHA is plotted using the delay formula for multipacket messages in [LAM 74]. For this traffic model, the reservation protocols have the best performance except at a channel throughput of less than 0.2, where slotted ALOHA is better. Slotted ALOHA, as we know, was not designed to take advantage of the presence of multipacket messages. Simulations also showed that when a large number of multipacket messages are present in the input traffic, the slotted ALOHA channel becomes more unstable [LAM 74].

Some protocols are designed to take advantage of a short-propagation-delay environment. They include CSMA protocols that are contention-based, the reservation protocols MSAP and MLMA, as well as polling protocols. Reservation protocols that are not contention-based and polling protocols have similar delay-throughput characteristics since the conflict resolution overhead in each case is proportional to N, the number of users. In particular, MSAP and polling are characterized by essentially the same delay formula; any difference in performance is just a consequence of different values for the minislot duration τ in MSAP and the corresponding average walk time $\bar{w}$ in polling [KLEI 77]. There are, of course, differences that do not show up explicitly in the delay-throughput performance, such as distributed control in MSAP versus centralized control in polling, and the need for time-synchronizing distributed users in MSAP but not in polling.

The delay-throughput performance of CSMA and roll-call polling are compared in Fig. 4.16 using the CSMA delay formula from [LAM 79B] and polling delay formula from [KONH 74]. The delay results shown for polling assume Poisson message arrivals and one packet per message. The ratio of propagation delay to the packet transmission time is $\alpha = 0.05$. The ratio of data to polling message length is $\bar{v} = 10$. Queueing of messages at individual users is assumed; hence the channel throughput approaches 1 when queues become very long under heavy traffic. Delay-throughput curves are shown for both 10 users and 100 users. The corresponding delay-throughput performance of CSMA at $\alpha = 0.05$ is independent of the number of users. Since the analysis in [LAM 79B] assumes that individual users handle one packet at a time, the maximum channel throughput is less than 1. As before, we observe that CSMA, being a contention-based protocol, is superior to polling when

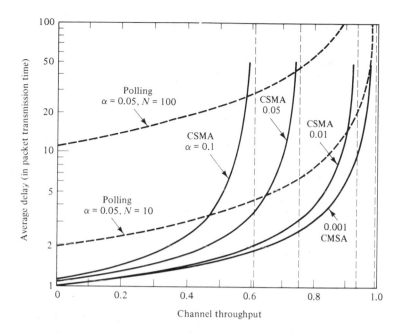

Figure 4.16. Comparison of CSMA and polling delay-throughout performance.

the channel throughput is low but becomes inferior when the channel throughput is increased to near 1. However, if queueing of messages is possible at individual users for CSMA, more than one message may be transmitted every time a user gains channel access; the amount of overhead per message is reduced. Hence as the network load is increased from 0 to 1, the delay performance of CSMA if first given by the $\alpha = 0.05$ curve at a small channel throughput but switches to the $\alpha = 0.01$ curve and then the $\alpha = 0.001$ curve and so on as the channel throughput increases and queues become long. The channel throughput of CSMA approaches 1 in the limit of infinitely long queues at individual users.

4.5 CONCLUSIONS

We considered the problem of interconnecting distributed users via a broadcast channel and surveyed a wide class of multiple access protocols. The throughput-delay performance characteristics of these protocols were examined and compared. Our emphasis has been on packet-oriented protocols. Channel-oriented protocols, however, are currently prevalent in existing systems and are in many cases more cost effective than packet protocols. Specifically, in broadcast networks with a large population of users, the total user interface cost, proportional to N, tends to dominate the network cost. Packet protocols become important only when the cost of user interface to a (shared) wideband broadcast medium is reduced to the point that a large population of users can be economically interconnected directly via the broadcast medium (i.e., without the user of a traffic multiplexor/concentrator to justify the cost of an interface). Trends in the costs of electronics and computing seem to be most encouraging toward packet protocols in the foreseeable future. Some specific observations follow.

With the current cost ($\geq$ $100,000) and size (antenna size $\geq$ 5 m) of satellite earth stations*, it would not be economical to install a separate earth station at a packet network node unless it has a substantial amount of traffic (100 kbps or more [ROBE 78]). At such a traffic level, traditional channel-oriented multiple access protocols will perform very well; there will be no need for the more complex packet protocols. However, the advent of satellite systems at the higher frequencies (e.g., 14/12, 30/20 GHz) than are currently available will facilitate the development of small, inexpensive earth stations (say, 1-to-3-m antenna size) that can be sited almost anywhere for low-rate users. The packet protocols described herein will be very important in this new environment. Other developments in satellite communications that will affect the development of multiple access protocols include multibeam satellites (thus the broadcast network assumption in this paper needs to be modified) and the availability of on-board processing capability [PRIT 77, JACO 78].

In recent years, packet communication has made significant advances to reduce the cost of long-distance backbone networks. Local distribution and collection of data (between a central site and a population of terminals), however, remains by far the most expensive portion of many communication networks. We are addressing local area networks which, although outside the computer room, are confined to local environments, such as office complexes and manufacturing plants, without the use of common-carrier facilities. Local area networks serve several functions: for local interconnection, for access to local computing facilities, for access to a gateway into a backbone network, and so on. The broadcast media of interest here include CATV, optical fiber, and radio. All of these are currently under intensive research and development. In this environment, packet protocols will again be important in networks that can economically interconnect a large population of users. With the availability of inexpensive microprocessors, the key to implementing such packet broadcast networks reduces to the development of inexpensive transceivers for the specific broadcast medium. The economic viability of packet broadcast networks using CATV-based technology has already been demonstrated at data rates of several Mbps [DEMA 76, METC 76, CLAR 78, WEST 78].

In conclusion, we have examined the basic principles and performance trade-offs of multiple access protocols for broadcast networks. For the sake of clarity, we have often omitted specific implementation details. Therefore, the protocols described herein form the basic elements of more sophisticated operational protocols. In the future, more flexible and reliable protocols will be needed to accommodate the increasing volume and diversity of data traffic, including digital voice, facsimile, and

---

*These are 1978 figures when this chapter was first written [LAM 79C].

word processing systems, in addition to the present transaction-based terminal and file transfer traffic.

ACKNOWLEDGMENTS

The final manuscript has benefited tremendously from the comments and suggestions of the editor. This work was supported by the National Science Foundation under Grant ECS78-01803.

REFERENCES

ABRA 70 Abramson, N., "THE ALOHA SYSTEM—Another Alternative for Computer Communications," *AFIPS Conf. Proc.*, Vol. 37, AFIPS Press, Montvale, N.J., 1970, pp. 281–285.

ABRA 73 Abramson, N., "Packet Switching with Satellites," *AFIPS Conf. Proc.*, Vol. 42, AFIPS Press, Montvale, N.J., 1973, pp. 695–702.

ABRA 75 Abramson, N., and E. R. Cacciamani, "Satellites: Not Just a Big Cable in the Sky," *IEEE Spectrum*, Vol. 12, September 1975.

BALA 79 Balagangadhar, M. M., and R. L. Pickholtz, "Analysis of a Reservation Multiple Access Technique for Data Transmission via Satellites," *IEEE Trans. Commun.*, October 1979.

BIND 75A Binder, R., et al., "ALOHA Packet Broadcasting—A Retrospect," *Nat. Comput. Conf., AFIPS Conf. Proc.*, Vol. 44, 1975, pp. 201–215.

BIND 75B Binder, R., "A Dynamic Packet-Switching System for Satellite Broadcast Channels," *ICC 75 Conf. Rec.*, IEEE, New York, 1975, pp. 41-1 to 41-5.

BORG 77 Borgonovo, F., and L. Fratta, "A New Technique for Satellite Broadcast Communication," *Proc. 5th Data Commun. Symp.*, Snowbird, Utah, September 1977.

BORG 78 Borgonovo, F., and L. Fratta, "SRUC: A Technique for Packet Transmission on Multiple Access Channel," *Proc. ICCC*, Kyoto, Japan, September 1978.

BUTT 74 Butterfield, S. C., R. D. Rettberg, and D. C. Walden, "The Satellite IMP for the ARPA Network," *Proc. 7th Hawaii Int. Conf. Syst. Sci.*, Computer Nets Supplement, January 1974.

CAPE 77 Capetanakis, J. I., "The Multiple Access Broadcast Channel: Protocol and Capacity Considerations," Ph.D., dissertation, Department of Electrical Engineering and Computer Science, M.I.T., August 1977.

CAPE 79 Capetanakis, J. I., "Generalized TDMA: The Multi-accessing Tree Protocol," *IEEE Trans. Commun.*, October 1979.

CHOU 78 Chou, W., "Terminal Response Time on Polled Teleprocessing Networks," *Proc. Comput. Networking Symp.*, December 1978.

CHU 78 Chu, W. W., and W. E. Naylor, "Measurement and Simulation Results of C-PODA Protocol Performance," *NTC 78 Conf. Rec., Natl. Telecommun. Conf.*, Birmingham, Ala., December 1978.

CLAR 78   Clark, D. D., K. T. Pogram, and D. P. Reed, "An Introduction to Local Area Networks," *Proc. IEEE*, Vol. 66, November 1978.

CROW 73   Crowther, W., et al., "A System for Broadcast Communication: Reservation-ALOHA," *Proc. 6th HICSS*, University of Hawaii, Honolulu, January 1973.

DEMA 76   DeMarines, V. A., and L. W. Hill, "The Cable Bus in Data Communications," *Datamation*, August 1976.

ELLI 73   Ellingson, C., and R. Kulpinski, "Dissemination of System Time," *IEEE Trans. Commun.*, Vol. COM-21, May 1973.

FAYO 77   Fayolle, G., et al., "Stability and Optimal Control of the Packet Switching Broadcast Channel," *J. ACM*, Vol. 24, July 1977.

GARD 80   Gardner, F. M., and W. C. Lindsey, eds., *Special Issue on Synchronization, IEEE Trans. Commun.*, August 1980.

GERL 77A   Gerla, M., and L. Kleinrock, "Closed Loop Stability Controls for S-ALOHA Satellite Communication," *Proc. 5th Data Commun. Symp.*, Snowbird, Utah, September 1977.

GERL 77B   Gerla, M., L. Nelson, and L. Kleinrock, "Packet Satellite Multiple Access: Models and Measurements," *Conf. Rec. Natl. Telecommun. Conf.*, Los Angeles, December 1977.

HANS 77   Hansen, L. W., and M. Schwartz, "An Assigned-Slot Listen-before-Transmission Protocol for a Multiaccess Data Channel," *Conf. Rec. Int. Conf. Commun.*, Chicago, June 1977.

HAYE 78   Hayes, J. F., "An Adaptive Technique for Local Distribution," *IEEE Trans. Commun.*, Vol. COM-26, August 1978.

HSU 78   Hsu, N., and L. Lee, "Channel Scheduling Synchronization for the PODA Protocol," *Conf. Rec. ICC 78*, Toronto, June 1978.

JACO 74   Jacobs, I. M., "Practical Applications of Coding," *IEEE Trans. Inf. Theory*, Vol. IT-20, May 1974.

JACO 77   Jacobs, I., et al., "CPODA—A Demand Assignment Protocol for Satnet," *Proc. 5th Data Commun. Symp.*, Snowbird, Utah, September 27–29, 1977.

JACO 78   Jacobs, I. M., R. Binder, and E. V. Hoversten, "General Purpose Packet Satellite Networks," *Proc. IEEE*, Vol. 66, November 1978.

KAHN 77   Kahn, R. E., "The Organization of Computer Resources into a Packet Radio Network," *IEEE Trans. Commun.*, Vol. COM-25, January 1977.

KAHN 78   Kahn, R. E., et al., "Advances in Packet Radio Technology," *Proc. IEEE*, Vol. 66, November 1978.

KLEI 73   Kleinrock, L., and S. S. Lam, "Packet-Switching in a Slotted Satellite Channel," *AFIPS Conf. Proc.*, Vol. 42, AFIPS Press, Montvale, N.J., 1973, pp. 703–710.

KLEI 74   Kleinrock, L., and S. S. Lam, "On Stability of Packet Switching in a Random Multi-access Broadcast Channel," *7th Hawaii Int. Conf. Syst. Sci.*, Honolulu, January 1974; *Proc. Spec. Subconf. on Comput. Nets*, 1974.

KLEI 75A   Kleinrock, L., and S. S. Lam, "Packet Switching in a Multiaccess Broadcast Channel: Performance Evaluation," *IEEE Trans. Commun.*, Vol. COM-23, April 1975, pp. 410–423.

KLEI 75B   Kleinrock, L., and F. A. Tobagi, "Packet Switching in Radio Channels, Part 1: Carrier Sense Multiple Access Modes and Their Throughput-Delay Characteristics," *IEEE Trans. Commun.*, Vol. COM-23, No. 12, December 1975, pp. 1400-1416.

KLEI 76   Kleinrock, L., *Queueing Systems*, Vol. 2: *Computer Applications,* Wiley-Interscience, New York, 1976.

KLEI 77   Kleinrock, L., and M. Scholl, "Packet Switching in Radio Channels: New Conflict-Free Multiple Access Schemes for a Small Number of Data Users," *Conf. Rec. Int. Conf. Commun.*, Chicago, June 1977.

KLEI 78   Kleinrock, L., and Y. Yemini, "An Optimal Adaptive Scheme for Multiple Access Broadcast Communication," *Conf. Rec. ICC 78*, Toronto, June 1978.

KONH 74   Konheim, A. G., and B. Meister, "Waiting Lines and Times in a System with Polling," *J. ACM*, Vol. 21, July 1974.

LAM 74   Lam, S. S., "Packet Switching in a Multi-access Broadcast Channel with Application to Satellite Communication in a Computer Network," Ph.D. dissertation, Computer Science Department, University of California, Los Angeles, March 1974.

LAM 75A   Lam, S. S., and L. Kleinrock, "Packet Switching in a Multiaccess Broadcast Channel: Dynamic Control Procedures," *IEEE Trans. Commun.*, Vol. COM-23, September 1975, pp. 891-904.

LAM 75B   Lam, S. S., and L. Kleinrock, "Dynamic Control Schemes for a Packet Switched Multi-access Broadcast Channel," *AFIPS Conf. Proc.*, Vol. 44, AFIPS Press, Montvale, N.J., 1975, pp. 143-153.

LAM 77A   Lam, S. S., "Satellite Multiaccess Schemes for Data Traffic," *Conf. Rec. Int. Conf. Commun.*, Chicago, June 1977, pp. 37.1-19 to 37.1-24.

LAM 77B   Lam, S. S., "Delay Analysis of a Time Division Multiple Access (TDMA) Channel," *IEEE Trans. Commun.*, Vol. COM-25, December 1977, pp. 1489-1494.

LAM 78A   Lam, S. S., "A New Measure for Characterizing Data Traffic," *IEEE Trans. Commun.*, Vol. COM-26, January 1978.

LAM 78B   Lam, S. S., "An Analysis of the R-ALOHA Protocol for Satellite Packet Switching," *Conf. Rec. ICC '78, Int. Conf. Commun.*, Toronto, June 1978.

LAM 79A   Lam, S. S., "On Protocols for Satellite Packet Switching," *Conf. Rec. Int. Conf. Commun.*, Boston, June 1979.

LAM 79B   Lam, S. S., "A Study of the CSMA Protocol in Local Networks," *Proc. 4th Berkeley Conf. Distributed Data Manage. Comput. Networks*, San Francisco, August 1979.

LAM 79C   Lam, S. S., "Satellite Packet Communication—Multiple Access Protocols and Performance," *IEEE Trans. Commun.*, October 1979.

LAM 80A   Lam, S. S., "A Carrier Sense Multiple Access Protocol for Local Networks," *Comput. Networks*, February 1980.

LAM 80B   Lam, S. S., "A Packet Network Architecture for Local Interconnection," *Conf. Rec. Int. Conf. Commun.*, Seattle, June 1980.

LAM 80C   Lam, S. S., "Packet Broadcast Networks—A Performance Analysis of the R-ALOHA Protocol," *IEEE Trans. Comput.*, July 1980.

MARK 78   Mark, J. W., "Global Scheduling Approach to Conflict-Free Multiaccess via a Data Bus," *IEEE Trans. Commun.*, Vol. COM-26, September 1978.

MARK 79   Mark, J. W., and S. F. W. Ng, "A Coding Scheme for Conflict-Free Multiaccess Using Global Scheduling," *IEEE Trans. Commun.*, September 1979.

MART 72   Martin, J., *Systems Analysis for Data Transmission*, Prentice-Hall, Englewood Cliffs, N.J., 1972.

METC 73   Metcalfe, R. M., "Steady-State Analysis of a Slotted and Controlled ALOHA System with Blocking," *Proc. 6th Hawaii Int. Conf. Syst. Sci.*, Honolulu, January 1973.

METC 76   Metcalfe, R. M., and D. R. Boggs, "Ethernet: Distributed Packet Switching for Local Computer Networks," *Commun. ACM*, Vol. 19, No. 7, July 1976.

NG 77   Ng, S. F. W., and J. W. Mark, "A Multiaccess Model for Packet Switching with a Satellite Having Some Processing Capability," *IEEE Trans. Commun.*, Vol. COM-25, January 1977, pp. 128–135.

PRIT 77   Pritchard, W. L., "Satellite Communication—An Overview of the Problems and Programs," *Proc. IEEE*, Vol. 65, March 1977.

PUEN 71   Puente, J. G., W. G. Schmidt, and A. M. Werth, "Multiple-Access Techniques for Commercial Satellites," *Proc. IEEE*, Vol. 59, February 1971.

ROBE 72   Roberts, L. G., "ALOHA Packet System with and without Slots and Capture," ARPANET Satellite System Note 8, (NIC 11290), June 1972; reprinted in *Comput. Commun. Rev.*, Vol. 5, April 1975.

ROBE 73   Roberts, L., "Dynamic Allocation of Satellite Capacity through Packet Reservation," *AFIPS Conf. Proc.*, Vol. 42, AFIPS Press, Montvale, N.J., 1973, pp. 711–716.

ROBE 78   Roberts, L., "The Evolution of Packet Switching," *Proc. IEEE*, Vol. 66, November 1978.

ROTH 76   Rothhauser, E. H., and D. Wild, "MLMA: A Collision-Free Multi-access Method," IBM Research Report RZ802, November 1976.

SCHW 73   Schwartz, J. W., and M. Muntner, "Multiple-Access Communications for Computer Nets," *Computer-Communication Networks*, N. Abramson and F. Kuo, eds., Prentice-Hall, Englewood Cliffs, N.J., 1973.

SCHW 77   Schwartz, M., *Computer-Communication Network Design and Analysis*, Prentice-Hall, Englewood Cliffs, N.J., 1977.

THOR 75   Thornton, J. E., et al., "A New Approach to Network Storage Measurement," *Computer Design*, November 1975.

THUR 79   Thurber, K. J., and H. A. Freeman, "A Bibliography of Local Computer Network," *Comput. Commun. Rev.*, April 1979.

TOBA 74   Tobagi, F. A., "Random Access Techniques for Data Transmission over Packet Switched Radio Networks," Ph.D. dissertation, Computer Science Department, University of California, Los Angeles, Calif., December 1974.

TOBA 76   Tobagi, F. A., and L. Kleinrock, "Packet Switching in Radio Channels: Part III. Polling and (Dynamic) Split-Channel Reservation Multiple Access," *IEEE Trans. Commun.*, Vol. COM-24, No. 8, pp. 832–845, August 1976.

TOBA 77   Tobagi, F. A., and L. Kleinrock, "Packet Switching in Radio Channels: Part IV—Stability Considerations and Dynamic Control in Carrier Sense Multiple Access," *IEEE Trans. Commun.*, Vol. COM-25, October 1977.

TOBA 79   Tobagi, F. A., and V. B. Hunt, "Performance Analysis of Carrier Sense Multiple Access with Collision Detection," *Proc. Local Area Commun. Network Symp.*, Boston, May 1979.

WEIS 78   Weissler, R., et al., "Synchronization and Multiple Access Protocols in the Initial Satellite IMP," *Proc. Fall COMPCON '78*, Washington, D.C., September 1978.

WEST 72   West, L. P., "Loop-Transmission Control Structures," *IEEE Trans. Commun.*, Vol. COM-20, No. 3, Part II, June 1972, pp. 531–539.

WEST 78   West, A., and A. Davison, "CNET—A Cheap Network for Distributed Computing," Department of Computer Science and Statistics, Queen Mary College, University of London, Rep. TR120, March 1978.

WILL 74   Willard, D. G., "A Time Division Multiple Access System for Digital Communication," *Comput. Des.*, June 1974.

YEMI 78   Yemini, Y., "On Channel Sharing in Discrete-Time Packet Switched, Multi-access Broadcast Communication," Ph.D. dissertation, Computer Science Department, University of California, Los Angeles, Calif., 1978.

5

Wideband Transmission Media I: Radio Communication

R. ANDREW PICKENS
Continental Page Communications, Inc.

INTRODUCTION TO WIDEBAND TRANSMISSION MEDIA (CHAPTERS 5, 6, 7)

Chou, in Chap. 1, has constructed a modular profile of computer communications. Clearly, transmission media are an essential ingredient of the profile, for without them no communication would be possible. Rather than treating all possible transmission media, we have elected to describe only those that will have major impact on the wideband computer communication system designs of the near future. These same media constitute the underlying transmission technologies necessary for Integrated Services Digital Networks (Chap. 17). In Chaps. 5 and 6 we examine "wireless" transmission — radio and satellite communications (which is really a special case of radio). In Chap. 7 we consider guided media —wirelines, coaxial-cable, and fiber-optic systems — which have in common the fact that they require a physical path between the communication terminals.

Fig. 5.1 shows a rough comparison of three media we consider, indicating their positions in the spectrum of cost, distance, and bandwidth for which they have been found to be most useful. Because the cost of satellite communication is not a function of distance, it has not been plotted.

It is assumed that the reader is not familiar with basic communications technology, and that his primary motivation is to possess some understanding of the characteristics of available transmission media as applicable to computer communication networks. He may be interested in ordering his communications needs from a common carrier, procuring a custom-built package from a system contractor, or designing and implementing his own system. In each case, the level of technical detail and the issues of economics and regulations assume varying degrees of importance. It is the intention of these chapters to touch on each of these issues by presenting, in an

© 1980 R.A.P. All rights reserved.

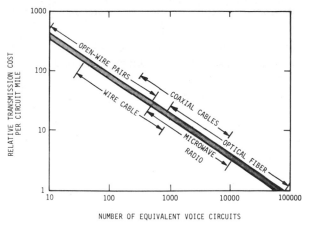

RELATIVE TRANSMISSION COST PER CIRCUIT MILE

OPEN-WIRE PAIRS

WIRE CABLE

COAXIAL CABLES

MICROWAVE RADIO

OPTICAL FIBER

NUMBER OF EQUIVALENT VOICE CIRCUITS

79-123-01-007

Figure 5.1. Relative costs of terrestial communications media versus band-width expressed as the equivalent number of voice-grade circuits (about 4 kHz). Satellite circuit costs are not sensitive to distance,thus are not plotted. (After [HAND 78].)

integrated fashion, an overview of the history and current state of the art of wideband transmission, a review of the underlying technical considerations, and discussion of the key issues and future outlooks.

To compress so much territory into three short chapters, it was necessary to make numerous generalizations and approximations, and also to omit much of importance. Nevertheless, the technical treatment culminates in the development of methods of estimating performance, which are sufficient for purposes of determining feasibility and initial sizing. The performance estimates can also be used for rough validation of specific designs; any substantial variance should be investigated.

5.1 CHARACTERISTICS OF RADIO COMMUNICATION

It is estimated that 60% of today's telecommunications transmission is provided by terrestrial radio, measured in terms of circuit-miles. Particularly in the industrialized nations, the probability is very high that the medium of radio is involved in some portion of a communications circuit going beyond the local level. Radio is also extensively used for the establishment of point-to-point circuits in private networks, involving distances ranging from, say, a few hundred meters to global distances. In many instances, there was no viable alternative to terrestrial radio until the advent of satellite communications (which can be viewed as a special case of radio). To provide a wire or cable between two given points is economically infeasible in some cases, and physically impossible in others (e.g., communication with a mobile terminal). In fact,

157

in its early days, radio was referred to as "wireless transmission"; the possibilities first exploited around the turn of the century by Guglielmo Marconi literally pushed back the horizons of communications.

Some of the chief characteristics of terrestrial radio as a transmission medium are summarized below:

Advantages	*Disadvantages*
• No physical path between terminals, "wireless"	• Subject to interference and propagation anomalies
• No right-of-way is required for transmission path	• Requires space in crowded radio spectrum
• Can be quickly implemented	• Long-distance, wideband links can be expensive
• Transmitter and/or receiver can be mobile	• Requires considerable engineering effort
• Broadcast or point to point	• Licensing and design approval required from governmental regulatory agencies (e.g., FCC)
• Wideband capability (up to 10% of operating frequency in special cases)	

5.2 THE NATURE OF RADIO SYSTEMS

The most familiar forms of radio are the entertainment broadcast services: AM, FM, and TV. Generally, the transmitting station operates with an antenna having essentially omnidirectional characteristics, covering a roughly circular area with a signal strength inversely proportional to distance squared. If the receiver is also equipped with an omnidirectional antenna, it will be able to receive signals (and potentially, interference) from other transmitters (and noise sources) located at any bearing from the receiver. The signal strength presented to a receiver from its antenna (and consequently received signal quality) can be increased by using an antenna with higher gain. The higher the gain as compared with an omnidirectional antenna, the more pronounced is the directionality of its response; for example, it is necessary to provide a rotator for a high-gain TV antenna, in order to receive stations located in different directions. However, for a given transmitter power, the receiver can be at a greater distance from the transmitter, and the receiver will be less subject to interference from other transmitters and noise sources located outside the sector of the receiving antenna's principal response.

Similarly, it is possible to equip a transmitter with a directional antenna possessing gain. In this situation, only a receiver located in a sector corresponding to the transmitting antenna's "beam" will be optimally coupled with the transmitter. With a receiver so located, the transmitter power required for a given received signal quality is lowered by a factor equal to the gain of the transmitting antenna.

The use of highly directional, high-gain antennas for both the transmitter and receiver creates a situation in which the transmitter can be "heard" only in one quite narrow angular sector, and the receiver can "hear" signals emanating within a similarly narrow sector. At microwave frequencies (above 1 GHz), beamwidths are commonly of the order of 1°, analogous to a good flashlight. If the transmitting and receiving antennas are aimed at each other, a good communications link is established with relatively low transmitter power and minimized interference with other such links. The latter is a key point in consideration of conservation of the limited spectrum; frequencies can be reused in the same general vicinity. This is the basis for point-to-point communications links (so-called "fixed" as contrasted with "broadcast" service), wherein it is generally intended that only one transmitter site communicates with only one receiver site.

The great majority of commercial and private radio systems (e.g., intercity telephone trunks) are fixed service (i.e., used as point-to-point telecommunications). The major exceptions are the previously mentioned entertainment broadcast services, and the many other situations in which a general coverage to multiple and/or mobile outlying stations is desired. New radio system technologies are emerging, however, which will be important in computer communication networks. These technologies rely at least partially on the "all points" nature of broadcast radio, and are particularly applicable to providing solutions to the problems of wideband local distribution. Some of these techniques are discussed in Sec. 5.6.

Tab. 5-1 shows the portions of the radio-frequency spectrum in current usage and gives a rough indication of the digital transmission rates that can be achieved. Reliable wideband digital communication generally requires operation at frequencies in the UHF and SHF regions. For that reason, we concentrate on microwave radio (see Fig. 5.2).

5.2.1 Radio-Wave Propagation

In radio reception, electromagnetic radio waves in "free space" are intercepted and coupled into a receiver by an antenna. Conversely, the antenna (which is a reciprocal device) couples radio-frequency (RF) power from a transmitter into free space. Consider a distant transmitter in free space, which is feeding an isotropic (point source) antenna. The radiated power expands uniformly in all directions, such that the total power integrated over the surface of a sphere centered on the transmitter is equal to the transmitted power. Since our transmitter is in free space, there are no losses in our system; consequently, the total power intercepted by the sphere is independent of its radius. The power *density*, however, is inversely proportional to the sphere's surface area. This corresponds to our intuition that the larger an antenna, the higher its gain; that a receiver system is more sensitive if it incorporates a larger antenna. If the receiving antenna is located distance d from the transmitting antenna, the received power P_R expressed as a fraction of transmitted power P_T is given by the ratio of the receiving antenna's effective area A_R to the surface of a sphere of radius d, or

Table 5.1. *Characteristics of Radio-Frequency Communications Bands.*

Frequency Band	Principal Applications	Characteristics	Principal Modulation Methods	
			Analog	*Digital*
ELF, VLF, LF 30 Hz–300 kHz	Navigation, low-data-rate broadcast	Very long distance ground wave Very limited bandwidth Very noisy Very large transmitting antenna	Generally not practical for voice communications	ASK, FSK, MSK; 0.1–100 baud
MF 300 kHz–3 MHz	Broadcast, AM radio	Long-distance ground wave Limited bandwidth Noisy Large transmitting antennas	AM (voice quality)	ASK, FSK, MSK; 10–1000 baud
HF 3–30 MHz	Broadcast, point-to-point, short-wave radio, amateur and CB radio	Intermediate distances by ground Long distance by sky wave, but sporadic availability Bandwidth = voice frequencies or lower Noisy, high congestion and interference Moderate antenna sizes	AM, SSB (voice quality)	ASK, FSK, MSK; 10–3000 baud
VHF 30–300 MHz	Broadcast, point to point, VHF television, FM radio, land and air mobile	Line-of-sight range Bandwidth = 5 kHz–5 MHz Moderate to low noise and interference Small antennas	AM, SSB, FM (voice, music quality, TV)	FSK, PSK, others to 100 kbps
UHF 300–3000 MHz (microwave)	Local broadcast, point to point, UHF television, radar, space telemetry	Line-of-sight range Bandwidth to 20 MHz Low noise; local congestion in some regions Small antennas	FM, SSB (multiplexed voice, TV)	PSK, FM, others to 10 Mbps
SHF 3000–30,000 MHz (microwave)	Point to point, terrestrial and satellite communications, radar	Line-of-sight range Bandwidth to 500 MHz Low noise Narrow antenna beam widths Significant attenuation at high end	FM, SSB (multiplexed voice, TV)	FM, PSK, others to 100 Mbps

Frequency Band	Principal Applications	Characteristics	Principal Modulation Methods	
			Analog	*Digital*
EHF 30,000 MHz + (millimeter waves)	Point to point, experimental systems, radio astronomy	Line-of-sight range Bandwidths to 1 GHz+ Low noise High atmospheric attenuation Very small antennas	FM	FM, PSK, others

Figure 5.2. Typical remote microwave radio repeater station. (Courtesy of Page Communications Engineers, Inc.).

$$\frac{P_R}{P_T} = \frac{A_R}{4\pi d^2} \qquad \text{(isotropic transmit antenna)}$$

(5.1)

Indeed, the "larger" the receiving antenna, the better it performs the function of intercepting transmitted energy. At microwave frequencies, a practical antenna has an effective area equal to a substantial fraction (50 to 75%) of its physical area.

At radio frequencies, an isotropic antenna is hypothetical, and not even particularly desirable. A practical antenna exhibits a responsiveness greater than an isotropic antenna in some direction. The ratio of its greater responsiveness to that of an isotropic antenna is referred to as its *gain*, G, which is related to its *effective* area as $G = 4\pi A / \lambda^2$, where λ is the wavelength of the operating radio frequency (see Sec. 5.3.3 and [REFE 77]). Antennas are reciprocal — the gain in the receiving mode is the same as in the transmitting mode. Since the gain of an isotropic antenna is defined as unity, as implicit in the derivation of Eq. (5.1), we can substitute for the gain G_T or the effective area A_T of our transmitting antenna as follows:

$$\frac{P_R}{P_T}\text{(ideal)} = \frac{A_R(1)}{4\pi d^2} = \frac{A_R(G_T)}{4\pi d^2} = \frac{A_R(4A_T)}{4\pi d^2(\lambda^2)} = \frac{A_R A_T}{d^2\lambda^2}$$

(5.2)

With antennas of a given physical size, an interesting thing happens. From Eq. (5.2), received power decreases by the square of distance d as we would intuitively expect; but the ratio also decreases by the square of wavelength λ. Since λ is inversely related to frequency,[1] P_R/P *increases* by the square of frequency. Ideally, this indicates that it would be desirable to operate at as high a frequency as possible, which will be discussed later.

Equation (5.2) for receiver-to-transmitter power ratio can be rewritten in terms of antenna gains:

$$\frac{P_R}{P_T}\text{(ideal)} = \frac{\lambda^2}{4\pi d^2}G_R G_T$$

(5.3)

This is the fundamental formula used for radio link calculations. The first term involving λ and d is referred to as the *free-space path loss*.

5.2.2   Radio-Frequency Propagation

At frequencies below about 2 MHz, radio waves tend to follow the general contour of the earth's surface. The lower the frequency, the more pronounced is this effect, which is exploited in very long distance, beyond-line-of-sight communications such as in the long-wave bands. Up to about 30 MHz, propagation is also influenced by the ionized layers of the earth's atmosphere. Many readers are familiar with the sky-wave phenomenon sometimes present in the short-wave bands, such as citizen's band radio (approximately 27 MHz). Sky-wave propagation, or *skip*, is caused by the reflection of radio waves from distant stations by the ionosphere. These readers will also be familiar with the sporadic nature of "skip," which makes it undependable as a full-service, high-quality means of communication.

[1]$\lambda = c/f$ meters, where f is frequency in hertz and c is the velocity of light (3×10^8 m/sec in free space).

Above about 30 MHz, the ionosphere is transparent to radio waves, and line-of-sight propagation becomes the rule; for example, area coverage in the FM broadcast band (approximately 100 MHz) is limited to the horizon. Continuing an increase in frequency, the analogy to visibility becomes increasingly pronounced. The classical "smooth-earth" formula for line-of-sight distance D between two antennas of heights h_1 and h_2 feet is $D = \sqrt{2h_1} + \sqrt{2h_2}$ statute miles.[2] However, obstruction by intervening objects, such as mountains and buildings, must be accounted for.

Multipath Interference and Fading

Following the optical analogy, radio waves in the ultrahigh frequency (UHF) and microwave regions are subject to reflection, refraction, and diffraction. Reflections from the earth's surface and natural or man-made objects, can create multiple paths between two antennas. Consider a receiving antenna responding to comparable signal amplitudes arriving via a direct path and also via a reflected path from a transmitter. Depending on the relative path distances and hence time delays, the reflected energy is shifted in phase with respect to the direct energy, which may result in constructive or destructive interference. Further, since the phase shift is a function of frequency, the composite received signal strength is frequency dependent, which can lead to serious problems in wideband transmission. Multipath fading in a dynamic situation is illustrated by the occasional "flutter" produced in TV or FM reception by an airplane. In fixed installations, multipath interference can be reduced by the use of antennas having narrow beamwidths and by other techniques discussed in Sec. 5.3.4.

Just as the density of the earth's atmosphere varies with altitude, there is a gradient of dielectric constant and, consequently, index of refraction. A "standard atmosphere" has the effect of bending radio waves toward the earth's surface, such that the effective radio horizon is extended. Equivalently, the earth's surface appears to be flattened; the earth's apparent radius is increased by a K factor of $4/3$. Abnormal distributions of temperature and humidity, however, cause the effective K factor to decrease—in some extreme cases, to as low as $1/2$. Clearly, such a change will have a pronounced impact on the received signal strength of a radio link operating near the radio horizon, or one using very high gain (and hence very narrow beamwidth) antennas.

The phenomenon of time-varying signal strength is called *fading*. The most common cause of fading in a fixed-service microwave link is also related to anomalies in atmospheric refractivity. Especially in early morning or evening hours, steep gradients in the dielectric constant occur, which give rise to another form of multipath propagation. Multipath-induced fading, being frequency selective, is the most serious anomalistic phenomenon in wideband radio transmission, because of distortions introduced in the frequency and time domains.

The magnitude of fades in microwave radio can exceed 30 dB (a power ratio of 1000:1) for periods ranging from fractions of seconds to minutes. Obviously, such a

---

[2]This relation can be derived by computing the distance D along a tangent to the earth's surface to a point at height h above the surface. It is assumed that $h \ll r$ (the earth's radius), and that r is increased by the factor $4/3$ to account for the radio refractivity of the atmosphere.

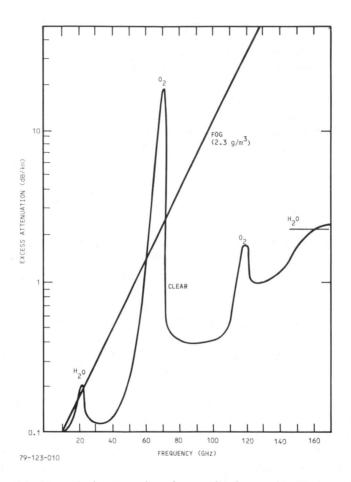

Figure 5.3. Atmospheric attenuation of super high frequencies. The curve for heavy fog should be taken as additive to the clear atmosphere attenuations (from [BENO 68].)

factor must be accounted for in the design of a radio link. Methods used to combat fading are space diversity (use of multiple transmit and/or receive antennas) and frequency diversity. These techniques depend on the space/frequency independence of the fading mechanisms (see Sec. 5.3.4).

Atmospheric and Precipitation Losses

At microwave frequencies, path losses due to the atmosphere and precipitation becoming increasingly important as frequency increases. Fig. 5.3 shows the excess attenuation suffered over each kilometer of the radio-link path in a clear atmosphere. This loss can usually be ignored for frequencies below 18 GHz.

A much more severe loss is experienced due to precipitation, as displayed in Fig. 5.4 for a range of rainfall rates. The loss can become very significant at frequencies

164

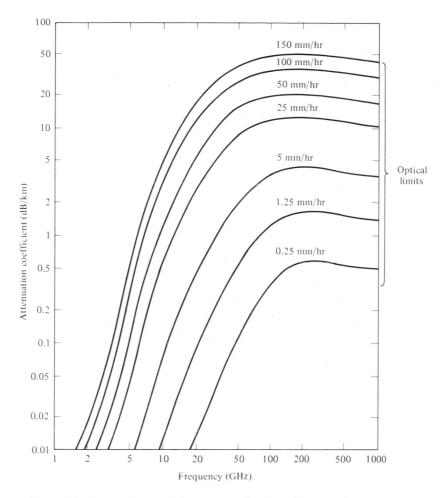

Figure 5.4. Attenuation coefficient due to rain. (From [CCIR 78].)

above about 4 GHz. In temperate climates, it is unlikely that an area experiencing rainfall rate over 25 mm/hr will exceed a diameter of 7 km. Total expected path attenuation for a given regional rain rate can be estimated by using an effective path length of $(7 + D/3)$ km when path length D is greater than 7 km. For example, using data from Fig. 5.4, the precipitation loss over a 25-km path at a heavy rainfall rate of 40 mm/hr would be (1.5 dB/km) (7 + 25/3 km) = 23 dB, the equivalent of a power ratio of 1/200.[3]

Path losses due to fading and meteorological phenomena are handled in

---

[3]Much more precise predictions are possible using recently developed models; see, for example, [CRAN 78, CRAN 79, ANAN 80]. The simplified estimation method given above can lead to substantial error at high attenuation levels.

radio-link design in a probabilistic manner. Empirical data have been collected under widely varying atmospheric and terrain conditions, in many different locales. The U.S. National Bureau of Standards (NBS) and the International Comité Consultative Internationale de Radio (CCIR) publish recommended methods of accounting for propagation anomalies, using expected characteristics of the region in which a radio link is to be located, and scaling factors for accommodating the predicted variations [DOUG 78, CHAS 75, WHIT 75]. Application of these methods leads to reasonable estimates for a loss margin and a corresponding percentage of the time (termed *path availability*) that the actual loss is not expected to exceed that margin.

Frequency-selective fading follows the Rayleigh distribution, with a probability of a fade (P_F exceeding a given margin M) given by

$$P_F \simeq 10 \exp(-M/10) \tag{5.4}$$

where M is expressed in dB and is larger than 10 [BULL 57]. For example, it would not be expected that a link with a fade margin of 30 dB would drop more than 30 dB below the "normal" signal level for more than 0.1% of the time (8.8 hr/yr). Normally, Rayleigh fading probability is conservative; numerous modification factors have been proposed, based on empirical observations, involving such parameters as terrain roughness, climate, path length, and frequency (see, e.g., [BARN 70, VIGA 75]).

From the earlier discussion of microwave propagation, it can be appreciated that these parameters would have a substantial influence on fading. The following factors can be applied to the results of Eq. 5.4 for a very rough adjustment for specific link conditions (after WHIT 75):

Parameter	Scaling Factor
1. Terrain/Climate	
a) Average	X1
(some roughness, inland/temperate)	
b) Worst Case	X10
(smooth/hot and humid)	
c) Best Case	X0.1
(very rough, mountainous/dry)	
2. Frequency	
a) $f \geq 10\text{GHz}$	X1
b) $f < 10\text{GHz}$	X1/f
3. Path Length d (km)	$X(\dfrac{d}{100})^{2.5}$
($5 > d > 100$)	

Precipitation losses should be treated in a similar manner. Maps and charts have been compiled which indicate the expected rainfall rates in various regions of the world (e.g., [OLSE 78, CCIR 78] as a function of time exceeded. Fig. 5.5 displays data from the CCIR recommendations.

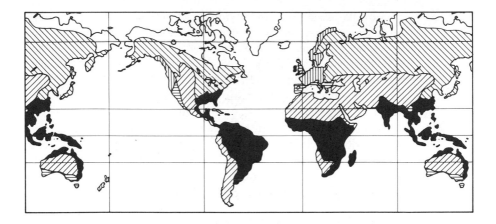

Region		0.001	0.01	0.1
■■■■	1	155	75	19
⬛	2	123	53	14
▥	3	82	37	11
▤	4	56	25	8
▨	5	32	14	5

Figure 5.5. Percentage of an average year for which rainfall rate (mm/hr) is exceeded in the indicated climatic regions. (After [CCIR 78].)

5.2.3 Signal-to-Noise Ratio

The primary criterion for establishing the performance of a radio link is the signal-to-noise power ration (SNR) of the received signal. Noise, considered as any unwanted signal, is superimposed on the signal by the following principal sources:

1. *Receiver noise.* A receiver adds a random (Gaussian) thermal noise power $N_R = KTF$ watts/Hz-bandwidth to the received signal; where K = Boltzmann's constant (1.38×10^{-23} J/Kelvin), T = temperature (in Kelvins; 1 Kelvin = $273°$C), and F = receiver excess noise factor. For terrestrial radio in temporate climates, it is customary to assume an operating temperature of $17°$ C (290 K), which leads to a value of 4×10^{-21} W/Hz, or -204 dBW/Hz, for the quantity KT. A typical value of F for a conventional microwave receiver is 10.

2. *Manmade noise* (e.g., from motors, power transmission, auto ignition). Below roughly 1000 MHz, noise from these sources can be much greater than the inherent receiver noise. At any frequency, interference from other transmitters must be considered.

3. *Atmospheric noise*, due to H_2O and O_2 molecules in the atmosphere; increases with higher concentration of H_2O such as in cloud, fog, or precipitation. Sometimes other noise sources, such as cosmic and solar, become important. Except for extremely sensitive systems, such as satellite receivers, atmospheric noise can be ignored between 1 and 10 GHz.

4. Noise due to imperfections in the radio equipment. In multichannel analog radio, a primary cause of noise is due to modulation products arising from nonlinearites in the transmitter and receiver chains. The levels of such noise are highly dependent on specific design and care in maintenance.

5. Interference from other sources, such as other radios operating on the same frequency or their harmonics. Although such interference contains information, if it is unwanted by a particular receiver, it is "noise" in the broad sense.

Basic terrestrial radio link calculations generally consider only receiver thermal noise. Separate attention is given to additional degradation from the other noise and interference sources because particular steps to reduce them to acceptable levels can possibly be taken. Possibilities include site relocation, change of operating frequency, and use of a different modulation technique or antenna.

The signal power available at the receiver's input was previously defined as P_R. We will define the effective input signal-to-noise ratio (SNR) as equal to P_R/N_R.[4] N_R is expressed above as a spectrum power density (W/Hz), and must be multiplied by the effective bandwidth B of the receiver to realize the equivalent noise power. Thus

$$\text{SNR} = \frac{P_R}{N_R} = \frac{P_R}{KTFB} \tag{5.5a}$$

or

$$\text{SNR (dB)} = P_R(\text{dBW}) - 10 \log B - 10 \log F \times -10 \log T - 10 \log K \tag{5.5b}$$

In accordance with Eq. (5.1), the value of -204 dBW is conventionally substituted for the terms $(10 \log T + 10 \log K)$.

5.2.4 Modulation and Demodulation

In any transmission link, the ultimate question is how faithfully the link's input signal is reproduced at the output. In an analog system, the signal-to-noise ratio is an end in itself. In digital systems, the criterion of transmission fidelity is usually expressed in terms of bit error rate (BER) or probability of bit error (P_e), which can be related to

---

[4]*Conventionally, this term and Eq. (5.5) are defined as *carrier-to-noise ratio* (C/N). *Signal-to-noise ratio* normally refers to the quality of the receiver output signal, after imperfections in the receiver and demodulator have been taken into account. For simplicity and expediency in these chapters, second-order effects have been ignored and the term SNR is used throughout. We also assume that noise is characterized by wideband stationary Gaussian statistics.

SNR. In either case, the modulation–demodulation process is the final determinant of a link's performance.

In a landmark paper [SHAN 49], Shannon expressed the information capacity C of a communication channel of bandwidth B perturbed by white Gaussian noise as

$$C = B \log_2 (1 + \frac{P}{N}) \qquad \text{bps}$$

For our present purposes, the quantity P/N can be taken to be P_R/N = SNR, the input signal-to-noise ratio previously defined. So defined, the channel capacity can be realized at an arbitrarily low error rate. This remarkable result tells us that bandwidth and SNR are the key measures of channel performance, but different practical modulation–demodulation techniques are variously effective in approaching the limit [COST 59].

The terms *modulation* and *demodulation* refer to the method of impressing intelligence to be communicated on the nominal carrier frequency of a radio transmitter, and the corresponding means of recovering the intelligence in the receiver. The unmodulated carrier of a transmitter can be represented as $A \sin (\omega t + \varnothing)$, where $\omega = 2\pi f$, the operating frequency. Modulation by a time-varying waveform can be effected by varying the amplitude term, the frequency term, and/or the phase term as a corresponding function of time. There are substantial differences between the various methods as regards their power requirements, performance in the presence of voice and interference, bandwidth efficiency, and ease of realization.

5.2.4.1 *Analog Modulation*

In analog radio, such as the entertainment services, AM (amplitude modulation) is normally the simplest to implement. FM (frequency modulation) requires more complex modulation–demodulation circuitry and imposes more stringent requirements on the characteristics of other portions of the transmitter and receiver; however, its superiority to AM is clear to the radio listener in terms of fidelity and relative freedom from interference. Another method, single-sideband, suppressed-carrier amplitude modulation (SSB), has a performance advantage over simple AM, which in many cases warrants the complexity of its implementation [PANT 65, REFE 77].

Conventional AM modulation is achieved by varying the amplitude of the transmitter's carrier frequency as a function of the amplitude of the information signal. The resultant spectrum comprises a carrier frequency component with a "sideband" on each side. One sideband is the mirror image of the other, and the spectral width of each corresponds with the bandwidth of the modulating signal. Hence the spectrum and consequently the receiver bandwidth, required with double-sideband AM is twice the information bandwidth. The amplitude envelope of either sideband (ideally) follows the amplitude of the modulating signal; this allows very easily implemented demodulation with an envelope detector, which can consist of a simple diode and low-pass filter. Envelope detection, however, exhibits poor performance at low SNR; much more elaborate schemes, such as synchronous detection, are possible to improve performance in the threshold region.

SSB can be regarded as a special case of AM. Since both sidebands in conventional AM carry the same information, nothing is gained by transmitting and processing both. Further, some transmitter power is expended in transmitting the carrier frequency, which carries no information *per se*. SSB modulation can be effected by filtering the output of an AM modulator, removing one sideband and the carrier — hence "single sideband, suppressed carrier." The transmitted spectrum and receiver bandwidth required now equal those of the modulating signal. Demodulation is considerably more complex than envelope detection because the carrier that serves as a reference in AM is absent in SSB and must be effectively reinserted by the receiver. For this reason, SSB requires extremely tight frequency stability in both transmitters and receivers, further adding to cost. Nevertheless, the power and bandwidth efficiencies of SSB have made it a very attractive modulation method.

FM modulation is accomplished by varying the *frequency* of the transmitter carrier as a function of the *amplitude* of the information signal. The frequency of the information signal is translated into the rate of change of the carrier frequency. Thus there is no information carried in the amplitude of the carrier. This is one of the major advantages of FM — above a given threshold, it is insensitive to amplitude variations in the transmitter, the propagation path, or the receiver. In fact, one of the functions of an FM receiver, in the course of its signal processing, is to limit the signal to a constant amplitude prior to demodulation. Limiting removes many of the perturbations that may have been imposed on the signal in its path to the receiver, and accounts for much of the quality improvement apparent in entertainment FM radio. FM's insensitivity to amplitude also allows the use of more efficient transmitters, which tend to be nonlinear in their amplitude transfer characteristics. FM demodulation employs a form of frequency discriminator or phase detector, the function of which is to retranslate frequency variation back into an amplitude variation.

Fig. 5.6 compares output SNR versus input SNR for typical cases of the various modulation schemes. At a threshold SNR_i of about 10 dB, a significant increase in SNR_o occurs for FM. The FM improvement factor above the threshold is related to the modulation index (how much the carrier frequency swings, compared to the highest modulating frequency), which can be made arbitrarily large. One way to view this phenomenon is that FM advantageously trades bandwidth for power. Additional SNR improvements of 3 to 5 dB are possible with FM by use of preemphasis of higher modulating frequencies in the transmitter.

The vast majority of extant radio links are analog in nature, because they were intended to carry voice circuits. Multichannel analog radios are based on frequency-division multiplex (FDM) hierarchies that have grown up over the years in telephony. The first level combines twelve 4-kHz channels into a "basic group" of 48-kHz bandwidth, by appropriate frequency translation of each of the channels. Five basic groups are translated into a "supergroup" of 240-kHz bandwidth containing 60 voice channels, and so on [FREE 75]. Imperfections in the multiplexing process itself, as well as in the modulation–demodulation process, give rise to

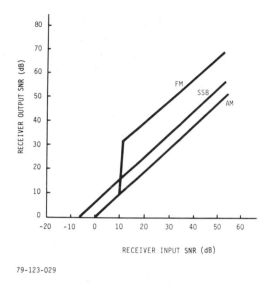

79-123-029

Figure 5.6 Representative output SNSR versus input SNR curves for analog modulation techniques.

additional noise and distortion products, such as intermodulation noise and cross-talk. In general, the objective of the telephone networks is to provide the subscriber with a signal-to-noise ratio of better than 30 dB for voice service. However, the performance of digital modems over these circuits is not what one would expect from that equivalent analog signal-to-noise ratio, because of the steps required to achieve the analog objective, such as control over individual channel energy levels (which limits signal power), sharp filters for band edges (which introduce phase distortion), and intersymbol interference.

5.2.4.2 Digital Modulation

A radio intended for analog service can be used to transmit digital information by adding a digital modem (*mo*dulator–*dem*odulator) to an analog channel. This can be done on each voice channel, by use of modems similar to the familiar telephone line data sets. Higher data rates can be accommodated by wider-band modems, operating in the bandwidths available for groups, supergroups, and so on. For all-digital transmission, however, the most efficient application of equipment is to use a radio specifically designed for direct digital modulation, in conjunction with time-division multiplexers.

Conceptually, the simplest form of digital modulation is amplitude-shift keying (ASK), or on–off keying (OOK) of the radio carrier frequency—"all or nothing" AM wherein, say, carrier-on represents a 1; and carrier-off, 0. This is the familiar CW or "Morse code" radiotelegraph modulation technique. A major drawback of OOK is that one of the two decisions required at the demodulator (was a 0 transmitted?) by definition must be made in the absence of any signal (and, consequently, in the full presence of only noise and interference). It can be shown that optimum demodulation of OOK requires that the decision threshold be a function of signal-to-noise ratio. Further, a comparable system's transmitter must provide a peak power twice that of other modulation methods. The resultant implementation problems coupled with poor performance and high interference potential have precluded the use of OOK as a practical modulation technique in wideband systems.

A very useful form of digital modulation is frequency-shift keying (FSK). In binary FSK, the carrier frequency assumes either of two values, f_1 or f_2, corresponding to a 1 or a 0. This is simple in both concept and implementation. In effect, the carrier is frequency modulated in steps between two (or more) values. The deviation $(f_2 - f_1)$ can be increased for better noise immunity at the expense of increased requirements for spectrum and power. Numerous variations are possible. For example, f_1 and f_2 can be forced in the transmitter to maintain phase coherence (coherent FSK); the resulting increased *a priori* knowledge of the signal in the receiver affords lower error rates for a given SNR. Coherent detection techniques, however, are considerably more expensive to implement, and FSK has found widest application in low-speed transmission ($\leq$ 300 bps) over voice-grade telephone circuits and HF radio.

The most widely used digital modulation technique is phase-shift keying (PSK), wherein the phase $\varnothing$ of the carrier frequency is shifted at the keying rate—say, 0° and 180° for binary PSK. Coherent PSK is possible. A useful variation is differentially coherent PSK (DPSK), wherein the information is conveyed by whether or not a phase transition occurs; with this technique, it is not necessary for the receiver to be in phase lock with the transmitter.

The modulation techniques described so far are binary-encoded schemes: one bit of information is transmitted per keying (signaling) interval, or baud.[5] With M-ary schemes, it is possible to convey $\log_2 M$ bits of information in each signaling interval. The basic idea is easily visualized by considering the previous example of PSK. Suppose that any one of four relative phases (rather than two) can be transmitted during any one signaling interval. It can be arranged that the incoming bit stream to be modulated is examined in groups of 2 bits rather than bit by bit. If a group of 2 bits represents say, 00, phase $\varnothing_1$ can be selected for transmission during that signaling interval; similarly, assign $01 = \varnothing_2$, $10 = \varnothing_3$, and $11 = \varnothing_4$. Clearly, with such a fixed code, demodulation on the receiving end can be accomplished without ambiguity. The resultant scheme is called 4-ary, or quarternary PSK (QPSK), and achieves an efficiency of $\log_2 4 = 2$ bits of information per signaling interval. Theoretically, the principle can be extended for $M = 8, 16, \ldots$. M-ary schemes can also be applied to any of the basic modulation techniques; QPSK is a particularly useful and popular modulation scheme, for reasons that we shall explore presently.

Many other digital modulation schemes have been proposed and used, which offer relative advantages in particular sets of circumstances involving signal strength, fading, multipath distortion, type of interference, special bandwidth constraints, and

---

[5]The term *baud* is defined as the inverse of the keying interval; the baud is the signaling rate. However, several bits of information can be conveyed in one signaling interval. Thus baud is equivalent to bits per second only in the case of binary-encoded signaling.

so on [FEHE 77]. Such methods include vestigial sideband (VSB), a form of AM wherein one of the two (redundant) spectral sidebands is essentially removed by filtration; and quadrature AM (QAM), wherein the carrier comprises two orthogonal components (90° phase shift), each of which is independently modulated. In the quest for more efficient modulation schemes, APK (a combination of amplitude and phase-shift keying) has received considerable recent interest, and can be expected to enjoy some use in the future.

The two primary characteristics of importance in considering digital modulation schemes are: (1) probability of bit error (P_e) as a function of signal-to-noise ratio, and (2) bandwidth efficiency (bandwidth required to convey a given information rate; bps/Hz). The analysis of digital modulation performance is quite complex, particularly giving consideration to practicable filtration and real-world implementation [PANT 65, LUCK 68, DAVE 72, SCHW 70, TAUB 71, SHAN 79]. With the understanding that the following treatment is highly idealized and simplified, it is possible to establish some useful rules.

By Nyquist's theorem [NYQU 28], a baseband signal[6] containing a maximum frequency component f_m can be sampled at a minimum sampling rate $f_s = 2f_m$, with no ambiguity or loss of information. Conversely, let the signaling interval T_s of an encoding waveform be $T_s = 1/f_s$; then $T_s = 1/2f_m$. If the spectrum is modulated on a carrier frequency f_c, the spectrum is translated from zero frequency to center on frequency f_c, and the resultant spectrum occupies the frequency band from $f_c - f_m$ to $f_c + f_m$ (i.e., the spectral width is $2f_m$). If we assume an ideal filter of bandwidth $B = 2f_m$ that will pass all frequency components from $f_c - f_m$ to $f_c + f_m$ but completely reject all others, then we have a band-limited transmission system of bandwidth $(f_c + f_m)$ $-(f_c - f_m) = 2f_m = B$, and which also occupies a spectral width of B. Further, $B = 2f_m$ $= 1/T_s = f_s$, so the system will support a maximum signaling rate of f_s.

Using the basic binary digital modulation schemes (ASK, FSK, and PSK), one bit of information is conveyed in each signaling interval; equivalently, 1 bps is transmitted in each baud, or signals per second. Thus binary modulation can (ideally) be accomplished at a bit rate R_b bps, in a bandwidth $B = R_b$ Hz, and with a spectral efficiency $R_b/B = 1$ bps/Hz. The M-ary variations of these techniques, compressing $\log_2 M$ bits of information per signaling interval, require bandwidth $B = R_b/\log_2 M$ Hz and achieve a spectral efficiency of $\log_2 M$ bps/Hz. In practice, the ideal bandwidth characteristic assumed earlier cannot be realized, and approaching the ideal requires increasing complexity and expense. Nevertheless, as demand for digital transmission capacity grows and the radio spectrum becomes more crowded, it is increasingly worthwhile to achieve spectral efficiency. Older radio transmission equipments commonly required 50 to 100% more bandwidth as compared with the theoretical; some newer designs are appearing that are in the range 15 to 30%.

The idealized error performance of the more popular modulation schemes is displayed in Fig. 5.7. Because of our emphasis on occupied spectrum and bandwidth,

---

[6]By *baseband signal* it is meant that the theoretical spectrum of the signal is symmetrical about zero frequency (i.e., extends from $-f_m$ to $+f_m$).

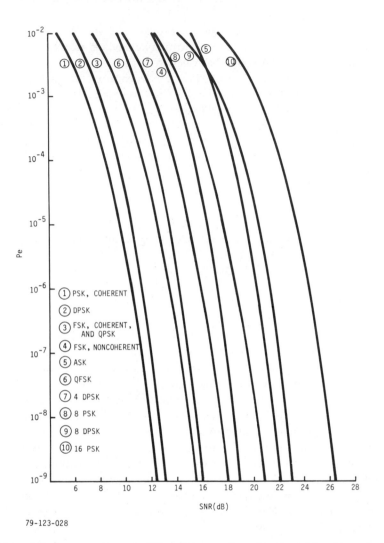

Figure 5.7 Approximate probability of bit error P as a function of signal-to-noise ratio (SNR) for popular modulation techniques. SNR is defined in the text.

signal-to-noise ratio (SNR) is defined for an idealized bandwidth equal to the signaling rate.[7] Generally, in practice, modern systems approach the ideal within 1 to 3 dB; the discrepancy is often specified. In the region $P_e = 10^{-9}$, the error rate becomes

[7]Normally, error performance is expressed in terms of P_s, probability of symbol error, and SNR is expressed in terms of E_b/N_0, the ratio of energy per bit to noise spectral power density. This allows for more precise analysis of the behavior of digital modulation systems, particularly for complex modulation schemes. Certain assumptions and approximations were used to produce the simplified and generalized curves shown in Fig. 5.7.

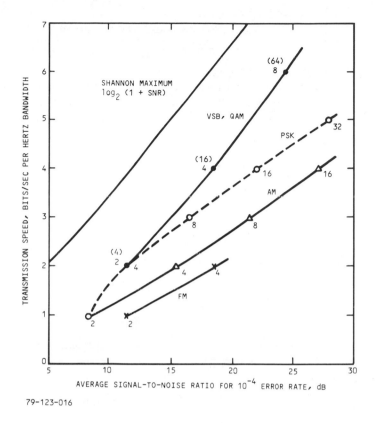

79-123-016

Figure 5.8. Ideal bandwidth efficiency of several digital modulation techniques. The points in the curves indicate the order (M) of information rate to signaling rate; for example, binary QAM ($M = 2$) and quartenary PSK (QPSK, $M = 4$) are the same point and can achieve 2 bits/Hz. (After [DAVE 72].)

dominated by factors other than SNR; increasing SNR alone will do little to improve P_e beyond this region.

Fig. 5.8 shows a comparison of modulation schemes with respect to both key criteria—required SNR and spectral efficiency—for a given P_e. This figure reveals a special property of QPSK modulation; with the proper selection of encoding of 2 bits per signaling interval (e.g., Gray code), the spectral efficiency ideally can be doubled with substantially the same SNR. The figure also illustrates that, even in theory, our current modulation techniques fall short of the bound predicted by Shannon.

5.2.5 Radio-Link Performance Calculations

We are now in a position to make a first-order estimate of the performance of a radio link. Combining Eqs. (5.3) and (5.5b) in dB form, we obtain

Box 5.1. **Typical Microwave-Radio SNR Calculation.**

Term	Description	Factor
P_T	Transmitter power, 5 W = 7.0 dBW	7.0 dBW
$+G_t$	Same antenna used for transmit and receive; diameter = 6 ft, efficiency = 55%, A = 1.4 m²; from Sec. 5.2.1,	43.8 dB
$+G_R$	$G = 4\pi A/\lambda^2 \simeq 24{,}000$ = 43.8 dB; frequency = 11 GHz, λ^2 = 0.027 m	43.8 dB
$+\alpha$	Path = 30 km, $\alpha = 20 \log \lambda/4\pi d$	-142.9 dB
$-B$	Bandwidth = 40 MHz = 76 dBHz	-76.0 dBHz
$-F$	Receiver system noise figure, typically 10 dB for terrestrial microwave radio	-10.0 dB
$-L_i$	Miscellaneous and incidental losses; assume 10 dB	-10.0 dB
$-kT$	Reference thermal noise at 17°C (290 K) temperature per hertz of bandwidth (Sec. 5.2.3)	-(-204.0 dBW/Hz)
SNR_B	Base signal-to-noise ratio = total of above	+59.7 dB
$-M$	Margin allowed for fading, etc.	-40.0 dB
SNR	Signal-to-noise ratio used for minimum performance under design conditions	+19.7 dB

$$\text{SNR}_{\text{ideal}} = P_T + \alpha + G_R + G_T - B - F - kT \tag{5.6a}$$

where $\alpha = 20 \log (\lambda/4\pi d)$, the free-space path loss.[8] Accumulating the additional losses experienced in a practical system and substituting the conventional 204 dBw for kT yields

$$\text{SNR} = P_T + \alpha + G_R + G_T - B - F - L_m + 204 \text{ dBW} \tag{5.6b}$$

where L_m accounts for miscellaneous system and component losses (usually about 10 dB), such as RF lines and nonideal demodulators.

A typical radio link SNR calculation is displayed in Box 5.1 for a link with radios having the following characteristics:

Link distance and path	= 30 km, average terrain and climate
Antenna diameters	= 6 ft. (1.8 m)
Antenna efficiency	= 55%
Frequency	= 11 GHz
Transmitter power	= 5 W
Receiver noise figure	= 10 dB
Bandwidth	= 40 MHz (90 Mbps using 8 PSK)

From the calculations of Box 5.1, the $\text{SNR}_B = 59.7$ dB. From the data in Sec. 5.2.4, it can be estimated that 90 Mbps/40 MHz = 2.2 bits/Hz could be achieved with 8 PSK at $P_e = 10^{-7}$ for a SNR of about 19.7 dB. We then have an excess SNR of 59.7 - 19.7 = 40 dB, which is the system margin(M). From the discussion of Sec. 5.2.2,

---

[8]Some may prefer to calculate $\alpha = -32.44 - 20 \log f - 20 \log d$, where f is frequency in MHz and d is distance in kilometers.

176

a margin of 40 dB corresponds to an average path availability of 0.9999. We can conclude that the radio link will provide a P_e of worse than 10^{-7} only 0.01% of the time, or 53 min/yr (however, see Sec. 5.3.4).

One further factor must be considered. If a lower operating frequency had been chosen, say 6 GHz, the path attenuation due to precipitation in region 2 would have increased by 3.3 dB for 0.01% of the time in region 2, in accordance with Sec. 5.2.2. Normal design practice would accept this loss under the assumption that it would be covered by the link margin of 40 dB, since it is unlikely that such heavy rain and worst-case fading conditions would occur simultaneously. In our case of an 11-GHz link, however, the calculated precipitation loss of 29 dB (0.01%) cannot be shrugged off so easily. There is still some controversy as to how such a situation should be handled. The conservative approach would add the outage times due to fading and precipitation, each calculated for the designed link margin.

5.3 MICROWAVE RADIO

The most common form of point-to-point radio telecommunications in the United States is microwave radio. Current frequency assignments in the United States are shown in Tab. 5.2; some of the indicated bands are shared with other services, such as mobile and satellite.[9]

FCC Rules and Regulations applicable to digital microwave radio transmission are Part 21 for common carriers and Part 94 for private users. Both require that transmission be accomplished with a minimum spectral efficiency of 1 bps/Hz. Part 21, however, further specifies a minimum voice-channel loading of 1152 equivalent voice circuits for carriers in the bands located between 3 and 15 GHz. Tab. 5.2 indicates the effective spectral efficiency that results from this requirement, assuming the conventional PCM multiplex hierarchy (see Sec. 5.3.2).

In the United States, radio links in the 4-GHz band (3700 to 4200 MHz) are most frequently found, followed by the 6 GHz and, more recently, the 11-GHz bands. Technically, the lower-frequency bands are the "easiest" to use; movement upward in frequency has been spurred by congestion in the lower bands, and made possible by improvements in technology.

At these frequencies, propagation is essentially line-of-sight, requiring repeaters to extend a circuit over long distances. Depending on terrain, losses, and other factors, a single hop may cover a distance of 100 km or more, or could be as short as 10 km. Consequently, the cost of long-haul terrestrial microwave circuits is distance sensitive, increasing roughly in proportion to distance.

Some early experimental microwave radio links were established in the mid-1930s. The principal impetus for development, however, was due to the overriding military requirements for reliable, high-quality communications between terminals

---

[9] Among the proposed changes being investigated at this writing (1979) are the addition of frequencies in the region 10.57 to 10.68 GHz, which would be allocated specifically for local digital microwave distribution networks.

Table 5.2. *Principal Microwave Bands Authorized for Fixed Telecommunications in the United States*[a] (1979).

Band Name	Range (GHz)	Maximum Channel Bandwidth (MHz)	Necessary Spectral Efficiency (bits/Hz)	Type of Service
2 GHz	1.71 – 1.85	—		Federal government
2 GHz	1.85 – 1.99	8		Private; local government
2 GHz	2.11 – 2.13	3.5	2	Common carrier (shared)
2 GHz	2.13 – 2.15	0.8/1.6		Private; local government
2 GHz	2.15 – 2.16	10		Private; multipoint
2 GHz	2.16 – 2.18	3.5	2	Common carrier
2 GHz	2.18 – 2.20	0.8/1.6		Private; local government
2 GHz	2.20 – 2.29	—		Federal government
2 GHz	2.45 – 2.50	0.8		Private; local government (shared)
4 GHz	3.70 – 4.20	20	4.5	Common carrier; satellite
6 GHz	5.925– 6.425	30	3	Common carrier; satellite
6 GHz	6.525– 6.875	5/10		Private; shared
7–8 GHz	7.125– 8.40	—		Federal government
10 GHz	10.550–10.680	25		Private
11 GHz	10.7 –11.7	50	2.25	Common carrier
12 GHz	12.2 –12.7	10/20		Private; local government
13 GHz	13.2 –13.25	25		Common carrier; private
14 GHz	14.4 –15.25	—		Federal government
18 GHz	17.7 –19.7	220		Common carrier; shared
18 GHz	18.36 –19.04	50/100		Private; local government
22 GHz	21.2 –23.6	50/100		Private; common carrier
31 GHz	31.0 –31.2	50/100		Private; common carrier
38 GHz	36.0 –38.6	—		Federal government
40 GHz	38.6 –40.0	50		Private; common carrier
	Above 40.0	—		Developmental

[a]There are many footnotes and qualifications within each band; reference should be made to Federal Communications Commission Rules and Regulations, Part 21 for common carriers and Part 94 for private usage. Spectral efficiency requirements apply only if digital modulation is employed.

that could be rapidly redeployed. The first production system, AN/TRC-1, appeared in 1943, which was capable of establishing four voice circuits over a distance of 40 mi. This was quickly followed by the AN/TRC-6 which provided for eight circuits over 40 mi at 2 GHz. The first commercial system was introduced in 1949 by Western Union; this system still carries traffic over the New York City–Boston route. Microwave radio designed specifically for digital transmission appeared in commercial service in Japan during the late 1960s and in the United States in the early 1970s.

5.3.1 Modern Digital Microwave Radio

Currently, the majority of digital transmission by microwave radio is accomplished by hybrid techniques, involving modifications to the extensive existing analog transmission plant. Numerous schemes have been employed, including the obvious device of employing modems operating with portions of the analog multiplex spectrum.

Another particularly clever technique has also enjoyed widespread use in North America, Europe, and Japan. This technique, called *data under voice* (DUV) in the United States, takes advantage of the relatively lower SNR required for acceptable error rates in digital transmission, and uses portions of the existing radio baseband spectrum that are unsuitable for analog transmission. Thus digital circuits can be added on previously all-analog routes, without subtracting from the analog capacity. A typical DUV implementation adds a T1 digital carrier (1.544 Mbps) using partial-response signaling below the spectrum of an 600-channel (analog) FDM master group.

As new routes are being built and radio equipment on older routes is being replaced, all-digital radios are appearing with increasing frequency. Even for telephony, the motivations are numerous — increased fidelity of transmission, lower operating costs, direct interface with digital switching, and local digital loops, to name a few. Manufacturers of microwave radios have responded with equipment suitable for truly wideband digital transmission.

Some characteristics of typical second-generation digital radios are listed in Tab. 5.3. These radios are used in both commercial common-carrier and dedicated private networks. In terms of required SNR to achieve a given error rate and bandwidth efficiency, these radios provide a performance level within 2 to 3 dB of that predicted by theory. Other digital radio equipments, along with detailed link design information, are summarized in [CUCC 79] and [DIGI 80].

The radio input–output is a digital data stream at the defined rate. Normally, the modem section of the radio also contains scrambler–descrambler and/or encoding–decoding circuitry. Scrambling in this sense is not to be confused with encryption. The function of the scrambler is to randomize the incoming bit pattern to maintain the transmitted power spectrum's independence from the bit pattern (see Chap. 7); for example, a string of continuous 1's or 0's would otherwise produce a strong low-frequency component in the baseband spectrum. The encoding process (here, *not* error coding) is related to the particular modulation method employed, and frequently also inserts additional operational information such as clock, framing, fault alarms, and service channels. Of course, the encoding function can also perform the scrambling function.

In Tab. 5.3, the receiver threshold is expressed in terms of dBW threshold necessary to achieve the given error rate, as is usually found in specification sheets (sometimes expressed in dBm, referred to 1 mW; dBW = dBm - 30). This number takes into account the bandwidth, receiver noise figure, type of modulation used, and internal losses. It is the qualified equivalent of P_R of Eq. (5.3), and can be substituted for the sum of B, F, 204 dBW, and SNR in analyses of the form of Eq. (5.6a) and Box 5.1 to calculate directly the required transmitter power and antenna gains.

The sizes given in Tab. 5.3 are for the single radio equipment alone; considerably more must be added to achieve a workable radio link. Multiplexers are required to form and break down individual channels. The radio and multiplex equipment require dc power, which must be supplied from some form of power supply: line-operated power supplies, batteries, solar cells, fueled generators, and so on. Usually, combinations are used to provide backup in case of failure of the primary power

Table 5.3. *Typical Digital Microwave Radios.*

	2 GHz	6 GHz	11 GHz	18 GHz
Frequency band	Farinon	Raytheon	Collins	NEC
Manufacturer				
Model	DMI-2C	6200	MDR-11	TRPI8GD274MB-1
Capacity (voice channels)	192	1344	1344	4032[a]
Data rate (Mbps)	2 x 6.132	90.148	90.258	274[a]
Occupied bandwidth (MHz)	7	30	40	220
Spectrum utilization (bps/Hz)	1.8	3	2.25	1.25[a]
Type of modulation	16 QAM	8 PSK	8 PSK	QPSK
Transmit power (dBm)	+33	+38	+40	+29
Receiver sensitivity for 10^{-6} BER (dBm)	-82	-67	-68	-68
Power requirements (VA or W)	-24 V dc 10.5 A -48 V dc 6.5 A	-24 V dc 28 A -48 V dc 14 A	-24 V dc 26 A term -24 V dc 44 A rep.	-48 V dc 1.8 A term -48 V dc 1.4 A rep.
Size	19 in. x 12 in. x 7 ft.	20.5 in. x 15 in. x 9 ft.	20.5 in. x 8.85 in. x 7 ft.	1875 mm x 112 mm x 445 mm
Weight (lb)	290	375	330	320

[a]Requires dual polarization to achieve these capacities.

supply. Antennas and their supporting structures must be provided — a major expense item if a tower must be erected. Normally, multiple radio and multiplex units are used for redundancy and diversity. These requirements are discussed in the following paragraphs of this section.

The estimated cost of one typical complete site (terminal or repeater) in a fixed-service wideband radio link system might break down as follows:

Dual radio, alarms, MUX, and associated electronic equipment	$120,000
Power and HVAC equipment	45,000
Tower, antennas, transmission lines, etc.	65,000
Civil works: shelter, fencing, access road, etc.	65,000
Land, erection rights, etc.	25,000
Allocated spares and test equipment	30,000
	$350,000

These estimates are inclusive in the sense that management, engineering, planning, installation, and test costs have been allocated. For any specific site, however, these costs could vary by a factor of 2 or more, depending on numerous factors. For example, site location can be the largest variable, since it determines the cost of land or erection rights, ease of access for construction and maintenance, the requirements for antenna tower and equipment housing, tower height, environmental control of the equipment, kinds of power supplies, and even difficulties in technical engineering such as frequency planning, interference avoidance, and required system margin.

Another variable, of course, is the equipment cost. In the example, dual-redundant radios with space diversity and multiplex to the DS2 level have been assumed. Different arrangements, such as frequency diversity and multiplex to the individual channel level, would modify equipment costs and would also affect power and HVAC requirements. However, a major point to be derived from the example is based on the observation that the radio equipment itself accounts for less than one-third of the total cost of this particular example—significant changes in equipment configuration and even bandwidth will have a relatively small impact on total cost.

5.3.2 Digital Multiplex

The radios described above accept a synchronous data stream at the indicated rates. Because these radios are normally used in commercial telephone networks, multiplexers used with them follow the practices that have grown up in that industry, and are related as much to cable and wireline transmission as to radio. Figure 5.9 illustrates the three principal muliplex hierarchies in wide use today to build up digitized voice [pulse-code modulation (PCM)] channels into high-speed data streams. Note that the output line rates are greater than the sum of the input-line rates.

REGION	Equivalent Channel	MULTIPLEX LEVEL			
		1	2	3	4
North America		(24)	(4)	(7)	(6)
Output Line Rate (Mbps)	0.064	1.544	6.312	44.736	274.176
Number of Voice Channels	1	24	96	672	4032
Designation		DS-1 (T1)	DS-2 (T2)	DS-3 (T3)	DS-4 (T4)
Conference Europeene des Postes et Tele-communicacions Consortium (CEPT, Europe)		(30)	(4)	(4)	(4)
Output Line Rate (Mbps)	0.064	2.048	8.448	34.368	139.264
Number of Voice Channels	1	30	120	480	1920
Japan		(24)	(4)	(5)	(4)
Output Line Rate (Mbps)	0.064	1.544	6.312	32.064	97.728
Number of Voice Channels	1	24	96	480	1440

Figure 5.9. The three principal PCM multiplex hierarchies in use throughout the world. Occasionally, in the North American hierarchy one finds intermediate levels made up of two lower-level streams; for example, T1C is 2 x 1.544 = 3.088 Mbps.

At the higher multiplex levels, this is due to the additional bits needed for framing, synchronizing, and alarms.

The same mechanisms are used in the lowest multiplex level, but additional information is also inserted in the data stream. For example, in the CEPT first level, a maximum of 30 channels (64 kbps each) is available, which would require an aggregate rate of 1.92 Mbps. Compared with 2.048 Mbps, the difference is 128 kbps, the equivalent of two more channels. In addition to synchronization and framing, these two "surplus" channels are used to carry channel signaling (call status) information, hence the name "30 + 2" commonly used to designate this level.

In the United States, it is not yet possible for a customer to take complete advantage of public network T-carrier transmission, or even have direct access at the indicated levels. The one exception is that, within a radius of a few miles from those central offices equipped with T-carrier, it is possible to obtain a "T1 line." However, those offices are generally confined to the larger cities, are sparse even within these cities, and the transparent data rate available to the customer is only 1.344 Mbps. The remaining 200 kbps is devoted to the carrier's timing and synchronization. At central offices in larger cities, direct digital service at the 56-kbps input rate is available. Elsewhere, service usually involves a modem-based unit operating on the equivalent of a 48-kHz analog "group" which would normally contain 12 analog voice channels. Of course, in a privately owned system, the designer is free to utilize the available multiplexer ports as best fit the system requirements.

5.3.3 Microwave Radio-Link Antennas

By far the most common type of microwave antenna is the "dish" type, so-called because the paraboloidal reflector resembles the shape of a dish. The flashlight analogy used earlier can be continued—the reflector is illuminated by a "feed," which is analogous to the filament of the flashlight bulb. The shape of the beam and its secondary responses (side lobes and backward response) are controlled by a nonuniform feed illumination pattern and reflector shape, using the same mathematics as in filter theory.

The gain of an antenna was defined in Sec. 5.2.1. The effective area of a dish antenna (the term A) is the physical area of the reflector, reduced by an efficiency factor related to the illumination pattern and the slight shadowing by the feed structure. Normally, the ratio of effective area to physical area is about 6/10. The beamwidth is approximately $1.2\lambda/D$ radians, where D is the diameter and λ is the operating wavelength. A typical antenna for the 6-GHz band has a diameter of 8 ft (2.5 m), gain of 41.5 dB, beamwidth of 1.4°, and maximum off-axis response (side lobe level) of -22 dB with respect to the main beam.

Disregarding other factors, one would be inclined to use the highest gain antenna available: transmitter power would be low, receiver SNR would be high, and interference would be minimized. Obviously, at some point in increasing gain, the physical size of the antenna would become a problem. The most important considerations, however, are associated with the inverse relationship of gain and beamwidth. Even assuming that two very high gain, extremely narrow beamwidth antennas can be initially aligned, maintaining that alignment could be a problem. Torsion and sway of an economically feasible tower (or building) could result in complete decoupling of the antennas. Further, it will be recalled from Sec. 5.2 that atmospheric anomalies can substantially change the beam position. These considerations lead to at least one case where more gain is not necessarily better.

On the other hand, the Federal Communications Commission effectively limits the *minimum* gain of an antenna for fixed-service radio. The intention is to restrict interference with other radio links (including satellite) that may be in the same area, by reducing the area illuminated by a given transmitter. For example, FCC Regulations

Part 94 for Fixed Private Service Microwave limits the maximum beamwidth in the 12-GHz band to 1° in congested areas, or 2° in less congested areas. The corresponding antenna gains are approximately 45 and 39 dB, respectively.[10]

Antennas are available that are sensitive to the polarization of the radiated/incident electromagnetic energy. A linearly polarized antenna mounted in one particular way may radiate and receive only horizontal polarization; rotated axially by 90°, that antenna would respond only to vertical polarization. Dual polarization antennas are available, which combine two separate feeds maintaining such an orthogonal relationship. The decoupling between the feeds is 25 dB or more, quite sufficient for digital transmission. It is thus possible to reuse the same radio frequency and associated spectrum for another independent channel. This is frequently done to provide for an independent backup channel, or even to double the capacity of an established path.

Microwave radio-link antennas are usually placed at considerable heights above ground level, to extend the radio horizon and thus the range of the link. The decisions as to location and height of antennas are made by path profiling, considering the topography of the intervening terrain and the various propagation factors discussed earlier. Normally, antenna heights are chosen to provide first Fresnel zone clearance of any intervening obstacle and to minimize super-refractive multipath fading [REFE 77, FREE 75].

The first Fresnel zone is defined as that contour between two antennas, on which a reflecting point establishing a secondary path would reflect signal energy one-half wavelength (180°) out of phase with respect to the received energy via the primary path, as illustrated in Fig. 5.10. Clearance of an obstacle is taken as 0.6 times the first Fresnel zone radius (R), defined as

$$R = 17.3 \left(\frac{d_1 d_2}{f(d_1 d_2)} \right)^{\frac{1}{2}} \quad \text{meters}$$

(5.7)

where f = frequency (GHz)

d_1 = distance from transmitter to path obstacle (km)

d_2 = distance from obstacle to receiver

The transmission line which carries the expensively produced and preciously conserved radio-frequency signals to and from a high antenna is of considerable importance. Waveguide is the lowest-loss transmission line, but lower-cost coaxial cable is often used. Special steps can be taken to maintain minimum loss, such as pressurization with inert gas or dried air to preclude H_2O absorption. Occasionally, a periscope antenna system is used—the antenna is located near ground level; a flat reflector mounted on the tower serves to aim the beam from the desired height.

Given the requirements for towers with the necessary rigidity, it is not unusual

[10]By the same token, maximum transmitter power *and* effective isotropic radiated power (EIRP) are limited. Transmitter power is 20 W maximum, 512 MHz to 10 GHz; 10 W, above 10 GHz. EIRP = transmitter power x antenna gain, and is limited to +55 dBW; thus *maximum* antenna gain is also constrained.

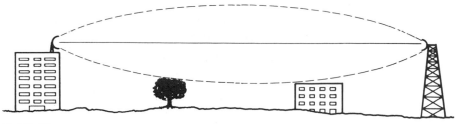

79-123-022

Figure 5.10. Path clearance for a microwave radio link.

for the overall antenna structure to be more costly than the actual radio equipment. Also, because of the many factors to be considered and the necessity for path surveys, the majority of the engineering costs of radio-link design can be associated with the antenna system. Adding the costs of a shelter building and associated costs of the land and power can result in support costs that overwhelm the cost of the radio equipment alone.

5.3.4 Radio Path Availability: Redundancy and Diversity

The availability of a radio link is affected both by the conventional considerations of equipment reliability and maintenance, and by anomalistic characteristics of the radio propagation path as outlined in Sec. 5.2.2. In the sense of protecting against equipment failure, availability can be improved substantially by appropriate system designs based on use of redundant equipments. Radio system design practices have also evolved which make major improvements in path availability; these techniques are also based on the ideas of redundancy since both equipment and path failures are probabilistic in nature. A current practice in radio-link engineering allows, of the total objective outage time, 50% for equipment failures, 25% for rain, and 25% for multipath fading.

As discussed in Sec. 5.2.2, fading in a radio channel is most commonly caused by the constructive or destructive interference resulting from a given multipath propagation situation. The relative phase shift of the received signal energy over each of the paths is related to the radio frequency, polarization, and relative positions of the transmitter antenna, receiver antenna, and intervening reflective or refractive objects. A familiar example of multipath fading is the "flutter" seen and heard on a television receiver when an airplane reflects some of the transmitted signal, which in turn interferes with the direct path signal. Another example indicative of the special problems experienced by mobile radio users is the sporadic multipath fading heard on an FM car radio as the automobile moves, changing its position with respect to direct and reflected paths.

With microwave radio, reflective multipath from the earth's surface is usually not severe on overland paths of average terrain, when adequate Fresnel-zone clearance has been provided. Fading on overwater paths, however, can be particularly severe. Coastal regions, combining smooth, flat terrain with high atmospheric humidity, can also be very troublesome. Fading also is a function of path length and frequency [RUTH 71].

A simple but effective method of combating multipath is the use of larger antennas, which provide smaller beamwidths. A larger antenna on the transmitter illuminates a smaller volume of space, thereby lessening the probability of creating a multipath situation. Similarly, a larger receiver antenna responds to fewer possible alternative paths. However, as previously discussed, there are practical limitations on antenna size, meaning that other methods usually must be employed on radio links having high availability requirements.

Fixed Radio Diversity Techniques

Consider two receivers, each equipped with an independent antenna. The temporal correlation between multipath-induced fades in each receiver will approach zero as the spacing between the antennas is increased, meaning that it is unlikely that a fade will occur simultaneously in both receivers. This is a form of space diversity — two diverse paths are established by positioning differences. Because most multipath occurs in the vertical plane, vertical spacing of antennas is normally used. Various techniques exist which allow the better channel to be used at a given time; often, rather elaborate combining techniques are employed to provide a continuous output. In line-of-sight paths, vertical space diversity can also protect against some fades resulting from changes in the atmosphere's refractive index (K factor).

Frequency diversity is an alternative method of protecting against fades. It is unlikely that a multipath fade will be simultaneously experienced at a frequency sufficiently far removed from that at which a fade is currently in progress. When this technique is used alone, it is most commonly implemented with the same antennas, but of course with transmitters and receivers equipped to communicate simultaneously on different frequencies. A major disadvantage of frequency diversity is the increased spectrum occupancy required.

A third possibility of diversity is polarization diversity, mentioned in Sec. 5.3.3. Although polarization diversity is useful, the degree of decorrelation is not complete in most cases. Also, at microwave frequencies, precipitation tends to scramble the sense of polarization, further reducing the degree of orthogonality.

Diversity techniques can be both repeated and combined, which increases the order of diversity and consequently the degree of protection against anomalistic behavior of the radio path. Although much theoretical work has been directed toward prediction of the "improvement factor" to be expected from diversity, the most useful information derives from curve fitting of empirical data [WHIT 75, BARN 70, VIGA 75]. These curves are fairly complex functions of numerous variables, including the design fade margin itself. Typical values for I_{fd} (improvement factor for frequency diversity), and I_{sd} (for space diversity) are shown in Box 5.2.

To calculate the effect on path availability A, the factor is used as a divisor for the "unavailability" U in the relation $A = 1 - U/I$. Thus if the nondiversity availability

Box 5.2. *Typical Microwave Diversity Improvement Factors.*

Given:	Frequency	=	6-GHz band
	Path length	=	50 km
	Fade margin	=	40-dB design

Frequency Diversity	Space Diversity
Frequency difference = Δf = 125 MHz	Vertical antenna spacing = 12 m
Improvement factor = $I_{fd} \simeq 50$	Improvement factor = $I_{sd} \simeq 200$
Scaling	Scaling
With frequency: $f^{0.8}$	With frequency: f
With Δf: Δf	With spacing: S^2

of the radio path of Box 5.2 were 0.999, the application of space diversity would raise availability to $A = 1 - 0.001/200 = 0.999995$ — a major improvement.

In the example of Box 5.2, space diversity gives an improvement factor significantly greater than frequency diversity. Operationally, space diversity is also more desirable because of spectrum conservation considerations. Space diversity is more expensive in implementation, however, due to the necessary additional antennas and feed lines. The additional tower height and strength required to support the antennas can also increase costs substantially.

Digital Radio Path Considerations

Until recently, almost all treatments of microwave radio path availability have been based on observations with analog FDM radio. Recent data indicate that extrapolation to wideband digital modulation is not necessarily in order [BARN 78, SHAR 78]. The frequency-selective nature of multipath is manifested in amplitude and phase distortion over the spectral width of the modulated carrier. To the first order, FDM-FM analog systems are not much affected by these characteristics because the portion of the spectrum occupied by an individual channel is relatively small. However, with digital modulation, such discreteness does not obtain because a bit of information representing *any* channel can occupy the entire transmitted spectrum. A constant-slope amplitude characteristic that varies only a small amount over a small portion of the spectrum can amount to a substantial variation over a 20-to 90-MHz digitally modulated spectrum, and result in a substantial error rate. An amplitude slope of as little as 0.2 dB/MHz over the system bandwidth can degrade the error rate to 10^{-3} [BARN 78]. One set of empirical data [GIGE 80], obtained on a radio link operating at 4 GHz within a 45 Mbps, 8-PSK signal, shows that an error rate of 10^{-3} was reached long before the traditionally defined 41-dB fade margin was exhausted. In some cases, fade depths as low as 19 dB produced an error rate of 10^{-3} or greater.

To combat the "nonflat" fading of multipath, digital microwave radios are becoming available equipped with adaptive equalizers. Fortunately, relatively simple circuits can effectively compensate for the time-varying distortion characteristic of multipath [HART 80]. Using adaptive equalizers alone, improvement factors (defined previously) ranging from 6 to 20 have been reported. When combined with space diversity, surprisingly, improvement factors increase dramatically, exceeding by several times the product of the separate improvement factors. A combined space diversity/adaptive equalizer improvement factor of over 700 on a 90-Mbps radio operated at 8 GHz over a 50-km path has been reported [ANDE 78].

Special Situations

When either the transmitting or receiving antenna (or both) must have a large beamwidth, multipath interference can become a severe problem. Obviously, this can be the case in omnidirectional or cellular broadcast services and mobile radio communications. It is frequently impossible to use either space or frequency diversity in such situations.

In wideband digital radio systems, the bandwidth can be large enough to resolve the signals received via the separate, multiple paths. For instance, a transmitted 10-nsec pulse would appear to a receiver as three pulses, if the delays over two secondary paths were larger than 10 nsec (3 m). A form of diversity can be built into the waveform in such cases, as discussed by Nielsen in Volume II.

5.4 MILLIMETER RADIO

The International Telecommunications Union defines the region of radio-frequency spectrum from 30 to 300 GHz (wavelength 10 to 1 mm) as millimeter waves. Some, however, regard operating frequencies above the 14-15 GHz band as being in the millimeter region, because of similarities in propagation characteristics.

Interest in millimeter radio is high for several reasons. For one, if practicable bandwidth is taken to be 10% of operating frequency, then bandwidths of 1.5 to 30 GHz could be available. Further, equipment sizes (in particular, antennas) would be expected to scale inversely with frequency. Perhaps most important, congestion in the lower frequencies continues to force the utilization of new, unused portions of the spectrum.

There are two major obstacles to exploitation of millimeter radio. One obstacle is fundamental — the propagation characteristics of millimeter waves are greatly affected by the atmosphere. In the microwave region, excess path loss is measured in small fractions of a dB per kilometer in the normal atmosphere (no precipitation). In the millimeter-wave region, losses can be greater by several orders of magnitude. Fig. 5.3 displays typical data for average atmospheric conditions. Attenuation is very high at frequencies corresponding to the molecular resonances of water vapor (about 22 and 183 GHz) and the oxygen lines (around 60 and 119 GHz). This curve suggests several natural atmospheric windows for radio transmission where attenuation is lower: viz., the bands in the range 30 to 40, 75 to 95, and 125 to 140 GHz. The FCC has allocated 28 channels at 50 MHz each, at 38.6 to 40.0 GHz, for fixed radio service.

At 35 GHz, moderately heavy rainfall (25 mm/hr) adds a path loss of about 5 dB/km. In the next-higher band, around 85 GHz, rain loss would be around 12 dB/km. One important consequence derives from the fact that these quantities express differences in path loss over time; it is necessary that the receiver be able to accommodate a large range of signal levels between threshold and saturation, to avoid the introduction of distortion products.

Atmospheric anomalies also produce more substantial effects in the millimeter-wave region. At these short wavelengths, fluctuations are rapid, having a period in the order of seconds. A very rough, but conservative estimate for scintillation fading (after data from [LANE 68]) is $\pm df/160$ dB, where d is the path distance (km) and f the frequency in GHz. Scintillation fading at 85 GHz over a 10-km path would be about ± 5 dB. Because scintillation tends to be frequency selective, a major problem can exist with distortion of wideband signals.

These propagation losses are large numbers, which suggest relatively high transmitter power, high antenna gain, and low receiver noise factor. This leads to the second obstacle in exploiting the millimeter region. As happened in the microwave region, much of the development of millimeter technology has been spurred by military requirements. However, very few commercial millimeter-wave equipments are yet available. Further, the propagation losses tend to negate the expected reduction in equipment size and power. The resultant cost/performance ratio, compared with microwave, is not yet attractive. Nevertheless, as the demand for spectrum increases, a larger commercial market will appear.

Evidence of very recent and rapid progress in millimeter-wave technology is appearing for both military and commercial applications [TAUB 80, MICR 79]. Exotic solid-state devices are appearing to perform the necessary functions of oscillators, amplifiers, and mixers. Devices well known in microwave technology — such as field-effect transistors; Gunn-effect, Schottky-barrier, and tunnel diodes — are being successfully scaled up in operating frequency. New types of components will play an important role — IMPATT, Barritt and Josephson devices, Mott profile diodes, and so on. Although silicon is still being used as a basic semiconductor material, emphasis is being placed on newer materials, such as gallium–aresenide (GaAs) and indium–phosphide (InP). Particularly at the shorter wavelengths, quasi-optical techniques are being used for signal routing and processing. Using such new technology, exploration of even the submillimeter region — 300 GHz and beyond — is well under way.

Also recently announced is the completion of widest-bandwidth transmission system of the author's knowledge [KUNO 79]. The Nippon Telephone and Telegraph Company has installed a 23-km test link operating at 43 to 87 GHz. The system has 28 channels, each carrying a 750-Mbps data rate using QPSK modulation, for a total of 21 Gbps — the equivalent of 13,000 T1 circuits. Initial reports indicate achievement of bit error rate of 10^{-7} or better. Using current signaling techniques, this system could carry 312,000 telephony, 624 black-and-white TV, or 208 color TV channels.

A currently available, off-the-shelf millimeter radio equipment is depicted in Fig. 5.11. This radio, operating in the 38-GHz band, exemplifies the compactness that can be realized at these frequencies; the transmitter, receiver, and antenna are

Figure 5.11. Current 38-GHz radio. The masthead unit contains all RF components: antenna, transcatter, and receiver. The auxiliary unit contains power supplies, modem, and external interface circuitry. (Courtesy of Norden Systems.)

contained in one integral 20-lb masthead package. The radio can carry a single video channel, or full-duplex data at the 1.544-Mbs rate, over a range up to 25 km in a clear atmosphere. A similar radio is available for operation at 60 GHz.

The Nippon Electric Company is offering a 40-GHz radio, intended for radio-link service. It supports one video signal and audio program, or one T1 (6.3-Mbps) data rate in a 50-MHz regulated bandwidth. The system is also of integrated design for pole mounting. The General Electric Company is working with prototypes of an integrated, potentially low-cost unit intended for communication up to 5 km in the newly opened 23-GHz band. Similar systems are beginning to appear from other manufacturers.

Assuming a continuation of the current trend in availability of millimeter-wave equipment, the remaining obstacle in the future will be the problems resulting from natural propagation phenomena. Since propagation variances are largely proportional to path length, their effects are ameliorated by shortening the path. For long-haul circuits, the implication is shorter repeater hops, robust modulation waveforms, and larger orders of diversity — all requiring more equipment and, therefore, higher costs. This is economically disadvantageous except for extreme bandwidth requirements or situations where the lower portions of the spectrum are saturated. However, for short paths such as in local distribution networks, millimeter radio is already an attractive alternative to microwave radio and cable transmission.

5.5 TROPOSPHERIC SCATTER RADIO

Prior to the advent of satellite communication, troposcatter radio was unique in its ability to provide beyond-line-of-sight, point-to-point transmission of high quality and relatively wide bandwidth. "Tropo" remains as the only alternative to satellite links in many situations. The operation of troposcatter radio depends on the forward-scattering properties of the earth's troposphere at certain frequencies, usually 350 to 5000 MHz. The actual scattering mechanism is not completely understood, but is generally thought to be due to a large population of discrete inhomogeneities in the troposphere. Extensive empirical data have been collected, generalizations of which allow quite accurate predictions of performance.

There are a number of troposcatter radio links in service throughout the world, providing commercial telephone service over distances ranging from 100 to 1000 km. Again, the special requirements of the military have been responsible for most of the research and development in the area, and account for the majority of currently active links.

Path losses are quite high, due to the inefficiency of the forward-scattering mechanism. Consequently, very large antennas (5 to 40 m) and high-power transmitters (0.5 to 50 kW) are common, while considerable effort is warranted in producing very low noise receivers. These factors exacerbate interference problems, thus making frequency assignment more problematical.

Because of propagation anomalies, most troposcatter systems use diversity techniques (usually combining space and frequency diversity) to improve availability. Availabilities of 99.5% and better are commonly achieved.

The troposcatter mechanism leads directly to a multipath situation. The individual scattering points within the common volume illuminated by the transmitting and receiving antennas creates paths of varying delay, resulting in an inherent bandwidth limitation. Most systems use analog FM-FDM modulation and multiplexing, and carry a maximum of about 120 voice channels, or an equivalent bandwidth of about 500 kHz. Within the last few years, very sophisticated digital modems and radios have been developed for the U.S. Department of Defense, which allow reliable transmission of data rates to 5 to 10 Mbps [CYBR 77, OSTE 77].

5.6 NETWORK RADIO OPERATION

5.6.1 Conventional Simplex/Duplex Radio Networking

Chapters 3 and 4 contain a discussion of the various access and protocol techniques useful for network operations. Generally, with suitable designs these techniques are applicable to any of the various transmission media. There are some special characteristics of radio, however, that may modify the systematic implementation of communication networks linking many users. In this section we relate the fundamental networking techniques to radio by analogy with citizen's band (CB) radio, which is familiar to many readers; and explore some other special techniques of employing radio, which will be of particular importance in future digital communication systems.

Protocols are necessary for successful operation of CB radio; many of us are aware of the chaos that results from the breakdown of the protocol's disciplines. Mobile terminals and the majority of fixed "base station" terminals operate with omnidirectional antennas; when transmitting, a terminal can be heard by (or interfere with) all other omnidirectional receivers tuned to the same frequency, within a radius of several miles. Within that area, simultaneous communication between two sets of terminals is possible if one set, by mutual agreement, selects another, unoccupied channel frequency — a form of frequency-division multiple access (FDMA). Alternatively, one set of terminals can "give the break and standby" while the other set communicates — a form of time-division multiple access (TDMA). If fixed terminals are equipped with "beam antennas," directed toward each other, the area of mutual interference is reduced — this is the basis of point-to-point radio discussed in Sec. 5.2, and can be viewed as space-division multiple access (SDMA). A further reduction in interference is possible by polarization diversity; many base station beam antennas are capable of being switched from vertical polarization to the "flat side" (horizontal polarization), which significantly reduces the coupling between antennas of the opposite (orthogonal) sense.

The analogy can be carried further. If a CB operator wishes to be certain that his transmission is heard, he must wait until there is no activity from any of the other potentially interfering transmitters. This is true whether his transmission is a short request for channel-time allocation, "break," or a longer transmission containing considerable information. The decision to transmit is based on a carrier-sense multiple-access (CSMA) protocol. [Strictly speaking, channel activity cannot always be related precisely to the presence or absence of a carrier, because some important modulation methods (e.g., single-sideband) do not contain a carrier *per se* — other means of detecting activity are necessary.] Sometimes out of frustration or lack of courtesy, an operator may resort to a perverse form of the ALOHA technique —simply repeating his transmission in the face of interference, hoping that one of them "gets through." Occasionally, formalized networks are established, using either a master net controller or a round-robin technique wherein the current transmitter designates who the successive transmitter should be.

A CB radio transmits and receives on the same frequency, but not simultaneously. In radio terminology, this is called *simplex operation*. In the same sense of network operation, however, the necessary protocol follows that of a half-duplex, multidrop broadcast configuration (because any terminal can potentially hear and respond). A particular terminal can be addressed by name or call sign (polling or TDMA), and/or previously known operating frequency (FDMA), and/or antenna aiming (SDMA).

A terminal's transmitter and receiver cannot operate simultaneously on the same frequency, because the transmitter blocks the receiver. Gating of receiver-on and transmitter-off, and vice versa, can be accomplished to arbitrarily short cycle times with exotic designs; nevertheless, the operation is still half-duplex, with the total available bandwidth split by some proportion between directions of transmission.

Full-duplex operation between two points requires two channelized frequencies, each operating in a full-time simplex mode, sufficiently offset to preclude transmitter interference in the receiver. Further isolation of transmitter and receiver can be accomplished by installing preselector filters just ahead of the receiver's front end, and by using separate transmit and receive antennas so located as to achieve a high degree of decoupling. Microwave radio links commonly use the same antenna for transmit and receive; decoupling is provided by filters and circulators that properly "steer" transmitted and received signals. In all cases, the transmit and receive frequencies must be chosen such that secondary responses characteristic of the receiver are avoided.

5.6.2 Cellular Radio

Cellular radio is a system concept intended to ameliorate spectrum congestion problems associated with the use of radio for local distribution purposes. While the original intent was to provide for mobile telephone services in an urban environment, the same concepts are useful for wideband communications for multiple fixed terminals.

Mobile telephone service is currently provided by a maximum of 25 channels in the UHF band, broadcast by a single high-power base station serving an entire city. Only one channel can be used at a time. Frequency reuse is possible only beyond the radio horizon — say, 50 mi. Thus only 25 channels are available in an area of about 8,000 mi^2, making large-scale service impractical and imposing a poor grade of service on even a very limited set of subscribers.

The cellular concept divides the served area into considerably smaller cells. Each cell is allocated a set of frequencies, and is served by a cell node, comprising a low-power transmitter, receiver, and control unit. A cell sufficiently distant can reuse a frequency assigned to a given cell; it is expected that a frequency can be reused 20 or more times within the area, thus increasing the network capacity by a substantial amount. As the number of subscribers grows, the cells could be split into subcells, allowing a potential of several hundred thousand subscribers to be served [BLEC 80].

A mobile terminal could transit several cells during the course of a single call. The control units "track" the terminal, handing it off to the appropriate cell site as a boundary is crossed. Because a frequency change is involved, command information must be transmitted to the terminal, and tight coordination is necessary between the two cell nodes and the terminal, to effect the switchover while maintaining the call. Obviously, such procedures would not be necessary with fixed terminals.

Variations on this SDMA/FDMA theme are possible. For example, cells could be covered by sector antennas rather than omnidirectional antennas. Four centrally located antennas, each having a 90+° beamwidth, could each cover a quadrant of a circularly shaped cell (or wholly different cell shapes could be adopted). It would be possible to reuse frequencies between the new "quarter-cells," or time-division and code-division multiple-access (TDMA or CDMA) techniques could be applied (see Sec. 5.6.4 and Chap. 6).

A trial of the cellular technique for mobile telephone service is being conducted by the Bell System in Chicago, using 10 cells covering a 2100 mi^2 area, in the new 800-MHz mobile band [BELL 79]. In the second phase, commencing in July 1979, up to 2500 terminals were into the system. Another system, operated by American Radio Telephone Service and using Motorola equipment, began trials in the Baltimore–Washington area in 1981.

The XTEN electronic message network proposed by Xerox [WILE 78, SATE 78] is unique in that the local distribution problem would be solved by a digital, cellular, fixed radio technique. Digital transmission links between a regional satellite earth station and several local cell nodes would be established by conventional point-to-point radio in the 10.6-GHz band, with a full-duplex data rate of 15 Mbps. The local nodes would have omnidirectional transmit/receive coverage for their assigned cell frequencies, also in the 10.6-GHz band. Cells would have a 6-mi radius. Since the subscriber terminal antennas are fixed (normally on the rooftop) and communicate only with its assigned cell node, they would be high-gain, directional antennas aimed at the node. Consistent with the broadcast nature of the node-to-subscriber link, downstream transmissions would be segregated by a combination of frequency and packet-address division (requiring encryption to assure privacy). The subscriber-to-node link would operate on a TDMA, demand-assignment basis in increments of 256 kbps. It is noted that polarization diversity could also be used for further segregation and frequency reuse, because all antennas are fixed.

Although Xerox abandoned the XTEN project in 1981 for financial reasons, its innovative concepts remain both technically sound and economically viable. The existing means of local distribution to individual subscribers, being dependent on the analog public telephone networks, is limited essentially to 9.6 kbps—hardly suitable for wideband computer communication or other integrated digital services (see Chap. 17). Circumventing this bottleneck with technologies similar to the XTEN fixed-service cellular radio concept is essential to the rapid development of wideband, shared-usage transmission to subscriber's premises. In 1981, the FCC invited first applications for such services, now called Digital Termination Service, in the frequency band of 10.55 to 10.68 GHz.

5.6.3 Packet Radio

During the past decade, new techniques of using digital radio have emerged, which are having a profound impact on networking concepts. Work began at the University of Hawaii in 1968 on the ALOHA system, employing a powerful means of taking advantage of the broadcast nature of radio [KUO 73, ABRA 73]. In its original concept, the ALOHA system implemented a star network, comprising central host computers connected to an omnidirectional base transmitter–receiver at the hub; and numerous terminals located throughout the Hawaiian islands, each equipped with an inexpensive transceiver. Two 100-kHz channels are used in the UHF band—407.350

MHz for the computer-to-terminal link, and 413.475 MHz for terminal-to-computer link. Data to be transmitted to a terminal are formatted into fixed-length packets, preceded by a header containing the intended terminal's address, and appended by a trailer containing an error detection checksum. Each terminal receives a transmitted packet and discards those not addressed to it. Any corruption during transmission is detected when the terminal checks the error-detecting code; if an error is detected, the terminal does not acknowledge receipt of the packet, which causes the base to retransmit that packet. Thus the computer-terminal link operates much like a conventional multipoint line.

The common terminal-computer link, however, operates in a most unconventional manner. A terminal's transceiver formats data intended for the computer into a packet, made up as before, and simply transmits it on the common channel. Since the channel is shared by many terminals, it is possible that two or more terminals may transmit simultaneously, a condition referred to as *packet collision*. When such a situation occurs, the base receiver does not send acknowledgments for those packets; it may not even be able to recognize the originator. If, after a suitable time, the terminal does not receive an acknowledgment from the base, it reschedules the packet for retransmissin at a random time. Eventually, all packets will be correctly received at the base and acknowledged. Although maximum utilization of the channel is $1/2e = 18.4\%$, the payoff is a multiple-access technique that is extremely simple to implement and conservative of spectrum. Chapter 4 contains a detailed discussion of the ALOHA protocols and numerous variants.

The DARPA[11] Packet Radio technology currently in development is based on techniques derived from the ALOHA and ARPANET systems [KAHN 75]. In the original ALOHA System, there is a master–slave relationship between a single base and its terminals. DARPA Packet Radio is intended to provide equal status to any member of the network, and to allow direct intercommunication between the members. Terminals can join or quit the network at will, and can be mobile.

Another distinguishing feature of Packet Radio is that a single-channel allocation is used for *both* transmit and receive functions. Operating in the vicinity of 1800 MHz (an available frequency reserved for government use), the experimental Packet Radio Network can support peak user data rates up to 1000 kbps. The actual occupied spectrum is considerably larger, because spread-spectrum techniques are used. Chapter 14 treats Packet Radio in detail.

5.6.4 Spread-Spectrum and Code-Division Multiple Access

A spread-spectrum system is loosely defined as one that employs considerably more spectrum width than would normally be required to convey the transmitted information [DIXO 76]. Spread-spectrum techniques in radio transmission have recently been receiving considerable attention, and they undoubtedly will have a profound

---

[11]Defense Advanced Research Projects Agency, an agency of the U.S. Department of Defense.

effect on future applications of radio. Spread spectrum offers one path toward relief in the crowded radio spectrum and creates a new dimension in multiple-access technology. Military interest is high for the same reasons; additionally, desirable characteristics such as antijam properties and low detectability of transmitters are available.

Suppose that there were only one television station in your area, and that you desire to watch a 1-hr program that starts at 8:00 on channel 2. Further suppose that the station publishes a schedule that calls for it to switch transmission from channel 2 to channel 3 at 8:05, from channel 3 to channel 4 at 8:10, and so on. Knowing the schedule, you simply switch your channel selector to the appropriate channel at the correct time. Except for a small "switching transient," you would enjoy continuous reception. A timer could be programmed to do the channel switching for you, eliminating the inconvenience.

Over the course of the hour, the transmitter (and your receiver) would cover all 12 channels of the VHF TV spectrum. However, at any given time, only one channel is occupied. The other 11 channels could also be used by other transmitters following different schedules, so nothing is lost and there is potential gain, as outlined below.

The foregoing is a simple example of a frequency-hopping spread-spectrum technique. In actual implementation, the transmission is usually in digital form, the dwell time (T) on any one frequency is much shorter, and the choice of frequencies (N) larger. Such a system has several very useful characteristics:

1. The frequency-versus-time program can be a pseudo-random sequence or code, making it extremely difficult for an unintended receiver to derive any information.
2. Multiple transmitters and receivers can be accommodated within the same overall assigned portion of spectrum by assignment of different codes. Multiple access can be effected by code selection — this is called code-division multiple access (CDMA).
3. If the frequencies are spaced at least as far apart as the bandwidth required to support the information rate, the hopped transmissions will not overlap in the spectrum and the "processing gain" is $G_P = 1/N$.
4. If the spectrum of interference or jamming is less than the information bandwidth, the system's performance will be improved by the processing gain. This is because the interference enters the receiver only during the dwell time on its discrete portion of the spectrum; hence interference is reduced by the processing gain G_P (see, however, [HOUS 78]).
5. The converse is also true—the time-averaged interference caused by a frequency-hopping transmitter to a fixed-tuned (conventional) receiver will also be reduced by G_P. Interference between transmitter–receiver parts, or even networks, operating in the same spectrum space can be kept negligible, or zero, by managing mutual intersections of the codes.
6. Note that, to produce the same signal-to-interference power ratio in a frequency-hopping receiver, a fixed jammer would have to increase *both* its bandwidth *and* power by factor of $1/G_P = N$.

These characteristics can be, and have been, carried to useful extremes. For instance, consider the fifth point above — suppose that the transmitted energy (power multiplied by time) on any one frequency is less than that necessary for detection by even the most sensitive receiver (which receiver does not know the code). One way that this can be accomplished is to make the spread-spectrum code rate higher than the information data rate. As far as that receiver is concerned, only a slight increase in the background noise level has occurred. Consequently, the receiver could not even determine that a transmission exists. Neither increasing or decreasing detection bandwidth *per se* will help, because this would do nothing to improve the match between transmission and reception. Reliable communication between synchronized terminals is made possible by reducing the tranmitted information rate to a fraction of the hopping rate; thus the integrated signal energy over the same number of hops, combined with the lower noise energy resulting from the implied smaller bandwidth, provides a sufficiently large SNR.

Several other spread-spectrum techniques are possible. "Time hopping" has analogous attributes, but is implemented by reducing duty factor (ratio of transmitter "on" time to "off" time) below unity and using an artificial modulating waveform correspondingly greater in bandwidth than the information rate. "Direct sequence" techniques can be used to generate spread-spectrum waveforms; these take advantage of the fact that an arbitrary spectrum can be synthesized in the time domain.

Recently, spread-spectrum techniques have been applied in radio network situations in which important considerations have included interference, antijam protection, multiple acessibility, and necessity. Examples are the Packet Radio Network (see Chap. 14), the TDRSS satellite data relay system (see Chap. 6), and proposals for relieving congestion in land-mobile radio services [COOP 79]. An excellent overview of the subject, supplemented by reprints of important papers, is contained in [DIXO 76]. A compact treatment of technology is provided in [BIRC 75, SCHU 77], as applied to radio data links [FEDE 75] and to satellite communication [LARU 75].

5.7 PIGGYBACK PUBLIC RADIO SERVICES

The preceding sections of this chapter have focused primarily on dedicated telecommunication applications or radio technology. In the introduction we used the more familiar forms of radio — the AM, FM, and TV entertainment services — to lay the conceptual groundwork for the specialized applications that followed. It is fitting that we close the chapter by briefly noting that these same old familiar forms of radio are poised as some of the newest alternatives to mass digital data communications.

5.7.1 Television Piggyback — Teletext

Television broadcasts can carry piggyback data services by a form of time-division multiplexing. In the television modulation format, it is necessary to provide a short vertical blanking interval between successive picture frames, which occur at a rate of 30 per second.[12] The vertical blanking interval contains various information necessary for television transmission, but enough time is unused in the interval to transmit at least 200 bits[12] of information over the TV channel bandwidth of several megahertz. Consequently, a data channel with an effective rate of about 6 kbps or more can be established, which can be used to transmit pages of alphanumeric and graphics information on a TV receiver. Systems exploiting this possibility have become known generically as Teletext.[13]

Teletext systems were pioneered in the United Kingdom by the BBC (the CEEFAX system) and the IBA (the ORACLE system). CEEFAX/ORACLE was conceived as a home information-providing system using conventional television receivers equipped with adapter circuitry and a simplified keyboard control unit. The adapter circuitry contains signal processing, decoding, a character generator based on the ASCII character set, and a display memory. The control unit is used to select the page to be displayed.

To keep costs low for the mass market, only one page of memory is provided. The control unit programs the adapter circuitry to look for and "grab" the particular page desired. This situation creates a trade-off between the number of pages accessible and the access time. In the British version of CEEFAX, each page comprises 24 rows of 40 characters, requiring approximately 1/4-sec transmission time. Thus if an average waiting time for a selected page of 12 sec is deemed acceptable, a cyclically transmitted "magazine" would be limited to 100 pages. Of course, the magazine can be changed on a time schedule, just as conventional programming, with perishable information such as news flashes and stock market reports interleaved on a frequent basis. The adapter works continuously; if normal TV programming is being viewed, the adapter continues to search for and grab the latest version of the selected page.

Trials of CEEFAX commenced in the United Kingdom in 1974; public service has been available since 1976. By 1980, full-scale trials of Teletext systems were under way in most industrialized countries of the world. In the United States, tests of various versions are being conducted in St. Louis, Salt Lake City, Philadelphia, and elsewhere. A modification of the technique has been used on national network television to provide "closed captions" of programs for the deaf.

The greatest advantage of Teletext technology will be enjoyed by subscribers to cable TV systems, in which a full-bandwidth channel can be devoted to transmission. This will allow the number of pages and/or access time per page to be improved by a factor of about 250. Further, cable systems with two-way capability can provide for subscriber interaction — the equivalent of a wideband Videotex system.

---

[12]The actual number varies with different TV broadcasting standards (e.g., NTSC in the United States, PAL or SECAM in Europe) and the specific Teletext system design.

[13]Teletext, being piggybacked on a conventional TV broadcast, obviously does not provide a return channel. Another technique allowing home subscriber interaction is known generically as Videotex, also pioneered in the United Kingdom as the VIEWDATA/PRESTEL system. Videotex also employs an adapted home TV receiver and keyboard but transmits data over telephone lines at 1200 bps. See [SPEC 79] for discussions of Teletext, Videotex and related techniques.

5.7.2   FM Radio Piggyback

FM radio broadcast service allows the transmission of an essentially frequency-multiplexed carrier called the *subsidiary communications authorization* (SCA). The SCA carrier is not audible on a conventional FM receiver but is capable of providing a completely independent channel on specially designed receivers. Typically, the SCA channel carries subscription background music to stores, restaurants, and so on, but the same channel is capable of digital transmission at 9600 bps.

In Woodside, California, the wireless digital Datacast service uses a SCA channel to broadcast an "electronic newspaper" similar to Teletext to owners equipped with modified FM receivers and microcomputer terminals. The channel provides a capacity the equivalent of 2500 newspaper pages per day. The microcomputer is used to select and store the subject-coded data that is of interest to the subscriber. Although the access time is slow, the potential volume of human-consumable information is enormous.

The Digital Broadcasting Corporation Infocast service, scheduled for trials in several large U.S. cities, uses a similar technical approach, but with an additional focus on an electronic message service for business and industrial subscribers. Messages (e.g., changes in inventory or item prices) are relayed from the Infocast central office to the broadcast station by telephone lines, then broadcast on the SCA channel in a block format containing the address of the intended recipient. A given receiver terminal responds to and prints only those messages addressed to it. A 300-word message reportedly can be transmitted for a cost of 13 to 29 cents, including the costs of sending and receiving terminals [INGL 79].

5.8   FUTURE OUTLOOK FOR RADIO TRANSMISSION

As we have seen, there are many diverse forms of radio serving in a large diversity of applications. The relative ease of establishing a wireless communication link will certainly remain as the primary attraction to the transmission medium of radio. Construction of long-haul microwave systems, and conversion of existing analog links to digital transmission, will continue unabated. New uses of older services, such as Videotex, Teletext and Infocast, will increase substantially.

The greatest obstacle to the growth of radio is the limited spectrum. In many areas of dense population and development, the most desirable parts of the spectrum are already saturated. The orderly reassignment of frequency bands to services that can best utilize their respective characteristics will help; such work is being undertaken at the national (e.g., FCC) and international (e.g., WARC) levels. Advances in technology, however, are prerequisite and forthcoming. Among the more important developments are:

- Exploitation of higher frequencies, in the microwave and millimeter-wave regions

- Improvements in solid-state devices and integrated circuits operating at RF frequencies
- New antenna design and deployment techniques
- Advances in modulation methods affording greater bandwidth efficiency and reduced interferences
- System architectures employing multiple-access techniques.

Of particular importance to computer communication networks are the fledgling packet radio, cellular radio, and millimeter-wave radio systems. Millimeter-wave systems promise a low-cost, easily implemented solution for point-to-point links spanning short-to-intermediate distances (say, 15 km). Cellular radio, embodying FDMA and SDMA principles, and packet radio, based on TDMA and CDMA techniques, offer very attractive possibilities for local distribution networks (Chap. 17 and [SHOC 79]). It is most likely that cross-fertilization between these developments will occur, and that prototype equipment for commercial applications will appear in the early 1980s.

The competition for terrestrial radio is satellite communication for the greater distances, and coaxial/fiber optic cable for the shorter distances. Each has certain advantages in a given situation, as discussed in subsequent chapters. Radio, however, will always play a major role in telecommunications.

Acknowledgement

The author wishes to acknowledge J. S. McLeod and J. E. Frey of Continental Page Communications, Inc., whose review and comments have been particularly helpful.

REFERENCES

ABRA 73 Abramson, N., and F. F. Kuo eds., "The ALOHA System," in *Computer Communication Networks*, Prentice-Hall, Englewood Cliffs, N.J., 1973, Chap. 14.

ANAN 80 Ananasso, F., "Coping with Rain above 11 GHz," *Microwave Sys. News*, Vol. 10, No. 3, March 1980, pp. 58–72.

ANDE 78 Anderson, C. W., S. Barberand, and R. Patel, "The Effect of Selective Fading on Digital Radio," *ICC '78 Conf. Rec.*, Vol. 2, Toronto, June 1978, pp. 33.5.1–6.

BARN 70 Barnett, W. T., "Microwave Line-of-Sight Propagation with and without Frequency Diversity," *Bell Syst. Tech. J.*, Vol. 49, No. 8, 1970.

BARN 72 Barnett, W. T., "Multipath Progation at 4.6 and 11 GHz," *Bell Syst. Tech. J.*, February 1972.

BARN 78 Barnett, W. T., "Measured Performance of a High Capacity 6 GHz Digital Radio System," *ICC '78 Conf. Rec.*, Toronto, pp. 47.4.1 to 47.4.6.

BELL 79 *Bell System Technical Journal*, Special Issue on Advanced Mobile Telephone Service, January 1979.

BENO 68   Benoit, A., "Signal Attenuation Due to Neutral Oxygen and Water Vapor, Rain and Clouds," *Microwave J.*, November 1968, pp. 73–80.

BIRC 75   Birch, J. N., "Spread Spectrum Technology Applications," *Signal*, August 1975, pp. 61–62.

BLEC 80   Blecher, F. H., "Advanced Mobile Phone Service," *IEEE Trans. Vehicular Technol.*, Vol. VT-29, May 1980, pp. 238–244.

BULL 57   Bullington, K., "Radio Propagation Fundamentals," *Bell Syst. Tech. J.*, Vol. 36, No. 3, 1957.

CCIR 78   International Telecommunications Union, Comité Consultatif International Radio (CCIR), Vol. V, Kyoto, 1978.

CHAS 75   Chasek, N., "How to Optimize Urban Microwave Density," *Telecommunications*, McGraw-Hill, New York, 1968.

COOP 79   Cooper, G. R., R. W. Nettleton, and D. P. Grybos, "Cellular Land-Mobile Radio: Why Spread Spectrum?" *IEEE Commun. Mag.*, March 1979, pp. 17–23.

COST 59   Costas, J. P., "Poisson, Shannon, and the Radio Amateur," *Proc. IRE*, Vol. 47, December 1959, pp. 2058–2068.

CRAN 78   Crane, R. K., "A Global Model for Rain Attenuation Production," *EASCON 78 Proc.*, Arlington, Va., September 1978, pp. 391–395.

CRAN 79   Crane, R. K., "Prediction of Attenuation by Rain" (submitted to *IEEE Trans. Commun.*), August 1979.

CUCC 79   Cuccia, C. L. (comp. and ed.), *The Handbook of Digital Communications*, EW Communications, Palo Alto, Calif., 1979.

CYBR 77   "Digital Tropo Modem" *Proc., AFCEA Interface Symp.*, Ft. Monmouth, N.J., 1977, pp. 65–84.

DAVE 72   Davey, J. R., "Modems," *Proc. IEEE*, Vol. 60, No. 11, 1972, pp. 1284–1292.

DIGI 80   "Digital Radio Future Bright — Probably," *MSN (Microwave System News)*, June 1980, pp. 91–108.

DIXO 76   Dixon, R. C., *Spread Spectrum Techniques*, IEEE Press, New York, 1976.

DOUG 78   Dougherty, H. T., "Atmospheric Limitations on Telecommunications Systems Performance — Recent Advances," *NTC 78 Conf. Rec.*, Vol. 2, pp. 18.1.1 to 18.1.5.

FEDE 75   Federhen, H. M., "RPV Command and Control," *Signal*, August 1975, pp. 64–67.

FEHE 77   Feher, K., *Digital Modulation Techniques in an Interference Environment*, Don White Consultants, Inc., Germantown, Md., 1977.

FREE 75   Freeman, R. L., *Telecommunication Transmission Handbook*, Wiley, New York, 1975.

GIGE 80   Giger, A. J., and W. T. Barnett, "Effects of Multipath Propagation on Digital Radio," *1980 Int. Zurich Semim. Digital Commun.*, Paper D2.

HAND 78   *Handbook and Market Guide, Fiber Optics 1978*, Information Gatekeepers, Inc., Brookline, Mass. 1978.

HART 80   Hartmann, P., and B. Bynum, "Adaptive Equalization for Digital Microwave Radio Systems," *ICC 80 Conf. Rec.*, pp. 8.5.1 to 8.5.6.

HOUS 78   Houston, S., "The Effect of CW Interference on Frequency-Hopped Waveforms," *Natl. Telecommun. Conf. '78 Record.*, pp. 43.1.1–43.1.3.

INGL 79   Ingles, K., "Two Startups, One Entrepreneur," *Venture*, June 1979, pp. 65–67.

KAHN 75   Kahn, R. E., "The Organization of Computer Resources into a Packet Radio Network," *NCC 1975 Proc.*

KUNO 79   Kuno, J., "Devices Ready for Millimeter Systems," *Microwave Syst. News*, May 1979, pp. 71–77.

KUO 73   Kuo, F. F., and N. Abramson, "Some Advance in Radio Communications for Computers," The ALOHA System Tech. Rep. No. B73-1, March 1973.

LANE 68   Lane, J. A., "Scintillation and Absorption Fading on Line-of-Sight Links at 35 and 100 GHz," *IEE Conf. Tropospheric Scatter Propagation*, London, October 1968.

LARU 75   LaRue, G. D., "The Evolution of Spread Spectrum Equipment for the Defense Satellite System Communication," *Signal*, August 1975, pp. 72–75.

LUCK 68   Lucky, R., J. Salz and E. Weldon, *Principles of Data Communications*, McGraw-Hill, New York, 1968.

LUCK 73   Lucky, R. W., "Common Carrier Data Communication," in *Computer Communication Networks*, N. Abramson and F. Kuo, eds., Prentice-Hall, Englewood Cliffs, N.J., 1973, Chap. 5.

MICR 79   *Microwave Syst. News*, Special Issue on Millimeter Waves, Vol. 9, No. 5, May 1979.

NYQU 28   Nyquist, H., "Certain Topics in Telegraph Transmission Theory," *AIEE Trans.*, Vol. 47, April 1928, pp. 614–644.

OLSE 78   Olsen, R. L., D. V. Rogers, and D. B. Hodge, "The aR^b Relation in the Calculation of Rain Attenuation," *IEEE Trans. Antennas Propagation*, Vol. AP-26, No. 2, 1978, pp. 218–239.

OSTE 77   Osterholtz, J., "Combined U.S./NATO Digital Tropo Test Program," *Proc. AFCEA Interface Symp.*, Ft. Monmouth, N.J., 1977, pp. 85–104.

PANT 65   Panter, P. F., *Modulation Noise and Spectral Analysis, Applied to Information Transmission*, McGraw-Hill, New York, 1965.

REFE 77   *Reference Data for Radio Engineers*, Howard W. Sams, Indianapolis, Ind., 1977.

RUTH 71   Ruthroff, C. L., "Multiple Path Fading on Line-of-Sight Microwave Radio Systems as a Function of Path Length and Frequency," *Bell Syst. Tech. J.*, September 1971, pp. 2375–2398.

SATE 78   *Satellite News*, Vol. 1, No. 8, Washington, December 1978.

SCHU 77   Schultz, R. A., "Spread Spectrum Concept," *IEEE Trans. Commun.*, August 1977, pp. 748–755.

SCHW 70   Schwartz, M., *Information Transmission, Modulation and Noise*, McGraw-Hill, New York, 1970.

SHAN 49   Shannon, C. E., "Communication in the Presence of Noise," *Proc. IRE*, Vol. 34, January 1949, pp. 10–21.

SHAN 79   Shanmugam, K. S., *Digital and Analog Communication Systems*, Wiley, New York, 1979.

SHAR 78   Sharma, J. S., "6/11 GHz Digital Overbuild of Analog Radio Systems," *ICC 78 Conf. Rec.*, Toronto, June 1978, pp. 33.2.1 to 33.2.6.

SHOC 79   Shock, J. F., and L. Stewart, "Interconnecting Local Networks via the Packet Radio Network," 6th Data Commun. Symp. Proc., Asilomar, Ca., November 1979, pp. 153–158.

SPEC 79   Special Issue on Consumer Text Display Systems, *IEEE Trans. Consumer Electronics*, Vol. CE-25, No. 3, July 1979.

TAUB 71   Taub, H., and D. Schilling, *Principles of Communication Systems*, McGraw-Hill, New York, 1971.

TAUB 80   Taub, J., "Will Component Advances Finally Yield Millimeter Systems?" *Microwave Syst. News*, January 1980, pp. 62–71.

VIGA 75   Vigants, A., "Space Diversity Engineering," *Bell Syst. Tech. J.*, January 1975, pp. 103–142.

WHIT 75   White, R. F., *Engineering Considerations for Microwave Communications Systems*, GTE Lenkurt, Inc., San Carlos, Calif., 1975.

WILE 78   Wiley, R. E., et al., *Xerox Corporation Petition for Rule Making*, Before the Federal Communications Commission, Washington, D.C., November 1978.

6

Wideband Transmission Media II: Satellite Communication

R. ANDREW PICKENS
Continental Communications, Inc.

Probably the single most important happening in communications during the last half of this century will be judged to have been the advent of satellite communications. For good reason—consider the following:

- A single satellite is visible to roughly a quarter of the earth's surface
- The cost of transmission is insensitive to distance, within that area
- Network connection can be effected simply by pointing an antenna at the satellite
- The communication channel can be either broadcast or point-to-point in nature
- Very wide bandwidths are available
- The quality of transmission is high.

Although it is still true that something for nothing is as elusive as the grail, the rapid advances in satellite technology have certainly led us to the land of more for less.

6.1 BACKGROUND

The first message was transmitted from a satellite in 1958 as part of Project Score, which broadcast a recording of a Christmas message by President Dwight D. Eisenhower. Subsequent early experiments in satellite communications involved passive reflectors of transmissions from earth. Examples are Echo (a giant metallized balloon, 100 ft in diameter) and West Ford (an earth-circling ring comprising millions of inch-long wires). It was soon realized, however, that substantial communications would require active satellites, with the ability to receive transmission from earth,

©1981 R.A.P. All rights reserved.

amplify them, and retransmit them to earth. The first active satellites included Relay, Telstar, and Syncom.

The practical beginning of commercial satellite communications was signaled in the early 1960's by events both technological and organizational. The National Aeronautics and Space Administration (NASA) demonstrated three key technologies:

- Earth stations with high-gain antennas and low-noise receivers
- Space-qualified hardware necessary for active satellites (in particular, reliable microwave transmitters and power supplies)
- Launch capability for emplacing satellites of significant size and weight in geostationary orbit.

During the same period, two organizations were established which played the principal roles in developing commercial satellite communications systems:

- Communications Satellite Corporation (COMSAT), a quasi-public corporation authorized by the U.S. Congress in 1962 to develop and operate the system
- International Telecommunications Satellite Organization (INTELSAT), a consortium initially comprising 14 member countries, organized in 1962 to own and operate an international telecommunication satellite system

COMSAT, under contract to INTELSAT, has developed and managed the INTELSAT system. In 1965, COMSAT's Early Bird, later renamed INTELSAT-1, was launched. This first commerical communications satellite had a usable bandwidth of 50 MHz, providing transatlantic telephone (240 two-way voice circuits) and television services, with a design lifetime of 1.5 years. By contrast, the present-day INTELSAT IV has a design lifetime of 7 years and a total bandwidth of 600 MHz. In December 1980, the first of a new generation, INTELSAT V, was launched. Each satellite in this series will provide a total bandwidth of 2100 MHz.

Currently, over 100 nations are members of INTELSAT, 90 of whom own and operate at least one earth station. There are over 300 INTELSAT earth stations throughout the world, interconnected by satellites orbiting over the Atlantic, Pacific, and Indian oceans. The resounding success of INTELSAT is one of the bright spots in the tableau of universal communication.

As technology progressed, it became economically feasible to employ satellite systems for "short-haul" communications and more specialized services. The first domestic commercial satellite system was instituted by TELESAT Canada by the launch of ANIK-1 in 1972; together with two subsequent launches, the system carries network television and both heavy- and thin-route telephony on a national basis. An all-Indonesian regional system (PALAPA) was inaugurated in 1976, as was MARISAT, a U.S. based global maritime system providing telephone and telex services to ships at sea. An excellent historical overview of communication satellites can be found in [MARS 78].

Counting the Soviet MOLNYA/STATSIONAR system, there were eight commercial satellite communication systems operating by 1980, having approximately 30 dedicated satellites in orbit. Many more communication service organizations exist, who lease capacity on these satellites. And, as Al Jolson said at an early stage in the development of another communication medium, "you ain't heard nothin' yet." Projections have been made (MCEL 78) that, in the year 2000, demand for satellite communication capacity will reach the order of magnitude of 100,000 Mbps. In the United States alone, the decade of the 1980s opened with authorizations for more than 5000 earth stations (DIRE 80); over 70,000 may be in operation by 1990. The present frequency band (4/6 GHz) and geostationary orbit space will be saturated within four years. The "new" frequency band of 12/14 GHz has at present limited commercial service, yet it will be saturated by 1990.

6.2 THE NATURE OF SATELLITE COMMUNICATION

Although satellite communication is a microwave radio technique and, in fact, uses many of the same frequencies, there are some substantial differences as compared with terrestrial radio. In this section we examine the distinctive nature of satellite communications and establish the groundwork for the subsequent sections.

6.2.1 Satellite Positioning and Coverage

Almost all communication satellites are geostationary; the major exceptions are those in the MOLNYA system. A geostationary satellite is one whose period is 24 hr (i.e., synchronized with the earth's period of rotation about its axis). Thus the satellite remains fixed with respect to any point on the earth's surface. This is important to a wideband communications system; otherwise, very expensive tracking antennas are required and the transmitted/received signals are subject to considerable variation.

Physics dictates that a geostationary orbit be in the equatorial plane approximately 35,900 km above the earth's surface. Consequently, satellite separation can be achieved only by relative angular displacement in the geostationary arc. Separation is necessary to prevent interference from an adjacent satellite within the field of view of a given earth station antenna. Current standards require 4° spacing in the 4/6-GHz band, and 3° at 12/14 GHz. The usefully visible portion of geostationary arc is limited for any given point on the earth's surface, and is further reduced with increasing latitude. For the coverage of the 50 United States, the usable segment is about 40°, leading to a maximum of 10 satellites at 4/6 GHz. Prime slots, which do not require low antenna elevation angles with the attendant deterioration of signal quality, are even fewer — about six. Further, coverage of South America and the balance of North America requires some of the same slots. This is the reason for the impending saturation of communications satellites using present-day technology. The situation is depicted in Fig. 6.1.

The field of view of a geostationary satellite positioned at 50° west longitude is shown in Fig. 6.2. An earth station antenna located directly underneath the satellite

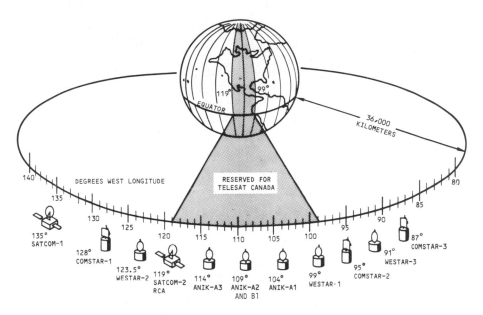

Figure 6.1. Geostationary positions of 4/6-GHz general service domestic communications satellites providing North American coverage (1980).

(approximately at Belém, Brazil) would have to aim its antenna at the zenith, or 90° elevation angle. The shaded outline of the figure shows where the satellite would just be visible at 0° elevation angle, assuming no obstruction such as hills, trees, or buildings. For reasons that will become clear later, it is not desirable, and sometimes not feasible, to operate earth station antennas at low elevation angles, say less than 10°, corresponding to the hashed area of the figure. Nevertheless, a very substantial portion of the earth's surface can be provided with good coverage from the single satellite — most of the continental United States, Canada and western Europe, all of Central and South America, and a substantial part of Africa.

Satellites in geosynchronous orbit are not completely stationary but are subject to drift and daily positional variations due to the influences of the sun, moon, earth, and solar radiation pressure. Part of the maintenance required in a satellite system is "station keeping," an occasional firing of on-board motors to correct for long-term drift. However, diurnal variations persist and are of magnitude comparable with the 0.2° beamwidth of very large earth station antennas. Every decibel counts in a satellite link; consequently, large antennas must have provisions for continuously moving the large structure in order to track the satellite.[1]

[1]One reason for the significant cost difference of smaller antennas is that expensive tracking subsystems are not needed because the beamwidth is larger. Alternatively, the need for tracking with high-gain antennas can be obviated by "tighter" satellite station keeping, which requires more satellite motor fuel, hence weight — another of the many system design trade-offs. In all cases, however, the satellite's short-term meanderings cause a Doppler shift in frequency which must be accounted for in transmitter and receiver designs. Also, the positional variations cause differences in path delay, which becomes important in wideband transmission (see Sec. 6.5.2).

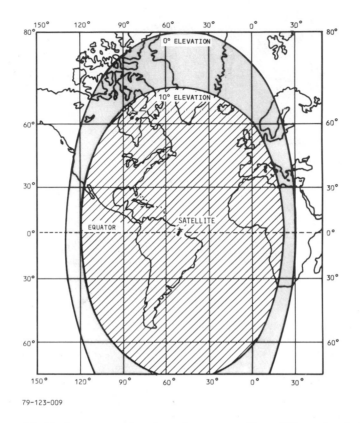

Figure 6.2. Earth coverage of earth-synchronous satellite at 50° west longitude earth station antenna elevations of 0° and 10°. (From [SCHW 73].)

6.2.2 Economics of Satellite Communication

A satellite system is very expensive, but the available bandwidth offers attractive economies. The initial cost of designing and fabricating three WESTAR satellites in the early 1970s was about $50 million. Two WESTAR's were launched; costs (launch vehicle, NASA facilities, and insurance) added another $20 million. Each WESTAR had an equivalent capacity of 6000 voice circuits. Thus the initial investment in the space segment amounted to $6000 per voice circuit. Assuming a 7-year satellite lifetime, and making allowances for the cost of capital, the cost of a voice-circuit space segment was about $1500 per year. To this must be added the costs of five earth stations — including building costs, switching and terminating equipment, and so on, about $5 million each in initial investment. The fully allocated cost of a point-to-point voice circuit, then, was approximately $2000 per year. Compared with tariffs for a long distance leased private line voice-grade circuits from New York to San Francisco, costing $13,000 per year, there was room for substantial net revenue after making allowances for local distribution and operating costs. Costs for the next generation of domestic satellite systems, to be coming into service in the 1980's, will be considerably higher. An equivalent system comprising two in-orbit satellites, plus one held on ground as a spare, costs about $200 million today. On the other hand, advances in technology are providing an offsetting increase in capacity, which results in roughly equivalent fully-allocated cost per circuit.

Of particular importance in the consideration of satellite communication is its cost insensitivity to distance. It makes no difference to circuit-allocated cost whether the earth station terminal points are across town or 6000 mi distant. For reliable, high-quality communication, within a global or even a small regional area, this has never before been true. Combined with the large bandwidths available, this has enormous ramifications, as we shall see later.

Another point to be derived from the previous discussion is the large proportion of circuit cost contributed by the launch of the satellite. Rocket launch vehicles are themselves expensive, and limited in the size and weight of payload to be carried. For the previous example of WESTAR, it cost about $30,000 per kilogram to orbit the satellite — an obvious premium on mass, which is particularly acute in the area of power supplies. Such considerations are the motivation for the NASA Space Shuttle, use of which will substantially lower the cost of future communication space segments.

Because of the size and weight of power supplies, on-board power is a precious resource. Taking rather heroic steps to increase the earth station's sensitivity (G/T ratio, defined in Sec. 6.4.2) by increasing its size would lower the required effective radiated power to the satellite's transmitter, and probably would be worthwhile if few earth stations were to be used in the system. Alternatively, the bandwidth could be decreased, but potential system revenues would fall correspondingly. Power on the earth's surface is much less costly than that on a satellite, so the downlink power budget is more critical than the uplink. Further, the effective satellite radiated power is limited by international agreement to preclude interference with other services such as terrestrial microwave radio links. These considerations are examined in later sections.

6.2.3 Satellite Communication Channels and Access

The early concept of communications via satellite viewed the satellite as a broadcast radio repeater on a very high tower, linking various terminals on earth — a kind of "pipeline in the sky." Because the vast majority of commercial communications was (and still is) concerned with telephony,[2] it was natural that telephone standards and techniques were applied to satellite transmission. This state of affairs is reflected in the general use of the term "equivalent voice circuits" when speaking of a satellite's bandwidth. Satellite system designs have been dominated by the analog-oriented technology that evolved in point-to-point cable and microwave radio systems within

---

[2]To date, the vast majority of revenue-producing traffic derives from telephone, telex, and television services, in that order.

the telephone industry. This technology includes frequency modulation (FM) and frequency-division multiplexing (FDM). Since a satellite serves a number of earth station terminals, within the field of view of its antenna beamwidths, some means of sharing access is necessary. Given the technology, the natural result was frequency-division multiple access (FDMA), a scheme whereby circuits established between individual stations are separated by differing frequency assignments within the available bandwidth. Unfortunately, linearity must be traded for power output in a satellite transponder, which leads to intermodulation distortion of the many discrete spectra if efficient power output is achieved, or inefficiency if the power output is backed off to achieve low distortion. The current generation of communication satellites uses channelized FDMA to alleviate the problem somewhat.

A channelized FDMA frequency plan divides the transponder bandwidth into discrete portions. Included in this plan is use of the single channel per carrier (SCPC) technique, whereby a discrete, modulated carrier representing one communication channel can be inserted in (or removed from) the aggregate spectrum of a transponder by an individual terminal. It is noted that the bandwidth available in the SCPC spectral "slot" is about 38 kHz, which is established by the peak deviation of the FM/FDM signal required for good-quality analog transmission. This bandwidth easily supports a phase-shift keyed (PSK) digital signal of 64 kbps, which corresponds to digitized voice. Obviously, the digital signal can just as well be a data stream from some other source, such as a computer.

A further advance in flexible utilization of satellite resources was made possible by the introduction of SPADE (single channel per carrier PCM multiple-access demand assignment equipment) [PUEN 71, SALA 78], a demand assignment multiple-access (DAMA) technique. SPADE operation takes advantage of the fact that any earth station can insert the carrier and its modulation in a given SCPC slot. In the INTELSAT network, for example, a number of SCPC channels is made available as a pool of channels that can be used on a demand basis by up to 50 stations. One channel is designated as the Common Signaling and Control Channel (CSC) and is monitored by all stations in the SPADE network. The CSC monitoring equipment at each station then knows the busy/idle status of each SPADE channel in the pool. A station desiring to use an idle channel transmits its intention to do so on the CSC, thereby changing the channel status from idle to busy in all stations. The CSC operates with digital information at a bit rate of 128 kbps. Discrete time slots in a CSC frame are assigned to each station; consequently, the SPADE CSC is really the first commercial communication satellite application of time-division multiple access and the SPADE technique itself is the first demand assignment scheme in common usage.

Time-division multiple access (TDMA), in its simplest form, allows shared use of the entire bandwidth of a satellite channel by allocating durations of time among the users. Thus a user requiring more communication capacity could be assigned a greater proportion of time. TDMA is fundamentally different than FDMA, and requires a quite different complement of equipment. However, TDMA has several major advantages in operation, and is being made practical by the

Table 6.1. *Primary Frequency Bands for Satellite Communications in Region 2*
(North and South America) (after [MCEL 78]).[a]

Frequency (GHz)

Service	Downlink	Uplink	Shorthand Nomenclature
Fixed	2.50–2.69		
	3.7–4.2	5.925–6.425	4/6 (C band)
	11.7–12.3	14.0–14.5[b]	12/14 (Ku band)
	17.7–20.2	27.5–30.0	20/30
	40.0–41.0	50.0–51.0	40/50
	102.0–105.0	92.0–95.0	
Broadcast	2.50–2.69	—	2.5
	12.1–12.7	14.0–14.5	12/14 (Ku band)
	41.0–43.0	—	
	84.0–86.0	—	
Intersatellite	54.25–58.20		
	59.0–64.0		
	105.0–130.0		
	28,000		
	560,000		
Satellite mobile			
Military		0.24–0.40	
Aeronautical			
and maritime	1.5350–1.5585	1.6365–1.6600	1.5/1.6 (L band)
	43.0–48.0		
	66.0–71.0		
	95.0–101.0		

[a]Some bands (particularly 12/14 GHz) reflect expected actions of the 1979 World Administrative Radio Conference (WARC) and its subsequent regional planning conferences. Also, some subbands are variously reserved for, or shared with, specialized services.

[b]14.0 to 14.5-GHz uplink is shared among fixed, broadcast, and mobile services.

accelerating shift to digital transmission techniques in all communications media. Section 6.6 treats TDMA in greater detail, as a most important ingredient in computer communication networks.

6.2.4 Frequency Allocations

The current frequency allocations for satellite communications in Region 2 (encompassing North and South America) are shown in Tab. 6.1. As previously mentioned, present-day systems are almost exclusively in the 4/6-GHz band, which is already congested because it is shared with terrestrial microwave radio-link transmission. The 12/14-GHz band will experience rapid growth in the 1980s as the new generation of satellites (e.g., Advanced WESTAR, INTELSAT V, SBS) comes into service. The 1979 World Administrative Radio Conference (WARC), approved the additional downlink band of 12.2-12.7 GHz for direct broadcast satellite (DBS) television services in Region 2 (comprising essentially the Western Hemisphere). Detailed deliberations of subsequent regional conferences, may result in some modifications to existing agreements concerning frequency assignments available in the various world regions, which actions may ameliorate somewhat the more serious problems of impending congestion. Of currently used bands, agreements are expected on frequency allocations for the 20/30-GHz band, which will be developed in the future, and perhaps expansion of the 12/14-GHz bands.

6.3 PRESENT-DAY SERVICES AND TECHNOLOGY — SOME EXAMPLES

The following examples illustrate the current status of satellite communications technology and available services.

6.3.1 International Satellite Communications

By far the majority of today's commercial satellite communications traffic is carried by the global INTELSAT network, which in 1980 provided 40,000 full-time and part-time half-circuits, 500 SPADE circuits, and 28,000 channel-hours of television through a total of 300 earth stations. The consumer cannot obtain private circuits directly from INTELSAT; arrangements must be made through the recognized telecommunications authority in each country in which a terminal or transit point is desired. With the notable exception of the United States and Canada, the authority is in the form of a government agency, such as a PTT (posts, telephone, and telegraph) or a ministry of communications. In the United States, arrangements for international communication must be made through one of the FCC-recognized international record carriers (IRC); viz., Western Union International, RCA Globecom, ITT Worldcom, and TRT. At this writing, the entry of AT&T and Western Union Telegraph into international private line service is still at issue. The primary U.S.— International gateways are operated by COMSAT, and are located in Etam, W. Va., and Calaveras, Calif.

Availability of kinds of services varies from country to country, as do the tariffs for these services. Generally, leased private line telex (50 to 75 baud) and voice grade circuits are available. On the other hand, it may be easier to make arrangements for a television channel (about 5 MHz) than for a 50-kbps data channel, because the appropriate facilities for data transmission, even today, are not universal. Where they are available, the quality is often also variable, especially because the tail circuits from the earth station to the terminal location are often provided by existing telephone facilities which may be subpar.

There are a number of very large and completely equipped INTELSAT earth stations providing the services one would expect in the commercial centers where they are found. The earth station located at Umm Haraz, Republic of Sudan, is a good example of the economic extension of communications services by satellite. Opera-

Figure 6.3. INTELSAT Type A earth station at Umm Haraz, Republic of
Sudan. (Courtesy of Page Communications Engineers, Inc.)

tional in November 1974, it had the distinction of being the first all-digital earth
station, and of having established network engineering procedures fully exploiting the
potential of demand assignment multiple access (SPADE) techniques [BLAC 77].

The Umm Haraz earth station, pictured in Fig. 6.3 is a Standard-A design
operating in the $4/6$-GHz band, using a 32-m antenna which provides as G/T of 41.7
dB / Kelvin. Communications at present are with the Atlantic satellite. The transmitter comprises redundant 400-W, two stage, traveling-wave tube amplifiers. The
channel plan is based on the SCPC described previously, using PCM / PSK modulation exclusively. In addition to the equipment necessary for satellite communication, the facility contains a 200-line computer-controlled telex switch, microwave
links to the remote International Traffic Center (Khartoum) and Television Center
(Omdurman), power generators, operations and maintenance facilities, and administrative offices.

The 1975 traffic plan comprised five telephone channels and 24 telex circuits.
Initially, all communications were limited to three locations—international traffic
centers in the United Kingdom, Switzerland, and Italy—which served as correspondent transit points for circuits to foreign locations. It is interesting to note that the initial
cost of the entire complex (about $7 million) was justifiable on the basis of this traffic
alone.

In 1977, the DAMA equipment was added, and the necessary operational procedures were approved by INTELSAT and the correspondent countries, allowing direct dialing to 56 countries. The quantity of traffic to six countries justifies the continuation of dedicated channels. If there were demand, any of the existing SCPC channels could be easily converted for 50-kbps data transmission. This could also be done on a DAMA channel if appropriate protocols and procedures were worked out. However, neither service presently exists.

Several recent actions by INTELSAT will have the effect of further increasing the possibilties of international networking via satellite. The specifications of a Standard-B earth station were issued in 1973. Basically, Grade B service allows smaller earth stations (11-m antennas, $G/T = 32.7$ dB/K) to join the INTELSAT system, with the possibility of using SCPC and DAMA equipment. The concomitant lower costs have triggered a proliferation of stations at points where traffic loading was too light for the economic viability of the earlier, larger earth stations.

INTELSAT has also agreed to lease satellite capacity for the purpose of a domestic satellite communication network. Increments of full, half, and quarter transponders are available; corresponding nominal bandwidths are 36, 18, or 9 MHz with, of course, corresponding fractions of total power. Global or hemispheric coverage can be chosen, as can grade of service—single transponder only, or standby backup capacity to provide continuity of service should the primary transponder experience problems. Capacity can also be leased on an as-available basis, subject to preemption by a higher–priority service need. A full global beam transponder in this category costs $1 million per year on a 5-year lease [PART 78]. Algeria was the first to utilize such a system, using 15 earth stations of $G/T = 31.7$ dB/K to provide television and telephone services between its major cities. Other countries now include Brazil, Chile, Oman, Nigeria, Norway, Saudi Arabia, and Spain. In the early 1980's, as many as 30 countries may be using this service.

In December 1980, the first of the new INTELSAT V series of satellites was launched. INTELSAT V is capable of operation with higher power and more efficient use of the spectrum through spot and regional as well as earth-coverage beams. Operations in the 4/6 GHz band are enhanced by frequency reuse via cross-polarized antennas (see Chap. 5, Section 5.3.3). More importantly, INTELSAT V provides a full complement of transponders and beams for the new 12/14 GHz band. These features give INTELSAT V a usable bandwidth in excess of 2100 MHz.

A third recent INTELSAT action was the release of specifications for TDMA operation in all services, thus opening the way for highly efficient networking on a global basis. International 120 Mbps TDMA service is scheduled to begin in 1983.

6.3.2 Domestic U.S. Systems

WESTAR, initially launched in 1974 by the Western Union Telegraph Company, was the first domestic U.S. satellite system. AMERICOM (RCA SATCOM) and COMSTAR (Comsat General/ATT/GTE) followed in 1975 and 1976, respectively. All provide coverage of the continental United States; SATCOM II also covers

Alaska; and the WESTARs, Hawaii, Alaska, and Puerto Rico. All systems operate in the 4/6-GHz band. Their satellites carry transponders quite similar to the INTELSAT IV series, each having a bandwidth of 36 MHz. Earth stations closely resemble those found in INTELSAT. Frequency plans, modulation, and access methods are also similar; in many cases, the same equipment can operate in any of these systems. SCPC and SPADE DAMA are used extensively. The COMSTAR system is unique in that it was the first to employ orthogonally polarized antennas in both satellites and earth stations, permitting frequency reuse for twice the effective bandwidth within a given spectrum allocation.

Each system has several earth stations, strategically located in the major population centers. WESTAR stations, for example, employ 16-m antennas (G/T = 37.4 dB) and are located near New York City, Atlanta, Dallas, Los Angeles, San Francisco, Phoenix, Seattle, and Chicago. Western Union tariffs offer a wide variety of services on a full-time lease basis. Conditioned voice-grade circuits are available, as are television and high-quality audio program channels. A typical charge for voice-grade service, New York–San Francisco, is $1100 per month, with a discount structure ranging to 30% for more than 24 channels. Pricing tends to follow the long-established distance-sensitive terrestrial transmission structure; the minimum charge for a voice circuit is about $600 per month, applicable to such routes as Chicago–Dallas and Washington–Atlanta.

Data service at subvoice rates is available at 75, 150, 300, 600, and 1200 bps. Wideband services range to 56 kbps, and higher by special arrangements. In all these instances, there is little to distinguish satellite transmission from any other medium, other than delay and some cost advantage (see, however, Sec. 6.2.4). In fact, links connecting the earth station with the customer's premises are usually conventional wireline circuits supplied by the local telephone operating company.

In addition to providing their own specialized services, the owners of domestic satellites can lease portions of satellite capacity to other commercial common carriers and private users. In these cases the potential of satellite communications is beginning to be realized. The radio, television, and news industries, being much concerned with distribution of their product, have been quick to capitalize on the possibilities. The Public Broadcasting Corporation (public television) has procured 6 transmit/receive and 160 receive-only earth stations colocated at member's studios for networking at the regional and national levels. Similarly, the National Public Radio network comprises 17 transmitter and over 200 receiver terminals. The antennas range in size from 4.5 to 10 m. The Mutual Broadcasting System (radio) is installing fifty, 4.5-m receive-only terminals, located at its members' premises. The one-way network is fed conventionally through commercial earth stations.

RCA AMERICOM is providing 10 channels of television services for Home Box Office, Inc., a supplier of special programming to CATV systems. Over 300 receive-only earth stations, both 10-m and 4.5-m, are in use. RCA implemented a service for receive-only volume users, such as press services, based on a 56-kbps channel with BER = 1 x 10^{-7} using 2- and 3-m antennas. The larger size would be used to obtain adequate signal-to-noise ratio in Florida and the southern tip of Texas, which lie in the diminishing area of the RCA satellite's antenna beam pattern (LAMS 78). An average installation, including ancillary equipment, initially cost about $35,000. The growth of television program distribution has been so rapid that RCA greatly accelerated its schedule for procurement and launch of satellites, some to be dedicated exclusively to television services.

The press services AP and UPI are experimenting with several receive-only earth station designs in the 2- to 3-m range, which would be located at subscriber's premises. Present plans are to select one or two standard designs, of which several thousand could be procured. With such a quantity buy, it is projected that the per-terminal cost may fall below $4,000.

The American Satellite Corporation (ASC) on a long-term basis, leases five transponders on WESTAR I, with full backup available from WESTAR II. ASC, however, constructs and operates its own earth stations, completely independent of the Western Union system. In addition to providing common-carrier services competitive with the space-segment owners, ASC supplies a number of dedicated and specialized services. For example, a network of 12 dedicated 10-m ($G/T = 33$ dB/K) earth stations located from Hawaii to Maine provides communications for the U.S. Department of Defense at rates to 6.3 Mbps. A private system for Dow Jones transmits high-resolution 3.5-min-per-newspaper-page facsimile from South Brunswick, New Jersey, to dedicated earth stations located at *Wall Street Journal* printing plants in Los Angeles, Orlando, and Wichita. Dedicated, nationwide data transmission systems for Sperry-Univac Corporation and Boeing Computer Services are in service [EDWA 78]. ASC was the first to operate a satellite TDMA network in the U.S.; the initial (1980) system comprised four nodes working at 64 Mbps.

In 1978, ASC announced its Satellite Data Exchange (SDX) Service based on less expensive 5-m antennas which can be placed on the user's rooftop. Prior to the commencing of SBS services in 1981 (see Sec. 6), SDX was the only available digital, rooftop-antenna private satellite communication service. An SDX terminal provides for data, facsimile, freeze-frame video, and voice, and for encryption using the NBS Data Encryption Standard. The nominal transmission rate is 56 kbps, although available data rate can be extended to 1.544 Mbps by use of a 10-m antenna and advanced electronics. Costs are in the vicinity of $1,100 per month per terminal end for a basic 56-kbps transmission channel.

As an indication of its pervasiveness, satellite communication is entering the realm of the individual citizens. For example, radio amateurs have been communicating for some years via the OSCAR series of satellites. Recently, articles have been appearing in popular publications catering to the do-it-yourself community; one series contains plans for your own backyard and satellite TV earth station [COOP 80]. Packaged systems are available in the consumer retail market for about $6,000.

As the decade of the 1970's closed, communication by satellite as a substitute for and supplement to terrestrial transmission was proved and became almost commonplace. Innovative services such as the above are appearing and will continue to burgeon. This will be made possible both by improvements in satellite system design and by the imagination of system architects who understand the special characteristics of satellite transmission. In the next sections we examine some of the key technical considerations, with examples relevant to computer communication, followed by a brief view of the future.

6.4 A SATELLITE CHANNEL AS A RADIO LINK

A communication channel established via satellite is basically a radio link; further, current frequencies used for commercial services are the same as for microwave radio. Expected performance can be calculated in a manner similar to that used for terrestrial radio links in Chap. 5. However, there are some significant differences in scale which must be outlined first. For one thing, the distances between transmitter/receiver sites is far greater; and both economic and technical considerations force substantial differences between the satellite station and the earth stations. Different constraints also operate on the uplink and downlink.

6.4.1 The Satellite

Commercial satellites of the current generation (e.g., INTELSAT IV, WESTAR, ANIK-A) typically carry 12 transponders. Each transponder is equipped with its own receiver, transmitter, frequency converter, and filters. Normally, each transponder has a bandwidth of 36 MHz and has fixed receive and transmit frequencies in the assigned uplink and downlink bands, respectively. Thus each transponder can be treated as a microwave radio repeater.

All transponders can share a common antenna, or can be associated with separate antennas provided regional or spot coverage. They can also be cross-strapped between beams, and even frequency bands as in the case of the upcoming INTELSAT V. Later satellites, notably RCA SATCOM and the new INTELSAT V, allow frequency reuse by polarization diversity.

The point was made earlier that weight is at a premium in a satellite, imposing major constraints on its design. Further, one cannot yet send maintenance technicians to retune circuits or repair failed equipment — reliability must be high. The motivations in satellite design are to keep it light and simple, and trade off as much as feasible in a given system design toward earth station complexity.[3]

Fundamentally, the gain of a satellite's antenna is limited by the minimum beamwidth that will give coverage for the desired portion of the earth's surface. In the case of global coverage satellites such as in the INTELSAT series, the earth subtends an angle of 17.5°. This corresponds to a nominal antenna gain of about 19 dB which, of course, will hold true regardless of frequency band. In domestic or special-purpose

---

[3]However, there are potentially many more earth stations than satellites, with a concomitant greater quantity leverage militating against earth station complexity. The trade-offs are complex and almost never immediately apparent. See Sec. 6.5.3.3 for an example.

applications, more restricted coverage allows spot-beam antennas to have higher gains, perhaps up to 50 dB. For example, CONUS coverage can be provided with 30-dB gain, while Alaska or Hawaii can be covered with about 36 dB. The same considerations apply for receive and transmit.

In either case, the receive antenna's beam is filled with the earth, which has an apparent noise temperature of about 250 K. This, combined with reliability, weight, and other considerations, make it not attractive to build satellites with very low noise figure receivers (besides, for the uplink, RF power is relatively cheap to produce on earth). Typically, noise figures correspond roughly with their terrestrial radio counterparts, about 8 dB.[4] Considerable care is exercised in design and layout to keep losses as low as possible — in the area of 1 dB.

In satellite design, much attention is paid to the transmitters and power supplies because they account for a major portion of the weight and cost. For power to be transmitted, it must be produced. Today's satellites use solar cell arrays with backup batteries to sustain operation during solar eclipses. The INTELSAT IV power supply produces about 500 W. Suppose that three-fourths of this power is available for use by the satellite's 12 transmitters which have an overall dc-to-RF power conversion efficiency of 25% — each transmitter then can produce about 8 W (9 dBW). WESTAR, COMSTAR, and ANIK transmitters are similar; each 4-GHz transmitter (and associated 6-GHz receiver) handles a bandwidth of 36 MHz.

A satellite's transmitted power is frequently expressed in terms of effective isotropic radiated power (EIRP). The quantity is simply the transmitter power in dbW, added to the antenna gain in dB. For link calculations based on the method outlined in Chap. 5, EIRP replaces the terms P_T and G_T. For the preceding case of an INTELSAT global beam, EIRP = 9 dbW + 19 dB = 28 dBW at beam center. The more restricted coverage of the United States provided by WESTAR allows higher antenna gain, leading to an EIRP of about 33 dBW.

An important point must be kept in mind regarding the character of current-generation transponders. Because the transponders have been designed to operate primarily with analog FM/FDM techniques, they function as a frequency-converting amplifier; the uplink signal is received, shifted to the proper downlink frequency, and amplified to the level necessary for downlink transmission. Thus the signal transmitted on the downlink has a finite SNR, determined by the parameters of the earth transmitter–uplink path–satellite receiver link. Unlike a digital radio repeater, in which the data stream can be regenerated, a current transponder passes through the uplink signal in analog form. This means that the quality of the signal received at a terminal earth station is determined by both the uplink and the downlink performance.

In the future, for all-digital transmission, on-board processing will be accomplished. At a minimum, this will allow digital regeneration of the bit stream, thereby improving performance over that currently achieved in the two tandem analog links. More advanced on-board processing may also incorporate error control on individ-

---

[4]Frequently, satellite receiver sensitivity is expressed in the same *G/T* form used for earth stations, explained in Sec. 6.4.2.

ual links, as well as such functions as reformatting, switching, routing, and store-and-forward.

6.4.2 Earth Stations

Some typical earth stations were described in Sec. 6.3. Generally, antenna diameters range from 10 to 30 m for wideband transmit/receive stations, although diameters as small as 4 to 6 m are being used for more restricted bandwidths. Earth stations do not suffer the tremendous weight penalties imposed on a satellite; sufficient transmitter power can be made available as necessary for the uplink. It is technically desirable to operate with the very high antenna gains associated with the large antennas possible on earth, from the point of view of both the up- and downlinks.

As with terrestrial radio antennas, the design and selection of satellite communication antennas is governed both by link performance considerations and by regulations [CUCC 80]. With earth stations, however, the constraints are even more meaningful because of their impact on the generally much larger, hence more expensive antennas, and concerns with side-lobe levels governing interference with terrestrial and other satellite communication systems.

As in any other form of radio, the quality of transmission depends on the receiver signal-to-noise ratio. Because the satellite transmitter power and antenna gain are limited, even the very large earth stations require much more sensitive receivers as compared with their terrestrial radio counterparts. Great care is taken to maximize antenna efficiency and to minimize RF loss and receiver noise figure. In most cases, very low noise receiver "front ends" are mounted directly on the antenna at the feed point; sometimes the receiver is actually refrigerated to reduce noise factors. Such measures are justified because sensitive earth station sites are located to minimize human-made noise and interference, and because they look upward into the cooler, lower-noise sky.

For earth station receiver/antenna combinations, a figure of merit (G/T) is used, because it is more appropriate in dealing with the low-noise cases. G/T expresses the ratio of the effective antenna gain to the effective noise temperature of the antenna/receiver combination. In link performance calculations of the form developed in Chap. 5, G/T in dB/Kelvin (dB/K) replaces the terms F and T of Eq. (5.5) and G_R and L of Eq. (5.6). The effect is to normalize system gain and noise to 0 K. Noise from other sources is subtracted (in dB form) in the same manner as path losses. Another reason that G/T is a popular expression is that it correctly implies a trade-off in the actual design of the earth station — for a given required sensitivity, a designer might choose to offset the effects of a somewhat smaller (hence lower gain and cost) antenna with a lower-noise-figure receiver (of higher cost).

Earth station transmitters working with an entire satellite transponder (36 MHz bandwidth) typically provide 300 to 3000 W of power to the antenna, depending on antenna size and site location. Transmitters working with portions of a transponder, such as with SCPC and SPADE channels, would transmit powers proportionally lower. In some cases, earth station transmitted power is expressed as EIRP, defined earlier in Sec. 6.4.1.

6.4.3 Propagation Losses

A satellite circuit is a form of radio channel and is subject to some of the same anomalies. Fortunately, multipath fading, the most severe anomaly with an overland radio path, is not of concern in an upward-looking satellite path with a narrow-beam antenna.[5] However, there are other effects that are peculiar to a satellite circuit.

One such effect is ionospheric scintillation fading, which is of greatest concern at lower frequencies. Measured data at various frequencies for a 95% confidence of fading less than a given value is: 250 MHz, 22 dB; 2.3 GHz, 2 dB; 7.3 GHz, 0.5 dB [SPIL 77]. Above the X-band, ionospheric scintillation fading can be neglected.

On a satellite circuit, propagation losses due to the atmosphere and precipitation generally have an effect lower in absolute magnitude than a long terrestrial radio path, because the path is upward looking, traversing less of the atmosphere. The sensible troposphere exists to a height of about 10 km above the earth's surface — a 12/14-GHz earth station directly under a satellite (90° elevation angle) would experience, from Fig. 5.7, about 0.2 dB attenuation due to clear atmospheric attenuation. At an oblique elevation angle of 5°, the path covers about 10 times more atmosphere, leading to an atmospheric attenuation of 2 dB. At lower frequencies, the loss is negligible; higher frequencies can be scaled from Fig. 5.7.

Path attenuation in an unclear atmosphere obviously is much greater. In conditions of heavy fog or cloud cover, the attenuation suffered by a vertical path would be approximately

$$A_{cv} = \frac{f^2}{160} \text{ dB, (f in GHz)}$$

(6.1)

or about 0.9 dB at 12 GHz [MART 78]. Attenuation for other sitings can be conservatively scaled by dividing by the sine of the elevation angle (greater than 10°).

The most serious propagation problem is precipitation attenuation. Very heavy rain cells, in cloudbursts, can produce rain rates exceeding 100 mm/hr; however, these cells are usually very localized, less than 5 km in diameter [SPIL 77]. Empirical results from the Application Technology Satellite series indicate that the path subject to precipitation at an elevation angle of 90° is effectively 4.8 km (the mean height of the 0° C isotherm) at low latitudes. Thus the vertical downlink path attenuation for a 4-GHz downlink could be (4.8 km)(0.11 dB/km) = 0.5 dB. At lower elevation angles, the atmospheric path traversed is greater, but it is less likely that such a heavy rainfall rate will exist over its entire length. At 10° elevation angle, for example, the slant range to a height of 4.8 km is about 25 km. Using the rough method of Sec. 5.2.2, the effective path length is about 15 km, leading to a loss of 1.7 dB at 100 mm/hr. A 12/14-GHz satellite system, however, would experience about 24 and 75 dB, respectively, under the same conditions. A secondary effect of atmospherics is an increase in effective antenna temperature with higher humidity or precipitation; this, too, becomes significant at low elevation angles and higher frequencies.

---

[5]With the trend toward even smaller antennas, multipath could become a problem in certain siting situations. The extreme case will be when direct satellite to mobile user links are considered.

6.4.4 Typical Satellite Path Calculation

The method for estimating the performance of a particular combination of radio equipment and path, developed in Chap. 5, can also be used for estimating satellite link performance. As outlined in the preceding paragraphs, satellite link engineering uses somewhat different terminology; collecting the factors defined in Secs. 6.4.1 and 6.4.2, Eq. (5.6b) can be rewritten as

$$\text{SNR} = \text{EIRP} + \alpha + \frac{G}{T} - M - K - B - L_i$$

(6.2)

where K is Boltzmann's constant = 1.38×10^{-23} J/K = -228.6 dBW/Hz/K, and L_m is replaced by L_i (incidental losses such as SNR degradation due to internal intermodulation products, RF losses not accounted for in G/T, etc.).

A typical downlink calculation is displayed in Box 6.1. In this case, Eq. (6.2) is solved for the satellite EIRP required for a specific SNR, derived from the earth station characteristics used for a network design example in Sec. 6.7. Because neither satellite transponder bandwidth nor power is fully utilized for this downlink design, it would be wasteful not to share the transponder with other users. Shared usage imposes two requirements: (1) a reduction (backoff) of total transponder power, to obtain operation in the linear region of the transponder's amplifier and thus to reduce intermodulation interference between users; and (2) establishment of "guard bands" between user's spectra, again to avoid mutual interference.

The caveat of Sect. 6.4.1 is repeated here. We have concentrated on the performance of the downlink, as it is usually more critical. The downlink received SNR is also a function of uplink performance, since a present-day analog transponder transmits what it has received. Normally, however, the uplink can be designed such that overall space-segment performance is effectively determined by the downlink. It is also necessary to calculate and control precisely the earth station's transmitted power, since the *transponder* output power follows its received power. This is particularly critical in SCPC and shared-use transponders, in order to maintain a fair share of power between users and to avoid the interference effects of nonlinearity. In consideration of the latter, shared-use transponders commonly operate at a total power level "backed off" about 5 dB below the maximum saturated power rating.

6.5 CHARACTERISTICS AND LIMITATIONS OF SATELLITE COMMUNICATION CHANNELS

As may have been gathered from the preceding section, there are many similarities between the characteristics of communication channels via satellite and those available by conventional terrestrial means. The suspicion that there also might be some characteristics that are peculiar to satellite channels is also correct. In this section we examine some more important characteristics that the communications system engineer should consider — various considerations of performance, availability, and cost.

Box 6.1 *Downlink Path Calculation for a Typical U.S. domestic Satellite and Small Earth Station Using Eq. (6.2) and Techniques Developed in Chap. 5.[a]*

Earth Station Characteristics

Antenna	7 m diameter; G_R = 47.5 dB; G_T = 51 dB.
Receiver	GaAs-FET low-noise amplifier, T = 120 K. Accounting for antenna noise temperature, the receiver/antenna combination provides a G/T = 25.3 dB/K.
Modem	QPSK modulation, performance within 1.8 dB of theoretical. From Fig. 5-6, $P_e = 10^{-7}$ requires SNR = 14.4 dB; thus net SNR needed = 14.4 + 1.8 = 16.2 dB. Required bandwidth B = 0.57 X data rate.
Error coding	Convolutional rate 1/2, processing gain = 5 dB. Thus operating SNR = 16.2 - 5.0 = 11.2 dB for $P_e = 10^{-7}$.
Data rate	Input/output at 1076 kbps. Rate 1/2 coding; thus transmission rate 2 x 1076 = 2152 kbps. Required transmission bandwidth B = (0.57)(2152) = 1227 kHz.
Incidental loses	0.5 dB, including redundancy switching, internal interference, pointing losses, etc.

Satellite Characteristics

Geosynchronous	Uplink at 6 GHz; downlink at 4 GHz.
EIRP	33 dBW at beam center, per transponder. For shared usage, backoff = 6 dB, thus total of 27 dBW (500 W) is available.
Bandwidth	36 MHz available per transponder. With shared usage, assume additional 15% of bandwidth is required for guard bands.

Downlink Path Calculation

Term	Description	Factor
SNR	Determined above for $P_e = 10^{-7}$	11.2 dB
$-\alpha$	At 45° latitude, d = 39,500 km α = 20 log λ $4\pi d$	196.4 dB
$-G/T$	Specified at left	-25.3 (K/dB)
$+K$	Boltzmann's constant, 1.38 x 10^{-23} J/K	-228.6 dBW/K-Hz
$+B$	Determined above 1227 kHz	60.9 dBHz
$+L_i$	Specified above	0.5 dB
$+M$	Desired operating margin	2.0 dB
EIRP	Required transponder EIRP	17.1 dBW (51 W)

[a]The earth station characteristics are those of a typical modern satellite communication terminal and are used as a design example in Sec. 6.7.

6.5.1 Satellite Circuit Availability Factors

The availability of a satellite communication circuit, like a radio circuit, is determined by the availabilities of both the hardware employed and the propagation path. Earth stations, although more sophisticated than most terrestrial radios, employ similar kinds of equipments and have demonstrated excellent reliability with conservative designs. After having survived the perils of launch and orbit emplacement, satellites themselves have turned in a remarkable performance record. That this is true, in view of the severe design constraints and hostile environment imposed, is a testament to the effectiveness of the extremely rigorous testing and qualification procedures in the manufacturing of satellites (which measures also account for the high costs).

Current-generation satellites have been designed for a service lifetime of 7 to 10 years, primarily limited by the degradation of power supply and station-keeping fuel with time. Nevertheless, individual transponders, and sometimes entire satellites, fail prematurely. Users concerned with high availability arrange for "protected service," whereby an equivalent bandwidth is made available on another transponder should the transponder in use fail. This can be accomplished either by reserving the additional capacity (which remains unused and is therefore wasted) or by allowing preemptible users to utilize the "spare" capacity as long as it is not needed for backup.

Users concerned with extremely high availability can arrange for backup capacity in an entirely separate satellite. Unless the reserve satellite is moved to the originally used orbital position, however, this would require repositioning of earth station antennas. (New antenna designs, such as the COMSAT "torus" antenna, can ameliorate the repositioning problem by providing multiple feeds which allow nearly instantaneous switch selection of pointing angles.)

Satellite channels are subject to periodic, short-term outages. For a 46-day interval during the vernal and autumnal equinoxes, all geosynchronous satellites experience solar eclipses part of each day. The duration of the eclipse peaks at 72 min at the equinox. During normal operation in sunlight, the satellite's power is provided by solar cell arrays; during an eclipse, the power must be derived from on-board batteries. Most satellites are nominally designed with sufficient battery power to carry full-power operation during the eclipse. However, because of the severe weight penalties and reliability problems associated with power supplies, the design must be "tight," leaving little margin for degradation. Over the satellite's lifetime, it is possible that full power may not be available during an eclipse. In fact, WESTAR is so designed that only 10 of its 12 transponders are available during solar eclipse (and are expected to be available at its end of life).

Another effect influencing satellite availability is fittingly exotic and mysterious. It is believed that the interaction of the earth's magnetic field, the plasma (charged ions) existing at a satellite's altitude, and the solar wind results in the buildup of high isolated charges (10 to 20 kV) on portions of a satellite's structure. These charges produce arc discharges, which in turn produce intense radio-frequency interference. In some cases, arcs may travel to wires carrying signals or to command lines. During the second week of April 1975, there was a period of unusually intense magneto-spheric activity. During this period, ANIK I suffered a 25-dB traffic loss for times ranging from 2 to 160 sec, and another communication satellite experienced gross errors in stabilization control. The mechanisms of, and countermeasures for, these phenomena are not well understood, but it is felt that they are responsible for many otherwise inexplicable satellite failures and anomalies [WADH 76].

Path Availability and Operating Frequency

In the discussion of radio transmission (Chap. 5), the notion of statistical availability of the transmission channel was introduced together with the concept of design margin, an excess of transmitter power and/or receiver sensitivity intended to allow for variations of SNR resulting from propagation anomalies. Following the consideration of propagation losses in Sec. 6.4.3, it can be seen that the system margin for a satellite link can be much lower than for a terrestrial radiolink at the same frequency. Typically, the downlink margin at 4 GHz is 2 to 3 dB, as contrasted with the 30 to 40 dB margin common for terrestrial radio. Satellite design systems can be much "tighter," which is particularly fortunate because of their considerably higher cost of margin.

At higher frequencies, however, more substantial margins are necessary, primarily to accommodate the higher losses in periods of precipitation. The next generation of satellite systems, operating in the 12/14-GHz band, are being designed with margins in the area of 8 to 12 dB. Consider an earth station in one of these systems, designed with a typical downlink margin of 8 dB, and sited with an elevation angle of 20°. From the information in Chap. 5 on precipitation losses, one can determine that the margin is nearly depleted at a spot rainfall rate of 14 mm/hr. If the earth station were located in the northeastern United States, the availability of the downlink *path* due to precipitation would be 0.999. *Path* is emphasized, since this availability can be ascribed to the downlink itself only if the satellite's EIRP remains constant. It will be recalled from Sec. 6.4.1 that the RF output power from current types of transponders is a function of the *uplink* power; and the uplink is subject to the same propagation losses as the downlink. Consequently, the total ground–satellite–ground circuit is susceptible to double jeopardy — it could become unavailable due to heavy precipitation in either the uplink or the downlink, or both.

As one means of coping with the problems attendant with operation in the higher-frequency bands, consideration is being given to multiple ground stations implementing a form of space diversity. If three earth stations are so located as to be at least 8 km apart, the probability of all simultaneously experiencing extreme path attenuation is quite small, due to the localized nature of heavy precipitation. Such an arrangement could prove to be less costly than other methods of obtaining high availability and the excess capacity during "normal" periods possibly could be put to additional use for low-priority traffic.

Alternatively, a lower worst-case link availability could be accepted with provisions for automatically "changing gears" to a lower bandwidth/data rate in periods of severe attenuation. Decreasing the data rate by a factor of 10 would compensate for an increased attenuation of 10 dB. The reduced bandwidth could be reserved for real-time needs, such as telephony and query–response transactions. Since such conditions exist for short times, measured in minutes, non-time-critical transmissions (e.g., electronic mail, bulk data transfers) would not be much affected.

Sun Transit Outages

A periodic outage peculiar to satellite systems is sun transit outage, which occurs when the sun comes within the field of view of an earth station's main beamwidth or major side lobes. To the antenna, the sun appears as a very high temperature (approximately 25,000 K) noise source in the beam center. The system noise temperature of a C-band earth station is typically 80 K, so the sun's effect is to increase the noise level and, consequently, reduce the signal-to-noise ratio by approximately 10 log (25,000 - 80) -10 log (290) = 19 dB. This is far in excess of the design margin; consequently, the received signal-to-noise ratio will be unusable during this condition. For a typical geosynchronous satellite system, sun transit outage occurs daily at apparent noon at the satellite's longitude, twice yearly, over a period of two weeks. The actual outage duration corresponds to the time and extent to which the beam intercepts the sun's disk—typically ranging from a few seconds to a peak of about 5 sec in the middle of the period. This is equivalent to a yearly outage time of 0.01% or an availability of 0.9999. To avoid sun transit outage at a given earth station, elaborate schemes have been proposed, involving diversity antenna feeds and multiple satellites; such schemes, however, would not be cost effective except for the most critical applications [SPIL 77].

Implications in Network Architecture

The various causes of unavailability of a satellite communication link are largely independent of those affecting a terrestrial link. For a network architecture in which extremely high availability of interconnectivity is important, one should consider a mixed-media network. For example, a properly designed network comprising a mixture of satellite and terrestrial links would afford both high availability of all circuits and high survivability of the network [HUYN 77]. Exact duplication of each circuit route is not necessary, because of alternate routing possibilities through the nodes. Traffic could be shared between types of circuits by any of numerous algorithms. Bulk file transfers, for example, normally can tolerate reasonably large delays, such as during a temporary outage or period of reduced throughput of the transmission system. On the other hand, even short transmission delays can prove troublesome in applications involving interactive or query–response traffic, or highly time sensitive network control instructions. For a network carrying such classes of traffic, one possible architecture is to carry time-sensitive traffic over terrestrial circuits (which normally afford less delay) and bulk traffic over satellite circuits (which carry large amounts of data inexpensively). If an outage were experienced in, say, a terrestrial link, the additional delay by transmission over a satellite link would be preferred to the alternative of no transmission at all during the outage period, which is usually measured in minutes. Similar reasoning can be applied to the case of traffic congestion in one of the circuits. Using such a multimode scheme, the implied class marking of data could be extended to cover the flexible assignment of priorities in the various circumstances.

A typical "raw" satellite channel provides a BER of 1 X 10^{-6} for 85% of the time, where no error detection/correction is used [OWIN 79]. By comparison, typical terrestrial voice-grade channels exhibit a P_e in the range 1 X 10^{-4} [CACC 75]. Even today, the majority of circuits via satellite use telephone lines to connect the user with an earth station. Consequently, the lower error rate routinely achieved on a satellite channel is often not apparent to the user, being corrupted by the terrestrial "tail" circuit. For this reason there is considerable motivation to co-locate the earth station in proximity to the user. Alternatively, specially designed tail circuits could be provided, such as fiber optics or dedicated microwave, which can achieve lower error rates.

For some types of traffic, such as voice or television, a $P_e = 1 \times 10^{-6}$ may be adequate or better. For most computer communication, however, a lower error rate is needed. This requires some form of error detection/correction in the transmission process. The delay experienced over a satellite link imposes special requirements on error detection/corrections, as discussed in the next section.

6.5.2 Effects of Delay

The most unique transmission characteristic of a satellite link is the delay that is introduced by the distances involved. For a satellite in geostationary orbit and an earth station located on the equator directly "under" the satellite, a signal transmitted from the earth station will be detected by the earth station 240 msec later. The satellite-to-earth station distance increases, however, for terminals located elsewhere; at the edges of the satellite's field of view, the additional delay experienced can be as much as 4 msec. Further delay is added by terrestrial tail circuits if the earth station is not located at the users' premises, and by signal-processing equipment, such as modems. Commonly, a figure of 270 msec is used for single-hop satellite circuit delay.

Satellite circuit delay is not constant, but varies due to changes in slant range resulting from orbital inclination and eccentricity. Normally, the variations are diurnal, and amount to approximately ±25 μsec [MART 78], although extreme cases of ±1 msec have been observed [SPIL 77]. Clearly, such variations must be accounted for in the design of wideband digital transmission; for example, in timing, buffers, and synchronization when using TDMA techniques [HARR 79]. These variations are insignificant, however, compared with the gross effects of the link delay.

With voice circuits, the delay's effect is most troublesome to a speaker if there is an echo of his own voice from the far end, which can result from telephone-line imbalance. The same problem exists with very long terrestrial circuits, such as on transoceanic cables, although the delays are shorter. Echo suppressors are used in both applications, which operate to reduce greatly the gain in the receive channel if "voice activity" is detected on the transmit channel. The result is very much like a half-duplex channel, with one major exception — if both users are speaking, as in an attempt to interrupt, neither will hear anything. It has been found that people will adopt a kind of CB radio protocol. Most echo suppressors can be disabled when a gated tone of 2025 Hz is applied to the line. To pass data over a satellite voice circuit, modems equipped with this disabling feature are necessary.

To alleviate the problems with echo suppressors, several firms are developing echo cancelers. These devices subtract from the "from-path" an estimate of the echo signal, thus obviating the valving effect of echo suppressors [HORN 77, DEMO 81]. It is not yet known whether certain echo canceler will have deleterious effects when modems are used on these voice circuits for data transmission. It is unlikely, however, that those placed in service cannot, at least, be disabled in the same way as echo supressors.

Effects of Delay on Error Control

In digital transmission, the effect of satellite channel delay must be considered with respect to the protocols employed. The distant-end response to any transmitted event cannot be received until two satellite hops, about 0.5 sec, later.[6] Such a delay can be a major factor in the operation of interactive or query–response communications. It must be accounted for in the application of line, link, and network protocol levels, and perhaps also at the process level [OWIN 79, BUX 78].

At the link or network protocol levels, satellite circuit delay has a major impact on throughput efficiency. The effect is most dramatically illustrated by a detailed examination of error control procedures. There are four popular schemes for error control:

- Stop-and-wait, with automatic-repeat-request (ARQ)
- Continuous, go-back-N ARQ
- Continuous, selective repeat ARQ
- Forward error correction.

The IBM Binary Synchronous Transmission Procedure (Bi-Sync) is an example of the stop-and-wait procedure. The transmitter sends a block of data appended with an error check, then waits for a positive acknowledgment (ACK). If an ACK is received, the next block is transmitted; if a NAK (negative acknowledgment) is returned, the block is retransmitted. With a terrestrial circuit, having a turnaround delay of some tens of milliseconds, the proportionate dead time at moderate error rates is relatively low, and the throughput efficiency is reasonable. However, we can immediately recognize that, if the probability of block error is the same, the much longer turn-around time in a satellite circuit will greatly increase the dead time, thus imposing a severe penalty in throughput.

The throughput efficiency (T) of a stop-and-wait (SAW) ARQ channel is

$$T_{SAW} = \frac{n(1 - P_n)}{n + B\tau} \tag{6.3}$$

where n is the number of bits per block; P_n the probability of block error = 1 - $(1 - P_e)^n$, where P_e is the probability of a bit error; B the transmission speed of the channel; and τ the round-trip delay (after [BURT 72]). The throughput is a sensitive function of both n and τ for error rates of 10^{-5} or less. On a terrestrial circuit[7] of BER = 10^{-4} running at 4800 bps using SAW-ARQ, a maximum throughput efficiency

[6]Effective end-to-end (and round trip) delays can be much greater in certain TDMA systems, due to buffering required on input and output. In some designs, frame time is an appreciable fraction of the satellite delay.

[7]Land-line circuits are better characterized by errors occurring in bursts, rather than randomly as assumed here for illustrative purposes. See, for example, [LUCK 73].

of 68% could be achieved with a block size of 1000 bits. On a satellite circuit, the peak realizable efficiency would be halved, and could be achieved only if block size were increased to about 3000 bits [CACC 75]. The situation deteriorates rapidly at higher data rates — clearly, SAW-ARQ is not useful for wideband satellite transmission.[8]

Go-back-N (GBN) protocols are exemplified by HDLC (high-level data link control) and IBM's similar SDLC (synchronous data link control). HDLC places a serial number on each block; in most implementations, the block count is modulo-8; thus the number of blocks that can be outstanding without ambiguity is $N = 7$. In the error control procedure, an ACK or a NAK is received for each block identified by serial number. Suppose that block 6 in a sequence is being transmitted, while a NAK is received for block 2, indicating that it was in error. After completing block 6, the transmitter goes back to block 2 (held in buffer), retransmits it, and continues to retransmit each subsequent block. The additional "cost" of an error is the retransmission of blocks 3 through 6, but this cost is usually much lower than the deadtime of SAW-ARQ, especially on satellite circuits. However, to avoid deadtime in the GBN scheme, even on a perfect channel with no errors, we must insure that we receive an ACK or NAK before the outstanding block count register is full. This can be expressed as the condition $n > B\tau/(N-1)$. For example, if $N = 7$, $B = 56$ kbps, and $\tau = 0.54$ sec, the block size (n) must be greater than 5040 bits. At a T1 line rate, the necessary (n) would be 140,000 bits, far greater than a block size desirable for other reasons. If the protocol's N were extended, say, to 127 (an 8-bit field), the block size could be as low as 6600 bits. Thus for high-data-rate satellite transmission, an HDLC-type protocol should have an extended block-count field.

For GBN-ARQ, the throughput efficiency is

$$T_{\text{GBN}} \geq \frac{1 - P_n}{1 + ZP_n} \qquad \text{where } Z = \left[\!\left[\frac{B\tau}{n} \right]\!\right] + 1 \leq N \tag{6.4}$$

The double bracket indicates that the quantity $B\tau/n$ is to be rounded to the next highest integer (after [BURT 72].). The condition $Z \leq N$ ensures no deadtime, as discussed above. In fact, this term establishes the block size for maximum transmission efficiency (again, neglecting overhead bits), occurring when $n = B\tau/(N-1)$. As n increases beyond that size, efficiency decreases relatively slowly, because of the increasing probability that a block will be in error.

Selective-repeat (SR) ARQ requires retransmission only of an identified block received in error. The throughput efficiency of this technique is approximately equal to the probability of *not* having to retransmit a block, which in turn is the complement of the block error rate: $T_{SR} = 1 - P_n$. If we again assume a binary symmetric channel with random bit errors,

---

[8]The American Satellite Corporation offers as part of its services a Satellite Delay Compensation Unit (SDCU) that allows the use of Bi-sync and similar protocols over satellite circuits with far lower efficiency penalties than described above. This is accomplished by immediately returning an ACK to the transmitting terminal from the *transmitting* SDCU at the end of a block, even though much time has yet to pass before the receiving SDCU and terminal receive that block. Error control is effected between SDCU's (including the satellite circuit) by buffering and using an HDLC-like protocol with go-back-N ARQ.

$$T_{SR} \simeq (1 - P_b)^n \qquad N \geq \frac{B\tau}{n} + 1 \tag{6.5}$$

In this case, and again ignoring overhead, the efficiency can be made arbitrarily large, approaching $(1 - P_b)$ as the block size is *decreased*. However, the block count field must be large enough to preclude deadtime, as in the case of GBN-ARQ. Further, at some point as block size is decreased, the relative overhead of the rapidly increasing block count field can no longer be ignored. The error control mechanisms also need to be "smarter" than with GBN. Nevertheless, efficient transmission of very high data rates on channels of even moderate error rates requires such steps.

Forward error-correcting (FEC) techniques, such as of BCH, Golay, and Viterbi constructions, can provide major gains in error rate performance, at the cost of transmission efficiency. Such codes are expressed in terms of a transmission rate, defined as the ratio of the number of information bits to the total number of bits transmitted after the encoding process. For example, an FEC encoder producing a bit stream containing as many redundant bits as information bits provides a rate $1/(1 + 1) = 1/2$ code, with an efficiency of $1/2 = 50\%$. A soft-decision Viterbi decoder of rate $= 1/2$, properly matched to the modulation process, can provide a coding "gain" equivalent to an increase of nearly 5 dB in signal-to-noise ratio, greater than the 3 dB implied by the rate. The FEC process itself effectively defines the throughput efficiency, and is not affected by round-trip delay as in the ARQ techniques.

6.5.3 Cost

The outstanding economic characteristic of satellite communication, as compared with any other medium, is its cost insensitivity to distance. The components of cost are those of the ground segment (at least two earth stations for a point-to-point link) and the space segment (the satellite itself and associated ground control equipment). As long as the earth stations are in the field of view of the satellite's antennas, it makes little difference where they are located. The transmitter powers, antenna sizes, and receive sensitivities required to establish a channel of a given quality remain substantially the same.

The qualifications in the preceding statements relate to a few second-order effects. As regards earth station location, there will be variations in the costs of the site itself and construction. Perhaps more important, frequency coordination problems (relating to interference) may preclude certain combinations of frequency and location. Also, earth station locations that require low antenna elevation angles (below about 10°) experience a higher noise factor and susceptibility to atmospherics, hence lower signal quality and availability. A station located near the edges of the satellite's beam may require a larger, more complex antenna, a lower-noise-figure receiver, and/or higher transmitter power to offset the effective loss of satellite antenna gain. Nevertheless, these factors are secondary to the basic point that satellite links are distance insensitive.

6.5.3.1 Services from Common Carriers

With advances in technology and increased utilization, the cost of satellite circuits continues to fall. In the INTELSAT system, annual charges for a half-circuit

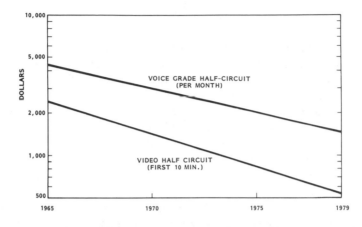

Figure 6.4. Cost trends of transmission via Intelsat. Those costs represent system costs charged to common carriers, as opposed to tariffs available to individual users, and thus reflect more accurately the trend of falling satellite communication costs: about 8 to 10% per year.

have dropped from $32,000 in 1965 to $5000 in 1979. Fig. 6.4 shows the historical user cost trend of satellite voice-grade and television channels between several points. By comparison, the cost of terrestrial transmission, when available, has also been decreasing, but not nearly as dramatically.

If satellite communication costs are distance insensitive, why does a voice-grade circuit from New York to Los Angeles cost more than one from New York to Chicago? The answer is one illustration of the powerful influence exerted by economic and regulatory issues, which are not necessarily consistent with what is technologically possible. The satellite circuit to Los Angeles costs more simply because it costs more to provide it by any other means. Or, to put it another way, a NYC–LA circuit can be sold for more than a NYC–CHI circuit. Prior to the possibility of satellite transmission, an extensive terrestrial network evolved, based on cable and microwave radio. Transcontinental networks were established using these facilities, the allocated cost of which is a direct function of distance. The existing terrestrial network represents a substantial investment that may not have been fully recovered through revenues. It is considered to be in the public interest to maintain and upgrade these facilities; not only do they provide services to the large number of intermediate points that will not be served by satellite for some time to come, but also the terrestrial facilities provide alternative paths in the event that the satellite services are not available. Consequently, governmental telecommunications policies allow, even encourage, tariff structures for satellite communications that reflect distance-sensitive rates, among other reasons, to preserve the maintenance of terrestrial facilities. Similar reasoning applies to intercontinental circuit pricing policies, as for example in considering satellite versus transoceanic cable.

230

Two trends will have major impact on the current situation: (1) the entry into the communications market of new, specialized satellite carriers having no investment in the plant of past technology; and (2) the eventual outcome of changes in the areas of policy and regulation, as exemplified by the current efforts to rewrite the Communications Act of 1934.

6.5.3.2 Private Satellite Links

Wholly owned private satellite communication systems can take full advantage of all cost advantages afforded by the technology. As discussed earlier, the space segment is very expensive; at present, ownership of a satellite for purely private (non-common carrier) purposes is probably not warranted economically. However, portions of a communications satellite's capacity can be leased on a dedicated, long-term basis at a price that is a reasonable approximation of its proportionate cost.

For example, part of a WESTAR transponder can be leased at a cost based on fractional bandwidth or power, whichever is greater. A transponder carrying some number of independent portions is called a *shared-use transponder* and is normally operated at "backoff" (reduced) power levels in order to minimize intermodulation interference between the users' channels that result from nonlinearities in the transponder circuitry. Typical backoff parameters are 8 dB on input and 4.5 dB on output, meaning that proportionately lower numbers are used in link design calculations of the form of Sec. 6.4.4. For the more critical downlink, a typical U.S. domestic transponder is rated for 36-MHz bandwidth and maximum of 28.5-dBW transmit power; shared usage would then be calculated on the basis of bandwidth required (including guard bands) as a fraction of 36 MHz, or power required as a fraction of 28.5 dBW (700 W). Sec. 6.7 contains an example of shared usage.

The costs of earth stations have reached the point where they are well within the range of consideration by substantial users of communications. Costs of representative types of earth stations are shown in Fig. 6.5. Cost is directly proportional to bandwidth, which for clarity of presentation has been normalized to that necessary for FM/FDM analog telephony to CCITT standards. The effect of a different signal structure or modulation method is to change the scale.

The economic attraction of dedicated satellite communication is considerable, and is becoming more favorable for even the more casual user. Some examples of current users who are taking advantage of the possibilities were discussed in Sec. 6.1.

6.5.3.3 Satellite Network Cost Considerations

From the potential user's point of view, a frequent question is: How does satellite transmission compare in cost with alternative (terrestrial) media? The fact that satellite transmission is insensitive to distance between terminals has given rise to the concept of break-even distance, that distance between terminals at which terrestrial transmission costs rise to equal satellite transmission costs. Figure 6.6 gives an indication of break-even distance at the highest data rates commonly available for both media [MCEL 78, STAM 78]. As one would expect, the figure also shows that break-even distance drops substantially as one moves from a point-to-point circuit to

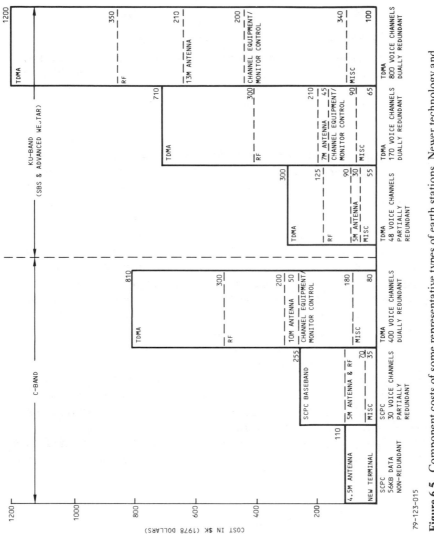

Figure 6.5. Component costs of some representative types of earth stations. Newer technology and increased production rates are putting great pressure on costs, particularly at the low end of earth station capacity. (After [MCEL 78].)

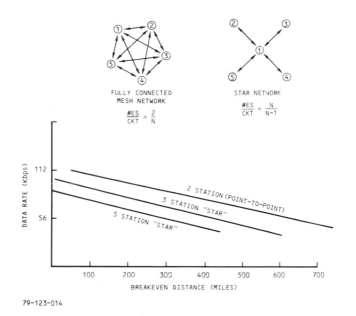

FULLY CONNECTED
MESH NETWORK

$$\frac{\#ES}{CKT} = \frac{2}{N}$$

STAR NETWORK

$$\frac{\#ES}{CKT} = \frac{N}{N-1}$$

79-123-014

Figure 6.6. Break-even distance for satellite communication as a function of data rate, showing the further cost advantage of network connectivity. Costs, hence break-even distance, will drop with the next generation of satellites incorporating advanced features such as on-board processing and switching. (After [MCEL 78].)

a multistation network that shares resources; further reductions would occur for fully connected (mesh) networks.

The cost of a network is a function of the efficiency of the resource-sharing mechanisms, and hence the access technique, as discussed subsequently. To set the stage, a comparison of the relative space segment costs for three important multiple-access techniques is shown in Fig. 6.7 for earth station sizes in the practical range of interest [ROSN 75]. The channel capacity in these cases is 16 kbps; the spread between TDMA and the other techniques would be expected to increase for wider bandwidths, showing a significant advantage even with small earth stations.

The reason for space segment costs being a function of earth station size is a reflection of the earlier sections of this chapter, which discussed the trade-offs between satellite size (and cost) and earth station size (and cost). In a network comprising a large number of geographically dispersed users, the total ground segment cost would dominate the network cost. Experience indicates that earth station cost scales approximately by the 2.4 power of G/T [DICK 74]. The space-segment cost for TDMA from Fig. 6.7 can be approximated as proportional to the -1.8 power of G/T. It is left as an exercise to examine the minimum network cost as a function of the number of earth stations in the system [CHOU 78].

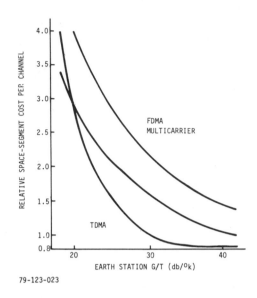

79-123-023

Figure 6.7. Relative space-segment cost for three multiple-access techniques. (From [DICK 74].)

6.6 EFFICIENT NETWORKING WITH SATELLITES

Given due attention to its particular characteristics, a point-to-point satellite channel can be employed in a network, just as any other transmission medium. The medium of satellites, however, has a very special property not shared by other media — a satellite is directly accessible by terminals located in a very large portion of the earth's surface. The implications are profound: it is possible for any terminal within view of a given satellite to establish a direct communication link with any other terminal visible to that satellite. Theoretically, if communication is desired with any geographic point, it is necessary merely to place an earth station terminal there.

The form of network topology naturally possible with communciation via satellite also has major impact on networking efficiency. Consider the network forms of Fig. 6.6. Using terrestrial transmission media, the tendency in network design is toward achieving economies of scale by concentration of traffic in few routes, because the cost of a route is proportional to distance; clearly, the transmission costs of a terrestrial mesh network would be substantially greater than the cost of a star network. With transmission via satellite, however, the opposite can be true. Consider the star network, wherein each link is established in a satellite. Suppose that terminal 2 has traffic for terminal 5 — it would be necessary to use the satellite twice (from 2 to 1, then 1 to 5) to transport the information. Since all terminals are in view of the satellite, it should be possible for terminal 1 to transmit directly to terminal 5 as in the mesh network diagram, thereby achieving greater efficiency in satellite usage. What is needed to accomplish this is some form of multiple access to the common satellite.

234

Preferably, such access should be on a demand-assigned nature: that is, access to and use of a network's resources would be granted only when required — "on demand."

Another benefit derives from a mesh network. If the central node of a star network were to become inoperative, no communication would be possible between any of the terminals. If any of the nodes in a mesh network were to fail, only communication with that node would be affected. This can be an extremely important consideration in network architecture requiring high availability and survivability.

A final consideration of satellite network topology concerns transmission delay. If the traffic matrix is such that communication is to be established between any pair of nodes, only a fully interconnected mesh network can provide a single-hop circuit delay (about 270 msec). Any other topology will require at least a two-hop delay for some circuits. For example, in a star network, communication between the hub and any outlying terminal will experience a one-hop delay, but communication between any pair of outlying terminals will suffer a minimum of two hop delays—from transmitting terminal to hub, plus another from hub to receiving terminal, plus the switching delay in the hub.

The earlier sections of this chapter briefly explained and gave examples of FDMA techniques which derived primarily from the needs of telephony. It was also shown that the more advanced of these techniques, such as SPADE, could be used effectively for moderate data rates and interconnectivity. Economical, richly interconnected networks carrying wide bandwidths for digital transmission, however, will require accessing and networking techniques based on time-division principles; the universal appearance of such techniques is inevitable.

As with any transmission system, the basic parameters susceptible to trade-off are power, bandwidth (or throughput), and time. Implicitly, we have been working with these parameters in the earlier discussions. The particular possibilities offered by digital transmission and processing lead to some very powerful techniques that are just now coming into use. These are briefly described in the following paragraphs (see [MART 78, ROSN 75, SPIL 77, WHIT 78]).

6.6.1 Basic Time-Division Multiple Access (TDMA)

The simplest form of time-division multiple access (TDMA) is illustrated in Fig. 6.8. Assume that all earth stations have synchronized clocks and that each is allocated a fixed time slot for transmission and reception that is known by all users. Then, during its assigned transmission slot time, station 1 transmits a burst of data intended for the other stations. Knowing the time at which station 2, say, is expecting to receive data, station 1 inserts its traffic for station 2 in the proper subslot in its transmissions. Similarly, traffic intended for other users is properly slotted; and other stations take their respective turns in transmitting and receiving. The depicted guard time allows for differences in transmission delay and prevents overlap of data bursts. If all stations are equipped with a properly synchronized system clock, gross differences in delay due to different slant ranges to the satellite can be accounted for, thereby reducing the guard time to that needed for satellite positional variations (Sec. 6.5.4).

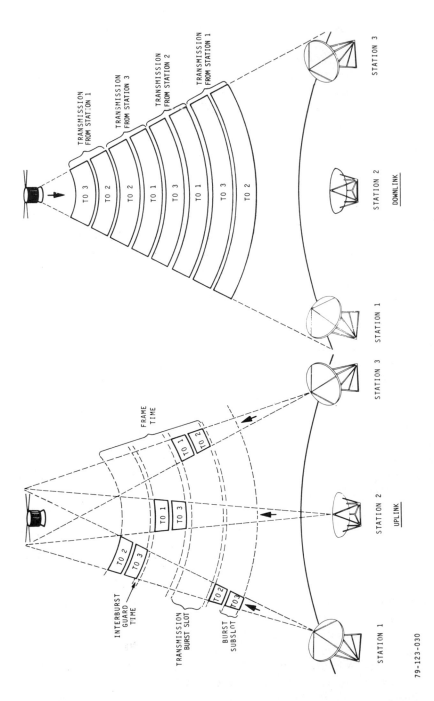

Figure 6.8. Basic TDMA satellite transmission and reception timing.

TRANSMISSION FROM STATION 1

TRANSMISSION FROM STATION 3

TRANSMISSION FROM STATION 2

TRANSMISSION FROM STATION 1

TO 3   TO 2   TO 2   TO 1   TO 3   TO 1   TO 3   TO 2

STATION 3

STATION 2
DOWNLINK

STATION 1

STATION 3   STATION 1

FRAME TIME

TO 1   TO 2

TO 1   TO 3

TO 2   TO 3

INTERBURST GUARD TIME

TRANSMISSION BURST SLOT

BURST SUBSLOT

TO 2   TO 3

STATION 2
UPLINK

STATION 1

79-123-030

236

In the basic TDMA scheme depicted in Fig. 6.8, it is assumed that the satellite antenna's beamwidth is broad enough to provide coverage of all user stations, in both transmit and receive modes. Thus the satellite is required to have only the simplest transponder; all system timing is provided in the earth stations. However, each station is limited in throughput to a fraction of the bandwidth with which the satellite transponder *and* the earth stations must operate. Assuming equal assignments of slot times to each station, the proportion of time, and hence bandwidth, available for any point-to-point circuit is $1/N(N - 1)$. In the case illustrated, if the earth stations and transponders were operating at a rate of 60 Mbps, the maximum throughput for the circuit, say from user 1 to user 3, would be $60/(3 \times 2) = 10$ Mbps. Note that, although the data port of a terminal can operate at a continuous data rate of 10 Mbps, the terminal actually transmits and receives in bursts at a data rate of 60 Mbps. In this case it is necessary for a terminal to have a buffer on input and output; alternatively, if the data source/sink can accommodate the higher-speed bursts, no buffer is required.

Of course, a similar situation could have been created with FDMA. Each station could be assigned an equivalent portion of the transponder's 36-MHz bandwidth, or $36/4 \times 3 = 3$ MHz, less some amount for frequency guard band. In general, however, the overhead of time guard bands with TDMA can be substantially less than the frequency guard bands with FDMA (requiring 10 to 20% more bandwidth per carrier).

A major operational advantage of TDMA, as compared with FDMA, is that the full available power of a transponder can be utilized. It will be recalled from the earlier discussions that multiple-carrier FDM operation with transponders of current design requires that the transmitter output power be "backed off" sufficiently to operate in the linear region, so as to avoid intermodulation interference between the multiple users. With TDM operation, such constraints are removed, allowing the transponder transmitter to operate at its most efficient point, which usually corresponds to maximum rated power.

6.6.2 Demand-Assigned TDMA

The full potential advantage of TDMA can be perceived by imagining a situation based on Fig. 6.8 wherein, say, user 2 has no traffic intended for user 1 at the time when the "2-to-1" slot rolls around. If nothing more were done in the system, the available throughput of 10 Mbps on that circuit would simply be wasted. Suppose that we were to add a capability in each station to do two things: (1) the transmitter inserts in the preamble of each burst an address identifying the intended recipient, and (2) the receiver is arranged to process only bursts which are addressed to it. Recall that user 2 has no traffic for user 1, but further suppose that user 2 has more traffic for user 3 than can be accommodated in the normal "2-to-3" subslot. Now, user 2 can readdress the burst occupying the normal 2-to-1 slot to user 3, thereby doubling its throughput and accommodating the additional traffic on that circuit. Thus we have the makings of a demand assignment TDMA (DTDMA) scheme[9] that can more efficiently utilize total channel capacity for multiple, noncontinuous users.

[9]In some system usages, the acronym stands for distributed or dynamic TDMA.

A further degree of flexibility is possible. Consider all time slots as forming a pool, from which individual users can draw, on an as-needed basis. Following the previous example, the maximum transmission throughput of any station is 2 x 10 = 20 Mbps. Suppose that user 2 needs 30 Mbps to transmit all of his instantaneous traffic, but all other stations need *at that instant* a combined total of 20 Mbps. The system has available six slots of 10 Mbps each; therefore, three slots can be temporarily assigned to user 2, two slots to the others, leaving one slot in the pool to satisfy another demand.

There is a basic analogy between DTDMA and the demand assignment technique (SPADE) used with FDMA systems, described in Sec. 6.2. Current SPADE usage, however, is limited to a 40 kHz/56-kbps channel, and requires several seconds of setup time. Consequently, SPADE is useful for such requirements as telephone calls. A satellite communications network equipped with DTDMA capability would have far greater flexibility; with appropriate station equipment, one could mix short, bursty terminal-to-computer communications with long data file transfers. Further, the frequency changing of transmitters and receivers necessary with DFDMA requires considerably greater complexity of equipment.

There are two fundamental methods of synchronizing and controlling a satellite TDMA system. The simplest method, often called "open-loop synchronization," requires only a simple clock at each station. By calculation or measurement, the gross path delay to each earth station can easily be determined to an accuracy of a fraction of a millisecond, which is the order of the constantly changing satellite positional variation (Sec. 6.5.4). Consequently, the interburst guard time can be sized to accommodate both the path delay indeterminancy and the positional variation—say, about 0.25 msec. If the frame length is much larger, say 50 msec or more, and the number of stations in the network is relatively small, the system capacity "wasted" during the guard time intervals is trivial.

Two major disadvantages exist in an open-loop system, however, when the number of stations is large and/or other constraints exist on the maximum frame time (such as to minimize system response time in a DTDMA network). When these conditions exist, the open-loop guard time overhead can be substantial; consequently, it may be necessary to implement a closed-loop system. Several techniques have been developed for accomplishing this; in general, they involve greater complexity in the earth station equipment to provide for much more precise real-time system timing [HARR 79].

Especially to systems carrying computer communications or mixed types of traffic, the distinction between the TDMA and DTDMA schemes just described are important. This is because of the bursty, noncontinuous nature of such traffic. In the literature, the basic TDMA described earlier is generally referred to as synchronous TDMA, which has the advantage of simplicity at the cost of flexibility [HUST 78]. Techniques capable of some form of adaptability to instantaneous traffic demands, and hence capable of more efficient utilization of system resources, are generally categorized as asynchronous TDMA (ATDMA). With ATDMA, the increased channel utilization is obtained at the expense of increased complexity in the earth station design, to provide for the necessary addressing, allocation, protocols, and buffering to handle statistical fluctuations of traffic. In extreme cases of ATDMA, such as ALOHA (see Chaps. 4 and 5), there may be no system timing whatsoever for control of bursts, or packets. Instead, reliance is placed on protocols, error checking, and acknowledgments to resolve conflicts arising when simultaneous demands are made on the system.

Among the more important ATDMA schemes utilizing packet switching concepts for satellite communication are those described in [ROBE 73, ABRA 73, KLEI 73, CROW 73, BIND 75, JACO 78]. [PICK 77] has described a scheme that adapts channel capacity in accordance with the recent history of channel utilization; a comparison with preassigned TDMA shows an order-of-magnitude improvement in packet delay. A more recent reservation multiple-access scheme, described in [BALA 79], appears to offer greater efficiency in adapting to cases in which all traffic can be treated asynchronously. As in terrestrial networks, there are complex interrelationships between key system parameters, such as the "peakiness" of the traffic, packet size, delay, utilization efficiency, and number of users, and overall system throughput and saturation point. The implications of these aspects are discussed in other chapters of this book.

6.6.3   TDMA Combined with Other Techniques

Further possibilities for satellite system TDMA open up with more sophisticated spacecraft. Figure 6.9 illustrates a TDMA system for point-to-point communication using a satellite equipped with rapidly switched spot beams (such as these produced by a phased-array antenna), and on-board processing. Bursts addressed to specific earth receivers are transmitted from the earth stations. These could be interleaved on a common channel, as in Fig. 6.8, but here we have assumed that individual channels (or transponders) are available. In a satellite having multiple beams, the switching of data from a given receive beam to the appropriate transmit beam can be accomplished on a fixed program basis. Alternatively, a more flexible system can be arranged with more complex processing in the satellite, which would read addresses in each burst and switch accordingly.

Combinations of techniques allow further flexibility. For example, a system could be designed to comprise regional subnetworks covered by area-coverage beams. Within each area, bursts from transmitting stations are interleaved, and are routed and switched in the satellite for relay to stations within the same subnetwork, or to another subnetwork, as desired [WHIT 78].

With such techniques almost complete flexibility in instantaneously optimizing the time/bandwidth/power trade-offs is possible. In addition to networking arrangements, some very real operational problems can be attacked. To illustrate, it will be recalled that a major deterrent to full exploitation of the higher-frequency satellite communication bands is the very high path attenuation suffered in periods and locales of intense precipitation. With appropriate processing, halving the transmitted information rate has the same effect as using twice as much power, thus adding another dimension to intelligent use of the total system resources made possible by TDMA.

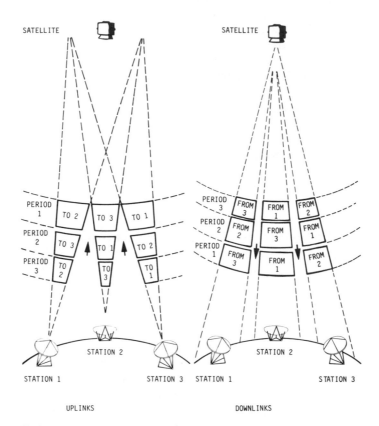

Figure 6.9. Satellite-switched TDMA with spot transmit beams. Satellites with such narrow beams and on-board switching will afford extremely high transmission efficiencies; however, some of the advantages of the broadcast mode of general-coverage wide beam will be lost in some network applications.

6.7 EXAMPLE OF A PRIVATE SATELLITE COMMUNICATION NETWORK DESIGN

In this section we consider some design issues for a private satellite communication network, using material previously covered in this chapter. The basis for the network design is the recently announced Digital Communications Corporation DYNAC Terminal, an integrated, low-cost earth station that can be used in various TDMA and DTDMA configurations in conjunction with leased transmission capacity in a 4/6-GHz satellite [SALA 79]. DYNAC terminals are available with various options, as summarized in Box 6.2.

240

BOX 6.2. *Basic and Optional Features of a DYNAC Terminal Package.*

Basic Terminal Configuration

Antenna	7 m diameter (G_R = 47.5 dB; G_T = 50.3 dB)
Receiver	GaAs-FET low-noise amplifier, 120 K (with 7-m antenna, G/T = 25.3 dB/K)
Transmitter	TWTA, 40 W (EIRP 66 dBW with 7-m antenna)
Modem	QPSK modulation, implementation margin = 1.8 dB
	Transmission rates—selectable at 269, 538, 806, 1613, 2048, 2152 kbps
	Occupied spectrum = 0.57 x transmission rate
	Error coding—rate 1/2 convolutional forward error correcting, selectable in or out
System reliability	MTBF = 3600 hr (nonredundant)

Options

Antenna	10 m diameter (G_R = 50.6 dB; G_T = 53.4 dB)			
	4.6 m diameter (G_R = 43.8 dB; G_T = 46.6 dB)			
Receiver	Parametric amplifier, 45 K			
Antenna/receiver combinations	4.6 m		7 m	10 m
	45 K	G/T = 24.5 dB/K	28.2	31.3
	120K	G/T = 21.6 dB/K	25.3	28.4
DTDMA network controller	Frame length — selectable, 50 to 250 ms			
	Overhead			
	Protocol	104 bits/burst		
	Signaling	512 bits/burst for control terminal		
		88 bits/burst per terminal, other than control		
	Guard time	0.3 msec/burst		
Multiplexer	Statistical type			
Full equipment redundancy	Available at approximately double price			
Modem	Rate 3/4 or 7/8 FEC			
Transmitter	TWTA, 75 W			
	Solid state, 4 W			

DYNAC terminals can operate in an adaptive demand-assigned TDMA mode, with the statistical multiplexer option in each terminal and the DTDMA controller option in one terminal designated as the network reference terminal. The network may be configured as either star or mesh topology. In a star configuration, the central hub normally would act as the network reference station; in a mesh configuration, any one of the terminals may be so designated. The network operation is based on a *network map*, a table containing assignments of slot time and length for each specific circuit; the network map is resident in each terminal. A request for more bandwidth (slot length), or release of excessive bandwidth, is determined in each terminal by a measure of buffer occupancy, then is transmitted to the reference station. The reference terminal is equipped with a minicomputer unit (DTDMA network controller) which computes a new network map as required. The algorithm for determining a new map can be customized to follow one's desired strategy in various situations (e.g., if the aggregate demand for bandwidth were to exceed network capacity, a proportionate reduction in each terminal's requested bandwidth might be made). After computation, the network map is transmitted to all terminals. Normally, the control station can make adjustments in the network map by a single control transmission per system frame time; in cases of extreme change of network traffic patterns, several transmissions may be required. After all terminals have acknowledged correct reception, the reference station sends an "enable new map" instruction to all terminals.

Several round-trip transmissions, and consequently 1 sec or more of time, are required for the network to adapt to changing demands. However, the DTDMA scheme is robust and easy to implement at low cost. The noninstantaneous response of the network makes possible the use of open-loop synchronization and a relatively long frame time (50 to 250 msec); these parameters are important in consideration of low cost.

Suppose that it is desired to provide a fully connected network linking six locations in the United States, and that studies show that the average one-way traffic between any two locations is 50 kbps. We will assume that all locations are within prime view of a typical domestic satellite, capacity in which can be leased at a cost of $R_{B/P} \times \$150,000$ per month, where R_P is the required power as a fraction of the transponder's EIRP of 27 dBW (500 W), *or* R_B is the required bandwidth as a fraction of the transponder's bandwidth of 36 MHz, whichever is greater.

Assuming the use of DYNAC terminals, the relevant downlink path calculations for this example are those presented in Sec. 6.4.4. The following steps typify a design scenario for the system:

1. There are $N(N-1) = (5)(4) = 20$ one-way circuits, each to carry an average 50 kbps of traffic. Thus required network data throughput is $(20)(50) = 1000$ kbps. Rate-$1/2$ coding is to be used; thus the minimum required transmission rate is $(2)(1000) = 2000$ kbps. Therefore, select the next highest available DYNAC rate of 2152 kbps.

2. The control terminal requires $104 + 512 = 616$ bits for protocol and signaling overhead, per burst. Each other terminal requires $104 + 88 = 192$ bits/burst. Each terminal transmits one burst per frame, so total protocol and signaling overhead is $(616) + (4)(192) = 1384$ bits/frame. At the 1076-kbps information rate, 1384 bits/frame = 1.3 msec/frame. Total guard time required is $(5)(0.3) = 1.5$ msec/frame. Therefore, total overhead is $1.3 + 1.5 = 2.8$ msec/frame.

3. The required throughput efficiency is 2000 kbps/2152 kbps = 0.93, from the required and selected bit rates, respectively. Efficiency E, overhead OH, and frame time F are related as $F = OH/(1 - E)$. Therefore, the minimum frame time is $F = 2.8/0.07 = 40$ msec, which provides close to the best system response

time. At the other extreme with a 250-msec frame time, efficiency would be improved: $(250 - 3.8)/250 = 0.985$, but network response to changes in traffic demands would be somewhat more sluggish.

4. Occupied spectrum is 1227 kHz (from Box 6.1). Assume that a 15% guard band is necessary: thus required transponder bandwidth is 1411 kHz, and $R_B = (1.411)/36 = 0.039$.

5. From Box 6.1 the required transponder EIRP is 51 W; thus $R_P = 51/500 \cong 0.1$. $R_P > R_B$; therefore, the system is power constrained. Space-segment cost is ($150,000/month)(0.1) = $15,000/month.

6. Consider the parametric amplifier option, assuming that the differential installed cost is $40,000. The difference in G/T is 28.2 - 25.3 = 2.9 dB = 1.9 : 1. The transponder power now required is $51/1.9 = 27$ W and $R_P = 0.054$, still greater than R_B, so space-segment cost is $8,100/month, a savings of $6,900/month. Assuming a 10-year system lifetime and real cost of capital of 5%, the present value (PV)[10] of $6,900/month is about $650,000. The cost of the parametric amplifiers is (5) ($40,000) = $200,000 so a clear PV saving of $450,000 results from electing this option, which will be used in the subsequent steps.

7. Consider the 10-m antenna option, assuming that the differential installed cost is $110,000. Assume that the terminal EIRP has been calculated to be 63.5 dBW (21 W with the 7-m antenna). Thus the 40-W transmitter is required. The 10-m antenna provides a G_T increase of 3.1 dB = 2 : 1, which would reduce necessary transmitter power to $21/2 = 11$ W — still more than the next-lower 5-W transmitter choice, so no possible savings in transmitters. For the downlink, G/T is improved by 31.3 - 29.2 = 3.1 dB = 2 : 1; thus R_P is halved to a value of 0.027. However, the bandwidth factor R_B remains at 0.039 and now becomes the controlling factor of space-segment cost, which is $(0.039)(150) = \$5,900$/month. A further savings over step 6 above of 8,100 - 5,900 = $2,200/month is possible, equivalent to a PV of $207,000. The total cost of antennas is (5)(110) = $550,000; therefore, there are no potential savings gained by using the 10-m antennas if the 40-K low-noise receivers are applied to the 7-m antennas.

8. It is left as an exercise to determine that the 7 m/40 K antenna/receiver combination is more cost effective than a 10 m/120 K combination; also, that fewer earth stations could change the balance.

9. From the viewpoint of availability, the network does not have all the attributes of a mesh network. This is because the control terminal is necessary for network control. However, it would be a simple matter to arrange for another terminal to serve as a backup network control. If both control terminals failed, other

---

[10]Recurring costs and initial investment costs can be compared when a cost of capital (interest rate) and lifetime of the purchase are assumed. The purchase cost can be "mortgaged" with periodic principal and interest payments over the lifetime. Equivalently, the present value (PV) of a stream of periodically recurring costs can be computed like an "inverse mortgage." Tax considerations are ignored here.

terminals would not receive updates. This situation could be covered by an additional arrangement, whereby terminals not receiving valid updates would revert to a predetermined network map, thus maintaining fixed TDMA network connectivity. Assuming a mean time to repair of 12 hr, the availability of a nonredundant terminal is 0.9967. Whether this is adequate depends on many factors beyond the scope of this example. It probably would be worthwhile to provide redundant equipment, at least for the control terminal.

6.8 NEW SATELLITE SYSTEM DESIGNS

As would be expected in a technology area as dynamic and profound in future implications as satellite communications, intense experimental activity has continued unabated. Among the most significant experimental programs have been ATS-6 (of the Advanced Technology Satellite Series), CTS (Communications Technology Satellite) and the Japanese CS project [OTSU 82], about which much can be found in the literature. Other systems have served as hosts for test and demonstration of important subsystem techniques (e.g., multiple-access and direct intersatellite communications).

The results of this work, coupled with the successes of extant systems, are defining the next generation of satellite communications systems. Of such future systems, two are highlighted to illustrate key trends: the SBS and Advanced WESTAR/TDRSS systems.

6.8.1 Satellite Business Systems

Satellite Business Systems (SBS) is a joint venture of International Business Machines (IBM), COMSAT General Corporation, and Aetna Life & Casualty Corporation. In 1977, the Federal Communications Commission granted authority to SBS for the construction of a domestic U.S. satellite system that would serve industrial, government, and public service organizations. Service began in mid-1981.

There are several technical and service features of the SBS system that are unique [BARN 77, MCCA 78]. The offering is aimed at the largest organizational users of communications, and will provide wideband channels capable of carrying *all* of a customer's communications needs — voice and image, as well as data over an integrated network. The service is to be provided by small earth stations located on the customer's premises: on the rooftop or parking lot.

Coverage of the 48 contiguous states is to be provided by each of two operating satellites; a third satellite will be held in reserve as an on-ground spare. In the central coverage regions, 5-m antennas (G/T = 30.4 dB/K) will be used. Locations in the coverage extremities (primarily central northwestern and extreme southern United States) will require 7-m antennas (G/T = 33.3 dB/K). These small sizes are possible because of the use of the 12/14-GHz bands.

Transmission is to be entirely digital. Each of 10 satellite channels will initially support a data rate of 43 Mbps, which can be increased to 48 Mbps as future experience permits. The nominal bandwidth of each channel (including guardbands) is 49 MHz. The RF channel has been designed to provide an intrinsic bit-error rate of 1 x 10^{-4}, 99.5% of the time. Forward error correction (FEC), operating at a coding rate of 2/3, is a customer option that will increase the performance to 1 x 10^{-7}.

Another distinguishing feature is that the SBS system design relies on time-division multiple access (TDMA) and demand-assignment (DAMA) techniques for its fundamental operation. The user of a given earth station will have access to ports including all standard data rates through 6.3 Mbps, and an aggregate bandwidth presumably approaching 43 Mbps. Even with the new services such an available bandwidth makes possible, it is not expected that an individual user would require (or could afford) full-time dedication of this bandwidth. Further, traffic destination loading varies as a function of local time. Thus the dynamic allocation of communication capacity in a customer's individual link, as well as in the overall network itself, is handled on an as-needed basis by DTDMA operation. Each earth station will contain a Burst Modem and a Satellite System Controller (SSC), which perform the necessary processing, buffering, switching, and control functions for the DTDMA operation.

The SSC will also perform the analog/digital and digital/analog conversions for voice signals. It is presently planned that voice signals will be transmitted by 32 kbps syllabically companded delta modulation, a technique that affords a 2:1 bandwidth advantage as compared with the pulse-code modulation (PCM) technique used in the telephone networks. Further reduction of digital voice bandwidth occupancy will be accomplished by digital speech interpolation (DSI), a technique that depends on the fact that voice activity on either half of a full-duplex circuit is, on average, about 50% of the time; that is, speakers in a telephone conversation (usually) employ a half-duplex protocol (see Chap. 17 and [WELT 77]).

SBS plans to offer a "total package" integrated-services approach for all existing intracompany communications, as well as taking responsibility for making all arrangements for connections to the public networks (telephone and telex) for "outside" calls. Clearly, this is of immense interest to AT&T, who perceive an encroachment on their historical turf. AT&T have answered with plans for the Advanced Communication Service (ACS), in which IBM perceives intrusion of their data-processing domain. The battle of giants has been joined, and with the FCC, the Justice Department, the Judiciary system and Congress wrestling with the issues opened by the advent of computer communication networks, the decade of the 1980s promises to be interesting indeed.

6.8.2 Tracking Data Relay Satellite System and Advanced WESTAR

In 1976, NASA entered into a leasing contract with the Western Union Telegraph Company[11] for the Tracking and Data Relay Satellite System (TDRSS), expected to

---

[11]The TDRSS program is now managed by the Space Communications Company, a partnership of Continental Telephone, Fairchild Industries and Western Union Telegraph.

be operational in 1983. Aside from the precedent-setting magnitude and nature of the leased offering of a major satellite communication system, TDRSS incorporates several technological innovations of major significance to future telecommunications networks.

Communications links will be provided at K-band (14/15 GHz) and at S-band (2.0 to 2.3 GHz). The frequencies are somewhat different from commercial communications bands; they are reserved for special-purpose government and NASA usage. The K-band ground-to-satellite link will support a bandwidth of 625 MHz, while the satellite-to-ground link will have a multiplexed capability of 650 MHz [POZA 77]. These bandwidths are considerably larger than current operational systems can provide.

The truly significant feat of TDRSS will be the capabilities for intersatellite communications. This is a principal *raison d'etre* for TDRSS; it will provide NASA with higher-quality, lower-cost communications with the space shuttle and other spacecraft and satellites, as compared with the current multiplicity of earth-bound stations located around the globe. Both single and multiple access to a satellite will be possible for a spacecraft. Single-access users will have data rates up to 12 Mbps at S-band, and 300 Mbps at K-band. Up to 20 simultaneous multiple-access users will be tracked by individual beams formed by a phased-array antenna, and will be provided 50-kbps service [HOLM 77, POZA 77].

The implications of direct wideband intersatellite communications are far-reaching. Since a single satellite cannot provide coverage of the entire earth's surface, unrestricted international links could be established via satellite relays without requiring hops back to intervening earth stations. More significant in the long term, internetworking between networks set up on different satellites could be accomplished directly, thus conserving satellite power requirements and reducing spectrum congestion problems with satellite–earth station links, and the attendant transmission delays.

Another significant feature of TDRSS is that spread-spectrum techniques (Chap. 5) will be used for some specified channels. A combination of code-division and time-division multiple access will be possible.

The TDRSS technology is also the basis for Advanced WESTAR commercial services. In addition to 12 conventional 4/6-GHz transponders, 12/14-GHz service will be available at TDMA rates to 250 Mbps. The 12/14-GHz service will be based on yet another innovation — switching of TDMA data in the spacecraft will be possible between 3 regional-coverage, 3 fixed spot beams and 2 steerable spot beams.

6.8.3   Other New Domestic Satellites

In 1980, the FCC imposed a deadline for early consideration of new U.S. domestic satellite applications. As permits are granted, and subsequent construction and launches are successful, these satellites will temporarily relieve the shortage of satellite capacity experienced in the early 1980s. Among the applicants are the existing carriers

(AT&T, RCA and Western Union) and the previously-approved SBS — all mentioned earlier. In addition, three new carriers have made applications.

Hughes Communications, Inc. (HCI) has proposed three satellites for the 4/6 GHz band. Hughes Aircraft designed and constructed the COMSTAR and WESTAR satellites previously described. The HCI satellite is similar, and would use cross-polarization for frequency reuse.

The GTE Satellite Corporation currently owns and operates 4/6 GHz earth stations, but obtains its space segment capacity by subleasing portions of the COMSTAR series. GTE has filed an application for two operational satellites in the 12/14 GHz band, which in turn would require the construction of new earth stations for those frequencies. The GTE design envisions 16 transponders primarily used for digital transmission at 60 Mbps each, with demand-assigned TDMA. Frequency reuse would be achieved by cross-polarization, resulting in a total capacity of 1920 Mbps per satellite. Coverage of all 50 states is planned.

The Southern Pacific Communications Company has proposed an ambitious system comprising four satellites operating in both the 4/6 GHz and 12/14 GHz bands. Uplinks in one band could be cross-strapped to downlinks in the other band, leading to expanded satellite capacity and a very flexible set of access possibilities. Transponders having a bandwidth of 72 MHz, rather than the usual 36 MHz, would be employed. Total capacity of each satellite would be 1728 MHz, or 2880 Mbps.

Mention should be made of Direct Broadcast Satellite (DBS), a new service in the planning stage as this is written. DBS is intended to provide broadcast television services, direct from satellite to home. Inexpensive, small (about 1 m) rooftop antennas are envisioned, which would be made possible by use of special frequencies in the band, and by very high EIRP (55 to 60 dBW) transmitted by the satellites. By July 1981, the FCC had received filings from 12 applicants including CBS, RCA, WU and a subsidiary of COMSAT Corporation. While the service is of wide general interest as an advancement in information distribution, and the technologies developed will be of even broader significance, DBS service *per se* is of little direct importance in the context of computer communication networks. This is because of the receive-only nature of the links with users.

6.9 THE FUTURE OF SATELLITE COMMUNICATIONS

During the course of the preceding discussions, we have explored the current state-of-the-art in the medium of satellite transmission, and have made some extrapolations into the future. Because of the immense importance of the medium to future communications, it would be well to review concisely the principal points:

- Circuits established via satellite systems of current technology can offer performance parameters equivalent to, and often better than, alternative media.
- Satellite circuits possess some fundamentally peculiar attributes, notably

transmission delay, instant accessibility to vast areas of the earth, and cost insensitivity to distance. There are also some special determinants of circuit availability, but these are amenable to control by system design.

- The broadcast nature of satellite communication lends itself naturally to exploitation in large-scale, resource-sharing networks by application of multiple-access techniques.
- The networking possibilities opened by satellite communication (just plug into the network) is creating new demand.
- Real costs are dropping and will continue to drop, both pushed by technological advances and pulled by increased utilization.
- The availablity of low-cost earth stations is greatly increasing the number of points directly served by satellite service. Coupled with the availability of portions of a satellite's capacity, low-cost earth stations are providing enhanced services from common carriers, and make possible completely dedicated private networks.
- Very real limits are visible on the horizon which could severely constrain the ability to meet demand; major advances in technology (e.g., higher frequencies) are needed to circumvent impending satellite space and spectrum congestion.
- Regulatory policies and issues are intermixed with technological considerations in determining the possibilities of services and applications.

The areas of technology that will have the greatest impact on future satellite communication services and applications include launch vehicles,[12] antennas, inter-satellite links, on-board processing, multiple and demand-assigned access, on-board beam switching, error control interfacing, networking, and higher frequencies. We have touched on each of these areas; a review and future outlook is contained in Tab. 6.2.

As a final note, the possibilities of communication by satellite, and in particular potentially universal connectivity, are receiving much attention. A recently completed study by NASA has concluded that revenues from U.S. space communications/information services could amount to $100 billion by the year 2000 [STIN 78]. A key aspect of the study was an examination of possible new services in both the industrial and private user sectors, based on projections made by sophisticated market analysis techniques. Of the candidates, several clear "winners" emerged, which are possible *only* if satellite communications technology is used:

1. *Personal portable communications.* A sort of "citizen's band satellite," which alone could produce $25 billion per year revenue 20 years after introduction

[12]The tremendous importance of the means of satellite orbit emplacement cannot be overlooked. As we have seen in Sec. 6.2.2, launch costs can account for about 40% of total space-segment cost, and launch vehicle limitations are the principal reason for size and weight constraints on satellite design. The next generation of high-capacity satellites depends on the availability of the NASA Space Shuttle. Furthermore, orbit insertion is a risky thing — witness the 1979 and early 1980 losses of SATCOM-III, AYAME-1, AYAME-2, and the ARIANE-2 test vehicle.

Table 6.2. *Assessment of Current and Future Communications Satellite Technology Areas (after [VANT 77]).*

Technology Area	Current Status	Possible Future (ca. 1985)
Intersatellite links	None (TDRSS in development)	1 Gbps; later higher rates via millimeter-wave or laser links
Multiple-access trunking	Mostly FDMA, 36 MHz	Extensive TDMA, 100 Mbps
Demand-assigned data and telephony	SPADE/SCPC, 40-kHz bandwidth	Continued SCPC, appearance of TDMA; TDMA on specialized carrier and private networks
Packet data and voice networks	Early experiments, ARPA	Development and use; reservation features
Data collection	Military CDMA; expensive	Low-cost CDMA, possibly ALOHA type
Computer communication	BER = 10^{-8}	BER = 10^{-12}; long, concatenated codes
Mobile applications	Mostly military; expensive	Reduced cost; applications of coding for multipath immunity
Digital voice	64 kbps PCM	16–32 kbps delta modulation; some 5–10 kbps LPC; use of DSI
Frequency bands	4/6 GHz (C-band)	Considerable 12/14 GHz in service; experimentation at 20/30 GHz
Satellite power	Limited in 4/6 GHz band due to coexistence with terrestrial microwave	Much higher EIRP in 12/14- and 20/30-GHz bans; adequate for direct-to-home TV broadcast
Satellite spacing	Every 4° of orbital are at 4/6 GHz	Possibly 3°, or every 2°, pending FCC decision

2. *Large-scale data transfer.* Involving both businesses and libraries, producing over $5 billion per year 10 years after introduction

3. *Locator system.* Button-sized transmitters that could be affixed to packages, vehicles, shipments, nuclear fuel containers, or even people; could produce $75 to $250 million per year 10 years after introduction.

REFERENCES

ABRA 73   Abramson, N., "Packet Switching with Satellites," *AFIPS Conf. Proc.*, Vol. 42, June 1973.

BALA 79   Balagangadhar, M. M., and R. L. Pickholtz, "A Reservation Multiple Access Technique for Data Transmission via Satellites," *Natl. Telecommun. Conf.*, Washington, D.C., October 1979.

BARN 77   Barnla, J. D., "The SBS Digital Communications Satellite System," *Proc. EASCON 77*, Washington, D.C., 1977, Paper 31/2.

BIND 75   Binder, R., "A Dynamic Packet Switching System for Satellite Broadcast Channels," *Proc. ICC 75*, San Francisco, June 1975.

BLAC 77   Black, S. T., "Sudan Digital Communications INTELSAT Earth Station," *Exposition Proc.*, Vol. 3, INTELCOM, Atlanta, 1977.

BURT 72   Burton, H. O., and D. D. Sullivan, "Errors and Error Control," *Proc. IEEE*, Vol. 60, No. 11, November 1972, pp. 1293–1301.

BUX 78   Bux, W., K. Kuemmerle, and H. L. Truong, "Results on the Performance of Balanced HDLC Procedures," *NTC 78 Conf. Rec.*, Vol. 2, pp. 28.3.1 to 28.3.7.

CACC 75   Cacciamani, E. R., and Kap S. Kim, "Circumventing the Problem of Propagation Delay on Satellite Data Channels," *Data Commun.*, July–August 1975.

CHOU 78   Chou, W., and M. Gerla, "Cost Impact of Satellite Technology on Future Large Data Networks," *Future Networks*, Infotech, Maidenhead, U.K. 1978.

CHU 74   Chu, W. W., "Optimal Message Block Size with Error Detection and Retransmission Strategies," *IEEE Trans. Commun.*, Vol. COM-22, October 1974, pp. 1516–1525.

COOP 80   Cooper, R. B., Jr., "Low Cost Backyard Satellite TV Earth Station," *Radio-Electronics*, February 1980, pp. 47.

CROW 73   Crowther, W., R. Rettberg, D. Walden, S. Ornstein and F. Heart, "A System for Broadcast Communication: Reservation ALOHA," *Proc. 6th Hawaii Intl. Conf. on System Sciences*, January 1973, pp. 371–374.

CUCC 80   Cuccia, C. L., "Regulations Direct Satcom Antennas," *Microwave Syst. News*, March 1980, pp. 45–57.

DEMO 81   "Round Trip Delay," Parts 1 and 2, *The Demodulator*, GTE Lenkurt Corp., San Carlos, Calif., July and August, 1981.

DICK 74   Dicks, J. L., "Domestic and/or Regional Services through INTELSAT IV Satellites," *COMSAT Tech. Rev.*, Vol. 4, No. 1, Spring 1974.

DILL 79   Dill, G. and A. Tomozawa, "Time Domain Multiple-Access from and Burst Synchronization for Spot-Beam Satellites," *EASCON 79 Conf. Rec.*, Washington, D.C., October 1979.

DIRE 80   *The 1980 Satellite Directory*, Phillips Publishing, Washington, D.C., 1980.

EDWA 78   Edwards, M., "Transmission Sources," *Commun. News*, May 1978, pp. 68–77.

HARR 79   Harrington, E. H., "Issues in Terrestrial/Satellite Network Synchronization," *IEEE Trans. Commun.*, Vol. COM-27, No. 11, 1979, pp. 1690–1695.

HOLM 77   Holmes, W. M. Jr., "TDRSS System Design," *NTC 77 Conf. Rec.*, Vol. 1, Los Angeles, December 1977, pp. 09:2-1 to 09:2-6.

HORN 77   Horna, O. H., *COMSAT Tech. Rev.*, Vol. 7, No. 2, Fall 1977.

HUST 78   Husted, J., and S. Dinwiddy, "Low Cost Satellite Data Transmission Networks Using Demand Assigned TDMA," *Proc. 4th Intl. Conf. Digital Satellite Commun.*, Montreal 1978.

HUYN 77   Huynh, D., H. Kobayashi, and F. F. Kuo, "Optimal Design of Mixed-Media Packet-Switching Networks: Routing and Capacity Assignments," *IEEE Trans. Commun.*, COM-75, No. 1, 1977, pp. 158–169.

JACO 78	Jacobs, I. M., R. Binder, and E. V. Hoversten, "General Purpose Packet Satellite Networks," *Proc. IEEE*, Vol. 66, No. 11, 1978, pp. 1448–1467.
KLEI 73	Kleinrock, L., and S. Lam, "Packet Switching in a Slotted Satellite Channel," *AFIPS Conf. Proc.*, Vol. 42, June 1973.
LAMS 78	Lamsey, R. M., and M. R. Freeling, "RCA's Satellite Distribution System for Small Dish Earth Terminals," *EASCON 78 Rec.*, Arlington, pp. 362–367.
LUCK 73	Lucky, R. W., "Common Carrier Data Communication," Ch., Computer Communication Networks, N. Abramson and F. Kuo (eds.), Prentice-Hall, Englewood Cliffs, N.J., 1973.
MARS 78	Marsten, R. B., "Satellites and Space Communication," *Telecommun. J.*, Part 1, June 1978, pp. 305–314.
MART 78	Martin, J., *Communications Satellite Systems*, Prentice-Hall, Englewood Cliffs, N.J., 1978.
MCCA 78	McCabe, R. W., "Satellite Business Systems — Innovative Services for Business Communications," *AFIPS Conf. Proc. (NCC)*, June 1978, Anaheim, Calif., pp. 721–725.
MCEL 78	McElroy, J. H., Study Manager, *Technological Priorities for Future Satellite Communications*, Goddard Space Flight Center, July 1978.
OTSU 82	Otsu, Y., *et al.*, "Japanese Domestic Satellite Communications Systems Experiments," *Microwave Journal*, January 1982, pp. 67–80.
OWIN 79	Owings, J. L., "Satellite Transmission Protocol for High Speed Data," *SBS Systems Briefs*, SBS, Inc., McLean, Va., 1979.
PART 78	Parthasarathy, R. and T. M. Kelley, "Leasing of INTELSAT Transponders for Domestic Services," *EASCON '78 Rec.*, Arlington, Va., 1978, pp. 310–315.
PICK 77	Pickholtz, R. L., and W. F. Vogelzang, "Dynamic Satellite Slot Allocations for Data Packets via Adaptive TDMA," *Proc. Natl. Telecommun. Conf., 1977*, pp. 48:2-1 to 48:2-6.
POZA 77	Poza, H. B., "TDRSS Telecommunications Payloads: An Overview," *NTC '77 Conf. Rec.*, Vol. 2, Los Angeles, December 1977, pp. 19:1-1 to 19:1-5.
PUEN 71	Puenti, J. G., W. G. Schmidt, and A. M. Werth, "Multiple Access Techniques for Commercial Satellites," *Proc. IEEE*, Vol. 58, February 1971, pp. 218–229.
ROBE 73	Roberts, L. G., "Dynamic Allocation of Satellite Capacity through Packet Reservation," *AFIPS Conf. Proc.*, Vol. 42, June 1973.
ROSN 75	Rosner, R. D., "An Advanced Communications System Concept Employing Demand Assignment Satellites," Technical Note No. 15-75, Defense Communications Engineering Center (DCA), March 1975.
SALA 78	Salamoff, S., "SPEC Is Efficient Satellite Technique," *Commun. News*, February 1978.
SALA 79	Salamoff, S., D. Roos, and J. Steinhorn, "DYNAC: A Low-Cost Data/Voice Communications Network," *Telecommunications*, August 1979, pp. 71–76.
SATE 78	*Satellite News*, Vol. 1, No. 8, Washington, D.C., December 1978.
SCHM 69	Schmidt, W. G., et al., "INTELSAT's Experimental 700-Channel TDMA/DA System," *Conf. Rec., IEEE Intl. Conf. Digital Satellite Commun.*, London, November 1969.

SCHW 73   Schwartz, J. W., and M. Muntner, "Multiple Access Communications for Computer Nets," in *Computer Communication Networks*, Norman Abramson and Franklin F. Kuo, eds., Prentice-Hall, Englewood Cliffs, N.J., 1973, Chap. 8.

SHAS 75   Shastry, A. R. K., "Performance of Hybrid Error Control Schemes on Satellite Channels," *IEEE Trans. Commun.*, Vol. COM-23, July 1975, pp. 689–694.

SPIL 77   Spilker, J. J. Jr., *Digital Communications by Satellite*, Prentice-Hall, Englewood Cliffs, N.J., 1977.

STAM 78   Stamminger, R., "U.S. Domestic Satellite Communications: A 10-year Forecast," Future Systems, Inc., Rep. No. 215, April 1978.

STIN 78   Stine, G. H., "The Economics of Future Space Communications Systems," *Satellite Commun.*, September 1978, pp. 20–25.

VANT 77   VanTrees, H. L., E. V. Hoversten, and T. P. McGarty, "Communications Satellite: Looking to the 1980's," *IEEE Spectrum*, December 1977, pp. 43–51.

WADH 76   Wadham, P. N., "Communications Satellite Outages Due to the Environment," *SMPTE Journal*, Vol. 85, February 1976, pp. 70–72.

WELT 77   Welti, G. R. and R. K. Kwan, "Comparison of Signal Processing Techniques for Satellite Telephony," *NTC '77 Conference Record*, Vol. 1, Los Angeles, December 1977, pp. 5.1-1 to 5.1-6.

WHIT 78   White, W. and M. Holmes, "The Future of Commercial Satellite Telecommunications," *Datamation*, July 1978, pp. 94–102.

7

Wideband Transmission Media III: Guided Transmission: Wireline, Coaxial Cable, and Fiber Optics

R. ANDREW PICKENS
Page Communications International, Inc.

In Chapters 5 and 6 we considered the two major "wireless" communications media, radio and satellite. In this chapter we examine the "wired" media capable of supporting large bandwidth transmission: wire, coaxial cable, waveguide, and fiber optics (Fig. 7.1). As we shall see, the term "wired" carries certain connotations that are irrelevant, and even antithetical, to the very special properties of fiber-optic systems; perhaps the term "guided" will come into general usage, to mean that the transmitted signal is intended to follow the physical path of the medium. This meaning is one of the few points, although a major one, that coaxial cable and fiber-optics systems have in common.

The common characteristic of guided transmission media is that a physical, tangible guide must be placed between the desired communicating points. This is not necessarily a disadvantage. For example, for security reasons one may desire that only certain points be able to receive one's transmissions. Guided media also are able to carry transmissions to places, such as building interiors, that are impenetrable by radio waves.

Each of the guided media have certain characteristics which may make them more or less suitable for a particular application. These are discussed in their individual sections. Since our concern in these chapters is with wideband transmissions, that emphasis will continue here. Figure 7.2 shows a comparison of typical

© 1981 R.A.P. All rights reserved.

Figure 7.1. Rugged cables containing multiple optical fibers are no longer than a single low-loss coaxial cable. In this photograph, individual connectors are being attached to each fiber of a 12-fiber cable. Each fiber can support a data rate of 274 Mbps over long distances; the cable can thus handle 13,104 digital telephone half-circuits. (Courtesy of Page Communications Engineers, Inc.)

examples of the three most important media. It also illustrates a characteristic common to the media—bandwidth of a medium is related to the transmission loss experienced over a given link distance. Conversely, the distance between the link terminals (or repeaters) is limited by the bandwidth required.

7.1 WIRE TRANSMISSION

Wires are ubiquitous. They are the essentially universal method of connecting components within equipments, and of interconnecting equipment to make up systems. Wirelines were the first, and for many years the only, communications transmission medium, and remain the most common. Over any but the shortest distances, however, wire transmission suffers from serious limitations in wideband transmission, as illustrated in the example of Fig. 7.2.

The first extensive electrical communication system, the key telegraph, originally used a single metallic wire between the transmitting and receiving instruments. The earth was used as the return path necessary to complete the electrical circuit. This was generally satisfactory, but some locations required rather heroic efforts to establish a good "ground." Especially as telephones came into use, the use of wire

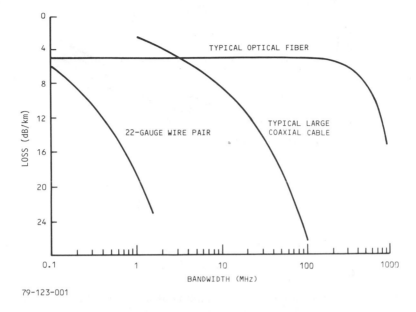

79-123-001

Figure 7.2. Effective loss of typical guided transmission media. (From [HAND 78].)

pairs became the accepted practice. Wire pairs provide a complete metallic circuit between the communicating points. For many years the wire pairs were strung openly on poles. An open-wire pair can carry a telephone conversation for 30 mi or more without amplification. With the growth of the telephone network, however, open-wire pairs became much too numerous and cumbersome to remain viable. Except in a few remote areas, about all that remains of open-wire pair transmission are the pole insulators, presently fetching incredible prices in antique shops. Today, most longer-distance wire transmission is accomplished by cables made up of multiple insulated wire pairs.

7.1.1 Common Characteristics of Wire Transmission

7.1.1.1 Loop Resistance

Almost all wires used for communication purposes use copper conductors. At dc and very low frequencies, the loss in a wireline is a function of its electrical resistance, which in turn is determined by its cross-sectional area and length. The resistance R of copper wire is approximately $R = 0.33 \times 2 \exp (G/3)$ ohms/km at 20° C, where G is the wire size expressed in American Wire Gauge (AWG). For example, a popular wire size is 22 gauge, the loop (go and return) resistance of which is 106 Ω/km.

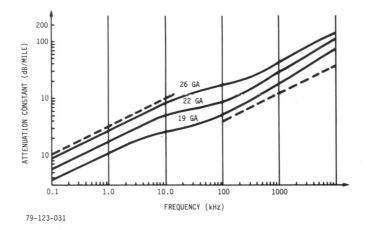

79-123-031

Figure 7.3. Attenuation of typical telephone cables at 55° F. Dashed lines indicate square-root dependence on frequency. (From [EVEN 79].)

Loop resistance determines the maximum transmission distance on wirelines at low frequency. For instance, consider the "current loop," an older method of providing a communication link for teletypewriter terminals. One common implementation for 75-baud circuits calls for a loop current of 20 mA, using a transmitter that is the equivalent of a 48-V source with an internal resistance of 100 Ω. By Ohm's law, 20 mA can be maintained with a total circuit resistance of $48/0.02 = 2400$ Ω, allowing a loop wire resistance of $2400 - 100 = 2300$ Ω. Thus the maximum transmission distance for a 22-gauge wire pair is $2300/106 \approx 22$ km.

In the telephone network [REFE 77, FREE 75], the maximum distance for a simple subscriber loop (wire wireline between subscriber's premises and central office) may be determined by the necessary supervisory signaling current (for bell ringing, off-hook detection, etc.). With modern instruments and central office equipment, the loop resistance objective is 1300Ω. For the 22-gauge wire pair, the loop resistance objective could be met with a link of 12 km.

7.1.1.2 Attenuation at Baseband Frequencies

Even at the relatively low frequencies associated with voice (up to about 3500 Hz), additional factors came into play that affect the attenuation of a wireline. In addition to resistance, the reactive components (inductance and capacitance) of the line contribute to signal loss at the distances being considered. *Skin effect*, the tendency of alternating currents to concentrate at the outer "skin" of the wire, becomes an important factor at frequencies of the order of 10^4 Hz and above for small-diameter wires. In general, wirelines exhibit an attenuation characteristic roughly proportional to the square root of frequency. Figure 7.3 illustrates the measured attenuation constant of typical telephone wire-pair cables.

In telephony, it is common practice to specify an "engineering loss" for a line at

1000 Hz, and to work with an objective maximum loop loss of 6 dB. For the 22-gauge wire pair of the previous example, voice-frequency loss is 1.05 dB/km. Thus the link would be limited to 6/1.05 = 5.7 km for voice frequencies—considerably less than the 12-km figured for dc loop resistance alone.

The line loss at voice frequencies can be decreased at the expense of higher frequencies by the use of line-loading coils, which insert additional series inductance in the line. One standard scheme (H-88) places a loading coil every 1830 m, which would reduce the effective loss of the line to 0.45 dB/km at 100 Hz. This would extend the range to 13 km, essentially equal to the dc signaling distance.

For digital transmission over wirelines, the rising attenuation versus frequency characteristic imposes a limit on the maximum baud rate that can be transmitted and interpreted by the receiver without intersymbol interference. The principal effect is manifested in a finite rise time (and fall time) of the pulses on the receiver end of the wireline. The rise time is a complex function not only of the wire characteristics, but also of the nature of the transmitter and receiver.

7.1.1.3 Wireline Circuit Impairments

Interference and Noise

Wires are quite susceptible to interference and noise, by virtue of their easy coupling with electromagnetic fields. Longer lengths of wire act as antennas that can intercept both intentional and unintentional radiation. For example, a long wire run parallel to an alternating-current power line will experience induction of a considerable amount of the power-line frequency (usually 50 or 60 Hz). Another example is low- to medium-frequency radio transmission. In the telephone network, these types of interference can be controlled by filtration, since they are outside the nominal 300-to 3500-Hz speech path bandwidth. With other wire systems, however, the interference may very well lie within the bandwidth necessary for the signal intelligence being transmitted.

Impulsive noise sources such as lightning, motors, and switches create high-energy, broadband interference that cannot be completely filtered. Even machinery in an ordinary office environment (e.g., electric typewriters, copying machines, fans) has caused severe interference problems. The best defense against this type of interference (and any interference, for that matter) is the use of cables and terminating equipment of special kinds. Shielding the wire with metallic braid or sheathing is one obvious ploy. The twisting of a wire pair effectively reduces induction at lower frequencies. A third technique is the use of a balanced transmission line—rather than operating with one wire at ground potential and the other wire "hot" (an unbalanced line), both wires of a pair can be above ground potential, carrying signals with equal amplitude but opposing phase. A balanced line requires a transformer or differential amplifier at the terminal ends to convert to the unbalanced signaling required by most circuitry. Combinations of the techniques are possible, and may be necessary for transmission involving low energy levels.

Clearly, other things being equal, the higher the level of signaling, the higher the received signal-to-noise ratio that can be expected. There are certain practical constraints, however. For one, higher signal energy requires greater power from the transmitting device, and may require a larger wire size for safe handling—both leading to increased cost. For another, a wireline is itself a radiator of potential interference with other wirelines or radio systems.

Security of communications is sometimes a major concern, and is a problem with wirelines because of their tendency toward radiation. Radiation can be reduced by using shielding, and by using transmission techniques that operate at lower current levels (but this, in turn, can decrease the data rate and increase susceptibility to external interference).

Crosstalk and Echo

Communication wirelines are normally packed in multipair cables, carrying a number of other circuits, for a considerable portion of their circuit length. The mutual inductance and capacitance of the wires results in coupled signals between wire pairs—crosstalk. In telephone usage, special precautions are taken in the manufacture of cables to reduce crosstalk; such measures include reverse layup to improve geometric balance and to preclude long-run contiguity of any wire pairs, and screening between go and return paths [NUTT 78]. Crosstalk levels are a direct function of line length.

Echo is a particular problem in duplex transmission. In the telephone network, echo is caused primarily by imperfect balances in two-wire to four-wire transitions,[1] but can also result from discontinuities in transmission-line impedance due to loading, bridging, and changes in wire gauge. Various telephony standards exist which specify and control the relative level of echo. It is standard practice to employ echo suppressors when the delay exceeds 50 msec; as a general rule, any satellite voice circuit, or a terrestrial circuit over 2400 km in length, will contain an echo suppressor. The echo suppressor must be disabled for data transmission, because the response characteristics are suitable only for voice (Chap. 5).

Crosstalk, like radiation from a wireline, tends to increase with frequency. In digital transmission, it is good practice to control the rise time of signaling pulses and hence the magnitude of their high-frequency components, in order to control crosstalk and interference with external devices. In some instances, crosstalk considerations rather than intrinsic bandwidth may be the limiting factor in signaling rate.

Environment

Environmental factors can have a substantial effect on wire characteristics. Resistance of copper wire changes roughly $0.3\%/°C$; other parameters determining

---

[1] In the telephone network, toll and interoffice wire trunks are normally four-wire circuits—the obvious arrangement where one pair is used for the transmit direction, and the other is used for receive. Because of the cost of local distribution, however, subscriber loops are almost always two-wire circuits. Duplex operation of a two-wire circuit is made possible by the use of "hybrid transformers," which sense the direction of signal flow and appropriately separate the signals for the transmitter and receiver at each end. Hybrids are critical in balance even over the limited range of voice frequencies [FREE 75, MART 76].

line impedance can change substantially more, depending on design. The presence of high-dielectric-constant materials, such as moisture in cables, can alter significantly the nominal transmission-line parameters. Obviously, overt physical damage will degrade or destroy altogether the usability of a cable. Successful wireline transmission of even modest bandwidths requires considerable attention to the environment.

7.1.2 Wireline Applications for Digital Transmission

Wire and wire cables are universally used for connection of components, devices, equipment, and systems. Since we are primarily concerned here with wideband digital transmission over significant distances, discussion is restricted to some examples that illustrate the applicability of wire for that usage.

7.1.2.1 Digital Interface Circuit Standards

Standards for digital interface circuits are based on the presumption of wireline interconnections (although wires need not necessarily be used). The older EIA Standard RS-232 contains provisions for transmitter and receiver characteristics which may limit data rate in specific instances, but does not uniquely determine wireline data rate versus transmission distance other than to recommend the use of cables less than approximately 15 m. RS-232 does specify a maximum capacitance of 2500 pF to be presented to the transmitter. Popular cables have a capacitance of about 50 pF/m; if all the capacitance load is allocated to the cable, a maximum length of 2500/50 = 50 meters could be used.

The new EIA standards and their CCITT counterparts contain specific guidelines for maximum cable lengths and data signaling rates, as displayed in Fig. 7.4.

During the past several years, a number of devices have appeared on the market that will permit the use of considerably greater wireline spans. These devices are called *short-haul modems* and *line drivers*, and are less expensive than conventional data modems intended for use with the telephone network. Typical distance limits over 22-gauge copper wire pairs are 24 km at 4800 bps and 10 km at 19.2 kbps.

7.1.2.2 The T1 Carrier System

As a result of the rapid expansion of telephone plant in the late 1940s and 1950s, operating companies felt an urgent need to provide economical means for increased transmission capacity. One particular bottleneck existed in the exchange trunks which interconnect switching centers in and around cities. These trunks were predominantly multipair wire cables, one pair carrying a single speech path in one direction, and additional pairs devoted to interoffice signaling. Not only were additional copper cables expensive, but the duct space carrying the cables was severely limited in many instances. New ducts could be more costly than the cable itself, especially in highly developed urban areas.

To satisfy these requirements, the Bell System began production and installation of the revolutionary T1 Carrier System in 1962. The T1 system was the first

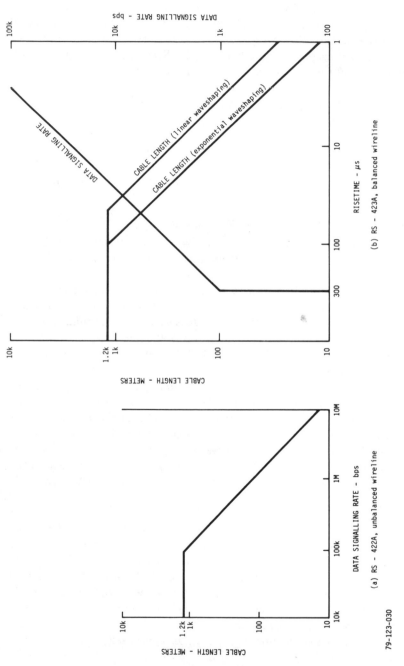

Figure 7.4. Data signaling rate versus cable length for (a) unbalanced and (b) balanced wireline transmission, using 24-AWG twisted-pair cable (EIA).

79-123-030

260

widespread application of digital transmission techniques, including pulse-code modulation (PCM) and time-division multiplex, in commercial telephony [HOTH 62]. With this system, it was determined that 24 one-way speech channels plus signaling and timing could be transmitted on a single pair of wires at a data rate of 1.544 Mbps.

Figure 7.3 displays the typical attenuation characteristic of unloaded exchange cables. A commonly applied constraint for wireline equalization is that the equalizer gain should not exceed 50 dB at the frequency band edge. By this criterion, a 22-gauge pair 1 mi in length can be equalized to about 2 MHz. Careful conditioning, matching, and use of alternating diphase coding and bipolar signaling allows the necessary transmission rate of 1.544 Mbps.

The T1 PCM speech digitalization and multiplexing techniques are described in Chap. 18. For present purposes, the important point is that it was found possible to transmit a relatively high data rate over significant distances of conventional wire cable by the use of carefully designed and matched equipment. The average length of interexchange trunk is about 6 mi; very few are longer than 25 mi. Most trunks are 22 gauge, although some are 19 and 24 gauge. Using conventional cable, it is necessary to use a repeater every 6000 ft on average (3000 ft, worst case), and crosstalk limits the number of pairs within a given cable that can be used with the system. Recently, improved cables, optimized for T1 transmissions with lower losses and screening between bundles of wires, have allowed an increase in repeater spacing to 8000 ft and a larger number of wire pairs to be used. In utilizing older cables originally in analog baseband service, it is necessary to remove loading coils to accommodate the T1 carrier.

7.1.2.3 Subscriber Loops

The most extensive transmission facilities existing are the local distribution networks providing telephone service to individual subscribers. Essentially all subscriber loops are wirelines, examples of which have been given previously. With the various telephone administrations poised to move toward direct digital services (Chap. 17), the question of the digital transmission capabilities of the subscriber loop plant assumes major importance.

Figure 7.5 displays an indication of digital performance bounds of subscriber loops [EVEN 79]. The dashed curve in the figure is derived from Fig. 7.3 using the following assumptions: (1) the characteristics of 22-gauge exchange trunk lines are generally representative of four-wire local loops; (2) T1-type conditioning, modulation, and signaling are used; and (3) the 50-dB equalizer constraint discussed in the preceding section is applied. The results indicate that four-wire local loops would be limited to a 100-kbps transmission rate if they are 30,000 ft or less in length. For comparison, Fig. 7.5 also displays the distance versus transmission rate limits for Dataphone Digital Service (DDS) and Local Area Data Service (LADS), in accordance with current Bell System standards.

The solid curve of Fig. 7.5 indicates the limit imposed by near-end crosstalk (NEXT). With all-digital signaling, the lower transmission rates are constrained by

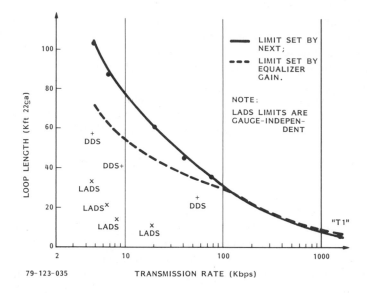

Figure 7.5. Loop-length limits for four-wire bipolar transmission. (From [EVEN 79].)

equalizer gain; crosstalk is the more constraining consideration at higher rates, but not by a substantial margin. If a given cable were also to contain wire pairs carrying analog speech, however, the much higher signal-to-noise ratio required of analog channels would result in more severe crosstalk constraints. During the transition to all-digital networks, such coexistence will be the rule.

The existing subscriber loop plant has, on the average, characteristics somewhat less favorable than the ideals assumed for Fig. 7.5. Older plant may have deteriorated due to moisture, temperature, and damage. More recently installed plant, while having improved cable designs, generally is made up of smaller wire sizes, such as 24 or 26 gauge. Further, the length and environment of the local loop plant subjects it to noise and interference.

Another major difference in assumptions so far is that four-wire service would be used. Almost all subscriber loops are two-wire, achieving full-duplex operation with the hybrid-balance techniques. Four-wire transmission would require halving the number of subscribers or doubling the plant—neither is a very desirable option. Investigations of two-wire techniques for digital transmission are continuing, including extension of hybrid balance, frequency-division multiplexing, and a time compression "ping-pong" method wherein the wire pair is periodically turned around for alternating one-way transmissions [EVEN 79].

7.1.3 Current Status and Outlook

Of all transmission media, wire was the first and still is the most pervasive. Under most conditions, wireline transmission remains the least costly communications medium for lower data rates and shorter distances. For new installations, the economy of wire transmission is largely due to the relative ease and low cost with which interfaces can be effected. For existing installations, particularly those representing a huge investment such as the telephone local distribution plant, there is considerable motivation to continue its utilization; but the costs of refurbishment and upgrade by application of new techniques must be traded off against the bandwidth and other advantages to be gained.

Wirelines share the physical characteristics of all guided transmission media— communication can be established in places impenetrable by radio waves, but a physical path must be established between all terminal points. Compared with the other transmission media we are considering in these chapters, wirelines are by far the most limited in terms of bandwidth, and distances spanned, susceptibility to interference, and proclivity for creating interference. Given current and likely future levels of technology, one should look to other media for transmission rates or span distances greater, say, than 1 Mbps and a few kilometers, respectively.

For numerous physical and economic reasons, copper is the best conductor material for wirelines. The cost of copper in recent years has been highly volatile. It is conceivable that the cost of copper wire may reach the level where other materials may be used, with substantial reduction in transmission capabilities, or where the cost tips the economic scales in favor of optical-fiber transmission even for low data rates and short distances.

7.2 COAXIAL CABLE (AND WAVEGUIDE)

In the quest for transmission bandwidth over longer distances, coaxial cable and waveguide systems have historically enjoyed several periods of intense interest. There are numerous advantages in their use, but several important deterrents exist as well:

Advantages
- Capable of wide bandwidths
- No propagation anomalies (but temperature variable)
- Reaches points impenetrable by radio waves
- Security
- Cost per subscriber is low where subscriber density is high.

Disadvantages
- Requires physical path between termini
- Requires frequent repeaters for long haul
- Repeaters are complex, requiring equalization for inconstant cable loss with frequency and temperature
- Right-of-way problems
- High initial and upkeep costs
- Slight leakage can create interference problems in some cases.

7.2.1 Characteristics and Applications

Coaxial Cable

A coaxial cable has a circular cross section and is made up of a wireline inner conductor, a concentric outer conductor, and an intervening dielectric material. Such a cable can be produced inexpensively and has some very useful properties. Its normal operation is as an unbalanced transmission line, with the outer conductor at "earth" potential. Thus, in addition to serving as one of the pair of conductors necessary for transmission of electrical energy, the outer conductor also serves as a shield against interference and to contain the internal energy.

A coaxial cable exhibits a characteristic impedance that is essentially constant over a very large frequency range—in some instances, well up into the gigahertz range. This permits relatively simple design of receivers and transmitters with wideband characteristics, and correct matching for minimum distortion and loss due to reflections. It is necessary, however, to ensure that the terminations of a coaxial cable (or any transmission line) closely match its characteristic impedance, in order to maximize signal power transfer and to avoid reflections. Reflections cause "standing waves" that adversely affect power transfer, and smearing of the signal waveform that can lead to intersymbol interference in digital transmission. Special techniques are required for multiple taps on a coaxial cable, such as in application to television distribution of local area network systems.

There are three principal areas in which the relatively inexpensive, low-loss, high-bandwidth properties of coaxial cable have found wide application:

- Telephone (and television) transmission
- Short-run system interconnects, both at video and radio frequencies
- Television distribution (CATV).

Starting in the late 1940s, coaxial-cable systems were developed for long-haul transmission of telephone and television signals. Wide bandwidths were needed for both applications. The Bell System L5 carrier system can carry up to 10,800 voice channels, or a mixture of voice and network television, on a single coaxial "tube" over transcontinental distances by analog frequency-division multiplexing (FDM). A typical cable system comprises 10 such tubes, affording an equivalent bandwidth of approximately 600 MHz. Coaxial cable is also used for wideband transmission in the larger telephone local distribution systems.

Prior to the advent of satellite communications, submarine coaxial cables were the primary means of reliable, high-quality intercontinental transmission. Even to-day, new cables are being laid, and plans are being made to replace and upgrade older transoceanic cables, as a backup and supplement to satellites.

Interconnections between system components are the most familiar application of coaxial cable; for example, the "coax run" between a citizen's band radio and its antenna. The more sophisticated home TV antenna systems also use coax, as do antenna distribution systems in apartment buildings. In high-speed computer installations, coaxial cable is commonly used to interconnect peripheral equipments, such as the IBM 3270 CRT local terminal, and also for intermodule connections within the processor cabinetry. In this application area, cable lengths are relatively short, ranging from several inches to perhaps a hundred meters.

The largest current market for coaxial cable is television distribution. The technology was originally developed to provide television signals to houses in outlying communities where high-quality reception with conventional household antennas could not be obtained. Such systems were called community antenna television (CATV), an acronym that persists even though the advantages of television-by-cable have led to its installation even in major metropolitan areas. "Cable television" is becoming a more accepted term; as we shall see later, however, even that is not entirely correct. The distances involved are usually restricted to a few tens of miles.

Waveguide

Radio-frequency waveguides look like hollow metallic tubes, with a circular, elliptical, or rectangular cross section. Such a structure when properly dimensioned will support and guide the transmission of radio-frequency waves, hence the name. The inside dimensions of a waveguide are of the order of one-half the wavelength of the frequency of operation, and thus tend to be considerably larger than coaxial cable even at high frequencies.

The principal waveguide characteristics of interest is the very much lower attenuation per unit length as compared with coaxial cable—from one to two orders of magnitude lower. Waveguides are commonly used as the connection between an antenna and transmitter/receiver where low loss and high-power-handling capabilities are important, as in microwave radios and satellite earth stations.

Because of their low-loss property, waveguides have received considerable attention as a medium of long-distance transmission. The bandwidth of a waveguide is limited to about 10 to 15%, but efficient transmission can be achieved into the millimeter-wave region, which would provide a useful bandwidth of several gigahertz. A waveguide system would be very expensive, however, because of the large content of costly metals and the relatively expensive terminals and repeaters. Waveguides require considerable precision in manufacture to achieve their low-loss characteristics. Installation is difficult because of their size and relative inflexibility, and great care must be taken to preclude potential physical distortion and leaks.

Because of these rather considerable disadvantages, interest in waveguide as a long-haul telecommunications transmission medium has waned. Fiber-optics technology has eclipsed waveguide as an extremely wideband transmission medium. Consequently, we will not consider waveguides further in this chapter.

7.2.1.1 Bandwidth, Losses, and Noise

Because of metallic and dielectric losses, coaxial cable exhibits a rising attenuation characteristic as a function of frequency, following an approximate square-root law. To illustrate, the attenuation of a popular cable (RG-58), properly terminated, is approximated by

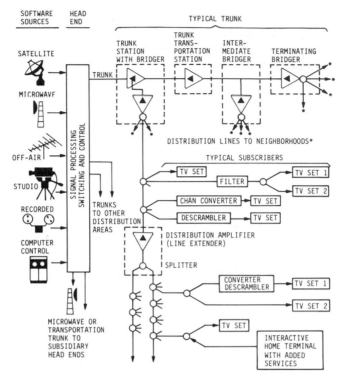

79-123-032

Figure 7.6. Typical modern CATV coaxial-cable system block diagram. The normal "downstream" direction of transmission is from the head end to subscriber. Since 1972, newly installed CATV systems have the potential for "upstream" communication, from subscriber to head end. (Courtesy of GTE Lenkurt.)

$$\alpha = 0.35\,f^{0.6} \qquad \mathrm{dB}/100\,\mathrm{ft} \tag{7.1}$$

where frequency f is expressed in MHz. For baseband signals, the intrinsic 3-dB bandwidth of a 100-ft section of this cable (without equalization) would be a 36 MHz, which is usually more than adequate for system interconnects and local links. For a 1-km length, however, the intrinsic baseband bandwidth would be about 110 kHz— hardly suitable for wideband, long-distance transmission.

Several techniques exist for extending baseband bandwidth. One is to increase the size of the coaxial cable; for a given characteristic impedance, attenuation is an inverse function of diameter. Another technique is to use a lower-loss dielectric material; low-loss cables are manufactured with just enough insulating material to support the center conductor, so that the majority of the dielectric consists of air. The improvement in attenuation in low-loss coaxial cables using these techniques is illustrated in Fig. 7.6.

266

A third technique is to equalize the attenuation versus frequency characteristics of a cable by using line drivers and receivers having gain characteristics which add up to the inverse of that characteristic. Within limits, preemphasis and equalization provide an overall system bandwidth that is essentially flat.

Singly or in combination, these techniques can be employed to realize very useful baseband bandwidths for computer networks contained within, say, a medium-sized building.

There is a fundamentally different method, however, for transmission of large bandwidths over large distances with coaxial cable. This method is based on modulation of a radio-frequency carrier, by means very similar to those used for radio transmission (Chap. 5). Consider a baseband signal occupying the spectrum from 0 to 10 MHz, and transmitted over a 1-km length of the cable example used earlier. By Eq. (7.1), the upper limit of the spectrum would be attenuated by 46 dB with respect to the lowest part of the spectrum; this is a power ratio of 36,000 : 1—rather difficult to drive and equalize precisely in the presence of other cable variables. Further, only one signal could be transmitted. Now, suppose that the signal were amplitude modulated on a carrier frequency of 50 MHz. The resultant spectrum would extend from 40 to 60 MHz, over which the differential attenuation would be 15 dB—much easier to equalize. A number of such signals could be modulated on different, individual carriers in an FDM fashion; precise equalization is not necessary between the individual spectral segments because they are not correlated. If TDM were used, however, equalization across the entire spectrum would be necessary.

The coaxial-carrier transmission technique naturally fits the analog FDM hierarchy of telephony, and many such transmission links are in service. The channelized television broadcast spectrum can also be viewed as an FDM carrier arrangement, also natural for this coaxial transmission technique in the CATV industry.

For extended long-distance runs, repeater amplifiers must be spaced periodically along the line, to build up and reequalize the signal amplitude for transmission over the succeeding section of cable. The spacing of repeaters is determined by the cable attenuation at the highest frequency of interest. Thus, for a given cable distance, the greater the bandwidth, the more frequently repeaters must be inserted.

Modern CATV systems routinely achieve a bandwidth of 400 MHz, carrying 50 or more television channels, with equalizing repeater spacing of about 600 m.

An example of current telephone usage is the Telletra ACX-10800 coaxial line system, which provides transmission for 10,800 voice channels, frequency-division multiplexed into a 60-MHz bandwidth. An additional digital channel with a rate of 17 Mbps can be accommodated above the analog FDM spectrum (data over voice). The cable attenuation is regulated and equalized by repeaters spaced at 1.55-km intervals. The repeaters are controlled by pilot signals placed at the upper and lower extremities of the FDM spectrum [BELL 78].

Noise on an analog coaxial-cable transmission system is normally lower, compared with radio transmission, because atmospherics and interference are avoided. However, noise and distortion are introduced by each repeater through which the signal must pass; the effect is more pronounced in the higher portions of the signal spectrum, where greater amplification is required. Telephone system practices employ design criteria leading to cable system noise factors approximately one-third of those in radio systems.

Propagation anomalies common to radio channels, such as fading and precipitation losses, do not exist in cable systems. The most significant transmission variable is an increase in cable loss as a function of temperature. The change is a function of frequency (approximately square-root law), amounting to 1.0 dB/mi at 100 MHz for a temperature difference of 20° F in a typical (3/8-in.) coax cable [FREE 75]. For a wideband system, compensation by simple automatic gain control is insufficient; the preemphasis and equalization characteristics must also be varied, adding to repeater and terminal costs.

7.2.1.2 Special Characteristics and Trade-offs

As previously mentioned, coaxial cable is much less susceptible than is radio to interference, distortion, and the effects of propagation anomalies. The other side of this coin also favors cable systems—since there is (ideally) no Hertzian emission as in radio, interference with other systems is negligible. This is one reason for the spread of cable television systems: many more TV channels can be transported into the home than could possibly be broadcasted. Similarly, the telephone companies have recognized cable (also waveguide and fiber optic) systems as an alternative to microwave radio, particularly in those areas where frequency congestion is severe.

In practice, coaxial cable can "leak" signals and can be susceptible to interference. Especially in analog systems,[2] crosstalk between long runs of paralleled coaxial cables and pickup of interference from nearby sources, such as power lines and motors, have caused problems. In CATV installations, the long coaxial cables can act as antennas, picking up signals broadcast by local transmitters. The FCC has launched an inquiry into possible interference in the aeronautical radio band (108 to 135 MHz) due to CATV systems. Common current practice is to use doubly, or even triply, shielded cable for the longer trunk lines.

There are several physical deterrents to the implementation of cable systems. One is the acquisition of rights-of-way, for the cable must physically exist along the paths between the terminal points—by burial, aerial suspension on poles, or installation in ducts. Some utilities have been reluctant to share existing facilities, particularly at reasonable rates. Federal legislation has been enacted (1978) that is a first step in establishing a "zone of reasonableness" rate structure for shared facilities. Nevertheless, the costs of installation are high,[3] as are costs associated with maintenance. Cables, simply by being there, are subject to damage; for example, construction crews may unintentionally dig up or sever a buried cable. A large metropolitan utility experiences about 10 such occurrences per week.

As discussed in Chap. 5, radio is a particularly effective transmission medium in

---

[2] Analog systems are sensitive to low-level signals; digital systems are relatively free from the effects of low-level signals, because of threshold detection methods.

[3] Typical current experience in metropolitan areas is about $5500 per mile [OVER 78]. Target costs per subscriber, including terminal devices, are in the range of $200 to $400. See also Sec. 7.2.5 for comparisons of coaxial cable and fiber optics.

situations in which the terminals are mobile. Broadcast radio allows the addition of terminals simply by erecting an appropriate antenna and attaching a receiver. Cable systems require a physical termination or tap into the transmission system. On the other hand, radio waves do not propagate reliably in enclosed areas, such as within buildings, or in areas containing a large number of obstructions, such as buildings in a city. In such instances, cable systems generally are preferred.

Security is an important consideration in military systems, and increasingly more so in commercial communication. Signals on cable systems are not so easily accessible by the casual eavesdropper, as they are with radio. Should a determined adversary gain access to a cable system, various techniques are available by which his presence can be detected. Encryption devices, of course, can be employed with cable, as with any other communication medium.

The trade-offs of cable versus point-to-point radio can be summarized as follows:

Coaxial Cable May Be Preferred When:
- Large bandwidth is required (greater than 40 MHz or 90 Mbps)
- Radio-frequency interference potential is high
- Noise is a great concern
- Points must be served which cannot be reached by radio waves
- Spectrum is congested
- Licensing and conformance to regulations would be difficult and/or expensive
- It is determined that system costs would be lower
- Special security measures are warranted.

Radio May Be Preferred When:
- Initial and operating/maintenance costs of cable are too high
- Right-of-way problems cannot be overcome
- A physical path between terminals is not desirable
- Mobile subscribers must be served
- Flexibility in relocating terminal points is required.

7.2.2 Cable Television

It is estimated that by 1980, there are 4000 CATV systems in operation in the United States, serving 16,000,000 subscribers. Some 22% of U.S. television households are on cable [SPEC 79]. In Canada, over half of the television households are connected to a coaxial-cable system; in some areas, cable television approaches ubiquity, but Canada is not yet a "wired nation."

The prospect of a total local distribution network, providing universal communication access to every conceivable user location, is exciting and has led to numerous books and articles outlining the increasingly less incredible possibilities of such a service [SMIT 72, MART 77]. The reader is referred to Chap. 17, which describes what is possible and also gives some appreciation of the resultant economic and sociological implications. Because of today's technology and economics, we are closer to realization of truly universal wideband networks through cable (and fiber optic) technology than by satellite or radio. Cable television today is based on mature technology, and because of the large quantities of coaxial cable and associated devices that are mass-produced for this industry, costs are at a relatively low level.

Recent government policy and regulation issues have been favorable to cable television systems, and have brought the future a large step closer. One of the most significant is the 1972 Federal Communications Commission decision to require newly installed systems to carry a minimum of 20 TV channels (minimum bandwidth of 120 MHz) and to have a potential capability for two-way communication (although at a greatly reduced bandwidth for the return path). The latter capability is a major distinguishing feature, setting cable systems apart from radio broadcast systems. Currently, the principal use of the "upstream" or return channel is for polling viewer preference and for billing purposes in pay-TV systems.

A typical CATV system is illustrated in Fig. 7.6 [DEMO 79]. Far beyond the simple off-the-air pickup of the original "community antenna" systems, the modern CATV system derives its signals from many sources, including local studios and satellites. The repeaters necessary for coaxial transmission are subdivided into several specialized types, termed "stations" and "bridges" according to their specific function in addition to amplification and equalization. Currently, all such systems operate with analog signals, arranged in an FDM hierarchy and allowing a 6-MHz bandwidth for each channel. Current systems operate between 50 and 300 MHz, and carry up to 35 TV channels plus FM radio. At this writing, new system designs are being announced in which the upper frequency is being extended to 400 MHz, thus providing for a 350-MHz bandwidth capable of carrying 52 channels. The available cable spectrum below 50 MHz is normally used for the upstream channel and/or special transmission services.

One domestic system showing a glimpse of the future is the Warner Cable Corporation's QUBE system in Columbus, Ohio. Subscribers are equipped with a terminal unit, from which programs can be selected, questions answered, and games played. The system employs four minicomputers for system control, billing, communications and generation of special programs such as games and tests. Initial services available include:

- 30 channels of TV programming: network, special events, new movies
- Ordering programs on an individual basis (from library)
- Interactive programs, including courses and individual tests
- Games.

The potential for TV catalog shopping, poll taking, test marketing, and new forms of entertainment already exist. By the fourth month of operation, 13,000 homes had subscribed to QUBE; in 1980, more than 30,000 subscribers are projected [OVER 78].

7.2.3   Computer Communication Applications

The two-way capability of cable system technology is one feature of interest in data transmission. Another is the wide-bandwidth, high-quality signal transmission avail-

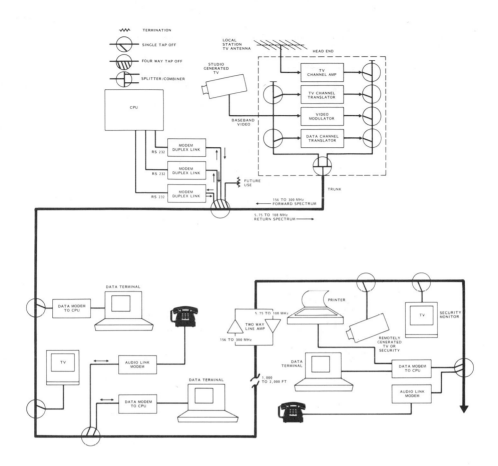

Figure 7.7. Illustration of the versatility of a broadband cable system, offering two-way video, voice, and data services. Here, video service includes both entertainment television and closed-circuit television such as that used for security surveillance. Addition of a CPU and appropriate modems to the "head end" of a conventional CATV system provides data services that can be used in businesses and homes. (After [BROA 80].)

able. Consider a single television channel, which with guard bands is allocated a spectrum width of 6 MHz. Current modem technology can offer a spectrum efficiency of up to 3 bps/Hz, leading to the possibility of up to 18 Mbps on the channel. Cable television systems now normally provide 30 channels, from which a potential data transmission rate of 540 Mbps could be derived. Furthermore, very low error rates would be expected, since the systems are designed for analog television signals requiring a signal-to-noise ratio in excess of 50 dB. The possibilities of such a communication capability linking every home and office are just beginning to be explored. The concept of a cable system providing integrated services (voice, video, and data) is depicted in Fig. 7.7 and expanded on in Chap. 17.

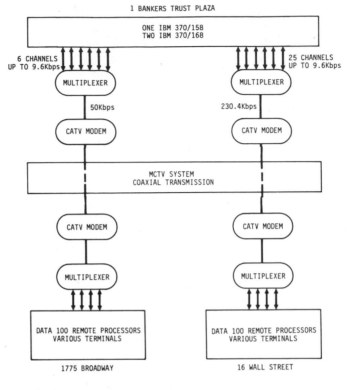

1 BANKERS TRUST PLAZA

ONE IBM 370/158
TWO IBM 370/168

6 CHANNELS
UP TO 9.6Kbps

25 CHANNELS
UP TO 9.6Kbps

MULTIPLEXER

MULTIPLEXER

50Kbps

230.4Kbps

CATV MODEM

CATV MODEM

MCTV SYSTEM
COAXIAL TRANSMISSION

CATV MODEM

CATV MODEM

MULTIPLEXER

MULTIPLEXER

DATA 100 REMOTE PROCESSORS
VARIOUS TERMINALS

DATA 100 REMOTE PROCESSORS
VARIOUS TERMINALS

1775 BROADWAY

16 WALL STREET

79-123-019

Figure 7.8. Bankers Trust data transmission system, using Manhattan Cable TV coaxial links between three locations.

Cable plant is well suited for dense metropolitan areas, because the potential demand for bandwidth is there. Virtually any building can be entered and cabled internally, making the system accessible to most business offices. By contrast, T1 (1.544 Mbps) service from telephone companies is expensive and difficult to obtain in all desired locations. Nevertheless, the possibilities of cable have been largely overlooked.

Manhattan Cable TV Company and Bankers Trust Company of New York were the first to use CATV facilities for computer communication at rates of 50 and 230.4 kbps. Manhattan Cable TV (MCTV) is franchised to operate in a major portion of New York City, which includes the midtown business district. Within this area, Bankers Trust uses MCTV cables for communications between three locations, as depicted in Fig. 7.8. In operation since November 1974, the network is enthusiastically praised by Bankers Trust. Reported uptime is 99.9%, with an intrinsic bit error rate of 10^{-8} [MALT 76, DICK 77].

The Banker's Trust system utilizes the CATEL/E-Com Model 159 data mo-

272

dem, especially designed for data transmission over CATV systems. The modem is capable of operating at data rates up to 1.5 Mbps (T1 rate) in the presence of interference that can often exist in a wideband FDM environment such as exists in CATV. The Computrol Corporation has recently announced a low-cost modem intended for transmission of synchronous data at a rate of 1.5 Mbps over coaxial cable distances up to 8 km. It is anticipated that similar units will appear in the market, perhaps containing additional circuitry providing for special networking protocol management.

7.2.4 Private Cable Systems

Privately owned coaxial cable systems intended for data transmission have been in use for some years in larger industrial complexes, including American Motors, Dow Chemical, General Motors, and Kellogg Cereal. In these plants, bidirectional CATV-type systems carry multichannel closed-circuit TV and voice communications, as well as digital data.

One of the most interesting cable systems is the Ethernet, a continuing development project at Xerox Palo Alto Research Center. The Ethernet is a baseband system intended to carry only digital signals at a data rate of 3 Mbps. It operates on contention packet-switching principles—a kind of wired ALOHA system (see Chap. 4). The original Ethernet connects 100 subscribers equipped with keyboard-display unit intelligent terminals. Each terminal is connected via a transceiver to a tap on the coaxial cable [METC 76]. Subsequently, several Ethernets have been constructed for separate buildings and interconnected with a Packet Radio Network [SHOC 79]. It is expected that a commercial version of Ethernet will be offered in the future, probably initially in conjunction with word-processing systems. As this section is written, Xerox, Intel, and the Digital Equipment Corporation have announced a joint program to develop and exploit the Ethernet technology.

The Mitre Corporation has developed a carrier coaxial-cable system, MITRENET, useful for intrabuilding and perhaps "campus" transmission for distributed subscribers' computers and terminals. Two parallel cables are used—one for each direction in full-duplex operation. The topology is dendritic (branched). A most interesting aspect of the MITRENET is that its basic transmission components are standard CATV devices, taking advantage of the cost advantage resulting from reasonably large scale production of such components. In contrast to Ethernet, the transmission is based on analog RF signals in the standard CATV frequency range of 5 to 300 MHz. By use of a modem on one of the 30 channels possible in a standard FDM CATV system, the current MITRENET provides a single-channel data rate of 307.2 kbps in 1 MHz of bandwidth. Experimental systems have been operated up to 7 Mbps. Other channels carry video, conventional TV, closed-circuit TV, FM radio, and voice telephone.

MITRENET requires a special interface device (Bus Interface Unit, or BIU) to attach digital terminals. The BIU contains the modem and microprocessor-based circuitry to control the ALOHA-like contention protocol used on the digital channel

[DEMA 76, DOLB 77]. An advanced version of the MITRENET, called CAB-LENET, is being designed to provide a complete range of protocol levels for varying subscriber needs [WOOD 79]. It is expected that the cost of a BIU, if produced in quantities of 1000, would be approximately $500.

The HYPERchannel is a commercially available coaxial-cable network offered by Network Systems Corporation. The system can operate with up to four coaxial data trunks, each capable of supporting a data rate of 50 Mbps for a 1000-ft distance, dropping to 1.5 Mbps for 5000 ft, using standard 0.3-in. cable. Distances can be increased by four times with 0.9-in. cable. CPUs, peripherals, bulk memory units, and terminals can access each multidrop trunk via buffered adapter units. Phase-modulated baseband is used as the transmission technique.

A bibliography and taxonomy of local computer networks, some of which are based on coaxial-cable technology and the above examples, is contained in [THUR 79]. Chapters 15, 16 and 17 develop more detailed application and design information.

7.2.5 Future Outlook

In the decade of the 1980s, wideband local distribution networks based on coaxial cable will become commonplace. Such networks, as well as providing for communication between the connected terminals, will concentrate long-distance demand and access satellite systems via one, or perhaps two, earth stations.

The levels of local distribution networks will devolve into three categories:

1. Area-wide distribution encompassing an entire small city, or segments of a larger city (e.g., a CATV system). Ranges of the order of 10 km.
2. "Campus" distribution (e.g., a university campus or large industrial complex). Ranges of the order of 1 km.
3. Internal, intrapremises distribution, within a building: "office of the future." Ranges from meters to hundred of meters.

Depending on the nature of the subscribers, each of these three categories could easily warrant satellite-system interconnections. For example, the area-wide system could serve primarily homes; the campus system, smaller businesses in an industrial park; and the internal system could be owned by a single, large, high-volume business user of communications.

For internal distribution, only cable systems are practicable. Packet cable systems exemplified by Ethernet and MITRENET are the harbingers of the future. Many computer manufacturers are developing architectures and software for cabled bus-distributed processing systems.

During the latter half of the 1980s, coaxial cable's competition will make some significant inroads. Radio, based on the developmental cellular system or packet radio, has attractive possibilities for area and campus distribution, and will appear in some specialized carrier's systems. Also, as we shall see in the next section, fiber optics is coming and possesses some characteristics compatible with cable systems.

Nevertheless, coaxial-cable technology and experience are well advanced. In the near term, economics is in favor of coaxial cable and does not favor rapid, widespread replacement of the major capital investments that will exist in cable transmission systems.

A likely development is a combination of technologies. For example, area-wide distribution from a common satellite earth station could be accomplished with cellular radio techniques. The terminal radio transceivers, located on each campus or building, would serve as a concentration point for further subdistribution to individual subscribers using cable (coaxial or fiber) techniques.

7.3 FIBER OPTICS

As satellites were the major transmission medium development of the 1960s, fiber optics was that of the 1970s. An optical fiber, sometimes referred to as a light waveguide, is a physical point-to-point transmission medium that in size and mechanical makeup resembles small coaxial cables. Consequently, many of the comments made in the preceding section concerning the use of cable systems apply also to fiber optics.

What, then, is all the excitement about? For one thing, cable itself is a very attractive medium for the computer communications engineer to consider. Compared with the composite of metallic conductors and dielectrics of coaxial cable, the fiber optic transmission medium is a single fiber (usually) fabricated of silica-based glass. Although it is an unfair oversimplification to observe that sand is cheaper than copper, it helps to make the point that fiber-optic cables are expected to be less expensive, with maturation of the technology and large-scale production under way. It is estimated that fiber-optic-system sales will grow from less than $40 million in 1978 to $1.7 billion in 1990.

For another thing, the potential bandwidth of a fiber-optic circuit is immense. A fiber-optic link operates with a carrier frequency in the infrared region of light (about 1 μm wavelength). The carrier frequency designer normally thinks in terms of bandwidth as a fraction of the carrier frequency—say, 5%. At fiber-optic frequencies, this would mean a bandwidth of 15,000,000,000,000 Hz. As we shall see, there are present-day limitations that limit practically achievable bandwidths, but bandwidths in excess of 1 GHz have been reported. It is the combination of lower cost, easier installation, and the bonus of larger bandwidth that is the primary motivation behind the intense activity in the field of fiber optics. Many feel that fiber optics is the medium that will bring realization to the promises of wideband, mass-distribution communications.

There are numerous attributes of transmission via optical fiber cables:

- Small size
- Light weight
- Very wide bandwidth
- Low cost potential

- Interference and noise immunity
- Complete electrical isolation
- Greater repeater spacing
- Low crosstalk
- No spark or fire hazard
- Security.

The possible disadvantages of fiber optics are largely temporal, and are being overcome as the technology matures and experience is gained in practical installation. Among the commonly expressed concerns are the following:

Ease of Installation

Being smaller, lighter, and usually more supple than metallic cables, installation should be greatly facilitated. Space in existing cable ducts and on poles is at a premium. However, there has been concern whether special handling or protection is required to avoid breakage of the fibers. Current fibers are routinely produced and proved to the order of 100,000 lb tensile strength (higher than steel), and conservatively designed cables have been installed without incident.

Fiber Degradation

There are some things that only time and experience will tell; among them are optical fiber's resistance to long-term degradation in a hostile environment. Concerns include moisture, cycling extremes in temperature, ice crushing, and effects of motion such as the swaying of aerial cables. Laboratory simulations of such conditions have been made using accelerated life techniques, which indicate that the potential problems are not as severe as had been feared. Fiber cables can be, and are, constructed with the same mechanical protection features as any other form of cable.

Coupling

Splices are necessary to join permanently fibers in extended runs, and often in terminations. Connectors are used, as with conventional wire cables, where removable couplings are desired. With standards emerging from the industry, coupling techniques and devices are becoming less of a problem. Fusion splice machines are entering the market claiming low losses and repeatable splices, but are expensive. New connectors have recently appeared which overcome a majority of earlier problems, but have not as yet been thoroughly field proven.

Interfacing

Means are needed for the conversion of electrical signals to light energy, and vice versa. This subject is subsequently treated in detail. Generally, several devices and application techniques work quite well, and are at a usefully high level of development. The principal remaining technical concern is the reliability of high-performance devices. Much progress remains to be made, moreover, in the areas of cost and size. At present, interface and coupling costs are the greatest detriment to the economic viability of fiber-optic systems.

7.3.1 The Transmission Medium

Fiber optics is the youngest of the transmission media we are considering in these chapters. The first postulation of the possibilities of long-distance transmission by guided light waves was made in 1966 by the Standard Telephone Laboratories in the United Kingdom [KAO 66]. In 1970, Bell Laboratories demonstrated a low-loss fiber, which was necessary for a viable system [KAPR 70]. Since that time, research and development activity has been intense, and much progress has been made in both the hardware and applications areas. Nevertheless, significant field trials of fiber-optic systems have only been undertaken during the last few years, and we are just entering the era of operational systems. Because of the youth of the techniques employed and the relative unfamiliarity of their potential uses, in this section we discuss fiber-optics technology in somewhat more detail than the other media.

A medium that can transport intelligence-carrying light energy can assume many forms. Analogous to radio, light energy can be broadcast in free space or the atmosphere, or can be focused by lenses that act as antennas. In fiber-optic technology, however, we are interested in "piped" energy. As in classical physics, light can be dealt with using ray theory, or pure electromagnetic theory using Maxwell's equations. Indeed, both approaches have been taken in application to fiber optics by Gallawa,[4] with equivalent results. A circular cross section is the easiest form to manufacture (hence "fiber"), but as with waveguides for radio frequencies, that form is not necessarily the "best" one.

The large intrinsic bandwidth of an optical fiber is one of its very special properties. A bandwidth of one gigahertz (10^9 Hz) in the scale of light frequencies (10^{14} Hz) is a tiny fraction, less than the width of a line used to draw the frequency response of a fiber (see Fig. 7.2). A key point is that over such a bandwidth, the *intrinsic* attenuation of the fiber is constant, as shown in Fig. 7.9. Fiber attenuation is not a function of signal frequency as is the case with coaxial cable; consequently, the cable preemphasis/equalization procedures necessary for coaxial cables, and their attendant contributions to signal deterioration, are not found in a fiber-optic system. In practice, the bandwidth of a fiber-optic system has an upper bound, determined by a combination of fiber and light-source characteristics. Up to this bound, however, the response is essentially flat.

7.3.1.1 Types of Optical Fibers

Many different types of fibers have evolved, representing various manufacturers' ideas as to appropriate trade-offs, as well as different characteristics most suitable for specific applications. For wideband transmission over medium to long distances, the construction is usually all glass. Plastic materials, however, have special properties useful in short runs, such as system interconnects. Generally, optical fibers can be classified in one of the four categories discussed below.

---

[4][GALL 76] is particularly commended to the reader as a source of material on the physics of optical fibers and associated interface devices. Much of the following material is extracted from that reference.

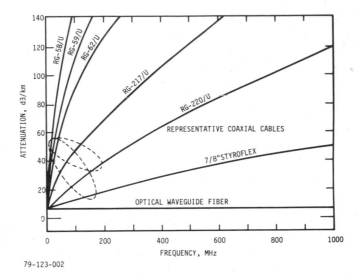

79-123-002

Figure 7.9. Comparison of the attenuation per unit distance of representative coaxial cables and optical fiber.

Step-Index Fiber

For long-distance, moderate-bandwidth transmission, the basic construction of a cladded optical fiber is shown in Fig. 7.10. The core material is usually a form of silica-based glass, with index of refraction n_1, while the cladding can be a similar or different material with index of refraction n_2. Since there is an abrupt boundary between the core and cladding, this type of fiber is referred to as step index. When $n_1 > n_2$, the structure acts as a waveguide. As a simple illustration, consider two light rays impinging on the end of an optical fiber as shown in Fig. 7.11. Ray a is reflected at the core-cladding boundary, while ray b, entering the core at a more oblique angle, is transmitted through that boundary. There is a critical angle (Brewster angle) at the boundary above which the ray will be transmitted into the cladding. This angle, in turn, establishes a maximum off-axis angle at which a ray can enter the core, and remain "guided" in the core by reflections at the boundary. By Snell's law,

$$\sin \theta = \quad n_1^2 - n_2^2 \overset{\Delta}{=} \text{NA} \qquad (7.2)$$

where NA is defined as the *numerical aperature*, a measure of the light-gathering properties of a fiber of given size. The larger the NA, the greater the angle of incident rays that will be captured and transmitted by the core. Numerical aperture (NA) is a characteristic widely found in specifications of optical fibers.

From Eq. (7.2) it might appear that it is desirable to maximize the ratio n_1/n_2, in order to maximize the numerical aperture, and hence the amount of light energy coupled into the fiber from a practical light source. As might be expected, however, this leads to other problems. As a simplistic approach, consider two rays, one entering

278

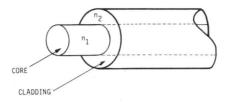

79-123-01-003

Figure 7.10. Basic construction of step-index optical fiber. The index of refraction of the core material (n_1) is slightly greater than that of the cladding material (n_2).

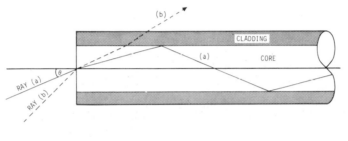

79-123-019

Figure 7.11. Numerical aperture (NA) of an optical fiber is defined as NA = sin Q, where Q is the maximum angle at which impinging light rays are captured within the core of a fiber-optic waveguide. Rays entering at an angle greater than Q escape through the cladding.

the core at an angle more oblique than the other. The former ray, during the course of many reflections throughout its traversal of the fiber, will travel a longer distance than will the other. Consequently, it will suffer more delay. If the light energy comprising these rays is thought of as a very short pulse, the fiber's output light energy is represented as a summation of pulses that have differing delays. The resultant is a smeared pulse; the mechanism leading to it is termed *modal dispersion.*

For those familiar with the notion of modes of propagation in a waveguide, it may be more convenient to think in terms of multimode propagation in the fibers. The number N of modes supported in step-index fiber is

$$N = 2\left(\frac{\pi a}{\lambda}\right)^2 \ (n_1^2 - n_2^2) \tag{7.3}$$

where a = core radius

λ = wavelength of the light energy

n_1 = core index of refraction

n_2 = cladding index of refraction.

279

Comparison with Eq. (7.2) reveals that N is proportional to $(NA)^2$—a strong motivation to design n_1 and n_2 for a small difference. The source energy captured by the fiber is related to its physical area, and hence to the square of its radius (a^2).

Single-Mode Fibers

If a, n_1, and n_2 in Eq. (7.3) are chosen so that $N = 1$, the result is a fiber that supports only a single mode of propagation, sometimes called a monomode fiber. In fiber manufacturing, the indices of refraction of core and cladding materials have been controlled with sufficient success to permit core diameters as large as 5 μ. From the preceding discussion, we would correctly suspect that a single-mode fiber has potentially the highest bandwidth. As always, however, there is a trade-off—a small difference between n_1 and n_2 gives a small value for NA, and practically achievable values for n_1 and n_2 force a small value for a. The combination of small a and NA (typically 0.1) makes it difficult to couple energy into a monomode fiber.

Graded-Index Fibers

Consider a fiber wherein the boundary between the core and the cladding, rather than being abrupt, is diffuse. The index of refraction decreases gradually in a graded fashion, as a function of radius in moving from the core material to the cladding material. Rays traversing at greater angles to the fiber axis (and thus a greater distance) will travel, on average, through a medium of lower index of refraction and therefore will experience less delay. The net effect is partial compensation for the different ray-path delays, affording up to two orders of magnitude lower pulse dispersion, or greater bandwidth, for a given fiber size and numerical aperture [GIAL 78]. Because of the favorable trade-offs, the majority of current wideband, long-run fiber-optic systems utilize graded-index fibers. Typically, NA for such fibers ranges between 0.2 and 0.3.

Special Profiles

Other fiber designs are possible. In Japan, considerable development effort is centered on "W-type" fibers, so named because the index-of-refraction profile resembles the letter W. In this type of fiber, the core and the outer cladding are separated by a third material of which the index of refraction is considerably less than either core or cladding. In some variations, the core itself is graded-index. Reported results are 1 dB/km loss and 1100 MHz-km bandwidth, but these are not achieved simultaneously [NAKA 77].

7.3.1.2   Attenuation

Optical-fiber losses are due to four causes [GALL 76]:

- Absorption
- Material scattering
- Waveguide scattering
- Bend losses

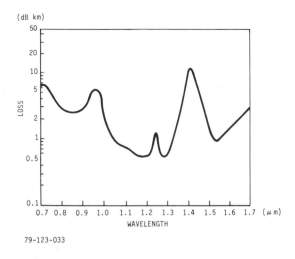

79-123-033

Figure 7.12. Loss characteristics of a typical low-loss, graded-index optical fiber.

A representative plot of graded index fiber attenuation versus wavelength is shown in Fig. 7.12. While light energy in the visible region can be used to illuminate optical fibers, it is seen that loss is lower at longer wavelengths (infrared region). The larger anomalies, such as in the vicinity of 950 nm, are attributable to absorption by the hydroxyl radical (OH) present to some degree in all fiber materials. Other ions, such as transition metals, may also exist and contribute to absorption loss at other wavelengths; to avoid large losses, these heavy ions must be held to concentrations of less than a few parts per billion.

Material scattering results from inhomogeneities in the fiber material. Losses are primarily due to Rayleigh scattering, following a λ^4 law. In fused silica, Rayleigh scattering loss is about 1 dB/km at $\lambda = 1\ \mu$. By referring to Fig. 7.11, it can be seen that material scattering loss is an important part of the intrinsic attenuation characteristic of fiber, in both magnitude and determination of the shape of the curve.

Variation in size and smoothness of boundaries of an optical waveguide causes waveguide scattering losses. For example, in the worst-case situation, a core radius deviation of $10^3\ \mu$m rms could cause a radiation loss of 10 dB/km. Losses experienced in present-day fibers are well below this figure, indicating that current manufacturing processes are quite good in this respect, and that variations that do exist are very gradual.

Packaging and installation can increase loss, by two mechanisms—bending and microbending losses. The latter arises due to the fact that the fibers are small in size, and hence are subject to axial distortion resulting from forces of relatively small magnitude. Such forces can be exerted by uneven pressures exerted on the cable and transmitted to the fiber. For example, the pressure of a fingernail on raw fiber can increase its attenuation by more than 1 dB. In practice, current cable designs protect the fiber from large pressure differentials and minimize microbending losses, and they can be considered to be small (less than 1 dB/km) in comparison with the nominal fiber attenuation characteristics.

Bending loss is an exponential function of the bend radius of a fiber. In practice, bending loss is usually negligible for bend radii that a prudent installer would permit with conventional coaxial cable: say, in the neighborhood of several centimeters. The minimum recommended bend radius is highly dependent on the refractive index contrast between the fiber and its surroundings. It is usually specified by the manufacturer of a particular cable. Cable manufacturers are devising ways to minimize these losses. One experimental cable utilizes a reverse-lay unit core which minimizes stress on the fiber, resulting in cable attenuation less than 3 dB/km at 850 μ.

When installed, variations of optical-fiber attenuation can occur due to the environment, but the magnitude of variation is generally much less than that experienced with coaxial cable. With regard to temperature, one set of data for a plastic-coated, graded index fiber shows that loss actually decreases with increasing temperature—7 dB/km at -40° C, 6 dB/km at -20° C, and 5 dB/km at +60° C [CHAN 78]. Another continuously monitored graded index fiber, spanning both buried and aerial installation in the vicinity of Montreal, has exhibited a peak-to-peak variation of ±0.5 dB/km from November 1978 through March 1979, implying a temperature coefficient of -0.03 dB/°C [ALEX 79]. In some earlier installations, fiber attenuation was observed to be actually modulated by cable sway and vibration; it is now known that this effect was due to bending and microbending losses as described above, and improved cabling techniques have eliminated the problem. The greatest variations in observed fiber attenuation are due to high irradiation levels, the effects of which are currently being investigated by NASA and the Department of Defense.

7.3.1.3   Bandwidth

The intrinsic bandwidth of a current optical fiber is determined by two principal mechanisms. With multimode step-index fibers, the dominant mechanism is modal dispersion, mentioned previously. The maximum spread τ of delays per unit length L is given approximately by

$$\text{(step index)} \qquad \frac{\tau}{L} = \frac{n_1 \Delta n}{c} \tag{7.4}$$

where $\Delta n = (n_1 - n_2)$ and c is the speed of light.

Calculations with common values for step-index fibers yields a result of the order of 10 nsec/km.

For parabolic graded index fibers, the delay spread τ is approximated by

$$\text{(graded index)} \qquad \frac{\tau}{L} = \frac{n_1 (\Delta n)^2}{8c} \tag{7.5}$$

Because typical values for n_1 and n_2 differ by the order of 1%, the modal dispersion in a graded index fiber can approach two orders of magnitude less than for a step-index fiber. Modal dispersion is an extremely sensitive function of the graded index profile, dipping sharply when it is square law (parabolic)—decreasing as an inverse function of the radius squared.

Although modal dispersion is expressed in the dimensions of time per unit length, the effect is not linear with fiber length. This comes about because the fiber attenuation is different for different modes, normally being greater for the undesired modes as compared with the dominant mode. Measurements indicate that the modifying power law of length ranges from nearly 1 to ½, depending on the particular fiber characteristics, test instrumentation, and measurement method. Until better specifications are developed, it is reasonable to use the compromise relation for effective length L:

$$L' = L^{0.75} \tag{7.6}$$

to estimate the modal dispersion in a fiber of length L, when L is greater than 1 km.

The second determinant of bandwidth is material dispersion (not to be confused with material scattering). Material dispersion is a chromatic aberration, arising from the fact that the indices of refraction of the fiber materials are nonlinear with wavelength. Most low-loss fibers use glasses of high-fused-silica content, for which the material dispersion is a very sensitive function of wavelength, becoming vanishingly small in the region of 1.3 μm. This is particularly significant because 1.3 μm is also the region of very low attenuation. Since single-mode fibers, by definition, are not subject to modal dispersion, they are intrinsically capable of low loss and enormous bandwidth at about 1.3 μm—potentially greater than 100 GHz. Material dispersion is essentially proportional to fiber length.

So far, we have considered only the intrinsic bandwidth of optical fibers. The high sensitivity of material dispersion to wavelength means that the choice of operating wavelength is critical to very wideband systems. Further, practical light sources (emitters) have spectral widths considerably broader than the modulation bandwidths we are considering, which fact has a pronounced effect on material dispersion. Thus practical fiber-optic transmission systems can be limited more by the combination of emitter and fiber than by the intrinsic fiber bandwidth itself [FELL 78]. The bandwidth actually realized can also be limited by the design techniques used in the receiver/circuitry. These situations are discussed in Sec. 7.3.2 and illustrated in Figure 7.14.

7.3.1.4 *Practical Fibers*

Table 7.1 contains a representative sample of fibers available in 1981. These fibers can be made up into equally diverse types of cable. The buffer material, not previously described, is usually a plastic outer coating of the fiber, the purpose of which is to provide further strength and protection during handling. Among these fibers are those suitable for short-run system interconnects at data rates below 1 Mbps, and those usable in long-haul systems capable of transmitting more than 100 Mbps over distances of several kilometers. As with other components, the technology and hence availability of fibers are advancing rapidly; source listings such as current versions of [IFOC 81, FIBE 78] should be consulted.

It will be noted from the data in Tab. 7.1 that there is a large variation in the physical parameters of fibers. In general, fiber core and cladding sizes tend to be grouped in ranges according to the fiber type and intended application, as discussed earlier. In particular, graded-index multimode "telecommunications grade" fibers, intended for long-haul, wideband transmission, now follow the recommendations of the EIA Standards Committee P-6 for 50 μm core and 125 μm cladding diameters. Commonality of dimensions makes possible the standardization of connectors and coupling methods, necessary for the widespread application of optical fiber systems.

Another observation to be made from Tab. 7.1 is that the attenuation of specific fibers is specified at various wavelengths. In a given region, such as 700 to 900 nm, this may be because the most advantageous wavelength for specifying attenuation may vary in accordance with a particular manufacturer's production technique; or because a manufacturer has "tuned" his process to match a particular light source. A few entries are specified in the newer micrometer wavelengths, where attenuation can be much lower and the usable bandwidth significantly greater. Additional manufacturers are expected to announce "dual window" fibers which can be used in both wavelength regions.

For wideband transmission over intermediate to long distances, all-glass fibers are used. Attenuation of present-day production fibers are such that bandwidths of the order of 10 Mbps are routinely achievable over distances in excess of 10 km, without repeaters. Recently reported figures for fibers in development indicate a continuing trend toward lower losses—one such fiber has been measured at 0.5 dB/km [OHR 79] and [MIYA 79] reports 0.2 dB/km at 1.55 μm. Extensive tests of a 32-Mbps, 53-km repeaterless link operating at 1.3 μm are described in [ITO 80].

Lower-cost fibers are available, based on a silica core and a plastic cladding [plastic-clad silica (PCS) fibers]. PCS fibers are useful for shorter distances (less than 1 km) and intermediate bandwidths (up to 10 Mbps). Attenuation of PCS fibers generally is of the order of 10 dB/km. One particular difficulty with PCS fibers has to do with coupling; the generally available connectors and splicing techniques are less satisfactory because of the plastic cladding, which does not exhibit good adhesion properties with glues and is difficult to clamp mechanically.

Inexpensive fibers of large sizes can be made from high-grade plastic materials. Practical all-plastic fibers are of the step-index type. Typically, attenuation figures are quite high, in the range 100 to 500 dB/km. The size of plastic fibers, however, provides very large NA figures, typically in the region of 0.5, leading to more efficient coupling with light sources. This, in turn, compensates somewhat for the high intrinsic attenuation, and allows all-plastic fibers to be quite useful for distances ranging up to some hundreds of meters. Compared with all-glass fibers, plastic fibers are much more limited in bandwidth-length product. However, their properties of high flexibility and strength, coupled with low cost, make them attractive for short-distance applications.

As in other parameters, there are as yet no generally accepted standards for measuring and specifying optical-fiber bandwidth. The situation is complicated because of the interaction between fiber and emitter characteristics (see Sec. 7.3.2.1). Some manufacturers' specification sheets express a nominal 3-dB bandwidth with the

Table 7.1. Typical Optical Fibers and Cables (after [OHR 79] and [IFOC 81])[a]

Fiber Type	Fiber Diameter (μm)		Numerical Aperture	Attenuation (dB/km)	Bandwidth (MHz-km) [or Dispersion (ns-km)]	Vendor	Cost/m (1-km)	Minimum Bend Radius (mm)	Tensile Strength	Type
	Core	Cladding								
All-plastic Step index	368	400	0.53	270 @ 790 nm	[50]	DuPont	$1.95	1.5	25 kg	PIFAX PIR 140 (cables)
	92	400	0.53	350 @ 650 nm	[50]	DuPont	1.45	1.5	25 kg	PIFAX P140 (cables)
Plastic-Clad	200	375	0.33	10 @ 850 nm	710	Maxlight	1.85	5	80 kgf	MSC200A
Silica Step Index Multimode	200	500	0.30	12 @ 800 nm	25	Valtec	0.70	6		PC-08
	250	550	0.30	12 @ 800 nm	25	Valtec	0.70	150	51 kg	PC-10
	200	380	0.27	5 @ 350 nm	25	Quartz Products	0.90	3	50 kg	QSF-A200
	125	300	0.27	5 @ 320 nm	30		0.52	2		QSF-A125
	200	600	0.40	25 @ 790 nm	[35]	DuPont	1.95	1.5	65 kg	PIFAX S-120, Type 30
	200	380	0.34	6 @ 850 nm	6	Belden	1.65	50	713 kg	22 0001
All-glass Large core Multimode	100	140	0.30	10 @ 800 nm	25	ITT	1.00	10	1×10^5 psi	T3001
	100	140	0.28	10 @ 840 nm	10	Fort				HP
	100	140	0.30	7 @ 850 nm	20	Corning	.70	50	50 kg	Siecor 144 Cable
All-glass Step index Single Mode	6	140	0.10	8 @ 850 nm	>500	Valtec	4.75	6	1×10^5 psi	SM05-B
	8	100	0.10	4 @ 1300 nm	[0.06]	American				3030
	10			~1 @ 1300 nm	~1000	Valtec				Under development
	4.5	80	0.10	4 @ 850 nm	>500	ITT	5.00			Other types under development
All-Glass, Graded	50	125	0.21	3 @ 850 nm	1500	Corning/Siecor	2.80	15	2.5×10^4 psi	3015 F (Siecor cable)
				3.5 @ 850 nm	600		1.10			3506 F (Siecor cable)
Index, Multimode Fiber			0.20	4 @ 850 nm	800		1.10			4008 F (Siecor cable)
	50	125		2.5 @ 850 nm	1000	Corning	3.00	15	2.5×10^4 psi	2510 D (double window)
				1.0 @ 1300 nm						
	50	125	0.20	0.7 @ 1300 nm	1300	Corning	1.30			(second window)
	50	125	0.20	1.0 @ 1300 nm	600	American				4090
	50	125	0.22	3.5 @ 850 nm	(0.3)	ITT	1.30	500	>400	T-1211
				3.5 @ 850 nm	(0.5)		1.00			T-1210
				8.0 @ 850 nm	(3.0)		0.20			T-1201
	50	125	0.16	5.0 @ 850 nm	400–600	TIMES	0.70	+30	100 kg	Double window fiber
				4.0 @ 1350 nm	800		0.80			
	50	125	0.20	4.0 @ 900 nm	500	VALTEC	0.95	1.50	51 kg	MG05

[a] With permission from *Electronic Design*, Vol. 27, No. 23, copyright Hayden Publishing Co, Inc., 1979, and Information Gatekeepers, Inc.

dimensions of MHz-Km.[5] Others relate more directly to digital signaling by providing a time-related quantity with the dimensions of nsec/km. The latter is frequently defined as "pulse rise time," "3-dB intermodal dispersion," "pulse dispersion," or some other parameter related to temporal smearing of a step function. One type of specification can be approximately converted to the other by the relationship:

$$\tau \text{ (rise time in nsec/km)} \cong \frac{400}{\text{bandwidth (MHz-km)}} \tag{7.7}$$

The error in this approximation could be as high as ±50% for unusual fiber types and/or measurement methods [HAND 78].

7.3.2 Electrical Interfaces

Figure 7.13 will help to visualize the functional components of a fiber-optic communication system and to establish the terminology for subsequent discussion. The fiber link is depicted as containing a coupler device, which would be necessary if an additional terminal(s) were to be added to the system by "tapping." For single point-to-point communication, the coupler would not be used.

The key component of the transmitter is the emitter, which converts electrical signals into the light flux carried by the optical fiber. Similarly, the key component of the receiver is the detector, which converts the incident light flux into electrical signals that can be processed by the subsequent circuitry.

7.3.2.1 Emitters

The two most widely used types of emitters are light-emitting diodes (LED) and injection laser diodes (ILD). Very roughly, the distinctions between the two follow an order-of-magnitude rule. Compared with LEDs, ILDs afford 10 times greater power, 10 times better spectral purity, and 10 times greater bandwidth. At the present time, unfortunately, ILDs also cost 10 times more and perhaps have 10 times greater failure rate.

While the familiar LEDs operating in the visible spectrum can be used for short-run, low-bandwidth fiber links, specialized devices such as Burrus and edge-emitting diodes operating in the infrared (IR) region are required for high-performance systems. The best IR LEDs (most efficient and having narrow spectral width) operate in the vicinity of 900 nm. Unfortunately, this is also in the vicinity of the OH absorption peak. Reasonable success has been realized in varying semiconductor material dopants and structures to achieve a shift in operating wavelength, to the range 800 to 850 nm. A primary concern in fiber-optic system design is the matching of emitter wavelength with the transmission characteristics of a particular fiber. Frequency stability of the emitter, such as variation with temperature, bias voltage, and age must be considered, lest the operating wavelength wander into an anomalous attenuation region.

[5]The figure of merit is expressed as a *product* of MHz and km. A common error is "MHz/km;" for this to be true, bandwidth would increase with greater distance!

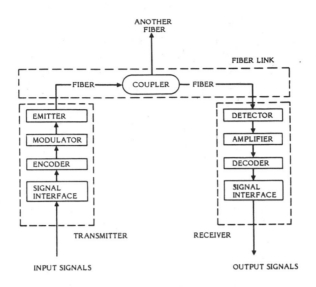

Figure 7.13. Functional representation of a fiber-optic communication system.

As mentioned in the previous discussion on the waveguide properties of optical fiber, material dispersion leads to highly wavelength-dependent losses. This situation is depicted in Fig. 7.14 [MCDE 78]. Because LEDs are incoherent light sources, the emitted spectral width is commonly in the range 30 to 50 nm, which generally limits system bandwidth to about 50 Mbps-km.

In contrast, the light-producing mechanism of an injection laser diode provides an essentially monochromatic emission (spectral width about 4 nm), and modulation to gigahertz rates is possible. Coupled with the higher optical powers available (1 to 10 mW and higher), this would make ILDs the ideal choice for emitters were it not for cost and questions concerning reliability. Present-day prices for IR LEDs are a few tens to hundreds of dollars, and valid extrapolation from long-term experience with visible LEDs indicates a mean time between failure (MTBF) of the order 10^5 hr. ILDs presently are priced from 500 to several thousand dollars, while loosely quoted figures for MTBF are in the order of 10^4 hr. In addition to the obvious concern of lifetime to outright failure, output power and frequency stability with age must be considered.

The physical interfacing of an emitter and fiber is critical, for only the energy coupled into the fiber is useful, and the modes that are coupled can have a significant effect on the performance of very wideband links. The previous discussion on optical waveguide physics will give some insight into the problems. LEDs generally display an area of luminance larger than can be accepted directly by the combination of size and NA of a high-performance fiber. ILDs, on the other hand, can be made with quite small lasing spots, hence efficient coupling can be achieved with care. With both devices, fiber positioning can be critical. One particularly useful form of emitter comes with a pigtail of fiber positioned and attached at the factory; physical interfacing by the user is then a matter of connecting or splicing the pigtail to the transmission fiber.

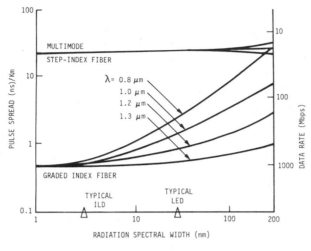

79-123-004

Figure 7.14. Pulse spreading in optical fibers limits the data rate that can be supported. The diagram depicts pulse spreading in 1-km lengths of typical optical fibers. In the step-index fiber, modal dispersion dominates pulse spreading effects. In graded-index fibers, material dispersion dominates if the emitter's spectral width is large. Material dispersion is also a sensitive function of the emitter's wavelength. (After [MCDE 78]; with permission from *Electronic Design*, Vol. 26, No. 22; copyright Hayden Publishing Co., Inc., 1978.)

Perversely, coupling between practical ILDs and fiber-cable installations can also cause anomalous behavior in systems operated at very high bandwidths (say, in excess of 100 Mbps). One investigator refers to such behavior as "a new kind of noise" [TANA 78] experienced in a 200-MHz link operated in both analog and digital modes using graded-index fiber, ILD emitters, and APD detectors. The observed effect is bursty in nature, occasionally (several times daily) degrading the long-term P_e of 10^{-9} to 10^{-6}, for periods of a few seconds. Qualitative observations of similar phenomena termed "model noise" are reported in [EPWO 79], which also relates the noise as inversely proportional to emitter coherence. The mechanisms involved are not well understood, but are believed to be related to wavelength-dependent reflections at impedance discontinuities in the optical path, such as could occur at splices or significant microbends. It is possible that such reflected energy returned to the laser can excite spurious modes of oscillation at a slightly different wavelength, leading to frequency-dependent constructive and destructive interference in a manner somewhat analogous to impedance mismatch problems experienced with tightly coupled oscillators at high radio frequencies. This is supported by the fact that the onset of the phenomenon has been correlated with fiber cable vibration and sway, and the further

288

observation that the effects of such mechanical perturbations diminish with increasing distance from the emitter (consequently, with increased decoupling due to fiber attenuation).

7.3.2.2 Detectors

Essentially all detectors currently employed in fiber-optic systems are based on some form of semiconductor diode junction. The photons of the incident light energy generate hole–electron pairs of carriers. If the junction is externally biased, the resultant electric fields sweeps the carriers through the junction and changes the current flowing through an external load. The differential current flow in the presence of light energy is termed *photocurrent.*

Detector efficiency is commonly characterized by one of two parameters: quantum efficiency η or responsivity S. Quantum efficiency η is simply a measure of the number of electrons produced per photon. Responsivity is related to quantum efficiency by $S = K\eta\lambda$ amperes/watt, where λ is the incident light wavelength (meters) and K is a constant.

Useful detector performance is related to the minimum discernible signal (MDS), which is limited by noise. The primary detector noise components are shot noise arising from leakage currents, and quantum noise, which can be thought of as the noise resulting from the discreteness of the photon/electron conversion process. Unlike the thermal noise basic to radio receivers, shot and quantum noise are best described by Poisson, rather than Gaussian, statistics [PATI 78]. A third source of noise is due to the thermal noise contributed by the front-end amplifier that follows the detector. Because of the very low signal level produced by the detector, the receiver thermal noise is a significant contributor. It has been shown that a Gaussian approximation to the total noise process affords reasonable accuracy but does not allow determination of optimum detector gain and decision threshold levels [PERS 77]. The optimum design of a receiver is not straightforward, but must consider many trade-offs between nominal light level, operating bandwidth, modulation method, and detector characteristics [PERS 73, MESI 78, TAKA 76], as well as the environmental characteristics.

Currently, the most popular choice of detector types is the silicon p-i-n diode (PIN), because its highest sensitivity is in the vicinity of 900 nm. It is a broadband device, however, having useful response in the range 700 to 1100 nm. Other PIN advantages include rise times (2 to 10 nsec) that are commensurate with bandwidths achievable with current emitter-fiber combinations, required bias voltage is easily obtained from commonly used power supplies, and dynamic range is large (about 60 dB). A representative, state-of-the-art analog PIN receiver has an MDS of -47 dBm at 10 MHz bandwidth [HAND 78].

Avalanche photo diodes (APD) exhibit an intrinsic gain characteristic due to the avalanche multiplication of carriers in a large electric field. To establish this field, APDs must be operated with a tightly regulated, high bias voltage (100 V or higher)—a major disadvantage. APDs are also more costly. Nevertheless, the net minimum detectable signal (MDS) using an APD can be two orders of magnitude

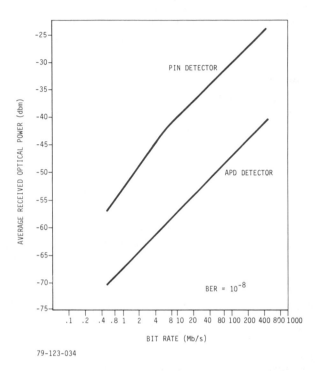

79-123-034

Figure 7.15. Required optical power versus bit rate for digital system implemented with PIN and APD detectors (for $P_e = 10^{-8}$). (Courtesy of
ITT.)

lower than a PIN. State-of-the-art analog receivers using APDs provide an MDS of
about -70 dBm at 10 MHz. A typical digital APD receiver design can operate at 10
Mbps and BER = 10^{-10}, for a received power level of -39.5 dBm [PATI 78]. One
peculiarity of APDs in analog receivers is that noise increases with the signal level due
to the quantum and excess noises, which are signal dependent. APDs display a
detector rise time in the region 0.5 to 2 nsec.

Curves relating required incident optical power to data rate for idealized digital
receivers employing PIN and APD detectors are shown in Fig. 7.15 [HAND 78]. At
data rates higher than about 10 Mbps, APD-equipped receivers enjoy a 16-dB
advantage over PIN receivers. However, the dynamic range of an APD receiver is
limited to about 25 dB; a wider range of signal levels will lead to waveform distortion
and deterioration of error rate. The curves shown are for $P_e = 10^{-8}$. Very roughly, and
for small changes, it can be estimated that a 1-dB change in optical power causes a
corresponding change of two orders of magnitude in P_e.

The smearing of pulse rise time in fiber transmission leads to intersymbol
interference and jitter in a digital receiver. Within limits, the resultant degradation in
error rate can be compensated by increasing optical power delivered to the detector.
For rough performance calculations, a factor of 2 to 3 dB is commonly used (e.g., Step

14 in Box 7.1). A more precise method of accounting for the degradation given specific characteristics of the link components can be found in [MURT 79].

7.3.2.3 *Modulators, Demodulators, and Coding*

Currently, modulation of intelligence on the light carrier in a fiber-optic link is almost universally accomplished by direct radiance intensity modulation of the emitter. With both LEDs and ILDs, radiance is a function of current, which offers the possibilities of analog, sampled-pulse analog, or purely digital signaling.

Analog intensity modulation is presently attractive for systems involving transmission of video information. Perhaps the greatest current demand for bandwidth comes from the television services, which are analog in nature. Well-developed and entrenched technology exists for analog TV transmission; further, the very wide band analog-to-digital (A/D) and digital-to-analog (D/A) converters required for digital transmission are currently quite expensive. Other cases exist wherein intensity modulation would impose fewer equipment requirements on a communication circuit: for example, applications best served by some form of frequency-division multiplexing. Intensity modulation, however, is hampered by the nonlinear radiance versus current characteristics of both LEDs and ILDs, and also by the detector characteristics, both of which can lead to serious intermodulation distortion products [MICH 79]. Linearization techniques based on feedback and predistortion have been employed. In high-performance systems, particularly those subject to environmental variations, elaborate circuits are used to set and maintain operating bias levels.

Because of these problems, sample-pulse and other quasi-analog modulation techniques have enjoyed a resurgence of interest. This type of modulation includes pulse-amplitude modulation, (PAM), pulse-width modulation (PWM), pulse-position modulation (PPM), and pulse-rate modulation (PRM) [SATO 78, SATO 79]. Frequently, they can be implemented more easily than can wideband, low-distortion D/A and A/D converters necessary for purely digital transmission. In the special case of television transmission, other techniques are also attractive, which can minimize the complexity of modulation/demodulation circuitry [MCDE 77, MONT 78].

Digital modulation overcomes some, but not necessarily all, of the linearity, bias point, and noise problems of analog modulation. Digital signaling is most easily implemented by simply turning emitter current on and off. In some instances it is desirable to maintain a lower, "almost-off" threshold current (and radiance) level to improve switching speed. In either case, the receiver should be ac-coupled to preclude dc drift errors, and the transmission should be unipolar, containing a transition for each bit to avoid shifts in average reference level. Consequently, conventional non-return-to-zero (NRZ) code is unsuitable, for both extremely low and high data rates; long strings of 0's and 1's cause changes in average level, and make clock recovery more difficult. Manchester (biphase) coding eliminates dc-level shifts because it has a transition for each bit, but requires twice the bandwidth to encode at an equivalent bit rate. The considerations are similar to those of digital transmission via other media, and the same coding schemes are applicable. Those most suitable for fiber-optic data links are compared in Tab. 7.2.

7.3.2.4   *Packaged Transmitters and Receivers*

As will have been gathered from the preceding paragraphs, the design of transmitters and receiver circuitry is not straightforward. Rarely can the circuitry be designed independently of the choice of specific emitters and detectors; efficient system designs further require consideration of the fiber characteristics. For these reasons, the user will normally prefer to work with integrated system components, or perhaps even prepackaged systems.

By 1979, numerous manufacturers had placed reasonably priced integrated system components and prepackaged systems on the market. Generally, the prepackaged systems are intended for applications requiring moderate data rates over relatively short distances, although some will operate up to 1 km over low-loss fiber cables. Prepackaged systems can be ordered with a specified length of fiber cable, preassembled with matching connectors. Figure 7.16 shows a typical system. Key characteristics of some typical systems are shown in Tab. 7.3, together with an independent evaluation of their data rate and bit-error-rate performance. Some prepackaged systems operate in effect as a pair of "optical modems," with a standard electrical interface such as RS-232. Other systems are designed for mounting on printed circuit boards and provide for electrical interface at TTL or ECL microcircuit signal levels—which require more effort to apply in system usage, but which allow the optimization of interfacing and coding for best performance in a specific application as well as providing better packaging.

Table 7.4 lists characteristics of some typical integrated transmitter/receiver pairs intended for high-performance applications. With these system components, much greater bandwidth and circuit length can be achieved, of course at considerably higher cost. To realize the maximum performance possible with these units, careful system design and choice of optical fiber are necessary.

7.3.3   Connectors and Splices

As with conventional wire cables, splicing is required to join fiber ends permanently, such as to make up long runs or to effect repairs of broken fibers. Connectors are used to mate ends of fibers to other fibers or fiber-optic devices when a permanent junction is not desired. Normally high performance devices such as emitters, detectors, and couplers, are provided with fiber "pigtails," so that connecting and splicing involves the mating of fibers.

Perhaps the greatest technological deterrent to the practical application and large-scale implementation of fiber-optic systems is the difficulty experienced with connectors and splices. The difficulties stem from losses, cost and utility of equipment and devices required, and unknowns concerning long-term performance.

Table 7.2. *Code Families Suitable for Fiber-Optic Modulation, and Some Salient Characteristics (from [LITT 78, BUCH 76, MORR 78]).*

Code Family	Bandwidth/Data Rate Ratio	DC Component	Error-Detecting Capability	Self-Clocking	Synchronizing Preamble
NRZ (non-return to zero)	1	Large	None	No	No
RZ (return to zero)	2 or more	Moderate	None	Partial	No
PE (Phase encoded)	2	Low to none	Some	Inherent	Yes
AMI (Alternate Mark Inversion)	1	None	None	No	Yes
Modified AMI (many variants)	2	None	Some	Inherent in most	Yes

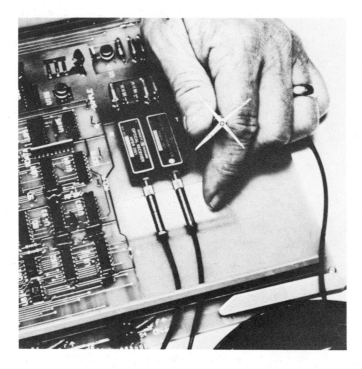

Figure 7.16. Printed circuit board mounting of medium-data-rate optical transmitter and receiver, typical of current technology (1980). (Courtesy of Hewlett-Packard, Inc.)

The predominant causes of loss in connecting and splicing can be analyzed from the viewpoint of how perfectly the ends of the fibers can be prepared and abutted. For details, the reader is referred to [KEEL 78] or [DAKS 77]; however, a few results will provide an idea of the dimensions:

- A 5% difference in core diameter (or numerical aperture) leads to a loss of 1 dB
- An end separation of 40 μm can cause a loss of 1 dB (can be reduced by index matching fluid)
- A 3° angle between planes of the fiber ends leads to a loss of 0.5 dB
- An axial misalignment of 10% of the core diameter leads to a loss of 0.5 dB.

One increasingly popular alignment technique involves precision V-shaped grooves in a mechanical fiber-holding device; this is particularly useful for mass-splicing (or connecting) fibers in a multifiber cable. With mechanical devices, the fibers are held in place by clamping arrangements, heat-shrinkable tubing, or adhesives such as epoxy glues. Splice losses can be reduced by the addition of an index-matching fluid

Table 7.3 *Key Characteristics of Some Typical Prepackaged Fiber-Optic Systems* [a]

Manufacturer and Model No.	Operating Wavelength (mn)	Nominal Link Length	Compatible Fiber	Special Features	BER Measured	Approximate Cost (No Fiber)
Hewlett-Packard HFBR Series	700	100 m	All-glass, 100/140 μm	Internal coding, three-level code capacity	$<10^{-9}$ @ 10 Mbps	$450
Burr-Brown 3712T, 3712R	670	20 m	All-plastic, 1016 μm	Bias adjustment possible	$<10^{-9}$ @ 25 kbps	$170
3713T, 3713R	660	20 m	All-plastic, 1016 μm	Interchangeable with 3712 for maximum efficiency	$<10^{-9}$ @ 250 kbps	$170
Canoga Data Systems CRS-100 and CSY-100	820	1 km	All-glass, 62.5/125 μm	RS-232C compatible; synchronous—CSY, asynchronous—CRS	$<10^{-9}$@ 9600 bps and @ 56 kbps	CRS—$625, CSY—$750
CCL-220	820	1 km	All-glass, 62.5/125 μm	RS-232C compatible; SMA connectors	$<10^{-9}$ @ 20 Mb/s	$700
Texas Instruments TXES, 485 C050 (emitter) TXED, 455 C050 (detector) TXEF, 402 M050 (cable assembly)	850	50 m	PCS 368/400 μm	All-plastic, AMP connectors	Not measured; but 10 Mbps data rate	$120

[a] Typical transmitter/receiver evaluated for application in fiber-optic lines. Unless otherwise indicated, the transmitters and receivers are not complete "optical modems," and require additional interface circuitry to match common interface speculations such as RS-232C. (Data courtesy of PAGE Communications Engineers, Inc.)

Table 7.4. Typical Transmitter/Receiver Combinations for Application to Long-Distance Fiber-Optic Links.

Manufacturer and Model No.	Emitter/Detector Types	Operating Wavelength (nm)	Maximum Distance (km)	Compatible Fiber	Maximum Bandwidth	Approx. Cost	Comments
Optical Information Systems (EXXON)	Laser/APD	820 (others available)	~ 10	All-glass, graded index, 50/125 μm	150 Mbps	$5500	Digital, TTL, or ECL Levels
Times Fiber Wideband Analog Analog OTL-1101, OR-211A	Laser/APD	830	≥ 3	All-glass, graded index, 50/125 μm	300 MHz	$5000	Multichannel capacity
Times Fiber TFM-6300	Laser/APD	830	≥ 5	All-glass, graded index, 50/125 μm	100 Mbps	$6000	Self-clocking
Digital Communications Corporation	Laser/APD	820	~ 10	All-glass graded index, 50 or 62.5 m/125 μm	90 Mbps	$16,000	Bell System compatible, two T3 channels
GTE Lenkurt FT3	Laser/APD	830	~ 10	All-glass graded index, 62.5/125 μm	45 Mbps	$16,000	Alarming provided, Bell System compatible
VALTEC VS-100	LED/PIN	820	3	All-glass, graded index, 50 or 62.5 m/125 μm	300 MHz		Multichannel analog, EIA-RS-440 compatible

between the fiber ends; in some cases, the same effect is achieved by the use of specially formulated glues. There is some controversy over such techniques; there is risk of contamination of fluids, and the long-term optical properties of glues are uncertain.

Another category of splicing techniques is based on the thermal fusion of fiber ends. High-temperature flames, electric arcs, and focused lasers have been used to create the relatively moderate temperatures necessary to melt the glass locally. Indications are that fusion techniques avoid the need for ultraprecise alignment and may also lower the long-term risk of contamination.

A wide variety of connectors is available, based on mechanical contrivances similar to those used for splicing. Obviously, the fiber ends cannot be glued or fused, and the two mating pieces of the connector must be separable. Further, the fiber faces should not touch, lest scratching or fracture of the fibers occur; consequently, some separation loss is inevitable. The use of index-matching fluid carries a high risk of contamination, with attendant high loss. Some of the more expensive connector designs incorporate lenses to reduce separation loss.

For both splices and connectors, the preparation of the fiber is crucial to achieving low loss. Various tools and techniques are available, some semiautomatic, to cleave and fracture a fiber so that a reasonably planar end face results that is perpendicular to the fiber axis. Those most successful maintain an axial tension on the fiber during the cleaving and fracturing processes. Particularly with connectors, marked improvement in losses can be achieved by careful polishing of the fiber face with a series of increasingly fine abrasives (grit size as small as 0.5 μm).

Generally, losses reported in use of the various splicing techniques range from 0.1 to 1.0 dB mean loss [DAKS 77, HATA 79, LARG 79]. As would be expected, connector losses are higher, currently falling in the range 1 to 3 dB, although somewhat lower losses have been reported [CHIP 80]. The problem is that the better results have been achieved in the laboratory, using cumbersome, sometimes delicate equipment and highly skilled technicians, whereas real splices and connector installations must be made in the field under less than ideal conditions. As this is written, a "second generation" of tools and techniques is appearing, which promises to make installation of fiber-optic communication systems economically viable.

It should be noted that not all of the splicing/connecting loss can be attributed solely to the device or techniques employed. The point was made earlier that until standards are universally adopted, there exist wide variations in fiber core diameter and concentricity, buffer material, or jacket design [CHAR 80]. Consequently, mechanical mating devices must be custom-designed for a particular fiber. Furthermore, quality control is often a problem. The author has had experience with one highly regarded fiber that exhibits quite good performance; however, its nominal outer diameter of 125 μm has been observed to vary as much as $\pm20\%$ over its length. Some connectors now on the market have been designed specifically to accommodate such variations; however, they are quite expensive.

Small fibers require considerable precision in connector alignment, and suitable connectors are accordingly expensive. Telecommunications-quality connectors currently cost in the range $40 to $100 per pair. In contrast, commercial-quality connectors for all-plastic and the larger PCS fibers are available for $3 to $10 per pair.

7.3.4 Couplers

Passive fiber-optic couplers are available in two configurations, somewhat analogous to those used in coaxial-cable systems: star couplers and directional couplers. The directional or Y coupler is favored where a tap or 1 : 2 power split is desired. One method of fabricating a Y coupler entails twisting and fusing two fibers together in such a manner that input light from one fiber is transmitted out to other fibers in a "Y" fashion at a desired ratio (e.g., 1 : 1). In addition to the splitting of the optical power, another 0.5 to 1 dB is lost in each path as excess insertion loss. Additionally, splice or connector losses must be included at all three ports of the "Y" to account for all the necessary calculations in determining coupling losses. While the procedure for manufacture of a "Y" coupler is straightforward, controlling the output ratio is difficult. As yet, low-cost manufacturing methods have not been perfected.

Star couplers, as they appear on the market today, provide one input port and a number of output ports (3 to 31). Distribution of the input power is accomplished by a reflective surface with approximately equal power being distributed to the output ports. Each port is accessed via a fiber-optic connector, and thus is subject to excess losses associated with such connectors. Each connector has an interface loss of 1.2 to 2.2 dB, and an excess insertion loss of 4 to 5 dB must be considered. In addition, the variation power of the output ports can range from 2 to 3 dB. Star couplers are presently the only available means by which tapping can be reasonably accomplished, in situations where a large number of passive taps is required.

Passive coupler technology has a long way to go to meet the needs of the present market. More efficient and less expensive multiport couplers need to be developed to make fiber optics economically attractive for multisubscriber distribution networks. Bandwidth restrictions must be overcome. Excess losses will be minimized in the next few years and cost will decrease as production increases (analogous to fiber itself). However, new methods for accomplishing the same results may yet surface to solve the existing problems.

7.3.5 Fiber-Optic Link Performance Analysis

The design and analysis of a wideband fiber-optic transmission system is a complex process, made even more difficult by the lack of standardization of definitions, measurement methods, and specifications. A detailed treatment of the process can be found in [PERS 73], while a somewhat simplified analysis is presented in [MIKI 78] for one specific use. It is possible, however, to perform a highly simplified analysis that provides a gross estimate of performance and gives good visibility of the important factors, using information contained in the preceding sections.

Suppose that a system of the form of Fig. 7.10 is designed to operate at a DS3 data rate (45 Mbps). The distance between the transmitter and the coupler is to be 1

Box 7.1. *Typical Power Budget Calculation for a Fiber-Optic Transmission System of the Form of Fig. 7.10.*

	Parameter	Factor
1.	Emitter average output power at T = 830 nm (specified peak power adjusted for modulation method; see the text) (ILD)	+4.0 dBm
2.	Emitter-fiber coupling loss (assume that the emitter power is coupled into a short "pigtail" fiber, the other end of which is used for connecting with the fiber link itself)	–8.0 dB
3.	"Pigtail"-to-fiber link termination connector	–1.0 dB
4.	First fiber link—1-km fiber @ 5 dB/km @ 830 nm	–5.0 dB
5.	Link-to-coupler input connector	–1.0 dB
6.	Coupler—equal power division between two output ports = –3 dB. Excess loss = 1.5 dB; thus overall loss to each output port = 4.5 dB	–4.5 dB
7.	Coupler-to-link connector	–1.0 dB
8.	Second fiber link—2-km fiber @ 5 dB/km @ 830 nm	–10.0 dB
9.	Splice between the two 1-km fiber sections making up the 2-km second link	–0.5 dB
10.	Fiber link termination connector (to detector pigtail)	–1.0 dB
11.	Detector coupling loss	–1.0 dB
12.	Optical power delivered to detector	–29.0 dBm
13.	System margin—allowance for degradation due to temperature and time	–2.0 dB
14.	Allowance for intersymbol interference and jitter	–2.0 dB
15.	Calculated usable detector power	–33.0 dB
16.	Required detector optical power for data rate = 45 Mbps and $P_e = 10^{-8}$ (PIN) (use Fig. 7.12)	(–33.0) dBm
17.	System excess margin	0 dB

km; and the distance between the coupler and the receiver is to be 2 km, made up of two 1-km sections of fiber joined with a splice.

Assuming that an ILD transmitter and a PIN receiver possessing average characteristics are used, the simplified link power budget analysis would appear as in Box 7.1. For step 1, an ILD *peak* output power of 10 mW (+10 dBm) at λ = 830 nm is assumed; however, it is *average* power delivered to the detector that we want to calculate. We also assume the use of alternate mark inversion (AMI) coding, to ensure reliable clock recovery. AMI coding provides an average power of 1/4 of the peak power; therefore, the average emitter power used is 10 dBm - 6 dB = 4 dBm.

As it happens, the completion of the analysis, step 16, indicates that the system design exactly matches requirements and possesses no margin other than that allowed for in step 13. If step 16 were to show a negative excess margin, at least this amount would have to be made up—perhaps by choosing a lower-loss fiber or a more sensitive APD receiver. A positive excess margin can be useful; for example, a higher-loss (and therefore less expensive) fiber could be used, or the drive to the ILD emitter could be reduced, thereby increasing its expected lifetime.

The power delivered to the "other fiber" from the second coupler port can be determined by totaling through step 7, giving -16.5 dBm. The "other fiber" link can be analyzed from that point onward in the same manner.

Box 7.2. *Simplified Digital Fiber-Optic System Bandwidth Analysis,*
for the Example of Box 7.1[a]

	Parameter	Rise Time (nsec)	Rise Time Squared (nsec²)
1.	Emitter: ILD at λ = 830 nm	2.0	4.0
2.	Fiber material dispersion: use excess pulse spreading from Fig. 7.11. For this example, pulse spread = (0.2 nsec/km)(3 km)	0.6	0.4
3.	Fiber modal dispersion: use Eqs. (7.6) and (7.7). For this example, assume that fiber is specified as 200 mHz-km; = ($\frac{400}{200}$) ($L^{0.75}$) = (2) (2.3) = 4.6 nsec	4.6	21.2
4.	Detector/receiver combined rise time For this example, assume 4 nsec	4.0	16.0
5.	Sum of squared rise times		41.6
6.	Square root of step 5	6.4	
7.	Calculated system rise time = 1.1 × step 6	7.0	
8.	Calculated system rise time (CSRT) must be $\frac{700}{\text{signaling rate (Mbps)}}$ nsec. For this example, AMI coding is used; thus signaling rate = 2 × data rate = 90 Mbps. Thus CSRT must be $\leq \frac{700}{(2 \times 45)} \leq$ 7.8 nsec. This condition is met by step 7.		

[a]The analysis is based on the root-sum-square addition of the various factors contributing to degradation of link rise time, hence to limitation of maximum link data rate.

Box 7.2 displays an analysis of the system rise-time budget, again using typical parameters for the components. Effects of the coupler have not been included, as these devices are not yet well specified. It is important to note that the system must support the signaling rate of twice the data rate, because AMI coding is used. In step 8, the system rise time must be less than 7.8 nsec. The calculated system rise time, step 7, is 6.7 nsec; therefore, it can be concluded that the system will perform satisfactorily.

7.3.6 Examples of Fiber-Optic Systems

The era of useful fiber-optic telecommunication system installations began in 1976. By 1980, over 200 systems were in service; their novelty had dissipated and the viability of the technology was clear. As would be expected, the majority of the larger systems have been implemented by common carriers and CATV system operators. Run distances average from 1 to 10 km, with some ranging to some tens of kilometers. A few of these systems have defined the current state of the art in various respects; these are summarized below.

7.3.6.1   London, Ontario, Digital CATV Supertrunk

The BCN Fiber Optics Group, London, Ontario, Canada, has installed the first digital fiber-optic video trunking system in North America. The system transmits 12 color-television channels and 12 FM stereo channels in one "downstream" direction, and provides for 3 video channels in the "upstream" direction. In the eight-fiber cable, five fibers are used for downstream transmission, one for upstream, and two fibers are reserved for expansion or as spares. Each fiber operates at a rate of 322 Mbps, made up as follows: a TDM multiplexer processes three input channels at a rate of 107.4 Mbps, for a total of 322 Mbps. Each input channel is a 10-bit word, for a word rate of 10.74 Mbps. The first 8 bits of each word carry video data, while the tenth bit is a parity bit. The ninth bit carries synchronization, a stereo FM channel, and the audio program associated with the video channel; the excess capacity can carry data services in the future.

The supertrunk run is over 7.8 km, using both aerial and buried cables. The cable diameter is 0.5 in., and each 125-μm fiber has less than 8 dB/km loss. Two repeaters are used. Transmitters employ 1 mW ILDS, and receivers use APDs. The system was designed for a bit error rate of 10^{-9}, while measurements have been typically 10^{-12} [COTT 78].

7.3.6.2   HI-OVIS: The Fiberized City

The most ambitious "wired city" undertaking to date, using fiber-optic transmission, is the HI-OVIS project in Japan (Higashi-Ikoma Optical Visual Information System). The system currently serves 168 subscribers, involving a total fiber length of 380 km. The "head end" transmission center contains facilities for TV retransmission, local TV origination, video tape recorders for playing requested programs, and still picture service equipment. Several 36-fiber trunks carry signals to and from regional junction boxes, from which subdivisions are made to the individual two-fiber cables connecting the individual subscriber terminals.

HI-OVIS is a truly full-duplex interactive system. A key feature is the home terminal, comprising a TV receiver, keyboard, camera, microphone, and a terminal controller. Both downstream and upstream channels support a full video bandwidth—a fact of great interest.

Each fiber carries one 4.5-MHz video baseband analog signal, plus subcarriers at 6.0 MHz for FM audio and 6.6 MHz for data. LEDs operating at 830 nm are used throughout, using direct AM intensity (analog) modulation. Detectors are PIN photodiodes. The fibers are plastic-clad step-index type, with a core diameter of 150 μm and attenuation of 5 to 8 dB/km. Such a fiber is satisfactory for the relatively small bandwidth, and the large NA allows the use of LEDs and PINs [KAWA 77, TAKE 78].

There are two reasons for the undertaking of HI-OVIS. One is the obvious development of a national high-technology industry—the project was sponsored by MITI (Ministry of International Trade and Industry). The second reason is the more interesting one, having major future implications. It is best put by a paraphrase of the Japanese spokesman:

> *Our principal natural resource in Japan is our people. We cannot increase them in numbers because of population constraints—the country just isn't big enough. . . . Therefore, our recourse is to increase productivity by enhancing the quality of life. We're going to do this by cultural and educational enrichment by means of a two-way, multimedia communication system encompassing the entire island of Japan. [ELIO 77].*

7.3.6.3   Bell System Lightwave Communications Projects

Following the favorable results of the earlier Atlanta experiment [KERD 78], the Bell System installed in Chicago a trial operational fiber-optic system carrying voice, data, and video [MAZU 78]. Fully operational in May 1977, one part of the system interconnects two central offices by a 1.6-km link; another 0.94-km link provides service to a customer location. Each link's cable comprises 24 graded-index fibers with an average loss of 5 dB/km. Each fiber operates simplex (one-way) and is backed up by a spare, resulting in six full-duplex circuits over each link. Each circuit is operated at a DS3 rate (44.7 Mbps). Voice and data signals are grouped at T1 rates (1.544 Mbps), which groups are then multiplexed to DS3. On each of the circuits, one T1 slot is used solely for test and monitoring. Picturephone video (4 MHz analog) is digitized directly to the T3 rate by exploratory differential PCM codecs.

One transmitter operates with a -20-dBm LED; all others utilize -3-dBm ILDs operating at 820 nm. The receivers incorporate APDs, providing a 10^{-9} error rate for received power of -54 dBm. Because of the high transmitter power and low fiber loss, attenuating jumpers are used to reduce the received optical power to the -30- to -40-dBm range.

As of November 1978, 18 months of operational data had been taken. The results show 99.98% error-free seconds, to be compared with the Bell System objective of 99.6% for T1 lines. Total outage time has been 39 sec, or 8×10^{-7}, compared with the guideline for short-haul trunks of 2×10^{-4}. (It must be noted that extensive protection and backup features were incorporated, which are normally applied to high-capacity trunklines.) No fiber failures have occurred; there has been one laser failure in the total cumulative 100,000 hr [JACO 79].

Similar prototype systems operating at the DS3 rate have been installed in Connecticut, the Manhattan (New York City) financial district, and Lake Placid, New York (in time to carry voice and television signals for the Winter Olympic Games in February 1980). The Manhattan installation is particularly interesting, in that its primary purpose is to provide high-speed communications for the many computer installations in the area. Further, nearly 100 telephone company employees are connected to the system to gather data on its operation in a local subscriber application. It is planned to upgrade the Manhattan system to DS4 operation (274 Mbps).

The Bell System has been quite impressed with their experiences with fiber-optic systems. At this writing, they have announced the introduction of the FT-3 Lightwave Transmission System. Bell intends to install this system for trunking between central switching offices at DS3 rates, for which application it is economic at current cost levels. The first FT-3 systems were in regular service by late 1980. Mention has also been made of planning internal fiber-optic connections in the large ESS No. 4 switch systems [JACO 79]. At the other extreme in distance, plans are being made for a long-haul fiber-optic transmission system spanning 611 miles from Washington, D.C., to Boston, Massachusetts [ELPH 80]. This "Northeast Corridor" system will carry 80,000 simultaneous telephone calls, interconnecting 19 supercapacity all-digital switching centers. Full service is expected by 1984.

7.3.7 System Economics

To date, the majority of system cost considerations have been concerned with comparisons between fiber-optic and metallic-cable CATV systems. They both are physical systems, use analogous components, and require similar installation techniques. As noted earlier, the dominant application for fiber-optic transmission will be as substitution for coaxial cable; however, there have been surprisingly few published studies of the subject.

One theoretical study [GALL 77] has analyzed the comparative costs in a multipurpose local information transfer system, concentrating on star and loop topologies. It is argued that the cost *per unit length* of a metallic cable system varies in proportion to the product of bandwidth and length, whereas the cost *per unit length* of fiber-optic cable varies only with bandwidth. This is because a fiber link does not suffer from the dispersion limitations of coaxial cable. For the purposes of the analysis, it is assumed that the base cost of fiber cable is 1.5 times that of metallic cable. However, for data rates above 450 kbps (a rather pessimistic figure), the normalized cost of fiber declines because of its extreme bandwidth capability.

Two of the scenarios considered in the study are reproduced as Figs. 7.17 and 7.18. In both cases, the distribution system serves 400 terminals, but the mixture of services and terminal data rates is quite different. The terminals are assumed to be randomly distributed in a rectangular coordinate system, in a service region of radius R. The terminals are tied to a distribution loop or radius D. A star topology exists in the special case $d/r = 0$. The parameter p is a measure of average terminal activity.

From the figures, some interesting observations can be made. Figure 7.14 reveals that the cost of a coaxial-cable ring network is highly sensitive to terminal activity, which can be related to network throughput. A fiber cable system, on the other hand, is relatively insensitive to throughput, even with an extreme topology ($D/R = 1$). In both cases, a star network ($D/R = 0$) is not sensitive to activity because lines are not shared—all terminals are connected by individual lines, by definition capable of supporting 100% activity.

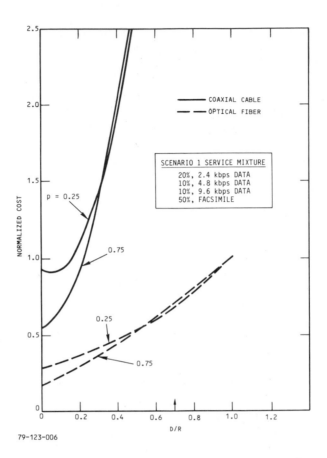

Figure 7.17. Normalized cost versus D/R ratio for network, scenario 1. Total connected capacity for 400 terminals is 6.2 Mbps, comprising the indicated service mixture. (From [GALL 77].)

Somewhat more broadly, it could be concluded that fiber networks are less sensitive to specific topology than are coaxial-cable networks. Figure 7.18 also supports this observation. Both scenarios demonstrate the general conclusion that fiber-optic systems are most cost effective in large-bandwidth, high-throughput situations.

Two studies of fiber optics as applied to mass communications systems are [GRAY 77] and [JULL 78], who have examined similar CATV-type systems. A comparison of the studies is presented in Tab. 7.5. Using Jull's costs for a coaxial-cable system, it could be concluded that a comparable fiber-optics system would be more expensive by a factor of 50 to 150%. Such a conclusion, however, must be approached with caution, for the following reasons:

1.   Although both studies have attempted a projection of fiber-optic component

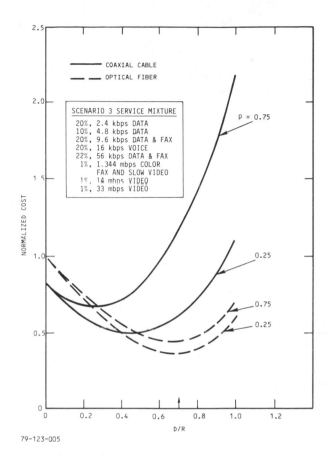

Figure 7.18. Normalized cost versus D/R ratio for network, scenario 3. Total connected capacity for 400 terminals is 242 Mbps, comprising the indicated service mixture. (From [GALL 77].)

costs, neither projected advances in fiber-optic *technology*. For example, Gray assigns one digital channel per fiber, and Jull limits individual fiber capacity to three analog channels (on the grounds that light sources exhibit nonlinear characteristics). In the light of current state-of-the-art, it is unreasonable to project yesterday's problems as a design constraint on a system to be implemented 10 years from now. Both analog and digital systems are being demonstrated currently with better performance.

2. Both network designs are based on coaxial-cable technology, with direct substitution of fiber cables and electrooptical devices for their coaxial-cable counterparts. The networks are quite complex, requiring many expensive devices, such as transmitters, receivers, switches, and couplers, the quantity and cost of which are related to the number of fibers.

3. The studies are not directly comparable. For example, Gray's optical hardware

Table 7.5. *Two Studies of Fiber-Optic Mass Communication System Costs.*[a]

	Gray (1977)		Jull and Bryden (1978)	
Time frame	Late 1980s		1990	
Transmission mode	All digital		Analog	
Trunk bandwidth	30 TV channels (one per fiber)		30 TV channels (but limited to three per fiber)	
Topology (first level/second level)	Star/tree		Star/star	
Second level hubs	Yes		Yes	
Remote switches	Yes		Yes	
Subscriber bandwidth				
Downstream	One TV channel		One TV channel (5–35 MHz)	
Upstream	Low-speed data		Low-speed data (1000 bits/60 sec)	
Assumed fiber cost (including power wires)	3 cents/m		3–10 cents/m	
Subscriber penetration	Two cases: 50% and 90%		Two cases: 63% and 100%	
Cable installation	Buried		Aerial and Buried	
Housing-unit density	1200/mi² (av.)	6800/mi² (av.)	3400/mi² (av.)	
Cable type	Fiber	Fiber	Coaxial	Fiber
Capital cost per subscriber (current dollars)				
50/63% penetration	573	411	250	
90/100% penetration	441	321	209	322–598
Incremental cost per added subscriber channel	~22%	~20%	~16%	—
Cost savings with integrated construction	40%	40%		

[a] Both networks are of the two-way CATV type, include subscriber termination and response unit costs, but exclude the display terminal (TV receiver). The subscriber-response return channels have very low bandwidth and high delay.)

costs are about 10% of the total; Jull's hardware costs cannot be separated, but appear to be substantially higher due to less optimistic projections. It should be noted that, if Gray's hardware costs were removed completely, the remaining cost would still be higher than Jull's. This suggests that there are substantial differences in construction and installation costs assumed; indeed, Gray's costs would be higher because of the assumption of the more expensive method of cable burial. In both cases, the construction and installation costs undoubtedly dominate total network costs, and the future projection of today's problems in these areas should be questioned.

4. Both studies assumed a return channel of extremely limited bandwidth, which is a reflection of current CATV cable system technology. With wavelength or time-division optical multiplexing techniques presently in development, it is possible that a return channel of substantial bandwidth (and low delay) could be provided for a small incremental cost with fiber optics.

One major point to be derived from these studies is that fiber-optic *network* costs cannot be scaled from a simple comparison of cost per unit length of fiber versus coaxial cable. The suggestion is that a single one-way TV channel insufficiently utilizes the cost-bandwidth product intrinsic to fiber optics. This is borne out by the conclusion of several users, including the Bell System [JACO 79], that point-to-point fiber links are more economic than metallic cable at data rates 45 Mbps and above, at near-term (ca. 1980) price levels. The observation is also reflected in conclusions that fiber optics is currently cost effective in the supertrunk and trunk levels of a CATV network, but situations reverse at the local loop and subscriber drop levels [LEIG 78].

Gray's study makes a further point. If other telecommunications services were integrated with the distribution of television, the marginal cost of providing additional services would be small, while the total cost could be allocated to the previously separate services. One obvious candidate for integration is telephone service. Other future possibilities for integrated services include data, alarms, meter reading, high-quality audio, and teletext. These ideas are further expanded in Chap. 17, and impacts on network costs are examined in [CHAN 79].

At current costs, point-to-point fiber-optic versus coaxial-cable cost crossover occurs somewhere between 6 MHz (one analog TV channel, or the DS2 PCM multiplex level) and 45 MHz (one DPCM digital TV channel, or the DS3 PCM level). In more complex networks, very substantial reductions in the costs of transmitters, receivers, couplers, and connectors will be necessary to bring the crossover point below the present-day region of hundreds of MHz. In addition to lower costs for components as currently defined, perhaps the answer lies in integrated electrooptical circuits and new network designs to exploit their properties.

7.3.8 Future Component Trends

Athough major strides have been made during the past 5 years, fiber-optic transmission is still an immature technology. Operational systems have only appeared during the past few years. Many improvements have yet to be made in the areas of system components, applications, and standards.

Table 7.6 contains a comparison of current component technology with a projection of the future state-of-the-art. Qualitatively, the primary areas for future improvements are:

- *Micron wavelengths.* Operating wavelength will move from the current region of 850 nm to about 1.3 μm and perhaps as high as 1.6 μm, resulting in lower losses, wider repeater spacing, wider bandwidth, and lower-cost systems.
- *Improved emitters and detectors.* During this writing, one firm had announced the availability of ILDs guaranteed for 100,000 hr of life; shortly thereafter, this offer was withdrawn. Nevertheless, 10^5 hr or better can be achieved. New semiconductor materials will make possible operation at longer wavelengths [HURW 78].

Table 7.6   *Trends in Fiber-Optics.*

	1980 Typical	1980 Best	1985 Typical	Unit
Fibers				
Attenuation	5–6	3–4	1–2	dB/km
Bandwidth	200	500	1500	MHz-km
Splice loss	0.6	0.3	0.2	dB
Connector loss	1–2	0.7	0.5	dB
Y-splitter loss	3–4	2	1	dB
Detectors				
PIN—responsivity	0.5	0.6	1.5	A/W
APD—responsivity	30	40	50	A/W
Emitters				
LED—power	-125 to -25	-25 to -15	-15 to -10	dBm
ILD—power	-10 to -5	-5 to $+10$	0 to $+6$	dBm
LED—life	10^5	10^5	10^6	hr
ILD—life	10^4	10^5	10^5	hr
Systems				
Operating wavelength	800–900	800–900	1100–1400	nm
Repeater spacing				
LED/PIN	2	3	5	km
ILD/APD	8	10	20	km

- *Improved fibers.* Advances in manufacturing processes will result in improvements in both physical and optical characteristics. Major advancements in system performance can be expected from monomode fibers operating at longer wavelengths.
- *Lower component costs,* a consequence of many factors, but primarily better processes for manufacture, and economies of scale attendant with larger production of both fibers and devices.
- *Satisfactory splices and connectors.* Reduction of losses and, more important, improvements in the field application of these physical interfaces.
- *Wavelength multiplexing.* Analogous to frequency multiplexing, individual carriers on different optical wavelengths will allow even greater bandwidths, easier drop-and-insert network access, and full-duplex operation on a single fiber.
- *Integrated optoelectronic circuitry.* This leads to easier signal interfacing; and low-cost, compact, and efficient transmitters, receivers, and repeaters.
- *Efficient couplers.* At competitive prices, both Y-splitters and multiport devices are necessary for multiple subscriber networks. Although passive, as opposed to active, couplers and taps are most commonly envisioned at the present time, major advances in integrated circuitry could alter the picture.
- *Standards.* As in any developing technology, the imposition of rigid standards could advance widespread application but stifle further devel-

opment. The standards organizations are proceeding cautiously. The EIA Committee P-6 has issued standards on terminology (e.g., RS-440 for connectors) and initial drafts for some test methods.

7.3.9 Future System Applications

In the next decade, the dominant fiber-optic-system applications areas will be these:

- *Telephone trunking.* Initially, applications will be for short-haul trunking such as for DS3 data rates between central offices. Later, as technology and cost factors improve, long-haul trunking applications will follow the lead of the Bell Northeast Corridor project (see Sec. 7.3.6.3).
- *CATV trunking.* Several examples have been mentioned previously. Fiber optics will also extend to the individual subscriber loop, as costs decrease subscriber demand for bandwidth grows and junction techniques are refined.
- *High-interference environments,* such as long-haul circuits paralleling electrified railroads and power lines, and shorter runs in the vicinity of high-power transmitters.
- *Military applications.* A relatively small but important market where security, light weight, interference immunity, isolation, and bandwidth are major considerations.
- *System interconnects.* Used where large bandwidth and low delay are important (e.g., large computers), or interference immunity and isolation are required (e.g., instrumentation, earth stations).
- *Local distribution networks.* Intra- and interpremises to take advantage of the noise immunity and very large bandwidths available.

REFERENCES

ALEX 79   Alexander, K., private communication, March 1979.

ANDR 79   Andrelev, N. "Fiber Optics, The Next Generation Prepares for a Long-Awaited Birth," *EDN*, January 5, 1979, pp. 48.

BARN 76   Barnoski, M. K., ed., *Fundamentals of Optical Fiber Communications,* Academic Press, New York, 1976.

BELL 78   Bellato, L., and C. Staffoli, "The 60 MHz Coaxial Line System," *Telletra Rev.*, No. 29, September 1978, pp. 3–15.

BROA 80   "Broadband Coax Cable Communications Comes On Strong," *Electron. Products*, Vol. 23, No. 9, 1980, pp. 25–26.

BUCH 76   Buchner, J. B., "Ternary Line Codes," *Philip Telecommun. Rev.*, No. 3412, June 1976, pp. 72–86.

CHAN 78   Chang, K. Y., E. Marthaler, and H. K. Basmadjian, "An Overview of a Fiber Optic Exploratory Trial in Montreal," *ICC '78 Conf. Rec.*, Toronto, June 4–7, 1978, pp. 6.1.1 to 6.1.6.

CHAN 79   Chang, K. W., "Fiber Optic Integrated Distribution and Its Implications," *Proc. ICC, '79*, June 1979, pp. 10.1.1 to 10.1.6.

CHAR 80   Charlton, D. "Optical-Waveguide Performance Hinges on Manufacturing Variables," *EDN*, April 5, 1980, pp. 109–112.

CHIP 80   Chipman, J. D., "Practical and Theoretical Considerations in the Design of Fiber Optic Connectors for a Tactical Environment," working paper No. WP-22688, Mitre Corp., Bedford, Mass., February 1980.

COTT 78   Cotton, W. W., "A Digital Television Fiber Optic Trunking System," *ICC '78 Conf. Rec.*, Toronto, June 1978, pp. 21.2.1 to 21.2.4.

DAKS 77   Dakss, M. L., "Review of Recent Fiber Splicing Techniques," *NTC '77 Conf. Rec.*, Los Angeles, Vol. 2, p. 23:5-1.

DEMA 76   Demarines, V. A., and L. W. Hill, "The Cable Bus in Data Communications," *Datamation*, August 1976, pp. 89–92.

DEMO 79   *Demodulator*, Vol. 28, Nos. 7 and 8, GTE Lenkurt, San Carlos, Calif., 1979.

DICK 77   Dickinson, R. V. C., "Digital Data Transmission on CATV Systems," *Can. Cable TV*, November 1977.

DOLB 77   Dolberg, C. E., "Multimode, Multiservice Local Networks," *Proc. INTEL-COM 77*, Atlanta, October 1977.

ELIO 77   Elion, H. A., "Fiber Optic Communications Needs of Developing Countries," *Exposition Proc. INTELCOM 77*, Vol. 2, Atlanta, October 1977, pp. 645–649.

ELIO 78   Elion, G., and H. A. Elion, *Fiber Optics in Communications Systems*, Marcel Dekker, New York, 1978.

ELPH 80   Elphick, M. "Fiber Optics: Short Links Now, Long Haul Coming Soon," *High Technol.*, March 1980, pp. 60–66.

EPWO 79   Epworth, R. E., "The Phenomenon of Modal Noise in Fiber Systems," *Tech. Dig., Optical Fiber Commun. Conf.*, Washington, D.C., March 6–8, 1979, pp. 20–23.

EVEN 79   Even, R. K., R. A. McDonald, and H. Seidel, "Digital Transmission Capability of the Loop Plant," *1979 Int. Conf. Commun.*, Vol. 1, June 10–14, 1979, pp. 2.1.1 to 2.1.7.

FELL 78   Fellinger, D. F., and H. F. Matara, "Fiber Optic Links Work Better When Matched with the Right Emitters," *Electron. Des.*, Vol. 26, No. 22, October 25, 1978, pp. 112–115.

FIBE 78   *Fiber Optics Handbook and Market Guide 1978*, Information Gatekeepers, Inc., Brookline, Mass., 1978.

FIBE 79   *Fiber Optics Commun. Newsl.* (Information Gatekeepers, Inc., Brookline, Mass.), Vol. 2, No. 1, February 1979.

FREE 75   Freeman, R. L., *Telecommunication Transmission Handbook*, Wiley, New York, 1975.

GALL 76   Gallawa, R. L., *A User's Manual for Optical Waveguide Communications*, U.S. Department of Commerce, Office of Telecommunications, March 1976, NTIS No. PB-252-901.

GALL 77   Gallawa, R. L., and W. J. Hartmann, *Operational and Cost Considerations in the Use of Optical Waveguides in a Local Information Transfer System*, U.S.

Department of Commerce, Office of Telecommunications, NTIS No.PB-275-291, November 1977.

GIAL 78   Giallorenzi, T. G., "Optical Communications Research and Technology: Fiber Optics," *Proc. IEEE*, Vol. 66, July 1978, pp. 744–780.

GRAY 77   Gray, M. B., "Cost Estimates for Urban Man-Communication System Employing Separately Constructed and Constructionally Integrated Optical Fiber Facilities," *Proc. INTELCOM 77*, Atlanta, October 1977, pp. 681–687.

HATA 79   Hatakeyama, I., and H. Tsuchiya, "Fusion Splices for Single-Mode Optical Fibers by Discharge Heating," *Rev. Elec. Commun. Lab.*, July–August 1978, pp. 532–542.

HOTH 62   Hoth, D. F., "The T1 Carrier System," *Bell Lab. Rec.*, November 1962, pp. 358–363.

HURW 78   Hurwitz, C. E., et al. "GaInAsP/InP Lasers and Detectors for Fiber Optics Communications at 1.0–1.6 Micrometer," *EASCON 1978 Rec.*, Arlington, Va., September 1978, pp. 25–27.

IFOC 81   "Fiber Matrix," *IFOC International Fiber Optics and Comm.*, November 1981, pp. 27-33.

JACO 79   Jacobs, I., "Lightwave Transmission in the Bell System," *Commun. Networks Conf.*, Washington, D.C., January 1979.

JULL 78   Jull, G. W., and B. Bryden, "New Broadband Home Services, Coaxial Cable or Optical Fiber Local Plant?" *ICC '78 Conf. Rec.*, Vol. 3, Toronto, June 1978, pp. 38.4.1 to 38.4.4.

KAO 66   Kao, K. C. and Nockham, G. A., "Dielectric Surface Waveguide for Optical Frequencies," *Proc. IEE*, July 1966, pp. 1151–1158.

KAPR 70   Kapron, F. P., D. B. Keck and R. D. Maurer, "Radiation Losses in Glass Optical Waveguides," *Appl. Phys. Lett.*, Vol. 17, November 1970, pp. 423–425.

KAWA 77   Kawahata, M., "Fiber Optics for Two-Way CATV in Higashi Ikoma New Town—HI-OVIS, *Exposition Proc., INTELECOM '77*, Vol. 2, Atlanta, October 1977, pp. 631–633.

KEEL 78   Keeler, P., "Alignment Is the Fiber Optic Connector's Main Job—But Accuracy Starts with the Fiber," *Electron. Des.*, October 28, 1978, pp. 104–108.

KERD 78   Kerdock, R. S., and D. H. Wolaver, "Results of the Atlanta Lightwave Systems Experiments," *Bell Syst. Tech. J.*, May–June 1978.

LARG 79   Large, S. F., *Fiber Optic Splicing Methods*, Vol. 1: *A Review*, WP-22497, Mitre Corp., Bedford, Mass., November 1979.

LEIG 78   Leigh, P., "The Developing Optical Transmission Industry," *ICC '78 Conf. Rec.*, Vol. 1, Atlanta, June 1978, pp. 6.4.1 to 6.4.3.

LITT 78   Little, W. E., and H. K. Clark, "PCM and Data Transmission Codes," *Teleph. Eng. Manage.*, August 1978, p. 6.

MALT 76   Maltz, A. C., "Cable Television—Its Role in Commercial Data Transmission," Bankers Trust Company, New York.

MART 76   Martin, J., *Telecommunications and the Computer*, Prentice-Hall, Englewood Cliffs, N.J., 1976.

MART 77   Martin, J., *Future Developments in Telecommunications* (2nd ed.), Prentice-Hall, Englewood Cliffs, N.J., 1977.

MAZU 78   Mazurgzyk, V. J., "Description and Performance Review of the Chicago Lightwave Communications Project," *ICC '78 Conf. Rec.*, Vol. 1, Toronto, June 1978, pp. 6.3.1 to 6.3.5.

MCCA 79   McCaskill, R. C., "Fiber Optics," The Connection of the Future," *Data Commun.*, Vol. 8, No. 1, 1979, pp. 67–73.

MCDE 77   McDevitt, F. R., N. Hamilton-Piercy, and D. F. Hennings, "Optimized Designs for Fiber Optics Cable Television Systems," *IEEE Trans. Cable Telev.*, Vol. CATV-2, October 1977.

MCDE 78   McDermott, J., "Emitters, Detectors on the Way for Longer Links, Lower Costs," *Electron. Des.*, Vol. 26, No. 22, 1978, pp. 55–59.

MESI 78   Mesiya, M. F., and J. C. Cartledge, "Analysis and Equalization of Digital Fiber Optic Transmission Systems," *ICC '78 Conf. Rec.*, Vol. 1, Toronto, June 1978, pp. 14.5-1 and 14.5-5.

METC 76   Metcalfe, R. M., and D. R. Boggs, "Ethernet Distributed Packet Switching System for Local Computer Networks," *ACM Commun.*, July 1976, pp. 395–404.

MICH 79   Michaelis, T. D., "Laser Diode Evaluation for Optical Analog Links," *IEEE Trans. Cable Telev.*, Vol. CATV-4, No. 1, 1979, pp. 30–42.

MIKI 78   Miki, T., H. Ishio, K. Nakagawa, and E. Yoneda, "Design and Performance of 32 Mb/s Repeated Line for Experimental Optical Fiber Transmission," *Rev. Elec. Commun. Lab.*, Vol. 26, Nos. 5–6, 1978, pp. 676–692.

MIYA 79   Miyashita, T., T. Miya and M. Nakahara, "An Ultimate Low Loss Single Mode Fiber at 1.55 μm," *Optical Fiber Communication* (Post-deadline Papers), Washington, 6–8 March 1979, pp. PD1-1 to PD1-4.

MONT 78   Monteith, D. G., "Design of a Digital Fibre Optic CATV Link," *IEEE Trans. Cable Telev.*, Vol. CATV-3, July 1978, pp. 120–126.

MORR 78   Morris, D. J., "Code Your Fiber Optic Data for Speed without Losing Circuit Simplicity," *Electron. Des.*, Vol. 26, No. 22, 1978, pp. 84–91.

MURT 79   Murty, S. S. R, and D. Derrington, "Intersymbol Interference and Timing Filter in a Fiber Optic Communications System," *NTC '79 Conf. Rec.*, Washington, D.C., November 1979, pp. 29.2.1 to 29.2.5.

NAKA 77   Nakagawa, J., et al., "Fiber-Optic Transmission Development in Hitachi," *INTELCOM '77*, Vol. 2, pp. 688–693.

NUTT 78   Nutt, W. G., and J. P. Savage, Jr., "Multipair Cables for Digital Transmission," *NTC '78 Conf. Rec.*, Vol. 2, pp. 21.1.1 to 21.1.5.

OHR 79   Ohr, S., and S. Alderstein, "Fiber Optics Is Growing Strong," *Electron. Des.*, Vol. 27, No. 23, 1979, pp. 42–52.

OVER 78   "Over 13,000 Houses Subscribe to QUBE Two-Way Cable TV Service," *Commun. News*, Vol. 15, No. 4, 1978.

PATI 78   Patisaul, C. R., "Performance Predictions for a High-Speed Digital Optical Cable Video Trunking System," *ICC '78 Conf. Rec.*, Vol. 2, Toronto, June 1978, pp. 21.1-1 to 21.1-7.

PERS 73   Personick, S. D., "Receiver Design for Digital Fiber Optic Communication System (I and II)," *Bell Syst. Tech. J.*, Vol. 52, 1973, pp. 843–886.

PERS 77   Personick, S. D., P. Balaban, and J. H. Bobsin, "A Detailed Comparison of

Four Approaches to the Calculation of the Sensitivity of Optical Fiber System Receivers," *IEEE Trans. Commun.*, Vol. COM-25, May 1977, pp. 539–541.

PHIL 79 *Philips Telecommunication Review*, Special Issue on Optical Communication, Vol. 37, No. 4, September 1979.

REFE 77 *Reference Data for Radio Engineers*, Howard W. Sams, Indianapolis, Ind., 1977.

SATO 78 Sato, M., M. Murata, and T. Namakawa, "Pulse Interval and Width Modulation for Video Transmission," *IEEE Trans. Cable Telev.*, Vol. CATV-3, No. 4, 1978, pp. 165–173.

SATO 79 Sato, M., M. Murata, and T. Namakawa, "A New Optical Communications System Using Pulse Interval and Width Modulated Link," *IEEE Trans. Cable Telev.*, Vol. CATV-4, No. 1, 1979, pp. 1–9.

SHOC 79 Shock, J., and L. Stewart, "Interconecting Local Networks via the Packet Radio Network," *6th Data Commun. Symp. Proc.*, Asilomar, Ca., November 1979, pp. 153–158.

SMIT 72 Smith, R. L., *The Wired Nation*, Harper & Row, New York, 1972.

SPEC 79 Special Report on CATV/CCTV, *Commun. News*, Vol. 16, No. 4, 1979.

TAKA 76 Takasaki, Y., and M. Maeda, "Receiver Designs for Fiber Optic Communications Optimization in Terms of Excess Noise Factors That Depend on Avalanche Gains," *IEEE Trans. Commun.*, Vol. COM-24, December 1976, pp. 1343–1346.

TAKE 78 Takeuchi, S., M. Ohashi, and K. Ohashi, "System Application of Optical Fiber Video Transmitter and Receiver," *ICC '78 Conf. Rec.*, Vol. 1, Toronto, June 1978, pp. 14.4.1 to 14.4.3.

TANA 78 Tanaka, M., et al., "New Kind of Noise Performance in Optical PCM 200 Mb/s Transmission System," *Natl. Telecommun. Conf. Proc.* 1978, Vol. 1, pp. 5.5.1 to 5.5.5.

THUR 79 Thurber, K. J., and H. A. Freeman, "A Bibliography of Local Computer Network Architectures," *Comput. Commun. Rev.*, Vol. 9, No. 2, 1979, pp. 1-6. See also Kenneth J. Thurber, *Tutorial: Distributed Processor Communication Architecture*, IEEE Catalog No. EHO-152-9, IEEE Computer Society, New York, pp. 41–44.

WOOD 79 Wood, D. C., S. F. Holmgren, and A. P. Skelton, "A Cable-bus Protocol Architecture," *6th Data Commun. Symp.*, Asilomar, Calif., November 1979.

8

Functions and Characteristics of Devices Used in Computer Communications

PATRICK V. McGREGOR
Network Analysis Corporation

8.1 INTRODUCTION

Understanding the fundamentals of network devices and their role in network architectures is a necessary step in achieving a practical perspective of the total network problem. Communications in a network may be a user service in itself, or may be an embedded capability of a different user service or services. In either case, current technology offers a wide range of networking alternatives for achieving the desired communications capability. Selecting an appropriate alternative is a complex problem that requires (practical, pragmatic) balancing of three major dimensions: cost, performance, and functionality. These three dimensions are strongly interdependent, with practical alternatives constrained in each dimension by available devices, facilities, and system technology. Historically, functionality has been minimal, performance specified, and cost the discriminating variable between alternatives. This perspective is changing as communications subnetworks become shared, common utilities that are viewed as an asset for developing broader services versus a cost component of a service. Similarly, development of devices for computer communications has been historically motivated by opportunities to reduce costs. Indeed, even with the communications subnetwork viewed as an asset, its cost remains a critical factor in the evaluation equation, and the role of many devices will be focused on their ability to reduce cost. However, the broader perspective requires that greater attention also be paid to the functionality of devices. This chapter differs from previous work in its focus on understanding the functions and characteristics of devices versus their role in reducing network cost.

The role of devices in cost reduction has been given considerable treatment [WHIE 79, CHOU 76, McGR 74]. Numerous techniques have been developed to ensure low cost of network designs through effective device usage [DYSA 78, McGR 77, HSIE 76, McGR 75, GREE 73, TANG 73, WOO 73, BAHL 72]. The role of devices in cost reduction is directly coupled to their functions and characteristics, and this coupling is examined. However, the primary focus of this chapter extends beyond the coupling of cost reduction and device functions to a broader base of understanding device functions in the context of alternative network architectures.

A network architecture may be viewed as the structure of a network, described by categorizing nodes based on their functions and characteristics, providing the rules by which different categories of nodes are interconnected, and defining the protocols by which processes at different nodes interact. To understand the roles of different devices in network architectures, it is helpful to introduce a structure of functions and characteristics within which to describe devices. Such a structure is introduced in Sec. 8.2 and is a modified version of a functional structure currently being given consideration in standards work. However, it should be noted that any such structure is essentially an arbitrary artifice to facilitate discussion: the reality of devices and what they do is the matter of substance. Many alternative structures of function and characteristics may be equally applicable as a framework for discussion of devices and their relation to network architectures.

Following introduction of the structure for discussing functions and characteristics, the next five sections discuss the different categories of devices in accordance with the structure. Section 8.3 discusses devices used for simple communications over a point-to-point link, and Sec. 8.4 discusses the extension of communications techniques into multipointing and multiplexing. Concentrating devices embodying the various communications techniques are discussed in Sec. 8.5, and switching in Sec. 8.6. Devices for user-oriented communications service are discussed in Sec. 8.7.

The problem of network management extends across all functions, and is discussed in Sec. 8.8. The shift in perspective of networks to that of an asset for service development is examined in the context of integrated services in Sec. 8.9. In view of this shift and the current networking thrust of distributed data processing, the role of devices in selecting an appropriate network architecture is formulated as a general network problem in Sec. 8.10.

8.2 FUNCTIONS, CHARACTERISTICS, FEATURES, AND DEVICES

A network device is a package of electronics that performs functions associated with its role in the architecture, is described in terms of its characteristics, and has features enhancing its practical application. Functions may be viewed as the fundamental capabilities of a device which make it useful for networking. As such, they are generic in nature and may be realized by many different device designs. Characteristics are the particular quantitative attributes of devices which govern their use in a particular network application or configuration. The characteristics of a device are directly

Keyboard/Display Terminal

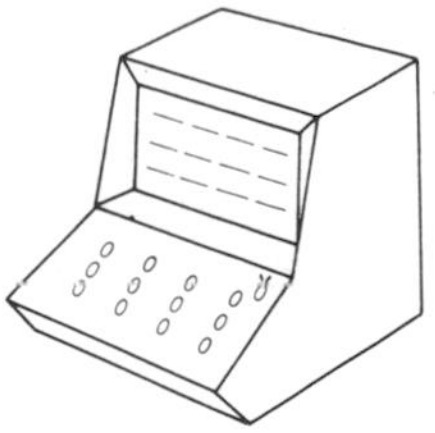

Functions:	(1)	Data input by translation of human actions into digital electronic signals
	(2)	Data output by translation of digital electronic signals into visual display characters readable by human beings
Characteristics:	(1)	Entry and display of all upper and lowercase alphanumeric characters and 12 special characters
	(2)	Buffers 2000 characters
	(3)	ASCII character coding
	(4)	Operates synchronously at 2400 bps
	(5)	Controlled by ADCCP protocol
Features:	(1)	Control knob for display light intensity
	(2)	Transmission error display light
Ingredients:	(1)	CRT tube with 5 by 7 dot matrix display
	(2)	Contact keyboard
	(3)	Protocol control by microprocessor with PROM program
	(4)	2000-byte semiconductor buffer memory

Figure 8.1. Functions, characteristics, features, and ingredients.

related to its design. Features are the ancillary capabilities of a device which enhance its application in a network implementation. Features often serve as a discriminatory base for selection of one device over another. The electronic ingredients of a device are its internal electronic components realizing its design.

The notions of functions, characteristics, features, and ingredients are illustrated by considering a common keyboard/display terminal as shown in Fig. 8.1. The functions are simply data input and output. The characteristics include the set of characters that can be entered and displayed, the size of buffering, its use of ASCII character coding, and its operation in accordance with the ADCCP protocol at a synchronized speed of 2400 bps. Its features may include a control knob for display light intensity and a transmission error display light. The electronic ingredients may include a CRT tube with 5 x 7 dot matrix display electronics, a contact keyboard, protocol control by a microprocessor with PROM programming, and a 2000-byte semiconductor memory. The functions of the terminal clearly establish its role as a user workstation. Its characteristics determine the specifics of communication support it requires. The features may or may not be significant in determining selection of this particular device versus others. The ingredients provide an insight into possible future developments with the terminal (e.g., a microprocessor control of protocol offers opportunities for easy change with future protocol developments).

The functions, characteristics, features, and electronic ingredients are used to discuss the devices used in computer communications.

8.2.1 Functions

The functions performed by a device determines its role in a network architecture; although there is no universal architecture for illustrating the role of all devices, the function levels identified in the ANSI reference model do facilitate discussion. The reference model defines seven functional levels to characterize communications employed in connecting computer systems into networks [DESJ 78]. The seven levels are:

- Level 1, physical control, concerns the actual means of bit transmission across a physical medium.
- Level 2, link control, enables logical sequences of messages to be exchanged across a physical data link.
- Level 3, network control, provides logical channels capable of transferring information reliably between two end points with single connection networks.
- Level 4, transport end-to-end control, provides reliable end point-to-end point transport of messages across an arbitrary topological configuration of several interconnected networks.
- Level 5, session control, provides for high-level connections supporting dialogue between pairs of workstation processes.
- Level 6, presentation control, provides required format transformation of the information being transferred.
- Level 7, application, is the level of the workstation process itself.

Functions identified with the first four levels are fundamental to the network providing basic transport service. The higher-level functions provide additional network capabilities. Applications in a primary host computer are viewed as level 7 functions, and are generally considered part of the network user domain. Level 7 functions identified as part of the network provider domain are considered network services. Transcending all levels are the general functions of network control. The reference model addresses communications functions from the perspective of computer-to-communications network interconnection: it does not address the many individual functions of the devices within the network. However, basic device functions can be similarly organized into the levels. In particular, functions associated with level 1 (physical), level 2 (link control), level 5 (session), and level 6 (presentation) may be used directly, and level 7 functions may be expanded as services (e.g., message switching, electronic mail). Levels 3 and 4 are (for purposes of this chapter) viewed somewhat differently as traffic concentrating functions and switching functions. Again, network control and management functions transcend all levels.

8.2.2 Characteristics

The characteristics of a device are its attributes of significance in properly incorporating the device in a network design. The characteristics of interest depend on the design aspects being considered (e.g., physical for space layout, power consumption for electrical wiring, traffic capacity for sizing) and the specific device role (e.g., line speed for modems, port capacity for multiplexors). Of primary interest here are the characteristics affecting the use of a device in a conceptual design sense. These characteristics include:

- *Interface speeds*. The transmission rates (bps) at which the device may be interfaced with communication facilities.
- *Port capacity*. The number of facilities that may be connected to the device.
- *Traffic capacity*. The amount of traffic of a given type the device may effectively handle in its normal role.
- *Service capacity*. The number of high-level service demands the device can perform while experiencing its normal traffic utilization.
- *Availability*. The percent time the device is operational in its normal operating environment.
- *Delay*. The amount of time traffic is delayed by the presence of the device.
- *Cost*. The purchase or lease price of the device.

Other particular characteristics can be of significance in particular design considerations.

8.2.3 Features

The features of a device are its ancillary capabilities, which enhance its application in a network implementation. Features may range from those considered incidental (e.g., choice of colors) to those considered necessary (self-diagnostic capabilities with LED display of trouble codes on a modem). The difference between characteristics and features is their relation to consideration of generic device capabilities and a conceptual network design. Characteristics are viewed as fundamental generic device capabilities, and features as ancillary capabilities. Characteristics are significant in the conceptual network design, determining number of devices, locations, interconnections, and performance. Features become significant in the actual operating environment of a network implementation.

Although there are many kinds of features, those associated with network maintenance are generally considered of a particular importance. These features are discussed separately in Sec. 8.8.4. Other typical features of devices of a generic type are discussed on an individual basis.

8.2.4 Device

A device is generally viewed as a package the electronic ingredients of which may be largely irrelevant to its use in a network; however, knowing such ingredients can provide useful insights into the limitations and developments of its capabilities. Device ingredients may be divided into the following types:

- *Analog electronics.* Signaling technique
- *Digital electronics.* Interfacing
- *Memory.* Buffering and program
- *Processor.* Micro-, mini-, midi-, mainframe, multiprocessor configurations
- *Peripherals.* Types and characteristics

Knowing the processor, memory, and peripheral ingredients of a device can provide many insights. At a strategic level, a minicomputer-based concentrator with good memory expansion may offer potential for user expansion with new capabilities, whereas a firmware-based microprocessor unit may be limited to catalog capabilities. At a tactical level, knowledge of particular characteristics of the ingredients may be necessary to analyze performance in various applications and loading scenarios. This is exemplified by the sizing analysis of a message switch to determine processor power adequacy, buffering requirements, disk storage needed for journaling, and tape storage needed for archiving. Typical ingredients of a generic device are discussed on an individual basis.

8.3 WORKSTATIONS AND LINKS
(Data Sets, Line Drivers, Modems, Biplexors)

A *workstation* is a configuration of hardware and software which can operate as a set of processes. A *link* is a configuration of communications media and hardware which can be used as a path over which information can be transferred between physically separated workstations. A *process* is an entity which, when active, is engaged in carrying out a predefined set of activities to accomplish a specific objective in accordance with established procedures and algorithms. In a computer system, processes essentially equate to active programs. At the terminal, human behavior may be viewed as a process (or multiple processes). A network architecture is a structure described by categorizing nodes based on resident processes, identifying associated node functions, providing the rules by which different categories of nodes are interconnected, and defining the protocols at which processes at different nodes interact. A very simple network architecture is one in which one node is a computer (also considered a very sophisticated workstation) and the other nodes are remote terminals (considered primitive workstations) connected to the computer by dedicated links. In this architecture the communication subnetwork includes only devices with level 1 functions enabling signaling over the communications media used in the link. All higher-level communication functions reside in the computer or the combined human being and terminal.

Even with the use of only devices of level 1 functions and simple links, there can be several variations of the network architecture from a distributed processing perspective. From this perspective the general network problem is determining what functions should reside at what workstations. Determining which communications functions should reside in communications devices within a separate subnetwork, and the design of the subnetwork, is only a part of the problem. This is made more evident by considering the range of possible workstations as discussed in Sec. 8.3.1. The focus in the remaining sections is on devices with level 1 functions, and subnetworks composed of only simple links are considered. The movement of more functions into a subnetwork leads to more complex subnetwork structures and devices with higher-level functions. This progression is pursued in the later sections.

8.3.1 Workstations

Workstations extend from simple interactive terminals to large mainframe computer complexes; they may be viewed as the particular capabilities at individual sites in realizing a selected network architecture. The following examples illustrate the range of workstations:

- The mainframe computer as the primary network resource
- A simple keyboard/display terminal
- A minicomputer-based data entry terminal system with multiple keyboard/displays, local storage, and line printer
- A high-speed bulk data transfer system with multiple tape drives connected through a microprocessor controller
- A sophisticated graphics terminal
- Another mainframe computer

The workstations described appear oriented to the general ADP support environment. However, they may in fact be applications-specialized products such as automatic teller machines, point-of-sale terminals, supermarket checkout terminals, and satellite data reporting devices.

In all cases, when workstations communicate over a simple link with only level 1 function communication devices, they must contain all the higher-level functional capabilities needed to effect their intended dialogue.

8.3.2 Links

Nominally, a link is a communications channel between two points, and is characterized by such attributes as transmission rate, error rate, and propagation delay; practically, there is a wide range of media and associated devices for realizing a link. The basic level 1 function is the connection of the workstation signal to the physical media in such a way that it can be received and reconverted into a signal acceptable to the destination workstation. The workstation signal is generally the output of a digital shift register creating a pulse stream of binary voltages representing a sequence of 1's and 0's (bits). This signal must be modified for effective transmission over the connecting medium by a level 1 function communications device.

The signal modifications required depend on the connected medium. It is assumed that once the signal is entered on the medium it will be propagated to the destination and received on the same form of medium as it was sent. (A similar level 1 function device at the destination provides the reconversion.) In its propagation from entry to exit the signal may pass through many interim transmission devices and media. This string of interim devices and media form an electronically continuous path which is considered the communications facility serving the workstation connection. The needed signal characteristics for propagation over this path and the path performance characteristics are essentially the lowest common denominator of all the interim devices and media. In general, these characteristics are well understood and defined relative to the facility as a whole. Consequently, the roles of the interim devices and media are essentially transparent to the facility use. They form part of the communications plant of the facility supplier, and are not usually of interest to the network designer.

Several different types of facilities are available to form links, including:

- Telephone lines, both dial and leased
- Coaxial cable
- Fiber optics
- Twisted-wire pairs
- Satellites

This range of alternatives is illustrated in Fig. 8.2.

The devices used for connecting workstations to the different kinds of facilities are discussed below. For reference purposes, the demarcation point between these devices and the workstation is referred to as the DTE/DCE [data terminal equipment (workstation), data communications equipment (device)] interface, and the demarcation point between the device and the facility as the DCE/facility interface.

The combination of level 1 function device and communications facility enables signals to be sent and received by the workstations. The physical nature of the communications path may introduce corruptions, making the received bit stream a less than exact replication of the sent bit stream. Processes within the workstations must be capable of forming the bit stream for sending, interpreting the data from the received bit stream, and coordinating the exchange, including correction of errors. These capabilities are structured into the six higher functional levels, with processes at each level viewed as connecting across the link with a peer process at the same level. The procedures and conventions used to regiment the progression required for orderly, mutually understood interaction between the processes is called a *protocol*. Thus processes at level 2 employ a protocol to ensure the basic transfer of a package of data across the link, whereas processes at level 5 employ a protocol to enable proper establishment of a dialogue (session) between the desired high-level processes. The link formed by level 1 functional device and facility essentially forms a connection enabling interaction between the higher-level processes via the associated protocols.

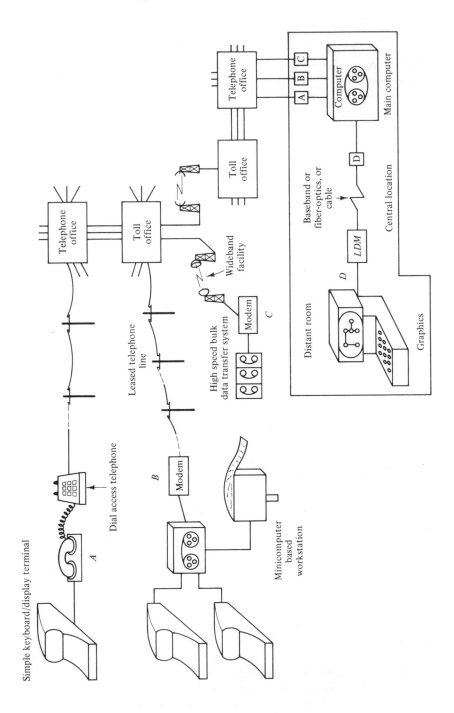

Figure 8.2 Workstations and links.

8.3.3 Baseband (Teletypewriters, Data Sets, Line Drivers)

Baseband signaling is the direct coupling of the workstation digital signal into the communications media. Long-distance baseband data communications signaling has a rich history, evolving from telegraphy into the ubiquitous teletypewriter devices used in such services as Telex. Facilities for this type of baseband signaling are available from the common carriers as sub-voice-grade (or low-speed) lines. They are generally limited to bit rates of less than 150 bps. The connecting media is essentially a pair of wires over which a (20 or 60 mA) current is generated by the telephone office when the wires are electrically closed. By electrically breaking and opening the wires, current pulses are generated as a bit stream. In teletypewriters, the breaking and opening of the wires is electromechanically achieved as an integral part of the device, and a separate level 1 function communications device is not used. The normal electrical state of the facility is a closed circuit (mark, or 0). The opening of the circuit is detected as a break (space, or 1). The electromechanical operation of the receiving teletypewriter detects the transition from the mark state to the space state as the beginning of a fixed-length pulse train of information bits. After completing each individual pulse train, the circuit is returned to the mark state long enough to ensure resynchronizing of the electromechanical equipment for recognition of a new pulse train. Thus the timing of the pulse train signal on the facility is determined entirely by the originating teletypewriter, and is present only when there are data in transmission. This type of signaling is termed *asynchronous*.

Higher-speed facilities are also available from the common carriers for baseband signaling. These digital transmission facilities generally require a signal in which the timing characteristics of the pulse train are tightly controlled, and in which there is a constant pulse train present on the facility even when data are not being sent. This is accomplished by encoding the facility signal as an idle condition in the absence of data. Control of the workstation output timing is by providing a synchronizing clock input. A level 1 function device is needed to provide the clock input to the workstation, encode the constant facility signal, and provide adequate power to ensure propagation of the facility signal. Such a device is typically referred to as a *data set*. Signaling based on providing a facility clock to the workstation is called *synchronous*. Basic characteristics of the data set are summarized in Tab. 8.1.

Baseband signaling can also be used over a common pair of wires provided by the telephone company as part of its local service plant. In this case, no interim telephone plant is involved; hence the constraining factor is simply the propagation characteristics of the wire pair. A device consisting of little more than electronics to provide higher output power than typically available in the workstation is used to provide the needed signal strength for local area (less than 10 mi) signaling. Such a device is termed a *line driver*. Essentially a transparent amplifier, it is used with asynchronous signaling. In limited-distance situations where twisted-wire pairs can be employed (versus common telephone local facilities), the better facility qualities can be used to achieve greater distance and greater speeds. Similarly, even greater

Table 8.1. *Typical Characteristics and Features of Signaling Devices.*

Device	Signaling Devices (Level 1 Functions)	
	Characteristics	*Features*
1. Data set (baseband)	Data rate bps: 4800, 9600, 50,000 Signaling technique: digital synch. Availability: MTBF = 5000 hr, MTTR = 1 hr, A = 0.9998 Cost: $2000	Typically provided in conjunction with common-carrier facility offering Standard DTE/DCE interface
2. Line drivers	Data rate: 0–56 kbps Signaling technique: digital asynch. or synch. Availability: MTBF = 10,000 hr, MTTR = 1 hr, A = 0.9999 Cost: $300	Typically provided as a special I/O Card in high-level function device
3. Modems—low speed (voice grade)	Data rate: 0–1800 bps Signaling technique: freq. shift key, asynch. Availability: MTBF = 2000 hr, MTTR = 2 hrs, A = 0.999 Cost: $500	Stand-alone/rack-mountable/acoustic-coupled Standard DTE/DCE interface Automatic answering Interface control signal display Loopback testing
4. Modems—medium-speed	Data rate (bps): 2400, 4800, 9600 Signaling technique Combined phase and amplitude modulation, synch. Availability: MTBF = 1000 hr, MTTR = 4 hr A = 0.996 Cost: $1800, $3800, $7500	Stand-alone/rack-mountable Standard DTE/DCE interface Split-stream multiplexing Secondary low-speed (150 bps channel) (typically used for remote monitoring and testing) Loopback testing Automatic answering
5. Modems—high-speed (wideband)	Data rate: 56 kbps Signaling technique: combined phase and amplitude, synch. Availability: MTBF = 2000 hr, MTTR = 2 hr, A = 0.999 Cost: $650	Typically provided in connection with common carrier wideband facility offering Standard DTE/DCE interface

Table 8.1. *Typical Characteristics and Features of Signaling Devices* (*cont.*)

	Signaling Devices (Level 1 Functions)	
Device	*Characteristics*	*Features*
6. Biplexor	Data rate: 19.2 kbps Signaling technique: use in conjunction with two modems to form one combined rate equivalent facility Availability; MTBF = 4000 hr, MTTR = 2 hr, A = 0.9995 Cost: $8000	Standard DTE/DCE interface to terminal and to modems Control signal monitoring and display

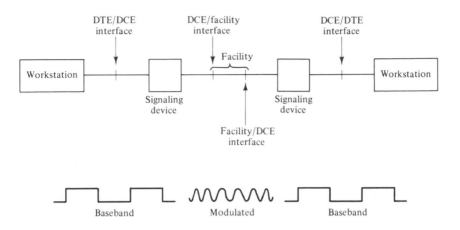

Figure 8.3 Baseband and modulated signaling.

performance can be achieved with line drivers coupled with coaxial cables. Typical characteristics and features of baseband signaling devices are summarized in Tab. 8.1.

8.3.4 Voice Grade (Modems)

Voice-grade signaling refers to the signaling techniques used for compatibility with the ubiquitous telephone plant. The primary role of the telephone plant is to support voice communications. By translating the acoustical speech waveform into an equivalent electrical waveform, voice information is transferred to a distant location where a reverse translation from electrical waveform to acoustical waveform is performed. The audio frequencies of conversational voice are generally within the range 300 to 3400 Hz, and thus the telephone plant has been designed to provide facilities of this bandwidth. However, the transmission plant does not care if the signal it is propagating is human originated, only that it is constrained to frequencies within the specified range. Thus by choosing two (reasonably separate) frequencies within the bandwidth to use as "tones," and assigning one tone to represent a 0 and the other to represent a 1, the output of a workstation shift register can be converted into a *frequency shift key* (FSK) signal on the facility. This elementary process of conversion is illustrated in Fig. 8.3. The level 1 device which performs such a conversion is known as a modem (modulator/demodulator). Modems based on the FSK technique are very simple, and generally operate asynchronously at speeds up to 1800 bps. Note that with the FSK technique, the states of the facility may include no tones and two tones as well as one (or the other) tone. The idle state can either be no tones or a designated one of the two tones, and during the transfer of bits there is generally shifting between the two tones, but both tones should never be present simultaneously.

The two tones used in FSK signaling are simply a pure frequency waveform. Changes in the waveform, known as a *carrier*, can also be used to code information, but also introduce other frequency components which may lie outside the allowed bandwidth. Theoretically, assuming the nominal bandwidth and only random noise, by employing proper techniques a maximum bit rate of about 20,000 bps can be achieved within the specified limits. However, the best practical techniques developed to date for real telephone facilities (with corruptions other than just random noise) achieve at most 9600 bps. Virtually all of the techniques for speeds from 2000 bps up to this practical limit employ waveform modifications (carrier modulations). Detection of these modifications at the receiving end requires constant knowledge of the waveform timing. This timing is embedded in the waveform itself, but requires seeing an extended part of the waveform to extract. This viewing of the waveform over time is essentially achieved by incorporating an analog equivalent of a shift register in the modem. The viewing is required only for timing information extraction, and hence there is no delay in bit decoding. However, if the carrier is not constantly present, a "training" delay is experienced in filling the shift register and extracting the timing information before bit decoding is begun. To facilitate this "training," the standard "idle" portion of the waveform is transmitted before the originating modem begins encoding data. Because the modem is so timing sensitive, it operates in a synchronous mode. That is, the modem provides the workstation with timing strobes for when it is encoding the next bit. In this manner the workstation bit-stream timing is synchronized with the modem transmission timing. Characteristics of voice-grade modems are summarized in Tab. 8.1, and tutorials on their operation are available [DICK 77, DAVE 72].

The telephone system also enables users to establish a facility for connection to a designated second station by dialing a telephone number. Use of this capability to acquire a facility for data communications is generally referred to as *dial access*. Because conversation is generally bidirectional, the telephone plant is designed to support transmission in both directions. However, because conversation does not work well when both parties are speaking, the local telephone plant generally includes only a single set of wires (two-wire facility) intended for sending signals in only one direction at a time. Furthermore, the local telephone plant often includes embedded devices aimed at actively suppressing signals propagating against the direction of the primary signals (echo suppressors). Consequently, not all the facility bandwidth is available for transmission in each direction, and generally dial connections are limited to transmitting in only one direction at a time (half-duplex). Alternatively, dedicated facilities (leased lines) may be acquired with two sets of wires (four-wire facility) to facilitate simultaneous transmission in both directions (full duplex).

Use of the dial access capability requires generation of the dialing operation and answering operation. The dial operation can be accomplished through the normal telephone instrument with the handset placed in a modem receptacle for acoustical coupling of the tones. The modem may also include features enabling electronic connection to the telephone instrument. In the former case, acoustic FSK signaling limits the modems to low speeds, whereas in the latter case synchronous techniques may also be used. Acoustically coupled modems frequently appear as an embedded part of portable terminals. For a computer installation with requirements for frequent dial access to remote sites, an automatic calling unit can be used to dial numbers generated by the computer.

The answering operation can also be done with human use of a common telephone instrument and acoustic coupling, or with an electrical coupling of the modem with the instrument. In the latter case the modem may also be equipped with features for automatic answering.

8.3.5   Wideband

Wideband signaling enables direct use of the higher-capacity telephone plant trunking facilities. Trunking facilities are the part of the telephone plant which interconnects the central office service locations where subscriber local access facilities terminate. The most primitive form of trunk is simply several pairs of wires bundled in a cable, each pair providing capability of a voice-grade connection. This is space-division multiplexing, as it allows several "channels" to share the same geographical path (or cable facility). However, to handle large numbers of conversations it is generally more cost effective to share a single medium by frequency-division multiplexing. In this mode each of the conversation channels receives its needed bandwidth as part of a wider-bandwidth medium. To understand this technique, recall the FSK signaling used shifting between two tones on the facility, whereas other techniques were based on modifying one tone (carrier). Now imagine a higher-bandwidth media allowing many distinguishable tones, or carriers. If rather than shifting between them, each is used as a separate carrier to be modified (or modulated) to encode the voice-grade signal, then frequency-division multiplexing is being used.

Propagation over a long distance with available media requires many stages of signal receiving and retransmitting. To achieve such distances economically, the transmission part of the telephone plant uses a variety of devices and techniques to combine several of the voice-grade signals into only one higher-bandwidth signal with transmission by a single modem. Thus all the modulated frequency-division multiplex carriers are used to modulate a single higher-frequency carrier of the transmission modem. Each stage along the transmission path can then be accomplished with only a single simple modemlike device. Similarly, different modem carrier frequencies can again be used to allow simultaneous transmission of several signals over the same medium (frequency-division multiplexor). Direct access to one of these single higher-speed transmission modems can also be used to form a data communications facility of higher bit rate than is available in a voice-grade facility. The first level of transmission modems usually serves the equivalent of 12 voice-grade channels [BELL 70]. Access to this part of the telephone plant is generally by leased line only, and requires use of an originating modem consistent in signaling technique with that of the transmission modem. Such a higher-bandwidth facility is generally called a "wideband" facility, and is available with synchronous modems at operating speeds of 56 kbps.

Wideband transmission rates (greater than 9.6 kbps) can also be achieved by installing dedicated transmission plant (sometimes cost competitive for geographically limited areas). Furthermore, as the telephone plant becomes digital transmission based, high-speed baseband facilities are becoming more readily available as tariffed offerings (such as the AT&T DDS service) [SNOW 75].

There is a large gap between the maximum voice-grade speed (9.6 kbps) and the smallest higher-speed leased facility (50 kbps). Current tariffs amplify the significance of this gap. It is attractive to use two 9.6-kbps voice-grade facilities to achieve an equivalent single 19.2-kbps facility. To accomplish this requires a level 1 function device to compensate for the delays and timing differences of using two physically separated facilities, each with its own modems. Such a device is the *biplexor*, with the basic characteristics shown in Tab. 8.1.

8.3.6 Satellite (Ground Stations)

Satellite facilities are an alternative to land-based transmission media with associated cost and capability trades often compensating for the long satellite propagation delay [ROSE 79, JACO 78, PODR 77]. Propagation delay of sending a signal to stationary satellite sites and its return to earth is approximately 250 ms. This is equivalent to 2500 bits when signaling at 10,000 bps, and it is a comparatively long delay. However, satellite facilities offer attractive economies for high-capacity channels. In this case the commonly available services include the needed level 1 function device as part of the facility package (which may use a terrestrial facility for access to the master satellite ground stations or a customer-site simple satellite ground station).

8.3.7 Cable (Modems and Line Drivers)

Coax cable, such as used in cable television, is an excellent medium that can be cost competitive for local sites with large intrasite requirements. The cable may be used for digital baseband signaling or with modulation of high-frequency carriers. In the former case, the level 1 function device is simply a line driver, and in the latter case, the level 1 function device is a simply a modem. However, the bandwidth of the cable allows this modem to operate with carrier frequencies in the megahertz range as opposed to voice-grade modems with carriers in the range 300 to 3400 Hz. Thus much-higher-capacity channels, or many more comparable voice-grade-capacity channels, can be achieved with the cable.

The attenuation and propagation characteristics of a cable require signal amplification for distances greater than 1 mi. Common cable television amplifiers and filters can serve this transmission requirement as an embedded part of the cable facility implementation.

8.3.8 Fiber Optics (LEDs)

Fiber optics is an excellent medium for high-capacity links, but its development (and deployment) is limited to large, point-to-point intrasite requirements [PERS 78]. The level 1 function device for signaling with fiber optics is simply a transmitting light-emitting diode (LED) and receiving photodetection unit. The signaling technique is simply to send a pulse of light corresponding to the bits of information. Such level 1 function devices are available with operating speeds in excess of 10 Mbps.

8.4 MULTIPOINT AND MULTIPLEXING (STUNT BOXES, DEVICE LOGIC, POLLING, RANDOM ACCESS, PORT SHARING UNITS, MODEM SHARING UNITS)

Links may be organized and operated to enable several separated workstations to share the same communications facility by frequency-division multiplexing and time-division multiplexing. A communications facility connecting more than two locations is called a *multipoint line*. Provided that the single facility can be used to serve the multiple locations adequately, it can offer one definitive advantage: cost. One facility properly configured can be substantially less expensive than individual point-to-point facilities for each location. There are numerous approaches available to enabling shared use of the facility, and different types of configurations which may be employed. The different approaches and configurations offer different functional capabilities and performance trades. The cost and capability trades of different topologies are examined first, followed by discussion of the different operating approaches. A key to several basic approaches is the level 2 function of link control. The role of devices in effecting this control for different types of configurations and media are then examined. Distinct from devices that use the facility are devices that can be used to configure the equivalent of a single facility. Two such devices, the Port Sharing Unit and the Modem Sharing Unit, are discussed. The devices described in this section are used to interface workstations to a shared-facility operating environment. Other devices serve to merge separate facilities into one shared facility. These latter devices are viewed as performing a concentrating function, and are discussed in the next section.

8.4.1 Topologies

Multipoint links appear most frequently as tree or ring topologies. A tree topology is a connection of n nodes with exactly $n - 1$ branches, whereas a ring topology is a connection of n nodes with exactly n branches in such a way that each node has exactly two branches joining it to other nodes. Examples of the two topologies are shown in Fig. 8.4. A leased line may be configured as a tree topology through bridging of the local access facility into the common trunk facility at the telephone office. The bridges may be used to form two wire (half-duplex) facilities, in which a signal entered by any workstation is received by all workstations, or four-wire (full-duplex) facilities in which signals sent by a central workstation are received by all remote workstations, and signals sent by a remote workstation are received by only the central workstation. This is also illustrated in Fig. 8.4. A tree topology may also be realized with an intralocation cable facility in which a tap into the cable is made for each workstation.

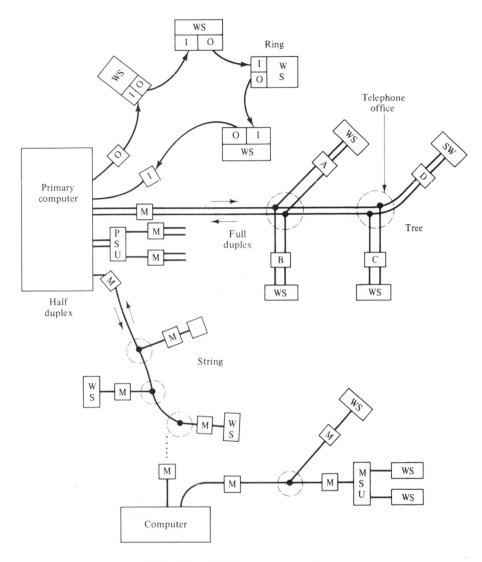

Figure 8.4 Multipoint configurations.

The primary advantage of a tree configuration is cost. The mileage of leased-line facilities connecting a set of *n* nodes can be minimized with an appropriately configured tree topology [CHOU 73]. However, this advantage must be balanced with the performance implications of sharing the facility, including a lower availability because of the longer, more complex (bridging) nature of the multipoint facility and the potential of a single device failure causing total facility disruption.

A ring topology is generally formed by the interconnection of point-to-point facilities by a device. Signals sent from the first workstation over the first facility are received at the second workstation and electronically coupled (through essentially a shift register) to a modem for transmission over the second facility. The process is repeated until the transmission is returned to the first workstation. If two-wire facilities are used, the ring is unidirectional (transmissions circulate in one direction only), and if four-wire facilities are used, the ring is bidirectional (transmissions may simultaneously circulate in both directions). A unidirectional ring is illustrated in Fig. 8.4.

A ring topology is generally less expensive than individual point-to-point lines, but more expensive than a tree topology. However, it can be used in operationally distinct ways from the tree topology, and has the availability attraction of simpler facilities and, with bidirectional configurations, the ability to retain connectivity even if any one facility fails. Ring topologies may be realized with leased lines, or with intrasite twisted pairs or cable [FARB 72, PIER 72].

A string topology may be viewed as a particular type of tree with all but two nodes interconnected by exactly two branches. Such a topology is shown in Fig. 8.4. The dotted line in the figure illustrates a possible configuration in which the string is terminated at a second central workstation. Such a configuration can be used to provide single-facility break tolerance by maintaining connectivity of all workstations to at least one of the central workstations.

8.4.2   Operations

Techniques for ensuring the equitable sharing of multipoint link capacity are based on frequency-division multiplexing and time-division multiplexing. Frequency-division multiplexing (FDM) enables sharing by dividing the capacity of the facility into multiple subchannels, each of lesser capacity, and each achieved by signaling on the facility at separate carrier frequencies.

Recall that one of the very simple voice-grade signaling techniques is frequency-shift keying (FSK), in which shifting between two "tones" is employed to encode the data. In fact, several distinct carriers can be present on the facility simultaneously. Thus two modems operating at one frequency pair can be used for signaling on the same facility, with two other modems operating at a distinct second frequency pair. This frequency-division multiplexing enables the shared multipoint facility to support multiple point-to-point links (or channels).

Modems used in the frequency-division multiplexing approach must have higher-quality control on the carrier frequency and detection capabilities than the usual FSK modem. The limited bandwidth requirements for reasonable carrier separations normally limit the aggregate rate of frequency-division multiplexing techniques to approximately 2000 bps on a voice-grade facility. Note than if all the links have a common termination point (central workstation), there will be several co-located modems (one for each channel). This leads to hardware configurations with much shared electronics and special provisions for the bridging of the multiple modem outputs onto a single access facility.

Whereas FDM may be viewed as electrically dividing the facility capacity into separate channels for each connection, time-division multiplexing (TDM) may be viewed as procedurally dividing the facility capacity into time slices for each connection. The simplest TDM analog to FDM is to view a primary station specifically sending a sequence of numbered control messages with a fixed interval of time between each message. A secondary station is associated with each number, and when it receives a control message with its number it knows it may transmit during the established interval. Thus the regular occurrence of the allocated time slot is a form of a separate channel for the designated workstation. Such an approach may be implemented on either two-wire (half-duplex) or four-wire (full-duplex) facilities. In the latter case (full-duplex), messages from the primary station for a particular secondary station are simply sent in a time slot immediately behind the control message having the number of the secondary station. In the former case (half-duplex), the control message must indicate if the time slot is available to the secondary station or has a message for the secondary station. There are countless variations of the TDM approach. Only the essential ideas of some of the more basic approaches are discussed here.

Polling is a TDM approach in which the length of time between the numbered control messages is varied to accommodate the length of message. If the workstation has no message, it returns a brief control message so indicating. The primary station then immediately sends the next numbered control message rather than waiting for the entire fixed interval. If the secondary responds with a message transmission, the primary station extends the interval until the transmission is completely received. Thus the control message enabling the next workstation to transmit data is delayed until it is clear that there will be no transmission interference.

If the topology is configured as a ring, the overhead of "no message" responses can be eliminated by use of a token (or *hub polling*). In this approach the primary station initiates the procedure by putting a control message, or token, on the ring. When the first station sees the token, if it has data to transmit, it removes the token and sends the data and then retransmits the token. After the first station retransmits the token, the second station receives the token. If it has no data to send, it simply retransmits the token. The third station may similarly respond to the token by its removal, data transmission, and token retransmission, or by simply passing the token by retransmission without use of the opportunity for data transmission. In this manner the token continuously circulates in the ring, sequentially providing each station its opportunity to transmit data.

The least disciplined TDM approach is *random access*. In this approach any workstation transmits whenever it has data to send. If the capacity of the facility is much greater than the throughput required, the probability of collision is small and may be acceptable. Practical variations of this approach involve control mechanisms to resolve collision, and are generally used to serve large numbers of low-speed terminals with a high-capacity facility (such as an intrafacility cable) [ABRA 72, RAPP 79].

Time-division multiplexing and its three basic variations of polling, hub polling, and random access may also be combined with FDM techniques and with each other (e.g., separate FDM channels may be operated with any of the TDM techniques). However, whereas FDM is achieved by somewhat special modems, TDM techniques involve the level 2 link control function and supporting level 2 function devices. Such devices do not usually provide the complete level 2 function, but rather must be combined with level 2 processes in the workstations. These devices are discussed in the following subsections.

8.4.3 Multipoint TDM Devices

Multipoint TDM approaches divide the facility capacity into fixed allocations for each subscriber workstation. If the facility signaling rate is the same as the workstation transmission rate, the per device subchannel capacity is reduced by a factor equivalent to the number of stations sharing the facility. Consequently, for such facilities, polling, with its variable-time-slot allocation, is much more attractive than the fixed allocation approach and is normally used to get better performance. However, if the facility signaling rate is much higher than the workstation transmission rate, a subchannel with capacity equal to or greater than the transmission rate of the workstation can be derived. Facilities supporting such higher-speed signaling are commonly cost competitive for intralocation networks, and use twisted-pair wires or coax cables [CLAR 78].

The workstation must enter its message on the facility in the allocated time slot, and hence the message must be transmitted at the facility's speed, not the workstation's speed. This requires a level 2 function device between the workstation and facility modem (or line driver). Such a device serves two level 2 functions:

- Speed conversion (buffering)
- Timing control

Speed conversion is accomplished by the device having a memory in which it can accept data from the workstation at the workstation transmission rate, store the data until its time slot is available, and then send the data through the modem at the transmission rate of the facility. Similarly, it must receive the higher-speed data from the facility, and store and then send the data to the workstation at its lower transmission speed.

Timing control is the detection of the numbered control message on the facility, and the sending and accepting of data in accordance with the allocated time slot. Timing control can be achieved by many implementations, including separate special FDM channels.

Other level 2 functions, such as error detection and retransmission, can be provided by the communications device or as part of the workstation (in hardware and/or software).

Implementations of this type of device are still largely prototypical and thus characteristics and features are not discussed.

8.4.4 Polled Devices

Polling requires each workstation to be capable of receiving messages with its address, distinguishing control messages from data messages, and responding to control messages with a control message or data message. The transmission rate of the workstation is generally the same as that of the facility, and hence speed conversion is not required. However, because data must wait for transmission until the workstation is polled, the workstation must be buffered.

These level 2 functional capabilities of address recognition, control message recognition, and buffering are normally embedded in the workstation and do not require a separate communications device. In teletypewriters, address recognition is accomplished electromechanically by a "stunt box" and buffering is via a punched paper tape. In keyboard/display terminals and other more sophisticated terminals, the functions are realized with relatively simple digital electronics and semiconductor (or core or magnetic bubble) memory.

8.4.5 Ring Devices

Devices used in a ring approach must be capable of recognizing the token, and removing it from the ring if data is to be sent, sending the data, and replacing the token on the ring after completion of the data transmission. These level 2 functions generally are accomplished by putting the received bit stream through a shift register with the output being transmitted as a continuation of the ring. When the token is seen in the shift register, the register is stopped and data transmission is begun. After the transmission is completed, the register is started again.

Because traffic must wait for the arrival of a token, buffering is required. If the ring speed is the same as the workstation speed, the buffering may be part of the workstation and is not needed in the level 2 function ring device. If the transmission speed of the ring facility is greater than the transmission speed of the workstation, the ring device must also perform speed conversion and hence have its own buffering.

Implementations of the general-purpose level 2 function ring device are still prototypical. However, particular application products with the ring functions embedded in the workstation are available.

8.4.6 Random Transmission Devices

Devices used in the random-access approach are the simplest in concept, but may be the most complex in practice. If the facility transmission speed is the same as the device speed, theoretically no device is required. The needed level 2 control function for responding to collision notification messages can be presumed embedded as part of the workstation. However, the random-access approach is not considered practical unless the facility capacity is substantially greater than the workstation rate. This means that transmission on the facility must be at a higher rate than for the workstations. Hence speed conversion is required, and thus a separate level 2 function device with buffering is used. The speed conversion also implies that the device must be able to recognize messages intended for the workstation, and hence have address recognition capability. However, theoretically, these functions and collision resolution (ability to recognize a received control message and retransmit after random delay to prevent recurrence of the collision) are the only functions required.

Practically, many variations of the random-access approach are used to maintain its basic character while achieving greater efficiency and operational effectiveness. A typical variation is to combine a TDM structure in which one slot is designated for random requests of a fixed slot allocation. The designated slot is available for random access with short control messages requesting a TDM slot allocation. After a fixed slot is allocated, future transmissions are always in the same slot. The level 2 function device complexity for these variations is considerably greater. These devices are still prototypical, and thus characteristics and features are not discussed.

8.4.7   Port Sharing Unit

The Port Sharing Unit (PSU) enables multiple facilities to appear as a single multipoint facility to a device port. The PSU connects several (typically up to six) modems to a single workstation (computer) port. The PSU broadcasts data from the port to all the modems and delivers data to the port from the first modem to generate an appropriate response. Thus in an environment of several simultaneously polled multipoint lines terminating at the workstation, the PSU is functionally transparent. In general, cost effectiveness is achieved by using only one multipoint line rather than several simultaneously polled lines, thereby saving local access cost and port cost. However, occasionally telephone plant performance results in an operational restriction on the number of points acceptable on a single multipoint line. Similarly, reliability considerations may also require multiple lines. In such circumstances, a PSU may find effective use.

8.4.8   Modem Sharing Unit

The Modem Sharing Unit (MSU) enables multiple devices to interface to a single modem as though each device had its own modem on the same communications facility. The MSU, or multiple-access coupler, connects several (typically up to six) terminals to a single modem. The terminals are usually restricted to be in the same location (within 50 ft of the MSU). Information received over the modem is "broadcast" to all terminals connected to the MSU, and the first terminal to respond appropriately gains access to the modem. Thus in a polled terminal environment, the MSU is functionally transparent.

In general, terminals at one location are bridged onto a multipoint facility with multiple local access facilities from the telephone central office. The purpose of an MSU is to replace the multiple local access facilities with only one access facility. The MSU effectively bridges the terminals onto the multipoint line at the user's location rather than at the telephone company's central office.

8.5 CONCENTRATING (FEPS, CONCENTRATORS, ITDMS, TDMS, FDMS)

Devices with communications control capabilities enable hierarchical network structures with economies in facility and computing resources, and with extension of service capabilities. Discussion of the level 2 link control functions as used in multipointing frequently noted the role of a primary station in providing overall control. This control is realized as a level 2 process which generally requires greater device intelligence than is needed for devices serving the secondary workstations. The complexities of the level 2 control processes generally lead to its implementation as software on a computer. However, comparatively speaking, the processes are computationally simple, operationally stable, and constantly active. Early in network development it was recognized that use of the primary computer resource for support of these processes was not as cost effective as using a separate, specialized device, and hence front-end processors (FEPs) evolved. The role of the FEP has been considerably extended with numerous features, and is discussed in the first subsection below.

Separation of the communications control functions into the specialized communications device enables hierarchical networks in which the centralized traffic flow is effected by distributed communications control. The level 2 functions of the FEP, now separated from the workstation, can also be remotely located in a device supporting the needed processes. To be cost effective, the distribution of control into a remote device must offer some form of economy: this is achieved by efficiently using one higher-speed link to the FEP for sending all the traffic from the large number of remote terminals served by the device. Thus the device essentially concentrates the traffic from several facilities onto one facility, and hence is called a *concentrator*. The nature of the economies is shown in Fig. 8.5. Concentrators are discussed in Sec. 8.5.2.

The concentrator must logically interact with the FEP to coordinate efficient use of the single trunking facility. This coordination is viewed as the interaction of distributed level 3 communication control processes. The economies of the single trunking facility can also be achieved in a manner transparent to the front-end processor. This is accomplished by using a second device co-located at the front-end processor to unmerge traffic received on the shared trunking facility into a reproduction of the original terminating facilities. This can be cost effective if the remote device and central device are comparatively simple. Hence these devices are normally limited to simply providing the level 3 communication control coordination necessary for efficient trunk usage; they do not normally support the level 2 communication control functions of the FEP at the remote site. If the merge/unmerge technique is a variable-slot-assignment TDM approach, the devices are called intelligent time-division multiplexors (ITDMs). These devices are described in Sec. 8.5.3. If the merge/unmerged technique is based on a fixed-capacity allocation approach, the devices are called *multiplexors*. To achieve the fixed-capacity allocation, either time-division multiplexing or frequency-division multiplexing may be used. These two types of multiplexing devices, called time-division multiplexors or frequency-division multiplexors, depending on the technique, are discussed in Secs. 8.5.4 and 8.5.5.

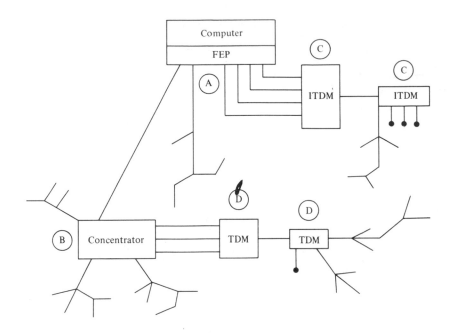

Figure 8.5   Hierarchical networks.

The devices discussed in this section are focused on the concentration of multiple facilities into one shared facility. The operating modes of the shared facilities are the same as those discussed in the preceding section. However, the devices discussed in the preceding section differ in their role of interfacing workstations to such a shared facility, as opposed to facility concentration. This difference in role is largely conceptual, and various particular devices may appear in particular configurations where the nature of role cannot be so easily partitioned.

8.5.1   Front-End Processors

Primary computing resources are conserved by moving communications control functions into a separate, specialized front-end processor (FEP). The FEP communications control functions include level 2 (link control) and level 3 (concentrating). Link control procedures (level 2 protocols) enable transfer of information packages over a common link. Understanding the need for such procedures and their complexity is facilitated by considering the intrinsic issues of human conversation.

- *Line discipline.* How do you know if you can start a new conversation?
- *Exchange coordination.* How do you know if it is your turn to speak in a conversation?
- *Error detection.* How do you know if you heard it correctly?
- *Error correction.* How do you correct garbled reception?

338

- *Failure detection.* How do you know if the other party cannot hear you—or you them?
- *Failure response.* What do you do in the event of a failure?
- *Information coding—transparency.* How do you know what part of what is said pertains to the conversation and what part pertains to the subject?
- *Performance.* How do you manage to say what must be said within the time available?

In human conversation each of these questions is answered by basic skills learned through experience and are adaptably and creatively applied in particular situations. Only infrequently, under "exceptional" circumstances, is there a conscious awareness of the answers and the process of determining answers. However, computers are not human, are not creative, and are not adaptive to situations (although they may be adapted to situations), and have not grown up in an environment of communications in which to learn basic skills. Rather, for two (or more) workstations to communicate over a communications link, an explicit procedure enabling answers to each of these questions must be incorporated in part of the workstation operation. The procedural conventions used to regiment the exchange of data over the link is called the link *protocol*. The particular structure and design of messages enabling conduct of the conventions are their *format*. Getting messages transmitted over the link by the level device requires an *interface*. These concepts are exemplified as follows. Sending a negative acknowledgment upon detection of an error in a received message and a resultant retransmission of the data is a protocol factor. The negative acknowledgment is a control message and to be recognized as such must be in a prescribed format. The level 1 function transmits a bit stream. The bit stream is drawn from designated storage by the level 1 interface hardware of the workstation. The level 2 process interfaces with the level 1 process by placing the message formatted as an appropriate bit sequence in the designated memory locations. Protocol considerations are currently a major area of network technology development [SCHN 79].

A workstation effects the communication control function for the link over which it communicates. However, the computer typically communicates with numerous workstations over several links, possibly involving many different protocols, formats, and interfaces. The protocols, and related formats and interfaces, are computationally simple, operationally stable, and require processes to be present continuously even though they act on data for any one link only occasionally. Consequently, it was recognized quite early that the level 2 link control functions could be more efficiently performed by a specialized communications device than by the mainframe computer. However, such a specialized device can only be cost effective if its interaction with the computer is made more efficient than the computer interacting with separate communication facilities. This is accomplished by interconnecting the device to the computer through a high-speed direct-access interface. This introduces the concept of the level 3 function—concentration. The FEP concentrates traffic for the multiple communication lines into one high-speed interface to the computer. Thus the FEP has two functions:

- Level 2 link control
- Level 3 concentrating

The evolution of FEPs has led to devices with a great range of capabilities. Early devices performed only the simplest form of the two functions, and were essentially based on hardwired logic (versus the currently most common minicomputer). These devices were called line interface units, or line control units. Their capabilities included modem interfacing, character timing (character buffering), special character recognition, parity construction and checking, and polling (based on computer supplied commands). Many computer-based FEPs (from which the processor part of the FEP terminology is derived) perform all these functions plus handle all the level 2 protocol and format requirements, including:

- Polling, with complete control in the FEP
- Message assembly with buffering for use of the high-speed computer interface with whole block transfers and its comparative efficiency
- CRC error detection and error correction by protocol capabilities [Automatic Retransmission reQuest (ARQ)]
- Line initialization
- Mapping of logical addresses and messages given by the computer to physical addresses of ports for transmission
- Traffic spooling for messages arriving when the computer is unavailable
- Failure detection and isolation

Typical characteristics and features of a front end processor are shown in Tab. 8.2. As noted above, the ingredients of a front-end processor are generally minicomputer based. However, it is interesting to note than many front-end processors, like many computers, have the equivalent of a line control unit for interfacing with the communication facilities as part of their architecture.

8.5.2   Concentrators

Economies in facility and computing resources are achieved by remotely locating communications control capabilities in concentrators which store and forward traffic from many workstations served by several facilities onto one shared trunking facility. As discussed in Sec. 8.5.1, putting the level 2 communications control functions in a specialized communications device rather than in the mainframe computer can be cost effective. However, to achieve such cost effectiveness required an efficient interface to the computer. Additional savings can be achieved by placing the specialized communications device in a remote location, but again, an efficient interface is required. In this case, the interface must be achieved over a communications facility between the remote device and a central computer. If the remote device can merge the traffic from several separate facilities onto one shared facility connecting it to the computer, the required efficiency may be achieved. The merging of the traffic from several facilities onto one shared facility is called *concentration*, and the shared facility connecting the remote device to the computer location is called the *trunking facility* (or *trunk*).

The economic benefit of concentrating can be readily established. Consider a requirement to serve a population of terminals in a remote region. The terminals operate at 1200 bps, and some can be polled, whereas others cannot. Without concentration, several long-distance facilities are required for connecting the terminals to the central location. With concentration, the long facilities are exchanged for much shorter facilities terminated at the concentrating device, saving many facility miles. If the cost of the trunk facility (plus device cost) is less than the savings in direct access cost, a net savings is achieved. Thus the leverage of concentrating is in the ability to use a single trunk facility with less cost than several individual facilities.

Several techniques are available to gain use of a single facility for economically serving the same traffic of several individual facilities. Recall the use of frequency-division multiplexing (FDM) and time-division multiplexing (TDM) techniques for multipoint facilities. The same techniques can be applied on a point-to-point basis to give the logical appearance of separate channels to the remotely terminated individual facilities. With FDM and the simplest TDM variation (with fixed time-slot allocation), the capacity (bit rate) of each individual facility must be replicated on the trunk. Although there can be economies of scale in facility bandwidth offerings, as discussed in Sec. 8.3.5, they are not often adequate for significant cost leverage. However, recall that a single voice-grade facility can support several FDM low-speed channels (up to 1200 bps aggregate bit rate), and can be operated with sophisticated modems at a rate up to 9600 bps. Thus one voice-grade facility operating at 9600 bps can serve eight 1200-bps facilities in a transparent mode. Devices that use these transparent techniques simply to achieve the related concentrating economy, without remote performance of the level 2 control functions, are called *multiplexors* and are discussed below. The intelligence required for remote level 2 functions generally requires a more sophisticated device. The greater sophistication involves greater cost, and hence requires greater trunk economy leverage.

The greater leverage is achieved by dynamically allocating facility capacity to serve the traffic from the remote facilities as opposed to a fixed allocation matching their individual capacities. Typically, the traffic from remote terminals is sporadic, and hence the utilization of the facility capacity serving the terminals is low. If the trunk capacity exceeds the aggregate traffic requirement, then presumably all the facilities can be served. Thus, if each of the 1200-bps terminal facilities are only 10% utilized, a single 9600-bps trunk can theoretically serve the traffic from 80 terminal facilities, a considerable increase in concentrating leverage. However, the traffic is generally random in nature (stochastic) and is not generated to accomplish efficient trunk usage. Indeed, although the average facility utilization may be accommodated, at any one instant the traffic input to the concentrating device may be substantially greater than the trunk capacity. To accommodate this situation, the device includes storage to accept traffic as required, with retransmission over the trunk as capacity becomes available (i.e., it stores and forwards the traffic).

Table 8.2. Typical Characteristics and Features of Concentrating Devices.

Device	Concentrating Devices (Level 3 Function)	
	Characteristics	*Features*
1. Front-end processor	Trunk interface: host channel Port configuration: 80 asynch./0–1800 bps, 30 synch./2400–4800 bps, 6 synch./9600–19,000 bps Throughput: 100 kbps Delay: ~2 × block transmission time Memory: 104K bytes program, 64K bytes buffer = 168K bytes total Availability: MTBF = 750 hr, MTTR = 2 hr, A = 0.9973 Cost: $150,000	Polling and link control for numerous terminal disciplines Traffic spooling Operator configuration control Statistics gathering and reporting Modularly extendable from small configurations (32 terminals @ $72,000) to large configurations (256 terminals @ $195,000) Buffer memory expandable
2. Concentrator	Trunk interface: voice grade or wideband synchronous, variable slot (block) interleave Port configuration: 32 asynch./0–1800 bps, 12 synch./2400–4800 bps, 2 synch./9600 bps Throughput: 35 kbps Delay: ~2 × block transmission time Memory: 96K bytes program, 32K bytes buffer = 128K bytes total Availability: MTBF = 1000 hr, MTTR = 4 hr, A = 0.996 Cost: $90,000	Polling and link control for numerous terminal disciplines Traffic spooling Operator configuration control Dual homing/multitrunks Modularly extendable from small configurations (32 terminals @ $60,000) to large configurations (128 terminals @ $135,000) Buffer memory expandable Downline loading Remote diagnostics and monitoring CRC/ARQ error protection Transparent to terminal Operator configuration control
3. Intelligent time-division multiplexor (ITDM)	Trunk interface: voice-grade synchronous variable-slot (multichar.) interleave	

Table 8.2. *Typical Characteristics and Features of Concentrating Devices.*

	Concentrating Devices (Level 3 Function)	
Device	*Characteristics*	*Features*
	Port configuration: 24 asynch./0–1800 bps, 1 synch./2400 bps Throughput: 6200 bps Delay: ~2 x segment transmission time (few chars.) Memory: ROM proc program, 8K bytes buffer Availability: MTBF = 2000 hr, MTTR = 2 hr, $A = 0.999$ Cost: $14,000/unit = $28,000 per mirrored pair	Remote diagnostics Modularly extendable from small configurations (4 terminals @ $6000/remote and central pair) to medium configurations (64 terminals @ $48,000/remote and central pair) Xon/Xoff CRC/ARQ error protection
4. Time-division multiplexor (TDM)	Trunk interface: voice-grade synch, fixed-slot (char.) interleave Port configuration: 16 asynch./0–1800 bps Throughput: 9600 bps capacity—fixed allocation = 1200 bps, actual typical throughput Delay: ~1.5 x character transmission time Memory: 2 bytes/port character buffering Availability: MTBF=4000 hr, MTTR=1 hr, $A=0.9975$ Cost: $3200/unit = $6400 per mirrored pair	Transparent to terminal Remote monitoring Modularly extendable from small configurations (4 terminals @ $4000/remote and central pair) to medium configurations (32 terminals @ $20,000/remote and central pair)
5. Frequency-division multiplexors	Trunk interface: voice-grade asynch. frequency-division multiplexed Port configuration: 8 asynch./0–300 bps Throughput: 2000 bps capacity—fixed allocation = 300 bps actual typical throughput Delay: ~0 Memory: None Availability: MTBF=4000 hr, MTTR=2 hr, $A=0.9995$ Cost: $2400/unit = $4800 per mirrored pair (no modems needed for trunk)	Transparent to terminal Remote monitoring Modularly extendable from small configurations (4 terminals @ $2800/remote and central pair) to medium configurations (16 terminals @ $9000/remote and central pair)

The store and forwarding of traffic in concentrating involves delay: the nominal delay of receiving traffic and then retransmitting, and the more complex statistical delay of having to queue traffic until trunk capacity availability. This statistical delay, or *queueing delay*, can be substantial, and depends on the sizing of the trunk capacity relative to the traffic load. Indeed, theoretically, for the trunk to be 100% utilized, infinite delays must be tolerated. As a rule of thumb, a trunk capacity sizing giving a 50% average utilization amounts to a queueing delay approximately equal to the nominal transmission time of the traffic. This is generally an acceptable with regard to performance, and still yields substantial economic leverage for concentration.

The store and forward concentration of traffic is viewed as a level 3 control function, and requires a level 3 process at the remote device with a cooperating level 3 process at the computer. The level 3 process at the computer normally resides in the FEP. The requirements of the level 3 process for store-and-forward concentrating, memory (and memory management) for traffic queueing (and also serving speed conversion), and the level 2 processes for remote link control generally lead to minicomputer-based implementations of the device. Such a device, performing both a level 3 concentrating function and remote level 2 link control functions, is generically termed a *concentrator*. Typical characteristics and features are given in Tab. 8.2.

As a remote minicomputer-based device with independent level 2 link control capabilities, the concentrator offers (at least conceptually) considerable flexibility for introduction of other remotely located functions. Such functions may be clearly aligned with its communications role (e.g., message formatting and editing capabilities) or may extend into (more generally considered) distributed computing (e.g., local data-base support). The determination of functions to be supported by a concentrator, and the degree of communications versus computing separation, are strategic issues of network architecture. Device selection and implementation to support such capabilities are tactical issues of network design.

8.5.3 Intelligent Time-Division Multiplexors

Intelligent time-division multiplexors (ITDMs) are a simple form of concentrator based on limited communication control capabilities directed at transparent statistical interleaving of traffic from several facilities onto one shared trunking facility. The concentrator provided both the level 3 concentration function and remote level 2 link control functions. A device can also be used for simply the level 3 concentrating function. However, in this case the level 2 link control functions must be performed by another device, normally the FEP to which the remote device is connected (possibly a concentrator to which the device is connected). For the FEP to accomplish the level 2 link control, it must be able to communicate with the remote workstations as though on a dedicated facility. Thus the remote level 3 concentrating device must be transparent to the level 2 processes in the FEP. This can be accomplished by putting a mirror image of the device in front of the FEP to provide the needed level 3 cooperating processes at the central site, with the individual remote facilities replicated for interfacing with the FEP. Alternatively, the needed level 3 cooperating processes may reside within the FEP (known as software demultiplexing). This requires a software interface between the FEP-resident level 2 link control processes for the remote workstations and the level 3 concentrating process, and it also requires an FEP resident level 2 link control process for the trunk (also interfaced with a level 3 concentrating process). Because of the lack of standardization in the approaches to implementing the concentrating techniques, and the relatively low cost of the devices, the use of a mirrored image device is currently prevalent.

Provision of a level 3 transparent concentrating function is considerably simpler than its combination with remote level 2 link control functions. However, if the trunk facility efficiency of variable TDM allocations is to be achieved, there is still a requirement for buffering and a reasonably sophisticated protocol process. Consequently, devices of this type are generally microprocessor based, and are called intelligent time-division multiplexors (ITDMs).

The variable TDM allocation techniques used in ITDMs to achieve reasonable transparency with minimal complexity are generally based on interleaving small segments of traffic (one or a few characters) without regard to beginning or end of messages. This approach creates a transparent pipelining effect of traffic flow from any one facility, and requires minimal buffering, and hence minimal remote storage (and cost), with minimal store and forward delay. In general, the variable TDM allocation techniques of ITDMs use smaller interleaving segments than concentrators, and thus ITDMs typically have less local memory. Similarly, the transparency and delay minimization implies constraining trunk utilizations to lower values, and thus less aggregate concentrating leverage than possible with concentrators. When serving low speed, asynchronous, unbuffered terminals, this approach is quite attractive. The buffering is generally much more than adequate to handle the occasional nearly simultaneous arrival of characters from many active terminals. However, when serving higher-speed, buffered, bursty terminals, the statistical character of the traffic may be more demanding of interim storage. That is, even though the average characters per unit time may be the same as with low-speed, unbuffered terminals, when characters from the higher-speed, buffered terminals do begin to arrive, they arrive in a fast, steady stream. Although the chances of transmission overlap among busy terminals is less for the same traffic (because of the faster terminal speed), when such overlap does occur it requires greater buffering capacity. Whereas the concentrator, with local level 2 link control, can control traffic input, and with minicomputer technology is easily configured for large buffering capacity, the ITDM does not have level 2 link control, and as a microprocessor based device is not generally configured for large buffer capacity.

The microprocessor implementation of the ITDM provides adequate remote intelligence for support of many features (e.g., error control on the trunk facility, traffic monitoring, trouble reporting). Frequently, it is these features that are of greater consequence in the use ITDMs than the variable TDM allocation efficiency. Among the more attractive features are techniques for flow control. Using the XON/XOFF special characters, input traffic can be regulated to protect against buffer overflow. This is a limited level 2 link control capability. Typical characteristics and features of ITDMs are shown in Tab. 8.2.

8.5.4 Time-Division Multiplexors

Time-division multiplexors (TDMs) are a very simple form of concentrator in which the communications control capability is limited to deriving transparent, fixed-capacity subchannels from a single trunking facility by a fixed allocation of time slots per subchannel from the steady stream of time slots available in the trunk signaling. The TDMs provide a (comparatively) pure and simple level 3 concentrating function. The trunk facility is simply divided into time slots, with a fixed allocation matching the individual capacity of the remotely terminated facilities. Thus the TDM allocation is based on capacity merging, not traffic merging. That is, each facility gets its allocated time slot independent of whether or not actual traffic is present. Consequently, there is no need in the TDM for buffering to handle the statistical fluctuations of traffic; all facilities and associated traffic are handled in a nominal manner. However, because the trunk signaling is at a faster rate than the facility signaling, there is a need for buffering to accommodate speed conversion. The amount of buffering depends on the size of the time slots (segments allocated for traffic interleaving). Bit interleaving is typical in TDMs used as part of the transmission plant, whereas character interleaving more typical of dedicated data communication devices. Character interleaving is preferred because there is a trunk usage overhead associated with even the simplest level 3 concentrating function, and this overhead can be more than offset with capacity gains achieved by detecting and eliminating the always present start and stop bits of characters from asynchronous terminals. The buffering required is nominal (one or two characters per facility).

The limited buffering and simplicity of the TDM allocation generally has led to TDM implementations with hardwired logic. Such TDMs are very inexpensive, and were among the first concentrating devices to be developed. However, the hardwired logic implementation limits availability of features. Often ITDMs are used as TDMs with fixed allocations of capacity simply to gain the features available through their microprocessor-based implementations. Typical characteristics and features of TDMs are given in Tab. 8.2.

As noted above, bit-interleaved TDMs are generally used within the transmission plant where there is no knowledge about the connected workstations. Bit-interleaved TDM capability is now also available as a feature of many synchronous modems. That is, a 9600-bps modem may be configured to provide combinations of 2400-bps and 4800-bps logical channels. In this case each channel appears to the connecting workstation (or downstream facility modem) as if provided by a dedicated synchronous modem.

8.5.5 Frequency-Division Multiplexors

Frequency-division multiplexors (FDMs), as the name implies, provide concentration by dividing the trunk facility bandwidth into fixed allocations matching the individual capacities of the workstation facilities. As discussed in Sec. 8.4.2, frequency-division multiplexing requires little more than high-quality modems.

However, when the modems are collocated for concentrating, there are economies to be achieved by integrating their electronics and special provisions for bridging the multiple carriers onto a single trunk facility. These economies lead to an integrated device package identified as a frequency-division multiplexor.

The FDMs provide the level 3 function via analog electronics as opposed to hardwired logic or programmable processors implementing a level 3 process. In this case the functional equivalent of the cooperating level 3 process is simply the tuning of the transmitting and receiving modem element to operate as a separate channel. Typical characteristics and features of FDMs are given in Tab. 8.2.

8.6 SWITCHING (CIRCUIT, PACKET, HYBRID, RING)

Devices capable of establishing switched interconnections enable mesh networks giving users access to multiple geographically dispersed host workstations. *Switching*, for purposes of this chapter, is defined as a device capability of effecting transfer of data arriving over multiple input facilities onto multiple output facilities in accordance with the requirements to serve specified connections. A switching network is one in which multiple devices with switching capabilities are interconnected via trunks to enable efficient interconnection of dispersed user workstations (terminals) and resource workstations (computers). Switching networks typically employ topologies in which each individual node is interconnected with multiple other nodes. Such networks, based on their graphical appearance as a "mesh," are called *mesh networks* (as distinct from trees, rings, or strings).

Switching networks as defined above may be employed to serve permanent connections, in which the communicating pairs are always the same, or demand connections, in which the connection is formed as required to serve specific requirements on a demand basis. The demand connection capability is frequently considered an intrinsic part of the switching function. Certainly, it is most frequently supported in switching networks, and is considered an intrinsic part of the network requirement in this discussion.

Devices with switching capabilities may be employed in a network without interconnection as a switching network. For example, a concentrator may be dual-homed onto computing resources (i.e., it may be connected to each of two computers).

The dual homed connection enables access by users to either of the computers. However, of primary interest here are those situations in which several computers serve many terminals in such a way that interconnected switching configurations (mesh networks) offer an economic advantage in comparison to separate centralized networks or multiple multihomed concentrators. Switching is considered a level 4 functional capability, and devices providing the switching capability as their primary role in the network architecture are termed *switches*.

The switching capability may be effected by various techniques. The telephone system is based on *circuit switching*, in which (essentially) an electronically contiguous path is formed through the switch to connect the input and output facilities. In this case, once the connection is established, the switch is transparent to the data flow, and vice versa. With the development of ARPANET, packet switching was introduced as a new switching technology. Packet switching is the store and forward of small packages of data through computer-based packet switches. In this case, the data are segmented into packets to facilitate a store-and-forward pipelining effect of data transfer through the switching network. Hybrid switching combines circuit switching and packet switching to address mixes of traffic viewed as appropriately served by both technologies. Ring switching is quite similar to the technique of ring multipointing, with simply a shift in the purpose of the capability. Ring and mesh network topologies are illustrated in Fig. 8.6.

Each of these four switching techniques and associated devices is discussed below. However, there is a great variance in their current state of development [KAHN 78, NUSS 79]. Circuit switches have evolved through the telephone system, and a great number of production devices are available, both for use as part of the common-carrier plant and for smaller dedicated user networks. Packet switching and hybrid packet/circuit switching are newer technologies with limited production device availability, although many specially designed networks are in place. Ring switching is still largely prototypical. Because of the variance in the development status, the cited typical characteristics and features should be viewed with care.

8.6.1 Circuit Switches

Circuit switches serve requests for connection of two workstations by interconnecting transmission facilities to establish a single, transparent, dedicated link. Early circuit switches used electromechanical means to establish an electrically contiguous connection between facilities. Current approaches include a diverse range of technologies to effect the operational equivalent of a contiguous facility, although there may be several media and electronic transformations involved. In particular, as the transmission plant becomes digitally based, digital switching techniques are becoming more heavily used. A simple digital approach is the use of a high-speed TDM structure as a switching basis. In this approach a TDM internal switching facility interconnects all the external facilities (much like a high-speed cable system with multipoint multiplexing). When a connection is desired, a common time slot is assigned the two facilities to be connected. When the time slot is available, the input facility uses it to effect data transfer to the output facility. (This approach can be used to effect switching on any half-duplex facility or full-duplex facility with a central device for sending the received inbound signal back out on the outbound half of the facility.)

To provide the equivalent of a contiguous facility, digital circuit switches for voice circuits must operate with a high-speed digital internal TDM rate adequate to support sampling, transfer, and reproduction of the waveforms permitted within the nominal 3000-Hz bandwidth of the voice-grade facilities. This generally implies a bit-interleaved TDM approach. Circuit switches dedicated for data communications may be more tolerantly designed to achieve transparency relative only to the data

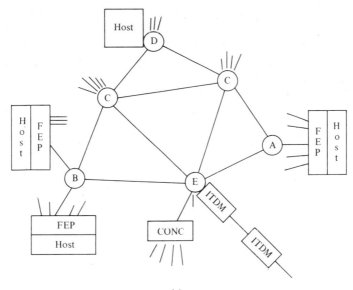

(a)

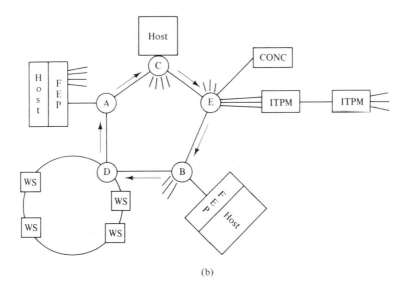

(b)

Figure 8.6 Mesh network: (a) mesh topology; (b) ring topology.

encoding (i.e., circuit switches for data communications can use character-interleaved TDM techniques).

Serving demand connections requires the capability to detect a service request, determine the desired connection, establish the connection, determine when the desired connection is to be terminated, and effect the termination. These capabilities are generally termed *call establishment* and *call termination*. In the telephone network, detection of a service request is through a signal to the switch indicating the handset has been taken "off-hook." Specifying the desired connection requires sending the dial code to the switch. Establishing the connection requires a routing of the call through the interim switches with associated interim facility interconnections, and then ringing the destination phone (with answering). Once the connection is established, the network is transparent to the signaling. When the connection is to be terminated, the "on-hook" replacement of the handset so indicates. The local switch then sends notice of this termination to the interim swtiches at which the interconnections are broken. The call establishment and call termination operations from the user perspective are quite simple. However, within the network, there are numerous approaches to effecting the needed interswitch control signaling and the routing of the call through the mesh network. If separate channels for the control signaling are used, it is called *out-of-band signaling*, whereas if the normal facility channels are used for the control signaling, it is called *in-band signaling*. The control signaling for call establishment and termination, and the call routing, are two of the principal capabilities needed for serving demand connections as part of the switching function.

In circuit switches dedicated to data communications (such as telex switches), the call establishment and termination approaches can be based on control messages originated by the user as opposed to separate signaling. Similarly, control messages between the switches can be used as a form of either in-band or out-of-band signaling. The requirements for call routing (connection routing) remain essentially the same. Typical characteristics of circuit switches are given in Tab. 8.3.

Note that circuit switches, effecting their transparent facility connection, provide essentially only the level 4 switching function. The level 3 concentrating function is provided by a lesser number of trunk channels than access facilities. Thus if the trunk channels are all interconnected to active facilities, new calls are blocked from service and receive a busy condition. The switch does not provide level 2 link control capabilities, and supports level 1 signaling in a transparent mode.

8.6.2   Packet Switches

Packet switches serve requests for connection of two workstations by store-and-forward routing of small packages of traffic (packets) through a path of switches interconnected by links. Conceptually, packet switch operation may be viewed as analogous to the digital circuit switch operation described in the preceding section, but with an internal variable TDM switching facility as opposed to an internal fixed TDM switching facility. In the circuit switch case, the fixed TDM allocation is used to connect the incoming facility to an outgoing channel of the same facility capacity (possibly derived from a trunk facility by fixed allocation TDM approach). In packet switches, as in concentrators, the stochastic nature of traffic is used to achieve greater efficiency of the trunk facility used. As incoming data are received, they are accumulated in a buffer until an appropriate-size segment is received (or a special character, such as a carriage return, is recognized). After the segment is formed, it is queued for transmission over the shared trunk. However, since the packet switch is interconnected in a mesh network, this requires the level 4 switching capability. Similarly, as the segment is received at interim switches, it must be switched to the queue for the appropriate outgoing trunk (or destination facility). To facilitate this routing, the segment is given a header relating to its destination, and thus becomes a packet. (In concentrators and ITDMs, the needed control information to associate the segments with corresponding facilities need not be provided in individual headers, but rather can be fixed in the sequencing of segments and characterized by a collective header since there is no interfering traffic from other trunks to perturb the sequence.)

The packet switch, like the circuit switch, serves demand connections through control and routing mechanisms for connection establishment and termination. Because of its data communications orientation, special control packets (or packets with control headers) are normally used for the establishment and termination operations. The determination of an appropriate data flow path through the mesh network is quite analogous to the similar circuit switching requirement. Indeed, if the variable TDM allocation on the trunks is viewed as providing logical channels which are interconnected by the switches, the routing operation may be viewed as establishing a "virtual circuit" connection. However, because each packet has its own header associating it with its destination, it may be routed independently from the other packets of the same connection. Establishing a fixed route path can simplify the interim switching operation by limiting the association of packet header with a fixed outgoing facility rather than having to make a complete connection routing determination for each packet of the same connection. Consequently, the fixed routing approach is desirable when the connection is going to be used for several packet exchanges, and is generally associated with a virtual circuit perspective of the network. However, if only one or a very few packets are going to be sent between the source and destination pair, the independent routing, without need of an interim switching control step to establish a route or destination availability, may be more attractive. This type of operation is frequently referred to as the *datagram approach*. Note that in cither case the transfer of packets in a store and forward manner may lead to packets arriving in a sequence different from the one in which they were originally sent. In the fixed-routing, virtual circuit approach, this can happen if individual packet error protection is provided with selective retransmissions (such as with satellite links). In a datagram approach different delays in packet transit time may occur by error protection techniques or different routing delays. Typically, networks employing a virtual circuit approach take responsibility for ensuring proper sequencing, whereas networks employing a datagram approach do not. Both approaches may be combined as alternative services in the same network.

The packet switch, like the concentrator, has historically been minicomputer based. Similarly, as an intelligent device economizing on the stochastic nature of traffic, it requires buffering for its store-and-forward operation, and provides level 2 (and level 1) link (and signaling) control capabilities. In addition to performing the level 4 switching function, its variable TDM allocation approach to trunk usage performs the level 3 concentrating function. Whereas the circuit switch provides a

Table 8.3. Typical Characteristics and Features of Switching Devices.

Switching devices (Level 4 Function)

Device	Characteristics	Features
1. Circuit switch	Access ports: 512 asynch./0–1800 bps, 32 synch./2400 bps Trunk ports: 6 synch. 19.2–56 kbps Simultaneous connects: 128 Throughput: capacity = 200 kbps Call set-up/termination delay: 300 ms Data transfer delay: ~0 Memory: 1024K bytes program and tables only Availability: MTBF = 2000 hr, MTTR = 4 hr, A = 0.998 Cost: $750,000	Typically provided with redundant configuration (combined availability A = ~0.99995, cost = $1,500,000 Small configurations—128 ports, 3 trunks, $170,000 Large configurations—4000 ports, 10 trunks, $2 million Self-diagnostics, monitoring, and control Can be configured for trunk interconnect only or access and trunks Camp-on busy Priority preempt Conference calls **Billing data capture**
2. Packet switch	Access ports: 128 asynch./0–1800 bps, 16 synch. 2400–9600 bps Trunk ports: 4 synch.—19.2–56 kbps Simultaneous connects: 64 Throughput: 100 kbps Call setup/termination delay: 300 ms Data transfer delay: ~0.5 sec in three tandem configurations Memory: 128K bytes program, 32K bytes buffer Availability: MTBF = 2000 hr, MTTR = 2 hr, A = 0.999 Cost: $125,000	Typically provided with redundant configuration (combined availability A = ~0.99995, cost = $200,000) Small configurations—32 ports, 3 trunks, $70,000 Large configurations—256 ports, 8 trunks, $200,000 Self-diagnostics, monitoring, and control Can be configured for trunk interconnect only or access and trunks Billing data capture Speed conversion CRC/ARQ error protection Wideband host interface for multiple logical channels

Table 8.3. *Typical Characteristics and Features of Switching Devices.*

Switching devices (Level 4 Function)

Device	Characteristics	Features
3. Hybrid packet/circuit switch	Access ports: 256 asynch./0–1800 bps, 32 synch./2400–9600 bps Trunk ports: 4 synch.—19.2–56 kbps Simultaneous connects: 64 Throughput: circuit capacity = 180 kbps, packet throughput = 60 kbps Call setup termination delay: 300 ms Data transfer delay: ~0 circuit, 0.5 sec—packet in three tandem configurations Availability: MTBF = 2000 hr, MTTR = 4 hr, A = 0.998 Cost: \$170,000	Typically provided with redundant configuration (combined availability A = ~0.99995, cost = \$300,000 Small configuration—64 ports, 3 trunks, \$125,000 Large configuration—512 ports, 12 trunks, \$325,000 Self-diagnostics, monitoring, and control Can be configured for trunk interconnect only or access and trunks Billing data capture Speed conversions for packet switching connections CRC/ARQ error protection for packet-switched connections Transparency for circuit switched connections Wideband host interface for multiple logical channels

transparent facility connection, the packet switch typically employs a level 2 link control capability on the interconnecting trunk facilities. In this way the interim trunk facilities appear as individual links over which the packets are simply data packages to be transferred. The link control function normally supports strong error detection with retransmission for correction, and thus leads to better error performance over the virtual circuit than over the equivalent single facility formed through circuit switches. This improved error performance can be significant for workstations without link control procedures providing their own protection, or when circuit switch facilities are established from a high-error-rate transmission plant.

The error protection and stochastic efficiency of packet switching is not achieved without a performance impact. As with concentrators, there is the nominal receive and retransmit delays and stochastic queueing delays to be considered. However, in packet-switched networks, these delays are compounded by the multiple-stage nature of the mesh network path. This delay impact is somewhat offset by an economy of scale achieved with serving greater traffic flows with a common switch backbone versus multiple separate networks: "twice the traffic at twice the rate gives half the delay."[1] Typical characteristics and features of packet switches are given in Tab. 8.3.

8.6.3   Hybrid Switches

Hybrid switches provide both packet-switching and circuit-switching capabilities to serve diverse traffic mixes containing some traffic viewed as best served by packet switching, and other traffic viewed as best served by circuit switching. Either circuit switches or packet switches can be used to serve virtually all classes of traffic, but possibly with very different economies. A continuous stream of data over a prolonged interval of time, such as in heavy file transfer, may essentially fully utilize a dedicated facility for the transmission interval. In this case it may be most appropriate to provide such a facility through a circuit switch. Alternatively, the stochastic nature of traffic from an interactive terminal may clearly favor the statistical economies of using a packet switch. Large data communication networks may be anticipated to serve a variety of applications having different traffic characteristics. For such networks, switches with both packet- and circuit-switching capabilities may be attractive, and are known as *hybrid packet/circuit switches.*

Hybrid structures, broadly defined, simply mean unified structures incorporating clearly distinct technologies. Several such structures exist today, as illustrated by:

- Telex "circuit switching" through use of intracomputer core-to-core real-time character transfers
- Digital transmission used for trunks in analog circuit switching networks
- Digital and analog broadband transmission mixtures (data under voice)
- Analog repeaters in digital transmission coaxial-cable systems

[1] $M/M/1$ queueing result: $W = 1/(\mu - \lambda)$; 2 @ 2 = ½ W.

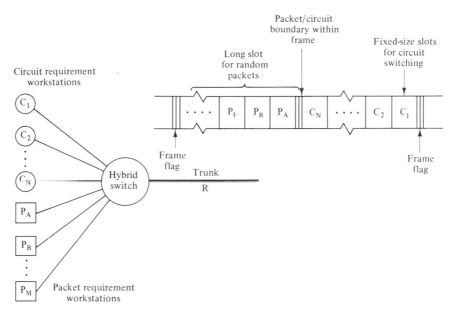

Figure 8.7 Hybrid packet circuit switching.

- Our nationwide telephone network with over 1700 separate interconnected telephone systems representing a broad range of technologies

However, these structures do not address the issue of economically satisfying the requirements for a broad mixture of traffic classes. Such a structure must be capable of dynamic adaptation to the continuum of requirements ranging from a fixed bandwidth (or data flow rate) between two given points to the effective use of channel capacity to support random bursts of information between arbitrary sets of points. Furthermore, any arbitrary collection of points on the continuum must be capable of being supported simultaneously.

A structural concept to satisfy the simultaneous requirements of the end points of the continuum is illustrated in Fig. 8.7. A fixed-bit-rate R trunk operates with a frame structure that is subdivided into a given number of fixed slots, N, followed by an unslotted time slice that can be used to transmit various size packets. The number of fixed slots determines the circuit capacity of the trunk, and the remaining time slot determines the capacity for packet transfers. This form of TDM multiplexing essentially defines two separate systems. However, several extensions are possible:

- The boundary may be adjusted depending on the offered circuit load
- The boundary may be adjusted to recover circuit slots unused because of actual gaps in circuit transmissions
- The size of circuit slots may be dynamically varied depending on demand, giving a capability of different levels of resolution for data encoding.

Other hybrid schemes of the same theme have been proposed, and analytical models of their performance characteristics have been developed and appear to suggest considerable effectiveness.

The hybrid packet/circuit switch provides the level 4 switching function in two distinct manners: as a transparent, fixed TDM allocation (circuit switching) and as a store-and-forward variable TDM allocation (packet switching). The switch may also provide the level 3 concentrating function both by connection blocking (circuit switching) and traffic merging (packet switching). The level 2 link control and level 1 signaling functions are clearly present for packet switching, but in this case may also be present for circuit switching as a consequence of the data communications orientation of the switch development. The switch may be structured as a combination of minicomputers, microprocessors, and internal high-speed TDM interconnections. Typical characteristics and features of the hybrid switch are given in Tab. 8.3.

8.6.4 Ring Interface Processors

Ring interface processors (RIPs) provide the communications control and service capabilities for efficiently using a ring network structure for general traffic transfer between any pair of nodes. As discussed in Secs. 8.4.2 and 8.4.5, multipoint facility sharing can be achieved with a ring topology operated with use of a token. Note that with addressing of each message on the ring to any of the other connected workstations, a basic switching capability is achieved. Achievement of the switching capability among connected workstations does not require a level 4 switching function, but rather is a part of the level 2 link control function for multipointing. However, the device on the ring network need not be simply a workstation, but rather can be a communications device serving interconnection of several facilities, possibly forming other rings, to the ring. In the case the level 4 switching function is present in the device, and it is appropriately termed a switch.

The ring switch must provide buffering to accommodate the stochastic character of the ring facility, and must perform routing of traffic from the ring to connected destination facilities. However, if the ring is unidirectional, the routing is no more than that required of a concentrator. If the ring is bidirectional, a choice must be made as to which direction to send the data (which may be arbitrary based on which direction becomes available first). In either case, the routing is relatively simple in comparison to more complex mesh switching networks.

Development of ring networks is still largely prototypical. Ring switches are generally minicomputer based and provide the level 3 concentrating function, level 2 link control function, and level 1 signaling function. Because of their prototypical status, typical characteristics and features are not cited.

8.7 SERVICE NODES

Communications services extending beyond the interconnection of workstations are viewed as higher-level functions and may be realized on processors also serving the interconnection role or on separate processors. The level 1 through level 4 functional capabilities enable data communication networks to serve transport of data from one workstation to another. The purpose for the data transfer is associated with the level 7 application. The processes comprising the application are generally on host workstations. Similarly, the host workstation employs level 5 (session) and level 6 (presentation) processes to facilitate user establishment of service process interconnection and compatible formatting of data exchanged in the dialogue. However, it should be noted that the levels 5 and 6 functions may also reside within intelligent network devices (e.g., concentrators and switches).

Several application processes have been historically associated with communications services. Such services include message switching, electronic mail, and facsimile switching. These services generally involve data storage and processing and hence are realized with computer-based systems. The communications service processor may also provide the lower-level functions, or may use separate devices for support of such functions. The application character of the three services noted above are discussed in this section.

8.7.1 Message Switching

Message switching is the store-and-forward transfer of formal message communications with a service focus of ensuring transfer integrity (e.g., intercept editing, journaling, backup). Message switching is one of the earlier forms of data communication service. The primitive basis of the service is essentially a switching capability: messages received from one workstation are routed to another in conformance with specified addressing. However, several service features are generally present, including:

- Creating journals for all traffic processed to ensure accountability and recoverability
- Holding messages for delivery until a destination workstation becomes available (overnight delivery)
- Providing an intercept capability to enable handling of improperly formatted messages
- Providing alternative routing to designated workstations if a primary workstation is incapable of accepting traffic
- Format conversion to enable communications between workstations with dissimilar operating modes
- Multiple routing of messages in which one message can be sent to multiple destination workstations
- Capturing traffic data for billing purposes

The focus of the message-switching service features is to ensure message transfer integrity. Such assurance is generally associated with the requirements of formal message communications. Support of these capabilities typically involves a computer complex with associated peripherals for storage and operator interaction, and with system redundancy to provide the highest possible level of availability.

8.7.2 Electronic Mail

Electronic mail is the store-and-access transfer of informal message communications with a service focus of features to facilitate use over a wide spectrum of applications (e.g., interoffice memos, letters, bills, document transfers). Electronic mail differs from message switching primarily in its service focus. Message switching targets its service to formal, formatted message communications. Electronic mail targets its service to supporting a wide range of information transfer capabilities with differing degrees of formalism, formatting, integrity, and delivery delay. Although neither is directed at real-time interactive dialogue between workstations, message switching usually implies the system initiates delivery of the message to the workstation as soon as possible. Electronic mail usually implies that the messages are stored within the system to be available to the destination on a demand-access basis. Typically, electronic mail applications may be characterized by the following functional division:

- *Create mail.* The user interacts with the application process to form the intended correspondence (with such features as editing support, screen prompting, etc.).
- *Deliver mail.* The completed correspondence is routed to a destination "mailbox" (repository for later access).
- *Read mail.* The destination user can access the correspondence in his mailbox, with such features as listing, selective output media, and scrolling.

Historically, the electronic mail application has evolved as a service within computer networks with implementation as an application process on host workstations. However, the market for more general, production-oriented services is leading to dedicated communication processors and associated networks for its provision.

8.7.3 Facsimile

A facsimile service enables users to transfer image reproductions of documents. Facsimile workstations form an electronic encoding of document images (versus character encoding for keyboard data transfer). The facsimile workstation typically does not have local capability to store the image, and hence the image must be transferred to a compatible destination device for reproduction as it is created. Consequently, circuit switching is usually employed to connect the devices. However, a communications processor can be provided to accept, store, and transfer the image as specified (including delayed delivery and copies to multiple destinations), and thus effect a switched facsimile service. Furthermore, such a processor can be used to provide speed and format conversion needed to enable transfers between dissimilar facsimile workstations. This service, with its storage, routing, and conversion capabilities, is viewed as a level 7 application function.

8.8 NETWORK MANAGEMENT

Network management functions with needs for network status information and controls for effecting operating changes transcend all devices, and generally require separate devices for operating problem isolation, compensation, diagnosis, and correction, and for trend-oriented network analysis and evaluation. The network management function may be divided into three parts:

- Operational control of the network resources
- Maintenance
- Planning and reporting

Operational control of the network resources extends from providing the logical coordination to match service demands with available resources (such as determining the routing of a connection in a switched network over a low-utilization path versus a high-utilization path) to effecting physical configuration changes to compensate for failed elements. The functions can be embedded as part of the basic implementation of the other network functions or can be separated with control focused in a Network Control Center (NCC).

The operational controls of the network resources provide for the orderly operation of the network under its varying demand conditions, and enables isolation of failed elements with limited local impacts. The maintenance function deals with problem diagnosis and compensation/correction. A wide range of special network devices are available to facilitate maintenance, including analog test equipment, digital test equipment, and patch panels. Several of the diagnostic and control capabilities needed in many cases are now provided as embedded network device features.

The planning and reporting functions deal with the longer-term management of network evolution as opposed to the immediate requirements of control and maintenance. In particular, they serve to quantify evolving system demand and performance as a basis to isolate inadequate resource allocation, and as a means to introduce engineering changes. Support of this functional capability is generally associated with an NCC.

Typical devices used in network maintenance are discussed first, followed by embedded features, and concluding with the NCC serving both operational control and planning functions. Considerable additional material is available for the interested reader [STIE 79, ARMS 79, HART 79, MCKE 72].

8.8.1 Analog Test Equipment

Analog test equipment is used to determine if the communications medium has the specified attributes required for effective signaling. The analog facility has many attributes which affect its performance as a media for signaling, including:

- *Loss.* The attenuation in signal strength as a consequence of propagation. The loss may vary depending on the frequency of signal, and hence must be characterized as a function of frequency over the entire facility bandwidth. The facility is specified as having a nominal loss over a prescribed frequency range, with rapid attenuation of signals outside this range. The edges of the range (bandwidth) is defined as that point where the attenuation becomes more than half the nominal power (3 dB) (e.g., the 300- and 3400-Hz frequencies in voice-grade facilities.

- *Noise.* The relative strength of sporadic interference on the facility, characterize in terms of the signal-to-noise ratio (SNR). It is generally this ratio that is of particular significance in the ability of the receiving modem to properly interpret the signal as opposed to absolute signal or noise strength.

- *Phase jitter.* The amount of random signal phase fluctuation. Phase jitter is essentially transparent in FSK signaling, but is very significant for higher-speed modems that modulate the carrier with phase shifts.

- *Impulse noise.* The occurrence of noise spikes such as those introduced by interference from electromechanical switching activities. Noise impulses essentially destroy the signal at the point of their occurrence, and hence duration and rate of occurrence are particularly important.

- *Phase hits.* The occurrence of random major phase shifts giving a loss in ability to identify intended signaling shifts.

- *Gain hits.* The instantaneous severe attenuation (loss) of the signal.

- *Dropouts.* The momentary complete loss of the signal.

- *Envelope delay.* Different frequencies may propagate with different delays. Most wave forms are composed of many frequency components, and hence are distorted by the different delays experienced by the different components.

In addition to the properties of the facility, for effective signaling the modem must also be operating properly. Analog test equipment is used to measure the facility attributes and the signals of the modem. Both manual and automatic test devices are available. Typical devices and characteristics are given in Tab. 8.4.

8.8.2   Digital Test Equipment

Digital test equipment is used to examine the digital inputs and outputs of the link to determine the net effect of facility performance and the proper operation of devices. The digital test equipment may provide a passive monitoring of the digital interface between the workstation (DTE) and modem (DCE), or it may actively simulate the workstation in a test mode. In either case, two distinct types of testing/monitoring are employed:

- *Control signals.* Focusing on the interface control signals exchanged between DTE and DCE

- *Data signals.* Focusing on the capture and display of (inserted) data signals sent across the facility.

Table 8.4. *Analog Test Equipment.*

Type of Test	Description	Typical Equipment
Signal level, noise level	Can be weighted or flat (in U.S.,C message wt.); selective voltmeter oscillator	Simple transmission test set at $2500
Distortion		
Amplitude	Stepped frequency sweep, envelope delay	Comprehensive
Phase	distortion	parameter measuring
Nonlinear		set ~ $10,000
Intermodulation	Mostly for wideband	
Par	Peak to average	
Phase jitter	Measures effect of local oscillator jitter in repeaters, MUX equipment	
Disturbances	Rapid changes due to switching in TELCO	Transmission transients
Impulse noise	plant, in-band signaling, microwave fading	measurement set
Amplitude hits		~ $8000
Dropout		
Phase hits		

The level 1 signaling interface provides for modem control via a number of status leads connected to the DTE. These leads indicate such conditions as modem ready and receive carrier detection, and provides such controls as clock and request to send. The control signal monitoring (and testing) provides for real-time display of the status of such leads.

The data signal monitoring provides for capturing and display of the data stream sent through the modem and received by the modem. In this way the net effect of modem and facility performance can be examined. Typical characteristics and features of devices available for digital monitoring and testing are given in Tab. 8.5.

8.8.3 Patch Panels

Patch panels facilitate configuration changes in the interconnection of device ports to modems and modems to facilities, and enables convenient insertion of test equipment for monitoring and testing. To employ the digital and analog test equipment described above, they must be connected to the devices and/or facilities to be monitored or tested. Patch panels facilitate such connections by eliminating the need to physically disconnect and reconnect the individual devices and facilities. Rather all facilities are terminated on an analog patch panel to which the analog output of all modems are connected. The patch panel provides the interconnection of each modem to its corresponding facility. However, the patch panel also provides a set of interim connection points through connected jacks which, via insertion of a cable, can be used to break the normal connection and establish a new connection to the other end of the cable in a manner quite analogous to a manual switchboard. Similarly, a monitoring

Table 8.5. *Digital Test Equipment.*

Type of Test	Description	Typical Equipment
Data domain		
Protocol testing	Check on character sequences, stimulus/ response capability, similar to logic analyzers but serial input	Serial data test and monitor ~ $7000
Time domain		
Error testing		Data error
Bit error rate	Typically uses pseudo-random pattern	test and analysis
Block error rate		~ $3000
Pattern sensitivity		
Code violation	Can be performed on line	
Timing		
Timeouts	Typical is RTS-CTS delay checking,	Timing test and
Jitter	measures effect of multiple regeneration	analysis ~ $3000
Control signals	RS-232 monitor	Embedded into modems

jack can be used to simply bridge the cable onto the normal connection for support of monitoring.

Digital patch panels provide the same basic capabilities for connections between the digital side of the modem and the workstation port (DCE/ DTE interface). Thus, with a combination of digital and analog patch panels, a spare modem can be conveniently inserted to replace a failed modem by performing the needed digital and analog (line) patches.

The patch panel is a manual operation to establish arbitrary configurations. Alternatively, configuration switches enable predefined substitutions of equipment/ facilities, and may be manual or automatic, local or remote. Configuration switches are generally employed to effect redundancy for high availability, whereas patch panels support a less demanding maintenance role.

8.8.4 Embedded Features

Many of the needed status reporting and control capabilities may be embedded as features of the individual devices. Facility testing generally requires cooperation of maintenance activities at both ends of the facility, and remote device testing and monitoring requires remote maintenance access. Many contemporary devices have embedded intelligence to perform self-monitoring and control functions facilitating centralized maintenance without need of remote site access. Modems generally have features for providing self-monitoring of control signals, and sending "snapshots" of the control signal status over the facility through a form of out-of-band signaling. This out-of-band signaling is essentially a low-speed FSK channel achieved by frequency-division multiplexing with the data carrier. Modem vendors providing such features also provide the necessary central equipment to receive and display the control signal status.

In addition to remote status monitoring, modems may also have features to facilitate centralized facility testing. These features center around the concept of "loopback" testing, in which the remotely received signal is looped back for return over the facility to the central. The loopback may be at the analog side of the modem or the digital side, and may be affected by control signals sent over the secondary control channel. Such loopback capabilities are also available in multiplexors, ITDMs, and concentrators, and can be extended through multiple levels of a hierarchy.

8.8.5 Network Control Center

The network control center (NCC) serves to focus high-level network management capabilities, including statistics gathering, processing, and reporting, trouble reporting and correction, and configuration change implementations. The NCC may be viewed as a network resource providing one or more of the following:

- Operational management of network resources to match demands
- Operational management of network resources to isolate failed elements and sustain (degraded) operations
- Event, status, and measurement data collection and reporting for staff review and action
- Statistics gathering, processing, and reporting for engineering and management use
- Support of centralized maintenance test and control activities
- Administrative network data storage and access
- Modeling and analysis of network performance and resource use
- Generation of network changes, software, and hardware

Operations and management of network resources to match demands may be distributed as an embedded part of the network functions, centralized as part of the NCC, or as a combination of distributed and centralized. The latter is more reflective of most practical network implementations, typically with local congestion control and isolation capabilities, and centralized network reconfiguration to accommodate failures with minimal impact. In either case, the operational control function is normally accompanied by the event, status, and measurement data collection and reporting to the operation staff. However, there is a wide variance in the completeness and usefulness of such reports.

Statistics gathering, processing, and reporting for engineering and management use also has wide variance in completeness and usefulness. Rare is the network implementation where these factors are adequately addressed.

The functions described above basically require a processor-based network resource interconnected with the other network devices. Such a processor may also serve the other functions or may be distinct. Support of maintenance test and control activities may be with a completely manual patch panel and test equipment, or automated (to varying degrees) with an NCC processor and local and remote configuration switching capability. Network administrative support, modeling and analysis, and development activities may be done off-line from the network (although presumably on a processor interconnected to the network).

8.9   INTEGRATED SERVICES

The extension of distributed processing as an embedded part of numerous applications and the continuing developments in communications technology tend toward networks providing a full range of integrated information services. *Service integration* simply means provision of multifarious services to comply with customer demands. In the information services context, an *integrated services network* means a common user system supporting a broad range of applications. Historically, individual applications have had many service features in common with other applications. However, as individual implementations, these overlapping features do not result in an economy of shared resources, but rather a plethora of user options as to the features of which service to use for which applications. Similarly, data communication networks were initially targeted in support of individual applications, and only recently have begun support of different services through the interconnection of multiple hosts. Concentrating devices have served to share (facility) resources, but primarily within a given service. Multiple services, even within the same organization, often have resulted in multiple communications subnetworks. Interconnection of multiple hosts offering multiple services has led to common utility communications subnetworks formed through switching devices.

Information services are rapidly becoming an embedded part of many application environments, with growing recognition by vendors that continued market growth requires making the computer more transparent to the user. That is, the application specialist must be the customer, not the computer specialist. However, as the computer extends into the broader range of applications, there becomes greater awareness of its capabilities and (albeit perhaps naive) questions of why it cannot do all that is desirable. Many of these questions relate to the extension of the applications service to incorporate general service features, and hence the need to provide such service features on an integrated system basis. For example, point-of-sale terminals capturing transaction data naturally lead to the question of why a separate device and activity is required to do credit checking. If it can do credit checking, why can it not also do order status inquiries? Theoretically, the full range of capabilities are possible. Practically, there are numerous operational and technical difficulties. These difficulties are focused primarily on the need for software design and implementation that can be integrated across the two dimensions of service and resources. Communications devices needed to form a transparent interconnection utility are readily available. Extension of the devices to support higher-level capabilities common to the services to be integrated remains a technological challenge of system design more than device design. However, as computing and communications becomes less and less expensive per unit resource, there will be continuing opportunities to extend the service range economically. Clearly, the opportunities arrive earlier if the economic leverage of resource sharing can be achieved. With such resource sharing, full-service networks are evolved. To understand the implications of full-service networking, the common functional ingredient services are first described. This is followed by discussion of alternative architectural approaches from the computer communications perspective, and then the role of devices is examined.

8.9.1 Services

Information services span the spectrum from classical ADP and voice telephone calls to office automation and security monitoring, and may be viewed as specific applications of data entry, storing, accessing, processing, reporting, and transferring functions. These six functions are the basic capabilities drawn upon to construct particular services. Application variations in each may appear immense: data entry devices for security monitoring may not appear at all like point-of-sale terminals for transaction capturing. However, both serve to convert the primitive application data into machine-understandable form, and once converted, can be operated on for storing, accessing, processing, reporting, and transferring in similar ways. Similarly, the terminal devices for correspondence creation and programming may appear quite similar, or even be the same device, but the associated storage and processing may be quite different. Typically, both may involve editing as a service feature, but the editing may be accomplished by different software editors associated with the particular applications. Identifying what service features to provide as common integrated capabilities is a major issue for both the user offering and the internal implementation. Similarly, the allocation of service feature implementations among network devices is a major issue. Implementations within distributed communications subnetwork devices may give the best responsiveness and result in the least communications cost. Implementations within centralized network resources may give the least maintenance difficulties and best resource utilization. As the communications devices become more functionally capable, these trades become less constrained and more a system architecture question.

8.9.2 Networks

The networks providing information services may be transparent to the user, but present major technical and managerial challenges to the supplier. With the rapid advances in computer and communication technologies comes a broad range of different architectures for realizing networks. To what extent should all processing and storing be centralized on a single large resource versus distributed among smaller resources closer to the user population? Should services be segmented into application—specialized functions and common utility functions, with each implemented on its own resource? In particular, should the data communications subnetwork be segmented as a transparent, common-user, data transport utility, or should the intelligence of its distributed devices also be used to support particular application features (e.g., should a concentrator support a local data base or should a separate computer at the concentrator site be used)?

Unfortunately, the architectural issue is not one of only extremes, but is rather a continuum. The question is not really if services should be segmented into application-dependent functions for separate resources or share one common resource, but rather to what extent which services and features should be separated and which should be merged. As the technical possibilities expand, so do the options and attendant confusion.

8.9.3 Devices

Although the menu of the devices for networking is large, it will continue to grow at a rapid pace, with new developments extending the range of applications and the alternatives for their support. "You can have it any color you want so long as it's black" are the famous words of Henry Ford in describing his approach to mass production of the Model T. Fortunately, technology and competition have combined to give a far broader range of automobiles than Mr. Ford might have ever had dreamed. Similarly, technologies and competition will continue to yield a growing family of communication devices differing in functional capabilities, characteristics, and features. Selection of appropriate devices to realize a particular network architecture in turn becomes a more complex problem.

8.10 NETWORK PROBLEM PERSPECTIVE

The general network problem is to determine what requirements should be served by what resources located where at what time, and how they should be interconnected. This computer-communications networking problem, from the perspective of devices and their functions and characteristics, may be posed as follows:

Given: a population with much need and use of information such as available through computers, and a willingness to pay—if the price is reasonable.

Determine:

1. The information services and features to be provided to what subsets of the population
2. The network(s) architecture(s) of service, feature, and function allocation to resources, and how the resources are to interconnect and interoperate
3. The network(s) design(s) of resource locations and interconnect topologies
4. Device selections for use as the individual resources

Unfortunately, although the problem appears nicely structured with distinct separation of issues, the reality is that all the issues interplay. Within this structure of the problem, it can be seen that the functions and characteristics of devices used in data communications determine a final design implementation, but the needed functions and characteristics are themselves to be determined by a much broader process of total problem considerations.

REFERENCES

ABRA 72   Abramson, N., "The ALOHA System," *Computer Communications Networks*, Prentice-Hall, Englewood Cliffs, N.J., 1972.

ARMS 79   Armstrong, T., "An Automated Network Management System," *Mini-Micro Syst.*, March 1979, pp. 79-84.

BAHL 72   Bahl, L., and D. Tang, "Optimization of Concentrator Locations in Teleprocessing Networks," *Proc. Symp. Comput. Commun. Networks Tele-Traffic*, Polytechnic Institute of Brooklyn, New York, April 4-6, 1972.

BELL 70   *Transmission Systems for Communications*, Bell Telephone Laboratories, Murray Hill, N.J., 1970.

CHOU 73   Chou, W., and A. Kershenbaum, "A Unified Algorithm for Design of Multidrop Teleprocessing Networks," *Proc. Data Networks: Anal. Des. 3rd Data Commun. Symp.*, St. Petersburg, Fla., November 13-15, 1973, pp. 148-156.

CHOU 76   Chou, W., and P. McGregor, "Computer Communications: Network Devices and Functions," *Comput. Commun. Rev.*, Vol. 6, No. 1, 1976, pp. 5-26.

CLAR 78   Clark, D., K. Pogran, and D. Reed, "An Introduction to Local Area Networks," *Proc. IEEE*, Vol. 66, No. 11, 1978, pp. 1497-1517.

DAVE 70   Davey, J., "Modems," *Proc. IEEE*, Vol. 60, No. 2, November 1972, pp. 1284-1294.

DESJ 78   des Jardins, R., and G. White, "ANSI Reference Model for Distributed Systems," *IEEE COMPCOM 78*, pp. 144-149.

DICK 77   Dick, G., "The Lowly Modem," *Datamation*, March 1977, pp. 69-73.

DYSA 78   Dysart, H., and N. Georganas, "NEWCLUST: An Algorithm for the Topological Design of Two-Level, Multidrop Teleprocessing Networks," *IEEE Trans. Commun.*, Vol. COM-26, No. 1, 1978, pp. 55-62.

FARB 72   Farber, D., and K. Larson, "The System Architecture of the Distributed Computer System—The Communications System," *Symp. Comput. Networks*, Polytechnic Institute of Brooklyn, Brooklyn, New York, April 1972.

GREE 73   Greenberg, D., "A New Approach for the Optical Placement of Concentrators in a Remote Terminal Communications Network," *Conf. Rec. Natl. Telecommun. Conf.*, Atlanta, Ga, November 26-28, 1973, pp. 37D-1 to 37D-7.

HART 79   Hartwig, G., "Network Control: Managing the Data Environment," *Data Commun.*, December 1979, pp. 41-52.

HSIE 76   Hsieh, W., M. Gerla, P. McGregor, and J. Eckl, "Locating Backbone Switches in a Large Packet Network," *Proc. ICC*, Toronto, August 1976.

JACO 78   Jacobs, I., R. Binder, and E. Hoversten, "General Purpose Packet Satellite Networks," *Proc. IEEE*, Vol. 66, No. 11, 1978, pp. 1448-1467.

KAHN 78   Kashn, R. ed., Special Issue on Packet Communication Networks, *Proc. IEEE*, Vol. 66, No. 11, 1978.

MCGR 74   McGregor, P., "Effective Use of Data Communications Hardware," *Proc. Natl. Comput. Conf.*, AFIPS Press, Montvale, N.J., Vol. 43, May 1974, pp. 565-575.

MCGR 75   McGregor, P. and R. Boorstyn, "Optimal Load Sharing in a Computer Network," *Proc. ICCC*, May 1975.

MCGR 77   McGregor, P. and D. Shen, "Network Design: An Algorithm for the Access Facility Location Problem," *IEEE Trans. Commun.*, Vol. COM-25, No. 1, 1977, pp. 61–73.

MCKE 72   McKenzie, A. B. Cosell, J. McQuillan, and M. Thorpe, "The Network Control Center for the ARPS Network," *Proc. First ICCC*, Washington, D.C., October 1972, pp. 185–191.

NUSS 79   Nussbaum, E., ed., Special Issue on Digital Switching, *IEEE Trans. Commun.*, Vol. COM-27, No. 7, 1979.

PERS 78   Personick, S., ed., Special Issue on Fiber Optics, *IEEE Trans. Commun.*, Vol. COM-26, No. 7, 1978.

PIER 72   Pierce, J., "Network for Block Switching of Data," *Bell Syst. Tech. J.*, Vol. 51, July–August 1972, pp. 1133–1143.

PODR 77   Podraczky, E., ed., Special Issue on Satellite Communications, *Proc. IEEE*, Vol. 65, No. 3, 1977.

RAPP 79   Rappaport, S., "Demand Assigned Multiple Access Systems Using Collision Type Request Channels: Traffic Capacity Comparisons," *IEEE Trans. Commun.*, Vol. COM-27, No. 9, 1979, pp. 1325–1331.

ROSE 79   Rosen, P., ed., Special Issue on Satellite Communications, *IEEE Trans. Commun.*, Vol. COM-27, No. 10, 1979.

SCHN 79   Schneider, G., ed., "Network Protocols," *Computer*, Vol. 12, No. 9, 1979.

SNOW 75   Snow, N., and N. Knapp, Jr., "Digital Data System: System Overview," *Bell Syst. Tech. J.*, Vol. 54, No. 5, 1975, pp. 881–832.

STIE 79   Stiefel, M., "Network Diagnostic Tools," *Mini-Micro Syst.*, March 1979, pp. 67–76.

TANG 73   Tang, D., "Network Optimization for Teleprocessing Systems," *Proc. 5th Annu. Southeast Symp. Theory*, Duke University, Durham, N.C., March 22–34 1973.

WHIE 79   Whieldon, D., "Data Communications Hardware: Modems, Multiplexers, and More," *Comput. Decisions*, Vol. 2, No. 10, 1979, pp. 62–71.

WOO 73   Woo, L., and D. Tang, "Optimization of Teleprocessing Networks with Concentrators," *Conf. Rec. Natl. Telecommun. Conf.*, Atlanta, Ga., November 26–28, 1973, pp. 37C1 to 37C5.

9

Security in Computer Communications Systems

HELEN M. WOOD
IRA W. COTTON[1]
Institute for Computer Sciences and Technology[2]
National Bureau of Standards
Washington, D.C.

9.1 INTRODUCTION

The pairing of computers and communications is rapidly becoming the norm rather than the exception. The result, teleprocessing and other forms of computer networking, is no longer solely a topic of research, but has developed into a set of vital, operational tools. Practically every business or industry today already uses or is fast becoming interested in computer communications systems. Computer communications systems are essential for such real-time control activities as air traffic control, banking and credit industries, wholesale and retail industries, and national health care and health insurance industries. Furthermore, computer networks provide the only practical means available for the sharing of expensive information and computing resources. The military has a long history of involvement with computer networking technology and has pioneered the field of computer communications security [BARAP 64]. However, with the increasing dependence on computer communications technology, the emphasis has shifted from a purely military concern to a widespread awareness of the need for security and privacy in public systems.

The Privacy Act of 1974 (5 U.S.C 552a), for example, imposes numerous requirements on federal agencies to prevent the misuse of information about individuals and assure its integrity and security. This has resulted in the creation of federal

---

[1]Formerly with the National Bureau of Standards. Dr. Cotton is currently employed by Booz, Allen & Hamilton Inc.

[2]Contribution of the National Bureau of Standards, not subject to copyright. Reference to any commercial product does not imply endorsement by NBS or any government agency.

guidelines and standards intended to assist federal agencies in their implementation of the act [FIPS 41, FIPS 46, FIPS 65]. Similar proposed legislation for the private sector is already stimulating much interest in securing systems. Additionally, reports on financial loss from computer-related crimes [PARKD 76A, PARKD 76B] have shown that it makes good business sense to incorporate protection mechanisms in computer systems.

The growing recognition of the need for computer and communications security has resulted in the design, development, and installation of "patches," packages, and even new operating systems intended to provide higher degrees of data and systems protection. Operating system structures have been identified to support both security and reliable software [LINDT 76]. Significant progress is currently being made in the secure operating systems area [POPEG 78A, POPEG 79, TASKP 73A, TASKP 73B]. With the increased utilization of computer networks and current developments in the area of network operating systems (NOSs) [THOMR 72, FORSH 77, KIMBS 76, KIMBS 78], the requirements for security in networking environments are also coming under investigation [KARGP 77, BRAND 75, COLEG 78, HEINF 78, WINKS 74, WOODH 79]. While research and development are still ongoing in the area, it is vital to ensure that requirements for the security and integrity of data are well specified and that mechanisms for achieving the needed levels of systems protection are included in the design of networking systems.

In this chapter we review methods and mechanisms that may be used to achieve required degrees of computer network security. Such methods include those aimed primarily at communications security (e.g., data encryption techniques), as well as access control techniques (e.g., authentication and authorization checking), physical security, and procedural controls. Emphasis is placed on those aspects of security that particularly relate to the communications environment in computer networks. We include many references to the open literature in order to guide the interested reader into the rapidly growing area of computer communications security.[3]

Before identifying particular security methods and techniques, however, we first identify some of the threats to the computer communications environment, describe vulnerabilities, and establish criteria for security goals.

9.1.1 Threats

Computer communications systems without adequate access controls are vulnerable to a variety of threats, including theft, fraud, and vandalism. Potential losses range from unauthorized use of computing time to the unauthorized access, modification, or destruction of valuable data. The ramifications of such actions, if unchecked, range from trivial to catastrophic. Perpetrators of such abuse may be otherwise honest individuals wishing to play a few computer games, or sophisticated corporate spies, hoping to learn trade secrets or perhaps acquire the list of a competitor's top 10 accounts. Extensive studies of computer crime [PARKD 73A, PARKD 73B, PARKD 76A, PARKD 76B] and frequent headlines reporting on computer-related

---

[3]A useful collection of general articles on computer security may be found in [ABRAM 77].

abuse are indicative of the need for increased protection of computer data and systems.

Ruth Davis, when Director of the Institute for Computer Sciences and Technology at the National Bureau of Standards, identified some of the real or perceived threats that stimulated the upsurge of interest in security [BRAND 78]:

1. Organized and intentional attempts to obtain economic or market information from competitive organizations in the private sector
2. Organized and intentional attempts to obtain economic information from government agencies
3. Inadvertent acquisition of economic or market information
4. Inadvertent acquisition of information about individuals
5. Intentional fraud through illegal access to computer data banks with emphasis in decreasing order of importance on acquisition of funding data, economic data, law enforcement data, and data about individuals
6. Governmental intrusion on the rights of individuals
7. Invasion of individual rights by the intelligence community

Clearly, not every threat is faced by every operating environment, so the first step in any security program is to specify the security requirements of the particular system or application so that the serious threats can be identified. Once the relevant security threats have been recognized, the next step is to identify specific vulnerabilities in the operating environment. Then appropriate countermeasures can be determined. In the following sections we consider only the vulnerabilities likely to be faced in the computer communications environment.

9.1.2 Vulnerabilities

Computer communications systems are vulnerable to many types of attacks, natural hazards (e.g., fire, flood), as well as malfunctions and failures resulting from faulty equipment and software. In order to identify vulnerabilities of a computer communications system, it is helpful to refer to a specific model of the environment.

9.1.2.1 Threats to Computer Communications Components

For our purposes, the computer communications environment shall be considered to consist of three components: (1) host systems, (2) user terminals, and (3) the communications subnetwork

Host systems are the general-purpose or special-purpose computer systems on the network. The host system may support terminals connected to it through means other than the communications network. *Browsing* is one of the types of communications-oriented attacks against host systems. This involves someone (who may be an authorized user of the host system) looking through other users' files or main memory locations. Another form of attack, *masquerading*, involves attempts to gain access to a system by posing as an authorized user [FIPS 39]. A person who successfully guesses another user's password and uses it to log on to a computer system is said to be masquerading. This is a more common form of attack, since the investment required for successful system penetration can be minimal if, for example, poor password techniques are employed by users [WOODH 77A, WOODH 77B, WOODH 77C].

User terminals may be of the conventional variety, such as "Teletype-compatible" printers and CRTs. Terminals with more logic capability are termed *intelligent terminals*. This category includes general purpose, programmable terminals, as well as more-special-purpose equipment such as point-of-sale (POS) and banking terminals. Regardless of the degree of sophistication, the terminal may be the origin of an attack on a host system. Such is the case for both masquerading and browsing.

The *communications subnetwork* encompasses the entire communications path from the host computer's interface to the network, up to (but not including) terminal equipment. Thus the communications subnet includes the transmission medium (e.g., coaxial cable, phone lines, satellite channels), as well as switches, terminal, and host interface processors. The subnet is particularly susceptible to attacks seeking to intercept information with little fear of detection [SANDC 77].

Wiretapping is one of several techniques that may be used to attack communications systems. Wiretapping may be passive or active. *Passive wiretapping* implies the monitoring and/or recording of data while the data are being transmitted over a communications link. While monitoring lines in this manner, an intruder can observe just the characteristics of the messages (e.g., message length, frequency). This type of attack is usually termed *traffic analysis*.

Active wiretapping involves attaching an unauthorized device, such as a computer terminal, to a communications circuit for the purpose of obtaining access to data through the generation of false messages or control signals, or by altering the communications of legitimate users [FIPS 39]. Any modification of valid communications is termed *message stream modification* [KENTS 76]. If messages are delayed in transit or destroyed then the attack is called *denial of service*.

Eavesdropping is the unauthorized interception of information-bearing emanations through the use of methods other than wiretapping [FIPS 39]. Thus the monitoring of electromagnetic emanations from computer, communications or terminal equipment would be eavesdropping.

Between-lines entry is access obtained through the use of active wiretapping by an unauthorized user to a momentarily inactive terminal of a legitimate user assigned to a communications channel [FIPS 39]. Here, for example, an attacker masquerades as the legitimate user currently connected to a host system, without having to discover the authorized user's password.

Piggyback entry is a somewhat similar technique by which unauthorized access is gained to a system via another user's legitimate connection [FIPS 39]. One opportunity for piggyback entry occurs when a legitimate user leaves an unattended terminal connected (logged on) to a remote system. An unauthorized person can gain access to the system simply by using the terminal. Alternatively, a special terminal could be tapped into the communications channel and used to intercept, modify,

Table 9.1. *Information Vulnerabilities.*

Attacks	Information			Denial of Service
	Disclosure	*Modification*	*Destruction*	
Browsing	×	×	×	
Masquerading	×	×	×	
Between-lines entry	×	×	×	×
Piggyback entry	×	×	×	×
Active wiretapping	×	×	×	×
Passive wiretapping	×			
Eavesdropping	×			

destroy, or insert spurious messages into the communications between a legitimate user and a system [PETEH 67]. Such an approach could be effective even if encryption were in use, since a valid message (e.g., "deposit $100") could be recorded in *encrypted* form and played back into the system.

9.1.2.2 Threats to Information

Because of the vulnerability of computer communications systems to these types of attack, information is exposed to four categories of threat: (1) disclosure, (2) modification, (3) destruction, and (4) denial of service. Table 9.1 associates these information vulnerabilities with the types of attacks previously identified.

Disclosure is the unauthorized acquisition of information. *Masquerading* is an example of a deliberate atempt to obtain information. Users or user processes could also acquire sensitive information through a series of nonsensitive queries of a file or data-base management system [DENND 78], [DEMIR 76, DEMIR 78]. Information may also be disclosed as a result of a user browsing through uncleared main memory in a host processor or an intelligent terminal. Other techniques that could be used to obtain information are eavesdropping, passive or active wiretapping, cross-talk between multiplexed channels, and piggyback or between-lines infiltration.

Modification of information is the unauthorized, accidental or deliberate changing of data. Data modification may occur as the data travel the communications path. For example, active wiretapping may be used to insert spurious messages onto the communications path. This category of vulnerability also includes the use of the communication system to modify information stored in a host or to interfere with normal processing of information to deceive authorized users.

The unauthorized *destruction* of data may be accomplished in a variety of ways. For example, while masquerading as an authorized user, an attacker may delete files or active wiretapping may be used to destroy data transmissions.

Denial of service includes the accidental or intentional prevention of an authorized user from making authorized use of system resources, including communications and host system services. An attacker could employ techniques such as tieing up all available communications ports to a particular host system, jamming or cutting communications lines, or altering or destroying routing tables.

9.1.3 Security Goals

The purpose of security methods and mechanisms in a computer communication system is the protection of information and equipment from the types of threats discussed. However, considering the costs involved, absolute security is rarely achievable in any environment [GAO 78].[4] Generally speaking, therefore, the goal in incorporating security in a system should be *to provide that degree of protection beyond which the cost of subverting the system becomes greater than the benefits or payoffs to be gained.* Systematically determining what is an "adequate" amount of protection for a given system is a part of the process of risk management [REEDS 74, REEDS 77, FIPS 65]. This process is discussed briefly in Sec. 9.5.

Although general security goals will vary across systems, the specific security objectives will still be the protection of information from unauthorized disclosure, modification, or destruction and the unauthorized denial of service. Practically speaking, it may be impossible to prevent the modification or destruction of data. In that case, detection of such an occurrence may suffice.

Network security requirements have been considered in a number of reports [BROWP 76, WINKS 74, BRAND 73, BRAND 75, BUSHA 75]. The suggested rules or techniques fall into several categories of protection or security mechanisms which are discussed next.

9.2 PHYSICAL SECURITY

Physical security provides a first line of defense for any computer system. For systems without data communications beyond the local site, physical security measures may be the principal protective measures. In the data communications environment, where new threats are introduced by the exposure of the communications facility, there is a tendency to forget physical security measures. This is a mistake! Physical security measures need to be a part of any security program, especially since when encryption is effectively applied to communications lines, would-be intruders will often revert to more familiar (and less sophisticated) means of accomplishing their aims.

Physical security measures are intended to protect against natural or environmental threats as well as against disruptive human acts, intentional or accidental. Physical security measures should be considered for all points in a data communications system through which information flows or can be accessed. This includes the terminals employed by human operators; the modems, multiplexers, and concentrators through which data enter the network; the communication lines (to the extent possible); any switching centers in the network; and the host computers being accessed.

Physical security can be broken down into four main areas: (1) access controls; (2) hazard protection; (3) personnel practices; and (4) backup, recovery, and disaster

---

[4]There is considerable doubt that "absolute" security is achievable at any cost!

planning. In the following sections we briefly identify how these areas should be applied to security systems for data communications systems.

9.2.1 Area Access Controls

As used in this section, *access controls* refers to imposed limitations on physical access of individuals to certain areas. (In later sections we discuss the various types of logical access that may be granted to remote computer users.) For highly centralized systems, it might be assumed that physical access to the host computer(s) and media libraries in the system is already quite limited. However, with the increasing trend to distributed processing resulting in computers being located at various decentralized sites, this may be an heroic assumption. Access control mechanisms of the type described in FIPS 31 are recommended for *all* host computers in a communications system [FIPS 31]. Furthermore, the level of sophistication of the access control mechanisms should be based not only on the sensitivity of the *data* stored in the system, but also accessible through it.

Access to the switching centers in data networks should always be quite severely limited, since these are shared facilities upon which many users depend. The trend in modern networks is to locate them off customer premises, with redundant power and environmental controls, in addition to access controls. The use of encryption on an end-to-end basis might tend to lessen somewhat the need for area access controls to protect against certain threats (e.g., unauthorized disclosure of information), but the need for such controls remains for other threats (e.g., malicious denial of service from tampering with the switching centers).

Limiting access to terminals may or may not be useful, depending on whether dial-in connections are supported. Where dial-in connections are not supported, as in private line or "hardwired" networks, then limiting access to terminals is a first-line measure to keep unauthorized users off the system.

9.2.2 Hazard Protection

Hazard protection refers to the measures taken to prevent or limit losses from environmental threats such as fire and flooding. These protective mechanisms apply to all components in a computer communications system, including the host computers, the switching computers, the communications equipment (modems, multiplexers, etc.) at both the central and any remote sites, and to secondary components such as the building itself, air conditioners, etc.

Fire and water are perhaps the two most serious environmental hazards, which are surprisingly often quite related. Protective measures for fire include alarm and extinguishing systems, structural isolation to limit the spread of fire, and good housekeeping to limit the accumulation of flammable materials. Too often, however, the efforts taken to extinguish a fire do more damage than the fire itself—water is particularly damaging to electronic equipment. Halon-gas-type fire extinguishers are preferred, but often are not cost justified at smaller remote locations. Where sprinkler systems are employed, they should be of a type not easily set off accidentally (as the

U.S. Census Bureau learned to their dismay [KIRCJ 79]). At a minimum, adequate drainage should be provided in equipment areas where water overflow is a possibility, and a modest investment should be made in plastic sheeting to cover equipment when not in use or when water damage is threatened.

Temperature and humidity controls customarily have been provided for large-scale computer installations. Terminals and minicomputers, however, often operate in much harsher environments, even on factory floors. Some consideration should be given to the special threats in such environments, such as excessive dust or metal filings that may infiltrate equipment cabinets. Vandalism may also become a threat when equipment is installed in factory environments. When entire assembly lines may be shut down as a result of one minicomputer or even terminal failure, instances of sabotage are not uncommon. In such environments, the physical ruggedness of terminal and computing equipment may be paramount, and special mechanical shielding may be employed.

9.2.3 Personnel Practices

In the context of computer security, good personnel practices include the hiring, training, and termination practices intended to enhance security and motivate security awareness among employees. With data communications serving to make computer services available to wider ranges of people in an organization, the importance of personnel practices in a computer security program is increasing.

Good hiring and organization practices include adequate background screening of system personnel and a separation of duties so that no single person can individually compromise the security of the system. Most medium-size to large organizations already have security and audit staffs; it is necessary, however, to educate them to the new threats posed by computer communications systems. Training and motivation for observance of security practices and prompt reporting of noted violations should be mandatory for all employees on hiring and perhaps at periodic "refresher" seminars as well.

Separation of duties, which is well understood by the financial and accounting communities and regularly applied as a control where handling of money is concerned, needs to be applied to the operation of computer systems as well. No single individual should have the authority to individually make system software changes, or access all files, or circumvent the system security features, as systems programmers too often do. This principle of dual control should extend to all aspects of system development and operation. No operator, for example, should be permitted to remain in the computer room or media libraries alone, and all system changes should be specifically authorized and reviewed.

Termination practices are especially important in computer security, since knowledgeable, disgruntled employees are in a position to do the most damage to the organization. It has already been suggested that management take special efforts to motivate the importance of security among all employees. As a corollary to this, it should be made clear that serious or continued violations of security rules are grounds for termination. In the event of termination for cause, the employee should be immediately escorted from the premises after surrender of all ID cards and access authorizations. The security and reception staff should be notified immediately, and all computer accounts and passwords to which the employee formerly had access should be changed.

9.2.4 Backup, Recovery, and Disaster Planning

Backup, recovery, and disaster planning refers to the procedures that must be implemented and regularly exercised to permit an installation to deal with failures both of a limited or catastrophic nature. While the principal objective of a security program is to *prevent* failures, prudent managers realize that some failures will occur anyway and plan for this eventuality in advance so as to minimize its impact.

9.2.4.1 *Vital Records Program*

First, a vital records program should be implemented to identify those data most essential to the continued operation of the organization and to ensure the recoverability of such data. Multiple duplicate copies will normally be maintained at different locations and updated at regular intervals. The computer communications system itself can be used to great advantage here, since the duplicate copies and regular updates can be transmitted through the system to secure locations, from which the information may readily be retrieved when necessary. The use of the computer communications system to store and retrieve backup copies also facilitates the testing of such backup copies, which should be a regular procedure.

9.2.4.2 *Emergency Action Program*

An emergency action program is necessary so that all personnel know the procedures to be followed to recover from failures of various types. These procedures should include recovery plans for both short-term (minutes to hours) as well as long-term (days or weeks) outages. The plans should provide for alternative communications facilities (e.g., dial-up lines as backup for leased lines), alternative processing facilities (e.g., prenegotiated arrangements for contingent computer time), and procedures for file recovery and integrity checking. In distributed processing systems where multiple active copies of files may be located at different locations, it is particularly important to ensure that the consistency of the various copies is maintained after recovery.

It may be worthwhile noting that the items with the longest lead times for replacement in the event of destruction are often not the processing or communications equipment. Common carriers and computer manufacturers are generally well able to provide replacement equipment on short notice by juggling delivery schedules for new equipment already in production. In contrast, the lead time for such mundane items as preprinted forms may well be measured in months, yet without them the system may be effectively nonfunctional. The identification and stockpiling of such critical items should be a part of the disaster plan.

Table 9.2. *Identification Problem Matrix.*

Element Being Identified \ Identifier	People	Terminal	Program	Data	Computer	O.S. Supervisor
People		×	×			×
Terminal					×	×
Computer		×	×		×	×
Program	×		×			×
Data			×			×
O.S. supervisor	×		×			×

Responsibility for backup, recovery, and disaster planning rests principally with management, not with the technical staff. A good checklist for disaster planning may be found in [GAADR 80]. Additional managerial responsibilities for system security are discussed in Sec. 9.5.

9.3 LOGICAL ACCESS CONTROL

The use of computer communications systems usually implies remote access by users. Consequently, control of remote user access privileges is a cornerstone of security in such systems. Access control techniques divide into two categories: (1) those dealing with authentication or verification of a claimed identity, and (2) those techniques which, once an identity has been accurately determined, may be used to check the access rights of the user to a particular object (e.g., file, computer, process).

A further access control consideration relates to who has the right (or discretion) to grant, deny, or modify access privileges to computing resources. In *discretionary* systems, "owners" of resources such as files can change the security classification of those resources. In *nondiscretionary* systems, however, access rights are assigned and changed only by a "higher" authority, such as the system security officer. The military security classification system is an example of the latter case. A scheme based on that system will be described in Sec. 9.3.3.1.

9.3.1 Authentication Techniques

When remote users are granted access to computer resources, authentication of the user's identity is critical. Automated identity verification techniques may be based on (1) something known, such as a password; (2) something possessed, such as a badge or key; or (3) a physiological or behavioral characteristic of the system user, such as a fingerprint or signature.

The authentication process takes place at least once at log-on time, and perhaps at other times throughout the user session (e.g., at file access time). In addition, not only users, but programs (processes), computers, and other elements involved in computer networking should be accurately identified. The matrix shown in Tab. 9.2 identifies the elements of a computer system that might require mutual identification and authentication. The checks indicate the entities that might reasonably require identity authentication in an automated environment [REEDS 74]. For example, an intelligent terminal might be programmed to require user and / or remote host computer identification prior to allowing further communications. Operating systems commonly require user authentication, usually through the use of passwords.

9.3.1.1 Passwords

Because of their relatively low cost and ease of implementation, passwords are the most commonly used mechanism to achieve personal identity authentication. Password schemes have been characterized according to (1) their method of selection, (2) lifetime, (3) size and the alphabet from which they are constructed, and (4) information contents (e.g., authorization levels, check digits) [WOODH 77A, WOODH 77B, WOODH 77C, WOODH 80]. Some of the advantages and disadvantages of various password schemes are summarized in Tab. 9.3. As will be discussed in Sec. 9.4, the possession of an encryption "key" can also be used for authentication.

Password Characteristics

A password may be chosen by the user or be assigned by the system. User-selected passwords are too often chosen on the basis of familiarity to the user and consequently are often easy to guess. The primary advantage of a user-chosen password is ease of recall, alleviating the need for writing down the word.

Passwords may be assigned to users by the system security officer or by the computer system itself. Although assigned passwords are generally more secure than user-selected codes, their benefits may be nullified if they are written down by the user, taken from a master list that is discovered [WINKS 74], or generated by an algorithm that is deducible [JOHNS 74].

The length of time that a password remains in effect is called the *password lifetime* or period. Current password schemes allow password assignments to be used for an indefinite period of time, for fixed intervals of time (e.g., 1 month), or for a single use only (one-time passwords). Passwords that remain in effect indefinitely (often called "fixed" passwords) are the most susceptible to compromise. Because of the length of time available, these passwords are especially vulnerable to exhaustive testing. Making the length of the password appropriately long, locking-out log-on attempts after several (e.g., three) tries [HELDG 76], and enforcing time delays between log-on attempts provide some defense against exhaustive password enumeration attempts [WEISC 69].

A password's physical characteristics include its size and makeup (i.e., the "alphabet" or set of characters from which it is made). The number of different passwords possible in a given scheme is called the password space. For example, given a password of length L that is formed using any of the 26 letters in the English alphabet, there are 26^L possible words of length L that could be generated. The

Table 9.3. *Password Characteristics.*

Password Scheme	Some Advantages	Some Disadvantages
Selection process		
User selected	Easy to remember	Often easy to guess
System generated	Difficult to guess	More difficult to remember; generating algorithm may be deducible
Lifetime		
Indefinite	Easy to remember	Most vulnerable to exhaustive enumeration and guessing attempts; difficult to tell if password stolen
Fixed	Easy to remember if time interval is fairly long (e.g., week or month); more secure than indefinite (the shorter time interval, the better the security provided)	Vulnerability depends on time interval
One-time	Useful for detecting successful penetration of system; short lifetime prohibits exhaustive testing	Difficult to remember unless written down; valid user locked out if successful penetration occurs
Size and alphabet	The larger the password and alphabet, the more difficult to guess; less need for duplication of passwords	The larger the word, the more difficult to remember and more storage required
Information contents (e.g., authorization information and check digits)	Could aid detection of penetration attempts if penetrator unaware of valid password structure	May cause passwords to be long and thus more likely to be written down; if scheme becomes known, passwords could be easy to deduce
Handshaking schemes (e.g., dialogues, user transformations)	Resistant to exhaustive enumeration attempts; provides some protection during transmission	May be time consuming; requires more storage space than single passwords

password space grows quite large for even modest values of L—the number of all possible words of length 8 is 26^8, or approximately 2.1×10^{11}. The password space becomes even larger if passwords of lengths *up to L* are permitted. Then the password space S becomes

$$S = \sum_{i=1}^{L} C^i$$

where C equals the number of characters in the alphabet [HELDG 76].

The introduction of constraints on acceptable passwords may significantly reduce the password space. When conditions such as pronounceability are added to the scheme, only a fraction f of the total number of possible words would comprise the password space. Once we know f, then for a total space S the usable or effective space S' is

$$S' = f \times S$$

For example, in their paper describing the evolution of the Unix password security scheme, Morris and Thompson [MORRR 79] recount an instance in which eight-character passwords were generated from an alphabet of lowercase letters and digits. Although the time to search the 36^8 (= 2^{40})-password space on the particular computer (a DEC PDP 11/70) was 112 years, all system-generated passwords were discovered in just 1 min of machine time because the random number generator only produced 2^{15} possible values.

The personal identification number (PIN) used in conjunction with banking transaction cards is typically a four- to six-digit number. Encryption keys can also be considered a type of authentication mechanism, analogous to passwords. However, a determination of adequate key size is based on additional considerations. For example, Shannon notes that the size of the key space should be as large as practical, not only to discourage trial-and-error approaches, but to permit the assignment of unique keys to large numbers of users and to allow frequent key changes [SHANC 49]. Furthermore, it should also be noted that the effectiveness of encryption as a protection mechanism does not depend solely on the encryption key chosen, as discussed in more detail in Sec. 9.4.

The password may provide information such as the user's authorization level, in addition to personal authentication. It has also been suggested that passwords could be constructed to contain check digits or some other sort of self-checking code.

Password Protection

Regardless of the password scheme implemented, protection of the password (or authenticating algorithm) during distribution, entry, storage, and transmission is vital. It is usually the practice that first-time users of a system make application in person for authorization to use the system resources. At that time a temporary password can be given to the user. The user then has the responsibility for logging onto the system and changing the password to one known only to him or her. When users are great distances from the computing facility, passwords may be transmitted by mail. PINs are normally distributed in this manner. If more assurance of receipt is required, registered mail or special messengers can be used. The use of the telephone to distribute passwords orally is specifically *not* recommended.

Password protection at entry is essentially a matter of destroying any visible copy of the password (e.g., terminal listings) and ensuring that the password is not displayed at the terminal where entered. As most password schemes employ the use of tables or lists which contain the current password for each authorized system user, efforts should be taken to protect them from browsers and masqueraders.

A protection scheme employing a "one-way cipher" was suggested by R.M. Needham as a mechanism for protecting stored password lists. Unlike conventional communications ciphers in which the enciphering and deciphering algorithms are of nearly equal complexity, this is a cipher for which no simple deciphering algorithm exists. In such a scheme the user's password is encrypted as soon as it is received by the system, and the transformed password is then compared with the encoded table entry [WILKM 75]. A discussion of Needham's system and the merits of various others can be found in [EVANA 74]. Purdy [PURDG 74] also describes the Needham scheme and discusses the selection of good one-way ciphers. A more recently proposed scheme involving the use of a microcomputer in conjunction with the user's terminal is described by Lamport [LAMPL 81].

Passwords are vulnerable to several threats during their transmission from terminal to computer. User-transformation schemes [HOFFL 69, CARRJ 70] are one way of effectively shielding the password in transit. Here the user, when presented with a random number, performs a predetermined transformation on it and transmits the result back to the computer for verification. Another method for password transmission can be found in Babcock's description of the RUSH time-sharing system [BABCJ 67]. Here mention is made of a "dial-up and call-back" system in which the user is directed to telephone the password to the computer system operator when access is requested to very sensitive files. Although this technique might afford a degree of protection for the password, it obviously would not be appropriate for a large, heavily used system. It also subjects the password to additional disclosure threats.

Of course, encryption of the communications link during the entire conversation can be used to protect the transmitted password. Communications systems incorporating such use of encryption are currently in use in the nonmilitary environment. The use of encryption as a protective measure is discussed in Sec. 9.4.

9.3.1.2   Physical Artifacts

Physical artifacts that must be in the possession of authorized individuals (such as a badge or key) are used frequently in daily life and have also been applied to security for computer systems. For example, interactive terminals have been built with physical locks on their keyboards for which keys are required, and various types of magnetically coded cards have been used to control access to computer areas. Readers for cards of this type can also be built into terminals.

The principal problem with all physical artifacts is that mere possession of them is adequate for intrusion by unauthorized individuals. Artifacts are subject to being stolen or in some cases (such as keys) duplicated. Artifacts are more effective when employed in combination with some other measure. Computer-controlled cash dispensing terminals, for example, require both possession of a magnetic stripe card plus knowledge of a special authentication code (the PIN or personal identification number) which is generally stored on the magnetic stripe in encrypted form.

9.3.1.3   Physiological or Behavioral
Techniques

Other automated techniques, including those based upon behavioral or physiological characteristics (e.g., dynamic signature verification, hand geometry, voice recognition, and fingerprints) are becoming available [CRANH 77, MUERJ 74, FIPS 48, HERBN 77, COTTI 75]. The main problem still is to find a technique that is powerful enough to provide effective protection yet economical enough to be incorporated in all devices providing remote access to users. Work is continuing on these techniques, and with remote access to computer services and resources steadily increasing, such automated personal authentication techniques will be used more widely. Guidelines to help users evaluate different authentication techniques have been issued by the National Bureau of Standards [FIPS 48].

9.3.2 Authorization Checking

Once the claimed identities of users have been authenticated, their rights to access and manipulate programs and data can be determined—a process called *authorization checking*. At the highest level, the right of a user or process to access an object (e.g., file, record, data item) can be determined by a set of rules and labels for determining what clearance is required in order to access an object at a given access class. Such rights are often called usage restrictions and define the "mode of access" permitted to the data. Sample modes of access include READ, WRITE, APPEND, and EXECUTE. Access of a user or process (subject) to a set of data (object) may be controlled by an access control list (ACL), as implemented in the Multics operating system [SALTJ 74] or other access control techniques [WILKM 75, FABRR 74, HOFFL 71].

9.3.3 Access Control in Networks

In a computer networking environment, it is important to consider the location at which authentication and authorization checking occur. If, for example, multiple computer systems are involved on behalf of a user, is it necessary for that user's identity to be authenticated at each computer? Although it may be more reliable to revalidate claimed identities at each processor, it may in fact be too costly or difficult to implement in some applications. To illustrate some of the complexity added to the access control problem in a networking environment, we now briefly consider two suggested approaches to network access control.

9.3.3.1 Security Lattice Model

A *lattice security model* [DENND 76] has been proposed to govern the flow of data among computer systems [KARGP 77, KARGP 78]. This model was derived originally from the military classification system and as such is intended to be enforced as a nondiscretionary access control system. Objects are assigned access classes and subjects (e.g., users, user processes) are assigned clearances. For a subject to gain access to an object (e.g., a file), it must be "cleared" for the object. A subject does not have the discretion to grant access to objects to other subjects who are not cleared for the objects. The basis of the lattice model is a set of partially ordered access classes from which subject clearances and object classifications are chosen. However, there must be a lowest access class that is strictly less than any other access class and a highest access class that is strictly greater than any other access class.

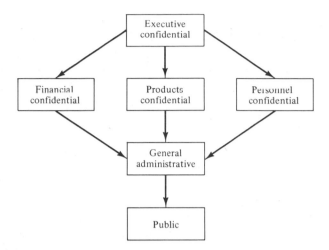

Figure 9.1   Security lattice.

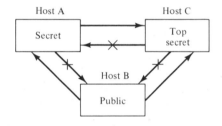

Figure 9.2   Network data flow control.

An example of a simple lattice would be the set of access classes [SECRET, PUBLIC]. In this case the ordering is a total ordering: PUBLIC < SECRET. The military security lattice, on the other hand, has two components: a sensitivity level and a category set. Sensitivity levels are [UNCLASSIFIED, CONFIDENTIAL, SECRET, and TOP SECRET]. Categories involve the further segmentation of sensitivity levels into collections of information requiring special access permission ("need to know"). Figure 9.1 shows a sample security lattice.

To ensure the integrity of the data, under this lattice structure an individual or process with a given clearance is not allowed to WRITE to a process or data file with a lower access class. READs from a set of data at a lower access class are allowed. Although these restrictions do not inhibit the flow of data from, say, an unclassified file to a process with secret clearance within an individual host, complications arise when data are being accessed across host boundaries. Figure 9.2 illustrates these data flow restrictions when applied at the host system level. In order for a process on HOST A to READ data from HOST B, HOST A must send a request for data to

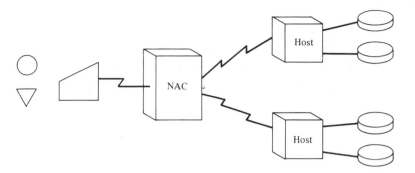

Figure 9.3   Network access controller.

HOST B. However, this request is analogous to a WRITE to HOST B; thus there is a violation of one of the rules of the lattice model [KARGP 77].

Acceptable solutions to this problem depend on the nature of the application and the security characteristics of the participating hosts. For example, if HOST A required update records from HOST B, then HOST B could perhaps send these records to HOST A whenever such records were created. Such asynchronous communications, however, result in still other possible problems (e.g., what if HOST A is not "ready" for a record when it is transmitted?).

Another solution approach would require that HOST B be a multilevel security host [SCHER 76]. Then a process B' could be created on B at the security level of HOST A. Process B' could accept the WRITE (request for data) from the HOST A process, READ the data from the lower-level process on HOST B and then transmit the data to HOST A. Karger discusses this type of problem and proposed solutions in some detail [KARGP 77].

9.3.3.2   Network Access Controllers

The use of network access controllers (NACs) has been suggested as one way to control access to network resources [BRAND 73, BRAND 75, HEINF 78, COLEG 78, LIPNS 74]. The idea is to place a computer system between the user and the rest of the network, as shown in Fig. 9.3. The user's identity must be authenticated before connection is allowed to any other network host. Of course, network hosts must likewise refuse connection attempted by anyone other than the NAC on behalf of the network users.

The cost of using this approach can be quite steep. For example, in addition to the cost of the NAC hardware (e.g., minicomputer with necessary interfaces), provision must be made for software and or hardware authentication not only of network users, but of network systems (e.g., the NAC must authenticate itself to network hosts). Finally, the NAC itself must be a trusted (i.e., secure) system.

Branstad's Network Security Center approach [BRAND 73, BRAND 75] is an example of a NAC. In this approach, dedicated minicomputers authenticate network users' identities and check access rights before establishing a secure (encrypted) communications channel between the user and the desired system. This approach is discussed in more detail in Sec. 9.4.

The implications of incorporating some of the access control features of a NAC in a support component of a network operating system [KIMBS 78] have also been investigated [WOODH 79]. By its very nature, a NAC must be a highly secure system. Ideally, the NAC code would be provably secure. As the combining of NAC functions with any additional software might compromise the security of the NAC functions, it appears that small systems dedicated to the NAC functions are the preferred approach.

9.4   DATA ENCRYPTION TECHNIQUES

Encryption provides a foundation upon which communications security may be built. Increasing reliance upon computer networks for the support of financial, industrial, transportation, and other systems, coupled with growing concerns for data integrity and security, have been driving forces behind the current civilian interest in data encryption. Interestingly, encryption techniques have been used for thousands of years to protect information, yet research is still ongoing in the field.

Encryption may be used to achieve the following:

1. To *prevent* unauthorized access to transmitted or stored data (disclosure)
2. To *prevent* the analysis of data traffic (disclosure)
3. To *detect* any modification of the data stream (including data destruction)
4. To *detect* the denial of transmission service
5. To *detect* unauthorized connections (authentication)

This section presents an overview of data encryption, describes modern encryption techniques and issues, and investigates the application of encryption to computer networks. The section is not intended to provide a comprehensive survey of cryptographic techniques. The interested reader should obtain David Kahn's comprehensive work, *The Codebreakers* [KAHND 67], which chronicles the history of cryptology in a highly readable fashion. As the facts are declassified, other books dealing with the vital role of cryptography during World War II are becoming available [STEVW 76, WINTF 74, LEWIR 78]. Tutorial introductions to contemporary cryptography are also available [DIFFW 76A, DIFFW 79]. Therefore, this section hopefully will serve to alert the reader to the vital function encryption can play in achieving secure communications and to provide direction into the ever-expanding literature on the subject.

9.4.1   Overview

Secret codes and transformations were used to protect information long before the advent of computers. Julius Caesar is said to have used a simple encryption algorithm, dubbed the Caesar cipher, by which he disguised each character in his messages by replacing it with the character that occurred three positions later in the alphabet [KAHND 67]. Cryptography was used by both the Confederate and Union armies during the Civil War and it played a very important role during World War II. However, its use has by no means been confined to the military. Lovers, artists, and scholars have also utilized cryptographic techniques.

Although codes and ciphers form the basis of the traditional forms of encryption, the power of computers has helped to make techniques that were too cumbersome or lengthy to execute by hand available for modern use in protecting data. Before discussing computer-oriented cryptography, however, it would be useful to establish some basic terminology.

Cryptography has been called the art of turning data into nonsense and then back again. More precisely, cryptography is the art or science that deals with the principles, means, and methods for rendering plaintext (also called "cleartext") unintelligible and for converting such encrypted messages back into intelligible form.

Cryptography includes the use of both ciphers and codes. A cipher is an algorithmic transformation that is performed on plaintext units of fixed length (e.g., symbol by symbol, three letters at a time). Codes, in contrast, operate on plaintext groups of variable length (e.g., words, phrases) [KAHND 67]. When discussing the uses of cryptography for the protection of computer systems and data banks, Horst Feistel distinguished the two techniques by noting that "with a cipher one can say things that have never been said before or even been anticipated as needing to be said. A code, on the other hand, is intrinsically semantic in character. A code can convey only meanings thought of in advance and provided for in a secret list such as a code book" [FEISH 73].

For example, if the phrase

SEND MORE MONEY

were encrypted using a Caesar cipher, the result would be

VHQG PRUH PRQHB

This same message could be encoded using the secret list shown in Tab. 9.4. The result is then

NO/ COLLECT/ CALLS

The terms *encipherment* and *encryption* are often used interchangeably, even though they are technically different. Throughout this chapter, we follow custom and use these terms without any implied distinction.

Early cryptographic schemes depended entirely upon the secrecy of the method or algorithm employed for "scrambling" or otherwise transforming the data. Once this algorithm was discovered, all communications could be compromised. In contrast, a modern encryption algorithm is a procedure for rendering information unintelligible by applying a series of mathematical transformations, controlled by a variable or *key*, to the cleartext. Thus modern cryptographic systems use both an

Table 9.4. *Secret List*

<BLANK>	/
★	+
APPLES	HOCKEY
BRANDY	WHITE
●	●
●	●
●	●
MONEY	CALLS
MORE	COLLECT
NICKEL	TIME
●	●
●	●
●	●
SEND	NO
SUN	COFFEE
●	●
●	●
●	●

algorithm and a key, which alters the "nature" of the algorithm so drastically that the use of different keys with the same encryption algorithm is much like using different algorithms.

Cryptography involves two basic transformations: transposition (or permutation) and substitution. In transposition, the order of the basic elements or characters of a plaintext message is changed; a simple example of a transposition of the message SECURITY would be ESUCIRYT. In substitution, the elements of a plaintext message are replaced by other elements (e.g., numbers, symbols). A substitution transformation of SECURITY might be 19 5 3 21 18 9 20 25. (A Caesar cipher is a simple substitution cipher.) Both transposition and substitution may be combined for additional protection.

In a key-based cryptographic system, a plaintext message and a key are both input to some device for encryption. The encryption device applies the encryption algorithm (in hardware, software, or firmware) to the cleartext message and outputs encrypted text that can be transmitted safely (see Fig. 9.4). An eavesdropper intercepting the data as they passed along the communications line would end up with the encrypted message, rather than the cleartext. The encrypted data are decrypted (returned to cleartext) at the other end of the line when they pass through a properly keyed receiving device.

9.4.1.1 *Attacks on Cryptosystems*

The goal in designing modern cryptosystems is to make the enciphering and deciphering operations inexpensive for the user while ensuring that any successful cryptanalytic attack would be too complex to be economical [DIFFW 76B]. As a part of the evaluation of system complexity (and hence system "strength"), the resistance of the cryptographic system to various types of attacks must be assessed.

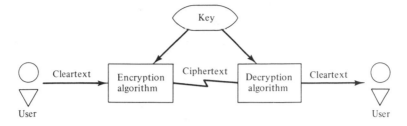

Figure 9.4   Conventional cryptographic system.

A cryptographic system that would succumb to an attack based on unlimited computational power is deemed "computationally" or "practically" secure if the cost of mounting such an attack is too great to be feasible. A cipher that is resistant to any attack of any magnitude is considered to be "unconditionally" or "theoretically" secure [SHANC 49].

For purposes of evaluating the resistance of a scheme to attack, it is assumed that the system attacker knows the type of cryptographic system being used. Cryptoanalytic attacks can then be classified as follows:

1. Attacks in which the cryptanalyst only possesses ciphertext
2. Attacks in which the cryptanalyst possesses both plaintext and the corresponding ciphertext
3. Attacks in which the cryptanalyst can submit plaintext messages of his own choosing and examine the resulting cryptograms

In the ciphertext-only attack, the cryptanalyst would typically require knowledge of the characteristic frequency distributions of the characters of the language being used. For example, an attack on an encrypted message that was known to be in English when in plaintext would make use of the fact that E is the most commonly used letter in English. With the more sophisticated encryption algorithms, however, such attacks are infeasible.

In the next type of attack, the cryptanalyst is able to obtain a string of plaintext and matching ciphertext. This is not too difficult to accomplish in a networking environment, since a given host system will usually "greet" a user who is just logging on with a "canned" message such as

HOST 123: ENTER USER NAME

Still, depending on the encryption technique employed, a fairly large quantity of matching plain and ciphertext may be required to mount an effective attack. Rather than using randomly acquired strings of matching plain and ciphertext, ideally a cryptanalyst would prefer to select the plaintext and acquire the corresponding ciphertext. Clearly, such threats must be considered when employing any encryption scheme. Furthermore, if the scheme is determined to provide inadequate resistance to attacks of type 1, another scheme should certainly be chosen.

9.4.1.2 Stream and Block Ciphers

Modern, computer-based encryption techniques are either stream or block ciphers. One implementation of a stream cipher is based on the use of a key which is actually a randomly ordered stream of bits, equal in length to the message to be encrypted. Such a system, sometimes called the *one-time pad* or Vernam system, is the only class of ciphers that can be proven to be totally unbreakable [SHANC 49]. Unfortunately, this class of cipher requires extremely long keys. Therefore, such ciphers are in most cases too expensive to be practical.

In practice, smaller, pseudo-random keys are used. The keys may be generated independently of the plaintext stream, say by a pseudo-random-number generator, or the key may be a function of the plaintext or the ciphertext and some initial (also called "priming" or "seed") key.

Block ciphers encrypt fixed-size blocks of data under the control of a key. When a block cipher is applied to a message block consisting of N bits, the resulting enciphered block is at least N bits in length. The strength of a given block cipher depends on such factors as the size of the block and the construction of the cipher itself (e.g., the mix of transformations). Additional discussions of stream and block ciphers can be found in [FEISH 73, FEISH 75, HOFFL 77].

9.4.2 Conventional Encryption Techniques

Customarily, unauthorized persons must know both the encryption algorithm and the key in order to decrypt intercepted messages. However, experts assert that a system which cannot be described safely in the open literature is not sufficiently secure to be used with confidence [BARAP 64]. Thus with the evolution of computers and the art of cryptanalysis have come techniques in which the encryption algorithm, and in some cases even the encryption key (but not the decryption key), may be known and still not compromise the security of the data.

In 1977, the Federal Data Encryption Standard (DES) was announced [FIPS 46]. As with other block ciphers, the DES is used in conjunction with an encryption/ decryption key. The DES algorithm is designed to encipher and decipher blocks of data consisting of 64 bits under control of the 64-bit key (of which 8 bits are used for error detection). The same key is used both for enciphering and deciphering; however, the use of the key bits is altered so that the deciphering process is the inverse of the enciphering process. A block to be enciphered is subjected to an initial permutation (IP), then to a complex key-dependent computation, and finally to a permutation which is the inverse of the initial permutation. The key-dependent computation can be simply defined in terms of a function f, called the cipher function, and a function KS, called the key schedule. To illustrate its complexity, the encipher computation of the DES is shown in Fig. 9.5. The complete algorithm is specified in [FIPS 46]. Additional discussion may be found in [BRAND 78, HOFFL 77].

The strengths and weaknesses of the DES have been the subject of much discussion [DIFFW 77, MEISP 76, BRAND 77, DAVID 78]. Criticisms of the standard have primarily centered around concern that the key size is insufficient to

ENCIPHERING COMPUTATION

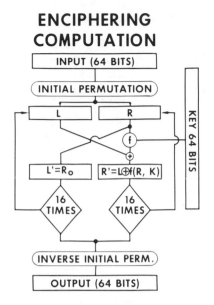

Figure 9.5 DES enciphering computation.

withstand elaborate brute-force attacks. The consensus at the time the standard was enacted was that the algorithm was at least acceptable for business applications and nonmilitary government applications. Commercially available implementations of the DES in integrated circuits and protocols for incorporating the DES in various network protocols are under development; several hardware implementations have been validated by the National Bureau of Standards [GAITJ 77]. Tab. 9.5 identifies successful validations as of February 1981. Because of the rapidly changing technology and advances in microminiaturization techniques, this standard will undergo periodic, critical review. However, for all practical purposes, the DES, combined with good key management techniques, should remain adequate for the intended purposes during at least the next 5 years.

9.4.3 Public Key Encryption

In conventional encryption systems it is essential that the encryption key, which is the same for both the sending and the receiving stations, be secret. Therefore, often elaborate schemes must be used to protect keys while they are being exchanged among users who wish to communicate over secure paths. Special couriers or registered mail may be used, or keys may be exchanged automatically over computer communications links using special techniques, some of which are described in the next section. Each of these key distribution methods has one aspect in common— users who wish to communicate securely must exchange encryption keys in advance of their communications.

Table 9.5. *Comparison of Validated DES Implementations.*

DES VALIDATIONS

COMPANY	DATE	DEVICE TECH.	ALGORITHM SPEED	COST OR APPLICATION
COLLINS	10/77	pMOS	40µs	COMM. SYSTEM
IBM	11/1/77	FET	32 CLOCKS 32µs@1MHz	TERMINAL SYSTEM
MOTOROLA	11/28/77	nMOS	320 CLOCKS 160us@2MHz	COMM. SYSTEM
INTEL	1/3/78	ROM	100 ms	$15-45
BURROUGHS	3/16/78	nMOS	32 CLOCKS 25.6µs@1.25MHz	$50-150
IBM	8/25/78	FET	32 CLOCKS 32µs@4.9MHz	COMM. SYSTEM
FAIRCHILD	12/20/78	I^3L	16 CLOCKS 4.8µs@5MHz	$30-100
GTE SYLVANIA	2/27/79	BIPOLAR LSI	6400 bps	VOICE SYSTEM
WESTERN DIGITAL	8/9/79	nMOS	25µs@2MHz	$75
IBM	9/21/79	TWO TTL CARDS	12 Mbps	COMPUTER SYSTEM
NIXDORF COMPUTER	1/7/80	TTL	*10-15 uS	COMPUTER SYSTEM
RACAL-MILGO	1/7/80	ROM FRMWRE	*8 MS	MODEM SYSTEM
UNIVAC	1/29/80	TTL	*5-10 uS	COMPUTER SYSTEM
MOTOROLA	2/11/80	nMOS	160 uS	*$100
ADVANCED MICRO DEVICES	1/28/81	MOS	6 uS	*$115

* ESTIMATED

A relatively recent development in the field of cryptography is an encryption system which does not require total key secrecy. This approach, suggested by Diffie and Hellman [DIFFW 76A] and, independently, by Merkle [MERKR 78A], employs different keys for encrypting and decrypting data, as shown in Fig. 9.6. Under this system, each user has two keys—a public key P and a secret key S. The keys are related in that the secret key is the decryption key for messages encrypted with the public key.

Suppose that user B wishes to send message M to user A. The message is encrypted using A's public key. The resulting encrypted message may be represented by $P_A(M)$. Upon receipt of such an encrypted message, user A applies his secret key S_A with the following result:

(1) $S_A(P_A(M)) = M$

In the design of public key cryptosystems it is important that both S and P be easy to compute and that S not be deduced easily from P. It is also possible to select the public and secret keys so that if a message M is first decrypted using S and then encrypted using P, the result is again M. That is,

(2) $P(S(M)) = M$

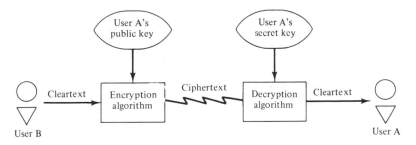

Figure 9.6   Public key system.

This last property is of special significance to the problem of message "signatures," which is discussed in the next section.

It should be noted that this example assumes that user A's public key is correctly transmitted to user B.

Since public key cryptosystems were first proposed, several implementations have been suggested [RIVER 78, MERKR 78B]. These approaches are all based on computationally difficult problems. The security of the Rivest–Shamir–Adleman (RSA) scheme is based on the difficulty of factoring large numbers [RIVER 78]. To use the RSA method, n is first computed as the product of two very large, "random," prime numbers, p and q. The number n is public, while the factors p and q are secret. Then the integer d is chosen such that d is a large, random integer, relatively prime to $(p - 1)(q - 1)$. Finally, the integer e is computed from p, q, and d to be the "multiplicative inverse" of d modulo $(p - 1)(q - 1)$.

To encrypt a message M, it is raised to the eth power modulo n. To decrypt the resulting ciphertext C, it is raised to the dth power modulo n. Thus we have the encryption and decryption algorithms E and D:

$$C = E(M) = M^e \bmod n$$
$$D(E(M)) = D(C) = C^d \bmod n$$

The scheme proposed by Merkle and Hellman is based on the "knapsack" problem, which involves determining a subset of a given set of positive integers with a proscribed value for the subset numbers [MERKRB 78]. Summary descriptions of these and other public key schemes are presented in [LEMPA 79], [DAVID 79A], [POPEG 78B].

9.4.4   Digital Signatures

As the use of computer communications for business transactions becomes more widespread, the need arises for a means of "signing" electronic messages in an unforgettable and verifiable way. The idea behind the concept is that a bit pattern could be used to prove to an impartial third party, such as a judge, that the message was genuine and originated with the claimed sender.

As proposed by Diffie and Hellman [DIFFW 76A] and shown in Fig. 9.7, to

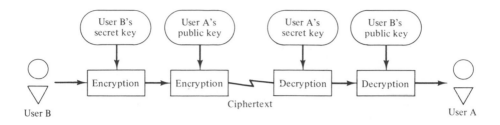

Figure 9.7   Digital signature using public key system.

send a "signed" message to user A, user B would encrypt the message M using his secret key S_B. Upon receipt of the encrypted message, and knowing that B allegedly sent the message, A would apply B's public key P_B to decrypt the message. Of course, anyone intercepting such a signed message, and knowing that B was the sender, could determine the message contents by simply applying P_B. Therefore, to protect the transmission from such threats, B could further encrypt the message, using A's public key. The message received by A would then be $P_A(S_B(M))$, to which A would first apply his secret key, and then B's public key to obtain M. In case B later denies sending the message to A, A can retain a copy of the encoded message $S_B(M)$ as proof to be presented to an impartial third party.

In their evaluation of public and conventional encryption methods, Kline and Popek [KLINC 79] note that for all digital signature schemes proposed to that date, the validity of a signature on a message is only as safe as the entire *future* history of protection of the signer's private key. For example, a message sender who later wishes to repudiate a message need only claim that his private key had been compromised. They propose a solution approach in which secret keys are maintained by a trusted, centralized key registry. Users never have access to their secret key, in such a scheme, since the registry would maintain and apply keys on the user's behalf, whenever necessary. Although the resultant signatures are still only valid as long as the secrecy of the private key is maintained, the user can no longer repudiate his signature at will. Consequently, this approach may prove an acceptable solution to the problem.

Needham and Shroeder [NEEDR 78] also considered the problems of digital signature verification. They proposed an approach incorporating conventional encryption methods and a "characteristic function" which is calculated on the message by a trusted third party (e.g., a key distribution center) which uses a key held only for that purpose. This approach thereby avoids in part the problem identified by Popek and Kline. However, when a third party is introduced, the trustworthiness of that party becomes very important. Meijer and Akl [MEIJH 81] describe four schemes involving a third party arbitrator which proport to reduce this dependency.

Kent [KENTS 79A] observed that in order for digital signatures to be accepted there must be provision for dating signed messages through either secure time-stamped archiving (wherein a copy of the dated and signed message is maintained at several archival sites around the network) or by centralized time-stamping facilities.

Although it may be desirable for users to be able to authenticate message senders in such a fashion, the ultimate test of the practicality of digital signatures is if they can "stand up in court." Such a capability, if recognized by law, could greatly reduce the time needed to engage in business transactions requiring signed agreements. A discussion on legalizing digital signatures is available in [LIPTS 78]. The use of signature systems based on conventional algorithmic techniques have also been proposed [DIFFW 76A, RABIM 78, SMIDM 79].

9.4.5 Comparison of Conventional and Public Key Cryptosystems

While proponents of public key systems claim superiority of that approach over conventional encryption methods, a study by Kline and Popek [KLINC 79] concludes that neither public key nor conventional key algorithms have any significant advantage over the other with respect to performance, simplicity, or safety. The need for strong encryption algorithms, regardless of their form, and reliable user authentication techniques are cited as being considerably more important than discussions of the relative strengths/weaknesses of public key and conventional systems.

Kent notes that several factors should be considered in the selection of cryptographic modes of use and protocols [KENTS 79A]. Furthermore, he asserts that any comparison of such systems must be made in the context of "specific application environments with well defined requirements and constraints." Upon examining both public key and conventional cryptosystems in the context of large-scale, connection-oriented communication networks, he concludes that public key systems appear to offer few advantages over conventional approaches.

Lempel observes that a major shortcoming of currently practiced cryptographic techniques, including the DES and public key schemes, is a lack of proof that they are as difficult to crack as they appear to be [LEMPA 79]. Rather than encourage the development of more schemes of uncertain absolute strength, he suggests the need for efforts to establish standard measures of "cryptocomplexity." Once such standards have been generated, efforts can be directed toward inventing schemes that provide a given level of protection.

9.4.6 Employing Encryption in Networks

Within a computer communications environment, encryption techniques provide mechanisms for authentication as well as secure communications. The former was investigated by Needham and Schroeder [NEEDR 78] for the case of large networks of computers. They presented protocols for decentralized authentication in such networks in which there is minimal reliance on network-wide services, such as a single network clock or name management authority.

The following authentication functions were considered:

1. Establishing authenticated, interactive communication between two entities on different machines

2. Achieving authenticated, one-way communications (e.g., for mail systems)
3. Signed communication (e.g., digital signatures)

The study considered both conventional and public key encryption algorithms as the basis for such protocols, and concluded that protocols using such techniques are "strikingly similar." Consequently, economy and cryptographic strength of the encryption techniques should be the basis for choosing between them, rather than their possible effects on the complexity of the authentication protocol.

Once the decision has been made to use encryption techniques for securing communications paths across computer communications networks, several practical issues must be addressed. These include such considerations as how much trust one can place in the various network components, which is a part of risk assessment; where to implement encryption services (i.e., at which communication level), and management-related concerns such as key distribution.

9.4.6.1 Communication Levels

As computer communications becomes more widespread, efforts are under way to facilitate the interconnection of systems. A distributed systems reference model has been developed under the auspices of the International Standards Organization (ISO) and the American National Standards Institute (ANSI) [BACHC 78, DESJD 78]. This model, shown in Fig. 9.8a, is based upon the concept of layering, where each layer performs a specific set of functions and provides a specified set of services to higher layers.

There are three basic elements to this model, which are illustrated in Fig. 9.8b:

1. The applications process
2. The local operating environment in which the process exists
3. Sessions that logically connect two applications processes, regardless of physical location

The lower four layers of the model are data communications oriented. The physical layer supports communications at the DTE-DCE level. The link layer controls data communications between two nodes on a network. The network layer is concerned with intranetwork communications, while the transport layer supports internetwork, end-to-end data exchange. The remaining three layers support data-processing-oriented functions: establishing, terminating, and controlling sessions; resolving data representation incompatibilities; and control of the applications processes themselves.

Support for the use of encryption for data protection, authentication, and access control must be provided within the distributed systems environment. Consequently, appropriate security functions must be included within the model. The inclusion of such functions, however, is intended only to imply a concern for maintaining the security of the local operating environment to at least the level that exists without the distributed systems or networking environment. No improvement of local security is implied.

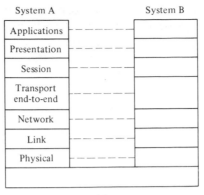

(a)

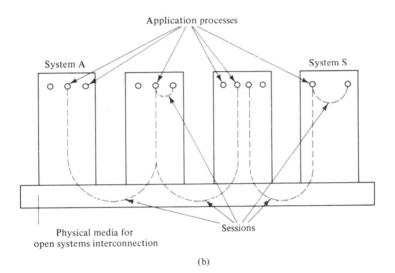

(b)

Figure 9.8　(a) Architectural reference model; (b) sessions within reference model.

Although the need for security functions in this model has been recognized, a number of issues remained to be resolved at the time this chapter was written. These include identification of the levels at which encryption is to be performed (e.g., link, network, transport), the level of control the application process should exert over the application of encryption, and the complex problem of key management functions. Similar issues exist for the provision of authentication and access control functions within this model.

Application of encryption at the link level versus from end-to-end on the communications subnet has been discussed extensively. In the former approach, messages are protected in transit between network nodes, but are in the clear within each node. This allows the node to examine needed header fields which contain such information as source and destination addresses, without exposure of these fields during transmission of the message. However, the security requirements for the node processor in this case are necessarily quite high.

In the end-to-end approach, the message contents are decrypted only at the destination host. For routing purposes, however, certain message header information must still remain in the clear. Karger [KARGP 77], among others, has noted potential vulnerabilities of this scheme. For example, tampering with unencrypted fields could go undetected.

Popek and Kline [POPEG 79] observed that, generally speaking, the higher the architectural level considered, the larger the number of identifiable and separately protected entities. For example, in a network with less than 100 host systems, there would likely be over 1000 concurrently operating processes, each controlled and secured separately. The large number of secure channels likely required in such an environment give rise to additional cost and complexity. They observe that when encryption is introduced at higher levels there can be a significant reduction in the amount of software for which correct functioning must be ensured, since all lower levels of protocol do not have to be trusted. They caution, however, that since the data must be in cleartext form in the machine in which they are being processed, there still remains a need for the more "classical" methods of protection. Thus there are limits to the security provided by high-level encryption. It is also difficult to perform communications processing operations such as character packing or control-character detection on encrypted data. These and other factors must be considered when selecting appropriate level(s) for encryption.

The current worldwide efforts to refine the architectural model for distributed systems promises a well-defined framework for the development of secure communications protocols. Initial work has already begun along those lines [DAVID 79B, NELSJ 79, POPEG 79, KENTS 79B].

9.4.6.2   Key Management

When the security of an encryption scheme depends upon the protection of the encryption key, as is the case with the DES and other secret key systems (including so-called "public key systems"), it is important that keys be properly managed.

There are three principal aspects to key management:

1.   Selection
2.   Lifetime
3.   Distribution

Selection relates to who chooses the key and how it is chosen (or generated). Encryption keys could conceivably be chosen by or assigned to a user. The latter is definitely not recommended. The concerns here are somewhat similar to those regarding the selection of passwords [WOODH 80]. Users could be expected to choose easily remembered strings of characters, numbers, or symbols, while automated key generation techniques could be programmed to choose more random strings which would be more difficult to guess. Furthermore, automated selectors could be directed to always generate nonblank character strings of maximum size, using the full set of available characters (including control and nonprinting characters). For example, if a 56-bit key was to be generated by a sequence of 8-bit ASCII characters, the selector routine would always generate strings seven characters in length. This would help thwart attacks based on exhaustive searching of the effective key space.

Ideally, a key should last no longer than necessary, to minimize the amount of data that would be compromised if a key is discovered. A single-usage or "disposable" key has a number of advantages. If, for example, message counters are used to help detect message stream modification (insertion, deletion, and replay) attacks, then at the start of a new terminal session, the message counter can be initialized with the result being that shorter counters are required [KENTS 76]. However, frequent key changes requires a satisfactory method for distributing and storing keys.

Keys may be distributed by manual or automated techniques. Selection of a distribution technique for a particular environment depends on several factors, including cryptoperiod, number of directly connected parties, and type of key. Manual methods, including registered mail and visits to the system security officer, may prove to be too time consuming for a networking environment. In such cases it may make sense to use the network itself for rapid key distribution. Data as important as the encryption key(s) for future transmissions must themselves be encrypted. There are two basic approaches that may be used to handle this situation: chained key and two-level key distribution systems [KENTS 76].

In the chained key approach, each successive key is encrypted using the last key. If an attacker discovers any one of the keys, then all successive keys in the chain are compromised as well. Under the two-level key distribution system, a special key is used solely for the transmission of new keys. The two ends of the connection must agree on some protocol to be used to signify when a new key, enciphered with the special "new-key" key, is going to be transmitted.

Kent [KENTS 76] suggests the use of both techniques, in the following manner. At the start of each terminal session, a PRIMARY key, used on a long-term basis by the particular user and system, is used to encipher a SECONDARY key which will control the encryption of all data subsequently transmitted during that session. Throughout the session, the SECONDARY key could be used to encipher replacement SECONDARY keys (key chaining), which would the take over for the remainder of the session or until the next SECONDARY key was transmitted, should even higher degrees of security be required.

Recovery from key exposure must be considered with key distribution techniques. As pointed out by Kent [KENTS 79A], the use of centralized key distribution centers (for conventional cryptosystems) or public files (for public key cryptosystems) greatly reduces the task.

Although formal guidelines for key management are not yet available, the following observations, arrived at during a workshop on the use of cryptography in support of computer security [BRAND 78], are a good starting point:

1.   Highest priority must be given to protecting the keys within a system, both to deny unauthorized access to the keys and to assure authorized access to keys used for long-term retention of encrypted data.
2.   It is essential that some element of the key be distributed to remote locations by a process which is outside the system that is being cryptographically protected. (The use of public key-based techniques to provide protection during the distribution of conventional encryption keys might satisfy this requirement.)
3.   More than one level of key management is acceptable and in some cases necessary.
4.   It is not advisable that a single key be used for all stations in a multistation cryptographic system.
5.   Key distribution systems will depend on the size, complexity, and topology of the cryptographic system.

9.4.6.3   Network Security Centers

An approach to network security utilizing dedicated minicomputers, termed the Network Security Center (NSC), establishes secure communications paths between users and network resources [BRAND 73, BRAND 75, HEINF 78, COLEG 78]. NSC responsibilities also include (1) user authentication, (2) authorization checking, and (3) the collection and/or distribution of appropriate information relative to this connection (e.g., audit data collected, user profile information supplied to host).

In this scheme, Intelligent Cryptographic Devices (ICDs) are used to establish protected connection between network entities after authentication and authorization checking have taken place. Each ICD must be capable of being remotely keyed—by the NSC only. Furthermore, whenever a dialogue is completed, the corresponding connection must be broken to ensure that other users do not have an opportunity to "piggyback" an authorized user and thus gain access to restricted resources. Figure 9.9 presents a simplified view of a network incorporating a Network Security Center.

In order for a user to gain access to a computer on a network which incorporates an NSC, the following steps must occur:

1.   The user must initially connect to the NSC.
2.   The NSC performs authentication and authorization checking.
3.   After validation of the user's claimed identity and successful authorization check, NSC then "keys" the ICD for the user's device (e.g., terminal) and the target host with a "one-time" session key.
4.   The user and target host may then communicate directly over encrypted lines.

In this type of environment, an additional reasonable requirement would be that the communications path used in step 1 be secure. This would prevent exposure

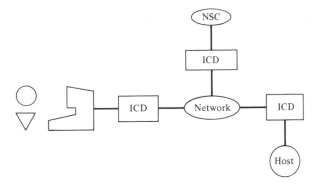

Figure 9.9 Network security center configuration.

of the user authentication information (e.g. user ID, password) transmitted to the NSC.

9.5 MANAGEMENT PRACTICES

It should go without saying that the most technically sound protective measures are worse than useless if they are not consistently enforced. Unfortunately, this is the case in far too many installations where lax management practices results in a false sense of security. *Managers, not technicians, are ultimately responsible for security!* Managers need to determine the level of protection they require in view of the risks they face; they need to organize a comprehensive and balanced set of protective measures of the type that have been discussed in this chapter; and they need to see that the protective measures they put in place are properly used and that security practices are enforced.

9.5.1 Security Planning

Managerial planning for security should begin with an assessment of the risks faced by the installation and the losses that would accrue to the organization in the event they took the risk and lost. Two key elements comprise such a process: (1) an assessment of the damage that can result from an undesirable event, and (2) the likelihood of such an event occurring. Thus the goal of a risk analysis is to "strike an economic balance between the impact of risks and the cost of protective measures" [REEDS 77].

Once risks are identified and quantified, countermeasures can be evaluated systematically. One simple rule of thumb is that a countermeasure is not employed unless it results in a reduction of risk exposure at least as great as the cost of the countermeasure. Ordinarily, the first countermeasures chosen will yield the greatest risk reduction at least cost; successive countermeasures cost more and more for less and less risk reduction. Since complete security is simply not achievable, each organization will have to decide for itself what constitutes an acceptable level of risk exposure for which no countermeasure will be taken.

9.5.2 Implementing Countermeasures

Advice on the implementations of the various countermeasures chosen is well beyond the scope of this discussion, since the details may differ from system to system. However, it can be advised that good security management practices be employed in these implementations. This includes review of all technical plans with a particular view to the impact on the overall security of the system, limitation of the details of the security system to those with a "need to know," separation of duties in the actual implementations, and full testing and audit to assure that the countermeasures work as intended and do not contain any "trapdoors."

9.5.3 Security Audit

Auditing is the final area in which good management practices are important to achieving and maintaining high levels of system security. A security audit is an organized assessment of the level and effectiveness of security measures in a given system. Audits may be performed by in-house staff, by consultants, or by independent auditing firms. The value of an audit is that it may highlight gaps in the protective measures that have been taken, as well as possibly uncovering specific instances in which the security of the system has been compromised. Security audits are facilitated if good implementation practices have been followed, such as structured programming and the provision of an audit trail for transactions that enter, retrieve, or modify data in the system. Any successful audit will also require the cooperation of operational personnel.

At the current time, the effectiveness of security audits are limited by the shortage of qualified security auditors. Far too many audits consist simply of going through a checklist rather than seeking to analyze the particular system to identify the likely weaknesses in security. In this case the audit is only as good as the list and its relevance to the system being audited.

Penetration testing is often employed as a means of testing the vulnerability of a system to sustained attack. Informed "tiger teams" are invited to seek to compromise the system in as many ways as possible. In a communications system, this may involve penetration attempts of all types, including active or passive wiretapping, or it may be restricted to trying to break into the system from a dial-in terminal. The results are often quite dramatic and most useful to alert a neglectful top management to the dangers they face. However, the failure to penetrate a system does not mean that the system is secure, so that penetration testing, although useful and often fun, should not supplant a more systematic, though perhaps less exciting, security audit.

9.6 CURRENT ASSESSMENT AND FUTURE TRENDS

Clearly, there exists a need for the intelligent incorporation of security mechanisms in today's computer communications networks. Numerous techniques already exist to help provide the required levels of security. The main question is: *How much is enough?* Hopefully, the information in this chapter has helped increase the breadth of understanding of the problems relating to computer communications security. This information, coupled with that referenced in the open literature, should at least equip managers with the appropriate questions needed to initiate a well-constructed analysis of the risks inherent in a particular system and to identify the appropriate mechanisms to help lessen that risk.

The following are perhaps the key conclusions that should be drawn from this chapter:

1. Absolute security is not attainable. The problem of security is the management of risk: identifying and assessing risks, devising countermeasures, and selecting then in view of the trade-off between cost and risk reduction.
2. A security program for computer communications systems should be a balanced one, addressing physical security (both area and logical), access controls, encryption, and good management practices as dictated by the threat environment.
3. Passwords are not by themselves an adequate security measure for remotely accessed systems. However, the effectiveness of password schemes can be improved by attention to good security practives for the assignment, duration, and use.
4. Encryption techniques are an effective measure for protecting information during transmission or in storage. However, good key management practices must be followed for encryption schemes to be effective.
5. Security is a management responsibility. Responsible managers will take the necessary steps to ensure that adequate security is provided for the information systems under their control.

Computer technology is rapidly providing hardware and software capable of meeting the increasing security requirements. Microminiaturization is resulting in the development of faster, cheaper, smaller logic elements which facilitates the incorporation of security provisions throughout the computer communications environment. Similarly, static and even dynamic access control features are beginning to find their way into data management systems. The nation's growing reliance on computer communications systems, coupled with the continuing pressures to ensure the privacy and integrity of information handled by these systems, will guarantee the continued relevance of this topic.

ACKNOWLEDGMENTS

The authors gratefully acknowledge the helpful comments and suggestions of Stephen T. Kent (Bolt, Beranek and Newman, Inc.), Frank Ferrante (Mitre Corp.), Dennis K. Branstad and Miles Smid (National Bureau of Standards) and Michael O'Brien (National Security Agency). Table 9.5 was contributed by Dennis K. Branstad.

REFERENCES

ABRAM 77   Abrams, M. D., D. K. Branstad, P. S. Browne, and I. W. Cotton, *Tutorial on Computer Security and Integrity*, IEEE Computer Society, New York, 1977.

BABCJ 67   Babcock, J. D., "A Brief Description of Privacy Measure in the RUSH Time-sharing System," *Spring Joint Comput. Conf.*, 1967, pp. 301–302.

BACHC 78   Bachman, C., "Domestic and International Standards Activities for Distributed Systems," *COMPCON 78*, September 1978, pp. 140–143.

BARAP 64   Baran, P., *On Distributed Communications: IX. Security, Secrecy, and Tamper-free Considerations*, Rand Corporation, AD-444 839, August 1964.

BRAND 73   Branstad, D. K., "Security Aspect of Computer Networks," *AIAA Comput. Network Syst. Conf.*, American Institute of Aeronautic and Astronautics, New York, April 1973.

BRAND 75   Branstad, D. K., "Encryption Protection in Computer Data Communications, " *4th Data Commun. Symp.*, October 1975, pp. 8-1 to 8-7.

BRAND 78   Branstad, D. K., ed., *Computer Security and the Data Encryption Standard*, National Bureau of Standards, Spec. Publ. 500-27. February 1978.

BROWP 76   Browne, P. S., "Computer Security—A Survey," *Nat. Comput. Conf.*, 1976, pp. 53–63.

BUSHA 75   Bushkin, A. A., *A Framework for Computer Security*, System Development Corporation, McLean, Va., AD-A025 356, June 1975.

CARRJ 70   Carroll, J. M., and P. M. McLelland, "Fast 'Infinite-Key' Privacy Transformation for Resource-Sharing Systems," *Fall Joint Comput. Conf.*, 1970, pp. 223–230.

COLEG 78   Cole, G. D., *Design Alternative for Computer Network Security*, National Bureau of Standards, Spec. Publ. 500-21, Vol. 1, January 1978.

COTTI 75   Cotton, I. W., and P. Meissner, "Approaches to Controlling Personal Access to Computer Terminals," *Comput. Networks: Trends Appl.*, 1975, pp. 32–39.

CRANH 77   Crane, H. D., D. E. Wolf, and J. S. Ostrem, "The SRI Pen System for Automatic Signature Verification," *Comput. Security Integrity: Trends Appl.*, May 1977, pp. 32–39.

DAVID 78   Davies, D. W., and D. A. Bell, *The Protection of Data*, National Physical Laboratory, Teddington, England, NPL Report COM98, January 1978.

DAVID 79A   Davies, D. W., W. L. Price, and G. J. Parkin, "An Evaluation of Public Key Cryptosystems," National Physical Laboratory, Teddington, England, March 1979.

DAVID 79B   Davies, D. W., and W. L. Price, "A Protocol for Secure Communications," National Physical Laboratory, Teddington, England, November 1979.

DEMIR 76   DeMillo, R., D. Dobkin, and R. Lipton, "Even Data Bases That Lie Can Be Compromised," University of Wisconsin-Milwaukee, TR-CS-76, 7, August, 1976.

DEMIR 78   DeMillo, R., D. Dobkin, and R. Lipton, "Combinatorial Inference," in DeMillo et. al., *Foundations of Secure Computation*, Academic Press, New York, 1978, pp. 27–37.

DENND 76   Denning, D. E., "A Lattice Model of Secure Information Flow," *Commun. ACM*, Vol. 19, No. 5, 1976, pp. 236–243.

DENND 78   Denning, D., "A Review of Research on Statistical Data Base Security," in R. DeMillo, D. Dobkin, and R. Lipton, *Foundations of Secure Computation*, Academic Press, New York, 1978, pp. 15–26.

DESJD 78   des Jardins, R., and G. White, "ANSI Reference Model for Distributed Systems," *COMPCON 78*, September 1978, pp. 144–149.

DIFFW 76A   Diffie, W., and M. E. Hellman, "New Directions in Cryptography," *IEEE Trans. Inf. Theory, Vol. IT-22*, November 1976, pp. 644–654.

DIFFW 76B   Diffie, W., and M. E. Hellman, "Multiuser Cryptographic Techniques," Nat. Comput. Conf., 1976, pp. 109–112.

DIFFW 77   Diffie, W., and M. E. Hellman, Exhaustive Cryptanalysis of the NBS Data Encryption Standard, *Computer*, June 1977, pp. 74–84.

DIFFW 79   Diffie, W., and M. E. Hellman, "Privacy and Authentication: An Introduction to Cryptography," *Proc. IEEE*, Vol. 67, No. 3, 1979, pp. 397–427.

EVANA 74   Evans, A., Jr., and W. Kantrowitz, "A User Authentication Scheme Not Requiring Secrecy in the Computer," *Commun. ACM*, Vol. 17, No. 8, 1974, pp. 437–442.

FABRR 74   Fabry, R. S., "Capability-Based Addressing," *Commun. ACM*, Vol. 17, No. 7, 1974, pp. 403–412.

FEISH 73   Feistel, H. "Cryptography and Computer Privacy," *Sci. Am.*, Vol. 228, No. 5, 1973, pp. 15–23.

FEISH 75   Feistel, H., W. A. Notz, and J. L. Smith, "Some Cryptographic Technique for Machine to Machine Data Communications," *Proc. IEEE*, Vol. 63, No. 11, 1975, pp. 1545–1554.

FIPS 31   Jacobson, R. V., W. F. Brown, and P. S. Browne, *Guideline for Automatic Data Processing Physical Security and Risk Management*, National Bureau of Standards, FIPS Publ. 31, June 1974.

FIPS 39   *Glossary for Computer System Security*, National Bureau of Standards, FIPS Publ. 39, February 1976.

FIPS 41   *Computer Security Guideline for Implementing the Privacy Act of 1974*, National Bureau of Standards, FIPS Publ. 41, May 1975.

FIPS 46   *Data Encryption Standard*, National Bureau of Standards, FIPS Publ. 46, January 1977.

FIPS 48   *Guideline on Evaluation of Techniques for Automated Personal Identification*, National Bureau of Standards, FIPS Publ. 48, April 1977.

FIPS 65   *Guideline for Computer Security Risk Analysis*, National Bureau of Standards, FIPS Publ. 65, August 1979.

FORSH 77   Forsdick, H. C., R. E. Schantz, and R. H. Thomas, "Operating System for Computer Networks," BBN Rep. No. 3614, Bolt, Beranek and Newman, Inc., Cambridge, Mass., 1977.

GAADR 80   Gaade, R. P. R., "Disaster Planning," *Datamation*, January 1980, pp. 113–118.

GAITJ 77   Gait, J., *Validating the Correctness of Hardware Implementation of the NBS*

406

Data Encryption Standard, National Bureau of Standards, Spec. Publ. 500-20, November 1977.

GAO 78   General Accounting Office, "Challenge of Protecting Personal Information in an Expanding Federal Computer Network Environment," LCD-76-102, April 28, 1978.

HEINF 78   Heinrich, F., The Network Security Center: A System Level Approach to Computer Network Security, National Bureau of Standards, Spec. Publ. 500-21, Vol. 2, January 1978.

HELDG 76   Held, G., "Locking Intruder Out of a Network," Executive Guide to Data Communications, McGraw-Hill, New York, 1976.

HERBN 77   Herbst, N. M., and C. N. Liu, " Automatic Signature Verification Based on Accelerometry," IBM J. Res. Dev., May 1977, pp. 245-263.

HOFFL 69   Hoffman, L. J., "Computer and Privacy: A Survey," Coput. Surv., Vol. 1, No. 2, 1969, pp. 85-103.

HOFFL 71   Hoffman, L. J., "The Formulary Model for Flexible Privacy and Access Controls," Fall Joint Comput. Conf., 1971, pp. 587-601.

HOFFL 77   Hoffman, L. J., Modern Methods for Computer Security and Privacy, Prentice-Hall, Englewood Cliffs, N.J., 1977.

JOHNS 74   Johnson, S. M., Certain Number Theoretic Questions in Access Control, Rand Corp., Rept. R-1494-NSF, Jan, 1974.

KAHND 67   Kahn, D., The Codebreakers, The Macmillan Co., New York, N.Y., 1967.

KARGP 77   Karger, P. A., "Non-discretionary Access Control for Decentralized Computing Systems," S.M. thesis, Dept. of Electrical Engineering and Computer Science, M.I.T., May 1977. (Also available as MIT/LCS/TR-179, Laboratory for Computer Science, M.I.T., May 1977, NTIS AD A040808.)

KARGP 78   Karger, P. A., "Non-discretionary Security for Decentralized Computing Systems," Distributed Processing: Trends and Applications, IEEE Press, New York, May 1978, pp. 33-39.

KENTS 76   Kent, S. T., "Encryption-Based Protection Protocol for Interactive User-Computer Communication," (Master's thesis), M.I.T., Cambridge, Mass., AD-A026 911, May 1976.

KENTS 79A Kent, S. T., "A Comparison of Some Aspects of Public Key and Conventional Crypto Systems," ICC '79, June 1979, pp. 4.3.1 to 4.3.5.

KENTS 79B Kent, S. T., "Protocol Design Considerations for Network Security," in Interlinking of Computer Networks, Kenneth G. Beauchamp, ed., D. Reidel, Dordrecht, 1979, pp. 239-260.

KIMBS 76   Kimbleton, S. R., and R. L. Mandell, "A Perspective on Network Operating Systems," Nat. Comput. Conf., 1976, pp. 551-559.

KIMBS 78   Kimbleton, S. R., H. M. Wood, and M. L. Fitzgerald, "Network Operating Systems—An Implementation Approach," Nat. Comput. Conf., 1978, pp. 773-782.

KIRCJ 79   Kirchner, J., "Flooding of Census Bureau DP Room Probed," Computerworld, October 8, 1979, p. 9.

KLINC 79   Kline, C., and G. Popek, "Public Key vs. Conventional Key Encryption," Nat. Comput. Conf., 1979, pp. 831-837.

LAMPL 81   Lamport, L., "Password Authentication with Insecure Communication," Commun. ACM, Vol. 24, No. 11, 1982, pp. 770–773.

LEMPA 79   Lempel, A., "Cryptology in Transition," *Comput. Surv.* Vol. 11, No. 4, 1979, pp. 285–304.

LEWIR 78   Lewin, R. *ULTRA Goes to War: The First Account of World War II's Greatest Secret Based on Official Documents*, McGraw-Hill, New York, 1978.

LINDT 76   Linden, T. A., "Operating System Structures to Support Security and Reliable Software," *Comput. Surv.*, Vol. 8, No. 4, 1976, pp. 409–445.

LIPNS 74   Lipner, S. A., "A Minicomputer Security Control System," *Compcon '74*, February, 1974.

LIPTS 78   Lipton, S. M., and S. M. Matyas, "Making the Digital Signature Legal—and Safeguarded," *Data Commun.*, February 1978, pp. 41–52.

MEIJH 81   Meijer, H., and S. Akl, "Digital Signature Schemes for Computer Communication Networks," *Seventh Data Communications Symposium*, 1981, pp. 37–41.

MEISP 76   Meissner, P. "Report of the 1976 Workshop on Estimation of Significant Advance in Computer Technology," National Bureau of Standards, August 30–31, 1976, NBS-IR 76-1189, December 1976.

MERKR 78A   Merkle, R., "Secure Communication over Secure Channels," *Commun. ACM*, Vol. 21, No. 4, 1978, pp. 294–299.

MERKR 78B   Merkle, R. C., and M. E. Hellman, "Hiding Information and Signatures in Trap Door Knapsacks," *IEEE Trans. Inf. Theory*, Vol. IT-24, September 1978.

MORRR 79   Morris, R., and K. Thompson, "Password Security: A Case History," *Commun. ACM*, Vol. 22, No. 11, 1979, pp. 594–597.

MUERJ 74   Muerle, J. L., C. Swonger, and C. Tona, "EDP Security through Positive Personal Identification," *Carnahan International Crime Countermeasure Conference*, University of Kentucky, 1974, pp. 246–253.

NEEDR 78   Needham, R. M., and M. D. Schroeder, "Using Encryption for Authentication in Large Network of Computers," *Commun. ACM*, Vol. 21, No. 12, 1978, pp. 993–999.

NELSJ 79   Nelson, J., "Implementations of Encryption in an Open System Architecture," *Computer Networking Symposium*, IEEE Computer Society, 1979, pp. 198–205.

PARKD 73A   Parker, D. B., *Threats to Computer Systems*, Lawrence Livermore Laboratory, UCRL-13574, March 1973.

PARKD 73B   Parker, D. B., S. Nycum, and S. S. Qura, *Computer Abuse*, Stanford Research Institute, PK-231 320, November 1973.

PARKD 76A   Parker, D. B., "Computer Abuse Perpetrators and Vulnerabilities of Computer Systems," *Nat. Comput. Conf.*, 1976, pp. 65–73.

PARKD 76B   Parker, D. B., *Crime by Computer*, Scriber's New York, 1976.

PETEH 67   Petersen, H., E., and Turn, R., "System Implication of Information Privacy," *Spring Joint Comput. Conf.*, 1967, pp. 291–300.

POPEG 78A   Popek, G., et al., "UCLA Secure Unix," *Natl. Comput. Conf.*, 1978, pp. 355–364.

POPEG 78B   Popek, G. J., and C. S. Kline, "Encryption Protocols, Public Key Algorithms, and Digital Signature in Computer Networks," in R. DeMillo and D. Dobkin, eds., *Foundations of Secure Computation*, Academic Press, New York, pp. 133–153.

POPEG 79   Popek, G. J. and C. S. Kline, "Encryption and Secure Computer Networks," *Comput. Surv.* Vol. 11, No. 4, 1979, pp. 331–356.

PURDG 74   Purdy, G. B., "A High Security Log-in Procedure," *Commun. ACM*, Vol. 17, No. 8, 1974, pp. 442–445.

RABIM 78   Rabin, M. O., "Digitalized Signatures," in R. DeMillo and D. Dobkin, eds., *Foundations of Secure Computation*, Academic Press, New York, 1978, pp. 155–168.

REEDS 74   Reed, S. K., and D. K. Branstad, eds., *Controlled Accessibility Workshop Report*, National Bureau of Standards, NBS Tech. Note 827, May 1974.

REEDS 77   Reed, S. K., *Automatic Data Processing Risk Assessment*, National Bureau of Standards, March 1977, NBSIR 77-1228.

RIVER 78   Rivest, R., A. Shamir, and L. Adleman, "On Digital Signature and Public Key Cryptosystems," *Commun. ACM*, Vol. 21, No. 2, 1978, pp. 120–126.

SALTJ 74   Saltzer, J. H., "Protection and the Control of Information Sharing in Multics," *Commun. ACM*, Vol. 17, No. 1, 1974, pp. 388–402.

SANDC 77   Sanders, C. W., G. F. Sandy, J. F. Sawyer, and A. Schneider, *Study of Vulnerability of Electronic Communication Systems to Electronic Interception*, 2 vols., The Mitre Corporation, MTR-7439, January, 1977.

SHANC 49   Shannon, C. E., "Communication Theory of Secrecy Systems," *Bell System Tech. J.* Vol. 28, No. 4, 1949, pp. 656–715.

SMIDM 79   Smid, M. E., *A Key Notarization System for Computer Networks*, National Bureau of Standards, Spec. Publ. 500-54, October 1979.

STEVW 76   Stevenson, W., *A Man Called Intrepid*, Ballantine Books, New York, 1976.

TASKP 73A   Tasker, P. S., and D. E. Bell, *Design and Certification Approach: Secure Communications Processor*, The Mitre Corporation, May 1973, AD-765 518.

TASKP 73B   Tasker, P. S., *Design of a Secure Communications Processor I: Overall Environment and Concept*, The Mitre Corporation, May 1973, AD-761 804.

THOMR 72   Thomas, R. H., "On the Design of a Resource Sharing Executive for the ARPANET," *Nat. Comput. Conf.*, 1972, pp. 155–164.

WEISC 69   Weissman, C., "Security Control in the ADEPT-50 Time-Sharing System," *Fall Joint Comput. Conf.*, 1969, pp. 119–133.

WILKM 75   Wilkes, M. V., *Time Sharing Computer Systems*, American Elsevier, New York, 1975.

WINKS 74   Winkler, S. and L. Danner, "Data Security in the Computer Communication Environment," *Computer*, February 1974, pp. 23–31.

WINTF 74   Winterbotham, F. W., *The Ultra Secret*, Dell, New York, 1974.

WOODH 77A   Wood, H. M., "On-Line Password Techniques," *Comput. Security Integrity: Trends Appl.*, May 1977.

WOODH 77B   Wood, H. M., *The Use of Passwords for Controlled Access to Computer Resources*, National Bureau of Standards, Spec. Publ. 500-9, May 1977.

WOODH 77C   Wood, H. M., "The Use of Passwords for Controlling Access to Remote Computer System and Services," *Natl. Comput. Conf.*, 1977, pp. 27-33.

WOODH 79   Wood, H. M., and S. R. Kimbleton, "Access Control Mechanism for a Network Operating System," *Natl. Comput. Conf.*, 1979, pp. 355-364.

WOODH 80   Wood, H. M., "A Survey of Computer-Based Password Techniques," *Advances in Computer Security*, Vol. 1, Heyden and Son Inc., Philadelphia, Pa., 1980, pp. 140-167.

10

Analysis of Data/ Computer Networks

W. CHOU
*North Carolina State University
Raleigh, North Carolina*

10.1 INTRODUCTION

Performance most commonly means how promptly a data/computer network responds to an input at a specific traffic volume or requirement. It may be measured by the blocking probability (the probability that an input cannot get into the network when it attempts to), end-to-end delay or response time, round-trip delay or response time, or the waiting time to get into the network.

Several elements contribute to delay or blocking. These include transmission time, propagation delay, device processing and reaction times (e.g., CPU processing time at the switch, modem turnaround time), and contention for a smaller number of resources (transmission facilities, ports) by a larger number of users. From the communication system's viewpoint the first three elements can be viewed as system parameters and are either given or can be easily determined or approximated. The elements that are difficult to determine are the delays and the blocking probabilities.

There are three ways to evaluate performance in terms of delay and blocking probability: analytic approaches, simulation, and measurement. Often, a combination, or hybrid, approach is necessary. In principle, measurement and simulation approaches are similar. Performance evaluation using measurement is based on experiments from real operating networks while performance evaluation using simulation is based on experiments from simulated networks, which may be modeled after real or hypothetical networks.

While results from measurement and simulation are generally more accurate than results from the analytic approach, measuring a real operating network does not have flexibility for varying network configurations and traffic environments. The simulation approach is generally time consuming to model and code and execution of simulation programs is generally expensive. Hence the analytic approach has been the most widely used, particularly during the network design stage.

Theoretically, analytic expressions can provide exact values of certain model parameters, but measurement and simulation cannot. For example, the exact mean response time can be determined for an analytic expression of a mathematical model while observations from measurement and simulation can never provide the value of average response time with certainty. On the other hand, even a very good analytic model does not fully represent a real network. So exactness of the value of any parameter is somewhat insignificant. Whether measurement and simulation approaches or analytic approaches are used, the exact true value of any parameter will not be determined. The right way to use analytic approaches is not to place too much significance on the exact values obtained. Instead, the results should be used as an indication of the trend of network behavior. The values observed from real networks would be expected to be in the neighborhood of the calculated values.

Since the waiting and blocking experienced in a data/computer communication network are caused by contention for resources, the analytic approach in determining the response times, blocking times, and waiting probability is essentially a direct application of queueing theory techniques. Some problems can be modeled by standard queueing models with readily available formulas or iterative procedures (for a list of these models, see [KLEI 75]). For other problems, application-specific formulas or iterative procedures must be developed. There are two schools of thought for how to derive such results: the "mathematical approach" and the "engineering approach." With the "mathematical approach" every step of the derivation must be rigorously carried out. The end result is a mathematically correct formula or iterative procedure. The rigorousness is obtained at the expense of the model not necessarily resembling the real network it is intended to represent. With the "engineering approach" the model must reasonably resemble the real network, but during the derivation process "seemingly reasonable approximations" are made in order to obtain closed-form formulas or iterative procedures. Although the latter approach may represent real networks better, it has the disadvantage that there is no guarantee that the seemingly reasonable approximations are really good ones and may require simulation models for verification and calibration. Note that these two approaches are not necessarily exclusive. There are models that can represent real networks well and can also be used to derive mathematically rigorous expressions. In this chapter analytic expressions for delays, response times, and blocking probabilities are presented. The approach leans toward the "engineering approach."

Any mathematical or queuing system terminology not defined in this chapter can be found explained in [MART 72, KLEI 75].

10.2 REPONSE TIMES ON POLLED NETWORKS AND RING-SWITCHING NETWORKS

10.2.1 Background

In many cases, mathematical models and analytic expressions for response times and delays experienced by terminals are the same on a multipoint polled network and a ring-switching network [SCHW 77, KLEI 76]. Since the polling procedures are much

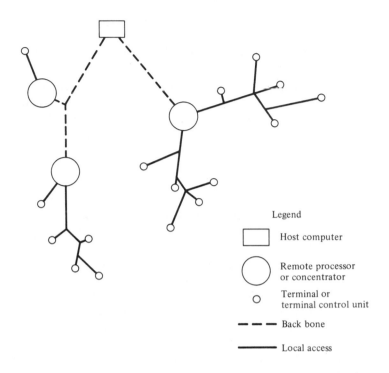

Legend

☐ Host computer

◯ Remote processor or concentrator

○ Terminal or terminal control unit

– – – Back bone

——— Local access

Figure 10.1 Tree-shaped hierarchically controlled data communication network architecture.

more widely used, the justifications, descriptions, terminologies, and examples used for the derivations and explanations in this section are all based on polling procedures.

Many papers have been published dealing with analytic problems and control procedures on ring networks. Some of their results are equivalent, even though the expressions and derivations may appear to be different. Most ring networks can be represented by a model similar to the one in this section. (A general model for ring networks, including control scheme with dissimilar mathematic models from polling, can be found in [NILS 80A].) Readers with a strong interest in ring networks may refer to Chap. 1 for a brief discussion on different control schemes and to [TROP 79, LIU 78] for more detailed discussions. Chaps. 1 and 13 also list other references on the topic.

Multipoint polled line configurations allow several terminals to share a line and save communication line costs. Line sharing is possible because the data input rate at terminals is typically much slower than the transmission rate of the communication line. The increasing number and size of data processing networks and distributed processing networks have led to an increase in the number of multipoint polled networks. Figure 10.1 shows a network with typical multipoint configurations.

As more terminals are added to a network, the accuracy of terminal response

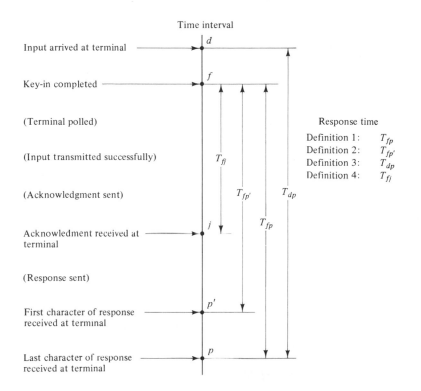

Time interval

Input arrived at terminal ———————— d

Key-in completed ———————— f

(Terminal polled)

(Input transmitted successfully) T_{fi}

(Acknowledgment sent) $T_{fp'}$ T_{dp}

Acknowledgment received at ———————— j T_{fp}
terminal

(Response sent)

First character of response ———————— p'
received at terminal

Last character of response ———————— p
received at terminal

Response time

Definition 1: T_{fp}
Definition 2: $T_{fp'}$
Definition 3: T_{dp}
Definition 4: T_{fi}

Figure 10.2   Points for defining the response-time interval.

time estimates becomes critical for assuring good performance with minimum costs. Control procedures, operating environment, system load, and other elements defined in Sec. 10.2.2. all affect response times.

A number of related terminal-response-time definitions exist. Any one can be used to calculate another as long as all the necessary response-time components are known. The difference in definitions is with the beginning and ending points for the response-time interval, which is illustrated in Fig. 10.2. The interval can begin with the arrival of a message at the terminal. In general, the message may queue at the terminal for its turn to be keyed in. The interval alternatively can begin with the completion of keying in a message at the terminal. The interval can end with the acknowledgment from the master station (usually the host computer, the front end processor or the concentrator) of correct receipt of the input message; or it can end with the appearance of the first or the last character of the response. These two beginning points and three ending points can be combined for six possible definitions of response time.

The following are the four most commonly used response-time definitions. They are listed in order of decreasing popularity.

Definition 1.   Response time is the time span from the key in of the last character of the input to the appearance at the terminal of the last character of the reply (or the last of the first page of the reply) to the input. This is the time between points f and p, or T_{fp}, in Fig. 10.2.

Definition 2.   Response time is the time span from the key in of the last character of the input message to the arrival at the terminal of the first character of the reply to the input, or $T_{fp'}$.

Definition 3.   Response time is the time span from the arrival at the terminal of the input message to the arrival at the terminal of the last character of the reply (or the last of the first page of the reply) to the input, or T_{dp}.

Definition 4.   Response time is the time span from the key in of the last character of the input message to the arrival at the terminal of the positive acknowledgment of the correct receipt of the input at the master station, or T_{fj}.

For any of the definitions, the terminal response time may be expressed in terms of an average value or a percentile value. One example is specification that the average response time be no more than 5 sec. Another is that the response times for 90% of the messages be no more than 7 sec.

The model given in this section for polling and response times is based on the work from [CHOU 78B]. Criteria and control procedures considered in the model development are specifically those applicable to real systems. The model has since been verified with detailed simulation [CHOU 79, CHOU 82]. (Other analytic models, which are developed for more idealized environments, can be found in [COBH 54, HAYE 71, CHU 72, MART 72, GREE 73, KAYE 73, KONH 74, CHAN 75, EVER 75, KONH 76, KLEI 76, SCHW 77].)

10.2.2   Elements Affecting Terminal Response Time

The performance of the multipoint line is governed by four elements: the data link control procedures or protocols, the line and node characteristics, the message dispatch disciplines, and traffic characteristics.

Data Link Control Procedures

This element is described in detail under the general model of a multipoint polled line in Sec. 10.2.4. The example in Sec. 10.2.3 leads into the general model.

Line and Node Characteristics

- Line speed
- Propagation delays
- Modem clear-to-send or turnaround delays

Message or Traffic Dispatch Disciplines

- *Half-duplex (HDX)*: The master station and terminals can transmit only one at a time.

- *Full-duplex (FDX)*: The master station and any one of the terminals can transmit simultaneously if required.
- *Single entry*: Only one outstanding transaction is allowed for each terminal (i.e., a terminal may not send an input message until the response to its preceding input is received).
- *Multiple entries*: Terminals are allowed to have multiple outstanding transactions (i.e., a terminal can send input messages even if responses have not been received for earlier inputs).
- *Interleaving*: The input and output are allowed to be interleaved (i.e., a terminal releases the line immediately after it sends its input message).
- *Noninterleaving*: The inputs and output are not allowed to interleave (i.e., a terminal holds the line after sending an input message until it receives the response).

Traffic Characteristics

- Input message's size and distribution; the output message's size and distribution
- The ratio between the input and output message size
- The total traffic on the line
- The traffic volume generated at different stations
- The number of devices controlled by terminal control units
- The number of terminals sharing the same line
- The master station's turnaround time

A discussion of the impact of these elements on response time/throughput can be found in [CHOU 79].

10.2.3   Polling Control Procedures: An Example

The two processes involved in the control of a multipoint polled line are "polling" and "select" or "addressing." Polling by the master or primary station (usually a concentrator or host computer) solicits input messages from the slave or secondary stations (usually terminals). Addressing by the master station delivers the responses to the input terminals.

In the polling process, the master station asks the terminals one by one whether they have a message to send. If a terminal has no message to send, it usually returns a "no" reply, and the next terminal is polled. When a terminal has a message to send and is polled, it sends one complete message and then, in general, the next terminal is polled.

When a response back to a terminal is ready at the master station, the terminal is "addressed" (or "selected"). Under some protocols, the master station sends the output together with the "addressing" sequence. Under others, the master station notifies the terminal and waits for a "yes" reply from the terminal, indicating its readiness to receive the output before it is sent.

There are many varieties of link protocols and within each protocol different

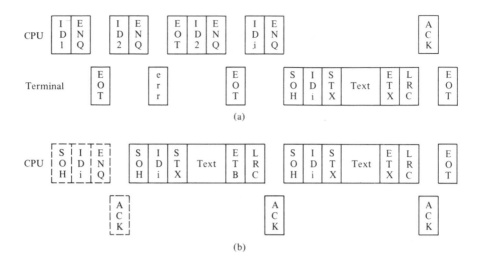

Figure 10.3 (a) Polling sequence in an ANSI procedure; (b) select (address) sequence in an ANSI procedure.

implementations are possible. Protocol examples include Binary Synchronous Communications (BSC) procedures [IBM 70], Synchronous Data Link Control (SDLC) procedures [IBM 75], and ANSI's asynchronous procedures [ANSI 76]. Chapter 3 contains further explanation and more examples. Figure 10.3 shows the polling and addressing (select) processes of the ANSI asynchronous procedure. It is the most commonly used link protocol for the multipoint polled lines. The entries ID_i, ENQ, and so or , each represent an ASCII character. ID_i is the identification terminal *i*. For specific meaning of the characters, see the references on link protocols listed above.

Polling (Fig. 10.3a)

The two-character set, ID_i and ENQ, form the polling sequence for inquiring whether terminal *i* has any data to send. If it has no data to send, the terminal sends an EOT character (stands for End of Transmission) on the transmission line inbound to the master station. If the polled terminal has data to send, it raises the carrier and transmits the data beginning with a SOH character and ending with a LRC character (stand for Start-of-Header and Longitude Redundancy Check, respectively).

If, by error, what the master station receives is not EOT or SOH, the master station responds EOT and polls the same terminal again. If an error is detected after SOH in the transmission of data from the terminal, the master station responds NAK. The terminal then retransmits the input. When the input is received without error, the master station responds ACK. The terminal sends an EOT after receiving the ACK. Once an EOT is received by the master station, it resumes its normal polling sequence.

Addressing (Fig. 10.3b)

When an output message to a terminal is ready for delivery, the master station sends a selection sequence to the terminal. The sequence follows one of two standard patterns. With acknowledged select, the selection sequence is SOH, ID_i, and ENQ. The terminal sends an ACK as the affirmative reply to its selection call or a NAK as its negative reply. If the master station receives a NAK or no reply, it will either retransmit the selection sequence or stop the call. Only if it receives an ACK will the master station send the message. The characters with dashed-line boxes in the figure show the acknowledged select control sequence.

With fast select, the SOH and ID_i in the prefix of an output message serve as the selection sequence but no reply is expected to the selection sequence. The ACK reply from the terminal acknowledges receipt of the message. An acknowledgment of message receipt is also required under the acknowledged select control sequence.

While Fig. 10.3 demonstrates the polling/select process of a specific data link control procedure, from the viewpoint of modeling, the polling/select process of other procedures is quite similar. (See [CHOU 80] for illustrations of SDLC and BSC and a performance comparison of the three procedures.)

10.2.4   A General Model of a Multipoint Polled Line

Figure 10.4a represents a general case of a complete polling and addressing sequence in the absence of errors. The effect from errors can be approximated by increasing the transmission times or reducing the line capacity. The concentrator or computer processor is called C and the terminal is called T.

Negative Polling Process

Time	Activity
a	C polls T.
(a,b)	Includes transmission time of polling sequence and propagation delay.
b	T receives the polling sequence but has no input message queued; so T sends an end of transmission message, EOT, to C.
(b,c)	Includes modem turnaround time, transmission time of an EOT, and propagation delay. (Modem turnaround time is the interval between the time a request-to-send signal is sent to a modem and the time the modem returns a clear-to-send signal.)
c	C receives the EOT from T.

Positive Polling Process

Time	Activity
d	The input message arrives at T.

Positive Polling Process (cont.)

Time	Activity
(d,e)	Includes waiting time for the input message to reach the head of the queue; this time can be zero if no other message was waiting at T.
e	The input message reaches the head of the queue at T.
(e,f)	Includes any processing and keying of the message by the terminal operator.
f	The input message is ready for transmission.
(f,g)	Time between keying completion and polling of T.
g	C polls T.
(g,h)	Like (a,b).
h	T receives the polling sequence and sends the input message to C.
(h,i)	Includes modem turnaround time, transmission time of the input message, and propagation delay.
i	C receives the input message from T (checks for correctness) and sends an ACK to T (since no error is apparent).
(i,j)	Includes modem turnaround time, transmission time of an ACK, and propagation delay.
j	T receives the ACK and sends an EOT to C.
(j,k)	Like (b,c)
k	C receives the EOT from T.

At this time, T might hold the line and no other terminal can input (the noninterleaving case); T might release the line (the interleaving case) but lock the terminal keyboard so that no other message can be entered at T (the single-entry case); or T might release the line and not lock the keyboard so other messages at T or at other terminals can be input (the multiple-entries case). C might have to wait for T's output to be ready before resuming polling in the noninterleaving case. In the interleaving case with single or multiple entries, C can poll or send output during the waiting time.

Addressing Process

Time	Activity
l	The outbound message has been processed and is ready to be queued for output.
(l,m)	Includes waiting time for the output message to reach the head of the queue at C. (The waiting time is zero in the noninterleaving case because no other message can be waiting for output.)
m	The output message reaches the head of the queue at C; C sends a selection sequence, represented by ENQ, to T.

Addressing Process (cont.)

Time	Activity
(*m*,*n*)	Includes transmission time of the selection sequence and propagation delay.
n	*T* receives the selection sequence and sends an ACK to *C*. (*T* is functioning properly and is connected to the line at the time of inquiry.)
(*n*,*o*)	Includes modem turnaround time, transmission time of an ACK, and propagation delay.
o	*C* receives the ACK and sends the output message to *T*.
(*o*,*p*)	Includes modem turnaround time, transmission time of output message, and propagation delay.
p	*T* receives the output message (sees no obvious error) and sends an ACK to *C*.
(*p*,*q*)	Like (*n*,*o*).
q	*C* receives the ACK and sends an EOT to *T*.
(*q*,*r*)	Like (*b*,*c*).
r	*T* receives the EOT.

If the line control is full duplex, the master station can be accepting input from one terminal while sending polling sequences and output messages to other terminals. Also, in the full-duplex case, the master station can interleave output and polling; the output is segmented and a polling sequence is inserted between output segments. The response to the polling, whether positive or negative, is sent through the terminals' transmitting channel and does not interfere with the output transmission. If there is a positive response to the polling sequence, the master station transmits the output without inserting polling sequences between the segments until the input transmission is completed.

Even though the model presented in Fig. 10.4 appears to represent a specific class of control procedures, it can be used for analytic or simulation modeling of almost any multipoint polled line. From the viewpoint of modeling, any polling/select procedure may be considered as consisting of five elements:

- Time associated with negative polling. In Fig. 10.4b, T_p denotes this time. It is the time interval (*a*,*c*). This time interval includes all time elements of a negative polling process. Thus in either simulation or analytic modeling, T_P denotes the time needed for a negative poll no matter how the sequence is carried out or how the line is synchronized.
- Time associated with a positive poll prior to the transmission of the input message. T_{PB} denotes this (*g*,*h*) time interval.
- Time associated with a positive poll after the transmission of the input. T_{PA} denotes this (*i*,*k*) time interval.
- Time associated with the addressing before the transmission of the output. T_{AB} denotes this (*m*,*n*) time interval.
- Time associated with signaling the end of transmission of output. T_{AA} denotes this (*p*,*r*) time interval.

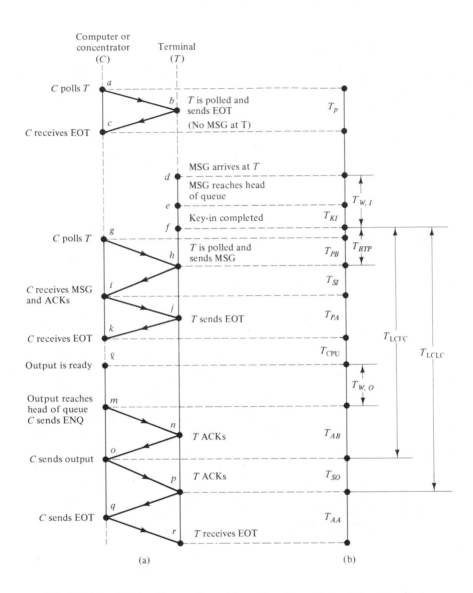

Figure 10.4 Timing diagram for polling addressing with stand-alone terminals.

Regardless of specific control procedures, the timing representations above can be used in the evaluation of the terminal response times to represent the different time elements in the control of a multipoint polled line. Fig. 10.5 is an extension of Fig. 10.4 to include the effects introduced by using terminal control units. Notations in the figures are explained in Tab. 10.1.

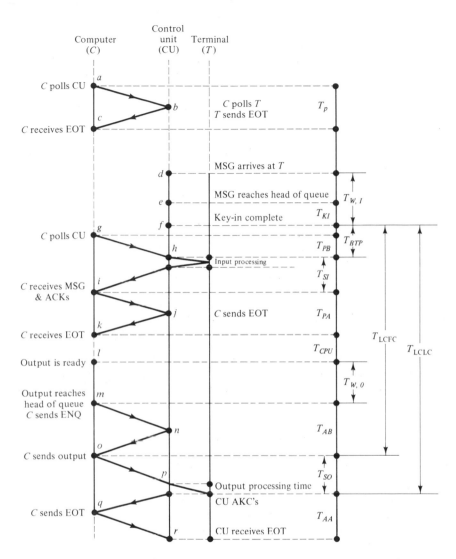

Figure 10.5 General timing diagram for a multidrop line with control units.

10.2.5 Analytic Expressions for Terminal Response Times

Among the definitions of response times, the most common one is the time duration from the key in of the last character of the input at the terminal to the arrival of the last character of the response or the first page of the response. This definition is used in this section. The random variable representing this response time is t_{LCLC}. The notation is explained in Tab. 10.1 and illustrated in Fig. 10.4.

Table 10.1. *Glossary of Notation.*

C	Line capacity or speed.
$E(\cdot)$	Expected value of the expression enclosed in parentheses.
λ	Input message arrival rate.
M	Number of terminals sharing a line.
ρ_{CPU}	Average line utilization contributed by CPU turnaround time, λT_{CPU}.
ρ_I	Average line utilization contributed by input messages, $\lambda T_{S,I}$.
ρ_O	Average line utilization contributed by outputs, $\lambda T_{S,O}$.
t	Lowercase t indicates the random variable for the time of the event indicated by the subscripts.
$T_{\text{BTP}}, V_{\text{BTP}}$	Mean and variance of the bid to poll time, the time between the key in of the last character of input and the polling of the terminal.
T_C, V_C	Mean and variance of the poll cycle time.
$T_{\text{CPU}}, V_{\text{CPU}}$	Mean and variance of the master station (computer or concentrator) turnaround processing time. This is the time span from the arrival of the input at the master station to the time the corresponding output is placed on the output queue.
T_{KI}	Average total time spent processing or keying an input message at the terminal.
T_{LC}	Average terminal response time from the key in of the last character of the input message to the arrival at the terminal of the positive acknowledgment of the receipt of the input at the master station.
T_{LCFC}	Average terminal response time from the key in of the last character of the input to the arrival at the terminal the first character of the output.
T_{LCLC}	Average terminal response time from the key in of the last character of the input to the arrival at the terminal the last character of the output.
T_{AA}	Average time associated with the signaling the end of the transmission of output.
T_{AB}	Average time associated with the addressing before the transmission of output.
T_P	Average total time associated with a negative poll.
T_{PA}	Average portion of total time associated with a positive poll after the transmission of the input message.
T_{PB}	Average portion of total time associated with a positive poll prior to the transmission of the input message.
$T_{S,I}, V_{S,I}$	Mean and variance of the output message transmission time, which is the input message size divided by line capacity. This time interval may also include other overheads associated with the transmission of the messages.
$T_{S,O}, V_{S,O}$	Mean and variance of the output message transmission time, which is the output message size divided by line capacity. This time interval may also include other overheads associated with the transmission of the messages.
T_T	Average terminal response time from the arrival of an input message at the terminal to the arrival at the terminal of the last character of the output.
$T_{W,I}$	Average total time an input message waits on the input queue at the terminal.
$T_{W,O}$	Average total time an output message waits on the output queue at the concentrator or the host computer.
$V(\cdot)$	Variance of the expression enclosed in parentheses.
$W(\rho, a^2, M)$	Normalized time on a single-server queue, on which the utilization is ρ, the coefficient of variance of the service time is a, the customer population size is M, and the arrival pattern is Poisson. No simple closed-form formula (quite cumbersome) exists for the general case but tables are available for the normalized waiting time given ρ, a, and M. In the limiting case where M is very large, there is a nice closed-form formula—the Pollaczek–Khinchin formula. The normalization is with respect to the transmission time.

$t_R = t_{LCLC} = t_{BTP} + t_{SI} + t_{CPU} + t_{WO} + t_{AB} + t_{SO}$
= time interval between key in of last character of input and the polling of the terminal
+ time duration of transmitting the input
+ turnaround time at the master station
+ time spent on the output queue at the master station
+ time associated with addressing before the transmission of output
+ time duration of output transmission (10.1)

The average of the response time is expressed as

$$T_R = T_{LCLC} = T_{BTP} + T_{SI} + T_{CPU} + T_{WO} + T_{AB} + T_{SO} \tag{10.2}$$

The quantities in this expression that require analysis are T_{BTP} and T_{WO}, since T_{SI}, T_{CPU}, T_{AB}, and T_{SO} can be viewed as system constants.

The Bid-to-Poll Time, T_{BTP}

This is the interval between the time the "send" key is hit and the time the terminal is polled and ready to transmit the input. Let T_C and V_C be the mean and variance of the poll cycle time; that is, the time the master station takes to poll every terminal once. It can be shown by using the residual life argument [FELL 66, EVER 75] that

$$T_{BTP} = \frac{1}{2}(1 + \frac{V_C}{T_C^2}) T_C \tag{10.3}$$

By assuming that the bid-to-poll time is gamma-distributed (see Sec. 10.4 for justification), it can be shown that [KLEI 76]

$$V_{BTP} = \frac{1}{3} \frac{E(t_C^3)}{T_C} - T_{BTP}^2 = \frac{1}{3} (1 + \frac{V_C}{T_C^2})(1 + \frac{2V_C}{T_C^2}) T_C - T_{BTP}^2 \tag{10.4}$$

These two expressions are in general valid only if the message arrivals at the terminal follow a Poisson pattern.

Thus in order to find an expression for T_{BTP}, we have to compute T_C and V_C.

1. *Average Poll Cycle Time, T_C*

    •   Case 1: HDX, noninterleaving

$$T_C = \frac{MT_p}{1 - (\rho_i + \rho_{CPU} + \rho_O)} \tag{10.5}$$

    •   Case 2: HDX, interleaving

$$T_C = \frac{MT_p}{1 - (\rho_i + \rho_O)} \tag{10.6}$$

- Case 3: FDX

$$T_C = \frac{MT_p}{(1 - \rho_i)(1 - \rho_O)}$$

(10.7)

2.   *Variance of Poll Cycle Time,* V_C

- Case 1: HDX, noninterleaving

$$V_C = \lambda T_C (V_{S.I} + V_{CPU} + V_{S.O}) + \lambda T_C (1 - \frac{\lambda T_C}{M})(T_{S.I} + T_{CPU} + T_{S.O})^2$$

(10.8)

- Case 2: HDX, interleaving

$$V_C = \lambda T_C (V_{S.I} + V_{S.O}) + \lambda T_C (1 - \frac{\lambda T_C}{M})(T_{S.I}^2 + T_{S.O}^2)$$

(10.9)

- Case 3: FDX

$$V_C = \frac{\lambda T_C (V_{S.I} + V_{S.O}) + \lambda T_C (1 - \frac{\lambda T_C}{M})(T_{S.I}^2 + T_{S.O}^2)}{(1 + \rho_i \rho_O)^2}$$

(10.10)

It can be shown by a more complicated analysis that a more exact formula, though still approximate, is obtained by modifying V_C as follows:

$$V_C \to V_C \left(\frac{T_C}{MT_\rho}\right)^2$$

(10.10a)

(See [CHOU 79].)

Output Waiting Time at the Master Station, $T_{W,O}$

In a multipoint polled-line environment, the output usually has priority over the input and the polling. However, the output does not preempt the input and the polling. By using a model that includes priority for a single-server queue with an infinite customer population, $T_{W,O}$ can be expressed as follows:

- Case 1: For HDX, non-interleaving

$$T_{W,O} = 0$$

(10.11)

- Case 2: For HDX, interleaving:

Let $W(\rho, a^2, M)$ be the normalized waiting time on a single-server queue where the utilization is ρ, the coefficient of variance of the service time is a, the customer population size is M, and the interarrival time is exponential. (See Tab. 10.1 and Sec. 10.2.6 for further discussion.)

$$T_{W,O} = W(\rho_O, V_{S,I} / T_{S,I}^2, M) \, T_{S,I} \, \frac{\rho_I}{\rho_O}$$

$$+ \, W(\rho_O, V_{S,O} / T_{S,O}^2, M) \, T_{S,O}$$

$$+ \, \frac{1 - \rho_I - \rho_O}{\rho_O} \, W(\rho_O, 0, M) T_\rho \tag{10.12}$$

- Case 3: For FDX

$$T_{W,O} = W(\rho_O, V_{S,O} / T_{S,O}^2, M) \, T_{S,O}$$

$$+ \, \frac{1 - \rho_I - \rho_O + \rho_I \rho_O}{\rho_O} \, W(\rho_O, 0, M) T_P \tag{10.13}$$

In the derivation and usage of these expressions, the following assumptions are made:

- Simplifications are made to keep the expressions from being unwieldly. The effects of these simplifications are discussed in Sec. 10.2.6.
- $T_{PB} = T_P, = T_{PA} = 0$, $T_{AB} = T_P$, $T_{AA} = 0$.
- Times to transmit control headers and trailers of the messages are included in $T_{S,I}$ and $T_{S,O}$.
- Every terminal has same arrival rate.
- Arrival patterns are Poisson.
- If the distribution of any particular time element is unknown, a gamma distribution is assumed (i.e., the bid-to-poll time).
- All nonoverlapping time elements are independent random variables. Therefore, the variances of the sum of any of these time elements are additive. [This assumption is needed for Eq. (10.10), but is not needed for Eq. (10.10a).]

More detailed discussions on material in Sec. 10.2.5 can be found in [CHOU 78B, CHOU 79].

10.2.6 Computational Considerations

- The assumptions used in Eqs. (10.5) through (10.13) that $T_{PB} = T_P$, $T_{PA} = 0$, $T_{AB} = T_P$, and $T_{AA} = 0$ serve only to reduce obfuscation. For practical systems, these assumptions actually have little impact on the results. If more accuracy is desired, the values of T_{SI} and T_{SO} in Eqs. (10.5) through (10.13) should be replaced by T_{SI}' and T_{SO}' with

$$T_{SI}' = T_{SI} + (T_{PB} + T_{PA} - T_p)$$
$$T_{SO}' = T_{SO} + (T_{AB} + T_{AA} - T_p)$$

The values of ρ_I and ρ_O should be changed to ρ_I' and ρ_O' with $\rho_I' = \lambda T_{S,I}'$ and $\rho_O' = \lambda T_{S,O}'$.

- The assumption that every terminal has the same arrival rate can easily be removed. The resulting expressions would be cumbersome. When the total arrival rate to the transmission line is kept constant, the variation of arrival rates among different terminals has been shown to have only a slight effect on the average response time and on the variance [CHOU 79].
- $W(\rho,a^2, M)$ in Eqs. (10.12) and (10.13) has a nice closed-form formula, the Pollaczek–Khinchin formula, when $M = \infty$.

$$W(\rho,a^2,\infty) = \frac{(1 + a^2)\rho}{2(1 - \rho)}$$

(For finite M, the expression is quite cumbersome; see [JAIS 68].)
- For practical problems, $W(\rho,a^2, \infty)$ is an adequate substitute for Eqs. (10.12) and (10.13) if $M \geq 10$. For $M \leq 5$, $W(\rho,a^2, \infty)$ can be used only if traffic load is light. Otherwise, the results would be on the pessimistic side.
- If the multiple entry discipline is used instead of single entry, $W(\rho,a^2, M)$ should be replaced by $W(\rho,a^2, \infty)$ in Eqs. (10.12) and (10.13).
- Figure 10.6 shows a comparison of results from analytic expressions given in this section and from simulations [CHOU 79].

10.3   RESPONSE TIMES IN PACKET/MESSAGE-SWITCHED NETWORKS

10.3.1   Background

Message-switched networks can be treated analytically as a special case of packet-switched networks. So without loss of generality, the discussion in this section is in the context of packet switching.

For most applications in the multipoint polled environment, the host computer and the network are managed by the same organization. The users may look at the combination of the computer and the network as one black box. Then, from the user's viewpoint, it is logical to think of response times as round-trip delays such as those described in Sec. 10.2. In the packet-switched network environment, the network and host computers are usually not managed by the same organization. Therefore, it is more logical to consider response times as end-to-end delays.

The end-to-end packet delay starts when a packet enters the network and ends when it arrives at the destination switch. For messages consisting of more than one packet, the message response time is of more interest. Expressions for average end-to-end message delays are given in Sec. 10.3.3.

Exact analytical solutions for response time in a distributed computer network have been shown to be all but impossible to determine, except for the limiting case in which the network is a tandem network [RUBI 74, RUBI 75]. The only alternative in

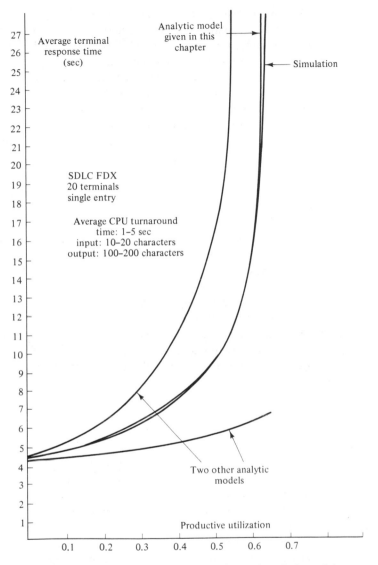

Figure 10.6   Comparing results of simulation and analytic models.

most cases is the use of approximate solutions. Much of the discussion in this section may be found in [CHOU 78A].

10.3.2   The Model

In a distributed computer communication network, the switches are interconnected by full duplex lines. If the network is packet switched, messages with length longer than a full packet length must be broken into packets before being transmitted into the network. Packets of the same message may be routed independently through the network according to certain routing algorithms [MCQU 74, MCQU 79]. The time span between the end of arrival of a packet at the destination switch and the beginning of the arrival of the next consecutive packet of the same message is called the interpacket gap. In an ideal situation, the gap is zero. But, in general, it is not. Therefore, in determining the message response time, both the packet response time and interpacket gap time must be known. In some applications, a logical or physical circuit must be established between the source and destination switches before the transmission of a message can be initiated. The maximum number of outstanding logical or physical circuits is limited by the number of bookkeeping blocks and buffers at the source and destination switches. (Usually, one bookkeeping block is used to keep track of information on each "circuit.").

Each full-duplex line on a packet-switching network can be modeled by two servers serving packets coming from two opposite switches. The network itself can be modeled as a network of interconnected queues. This is illustrated in Fig. 10.7. The network represented in Fig. 10.7a is modeled as a network of interconnected queues in Fig. 10.7b.

Queues on each communication link are characterized by the distribution of interarrival times between consecutive packets and the distribution of transmission times for packets. The traffic loads are determined by the external traffic requirements imposed on the network and the routing strategies used [CHOU 72, FRAT 73, FULT 72]. For the purpose of this chapter, the interarrival times on the links are assumed to have been determined and given.

10.3.3   Analytic Expressions for Response Times

Average End-to-End Packet Delay

This response time has already been defined as the time span starting when a packet enters the source switch and ending when it arrives at the destination switch. Different expressions have been derived for response time. They depend on assumptions about the packet-length distribution and on the number of priority classes for packets. Priority classes are groupings of traffic types based on the urgency of transmission. A packet in a higher-priority class is transmitted before waiting packets in lower-priority classes. For example, packets of data from interactive terminals are more sensitive to delay than packets of non-real-time data, such as RJEs (remote job entries), and might be assigned to a higher-priority class.

1.   *Exponential Packet Length, One Priority Class.* By using Little's result, the single packet response time can be expressed as [KLEI 76]

$$T_{sp} = \sum_{i=1}^{M} \left[\frac{\lambda_i}{\gamma} \left(\frac{1}{\mu C_i} + W_i + S_i + P_i \right) \right] \qquad (10.14)$$

with

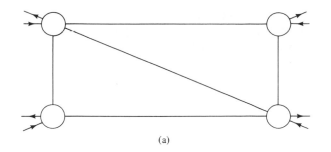

(a)

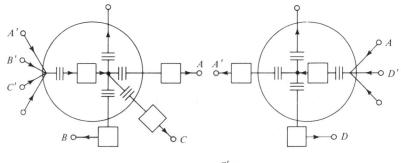

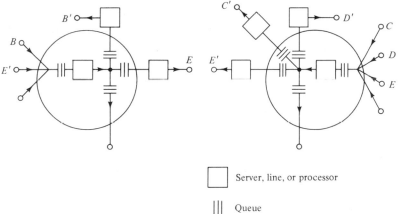

| | Server, line, or processor |
| | Queue |

(b)

Figure 10.7 Model of a distributed computer network.

$$W_i = \frac{\lambda_i / \mu C_i}{\mu C_i - \lambda_i}$$

where λ_i = mean arrival rate of packets to the ith link
γ = mean arrival rate of packets entering the network
W_i = mean time spent waiting for using the ith link

M = number of links in the networks

$1/\mu$ = mean packet size

C_i = capacity of the ith link

S_i = average processing and queueing delay at the switch to which link i is connected

P_i = propagation delay on link i

The formula used for W_i assumes the network is Markovian and every link can be modeled as an $M/M/1$ queue. The following conditions are necessary for this to be true [MUNT 73, JACK 63, KLEI 76]: the interarrival time of external traffic to the network is exponentially distributed (a Poisson process), the packet length (equivalent to service process) is exponentially distributed, the queue discipline in each switch is nonpreemptive and workconserving, the service and arrival processes are independent at every switch, and the number of buffers at each switch is infinite.

In the packet-switching environment, the infinite buffer space and the independence assumptions are definitely not true. However, for a well-designed switch, enough buffers should be available that the impact of finite buffers is negligible. The independence assumption has been verified by simulations and other arguments [KLEI 64, KLEI 70, FRAN 72]. Rubin [RUBIN 76] developed an approximate procedure for determining the average response time without the independence assumption in a limited network structure.

2.   *Arbitrary Packet Length, One Priority Class.* Exponentially distributed service time, which is equivalent to the exponential-packet-length assumption, is one of the conditions that must be satisfied for the average packet response time in Eq. (10.14) to be valid. Since the packet length is seldom exponentially distributed, a more realistic analysis would relax this assumption. A general distribution function can be approximated as a gamma distribution. That in turn can be approximated either as an Erlang or a hyperexponential distribution. (See [FELL 68] for an understanding on these distributions.) A server with an Erlang service process is equivalent to a chain of tandem servers with exponential service processes; and a server with a hyperexponential service process is equivalent to a set of parallel servers with exponential service processes. With these approximations and with the assumption of Poisson arrival, the network can be analyzed using Markovian queues [SAUE 75]. W_i of Eq. (10.14) can then take the following form (the Pollaczek-Khinchin formula):

$$W_i = \frac{(1 + \mu^2 C_i^2 V_{si}^2)\,(\mu C_i)}{2\,(\mu C_i - \lambda_i)} \tag{10.15}$$

where V_{si}^2 is the variance of the transmission time of line i. Simulation experiments have shown that this approximation fits the simulation results very well, much better than the use of exponential packet length assumption.

3.   *Arbitrary Packet Length, Multiple Priority Classes.* For the end-to-end packet

response time, priority considerations may be included by substituting W_{ij} as defined below for the average waiting time W_i in Eq. (10.14).

Let W_{ij} be the waiting time on ith link with jth priority. Then

$$W_{ij} = \frac{(1 + \mu^2 C_i^2 V_{si}^2)\rho_i \, (1/\mu C_i)}{2\left(1 - \sum_{k=1}^{j-1} \rho_{ik}\right)\left(1 - \sum_{k=1}^{j} \rho_{ik}\right)} \qquad (10.16)$$

where ρ_{ik} is the portion of the line utilization on link i that is contributed by priority k traffic [COBH 54].

Average End-to-End Message Delays

A message can consist of multiple packets. Two packets leaving the source switch consecutively may arrive at the destination switch with a time gap between them. This is called the interpacket gap time. By assuming the path between a source–destination pair is fixed for packets of the same message, the link capacity C for every link on the path is the same, and the link utilization is a constant ρ on the path, Cole [COLE 71] derived the following expression for the average interpacket gap time τ of a path consisting of n hops, or links:

$$\tau = \frac{\rho(1 - \rho^{n-1})}{1 - \rho} \frac{1}{\mu C} \qquad (10.17)$$

Kleinrock [KLEI 74] further extends the approximation by replacing τ, n, ρ, and $1/\mu C$ with $\tau, n, \rho,$ and S_F, which are averages over the whole network. τ is the average interpacket gap time, n the average number of hops, ρ the average line utilization, and S_F the average full-packet transmission time. The average path length, in terms of number of hops, traveled by a message is given by

$$\bar{n} = \frac{\lambda}{\gamma}$$

where

$$\lambda = \sum_{i=1}^{M} \lambda_i$$

The average link utilization is

$$\rho = \frac{\sum\limits_{i=1}^{M} (\lambda_i/\mu C_i)}{M}$$

Then the average time it takes to transmit a full packet over a link in the network is

$$\bar{S}_F = \sum_{i=1}^{M} \left(\frac{\lambda_i}{\lambda} \frac{1}{\mu_F C_i}\right) \qquad (10.18)$$

where $1/\mu_F$ is the length of a full packet. Finally, the following approximation can be used for average interpacket gap time, τ:

$$\bar{\tau} = \frac{\bar{\rho}(1 - \bar{\rho}^{\bar{n}-1})}{1 - \bar{\rho}} S_F \qquad (10.19)$$

The most crucial assumption used in obtaining Eqs. (10.17) and (10.19) is that the path between a source–destination pair is fixed for packets of the same message. Although the ARPANET definitely does not use a fixed path for the packets of a message, a majority of packet-switched networks do. Every public packet-switched network uses the same virtual or logical circuit for sending packets, (see chap. 14). GTE Telenet, which was originally modeled after ARPANET, initially used a dynamic adaptive routing approach but has since changed to a fixed path approach [TELE 79].

With the assumptions discussed earlier, the average message delay can be expressed in terms of the average single packet delay by adding in the average transmission times of the remaining packets in a message and their interpacket gap times. If the average number of packets per message is m and every packet, except perhaps the last one of a message, is of full length, then the average message delay is

$$T_{\text{MP}} = T_{\text{SP}} + (\bar{m} - 1)(\bar{S}_F + \bar{\tau}) = \text{average single-packet response time}$$
$$+ (\bar{m} - 1) \times \text{average transmission time of a full packet}$$
$$+ (\bar{m} - 1) \times \text{average interpacket gap time} \qquad (10.20)$$

T_{SP}, $\bar{S}_F$, and $\bar{\tau}$ were defined in Eqs. (10.14), (10.18), and (10.19), respectively. Equation (10.20) does not include, but can be easily extended to include the processing and associated delays at the destination switch.

10.4   PERCENTILES OF RESPONSE TIMES

A user is often more interested in worst cases than in averages. Such a user demands a limit on the percentage of packets or messages that have more than a prespecified delay. Interactive traffic cannot tolerate long delays between consecutive packets. The message response time for bulk traffic, even though it has lowest priority, should still be within a reasonable bound. Thus the distribution function of the response time, because it specifies percentiles, is often more significant than the average response time. The response-time distribution is typically defined by its type and variance, in addition to its mean. Except in some trivial cases, these cannot be easily determined. However, good estimates of percentiles often can be obtained with some or all of the following approximations:

- If both mean and variance can be determined, assume a gamma distribution.
- If there are not multiple (parallel) servers, assume that the waiting and service time of each server is independent of those of other servers and that the nonoverlapping time elements are also independent of each other.

- Assume that the cumulative distribution function of waiting times can be approximated by a biased negative exponential function; thereby the variance can be determined. (This is true, however, only if the probability that there is no waiting at all can also be estimated.)
- As a last resort, if variance cannot be determined for certain time elements, such as the intergap delays, assume the exponential distribution. (This usually results in somewhat conservative results.)

Experience has shown that in the data communication environment the service-time distribution, which includes transmission and processing times, and the response-time distribution are quite close to, or can be approximated by, a family of gamma distributions [MART 72, EVER 75, PAND 77]. Both the commonly used exponential distribution and the constant distribution are special cases of gamma distributions. A unique gamma distribution exists for each distinct pair of mean and variance values. Specification of the gamma-type distribution, its mean, and variance allows the percentile values to be determined.

Another advantage of assuming gamma-distributed service times is that gamma distributions are *almost* additive. (They are exactly additive if the distributions have the same mean.) The sum of two independent gamma-distributed random variables is still approximately gamma distributed. The mean of the sum of the variables is the sum of the individual means, and the variance of the sum of the variables is the sum of the individual variances. Although no analytic approach is available to prove this argument, experiments do verify this hypothesis. Let t_1 and t_2 be two gamma-distributed random variables with their means and variances to be T_1, T_2, V_1, and V_2. Let t be a gamma-distributed random variable with its mean and variance to be respectively $T_1 + T_2$ and $V_1 + V_2$. Nilsson [NILS 80B] plotted the distributions for $t_1 + t_2$ and for t with the same coordinates. For various arbitrarily chosen $t_1 t_2$, no distinguishable differences can be observed on the plot of the two curves. He did the same for the probability density functions. In most cases, there are still no distinguishable differences. Some do show differences, but only minor ones. An example that shows some observable difference for the density functions of $t_1 + t_2$ and t is given in Fig. 10.8. Figure 10.8a shows the two completely overlapping distribution functions; Fig. 10.8b shows the slightly different probability density functions; and Fig. 10.8c shows the numerical values of the differences between the two density functions. Note that in this example the maximum error for the two density functions is only 6×10^{-3}.

By assuming that gamma distributions are additive, and given that the transmission time of a packet on the link is gamma distributed, the time a packet spends in waiting for access to a line also will be approximately gamma distributed. This follows because the waiting time is the sum of the transmission times of independent packets which are gamma-distributed random variables.

With the independence assumption, the problem of determining an end-to-end message response time reduces to finding the means and variances of time elements that contribute to the total response time. The sum of the means and the sum of the variances of the contributing time elements will be the mean and the variance of a

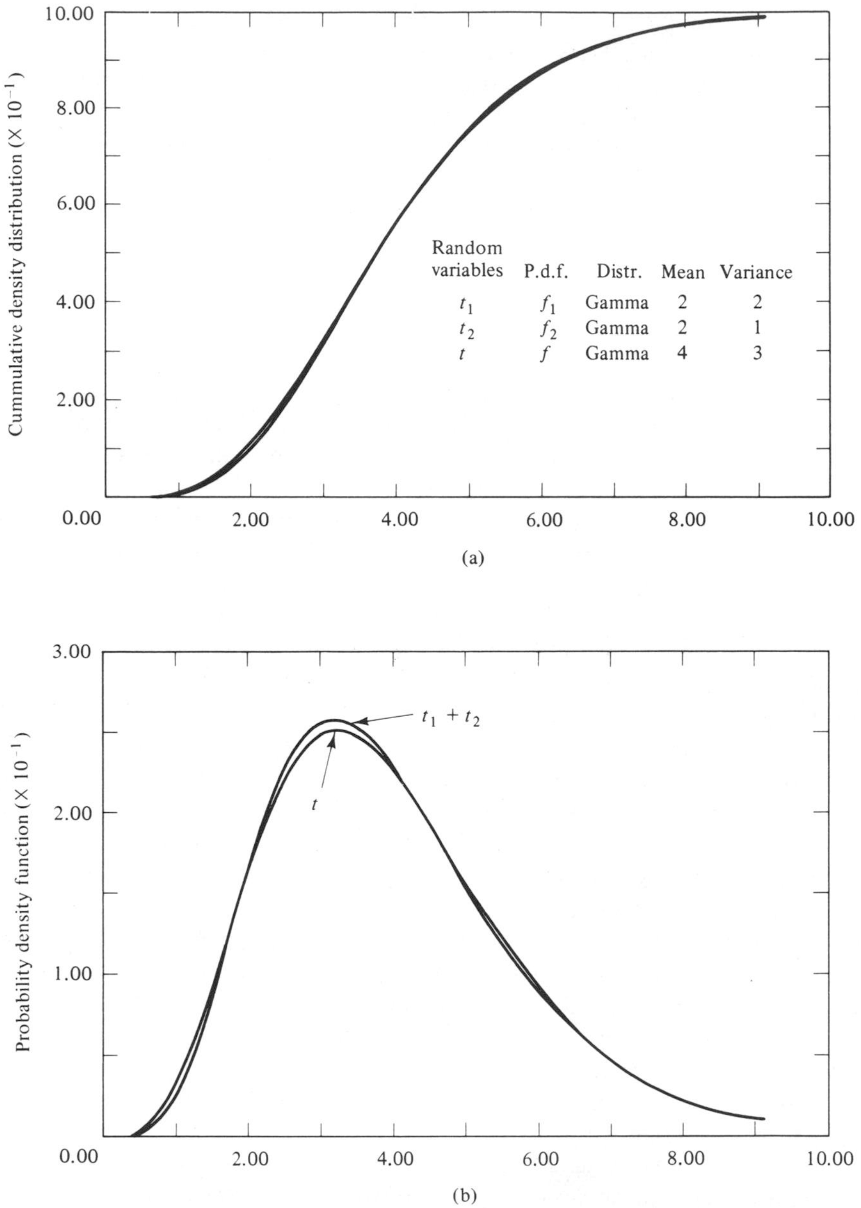

Figure 10.8 (a) Overlapped cumulative distribution function of $t_1 + t_2$ and t; (b) probability density function of $t_1 + t_2$ and t; (c) differences between the probability density functions of $t_1 + t_2$ and t.

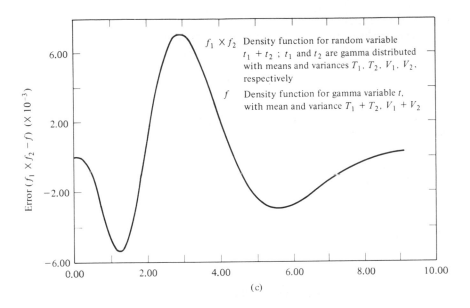

$f_1 \times f_2$ Density function for random variable $t_1 + t_2$; t_1 and t_2 are gamma distributed with means and variances T_1, T_2, V_1, V_2, respectively

f Density function for gamma variable t, with mean and variance $T_1 + T_2$, $V_1 + V_2$

(c)

Figure 10.8 (cont.)

uniquely defined gamma distribution approximation that characterizes the response time for the packets or messages concerned.

The components of the total response time for a multipoint polled line are given in Eq. (10.1). The components for a store-and-forward network, along the path between a specific source–destination node pair, include (1) waiting times for access to every line on the path; (2) transmission times of a packet and the associated overhead on every line of the path; (3) every interpacket gap time; (4) queueing times and service times contributed by processors and peripheral devices, if they are not negligible; (5) propagation delay, if it is not negligible; and (6) printing or displaying time, if it is to be included.

So far, the variances of all the time elements have been assumed to be known. Some of them are known. For example, the expression for variance of the cycle time on a polled line is given in Eq. (10.3). Expressions for the variances corresponding to the average waiting times given in Eqs. (10.14), (10.15), and (10.16) ($M/M/1$, $M/G/1$ without priority, $M/G/1$ with priority) are readily available from many textbooks, including [KLEI 75, MART 72]. However, for some time elements such as the interpacket gap time, the variances are not available. When variances are not known but means have been determined, approximation can be based on the observation that any cumulative distribution resembles a biased negative function. Then the cumulative distribution function, $F(\hat{t})$, for a time element t is expressed as

$$F(\hat{t}) \approx 1 - ae^{-(a/m)\hat{t}} \tag{10.21}$$

where $F(\hat{t})$ is the probability that $t \leq \hat{t}$, $1 - a$ is the probability that $t = 0$, and m is the mean or average value that has been determined. The corresponding variance, V_t, is

$$V_t = m^2 \left(\frac{2}{a} - 1 \right)$$

(10.22)

If t is a waiting time, then $1 - a$ is the probability that there is no waiting, and a is the same as the blocking probability, P_B, defined in Sec. 10.5. For a single-server queue, $1 - a$ becomes $1 - \rho$. For other situations, the value of a may need to be estimated. In the absence of better information, the value of a can be assumed to be 1; this corresponds to an exponentially distributed t.

10.5   GRADE OF SERVICE AND BLOCKING PROBABILITY

10.5.1   Packet-Switched Networks

In many packet-switched networks a logical connection between the origin and the destination must first be established before a message can be sent. The connection is analogous to establishing the dedicated physical channel between the end users in a regular telephony network (circuit-switching network). For an end-to-end logical channel, the route traversed by the message packets may vary with time. Part or all of the physical path may be shared with other logical channels through statistic time-division multiplexing. For a physically dedicated channel (circuit switching), the route is fixed and there is no sharing.

The total number of connections that can be accommodated at a packet switch is limited mainly by the bookkeeping blocks and buffers that are specified on the basis of network capacities. If all the bookkeeping blocks or buffers are in use, the maximum number of simultaneous logical channels allowed through the switch is reached and additional requests for a connection are blocked. The probability of blocking establishment of a logical channel is called *grade of service*. For example, a grade of service of P05 indicates a 0.05 probability that a request for a connection will be blocked.

If the end-to-end packet or message response time can be approximated as exponential, and if a blocked message is not lost but immediately queued, the situation fits the $M/M/m$ model and the results available for that queuing model are applicable. Of specific interest are the grade of service P_B (i.e., the probability all channels are busy), and the average time spent waiting in the queue, W (i.e., the waiting time for access to the network).

$$P_B = \frac{1 - A}{1 - \rho A}$$

(10.23)

where $A = \dfrac{\left[\displaystyle\sum_{N=0}^{m-1} (m\rho)^N / N!\right]}{\left[\displaystyle\sum_{N=0}^{m} (m\rho)^N / N!\right]}$

m = maximum number of simultaneous (logical) channels allowed

ρ = average message delay = average arrival rate at the switch $\div\ m$

This expression is called the Erlang C formula, which may be denoted as $E_C(m,\rho)$ (see [KLEI 75] or [MART 72]).

$$W = \frac{(1-A)/(1-\rho A)}{1-\rho}\ \frac{T}{m} \tag{10.24}$$

where T is the average end-to-end message delay.

If the end-to-end message delay cannot be assumed to be exponentially distributed, the problem fits an $M/G/m$ queuing model. There are no closed formulas for this model. For quick and rough estimations, the following can be assumed:

$$P_B \text{ (with general delays)} \approx P_B \text{ (with exponential delays)} \tag{10.25}$$

$$W \text{ (with general delays)} \approx \frac{(1+a^2)}{2} W \text{ (with exponential delays)} \tag{10.26}$$

where a is the coefficient of variance of the message delays. For more accurate approximations, diffusion approximation [NILS 79] or tables [HILL 71] may be used.

10.5.2 Port Contention

Port contention occurs for networks in which a number of terminal devices seek access to the network via a smaller number of common host computer or multiplexer ports. When a terminal device seeks access to the network, it is possible that no port is available and the terminal is blocked. An important part of network design is determining the number of ports needed to satisfy the grade-of-service requirements. (Note that, if all terminals are assumed to have same traffic profile, then the fewer the number of terminals sharing a set of ports, the greater the ratio of number of ports to number of terminals must be to maintain the same grade of service.)

Terminal devices may access the ports by dial-up arrangements or through connections to contention devices bridging the terminals and the host computer. When all ports are busy, a blocked call typically will be (1) queued; (2) lost; or (3) recalled.

1. *Blocked calls queued.* In this case, the call from the terminal user is placed in a queue. This fits exactly the same queueing model presented in Sec. 10.5.1. Of course, the meaning of m and ρ are slightly different. "m" now stands for the number of ports and ρ = average session time $\times$ average number of sessions

accessing all the ports per unit time ÷ m. With the adjustment in the meanings of ρ and m, all discussion on the grade-of-service and waiting times in Sec. 10.5.1 is applicable in this case, and Eqs. (10.23) and (10.24) can be used.

2. *Not queued, no recall.* This is the case in which an unsuccessful call is not queued and the terminal user will not make the same call again, i.e., all unsuccessful calls are completely lost. The grade-of-service for this case is

$$
\begin{aligned}
P_B &= \text{grade of service} \\
&= 1 - A \\
&= \frac{(m\rho)^m/m!}{\displaystyle\sum_{N=0}^{m} (m\rho)^N/N!}
\end{aligned}
\tag{10.27}
$$

This expression is called the Erlang B formula, which may be denoted as $E_B(m,\rho)$ (See [KLEI 75] or [MART 72]).

2. *Not queued, with recall.* For this case, a blocked call is not queued, but some or all of the blocked calls will try again at a later time. A first-order approximation for the blocking probability under this condition can be expressed as

$$
P_B \approx E_B(m,\rho')
\tag{10.28}
$$

where $\rho' = (1 + P_{rt}E_B(m,\rho)/(1 - P_{rt}E_B(m,\rho)))\rho$

P_{rt} = percentage of blocked calls that will retry at a later time

In an operational environment, the value of P_{rt} is likely to be self-adjusting. When traffic is light and the blocking probability is small, every blocked call is likely to retry. The value of P_{rt} is then almost 1. On the other hand, if the traffic is heavy and the blocking probability is large, many blocked calls will not retry. Furthermore, even if they do all retry at a "later time", the "later time" may no longer be a busy period. The value of P_{rt} during the busy period usually is less than 1. How much less it is than 1 depends on the traffic load.

For another approximate approach, see [RIOR 62].

10.6 DISCUSSION

In this chapter "engineering approaches" have been used to determine the performance of several data/computer communication network architectures. To obtain analytic expressions, some "seemingly reasonable" assumptions are made. If these assumptions do not seem to be reasonable for some systems, the same models used in this chapter for determining the analytic expressions can also be used as models for simulation. Simulations are not constrained by the assumptions that are necessary for analytic expressions and, therefore, more accurate results can be expected. As mentioned earlier, the additional accuracy is at the expense of substantially more effort for development of simulation programs and execution of the simulation programs. For many cases the additional complexity and expense may not be justified for the additional accuracy. Simulation can also be used for verifying and calibrating analytic models.

This chapter has not covered all possible cases. Nothing has been discussed on the delays or response time under multiple access schemes. Performance models and analysis for multiple access schemes is given in Chap. 4. This chapter has also not covered all the ring network architectures. From the viewpoint of response time models, the ring network can be classified into two categories. One of them is exactly the same as a multipoint polled network, which is discussed in Sec. 10.2. This is the case when the ring network is controlled by passing the token around the ring network (see Chaps. 1 and 13, and [LIU 78]). The performance model for the other general category that is not similar to a multipoint polled network can be found in [NILS 80A]. For readers who are interested in more references on these two problems, please also refer to the above mentioned chapters and references.

ACKNOWLEDGMENT

This work was supported by the National Science Foundation under Grant ENG-77-24110.

REFERENCES

ANSI 76 *"American National Standard Procedures for the Use of the Common Control Character of ASCII in Specified Communication Links,"* ANSI X3.28, 1976.

CHAN 75 Chang, J. H., "Terminal Response Times in Data Communications Systems," *IBM J. Res. Dev.*, May 1975.

CHOU 72 Chou, W., and H. Frank, "Routing Strategies in Computer Networks," *Proc. Symp. Comput. Commun., Networks Traffic*, Polytechnic Press of Brooklyn, New York, 1972.

CHOU 78A Chou, W., "Responsiveness Evaluation of Distributed Processing Networks," *Proc. Trends Appl.: Distributed Processing*, NBS, Gaithersburg, Md., June 1978.

CHOU 78B Chou, W., "Terminal Response Time on Polled Teleprocessing Networks," *Proc. Comput. Networking Symp.*, December 1978, pp. 1–10.

CHOU 79 Chou, W., A. Nilsson, and R. King, "Performance Evaluation of Multipoint Polled Teleprocessing Networks," *Proc. 1979 Comput. Networking Symp.*, NBS, Gaithersburg, Md., December 1979.

CHOU 80 Chou, W., and R. King, "Comparative Evaluation of Data Link Control Procedures under Multipoint Environment," *Proc. Trends Appl.: Protocols*, NBS, May 1980.

CHOU 82 Chou, W., and A. A. Nilsson, "A General Analytic Model for Polled Networks," Technical Report TR82-1, Computer Studies Program, N.C. State University, Raleigh, N.C.

CHU 72   Chu, W. W., and A. G. Konheim, "On the Analysis and Modeling of a Class of Computer Communication Systems," *IEEE Trans. Commun.*, Vol. COM-20, June 1972, pp. 645–660.

COBH 54   Cobham, A., "Priority Assignment in Waiting Line Problems," *Oper. Res.*, Vol. 2, 1954.

COLE 71   Cole, G. D., "Computer Network Measurements: Techniques and Experiments," Engineering Report No. UCLA-ENG-7165, University of California, Los Angeles, Calif., 1971.

EVER 75   Everling, W., *Exercises in Computer Systems Analysis*, Lecture Notes in Computer Science 35, Springer-Verlag, New York, 1975.

FELL 66   Feller, W., *An Introduction to Probability Theory and Its Applications*, Vol. 2, Wiley, New York, 1966.

FELL 68   Feller, W., *An Introduction to Probability Theory and Its Applications*, Vol. 1, 3rd ed., Wiley, New York, 1968.

FRAN 72   Frank, H., R. E. Kahn, and L. Kleinrock, "Computer Communication Network Design—Experience with Theory and Practice," *AFIPS Conf. Proc. 40*, SJCC, Atlantic City, N.J., 1972, pp. 255–270.

FRAT 73   Fratta, L., M. Gerla, and L. Kleinrock, "The Flow Deviation Method: An Approach to Store-and-Forward Comm. Network Design," *Networks*, Vol. 3, No. 2, 1973.

FULT 72   Fultz, G. L., "Adaptive Routing Techniques for Message Switching Computer Communication Networks," Engineering Report No. UCLA-ENG-7252, University of California, Los Angeles, Calif., 1972.

GREE 73   Green, P. E., and D. T. Tang, "Some Recent Developments in Teleprocessing System Optimization," *IEEE InterCommun. Conf. Rec.*, New York, March 1973.

HAYE 71   Hayes, J. F., and D. N. Sherman, "Traffic Analysis of a Ring Switched Data Transmission System," *Bell Syst. Tech. J.*, Vol. 50, November 1971, pp. 2947–2978.

HILL 71   Hillier, F. S., and F. D. Lo, "Tables for Multiple-Server Queueing Systems Involving Erlang-Distributions," Tech. Rep. No. 31, December 28, 1971, Stanford University, Stanford, Calif.

IBM 70   IBM Corp., *General Information-Binary Synchronous Communications*, GA27-3004-2, IBM, 1970.

IBM 75   IBM Corp., *IBM Synchronous Data Link Control-General Information*, GA27-3093-1, IBM, 1975.

JACK 63   Jackson, J. R., "Jobshop-like Queueing Systems," *Manage. Sci.* Vol. 10, 1963.

JAIS 68   Jaiswal, N. K., *Priority Queues*, Academic Press, New York, 1968.

KAYE 73   Kaye, A. R., and T. G. Richardson, "A Performance Criterion and Traffic Analysis for Polling Systems," *INFOR*, Vol. 11, June 1973, pp. 93–112.

KLEI 64   Kleinrock, L., *Communication Nets: Stochastic Message Flow and Delay*, McGraw-Hill, New York, 1964; reprinted by Dover, New York, 1972.

KLEI 70   Kleinrock, L., "Analytic and Simulation Methods in Computer Network Design," *AFIPS Conf. Proc., 36*, SJCC, Atlantic City, N.J., 1970, pp. 569–579.

KLEI 74   Kleinrock, L., and W. E. Naylor, "On Measured Behavior of the ARPA Network," *1974 NCC.*

KLEI 75   Kleinrock, L., *Queueing Systems,* Vol. I: *Theory*, Wiley, New York, 1975.

KLEI 76   Kleinrock, L., *Queueing Systems,* Vol. 2, *Computer Applications*, Wiley, New York, 1976.

KONH 74   Konheim, A. G., and B. Meister, "Waiting Lines and Times in a System with Polling," *J. ACM*, Vol. 21, No. 3, July 1974, pp. 470–490.

KONH 76   Konheim, A. G., "Chaining in a Loop System," *IEEE Trans. Commun.*, Vol. COM-24, February 1976, pp. 203–210.

LIU 78   Liu, M. T., "Distributed Loop Computer Networks," *Advances in Computers*, Vol. 17, Academic Press, New York, 1978, pp. 163–221.

MART 72   Martin, J., *Systems Analysis for Data Transmission*, Prentice-Hall, Englewood Cliffs, N.J., 1972.

MCQU 74   McQuillan, J. M., "Adaptive Routing Algorithms for Distributed Networks," Bolt, Beranek and Newman, Inc., Rep. 2831, May 1974.

MCQU 79   McQuillan, J. M., I. Richer, and E. Rosen, "An Overview of the New Routing Algorithm for the ARPANET," *Proc. 6th Data Commun. Symp.*, November 1979, pp. 63–68.

MUNT 73   Muntz, R. R., "Poisson Departure Processes and Queueing Networks," *Proc. 7th Annu. Princeton Conf. Inf. Sci. Syst.*, March 1973.

NILS 79   Nilsson, A. A., W. J. Stewart, and J. Seraj, "On the Use of Diffusion Approximation for Modeling Multiprocessor Systems," *9th Int. Teletraffic Congr.*, Spain, October 1979.

NILS 80A   Nilsson, A. A., and W. Chou, "A General Performance Model for Different Ring Network Protocols," Computer Studies Tech. Rep. TR 80-08, North Carolina State University, Raleigh, N.C., 1980.

NILS 80B   Nilsson, A. A., private consultation, February 1980.

PAND 77   Pandya, R. N., "Delay Analysis for Datapac—A Packet Switched Network with Two Priority Classes," *Proc. 5th Data Commun. Symp.*, September 1977.

RIOR 62   Riordan, J., *Stochastic Service Systems*, Wiley, New York, 1962.

RUBI 74   Rubin, I., "Communication Networks: Message Path Delays," *IEEE Trans. Inf. Theory*, November 1974.

RUBI 75   Rubin, I., "Message Path Delays in Packet-Switching Comm. Networks," *IEEE Trans. Commun.*, February 1975.

RUBI 76   Rubin, I., "An Approximate Time-Delay Analysis for Packet-Switching Comp. Networks," *IEEE Trans. Commun.*, February 1976.

SAUE 75   Sauer, C. H., and K. M. Chandy, "Approximate Analysis of Central Server Models," *IBM J. Res. Dev.*, Vol. 19, No. 3, May 1975.

SCHW 77   Schwartz, M., *Computer-Communication Network Design and Analysis*, Prentice-Hall, Englewood Cliffs, N.J., 1977.

TELE 79   Telenet Communications Corp., *Functional Description: Private Data Networks*, April 1979.

TROP 79   Tropper, C., "Models of Local Computer Networks," MTR-3783, MITRE-Bedford, May 1979.

Index